HUMAN COMMUNICATION

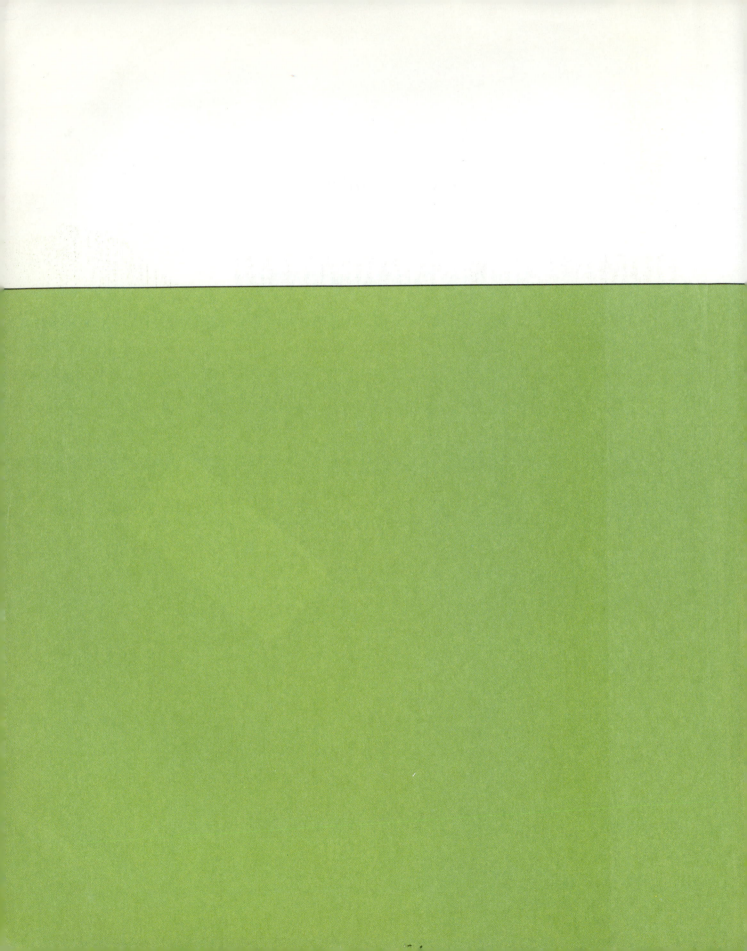

Colleen Kelley

seventh edition

HUMAN COMMUNICATION

the basic course

joseph a. devito

Hunter College of the City University of New York

An Imprint of Addison Wesley Longman, Inc.

New York • Reading, Massachusetts • Menlo Park, California • Harlow, England
Don Mills, Ontario • Sydney • Mexico City • Madrid • Amsterdam

Credits

Unless otherwise acknowledged, all photographs are the property of Scott, Foresman and Company.

9: Mary Kate Denny/PhotoEdit; *10:* David R. Frazier; *23:* Grunnitus Studios/Monkmeyer Press Photo Service, Inc.; *38:* John Coletti/Picture Cube, Inc.; *42:* Art Montes de Oca/FPG International Corp.; *58:* Joel Gordon; *64:* Stephen Jaffe/JB Pictures Ltd.; *73:* Gamma-Liaison; *78:* Myrleen Ferguson/PhotoEdit; *94:* Renato Rotolo/Gamma-Liaison; *95:* Sotographs/Gamma-Liaison; *108:* Bob Daemmrich/Stock Boston; *111:* Hugh Scott/Gamma-Liaison; *130:* Bob Daemmrich/Image Works; *137:* Rick Friedman/Black Star; *144:* P. F. Gero/Sygma; *148:* Roger Tully/Tony Stone Images; *159:* Jim Whitmer; *166:* Anna E. Zuckerman/PhotoEdit; *176:* Jim Whitmer; *196:* Jim Whitmer; *203:* Bob Daemmrich/Stock Boston; *212:* Jon Riley/Tony Stone Images; *234:* Cameramann International, Ltd.; *237:* Albert Trotman/Trotman, Allford & Assoc.; *259:* Tony Savino/Image Works; *276:* Jim Whitmer; *286:* Billy Barnes/PhotoEdit; *300:* Jim Whitmer; *305:* Jean-Marc Giboux/Gamma-Liaison; *319:* Okoniewski/Image Works; *341:* Joseph Nettis/Tony Stone Images; *359:* Michael Newman/PhotoEdit; *360:* Chuck Savage/Stock Market; *377:* Bob Daemmrich/Stock Boston; *380:* Bob Daemmrich/Stock Boston; *396:* Richard Hutchings/PhotoEdit; *401:* Franz Kraus/Picture Cube, Inc.; *410:* John Nordell/JB Pictures Ltd.; *414:* McLaughlin/Image Works

Senior Acquisitions Editor: Deirdre Cavanaugh

Developmental Editor: Dawn Groundwater

Supplements Editor: Diane Wansing

Project Editor: Lois Lombardo

Text and Cover Designer: Sandra Watanabe

Front Cover Braille Text: *Human Communication/ The Basic Course/* seventh edition/ Joseph A DeVito/ communication takes many forms/ this is not a braille book

Art Studio: Academy Artworks Inc.

Photo Researcher: Diane Kraut

Electronic Production Manager: Valerie A. Sawyer

Desktop Administrator and Electronic Page Makeup: Jim Sullivan

Manufacturing Manager: Helene G. Landers

Printer and Binder: Courier Kendallville, Inc.

Cover Printer: The Lehigh Press, Inc.

Library of Congress Cataloging-in-Publication Data

DeVito, Joseph A., (date)
Human communication : the basic course / Joseph A. DeVito. – 7th ed.
p. cm.
Includes bibliographical references and index.
ISBN 0-673-98081-2
1. Communication. I. Title.
P90.D485 1995
302.2–dc20 96-2247
CIP

ISBN 0-673-98081-2 (student edition)
ISBN 0-673-98529-6 (instructor's edition)

2345678910—ARH—99897

contents in detail

specialized table of contents

Media Watch

Introducing Research

Listen to This

preface

It is a pleasure to write a preface to a book that is now in its seventh edition and that has proven so popular with both students and teachers.

Human Communication: The Basic Course is designed for the introductory college course that surveys the broad field of communication. It covers classic approaches and new developments, delves into research and theory, and devotes attention to important communication skills.

The book is addressed to students with little or no prior background in communication. For those students who will take this course as their only communication course, it will provide a thorough foundation in the theory, research, and principles of this essential liberal art. For those who will take additional and advanced courses or who are beginning their majors in communication, it will provide the basis for more advanced and specialized study.

MAJOR FEATURES OF HUMAN COMMUNICATION

The seventh edition, revised in light of comments from a large number of instructors, builds on the successful features of previous editions but represents a major revision. Consequently, the major features of the text (especially those new to this edition) and how they are presented, need to be explained.

Comprehensive Coverage

Like its previous editions, this revision continues to provide broad coverage of the entire field—the preliminaries of human communication (principles, perception, listening, self, culture, and verbal and nonverbal messages) and the areas of human communication (interpersonal communication and relationships; small group, organizational, and interviewing communication; public speaking; and mass communication). In this edition, the major areas of human communication are presented in tables to illustrate the wide range of the field that we can only scratch the surface of in this text. See Units 1, 6, 12, 17, and 21.

Emphasis on Research and Theory

The seventh edition emphasizes the research and theory in human communication to a much greater extent than previous editions. Theories and theoretically rich concepts new to this edition include communication accommodation theory (Unit 2); the facial feedback hypothesis (Unit 9); protection, equilibrium, and expectancy violations theories of proxemics (Unit 10); relationship rules theory (Unit 12); cognitive restructuring (including performance visualization) and systematic desensitization in communication apprehension (Unit 19); power distances (Unit 21); and cultural imperialism, the spiral of silence, and knowledge gap theories of media (Units 6, 10, and 19).

In addition, approximately two hundred new research studies—most from the 1990s—have been carefully integrated into the text.

Another dramatic change in the coverage of research and theory is the addition of nine **Introducing Research** boxes, all addressed to the student who has no prior experience with any research concepts. This feature provides an introductory explanation of how we know what we know about communication and how researchers go about expanding our knowledge of communication in all its forms. Ideally, the research introduction in this basic text will be continued and expanded in depth and breadth by more advanced and more specialized communication textbooks. The Introducing Research boxes cover:

- the nature of theory (Unit 2)
- the general process of research (Unit 3)
- the three research methods: descriptive, historical/critical, and experimental (Unit 4)
- the process of conducting research from asking the question to drawing conclusions (Unit 7)
- a sample descriptive study (Unit 9)
- a sample historical/critical study (Unit 12)
- a sample experimental study (Unit 13)
- evaluating research methods and conclusions (Unit 17)
- ethics in research (Unit 21)

The last question at the end of the Unit "Thinking Critically About. . . ." section focuses on research and asks the reader how she or he would go about finding answers to a series of researchable questions. These questions can be integrated with the research boxes if a greater focus on research is desired, or with the text material if a greater focus on content is desired.

Because communication is simply an eminently useful body of knowledge, the skills of communication can never be totally excluded from considerations of theory and research. So, the skills of human communication are still present but are not highlighted as much as the theory and research aspects. A companion text, *Essentials of Human Communication,* focuses more on skills and less on theory and research.

Expanded Coverage of Cultural Issues

This edition—as did the previous edition—reflects the growing importance of culture in communication. There are few communications that are not influenced by culture in some way. Thus, a cultural consciousness is essential in any text in communication. In this seventh edition, this cultural consciousness and coverage is seen in two major ways:

- Unit 6 (Culture in Communication) covers the importance of culture to all communication, explains essential concepts and theories, and introduces intercultural communication and the principles for making such communications more effective. This Unit replaces the previous edition's Units 22 and 23. This change allows the introduction of culture much earlier in the semester and emphasizes culture as a foundation concept essential to all areas of communication. New material includes the areas of intercultural communication; cultural maxims; power distances; racist, sexist, and heterosexist listening; a self-test of one's own cultural values and how these influence communication; an improved organizational system for the principles of intercultural communication; and a consideration of cultural factors that influence listening.
- Numerous sections, many of which are major Unit divisions, discuss cultural variations in communication and appear throughout the text as well. Major ones that are new to this edition include: culture and human communication (Unit 1), cultural variation in implicit personality theory (Unit 3), listening and culture (Unit 4), nonverbal cultural taboos (Unit 6), cultural identifiers (Unit 7), the social clock (Unit 10), equity in cultural perspective (Unit 12), culture and relationships (Unit 13), cultural context of conflict (Unit 14), face and conflict (Unit 14), cultural differences in love (Unit 15), small groups and culture (Unit 17), membership and leadership in cultural perspective (Unit 18), culture and apprehension (Unit 21), and cultural differences in criticism (Unit 22).

Expanded Coverage of Listening

The coverage of listening has been greatly expanded. The listening unit remains but is supplemented by nine **Listen to This** boxes positioned throughout the text. These boxes, which build on the foundation for listening covered in Unit 4, stress the importance and skills of listening to specific areas of human communication. They cover the following:

- racist, sexist, and heterosexist listening (Unit 6)
- some difficult listeners (Unit 13)
- listening and gender (Unit 15)
- active listening (Unit 16)
- listening to new ideas (Unit 17)
- listening for groupthink (Unit 18)
- power listening (Unit 19)
- ethical listening (Unit 21)
- critical listening (Unit 23)

Integrated Coverage of Mass Media

The coverage of mass media, formerly Units 24 and 25, has been completely revised. Instead of separate units on mass communication, 17 **Media Watch** boxes are presented throughout the text. These boxes integrate mass media with the other areas of communication and sensitize the reader to the ever-present, ever-influential media. They also function to connect the concepts of interpersonal, small group, and public speaking with the concepts and theories in mass communication. These Media Watch boxes cover three major areas:

Media theories
- cultivation theory (Unit 3)
- cultural imperialism (Unit 6)
- spiral of silence theory (Unit 10)
- uses and gratifications theory (Unit 14)
- agenda-setting theory (Unit 18)
- the knowledge gap hypothesis (Unit 19)

Central concepts
- media ethics (Unit 1)
- outing (Unit 5)
- objectivity in the media (Unit 7)
- gatekeepers (Unit 15)
- media credibility (Unit 22)
- reversing the process of media influence (Unit 23)

Types and forms of media
- talk radio (Unit 4)
- human communication in cyberspace (Unit 8)
- legible clothing (Unit 11)
- parasocial relationships (Unit 12)
- the television talk show (Unit 20)

Expanded Interactive Pedagogy

As in the previous edition, this text continues to emphasize new and useful pedagogical aids, especially those that are interactive (at least as far as the print medium allows), to help the student master both the theory and the skills of human communication.

The most popular interactive component, the **self-tests,** have been increased in number from 22 to 28. These self-tests, designed to help personalize the material, appear throughout the text. Sixteen of these are research-based instruments and 12 serve a more purely pedagogical function.

Throughout the text are **interactive discussions** that ask the reader to respond to issues just discussed or about to be discussed. These interactive discussions—introduced in the previous edition—now cover approximately 70 issues and appear throughout the text, introduced by the title **"Think about."** Some of the applications, formerly at the end of each unit, have been recast into these integrated interactive components.

Those **exercises** that are better conducted in groups or with an entire class or as written assignments have been deleted from the text and now constitute a separate section of the Instructor's Manual.

Critical thinking questions appear at the end of each unit—replacing the end-of-part questions that appeared in the last edition. These questions will prove especially useful for expanding and evaluating the concepts, theories, and research findings discussed in the text. The questions ask the reader to interact with the material in different ways: (1) to personalize the material; (2) to apply the concepts and principles to other contexts, (3) to evaluate principles or conclusions, and (4) to identify ways to find answers to questions. The questions should thus serve four major critical thinking skills: self-analysis, application, evaluation, and discovery.

Other pedagogical aids include:

Unit openers identify the major topics covered in the unit and the learning goals that the reader should reach after reading the unit.

Suggestions for approaching each area continue to appear in the part openers and provide some general principles to keep in mind in reading the units.

Learning Aid Notes accompanying the first appearance of each of the major pedagogical aids explain how the reader can get the most benefit from them.

A **glossary** at the end of the book provides brief definitions of the significant terms in the study of human communication.

Coverage of Public Communication, Its Theory and Skills

Three units focus on public speaking. The first two (Units 21 and 22) cover the essential theories and principles of informative and persuasive speaking, apprehension, and criticism. Unit 23 provides a "how-to" guide to preparing and presenting a public speech. A separate booklet, "The Public Speaking Guide," available to users of *Human Communication,* at the option of the instructor and at no extra cost, provides more detailed coverage of the practical skills of preparing and presenting a speech.

Expanded Focus on Ethics

Ethics is given expanded coverage in this edition. Ethics is introduced in Unit 1, where its central role in communication is considered. An interactive discussion illustrates its relevance to all forms of communication. Media ethics is also considered in a separate Media Watch box in Unit 1. Focused discussions of ethical issues are also included in Unit 8, in which gossip and lying are considered, and in Unit 21, in which both the ethics of research and ethical listening are discussed. Ethics is naturally a part of all communication topics and therefore ethical issues are referred to repeatedly throughout the text.

New Organizational Structure

Those familiar with the previous editions will note a major organizational change. Especially significant organizational changes include: (1) the discussion of culture, formerly in Units 22 and 23, now appears as Unit 6; (2) the coverage of media, formerly Units 24 and 25, has been completely revised and is now presented in Media Watch boxes positioned throughout the text; (3) conversation is now discussed within the interpersonal area; and interviewing is now covered in the small group and organization area.

SUPPLEMENTARY MATERIALS

This text comes with a variety of supplementary aids to make using this book more effective and for helping students get the most out of the course experience.

Public Speaking Guide

A 116 page supplement, *The Public Speaking Guide,* covers the essential practical skills of public speaking. It is available with this text at the option of the instructor and at no extra cost.

Instructor's Manual and Test Bank

The Instructor's Manual prepared by Thomas Veenendall of Montclair State University includes unit planners containing suggested teaching approaches, sample syllabi, examination questions and answers, guidelines for using the application exercises, and transparency masters that highlight essential terms and principles. In addition, it contains a handbook of experiential vehicles in human communication with suggestions for coordinating these exercises with specific text units.

Transparency Packet

New to this edition is a set of 75 full-color transparencies. These transparencies reproduce the major figures and tables of the text and will prove especially useful for class lectures. They are free to qualified adoptors of the book.

TestMaster

The complete test bank, arranged by unit, is available on diskette for IBM PC, Mac, and compatibles. TestMaster allows complete customizing capabilities.

Grades

A grade keeping and classroom management software program for IBM PC, Mac, and compatibles that can maintain data for up to 200 students is available from the publisher.

The Addison Wesley Longman Communication Video Library

A wide variety of videos is available to users and cover such topics as effective listening, interpersonal relationships, interviewing, small group communication, and public speaking. Since these videos are updated regularly, talk with your sales representative about obtaining them.

ACKNOWLEDGMENTS

It is a pleasure to thank the many people who have had an influence on the writing and production of this book. My major debt is to those colleagues who reviewed the manuscript for this edition and the previous editions and have given freely of their insights, suggestions, criticisms, time, and energy. To those who reviewed previous editions and to whose insights I return repeatedly, I am most grateful. Thank you:

Steven A. Beebe, Southwest Texas State University; Ernest G. Bormann, University of Minnesota; Bernard Brommel, Northeastern Illinois University; Edward Brown, Abilene Christian University; Marcia L. Dewhurst, Ohio State University; Robert Dixon, St. Louis Community College at Meramac; Joseph R. Dominick, University of Georgia; Kenneth D. Frandsen, University of New Mexico; Fran Franklin, University of Arkansas; Ted Hindemarsh, Brigham Young University; Fred Jandt, California State University at San Bernardino; Stephen Johnson, Freed-Hardeman College; Robert Kastenbaum, Arizona State University; Albert M. Katz, University of Wisconsin, Superior; Kathleen Kendall, State University of New York, Albany; Elaine Klein, Westchester Community College; Joel Litvin, Bridgewater State College; Don B. Morlan, University of Dayton; Jon F. Nussbaum, University of Oklahoma; Dorman Picklesimer, Jr., Boston College; George Ray, Cleveland State University; Mark V. Redmond, Iowa State University; Armeda C. Reitzel, Humboldt State University; Thomas Ruddick, Edison State College; Robert M. Shuter, Marquette University; Gail Sorenson, California State University at Fresno; James S. Taylor, Houston Baptist University; Robert Worthington, New Mexico State University; and Christopher Zahn, Cleveland State University.

To those who reviewed the sixth edition and the manuscript for the present edition and shared many and valuable insights, I am most appreciative. Thank you:

Donald E. Baker, North Carolina Agricultural and Technical State University; Michael Bruner, University of North Texas; Dennis Doyle, Central College; Angela Gruppas, St. Louis Community College at Meramec; Michael Hecht, Arizona State University; Mary Hinchcliff-Pelias, Southern Illinois University; David D. Hudson, Golden West College; Edward Lee Lamoureux, Bradley University; Larry Z. Leslie, University of South Florida; Lisa Merrill, Hofstra University; Dreama Moon, Arizona State University; Jerry S. Phillips, Trinity Valley Community College; Henry L. Roubicek, The University of Houston—Downtown; Don W. Stacks, University of Miami; Gretchen Aggertt Weber, Indiana State University; and Doris Werkman, Portland Community College.

I also wish to thank the many people at Longman who together contributed their time and talents to make this book both attractive and functional. Thank you:

Cynthia Biron, immediate past editor, and Deirdre Cavanaugh, present editor, for all your hard work and goodwill; Dawn Groundwater, developmental editor, for securing and coordinating reviews, for your numerous suggestions for improvement, and for guiding the revision process at all its stages; Peter Glovin, marketing manager, for always useful advice; and Edith Baltazar and Lois Lombardo, project editors, for guiding the transition from manuscript to completed text with skill. I am in your debt.

JOSEPH A. DEVITO

HUMAN COMMUNICATION

one parT

Foundations of Human Communication

This first part of *Human Communication* looks at the basic concepts and principles of communication. Unit 1 considers the nature and areas of communication, its most important components, and its purposes. Unit 2 covers the basic principles of human communication and further explores how communication works. Units 3 and 4 focus on the processes involved in receiving messages: perception and listening. Unit 5 looks at the self—self-concept, self-awareness, self-esteem, and self-disclosure. The last unit in this part, Unit 6, focuses on the concept of culture and how culture influences all aspects of human communication.

In approaching the study of human communication, keep the following in mind:

- The study of human communication involves not only theory and research but also practical skills for increasing the effectiveness of communication. Seek to understand the theories, and through them, improve your skills.
- The ideas and principles discussed throughout this book relate directly to your everyday communications. Try, for instance, to recall examples from your own communications that illustrate the ideas considered here. This will help make the material more personal and easier to assimilate and internalize.
- The principles of human communication apply to you as both speaker and listener. See yourself and the principles from the perspectives of both sending and receiving messages.

one unit

Preliminaries to Human Communication

unit contents

unit goals

After completing this unit, you should be able to

1. identify the major areas of human communication
2. explain the nature of culture and its relevance to human communication
3. define *communication* and its components: communication context, sources-receivers, encoding-decoding, competence, messages, channel feedback, feedforward, noise, communication effect, and ethics
4. explain the five purposes of communication

Of all the knowledge and skills you have, those concerning communication are among the most important and useful. Communication will always play a crucial part in your personal and professional lives and its mastery will influence how effectively you live these lives.

THE AREAS OF HUMAN COMMUNICATION

In **intrapersonal communication** you talk with yourself. You talk with, learn about, and evaluate yourself; persuade yourself of this or that; reason about possible decisions to make; and rehearse the messages you intend to send to others.

Through **interpersonal communication** you interact with others, learn about them and about yourself, and reveal yourself to others. Whether with new acquaintances, old friends, lovers, or family members, it is through interpersonal communication that you establish, maintain, sometimes destroy—and sometimes repair—your personal relationships.

In **small group and organizational communication** you interact with others, solving problems, developing new ideas, and sharing knowledge and experiences. From the employment interview to the executive board meeting, from the informal social group having coffee to the formal meeting discussing issues of international concern, your work and social life are lived largely in small groups. Through an **interview** you secure information from those with special knowledge and present yourself as a valuable potential employee.

Through **public communication**, others inform and persuade you. And you in turn inform and persuade others—to do, to buy, or to think in a particular way, or to change an attitude, opinion, or value.

Through **mass communication** you are entertained, informed, and persuaded by the media—movies, television, radio, newspapers, and books. Also, through your viewing habits and buying patterns, you in turn influence the media's form and content.

With the exception of intrapersonal communication, all other forms of communication may be **intercultural,** in which you communicate with members from other cultures who follow different customs, roles, and rules. Perhaps most important, you come to understand new ways of thinking and new ways of behaving and begin to see the tremendous variety in human thought and experience.

This book, then, is about these types of communication and about your personal communications. Its major goal is to explain the concepts and principles, the theory and research central to these varied areas of human communications. Another goal is to provide the foundation and direction for learning the skills of human communication and increase your own communication competency. The relevance of these skills is seen throughout the communication spectrum; it is the difference between

- the self-confident and the self-conscious speaker
- the person who is hired and the one is passed over
- the couple who argue constructively and the couple who argue by hurting each other and eventually destroying their relationship
- the group member who is too self-focused to listen openly and contribute to the group's goals and the member who helps accomplish the group's task *and* satisfy the interpersonal needs of the members
- the public speaker who lacks credibility and persuasive appeal and the speaker audiences believe and follow

TABLE 1.1

human communication

This table identifies and arranges the forms of communication in terms of the number of persons involved, from one (in intrapersonal communicaions) to millions (in mass communication). It also echoes (in general) the progression of topics in this book.

Areas of Human Communication	Some Common Purposes	Some Theory-related Concerns	Some Skills-related Concerns
Intrapersonal: communication with oneself	To think, reason, analyze, reflect	How does one's self-concept develop? How does one's self-concept influence communication? How can problem-solving and analyzing abilities be improved and taught? What is the relationship between personality and communication?	Enhancing self-esteem, increasing self-awareness, improving problem-solving and analyzing abilities, increasing self-control, reducing stress, managing interpersonal conflict
Interpersonal: communication between two persons	To discover, relate, influence, play, help	What is interpersonal effectiveness? Why do people develop relationships? What holds friends, lovers, and families together? What tears them apart? How can relationships be repaired?	Increasing effectiveness in one-to-one communication, developing and maintaining effective relationships (friendship, love, family), improving conflict resolution abilities
Small group: communication within a small group of persons	To share information, generate ideas, solve problems, help	What makes a leader? What type of leadership works best? What roles do members serve in groups? What do groups do well and what do they fail to do well? How can groups be made more effective?	Increasing effectiveness as a group member, improving leadership abilities, using groups to achieve specific purposes (for example, solving problems, generating ideas)
Organizational: communication within a formal organization	To increase productivity, raise morale, inform, persuade	What makes an effective organization? What needs must an organization meet to ensure worker morale and productivity? How does communication work in an organization?	Improving efficiency of upward, downward, and lateral communication; using communication to improve morale and increase productivity; reducing information overload; structuring networks to increase efficiency
Public: communication of speaker to audience	To inform, persuade, entertain	What kinds of organizational structure work best in informative and persuasive speaking? How can audiences be most effectively analyzed and adapted to? How can ideas be best developed for communication to an audience?	Communicating information more effectively; increasing persuasive abilities; developing, organizing, styling, and delivering messages with greater effectiveness
Mass: communication addressed to an extremely large audience, mediated by audio and/or visual means	To entertain, persuade, and inform	What functions do the media serve? How do the media influence us? How can we influence the media? In what ways is information censored by the media for the public? How does advertising work?	Improving our ability to use the media to greater effectiveness, increasing our ability to control the media, avoiding being taken in by advertisements and tabloid journalism

***LEARNING AID NOTE.** This table is designed to give you a broad overview of the vast area of communication. More specific area tables appear in four other places in the text: Unit 6 (intercultural communication), 12 (interpersonal communication and relationships), 17 (small group and organizational communication), and 21 (public communication). All of these are designed to highlight the major areas of communication and not to establish rigid divisions between areas.

- the uncritical consumer of media who is influenced without awareness and the critical, watchful consumer who uses media constructively

The areas of human communication, some common purposes of each area, and some theory- and skills-related concerns are summarized in Table 1.1. This table will give you a broad overview of the field of human communication and will preview the entire text.

Communication is an enormous field and for many of you this is your first academic exposure to it. It will take a great deal of time and effort to even begin mastering the theories and principles of human communication. Fortunately, the energy that you will put into studying the material in this book and this course will be more than repaid by the knowledge you will gain and the skills you will acquire and improve.

Your beliefs about communication influence how you communicate (as both sender and receiver) and how you approach the study of communication. Before launching into the content of human communication, try examining these beliefs by taking the self-test, "What Do You Believe About Communication?"

CULTURE AND HUMAN COMMUNICATION

A walk through any large city, many small towns, and through just about any college campus will convince you that the United States is largely a collection of lots of different cultures (see Figure 1.1). These cultures coexist somewhat separately but also with each influencing the others. This coexistence has led some re-

SELF-TEST*
what do you believe about communication?

Respond to each of the following statements with T if you believe the statement is usually true and F if you believe the statement is usually false.

_____ 1. Good communicators are born, not made.
_____ 2. The more a couple communicates, the better their relationship will be.
_____ 3. Unlike effective speaking, effective listening cannot be taught.
_____ 4. Opening lines such as "How are you?" or "Fine weather today" or "Have you got a light?" serve no really useful communication purpose.
_____ 5. When two people are in a close relationship for a long period of time, one should not have to communicate his or her needs and wants, the other person should know what these are.
_____ 6. When verbal and nonverbal messages contradict each other, people believe the verbal message.
_____ 7. Complete openness should be the goal of any meaningful interpersonal relationship.
_____ 8. When there is interpersonal conflict, each person should aim to win even at the expense of the other person.
_____ 9. Like good communicators, leaders are born, not made.
_____ 10. Fear of speaking in public is detrimental and must be eliminated.

Thinking Critically About Your Beliefs About Communication. As you may have figured out, all ten statements are false. As you read through the text, you will discover not only why these statements are false but, more importantly, some of the problems that can arise when people act on the basis of such misconceptions about communication. You will also see that people from different cultures have very different beliefs about communication and thus very different ways of communicating.

***LEARNING AID NOTE.** Throughout this text there are 28 self-tests designed to help personalize the material discussed. They ask you to pause and reflect on your own thoughts and behaviors. In working with these self-tests, focus on the statements in the test, on the issues they raise, and on the thoughts they help generate. The number you get "right" or "wrong" or the score you get (some tests yield scores for comparison purposes) is far less important.

searchers to refer to these cultures as co-cultures (Samovar & Porter 1994, Jandt 1995). Try to see communication, in all its forms, within this cultural context.

The Relevance of Culture

There are lots of reasons for the cultural emphasis you will find in this book, and in many of your other textbooks. Most obviously, perhaps, are the vast demographic changes taking place throughout the United States. Whereas at one time, the United States was largely a country populated by Europeans, it is now a country greatly influenced by the enormous number of new citizens from Latin and South America, Africa, and Asia. The same is true to an even greater extent on college and university campuses throughout the United States. With these changes have come different communication customs and the need to understand and adapt to new ways of looking at communication.

We are also living at a time when people have become increasingly sensitive to cultural differences. American society has moved from an originally assimilationist perspective (people should leave their native culture behind and adapt to their new culture) to one that values cultural diversity (people should retain their native cultural ways). With some notable exceptions—hate speech, racism, sexism, homophobia, and classism come quickly to mind—we are now more concerned with saying the right thing and with ultimately developing a society in which all cultures can coexist and enrich each other. At the same time, the ability to interact effectively with members of other cultures often translates into financial gain and increased employment opportunities and advancement prospects. The increased economic interdependence of the United States and widely different cultures makes it essential to gain the needed intercultural communication understanding and skills.

The Aim of a Cultural Perspective

Because culture permeates all forms of communication, it is necessary to understand its influences in order to understand how communication works and master its skills. As illustrated throughout this text,

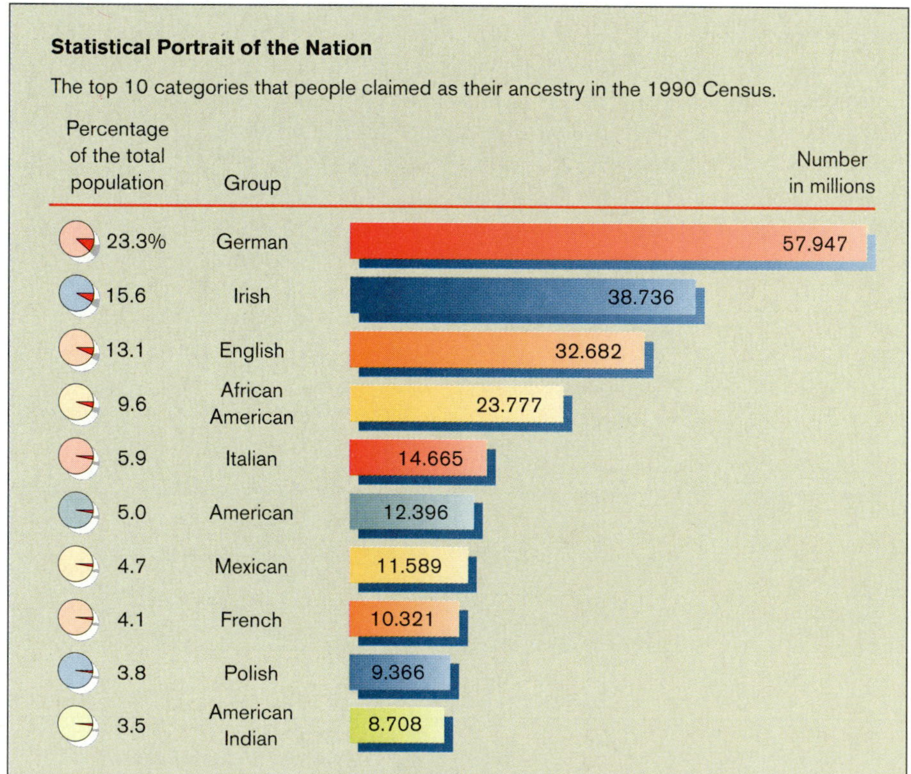

FIGURE 1.1 Ancestry of U.S. residents. With immigration patterns changing so rapidly, the portrait illustrated here is likely to look very different in the coming years. What do you think the top ten categories that people claim as their ancestry will be in the census for the year 2000? For the year 2020?

culture influences communications of all types. It influences what you say to yourself and how you converse with friends, lovers, and family every day. It influences how you interact in groups and how much importance you place on the group versus the individual. It influences the topics you talk about and the strategies you use in communicating information or in persuading. It also influences how you use the media and in the credibility you attribute to them.

A cultural emphasis helps distinguish what is universal (true for all people) from what is relative (true for people in one culture and not true for people in other cultures) (Matsumoto 1994). The principles for communicating information and for changing listeners' attitudes, for example, will vary from one culture to another. If you are to understand communication, then you need to know how its principles vary and how the principles must be qualified and adjusted on the basis of cultural differences.

Of course this cultural understanding is needed to communicate effectively in a wide variety of intercultural situations. Success in interpersonal, small group, or public speaking—on your job and in your social life—will depend in great part on your understanding of and your ability to communicate effectively with persons who are culturally different.

The cultural emphasis in this text will be seen in two ways. First, cultural issues are integrated into the text as they are appropriate. Thus, for example, when discussing self-disclosure, we also consider how different cultures view this form of communication very differently. Similarly, when considering criticism, we examine how members from different cultures see criticism differently. Second, a complete unit (Unit 6) is devoted to the role of culture in communication and introduces intercultural communication where the theories and principles of this rapidly growing area of human communication are considered.

THE COMPONENTS OF HUMAN COMMUNICATION

Communication refers to the act, by one or more persons, of sending and receiving messages that are distorted by noise, occur within a context, have some effect, and provide some opportunity for feedback. Figure 1.2 illustrates what we might call the universals of communication. It contains the elements present in every communication act, regardless of whether it is intrapersonal, interpersonal, small group, public speaking, or mass communication.

Communication Context

All communication takes place in a **context** that has at least four dimensions: physical, cultural, social-psychological, and temporal. The *physical context* is the tangible or concrete environment in which communication takes place—the room or hallway or park. This

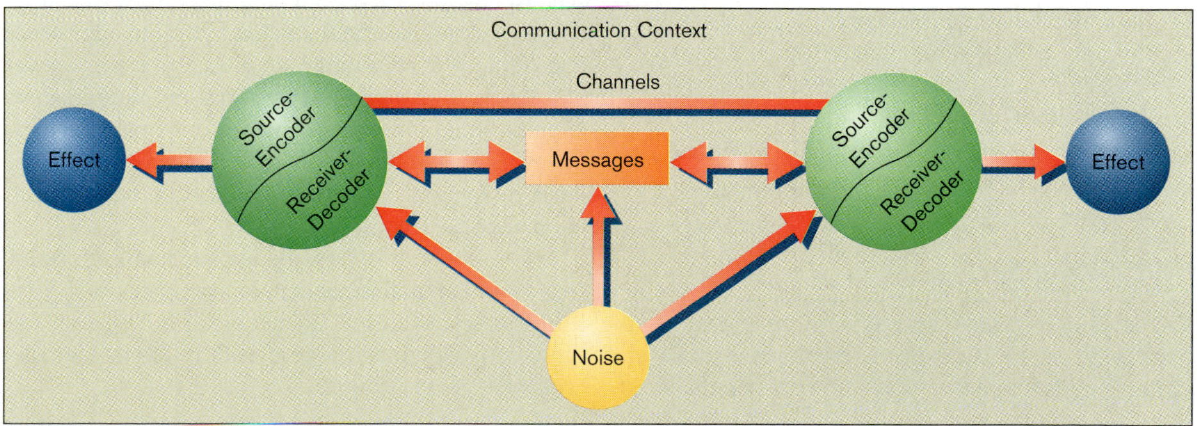

FIGURE 1.2 The universals of human communication. This is a simplified view of some essentials of human communication and their relationship to each other. Messages (including feedforward and feedback) are sent simultaneously through a variety of channels from one encoder-decoder to another. The communication process takes place in a context (physical, cultural, social-psychological, and temporal) and is subjected to interference by noise (physical, psychological, semantic). The interaction of messages with the encoder-decoder lead to some effect.

physical context exerts some influence on the content (what you say) as well as the form (how you say it) of your messages.

The *cultural context* refers to the communicators' rules and norms, beliefs and attitudes that are transmitted from one generation to another. For example, in some cultures it is considered polite to talk to strangers; in others, it is something to avoid. In some cultures, direct eye contact between child and adult signifies directness and honesty; in others it signifies defiance and lack of respect.

The *social-psychological context* includes, for example, the status relationships among the participants, the roles and the games that people play, and the cultural rules of the society in which they are communicating. It also includes the friendliness or unfriendliness, formality or informality, and seriousness or humorousness of the situation. Communication that would be permitted at a graduation party may not be considered appropriate in a hospital.

The *temporal (or time) context* includes the time of day as well as the time in history in which the communication takes place. For many people, the morning is not a time for communication; for others, the morning is ideal. Historical context is no less important because the appropriateness and impact of messages depend, in part, on the time in which they are uttered. Consider, for example, how messages on racial, sexual, or religious attitudes and values would be differently framed and responded to in different times in history.

Even more important is how a particular message fits into the temporal sequence of communication events. For example, consider the varied meanings a "simple" compliment paid to a friend would have depending on whether you said it immediately after your friend paid you a compliment, immediately before you asked your friend for a favor, or during an argument.

THINK ABOUT *

Think about how these four dimensions of context interact with one another. For example, how might arriving late for a date (temporal context) be influenced by the cultural context? How might arriving late lead to changes in the social-psychological context and how might these changes lead to changes in the physical context in which future communications take place? How might communicating in a large lecture course be influenced by the culture of the students or the instructor? How might communication in an organization be influenced by the social-psychological context?

Sources-Receivers

The hyphenated term *sources-receivers* emphasizes that each person involved in communication is both a **source** (or speaker) and a **receiver** (or listener). You send messages when you speak, write, gesture, or smile. You are a receiver of messages by listening, reading, smelling, and so on. As you send messages, however, you are also receiving messages. You are receiving your own messages (you hear yourself, you feel your own movements, you see many of your own gestures) and you are receiving the messages of the other person—visually, aurally, or even through touch and smell. You look at anyone you speak to for responses—approval, understanding, sympathy, agreement, and so on. As you decipher these nonverbal signals, you are performing receiving functions.

Source-Receiver Encoding-Decoding

In communication we refer to the act of producing messages—for example, speaking or writing—as encoding. By putting our ideas into sound waves or on paper we are putting these ideas into a code, hence **encoding.** We refer to the act of receiving messages—for example, listening or reading—as decoding. By translating sound waves or words on paper into ideas you take them out of code, hence **decoding.** Thus we refer to speakers or writers as encoders, and listeners or readers as decoders.

Like source-receiver, the hyphenated term *encoding-decoding* emphasizes that you perform these functions simultaneously. As you speak (encoding), you are also deciphering the responses of the listener (decoding).

***LEARNING AID NOTE.** View these **Think Abouts** as invitations to interact with the ideas presented here even more actively than you would with most textbook material. They are signals to personalize the material, to ask yourself what you would say or do in each of the cases cited. When you see these **Think Abouts**, pause and consider the situations and especially how you would communicate in them.

Why is it so important to include "culture" as part of communication competence?

Source-Receiver Communicative Competence

Communicative competence refers to a person's knowledge of the social aspects of communication (Rubin 1982, 1985; Spitzberg & Cupach 1989). It includes such knowledge as the role the context plays in influencing the content and form of communication messages—for example, the knowledge that in certain contexts and with certain listeners one topic is appropriate and another is not. Knowledge about the rules of nonverbal behavior, for example, the appropriateness of touching, vocal volume, and physical closeness, is also part of communicative competence.

You learn communicative competence by observing others, by trial and error, and by explicit instruction (for example, as in this course and this text). One of the major goals of this text and this course is to spell out the nature of communicative competence and to increase your own competence. By increasing your competence, you will have available a broader range of options for all your communications. The more you know about communication (the greater your competence), the more choices you will have available for your day-to-day communications. The process is comparable to learning vocabulary: the greater your vocabulary, the more ways you have for expressing yourself.

Culture and Competence

Competence is specific to a given culture. The principles of effective communication will vary from one culture to another; what will prove effective in one culture may prove ineffective in another. For example, in the United States business executives will get right down to business during the first several minutes of a meeting; in Japan business executives interact socially for an extended period of time and try to find out something about each other. Thus, the small group communication principle influenced by U.S. culture would advise participants to get down to the meeting's agenda during the first five or ten minutes. The principle influenced by Japanese culture would have participants avoid dealing with business until all members of the group had socialized sufficiently and felt they knew each other well enough to begin business negotiations. Of course, neither principle is right or wrong: each is effective within its own culture and each is ineffective outside its own culture.

Messages and Channels

Communication messages take many forms. You send and receive messages through any one or any combination of sensory organs. Although you may customarily think of messages as being verbal (oral or writ-

How many dimensions of context (physical, temporal, social-psychological, and cultural) can you identify as potentially influencing the interaction shown in this photo? In what specific ways might these dimensions influence the communications taking place?

ten), you also communicate nonverbally. For example, the clothes you wear, and the way you walk, shake hands, cock your head, comb your hair, sit, and smile all send messages. Everything about you communicates.

The communication channel is the medium through which the message passes. Communication rarely takes place over only one channel; you may use two, three, or four different channels simultaneously. For example, in face-to-face interactions you speak and listen (vocal channel), but you also gesture and receive these signals visually (visual channel). In addition you emit and detect odors (olfactory channel). Often you touch another person, and this too communicates (tactile channel).

Two special types of messages need to be explained more fully: these are feedback (the messages you send that are reactions to other messages) and feedforward (the messages you send as preface to your "main" messages).

Feedback Messages

Throughout the listening process, a listener gives a speaker **feedback**—messages sent back to the speaker reacting to what is said (Clement & Frandsen 1976). Feedback tells the speaker what effect he or she is having on the listener(s). On the basis of this feedback, the speaker may adjust the messages by strengthening, deemphasizing, or changing the content or form of the messages. These adjustments then serve as feedback to the receiver who, in response, readjusts his or her feedback messages. The process is a circular one, with one person's feedback serving as the stimulus for the other person's feedback, just as any message serves as the stimulus for another person's message.

In the diagram of the universals of communication (see Figure 1.2), the arrows from source-receiver to effect and from one source-receiver to the other source-receiver go in both directions to illustrate the notion of feedback. When you speak to another person you also hear yourself. That is, you get feedback from your own messages; you hear what you say, you feel the way you move, you see what you write.

In addition to this self-feedback, you get feedback from others, which can take many forms. A frown or a smile, a yea or a nay, a pat on the back or a punch in the mouth are all types of feedback.

Feedback can be looked upon in terms of five important dimensions: positive-negative, person focused-message focused, immediate-delayed, low monitoring-high monitoring, and critical-supportive. To use feedback effectively, then, you need to make educated choices along these dimensions:

Positive ___:___:___:___:___:___:___ Negative
Person-focused ___:___:___:___:___:___:___ Message-focused
Immediate ___:___:___:___:___:___:___ Delayed
Low Monitoring ___:___:___:___:___:___:___ High Monitoring
Supportive ___:___:___:___:___:___:___ Critical

It may be argued that, generally at least, your interpersonal relationships would be characterized as existing toward the left side of the diagram. This "feedback model of relationships" would characterize close or intimate personal relationships as involving feedback that is strongly positive, person-focused, immediate, low in monitoring, and supportive. Acquaintance relationships might involve feedback somewhere in the middle of these scales. Relationships with those you dislike would involve feedback close to the right side of the scales, for example, negative, message-focused, delayed, highly monitored, and critical.

Positive-Negative. Positive feedback (applause, smiles, head nods signifying approval) tells the speaker that the message is being well received and that he or she should continue speaking in the same general mode. Negative feedback (boos, frowns and puzzled looks, and gestures signifying disapproval) tells the speaker that something is wrong and that some adjustment needs to be made.

Person-Focused and Message-Focused. Feedback may center on the person ("You're sweet," "You have a great smile") or on the message ("Can you repeat that phone number?" "Your argument is a good one"). Especially in giving criticism (as in public speaking) it is important to make clear that your feedback relates to, say, the organization of the speech and not to the speaker himself or herself.

Immediate-Delayed. In interpersonal situations, feedback is most often sent immediately after the message is received. In other communication situations, however, the feedback may be delayed. Instructor evaluation questionnaires completed at the end of a course provide feedback long after the class began. When you applaud or ask questions of the public speaker, the feedback is also delayed. In interview situations, the feedback may come weeks afterward. In media situations, some feedback comes immediately through, for example, Nielsen ratings, while other feedback comes much later through viewing and buying patterns.

Low Monitoring-High Monitoring. Feedback varies from the spontaneous and totally honest reaction (low-monitored feedback) to the carefully constructed response designed to serve a specific purpose (high-monitored feedback). In most interpersonal situations you probably give feedback spontaneously; you allow your responses to show without any monitoring. At other times, however, you may be more guarded as when your boss asks you how you like your job or when your grandfather asks what you think of his new motorcycle outfit.

Supportive-Critical. Supportive feedback confirms the person and what that person says; it occurs when, for example, you console another, when you encourage the other to talk, or when you affirm the person's self-definition. Critical feedback, on the other hand, is evaluative. When you give critical feedback you judge another's performance as in, for example, evaluating a speech or coaching someone learning a new skill.

These categories are not exclusive. Feedback does not have to be either critical or supportive; it can be both. Thus, in teaching someone how to become a more effective interviewer, you might critically evaluate a specific interview but you might also express support for the effort. Similarly, you might respond to a friend's question immediately and then after a day or two elaborate on your response. Each feedback opportunity will, then, present you with choices along at least these five dimensions.

THINK ABOUT

Think about, for example, how you would give feedback (positive or negative? person-focused or message-focused? immediate or delayed? low-monitoring or high-monitoring? supportive or critical?) in these varied situations:

- your mother asks how you liked the dinner she prepared
- a friend—who you like but do not have romantic feelings for—asks you for a date
- your instructor asks you to evaluate the course
- an interviewer asks if you want a credit card
- a homeless person smiles at you on the street
- a colleague at work tells a racist joke

Feedforward Messages

Feedforward is information you provide before sending your primary messages (Richards 1951) revealing something about the messages to come. Feedforward includes such diverse examples as the preface or the table of contents to a book, the opening paragraph of a chapter, movie previews, magazine covers, and introductions in public speeches.

Feedforward messages are examples of metamessages—messages that communicate about other messages. Such information may be verbal ("Wait until you hear this one") or nonverbal (a prolonged pause or hands motioning for silence to signal that an important message is about to be spoken). Or, as is most often the case, it is some combination of verbal and nonverbal signals. Feedforward may refer to the content of the message to follow ("I'll tell you exactly what they said to each other") or to the form ("I won't spare you the gory details"). Feedforward has four major functions: (1) to open the channels of communication, (2) to preview the message, (3) to altercast, and (4) to disclaim.

To Open the Channels of Communication. Phatic **communion** refers to messages that open the channels of communication rather than communicate information (Malinowski 1923). Phatic communion is a perfect example of feedforward. It is information that tells us that the normal, expected, and accepted rules of interaction will be in effect. It tells us another person is willing to communicate. The infamous "opening line" ("Have you got a match?" or "Haven't we met before?") is a clear example of phatic communion. When such phatic messages do not precede an initial interaction, you sense that something is wrong and may conclude that the speaker lacks the basic skills of communication.

To Preview Future Messages. Feedforward messages frequently preview other messages. Feedforward may, for example, preview the content ("I'm afraid I have bad news for you"), the importance ("Listen to this before you make a move"), the form or style ("I'll be brief"), and the positive or negative quality of subsequent messages ("You're not going to like this, but here's what I heard").

To Altercast. Feedforward is often used to place the receiver in a specific role and to request that the receiver respond to you in terms of this assumed role. This process, known as **altercasting,** asks the receiver to approach your message from a particular role or even as someone else (McLaughlin 1984; Weinstein & Deutschberger 1963; Johnson 1993). For example, you might ask a friend, "As an advertising executive, what do you think of corrective advertising?" This question casts your friend into the role of advertising executive (rather than parent, Democrat, or Baptist, for example). It asks your friend to answer from a particular perspective.

To Disclaim. The **disclaimer** is a statement that aims to ensure that your message will be understood and will not reflect negatively on you. Disclaimers try to persuade the listener to hear your message as you wish it to be heard rather than through some assumption that might reflect negatively on you (Hewitt & Stokes 1975). For example, to ensure that people listen to you fairly you might disclaim any thought that you are sexist and say, for example, "I'm no sexist, but . . . ." (The disclaimer is discussed in greater detail in Unit 13.)

Noise

Noise is a disturbance in communication that distorts the message. Noise prevents the receiver from getting the message the source is sending. Noise is present in a communication system to the extent that the message sent differs from the message received. The noise may be physical (others talking in the background), psychological (preconceived ideas), or semantic (misunderstood meanings). Table 1.2 identifies these three major types of noise in more detail.

Noise is inevitable. All communications contain noise of some kind, and although you cannot eliminate noise completely, you can reduce noise and its effects. Making your language more precise, acquiring the skills for sending and receiving nonverbal messages, and improving your listening and feedback skills are some ways you can combat the interference of noise.

Communication Effects

Communication always has some effect on one or more persons involved in the communication act. For every communication act, there is some consequence. For example, you may gain knowledge or learn how to analyze, synthesize, or evaluate something. These are intellectual or cognitive effects. Or you may acquire or change your attitudes, beliefs, emotions, and feelings. These are affective effects. You may even learn new bodily movements, such as throwing a ball or painting a picture, as well as appropriate verbal and nonverbal behaviors. These are psychomotor effects.

TABLE 1.2
three types of noise

The concept of noise may be viewed more broadly than depicted here, for example, the concept of noise may be extended to cultural noise, political noise, emotional noise, or economic noise. How would you define such types of noise? Can you give specific examples to illustrate these noise types?

Type	Definition	Example
Physical	Interference with the physical transmission of the message	Screeching of passing cars, hum of computer, sunglasses
Psychological	Cognitive or mental interference	Biases and prejudices in senders and receivers, closed-mindedness
Semantic	Speaker and listener assigning different meanings	People speaking different languages, use of jargon or overly complex terms not understood by listener

Ethics and Individual Choice

Because communication has consequences, it also involves questions of ethics, of right and wrong (Bok 1978; Jaksa & Pritchard 1994). For example, while it may be effective to exaggerate or even lie in attempting to sell a product or in getting elected, it would not be ethical to do so.

The ethical dimension of communication is complicated because ethics is so interwoven with one's personal philosophy of life and the culture in which one is raised that it is difficult to propose guidelines for everyone. Nevertheless, ethical considerations need to be considered as integral to any communication act. The decisions you make concerning communication must be guided by what you consider right as well as what you consider effective.

Whether communications are ethical or unethical may be grounded in the notion of choice and the assumption that people have a right to make their own choices. Communications are ethical when they facilitate an individual's freedom of choice by presenting that person with accurate bases for choice. Communications are unethical when they interfere with an individual's freedom of choice by preventing that person from securing information relevant to the choice. Unethical communications, therefore, would be those that force people (1) to make choices they would not normally make, or (2) to decline to make choices they would normally make. For example, the corporate recruiter might exaggerate the benefits of working for General Dynamo and thus encourage you to make a choice you would not normally make (if you knew the facts) and to decline to make a choice you would have made (for example, to work for National Widget). The ethical communicator, then, provides others with the kind of information that helps them make their own choices.

In this ethic based on choice, however, there are a few qualifications. We assume that these individuals are of an age and mental condition to allow the reasonable execution of free choice. For example, children of 5 or 6 years of age are not ready to make certain choices (for example, to choose their own menu, time for bed, or type of medication to take).

In addition, the circumstances under which one is living can restrict free choice. For example, persons in the military will at times have to give up free choice and eat hamburger rather than steak, wear uniforms rather than jeans, and march rather than stay in bed. Finally, these free choices must not prevent others from making their free choices. We cannot permit a thief to have the freedom of choice to steal, because the granting of that freedom effectively prevents the victims from exercising their free choice—to own property and to be secure in their possessions.

Note too that many cultures throughout the world would not accept the idea that people do have a right to make their own choices and a right to the information bearing on these choices. For example, in many Asian and Arab countries, men, when compared to women, have a greater range of choices and

MEDIA WATCH*

MEDIA ETHICS

As noted in the text, ethics is relevant to all forms of communication; the media are no exception. Because of its great influence, media ethics is important to everyone who listens to the radio, watches television, surfs the Net, or reads a newspaper (Elliott 1993). Here are just a few questions that raise ethical issues relevant to the media. They are presented to stimulate you to think about these important topics and to watch the media more closely.

What do you think of checkbook journalism? Is it ethical for a news organization to pay someone for a story? For example, is it ethical to pay a juror from, say, the O.J. Simpson or Susan Smith trial to reveal what went on during deliberations? Can such payments lead people to distort the accuracy with which they present the events?

At what point, if any, does hate speech fall outside protection by the first amendment? Does a person have the right to say anything? If not, what (specifically) should people be prevented from saying?

Should anonymous speech (for example, writing and distributing social-action pamphlets without any name attached) be granted the same protection as speech that identifies the author? Recently, the Supreme Court upheld the protection of anonymous speech (*New York Times* April 24, 1995, A16). Do you agree?

What about sex, nudity, and violence? Should the media be allowed greater freedom? Should the regulations governing such portrayals be made more stringent? What standard should be used in making decisions about what is "too sexual," "too much nudity," and "too violent?" What do you think of the V-chip that will lock out programs rated as violent? Would you support an S-chip or an N-chip to lock out programs containing sex or nudity?

To what extent can the media be expected to be objective? To what extent can the media be required to give all points of view adequate coverage? If the media must serve the public interest by covering and reporting the news, might they also serve the public interest by withholding information (Merrill, Lee, & Friedlander 1994)?

What do you think of Shield laws—laws protecting reporters from revealing their sources if they promised anonymity in order to secure the information? What do you think of gag rules—rules prohibiting reporters from revealing certain information? What types of information, if any, should be covered by gag rules?

How accurate must advertising be? If misleading statements are made, what form must corrective advertising take? For example, how much corrective advertising should be required to correct a misleading $20 million campaign?

Should advertisers be allowed to appeal directly to children? Because children are especially susceptible to the appeals of advertisers and because they have not built up a sales resistance, should such advertising be limited or monitored (Elliott 1993)?

An advertising campaign for the Italian clothing conglomerate, Benetton, features scenes evoking extremely strong feelings. Scenes include a human body with "H.I.V. Positive" stamped on it and small Latin American children working in a stone quarry. A recent decision by a German court has ruled the ads illegal. A French court fined Benetton $32,000 for the H.I.V. ad (Nash 1995). Do you think the decisions of these courts were fair? Were the ads "a provocative exploitation of suffering" as the French court ruled? Or, are they designed to stimulate awareness and highlight social problems as Benetton argues? Do you think these decisions violate Benetton's (or any person's or company's) freedom of expression?

***LEARNING AID NOTE.** Seventeen Media Watch boxes appear throughout this text. These are designed to sensitize you to the ever-present, ever-influential communication media and to illustrate the close connections between the media and other forms of communication. These Media Watch boxes cover a wide variety of topics and will provide a broad and involving view of mass communication. They are designed to raise your consciousness about the media and its influence, so, interact with these discussions. Agree or disagree. Bring the evidence from your own experiences and from readings to bear on the theories and issues discussed in these boxes.

greater access to information (for example, men are more likely to attend college). Similarly, in many cultures (Hispanic and Southern European cultures are good examples), men are granted (without any written rule) greater freedom in their communications than are women. Slang, obscene, and generally strong (even aggressive) language, for example, is less acceptable coming from women than men. Many in these cultures might argue that different ethical standards should apply to men and women. Of course, throughout the world there are cultural groups that oppose equal choice and equal rights to information for other cultural groups.

The topic of ethics is returned to repeatedly throughout the text as well as in several special boxes: "Ethical Listening" (Unit 21), "Ethical Research" (Unit 21), and "Media Ethics" in this unit.

THINK ABOUT

Think about these few questions (in addition to those raised in the Media Watch box) that deal with ethical issues for each of several areas of human communication. What would you do in each case? What do you feel you should do? What general principle of ethics are you using in making these would/should judgments? Does the perspective of choice discussed here provide any useful guidelines in making such decisions?

- **Interpersonal Communication** Would it be ethical to exaggerate your virtues and minimize your vices in order to win someone's approval? To get a job? To get someone to love you? How much of your past are you ethically obligated to reveal to your relationship partner? How much of your present feelings are you obliged to reveal to this partner? Would it be ethical to reveal what someone else told you in confidence?
- **Small Group Communication** Would it be ethical to assume leadership of a group so that you can get the group to do as you wish? Do you have an ethical obligation to enhance the potential of group members?
- **Public Communication** Would it be ethical to present another's research as your own in a public speech? Are you morally responsible for informing your listeners of weaknesses in your evidence and arguments? Would it be ethical to persuade an audience to do something by scaring them? By threatening them?
- **Intercultural Communication** Do you have an ethical obligation for increasing intercultural understanding and communication? Are you morally responsible for responding to language that is offensive to, say, members of a particular race? Are you ethically obligated to protest negative cultural stereotypes?
- **Ethical System** How universal do you feel the ethic of choice presented here is? Do you agree or disagree with the idea that men and women should be governed by different rules for what constitutes ethical communication?

THE PURPOSES OF HUMAN COMMUNICATION

Five general purposes or motives of communication can be identified (see Figure 1.3). Purposes need not be conscious, nor must individuals agree about their purposes for communicating. Purposes may be conscious or unconscious, recognizable or unrecognizable. Further, although communication technologies

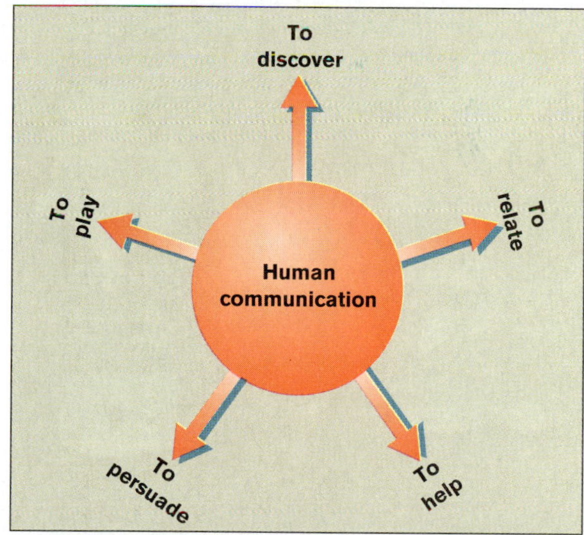

FIGURE 1.3 The purposes of human communication. A similar typology of purposes comes from research on motivating communicating. In a series of studies, Rubin and her colleagues (Rubin, Fernandez-Collado, & Hernandez-Sampieri 1992; Rubin & Martin 1994; Rubin, Perse, & Barbato 1988; Rubin & Rubin 1992; Graham 1994; Graham, Barbato, & Perse 1993) have identified six primary motives for communication: pleasure, affection, inclusion, escape, relaxation, and control. How do these compare to the five purposes shown here and discussed in the text?

are changing rapidly and drastically—we send electronic mail, work at computer terminals, and telecommute, for example—the purposes of communication are likely to remain essentially the same throughout the electronic revolution and whatever revolutions follow (Arnold & Bowers 1984; Naisbitt 1984). (The Media Watch box in Unit 8 discusses human communication in cyberspace.)

To Discover

One of the major purposes of communication concerns personal discovery. When you communicate with another person, you learn about yourself as well as about the other person. In fact, your self-perceptions result largely from what you have learned about yourself from others during communications, especially your interpersonal encounters.

Much as communication gives you a better understanding of yourself and the person with whom you are communicating, it also helps you discover the external world—the world of objects, events, and other people. Today, you rely heavily on the various communications media for information about entertainment, sports, war, economic developments, health and dietary concerns, and new products. Much of what you acquire from the media interacts with what you learn from your interpersonal interactions. You get information from the media, discuss it with other people, and ultimately learn or internalize the material as a result of thc interaction between these two sources.

This poster identifies just some of today's occupations that rely heavily on communication. Note that this poster is not meant to imply that communication is the only training one needs for these fields or even that communication is the most essential ingredient in such job preparation. Rather, its purpose is to suggest that communication is significant in a wide variety of fields, some of which we may not have even thought of as integrally involving communication. (This poster was prepared by Longman Publishers and was originally titled "What Can You Do with a Communication Degree?")

To Relate

One of our strongest motivations is to establish and maintain close relationships with others. The vast majority of people want to feel loved and liked, and in turn want to love and like others. You probably spend much of your communication time and energy establishing and maintaining social relationships. You communicate with your close friends in school, at work, and probably on the phone. You talk with your parents, children, and brothers and sisters. You interact with your relational partner. All told, this takes a great deal of your time and attests to the importance of this purpose of communication.

Of course, you may also use communication to distance yourself from others, to argue and fight with friends and romantic partners, and even to dissolve relationships.

To Help

Therapists, counselors, teachers, parents, and friends are just a few categories of those who often—though not always—communicate to help. As is the case with therapists and counselors, entire professions are built around this communication function (there are few professions that do not make at least some significant use of this helping function). You also use this function when you constructively criticize, express empathy, work with a group to solve a problem, or listen attentively and supportively to a public speaker.

To Persuade

The mass media exist largely to persuade you to change your attitudes and behaviors. The media survive on advertisers' money, which is directed at getting you to buy a variety of items and services. Right now you probably spend much more time as consumers than originators of these mass media messages. In the not too distant future, however, you will no doubt be originating messages. You may work on a newspaper or edit a magazine, or work in an ad agency, television station, or a variety of other communication-related fields.

A great deal of your time is also spent in interpersonal persuasion, as both sources and receivers. In your everyday interpersonal encounters you try to change the attitudes and behaviors of others. You try to get them to vote a particular way, try a new diet, buy a particular item, see a movie, read a book, take a specific course, believe that something is true or false, value or devalue some idea, and so on. The list is endless. Few of your interpersonal communications, in fact, do not seek to change attitudes or behaviors.

To Play

You probably also spend a great deal of your communication behavior on play. As viewed here, communication as play includes motives of pleasure, escape, and relaxation (Barbato & Perse 1992; Rubin, Perse, & Barbato 1988). For example, you often listen to comedians as well as friends largely because it is fun, enjoyable, and exciting. You tell jokes, say clever things, and relate interesting stories largely for the pleasure it gives to you and your listeners. Similarly, you may communicate because it relaxes you, allowing you to get away from pressures and responsibilities.

Although no list of communication purposes can be exhaustive, these five are the major ones. Further, no communication act is motivated by just one factor; communication is motivated by a combination of purposes. The discussions of the various contexts of communication (interpersonal, small group and organizational, and public communication) will identify more specific purposes that each of these forms fulfills.

SUMMARY*

In this unit we introduced the nature of human communication, explained the major areas, components, or elements, and its purposes.

1. Communication refers to the act, by one or more persons, of sending and receiving messages that are distorted by noise, occur within a context, have some effect (and some ethical dimension), and provide some opportunity for feedback.
2. Culture refers to the collection of beliefs, attitudes, values, and ways of behavior shared by a group of people and passed down from one generation to another through communication rather than through genes.
3. All communication is influenced by culture; hence, an understanding of the role of culture is essential for understanding communication and for mastering its skills.
4. The universals of communication—the elements present in every communication act—are: context, source-receiver, message, channel, noise (physical, social-psychological, and semantic), sending or encoding processes, receiving or decoding processes, feedback and feedforward, effect, and ethics.
5. The communication context has at least four dimensions: physical, cultural, social-psychological, and temporal.
6. Communicative competence refers to knowledge of the elements and rules of communication, which vary from one culture to another.
7. Communication messages may be of varied forms and may be sent and received through any combination of sensory organs. The communication channel is the medium through which the messages are sent.
8. Feedback refers to messages or information that is sent back to the source. It may come from the source itself or from the receiver and may be indexed along such dimensions as positive and negative, person-focused and message-focused, immediate and delayed, low-monitored and high-monitored, and supportive and critical.
9. Feedforward refers to messages that preface other messages and may be used to open the channels of communication, to preview future messages, to disclaim, and to altercast.
10. Noise is anything that distorts the message; it is present to some degree in every communication transaction.
11. Communication always has an effect. Effects may be cognitive, affective, or psychomotor.
12. Communication ethics refers to the rightness or wrongness—the morality—of a communication transaction and is an integral part of every communication transaction.
13. Communication may serve at least five general purposes: discovery, relating to others, help, persuasion, and play.

***LEARNING AID NOTE.** Each unit ends with a series of itemized summary statements. These are not substitutes for reading the unit, but they will prove useful in at least two ways. First, reading these statements before reading the unit will give you a good overview of the unit contents. It will take you less than five minutes. Second, reading these after completing the unit will help to reinforce what you have just read and will refresh your memory as you prepare for a test. Of course, you can use them as both preview and review. Try different systems to see which works best for you.

THINKING CRITICALLY ABOUT THE PRELIMINARIES TO HUMAN COMMUNICATION*

1. Do your college courses integrate a multicultural perspective? How is this reflected in your course textbooks? What would be the ideal multicultural curriculum for your college? Is this also reflected in the media, for example, in newspapers, magazines, and television? Are your local media more or less "culturally integrated" than the national media?
2. In what ways would communication (interpersonal, small group, or public speaking) between or among people from the same culture and people from widely different cultures be the same? In what ways would they differ?
3. When are you most likely to communicate intrapersonally? Are there certain topics that you communicate about intrapersonally a great deal and others that you won't talk about with yourself at all?
4. How would you describe this class in terms of its being a context for communication? How would you describe its physical, cultural, social-psychological, and temporal dimensions?
5. What kinds of feedforward can you find in this textbook? What specific functions do these feedforwards serve? Can you find examples of feedback in this text? What functions do these serve?
6. What arguments could you advance for the validity of the feedback model of relationships as explained on page 10? What arguments could you advance against this model's validity?
7. How would you describe your own tendencies in giving feedback to others in, say, conversation? In small group settings? In public speaking situations? For example, how positive are you? Do you focus more on the person or on the message? To what extent do you give immediate feedback? Are you a high self-monitor? How critical are you?
8. What ethical principles do you follow in communicating with others? What ethical principles do you wish others would follow more often when communicating with you? What would be the most unethical communication you can think of?
9. How will communication skills figure into your professional life? Which areas of communication are likely to be most important?
10. How would you go about finding answers to such questions as these:
    a. Are instructors who accurately read student feedback better liked than instructors who do not read feedback accurately? Is there a relationship between the ability to read feedback and the ability to communicate information or to motivate or persuade an audience?
    b. Is knowledge about communication related to the ability to communicate effectively? That is, are those who know more about communication more effective communicators than those who know less?
    c. Do people who watch more television feel less positively about themselves than do those who watch less television?
    d. Do sunglasses influence the effectiveness of a speaker's interpersonal, small group, and public communication?

***LEARNING AID NOTE.** At the end of each unit are questions designed to encourage you to exercise your critical thinking abilities. They focus on four critical thinking skills:

Self-analysis questions ask you to analyze yourself as a communicator and attempt to encourage you to personalize the material: What are your major strengths and weaknesses? What is your conflict style? How does fear influence your willingness to communicate?

Application questions ask you to apply the concepts and principles discussed in one context to other forms of communication (for example, interpersonal, interviewing, or small group) and to other contexts (for example, family, work, or school).

Evaluation questions ask you to make judgments about the principles and theories presented: When is lying unethical? Is the communication sexually harassing? Is the model of conversation useful?

Discovery research questions (the last question in each section) ask you to consider the ways in which you would go about finding answers to a variety of questions. They ask that you put on the researcher's hat and figure out how you might research a question.

two unit: Principles of Communication

unit contents

unit goals

After completing this unit, you should be able to

1. explain the packaged nature of communication
2. explain the principle of adjustment in communication
3. distinguish between content and relationship dimensions of communication
4. define *punctuation*
5. distinguish between symmetrical and complementary transactions
6. explain the transactional nature of communication
7. explain the inevitability, irreversibility, and unrepeatability of communication

The previous unit defined communication and explained some of its components and characteristics. This unit continues to explain the nature of communication by presenting seven principles. These principles are essential to understanding communication in all its forms and functions.

Although significant in terms of explaining theory, these principles also have very practical implications. They provide insight into such day-to-day issues as:

- why disagreements so often center on trivial matters and yet seem so difficult to resolve
- why you can never know exactly what another person is thinking or feeling
- how power works in communication
- why you and others may see issues in extremely different, even opposite ways

COMMUNICATION IS A PACKAGE OF SIGNALS

Communication behaviors, whether they involve verbal messages, gestures, or some combination thereof, usually occur in "packages" (Pittenger, Hockett, & Danehy 1960). Usually, verbal and nonverbal behaviors reinforce or support each other. All parts of a message system normally work together to communicate a particular meaning. You do not express fear with words while the rest of your body is relaxed. You do not express anger through your posture with a smile on your face. Your entire body works together—verbally and nonverbally—to express your thoughts and feelings.

In any form of communication, whether interpersonal, small group, public speaking, or mass media, you probably pay little attention to its packaged nature. It goes unnoticed. When there is an incongruity however—when the weak handshake belies the verbal greeting, when the nervous posture belies the focused stare, when the constant preening belies the expressions of being comfortable and at ease—you take notice. Invariably you begin to question the credibility, the sincerity, and the honesty of the individual.

Often contradictory messages are sent over a period of time. Note, for example, that in the following interaction the employee is being given two directives—use initiative and don't use initiative. Regardless of what he or she does, rejection will follow.

EMPLOYER: You've got to learn to take more initiative. You never seem to take charge, to take control.

EMPLOYEE: [Takes the initiative, makes decisions.]

EMPLOYER: You've got to learn to follow the chain of command and not do things just because you want to.

EMPLOYEE: [Goes back to old ways, not taking any initiative.]

EMPLOYER: Well, I told you. We expect more initiative from you.

Contradictory messages are particularly damaging when children are involved. Young children can neither escape from such situations nor communicate about the communications. They cannot talk about the lack of correspondence between one set of messages and another. They cannot ask their parents, for example, why they do not hold them or hug them when they say they love them.

These contradictory messages may be the result of the desire to communicate two different emotions or feelings. For example, you may like a person and want to communicate a positive feeling, but you may also feel resentment toward this person and want to communicate a negative feeling as well. The result is that you communicate both feelings, for example, you say that you are happy to see the person but your facial expression and body posture communicate your negative feelings (Beier 1974). In this example, and in many similar cases, the socially acceptable message is usually communicated verbally while the less socially acceptable message is communicated nonverbally.

THINK ABOUT

Think about how you would confront contradictory messages or messages that do not seem to ring true, how you would frame responses that are appropriate and supportive. Here are several statements that contain either mixed messages or messages that seem illogical or inconsistent with what you know about the individual. How would you respond to each of these statements:

- Even if I do fail the course, so what? I don't need it for graduation.
- I called three people. They all have something to do on Saturday night. I guess I'll just curl up with a good book or a good movie. It'll be better than a lousy date anyway.
- My parents are getting divorced after 20 years of marriage. My mother and father are both dating other people now so everything is going okay.
- My youngest child is going to need special treatments if he's going to walk again. The doctors are going to decide today on what kind of treatment. But all will end well in this, the best of all possible worlds.

COMMUNICATION IS A PROCESS OF ADJUSTMENT

Communication may take place only to the extent that the communicators use the same system of signals (Pittenger, Hockett, & Danehy 1960). You are able to communicate with another person to the extent that your language systems agree. In reality, however, no two persons use identical signal systems, so this process of adjustment principle is relevant to all forms of communication. Parents and children, for example, not only have largely different vocabularies but also have different meanings for the terms they do share. Different cultures, even when they use a common language, often have greatly different nonverbal communication systems. To the extent that these systems differ, meaningful and effective communication will not take place.

Part of the art of communication is identifying the other person's signals, learning how they are used, and understanding what they mean. Those in close relationships will realize that learning the other person's signals takes a great deal of time and often a great deal of patience. If you want to understand what another person means (by a smile, by saying "I love you," by arguing about trivia, by self-deprecating comments), rather than simply acknowledging what the other person says or does, you have to learn that person's system of signals.

This principle is especially important in intercultural communication, largely because people from different cultures use different signals and sometimes the same signals to signify quite different things. Focused

How does the principle of adjustment relate to communication between parents and children? Communication between students and teachers? Communication between members of different races or religions?

eye contact means honesty and openness in much of the United States. That same behavior, however, may signify arrogance or disrespect in Japan and in many Hispanic cultures if engaged in by a youngster with someone significantly older. An illustration of the same signals meaning quite different things in other cultures is provided in the photo of the four hand signals.

Communication Accommodation

An interesting theory largely revolving around adjustment is communication accommodation theory. This theory holds that speakers will adjust to or accommodate to the speaking style of their listeners in order to gain, for example, social approval and greater communication efficiency (Giles, Mulac, Bradac, & Johnson 1987). For example, when two people have a similar speech rate, they seem to be more attracted to each other than to those with dissimilar rates (Buller, LePoire, Aune, & Eloy 1992). Speech rate similarity has also been associated with greater immediacy, sociability, and intimacy (Buller & Aune 1992). Also, the speaker who uses language intensity similar to that of listeners, is judged to have greater credibility than the speaker who used intensity different from that of listeners (Aune & Kikuchi 1993). Still another study found that roommates who have similar communication attitudes (both were high in communication competence and willingness to communicate and low in verbal aggressiveness) were highest in roommate liking and satisfaction (Martin & Anderson 1995).

As illustrated throughout this text, communication characteristics are influenced greatly by culture (Albert & Nelson 1993). Thus, the communication similarities that lead to attraction and more positive perceptions are likely to be present in *intra*cultural communication but absent in many *inter*cultural encounters. This may present an important (but not insurmountable) obstacle to intercultural communication.

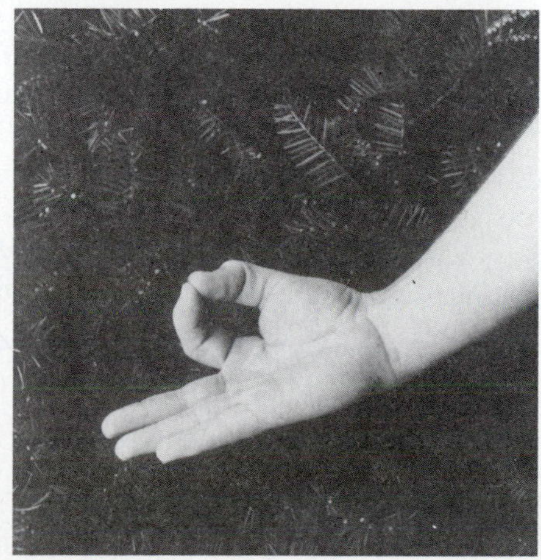

What do these nonverbal gestures mean to you? Do they all mean the same thing? Actually, they are all slightly different, and mean different things depending on their cultural context: (a) is American for "OK"; (b) is from the Mediterranean, and means "zero"; (c) is from Japan, and means "money"; (d) is from Tunisia, and means "I will kill you."

COMMUNICATION INVOLVES CONTENT AND RELATIONSHIP DIMENSIONS

Communications, to a certain extent at least, refer to the real world, to something external to both speaker and listener. At the same time, however, communications also refer to the relationships between the parties (Watzlawick, Beavin, & Jackson 1967). For example, an employer may say to a worker, "See me after the meeting." This simple message has a content aspect and a relational aspect. The content aspect refers to the behavioral responses expected—namely, that the worker see the employer after the meeting. The relational aspect tells how the communication is to be dealt with. Even the use of the simple command says that there is a status difference between the two parties: the employer can command the worker. This is perhaps seen most clearly when you imagine the worker giving this command to the employer; it appears awkward and out of place because it violates the expected communications between employer and worker.

In any communication situation the content dimension may stay the same but the relationship aspect may vary. Or, the relationship aspect may be the same while the content is different. For example, the employer could say to the worker either, "You had better see me after the meeting" or, "May I please see you after the meeting?" In each case the content is essentially the same; that is, the message being communicated about the behaviors expected is the same in both cases. The relationship dimension is very different, however. In the first it signifies a definite superior-inferior relationship and even a put-down of the worker. In the second, the employer signals a more equal relationship and shows respect for the worker.

Similarly, at times the content may be different but the relationship essentially the same. For example, a teenager might ask his or her parents, "May I go away this weekend?" and "May I use the car tonight?" The content of the two messages is clearly very different. The relationship dimension, however, is essentially the same. It is clearly a superior-inferior relationship in which permission to do certain things must be secured.

Ignoring Relationship Dimensions

Problems may arise when the distinction between the content and relationship levels of communication is ignored. Consider a couple arguing over the fact that Pat made plans to study during the weekend with friends without first asking Chris if that would be all right. Probably both would have agreed that to study over the weekend was the right choice to make. Thus the argument is not at all related to the content level. The argument centers on the relationship level. Chris expected to be consulted about plans for the weekend. Pat, in not doing so, rejected this definition of the relationship.

Let me give you a personal example. My mother came to stay for a week at a summer place I had. On the first day she swept the kitchen floor six times, though I had repeatedly told her that it did not need sweeping since I would be tracking in dirt and mud from outside—all her effort would be wasted. She persisted in sweeping, however, saying that the floor was dirty and should be swept. On the content level, we were talking about the value of sweeping the kitchen floor; but on the relationship level we were talking about something quite different. We were each saying, "This is my house." When I realized this (though only after considerable argument), I stopped complaining about the relative usefulness of sweeping a floor that did not need sweeping and she stopped sweeping it.

Consider the following interchange:

DIALOGUE	COMMENTARY
PAUL: I'm going bowling tomorrow. The guys at the plant are starting a team.	He focuses on the content and ignores any relational implications of the message.
JUDY: Why can't we ever do anything together?	She responds primarily on a relational level and ignores the content implications of the message, and expresses her displeasure at being ignored in his decision.
PAUL: We can do something together anytime; tomorrow's the day they're organizing the team.	Again, he focuses almost exclusively on the content.

This example reflects research findings that show that men focus more on content messages, whereas women focus more on relationship messages (Pearson, West, & Turner 1995). Once we recognize this gender difference, we may be able to develop increased sensitivity to the opposite sex.

Recognizing Relationship Dimensions

Here is essentially the same situation but with the added sensitivity to relationship messages:

DIALOGUE	COMMENTARY
PAUL: The guys at the plant are organizing a bowling team. I'd sure like to be on the team. Would it be all right if I went to the organizational meeting tomorrow?	Although he focuses on content, he shows awareness of the relational dimensions by asking if this would be a problem. He also shows this in expressing his desire rather than his decision to attend this meeting.
JUDY: That sounds great, but I'd really like to do something together tomorrow.	She focuses on the relational dimension but also acknowledges his content orientation. Note too that she does not respond as if she has to defend herself or her emphasis on relational aspects.
PAUL: How about meeting me at Luigi's for dinner after the organizational meeting?	He responds to the relational aspect—without abandoning his desire to join the bowling team—and seeks to incorporate it into his communications. He attempts to negotiate a solution that will meet both Judy's and his needs and desires.
JUDY: That sounds great. I'm dying for spaghetti and meatballs.	She responds to both messages, approving of both his joining the team and their dinner date.

Arguments over the content dimension are relatively easy to resolve. You may look something up in a book or ask someone what actually took place. Arguments on the relationship level, however, are much more difficult to resolve, in part because you (like me in the example of my mother) may not recognize that the argument is in fact a relationship one.

COMMUNICATION SEQUENCES ARE PUNCTUATED

Communication events are continuous transactions. There is no clear-cut beginning or ending. As a participant in or an observer of the communication act, you divide up this continuous, circular process into causes and effects, or stimuli and responses. That is, you segment this continuous stream of communication into smaller pieces. You label some of these pieces causes or stimuli and others effects or responses.

Consider an example: The students are apathetic; the teacher does not prepare for classes. Figure 2.1(a) illustrates the sequence of events in which there is no absolute beginning and no absolute end. Each action (the students' apathy and the teacher's lack of preparation) stimulates the other. But there is no initial stimulus. Each of the events may be regarded as a stimulus and each as a response, but there is no way to determine which is which. Consider how the teacher might divide up this continuous transaction. Figure 2.1(b) illustrates the teacher's perception of this situation. From this point of view, the teacher sees the students' apathy as the stimulus for his or her lack of preparation, and the lack of preparation as the response to the students' apathy. In Figure 2.1(c) we see how the students might divide up the transaction. The students might see this "same" sequence of events as beginning with the teacher's lack of preparation as the stimulus (or cause) and their own apathy as the response (or effect).

This tendency to divide up the various communication transactions in sequences of stimuli and responses is referred to as **punctuation** (Watzlawick, Beavin, & Jackson 1967). People punctuate the continuous sequences of events into stimuli and responses for ease of understanding and remembering, and, as the example of the students and teacher illustrates, people punctuate communication in ways that allow them to look good and that are consistent with their own self-image.

If communication is to be effective, if you are to understand what another person means from his or her point of view, then you have to see the sequence of events as punctuated by the other person. Further, you have to recognize that your punctuation does not reflect what exists in reality; rather, it reflects your own unique but fallible perception.

COMMUNICATION INVOLVES SYMMETRICAL AND COMPLEMENTARY TRANSACTIONS

Relationships can be described as either symmetrical or complementary (Watzlawick, Beavin, & Jackson 1967). In a **symmetrical relationship** the two individuals mirror each other's behavior. The behavior of one person is reflected in the behavior of the other. If one member nags, the other member responds in

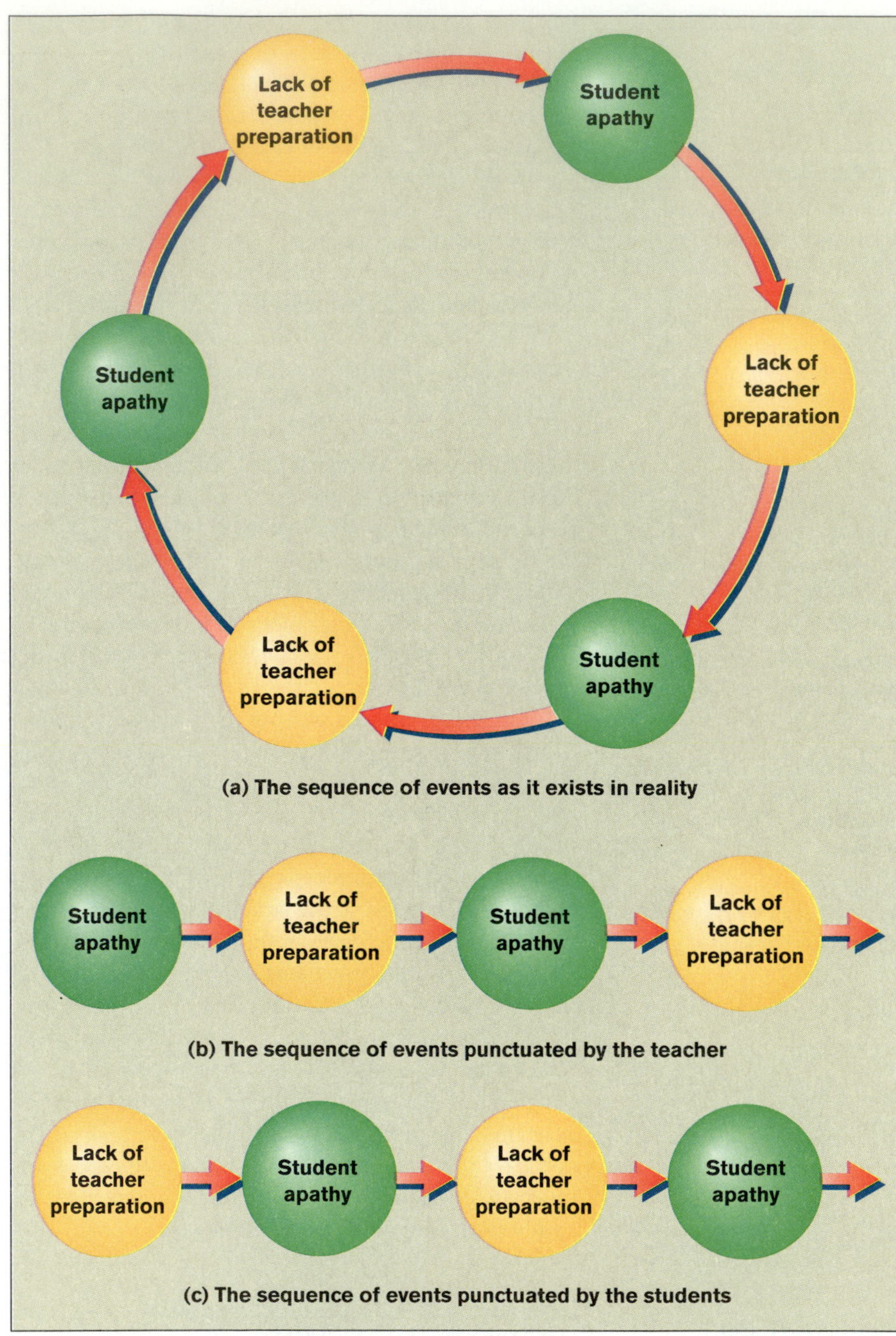

FIGURE 2.1 The sequence of events. Try using this three-part figure, discussed in the text, to explain what might go on when Pat complains about Chris's nagging and Chris complains about Pat's avoidance and silence.

kind. If one member expresses jealousy, the other member expresses jealousy. If one member is passive, the other member is passive. The relationship is one of equality, with the emphasis on minimizing the differences between the two individuals.

Note, however, the problems that can arise in this type of relationship. Consider the situation of a husband and wife, both of whom are aggressive. The aggressiveness of the husband fosters aggressiveness in the wife; the anger of the wife arouses anger in the husband. As this escalates, the aggressiveness can no longer be contained, and the relationship is consumed by aggression.

In a **complementary relationship** the two individuals engage in different behaviors. The behavior of one serves as the stimulus for the complementary behavior of the other. In complementary relationships the differences between the parties are maximized. One partner acts as the superior and the other the inferior, one passive and the other active, one strong and the other weak. At times cultures establish such relationships—as, for example, the complementary relationship between teacher and student or between employer and employee.

Early marriages are likely to be complementary relationships in which each person tries to complete himself or herself. Should these couples separate and form new relationships, the new ones are likely to be symmetrical and involve a kind of reconfirmation of their own identity (Prosky 1992). Generally, research finds that complementary couples have a lower marital adjustment level than do symmetrical couples (Main & Oliver 1988; Holden 1991).

A problem in complementary relationships familiar to many college students is one created by extreme rigidity. Whereas the complementary relationship between a nurturing and protective mother and a dependent child was at one time vital and essential to the life of the child, that same relationship when the child is older becomes a handicap to further development—the change so essential to growth is not allowed to occur.

An interesting perspective on complementary and symmetrical relationships can be gained by looking at the ways in which these patterns combine to exert control in a relationship (Rogers-Millar & Millar 1979; Millar & Rogers 1987; Rogers & Farace 1975). Such relationships may occur in interpersonal, small group, interviewing, or organizational communication settings. Nine patterns are identified; three deal with symmetry (similar type messages), two with complementarity (opposite type messages), and four with transitional (neither the same nor opposite type messages).

In *competitive symmetry* each person tries to exert control over the other (symbolized by an upward arrow, ↑). Each communicates one-up messages (messages that attempt to control the behaviors of the other person):

PAT: Do it now. ↑
CHRIS: I'll do it when I'm good and ready; otherwise, do it yourself. ↑

In *submissive symmetry* each person communicates submission (symbolized by a downward arrow ↓); both messages are one-down (messages that indicate submission to what the other person wants):

PAT: What do you want for dinner? ↓
CHRIS: Whatever you'd like is fine with me. ↓

In *neutralized symmetry* each person communicates similarly (symbolized by a horizontal arrow →) but neither competitively, one-up, or submissively, one-down:

PAT: Jackie needs new shoes. →
CHRIS: And a new jacket. →

In *complementarity* one person communicates the desire to control (one-up) and the other person communicates submission (one-down).

PAT: Here, honey, do it this way. ↑
CHRIS: Oh, that's great; you're so clever. ↓

In a reverse type of *complementarity,* the submissive message (one-down) comes first and is followed by a controlling (one-up) message:

PAT: I need suggestions for managing this new team of recruits. ↓
CHRIS: Oh, that's easy; I've managed similar groups for years. ↑

Transition patterns are those that do not involve stating the opposite of the previous message; they do not respond to a competitive message with submission, nor to a submissive message with a competitive one. There are four possible transition patterns:

- a competitive message (one-up) is responded to without either another competitive message or a submissive message:

PAT: I want to go to the movies. ↑
CHRIS: There surely are a lot of choices this weekend. →

- a submissive message (one-down) is responded to without either another submissive message or a competitive message:

PAT: I'm just helpless with tools. ↓
CHRIS: Lots of people have difficulty using a router. →

- a transition message (one-across) is responded to with a competitive (one-up) message:

PAT: We can do it in lots of ways. →
CHRIS: Well, here's the right way. ↑

- a transition message (one-across) is responded to with a submissive (one-down) message:

PAT: We can do it in lots of ways. →
CHRIS: However you do it is fine. ↓

THINK ABOUT

Think about these patterns in relation to your own interactions, whether among friends, loved ones, or family, or among colleagues at work:

- How rigid or flexible are these patterns? For example, do you and your friends or colleagues share control and submission or does one of you exercise control and the other respond with submission?
- Can you identify a relationship you have that makes use of one major pattern? What part do you play? Are you comfortable with this pattern?
- Can you identify a general pattern that you use in many or most of your interpersonal relationships? In most of your work relationships? How satisfied are you with your customary patterns of expression?
- Can you identify relationships you have that began with one pattern of communication and over the years has shifted to another pattern? What happened?
- Do these patterns have anything to do with the degree of satisfaction you experience? For example, do you derive greater satisfaction from an interaction that relies on one pattern than you do with an interaction that relies on another pattern?

COMMUNICATION IS TRANSACTIONAL

Communication is a transaction (Barnlund 1970; Watzlawick 1977, 1978; Watzlawick, Beavin, & Jackson 1967; Wilmot 1987). One implication of viewing communication as transactional is that each person is seen as both speaker and listener, as simultaneously communicating and receiving messages. Figure 2.2 illustrates this transactional view and compares it with earlier views of communication that may still influence the way you see communication.

Transactional also means that communication is an ever-changing process. It is an ongoing activity; all the elements of communication are in a state of constant change. You are constantly changing, the people with whom you are communicating are changing, and your environment is changing. Nothing in communication ever remains static.

In any transactional process, each element relates integrally to every other element. The elements of communication are interdependent (never independent). Each exists in relation to the others. For example, there can be no source without a receiver. There can be no message without a source. There can be no feedback without a receiver. Because of this interdependence, a change in any one element of the process produces changes in the other elements. For example, you are talking with a group of your friends when your mother enters the group. This change in "audience"

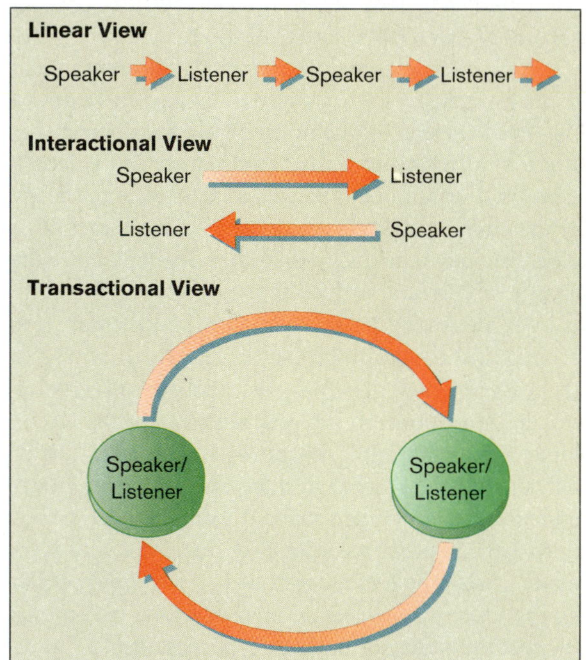

FIGURE 2.2 The transactional view of communication. The top figure represents a linear view of communication, in which the speaker speaks and the listener listens. The middle figure represents an interactional view, in which speaker and listener take turns speaking and listening; A speaks while B listens and then B speaks while A listens. The bottom figure represents a transactional view, in which each person serves simultaneously as speaker and listener; at the same time that the speaker sends messages, he or she is also receiving messages from his or her own communications and also from the reactions of the other person(s).

will lead to other changes. Perhaps you or your friends will adjust what you are saying or how you say it. The new situation may also influence how often certain people talk, and so on. Regardless of what change is introduced, other changes will be produced as a result.

Each person in a communication transaction acts and reacts on the basis of the present situation. This present situation, your immediate context, is influenced in great part by his or her history, past experiences, attitudes, cultural beliefs, self-image, future expectations, emotions, and a host of related issues. One implication of this is that actions and reactions in communication are determined not only by what is said, but also by the way the person interprets what is said. Your responses to a movie, for example, do not depend solely on the words and pictures in the film but also on your previous experiences, present emotions, knowledge, physical well-being, and other factors.

Another implication is that two people listening to the same message will often derive two very different meanings. Although the words and symbols are the same, each person will interpret them differently.

COMMUNICATION IS INEVITABLE, IRREVERSIBLE, AND UNREPEATABLE

Communication is a process that is inevitable, irreversible, and unrepeatable. Communication messages are always (or almost always) being sent, cannot be reversed or uncommunicated, and are always unique and one-time occurrences. Let us look at these qualities in more detail.

Inevitability

In many instances communication takes place even though one of the individuals does not think he or she is communicating or does not want to communicate. Consider, for example, the student sitting in the back of the room with an expressionless face, perhaps staring out the window. Although the student might claim not to be communicating with the teacher, the teacher may derive any one of a variety of messages from this behavior. Perhaps the teacher assumes that the student lacks interest, is bored, or is worried about something. In any event, the teacher is receiving messages even though the student may not intend to communicate. In an interactional situation, you cannot avoid communicating (Watzlawick, Beavin, & Jackson 1967); communication is inevitable. This is not to say that all behavior is communication. For example, if the student looked out the window and the teacher failed to notice this, no communication would have taken place.

Further, when you are in an interactional situation you cannot avoid responding to the messages of others. For example, if you notice someone winking at you, you must respond in some way. Even if you do not respond actively or openly, that lack of response is itself a response, and it communicates. Again, if you don't notice the winking, then obviously communication has not occurred.

Irreversibility

Notice that you can only reverse the processes of some systems. For example, you can turn water into ice and then the ice back into water. And you can repeat this reversal process as many times as you wish. Other systems, however, are irreversible. You can turn grapes into wine but you cannot turn the wine back into grapes—the process can go in only one direction. Communication is such an irreversible process. Once you communicate something, you cannot uncommunicate it. You can of course try to reduce the effects of your message by saying, for example, "I really didn't mean what I said" or "I was so angry I couldn't think straight." But regardless of how you try to negate or reduce the effects of your message, the message itself, once it has been sent and received, cannot be reversed.

This principle has several important implications. For example, in interpersonal interactions you need to be careful not to say things you may be sorry for later. Especially in conflict situations, when tempers run high, you need to avoid saying things you may later wish to withdraw. Commitment messages—the "I love you" messages and their variants—need to be similarly monitored, otherwise, you may commit yourself to a position you may not be happy with later. In public and in mass communication situations, where the messages are heard by hundreds, thousands, or even millions, it is especially crucial to recognize the irreversibility of your communications.

Unrepeatability

The reason communication is unrepeatable is simple: everyone and everything is constantly changing. As a

INTRODUCING RESEARCH*

INTRODUCING THEORY

Throughout this unit and throughout this book you will encounter a wide variety of theories. A **theory** is simply a generalization that explains how something works—gravity, blood clotting, interpersonal attraction, communication. In academic writing, the term is usually reserved for a well-established system of knowledge about how something works or how things are related. The theories you will encounter will vary from those concerned with explaining how communication (in general) operates (for example, a theory that explains communication as a transactional process or how people accommodate their speaking style to their listeners) to those concerned with more specific areas (for example, how communication works when relationships deteriorate, how self-disclosure operates in friendship, how problem-solving groups communicate, how speakers influence audiences, and how media have the effects they do). In reading about these theories, you may well ask yourself, "Why should I learn this? Of what value is this material to me?" Here are a few answers to these very legitimate questions (Griffin 1991; Infante, Rancer, & Womack 1993; Littlejohn 1996).

Communication theories help us understand the way in which communication operates. Theories provide general principles that help us understand an enormous number of specific events—how and why these events occur and how they are related to each other. Theories provide generalizations that will usually help you in understanding situations you never encountered before. As one communication theorist puts it, A good theory synthesizes the data, focuses our attention on whats crucial, and helps us ignore that which makes little difference" (Griffin 1991, p. 4).

Communication theories also help us to predict future events. The theories summarize what has been found and can therefore offer a useful and generally reasonable prediction for events that you have never encountered. For example, based on the theories of persuasion, you would be able to predict whether strong, medium, or weak appeals to fear will be more effective in persuading an audience. Or, based on the theories of conflict resolution, you would be able to predict which strategies will prove more effective in resolving the differences.

Communication theories also help to generate research. For example, if a theory predicts that audiences differing in education will be persuaded by different amounts of evidence, it suggests to the researcher to ask what other differences exist between educated and uneducated audiences (Infante, Rancer, & Womack 1993). Will they differ in their responses to credibility appeals? To dramatic stories? To motive appeals? In serving this "heuristic" or research-generating function, theories add to our knowledge of communication.

Theories do not, however, reveal truth in any absolute sense (Littlejohn 1996). Rather, theories reveal some degree of accuracy, some degree of truth. In the natural sciences, such as physics and chemistry, theories are extremely high in accuracy. If you mix two parts of hydrogen to one part of oxygen, you will get water—every time you do it. In the social and behavioral sciences (communication, sociology, psychology), the theories are far less accurate in describing the way things work and in predicting how things will work. One communication theorist offers this summary guidance: "So because a theory does not reveal truth, does not mean that it fails to communicate a kind of truth. An insight or useful way of classifying or explaining events is a kind of truth. Just don't make the mistake of believing too hard in one theory because every theory has its limits" (Littlejohn 1996, p. 361).

"Introducing Research" boxes later in this text address the research process (Units 3 and 7), the

***LEARNING AID NOTE.** Nine "Introducing Research" boxes are distributed throughout the text. These boxes are designed to give you a glimpse of the ways research is conducted. It is a way of explaining how the findings and conclusions reported in this book are discovered. Understanding the research process (and we only cover the surface here) will give you added insight into the concepts and theories of communication as well as into the general processes of scientific discovery. These processes and the research concepts generally will also prove to be valuable critical thinking tools that have application to all forms of thinking.

types of research (Units 4, 9, 12, and 13), the means for evaluating research (Unit 17), and research ethics (Unit 21). As you read through this text, you'll probably come across references to articles and books you'll want to look at in more detail. The complete texts of most of the research studies cited here are available in most college libraries. Abstracts (ranging from about 100 to 300 words) for most of these studies can be found in ERIC, PSYCHLIT, or SOCIOFILE databases, which are also available in most college libraries. Often the same study will be included in several different databases. Your librarian will help you locate and access the appropriate print sources and electronic databases.

result, you can never recapture the exact same situation, frame of mind, or relationship dynamics that defined a previous communication act. For example, you can never repeat meeting someone for the first time, making a first impression in an interview, or resolving a specific group problem.

You can, of course, try again, as when you say, "I'm sorry I came off as being so forward, can we try again?" Even when you say this you have not erased the initial impression. Instead you try to counteract the initial and perhaps negative impression by going through the motions again.

THINK ABOUT

Think about how you would use these principles to describe (not to solve) what is happening in each of the following situations. Do realize that these scenarios are extremely brief and are written only as exercises to stimulate you to think more concretely about the principles. Note, too, that the objective is not to select the one correct principle (each scenario can probably be described with several principles), but to provide an opportunity to think about the principles in reference to specific situations.

- A couple, together for 20 years, argues constantly about the seemingly most insignificant things—who takes the dog out, who does the shopping, who decides where to go to dinner, and so on. It has gotten to the point that they rarely have a day without argument; both are considering separating.
- In teaching communication skills, Professor Jones frequently asks students to role-play effective and ineffective communication patterns and offers criticism after each session. Although most students respond well to this instructional technique, Mariz has difficulty and has frequently left the class in tears.
- Pat has sought the assistance of a family therapist. The problem is simple: whatever Pat says, Chris says the opposite. If Pat wants to eat Chinese, Chris wants to eat Italian; if Pat wants Italian, Chris wants Chinese. And on and on. The problem is made worse by the fact that Chris has to win; Pat's wishes are invariably dismissed.
- In the heat of a big argument, Harry said he didn't ever want to see Peggy's family again: "They don't like me and I don't like them." Peggy reciprocated and said she felt the same way about his family. Now, weeks later, there remains a great deal of tension between them, especially when they find themselves with one or both families.
- Grace and Tom, senior executives at a large advertising agency, are engaged to be married. Recently, Grace made a presentation that was not received positively by the other members of the team. Grace feels that Tom—in not defending her proposal—created a negative attitude and actually encouraged others to reject her ideas. Tom says that he felt he could not defend her proposal because others would have felt his defense was motivated by their relationship and not by an objective evaluation of her proposal. He therefore felt it was best to say nothing.
- Joe, a police detective, cannot understand what happened. "All I did," he says, "was introduce myself and they refused to talk to me."

SUMMARY

In this unit we looked at some of the principles of human communication, principles that explain what communication is and how it works in a wide variety of situations and contexts.

1. Communication is normally a package of signals, each reinforcing the other. Opposing communication signals from the same source result in contradictory messages.
2. Contradictory messages may be created when there is a desire to communicate two different feelings or emotions.
3. Communication is a process of adjustment and takes place only to the extent that the communicators use the same system of signals.
4. Communication involves both content dimensions and relationship dimensions.
5. Communication sequences are punctuated for processing. Different people divide up the communication sequence into stimuli and responses differently.
6. Communication involves symmetrical and complementary transactions.
7. Communication is transactional. Communicators serve simultaneously as speakers and listeners. Communication is an ever-changing process with interrelated components in which message effects are influenced by the individual, not only by the words and gestures.
8. In any interactional situation, communication is inevitable; you cannot avoid communicating nor can you not respond to communication.
9. Communication is irreversible. You cannot uncommunicate.
10. Communication is unrepeatable. You cannot duplicate a previous communication act.

THINKING CRITICALLY ABOUT THE PRINCIPLES OF COMMUNICATION

1. How would you answer the questions posed in the introduction to this unit (page 21)? Which principles seem particularly useful in gaining insight into these questions? Can you think of other questions to which you might apply these principles?
2. It has been argued that both the therapist and the client with disabilities send contradictory messages that create "double-binds" for each other (Esten & Wilmot 1993). The client communicates both the desire to focus on the disability but also the desire to disregard it. What does the therapist do? If the therapist focuses on the disability, it is in violation of the client's desire to ignore it and if the therapist ignores it, it is in violation of the client's desire to concentrate on it. Regardless of how the therapist responds, it is in violation of one of the client's preferences. What guidelines would you offer the therapist or the client, based on your understanding of contradictory messages?
3. Do you accommodate to the communication styles of those with whom you interact? Do teachers and students or lawyers and witnesses or doctors and patients accommodate to each other's communication style? In what direction is there likely to be greater accommodation? For example, is the teacher or the student more likely to accommodate to the other?

4. Can you think of a specific example from your own experience where the differences between content and relationship messages caused a misunderstanding? Was this misunderstanding eventually clarified? If so, how?
5. Can you describe an argument that revolved around the difference in the way two people punctuate a sequence of events?
6. How would you explain the superiority of the transactional perspective as compared to the linear perspective? Can you think of situations in which the linear perspective would provide better insight into understanding communication?
7. Throughout this text, gender differences are discussed in a wide variety of contexts. Following Holmes (1995) we can distinguish three perspectives on gender differences in communication: (1) gender differences are due to innate biological differences; (2) gender differences are due to different patterns of socialization, which leads to different forms of communication; and (3) gender differences are due to the inequalities in social power; for example, because of women's lesser social power, they are more apt to communicate with greater deference and politeness than are men. What do you think of these three positions? Can you find arguments to support or contradict these positions?
8. Can you give a specific example of noncommunication occurring in an interactional situation? An example of a reversal of communication messages? An example of an exact repetition of a message?
9. How many principles discussed in this unit can you find operating in popular television sitcom interactions?
10. How would you go about finding answers to questions such as these:
    a. Is there a gender difference in the ability to appreciate the punctuation of another person?
    b. Does relative status influence who accommodates to whom?
    c. Does the higher adjustment evidenced by symmetrical couples (over complementary couples) hold for all age groups? Does it hold for homosexual as it seems to hold for heterosexual relationships?
    d. What is the most effective way to "take back" an unkind or culturally insensitive remark?

three unit
Perception

unit contents

unit goals

After completing this unit, you should be able to

1. define *perception*
2. explain the three stages in the perception process
3. explain how the following processes influence perception: primacy and recency, the self-fulfilling prophecy, perceptual accentuation, implicit personality theory, consistency, stereotyping, and attribution
4. explain the barriers to accurate perception that each process may create
5. explain how you can make perception more accurate

Perception is the process by which you become aware of the many stimuli impinging on your senses. Perception influences what stimuli or messages you take in and what meanings you give them. Perception influences the way you see people, and the evaluations you make of them and of their behaviors. Perception is therefore central to the study of communication in all its forms and functions. Here we look at (1) the process of perception, identifying its three main stages; (2) the processes that influence perception; and (3) how you can make your perceptions more accurate.

THE PERCEPTION PROCESS

Perception is complex. There is no one-to-one relationship between the messages that occur "out there" in the world—in the vibrations of the air and in the marks on paper—and the messages that eventually get to your brain. What occurs "out there" may differ greatly from what reaches your conscious mind. Examining how and why these messages differ is crucial to understanding communication.

We can illustrate how perception works by explaining the three steps involved in the process. These stages are not discrete and separate; in reality they are continuous and blend into and overlap one another (see Figure 3.1).

Sensory Stimulation Occurs

At this first stage the sense organs are stimulated. You hear a recording. You see someone you have not seen for years. You smell perfume on the person next to you. You taste a slice of pizza. You feel a sweaty palm as you shake someone's hand.

Even when you have the sensory ability to perceive stimuli, you do not always do so. For example, when you are daydreaming in class, you do not hear what the teacher is saying until he or she calls your name. Then you wake up. You know you heard your name, but you do not know why. This is a clear example of perceiving what is meaningful to you and not perceiving what is not meaningful.

Sensory Stimulation Is Organized

At the second stage, the sensory stimulations are organized according to various principles. One of the more frequently used principles is that of **proximity:** people or messages that are physically close to one another are perceived together, or as a unit. For example, you probably perceive people you often see together as a unit (such as a couple). Similarly, you perceive messages uttered one immediately after the other as a unit and assume that they are in some way related to each other. Another such principle is closure: you perceive as closed, or complete, a figure or message that is in reality unclosed or incomplete. For example, you see a broken circle as a circle even though part of it is missing. You would even perceive a series of dots or dashes arranged in a circular pattern as a circle. Similarly, you fill in the fragmented messages you hear with those parts that seem logically to complete the messages.

Proximity and closure are just two of the many organizing principles. In thinking about these principles, remember that whatever you perceive you also organize into a pattern that is meaningful to you. It is not a pattern that is necessarily true or logical in any objective sense.

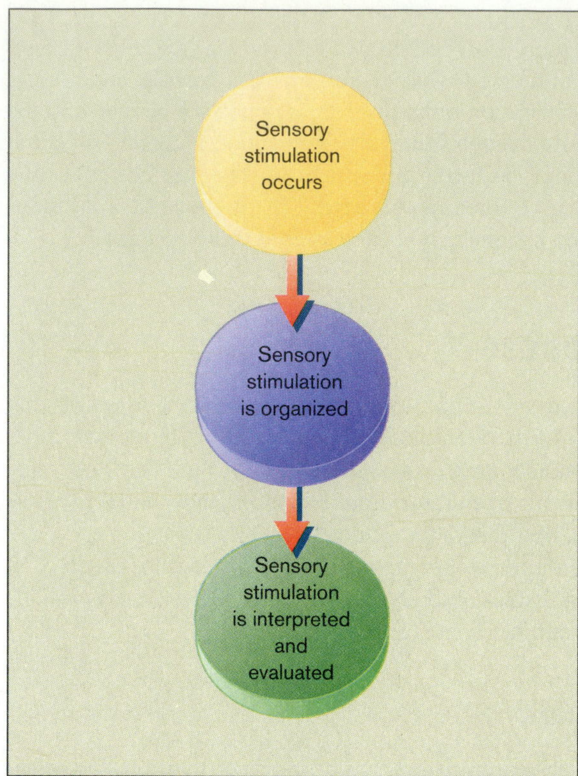

FIGURE 3.1 The perception process. The three circles are designed to illustrate the stages of perception. Do realize that as the process goes from sensory stimulation to interpretation and evaluation, the focus narrows; for example, you organize *part of* what you sensed and you interpret and evaluate *part of* what you organized.

Sensory Stimulation Is Interpreted-Evaluated

The third step in the perceptual process is interpretation-evaluation. This term is hyphenated to emphasize that its two parts cannot be separated. This step is a subjective process involving evaluations on the part of the perceiver. Your interpretations-evaluations are not based solely on the external stimulus. Like communication, perception is a transactional process (Unit 2) and as a result is greatly influenced by your past experiences, needs, wants, value systems, beliefs about the way things are or should be, physical or emotional states at the time, expectations, and so on.

It should be clear from even this very incomplete list of influences that there is much room for individual interpretation of a given stimulus and hence disagreements. Although we may all be exposed to the same message, the way each person interprets-evaluates it will differ. The interpretation-evaluation will also differ for the same person from one time to another. The sound of a popular rock group may be heard by one person as terrible noise and by another as great music. The sight of someone you have not seen for years may bring joy to you and anxiety to someone else. The smell of perfume may be pleasant to one person and repulsive to another. A sweaty palm may be perceived by one person to show nervousness and by another to show excitement.

PROCESSES INFLUENCING PERCEPTION

Between the occurrence of the stimulus (the uttering of the message, presence of the person, a smile, or wink of the eye) and the evaluation or interpretation of that stimulation, perception is influenced by a number of significant psychological processes. Before reading about these processes, take the self-test, "How Accurate Are You at People Perception," to determine your own customary ways of perceiving others. Regardless of what form of communication you are engaged in—interpersonal, small group, public speaking, or mass communication—the ways in which you perceive the people involved will influence your communications and your communication effectiveness.

Here follows a discussion of seven major processes involved in perceiving others (Cook 1971; Rubin 1973; Rubin & McNeil 1985): implicit personality theory, the self-fulfilling prophecy, perceptual accentuation, primacy-recency, consistency, stereotyping, and attribution. As you will see, each of these processes also contains potential barriers to accurate perception that can significantly distort your perceptions of others and your interpersonal interactions generally.

Implicit Personality Theory

Each person has a subconscious or **implicit personality theory** that says which characteristics of an individual go with other characteristics. This system of rules is well illustrated in the poem "Richard Cory" by Edward Arlington Robinson, in which the onlookers see certain characteristics of Mister Cory and then fill in the rest on the basis of their implicit or unstated personality theories.

SELF-TEST

how accurate are you at people perception?

Respond to each of the following statements with T (true) if the statement is usually accurate in describing your behavior. Respond with F (false) if the statement is usually inaccurate in describing your behavior. (Of course, when you take a test like this, you can often figure out the right answers and give these rather than really think about your own behaviors. Try to resist this very natural tendency to give the socially acceptable responses to this test as well as in similar tests throughout this text.)

______ 1. I base most of my impressions of people on the first few minutes of our meeting.
______ 2. When I know some things about another person I fill in what I don't know.
______ 3. I make predictions about people's behaviors that generally prove to be true.
______ 4. I have clear ideas of what people of different national, racial, and religious groups are really like.
______ 5. I reserve making judgments about people until I learn a great deal about them and see them in a variety of situations.
______ 6. On the basis of my observations of people, I formulate guesses about them (which I am willing to revise) rather than firm conclusions.
______ 7. I pay special attention to people's behaviors that might contradict my initial impressions.
______ 8. I delay formulating conclusions about people until I have lots of evidence.
______ 9. I avoid making assumptions about what is going on in someone else's head on the basis of their behaviors.
______10. I recognize that people are different, and I don't assume that everyone else is like me.

Thinking Critically About Perception. This brief perception test was designed to raise questions we will consider in this unit and not to provide a specific "perception score." The first four questions represent distortions of some common processes influencing perception. Ideally you would have responded "false" to these four questions. Questions 5–10 represent guidelines for increasing accuracy in perceptions. Ideally you would have responded with "true" to these six questions.

Whenever Richard Cory went down town,
We people on the pavement looked at him:
He was a gentleman from sole to crown,
Clean flavored, and imperially slim.

And he was always quietly arrayed,
And he was always human when he talked;
But still he fluttered pulses when he said,
"Good-morning," and he glittered when he walked.

And he was rich—yes, richer than a king—
And admirably schooled in every grace:
In fine, we thought that he was everything
To make us wish that we were in his place.

So on we walked, and waited for the light,
And went without the meat, and cursed the bread;
And Richard Cory, one calm summer night,
Went home and put a bullet through his head.

THINK ABOUT

Think about your own use of implicit personality theories to fill in missing parts about a person and if you, like the people observing Richard Cory, make mistakes. Consider, for example, the following brief statements. Note the word in parentheses that you think best completes each sentence:

- Juan is energetic, eager, and (intelligent, unintelligent).
- Mary is bold, defiant, and (extroverted, introverted).
- Joe is bright, lively, and (thin, fat).
- Kadisha is attractive, intelligent, and (likable, unlikable).
- Susan is cheerful, positive, and (attractive, unattractive).

MEDIA WATCH

CULTIVATION THEORY

An interesting perspective on perception—on how what you see influences what you think—is provided by **cultivation theory.** According to cultivation theory, the media, especially television, are the primary means by which you learn about your society and your culture (Gerbner, Gross, Morgan, & Signorielli 1980). It is through your exposure to television (and other media) that you learn about the world, its people, its values, its customs.

Cultivation theory argues that heavy television viewers form an image of reality that is inconsistent with the facts (Potter 1986; Potter & Chang 1990). For example, heavy viewers see their chances of being a victim of a crime to be 1 in 10; in reality the ratio is 1 in 50. The difference, according to cultivation theorists, is due to the fact that television presents crime to be significantly higher than it really is; that is, crime is highlighted on television dramas as well as in news reports. Rarely does television devote attention to the absence of crime (Williams 1992).

Heavy viewers also think that 20 percent of the world's population lives in the United States; in reality it is only 6 percent. Heavy viewers believe that the percentage of workers in managerial or professional jobs is 25 percent; in reality it is 5 percent.

Heavy viewers in the United States are more likely to believe that "hard work yields rewards" and that "good wins over evil" than are light viewers. Heavy sports program viewers were more likely to believe in the value of hard work and good conduct. Heavy soap opera viewers were found more likely to believe that "luck is important" and that "the strong survive" than are light viewers (Potter 1990). Television viewing has also been found to be related to attitudes and beliefs about which sex should do which household chores (Signorielli & Lears 1992). In Argentina, on the other hand, television viewing is related to antidemocratic attitudes. According to researchers television cultivates antidemocratic attitudes (Morgan & Shanahan 1991).

Of course, not all heavy television viewers are cultivated in the same way or to the same extent. Some are more susceptible to the influence of television than others (Hirsch 1980). For example, the influence will depend not only on how much a person watches television but also on the person's education, income, and sex. Low-income light viewers see crime as a serious problem but high-income light viewers do not; similarly, female heavy viewers see crime as a more serious problem than do male heavy viewers. That is, factors other than the amount of television viewing influence our perception of the world and how ready we are to take the world television portrays as the real world. Thus, although television is not the only means by which our view of the world is created—other factors, such as income and gender, are also important—it surely is one of the most potent. This seems especially true when exposure to television is heavy and when it occurs over a long period of time.

What do you think of this theory? Do you think it is a valid explanation of at least one aspect of the media's influence? How would you go about testing it? For example, how would you go about testing whether teenagers who watch lots of television violence are more apt to engage in violence than teenagers who watch significantly less television violence? Do heavy television viewers have a greater expectation that they will experience violence?

How would you go about discovering if heavy viewers of the O. J. Simpson trial had different attitudes about the United States' legal system than those who viewed it only occasionally or not at all? How would your findings relate to cultivation theory?

- Daryl is handsome, tall, and (flabby, muscular).

Certain choices in this list seem right and others seem wrong. What makes some seem right is your implicit personality theory. Most people's theories tell them that a person who is energetic and eager is also intelligent. Of course, there is no logical reason why an unintelligent person could not be energetic and eager. Or is there?

The widely documented "halo effect" is a function of the implicit personality theory. If you believe an individual has a number of positive qualities (for example, is kind, generous, and friendly), you make the inference that she or he also has other positive qualities (for example, is supportive or empathic). The "reverse halo effect" operates in a similar way. If you know a person has a number of negative qualities, you are likely to infer that the person also has other negative qualities.

Cultural Variation in Implicit Personality Theories

As might be expected, the implicit personality theories that people hold differ from culture to culture, group to group, and even person to person. For example, the Chinese concept *shi gu,* which refers to "someone who is worldly, devoted to his or her family, socially skillful, and somewhat reserved" (Aronson 1994, p. 190) is not easily encoded in English as you can tell by trying to find a general concept that covers this type of person. In English, on the other hand, we have a concept of the "artistic type," a generalization that seems absent in Chinese. Thus, although it is easy for speakers of English or Chinese to refer to specific concepts—such as socially skilled or creative—each language creates its own generalized categories. In Chinese the qualities that make up *shi gu* are more easily seen as going together than they might be for an English speaker; they are part of the implicit personality theory of more Chinese speakers than English speakers.

Similarly, consider the different personality theories that "graduate students" and "blue-collar high school dropouts" might have for "college students." Likewise, an individual may have had great experiences with doctors and so may have a very positive personality theory of doctors whereas another person may have had negative experiences with doctors and might thus have developed a very negative personality theory.

Potential Barriers

Two serious barriers may appear when you use implicit personality theories. Your tendency to develop personality theories and to perceive individuals as confirming your theory can lead you to perceive qualities in an individual that your "theory" tells you should be present when they actually are not. For example, you may see "goodwill" in the "charitable" acts of a friend when a tax deduction may be the real motive. Conversely you may see "tax deduction" as the motive of the enemy when altruism might have been the motive. Because you more easily remember information that is consistent with your implicit theories than you would inconsistent information, you are unlikely to revise or modify your theories even when you come upon contradictory evidence (Cohen 1983).

Implicit personality theories can also lead you to ignore or distort qualities or characteristics that do not conform to your theory. You may ignore (simply not see) negative qualities in your friends that you would easily see in your enemies.

The Self-Fulfilling Prophecy

A **self-fulfilling prophecy** occurs when you make a prediction or formulate a belief that comes true because you made the prediction and acted on it as if it were true (Insel & Jacobson 1975; Merton 1957). There are four basic steps in the self-fulfilling prophecy:

1. You make a prediction or formulate a belief about a person or a situation. *You predict that Pat is awkward in interpersonal situations.*
2. You act toward that person or situation as if that prediction or belief were true. *You act toward Pat as if Pat were awkward.*
3. Because you act as if the belief were true, it becomes true. *Because of the way you act toward Pat, Pat becomes tense and manifests awkwardness.*
4. You observe your effect on the person or the resulting situation, and what you see strengthens your beliefs. *You observe Pat's awkwardness, and this reinforces your belief that Pat is in fact awkward.*

If you expect people to act in a certain way or if you make a prediction about the characteristics of a situation, your predictions will frequently come true because of the self-fulfilling prophecy. Consider, for example, people who enter a group situation convinced that the other members will dislike them. Almost invariably they are proven right, perhaps because they act in a way that encourages people to respond negatively. Such people fulfill their own prophecies.

The Pygmalion Effect

A widely known example of the self-fulfilling prophecy is the **Pygmalion effect,** the condition in which one makes a prediction and then proceeds to fulfill it (Rosenthal & Jacobson 1992). In one study of this effect, teachers were told that certain pupils were expected to do exceptionally well, that they were late bloomers. The experimenters had actually selected the students' names at random. The students whose names were selected actually did perform at a higher level than the other students. The expectations of the teacher probably generated extra attention to the students, thereby positively affecting their performance.

Potential Barriers

The self-fulfilling prophecy may create two potential barriers. Your tendency to fulfill your own prophecies can lead you to influence another's behavior so it confirms your prophecy. Thus, if you and other students believe that Professor Crawford is a boring teacher and pay no attention and give no feedback, you may actually be creating a boring lecturer.

The self-fulfilling prophecy also distorts your perception by influencing you to see what you predicted rather than what is really there. For example, it can lead you to see yourself as a failure because you have made this prediction rather than because of any actual setbacks. It may lead you to see someone's behavior as creative because you have made this prediction and are expecting this person to act creatively.

Perceptual Accentuation

"Any port in a storm" is a phrase that appears in various guises throughout your communications. To the would-be actor, any part is better than no part at all. Spinach may taste horrible, but when you are starving, it can taste as good as pepperoni pizza. And so it goes.

This process, called **perceptual accentuation,** can lead you to see what you expect to see and what you want to see. You probably see people you like as being better looking and smarter than people you do not like. The obvious counterargument to this is that you actually prefer good-looking and smart people and therefore seek them out. But perhaps that is not the entire story.

In a study reported by Zick Rubin (1973), male undergraduates participated in what they thought were two separate and unrelated studies that were actually two parts of a single experiment. In the first part, each subject read a passage. Half the subjects read an arousing sexual seduction scene. The other half read about seagulls and herring gulls. In the second part of the experiment, subjects were asked to rate a female student on the basis of her photograph and a self-description. As predicted, the subjects who read the arousing scene rated the woman as significantly more attractive than did the other group. Further, the subjects who expected to go on a blind date with this woman rated her as more sexually receptive than did the subjects who were told that they had been assigned to date someone else. How can we account for such findings?

Although this experiment was a particularly dramatic demonstration of perceptual accentuation, this same general process occurs frequently. The thirsty person sees a mirage of water; the nicotine-deprived person sees a mirage of cigarettes and smoke.

Potential Barriers

Perceptual accentuation can create a variety of barriers. Your tendency to perceive what you want or need can lead you to distort your perceptions of reality; to make you perceive what you need or want to perceive rather than what is really there. At the same time it can lead you to fail to perceive what you do not want to perceive. For example, people frequently perceive politeness and friendliness from a salesperson as demonstrating personal liking for them, not as a persuasive strategy. Similarly, you may not perceive that you are about to fail your chemistry course because you focus on what you want to perceive.

Accentuation can influence you to filter out or distort information that might damage or threaten your self-image (for example, criticism of your writing or speaking) and thus make self-improvement extremely difficult.

It can lead you to perceive in others the negative characteristics or qualities you have, a defense mechanism psychoanalysts refer to as **projection.**

Also, accentuation can influence you to perceive and remember positive qualities better than negative ones (called the Pollyanna effect), and thus distort perceptions of others. In one study, for example, students who liked and who disliked Madonna viewed her video, "Open Your Heart." Those who liked Madonna saw it as the story of a dancer and her son. Those who disliked Madonna saw it as the story of sexual attraction between a young boy and an older woman (Brown & Schulze 1990).

Primacy-Recency

THINK ABOUT

Think about the following situation. You took a course in which half the classes were extremely dull and half were extremely exciting. It is now the end of the semester and you are reflecting on the course and the instructor. Would your evaluation be more favorable if the dull classes came during the first half of the semester and the exciting classes during the second half? Or would it be more favorable if the order were reversed? Consider similar situations in other contexts. For example, would you evaluate a job more favorably if your initial experiences were the positive or if your most recent experiences were the positive? Do you evaluate a friend on the basis of your early or your most recent experiences? If what comes first exerts the most influence, the result is a **primacy effect.** If what comes last (or is the most recent) exerts the most influence, the result is a **recency effect.**

In an early study on the effects of primacy-recency in interpersonal perception, Solomon Asch (1946) read a list of adjectives describing a person to a group of subjects and found that the effects of sequence were significant. A person described as "intelligent, industrious, impulsive, critical, stubborn, and envious" was evaluated more positively than a person described as "envious, stubborn, critical, impulsive, industrious, and intelligent." The implication here is that you use early information to provide yourself with a general idea of what a person is like. You then use later information to make this general idea more specific. The obvious practical implication of primacy-recency is that the first impression you make is likely to be the most important. Through this first impression, others filter additional information to formulate a picture of whom they perceive you to be.

Potential Barriers

Primacy-recency may lead to two major types of barriers. Your tendency to give greater weight to early information and to interpret later information in light of these early impressions can lead you to form a "total" picture of an individual on the basis of initial impressions that may not be typical or accurate. For example, you might form an image of someone as socially ill at ease. If this impression was based on watching this person at a stressful job interview, it is likely to be wrong. But, because of primacy you may fail to see accurately the later comfortable behavior.

Primacy may prevent you from seeing signs of deceit in someone who made a good first impression because of the tendency to avoid disrupting or revising initial impressions.

Consistency

People have a strong tendency to maintain balance or consistency among perceptions. Consistency represents people's need to maintain balance among their attitudes. You expect certain things to go together and other things not to go together.

THINK ABOUT

Think about your own attitudes in terms of consistency. Respond to the following sentences by noting the response you feel best represents your attitudes.

1. I expect a person I like to (like, dislike) me.
2. I expect a person I dislike to (like, dislike) me.
3. I expect my friend to (like, dislike) my friend.
4. I expect my friend to (like, dislike) my enemy.
5. I expect my enemy to (like, dislike) my friend.
6. I expect my enemy to (like, dislike) my enemy.

According to most consistency theories, your expectations would be as follows: You would expect a person you liked to like you (1) and a person you disliked to dislike you (2). You would expect a friend to like a friend (3) and to dislike an enemy (4). You would expect your enemy to dislike your friend (5) and to like your other enemy (6). All these expectations are intuitively satisfying. Or are they?

Further, you expect someone you like to have characteristics you like or admire; and you would expect your enemies not to possess characteristics you liked or admired. Conversely, you would expect persons you like to lack unpleasant characteristics and persons you dislike to have unpleasant characteristics.

Potential Barriers

Consistency can create three major barriers. Your tendency to see consistency in an individual can lead you to ignore or distort your perceptions of behaviors that are inconsistent with your picture of the whole person. For example, you may misinterpret Karla's unhappiness because your image of Karla is "happy, controlled, and contented."

Your desire for consistency may lead you to perceive specific behaviors as emanating from positive qualities in people you like and from negative qualities in people you dislike. You therefore fail to see both positive and negative behaviors.

Consistency can lead you to see certain behaviors as positive if other behaviors were interpreted positively (the halo effect) or as negative if other behaviors were interpreted negatively (the reverse halo effect).

Stereotyping

A frequently used shortcut in perception is stereotyping. Originally stereotype was a printing term that referred to the plate that printed the same image over and over. A sociological or psychological **stereotype** is a fixed impression of a group of people. Everyone has attitudinal stereotypes—of national groups, religious groups, racial groups, or perhaps of criminals, prostitutes, teachers, or plumbers.

If you have these fixed impressions, you might, upon meeting a member of a particular group, see that person primarily as a member of that group. Initially, this may provide you with some helpful orientation. It creates problems, however, when you apply to that person all the characteristics you assign to members of that group without examining this unique individual. If you meet a politician, for example, you may have a host of characteristics for politicians that you can readily apply to this person. To complicate matters further, you may see in this person's behavior the manifestation of various characteristics that you would not see if you did not know that this person was a politician. Although we often think of stereotypes as negative ("They're lazy, dirty, and only interested in getting high"), they may also be positive ("They're all smart, hardworking, and extremely loyal"). Whether negative or positive, stereotypes distort your ability to perceive other people accurately. They prevent you from seeing an individual as an individual rather than as a member of a group.

Consider, however, another kind of stereotype: You're driving along a dark road and are stopped at a stop sign. A car pulls up beside you and three people

How do you feel about the people in this photo? Are your feelings generally positive or negative? Did you have to think about it? Some research claims that you really didn't have to think about this before assigning these people or any perception a positive or negative value. This research argues that all perceptions have a positive or negative value attached to them and that these evaluations are most often automatic and involve no conscious thought. Immediately upon perceiving a person, idea, or thing, a positive or negative value is attached (*New York Times,* August 8, 1995, C1, C10). What do you think of this viewpoint? One bit of evidence against this position would be the ability to identify three or four or five things, ideas, or people about which you feel *completely* neutral. Can you do it?

jump out and rap on your window. There may be a variety of reasons for this: they need help, they want to ask directions, they want to tell you your trunk is open, or they may be in the process of carjacking. Your self-protective stereotype may help you decide on "carjacking" and may lead you to pull away and into the safety of a busy service station. In doing that, of course, you may have escaped being carjacked or you may have failed to help those who may have needed your help or who wanted to help you.

THINK ABOUT

Think about your own stereotypes. For example, what (if any) stereotypes do you have for:

- bodybuilders
- member of the opposite sex
- a racial group different from your own
- members of a religion very different from your own
- drug abusers or alcoholics
- college professors

What basis or evidence do you have for these stereotypes? How accurate generally are your stereotypes? What problems might these stereotypes lead to? Are there any benefits to these stereotypes?

Potential Barriers

Stereotyping can lead to two major barriers. Your tendency to group people into classes and to respond to individuals primarily as members of that class can lead you to perceive someone as having those qualities (usually negative) that you believe characterize the group to which he or she belongs (for example, all Venusians are lazy). Therefore, you fail to appreciate the multifaceted nature of all people and all groups.

Stereotyping can also lead you to ignore the unique characteristics of an individual and therefore fail to benefit from the special contributions each can bring to an encounter.

Attribution

Attribution is a process through which you try to discover why people do what they do and even why you do what you do (Fiske & Taylor 1984; Jones & Davis 1965; Kelley 1979). One way in which we try to answer this question (in part) is to ask if the person acted this way because of who the person is (their personality) or because of the situation. That is, your task is to determine whether the cause of the behavior is internal (due to who the person really is) or external (due to extenuating circumstances).

Internal behaviors are caused by the person's personality or some enduring trait. In this case you might hold the person responsible for his or her behaviors and you would judge the behavior and the person in light of this responsibility. External behaviors, on the other hand, are caused by a situational factor. In this case you might not hold the person responsible for his or her behaviors.

Consider an example. A teacher has given ten students F's on a cultural anthropology examination. In an attempt to discover what this behavior (assignment of the ten F's) reveals about the teacher, you have to determine whether the teacher was responsible for the behavior (the behavior was internally caused) or not (the behavior was externally caused). If you discover that a faculty committee made up the examination and that the committee set the standards for passing or failing, you could not attribute any particular motives to the teacher. You would have to conclude that the behavior was externally caused. In this case, it was caused by the department committee in conjunction with each student's performance on the examination.

On the other hand, assume that this teacher made up the examination and set the standards for passing and failing. Now you would be more apt to attribute the ten F's to internal causes. You would be strengthened in your belief that something within this teacher (some personality trait, for example) led to this behavior if you discovered that (1) no other teacher gave nearly as many F's, (2) this particular teacher frequently gave F's in cultural anthropology, (3) this teacher frequently gave F's in other courses as well, and (4) this teacher was free to give grades other than F. These four bits of added information would lead you to conclude that something in this teacher motivated the behavior. Each of these new items of information represents one of the principles you use in making causal judgments, or attributions, in interpersonal perception: consensus, consistency, distinctiveness, and controllability.

Consensus

When you focus on the principle of **consensus**, you ask, "Do other people behave the same way as the person on whom I am focusing?" That is, does this person act in accordance with the general consensus? If the answer is no, you are more likely to attribute the behavior to some internal cause. In the previous example, you were strengthened in your belief that the teacher's behavior had an internal cause when you learned that other teachers did not follow this behavior—there was low consensus.

Consistency

When you focus on **consistency** you ask whether a person repeatedly behaves the same way in similar situations. If the answer is yes, there is high consistency, and you are likely to attribute the behavior to internal motivation. The fact that the teacher frequently gives F's in cultural anthropology leads you to attribute the cause to the teacher rather than to outside sources.

Distinctiveness

When you focus on the principle of **distinctiveness,** you ask if this person acts in similar ways in different situations. If the answer is yes, you are likely to conclude the behavior has an internal cause. Low distinctiveness indicates that this person acts in similar ways in different situations; it indicates that this situation is not distinctive.

Consider the alternative: assume that this teacher gave all high grades and no failures in all other courses (that is, that the cultural anthropology class situation was distinctive). Then you would probably conclude that the motivation for the failures was external to the teacher and was unique to this class.

Controllability

THINK ABOUT

Think about a specific case as a way of looking at the judgments we make as to the extent to which the person was in control of his or her behavior (**controllability**). Say, for example, that you have invited your friend Desmond to dinner for seven o'clock and he arrives at nine. Consider how you would respond to the reasons he might give you for his lateness:

REASON NO. 1: Oh, I got to watching this old movie and I wanted to see the end.

REASON NO. 2: On my way here I witnessed a robbery and felt I had to report it. At the police station the phones were all tied up.

REASON NO. 3: I got in a car accident and was taken to the hospital.

Assuming you would believe all three explanations, you would attribute very different motives to Desmond's behavior. With Reasons 1 and 2, you would conclude that Desmond was in control of his behavior; with Reason 3, you would conclude that Desmond was not in control of his behavior. Further, you would probably respond negatively to Reason 1 (Desmond was selfish and inconsiderate) and positively to Reason 2 (Desmond did his duty as a responsible citizen). Because Desmond was not in control of his behavior in Reason 3, you would probably not attribute either positive or negative motivation to Desmond's behavior. Instead you would probably feel sorry that he had an accident on the way to your house.

THINK ABOUT

Think about your tendency to make similar judgments based on controllability in a variety of situations. Consider, for example, how you would respond to such situations as the following:

- Doris fails her midterm history exam.
- Sidney's car is repossessed because he failed to make the payments.
- Margie is 150 pounds overweight and is complaining that she feels awful.
- Thomas's wife has just filed for divorce and he is feeling depressed.

Very probably you would be sympathetic to each of these people if you felt they were not in control of what happened—for example, if the examination were unfair, if Sidney lost his job because of employee discrimination, if Margie has a medical problem, and if Thomas's wife were leaving him for a wealthy drug dealer. On the other hand, you might blame these people for their problems if you felt that they were in control of the situation—for example, if Doris partied instead of studied, if Sidney gambled his payments away, if Margie ate nothing but junk food and refused to exercise, and if Thomas had been repeatedly unfaithful and his wife finally gave up trying to change him.

In perceiving other people and especially in evaluating their behavior, you frequently ask if the person was in control of the behavior. Generally, research shows that if you feel people are in control of negative

TABLE 3.1
a summary of causal attribution

Situation: John was fired from a job he began a few months ago. On what basis will you decide whether this behavior is internally caused (and John is, therefore, responsible) or externally caused (and John is not responsible)?

Internal If:	External If:
No one else was fired. (low consensus)	Lots of others were fired. (high consensus)
John was fired from lots of other jobs. (high consistency)	John was never fired from any other job. (low consistency)
John has failed at lots of other things. (low distinctiveness)	John has always been successful. (high distinctiveness)
John could have been retained if he agreed to move to another shop. (high controllability)	John was not given any alternatives. (low controllability)

behaviors, you will come to dislike them, but you feel sorry for someone who you feel is not in control of negative behaviors, and you will not blame the person for his or her negative circumstances.

Low consensus, high consistency, low distinctiveness, and high controllability lead to an attribution of internal causes. As a result you praise or blame the person for his or her behaviors. High consensus, low consistency, high distinctiveness, and low controllability lead to an attribution of external causes. As a result you might consider this person lucky or unlucky. Table 3.1 summarizes these four principles of attribution.

Potential Barriers

Attribution of causality can lead to several major barriers. Your tendency to make judgments of others' behaviors can lead you to mind read the motives of another person and confuse guesses with valid conclusions. This tendency is common in a wide variety of situations (attempts to mind read are shown in italics): You forgot my birthday; *you don't love me.* You don't want to go to my parents' house for dinner; *you've never liked my parents.* You don't want to go to that interview; *you lack self-confidence.*

The Self-Serving Bias. The **self-serving bias** is another perceptual barrier and is generally designed to preserve or raise self-esteem. When you evaluate your own behaviors by taking credit for the positive and denying responsibility for the negative, you are committing the self-serving bias. You are more likely to attribute your own negative behaviors to uncontrollable factors. For example, you are more likely to attribute getting a D on an exam to the difficulty of the test rather than to your failure to prepare adequately for it. You are also more likely to attribute your positive behaviors to controllable factors, to your own strength or intelligence or personality. For example, after getting an A on an exam, you are more likely to attribute it to your ability or hard work (Bernstein, Stephart, & Davis 1979).

There is some evidence (though it is not overwhelming) that we explain the behaviors of in-group and out-group members differently (Taylor & Jaggi 1974; Berry, Poortinga, Segall, & Dasen 1992). For example, there seems to be a tendency to explain the negative behavior of members of one's own culture as externally or situationally caused but to explain the very same behavior of members of other cultures as internally motivated. Thus, for example, you would be more apt to attribute a high school dropout rate (a negatively evaluated behavior) to external sources (teachers who were not motivating or irrelevant educational programs) if this was shown to be true of your own cultural group. If, on the other hand, it were shown to be true of another culture then you would be more apt to attribute it to internal sources (the students aren't interested in education; they lack motivation).

Alternatively, we seem to explain members' positive behavior as internally motivated and nonmembers' positive behaviors as externally motivated. Thus, you would be more apt to explain, say, a high record of charitable contributions for your own culture with something like, "we're a charitable people; we believe in helping others." If shown for another culture, you would be more apt to say something like, "They're rich; they need tax deductions."

Sometimes we construct defensive attributions by which we try to explain behavior in ways that make us seem less vulnerable. One way we do this is with unrealistic optimism, the belief that good things are more likely to happen to us than to others. For example, most people think that they will ultimately experience more good things and less bad things than their peers (Aronson 1994). A similar belief is the just world hypothesis, the belief that bad things will happen only to bad people. Since we are good people, good things will happen to us. Of course, in our mindful state we know that good things often happen to bad people and that bad things often happen to good people.

The Fundamental Attribution Error. Perhaps the major difficulty in making accurate attributions is the **fundamental attribution error:** the tendency to conclude that people do what they do because that's the kind of people they are not because of the situation they are in. When Pat is late for an appointment, we are more likely to conclude that Pat is inconsiderate or irresponsible rather than attribute the lateness to the bus breaking down or to a traffic accident. When we commit the fundamental attribution error we overvalue the contribution of internal factors and undervalue the influence of external factors.

When we explain our own behavior we also favor internal explanations although not to as great an extent as we do when explaining the behaviors of others. In one study, managers who evaluated their own performance and that of their subordinates, used more internal explanations when evaluating the behavior of their subordinates than they did in evaluating their own (Martin & Klimoski 1990). One reason for giving greater weight to external factors in explaining our own behavior than we do in explaining the behavior of others is that we know the situation surrounding our own behavior. We know, for example, what's going on in our love life and we know our financial condition and so we naturally see the influence of these factors. We rarely know as much about others and, therefore, we are more likely to give less weight to the external factors in their cases.

This fundamental attribution error is at least in part culturally influenced. For example, in the United States people are more likely to explain behavior by saying that people did what they did because of who they are. When Hindus in India were asked to explain why their friends behaved as they did, however, they gave greater weight to external factors than did Americans in the United States (Miller 1984; Aronson 1994). Further, Americans have little hesitation in offering causal explanations of a persons behavior (Pat did this because . . ."). Hindus, on the other hand, are generally reluctant to explain a person's behavior in causal terms (Matsumoto 1994).

THINK ABOUT

Think about how you would explain such cases as the following in terms of attribution theory. For example, do you think the individual's behavior was due to internal causes—for example, personality characteristics and traits or various personal motives—or external causes—for example, the particular situation, the demands of others who might be in positions of authority, or the behaviors of others? The behavior in question appears in italics.

1. *Mita's performance in the race was disappointing.* For the last few days she had to tend to her sick grandfather and got too little sleep.
2. *Peter just quit his job.* No one else that you know who has had this same job has ever quit.
3. *Karla just failed her chemistry test.* A number of other students (in fact, some 40 percent of the class) also failed the test. Karla has never failed a chemistry test before and, in fact, has never failed any other test in her life.
4. *Juan earned a substantial income from real estate.* His brother made the investment decisions for both of them.
5. *Liz tasted the wine, rejected it, and complained to the waiter.* No one else in the place complained about the wine. Liz has complained about the wine before and has frequently complained that her food was seasoned incorrectly, that the coffee was cold, and so on.
6. *Russell took the schoolchildren to the zoo.* Russell works for the board of education in a small town, and taking the students on trips is one of his major job functions. All people previously on the job have taken the students to the zoo. Russell has never taken any other children to the zoo.
7. *John ran from the dog.* A number of other people also ran from this dog. I was surprised to see John do this because he has never run from other animals before and never from this particular dog.
8. *Donna received A's on all her speeches.* In fact, everyone in the class got A's. This was the first A that

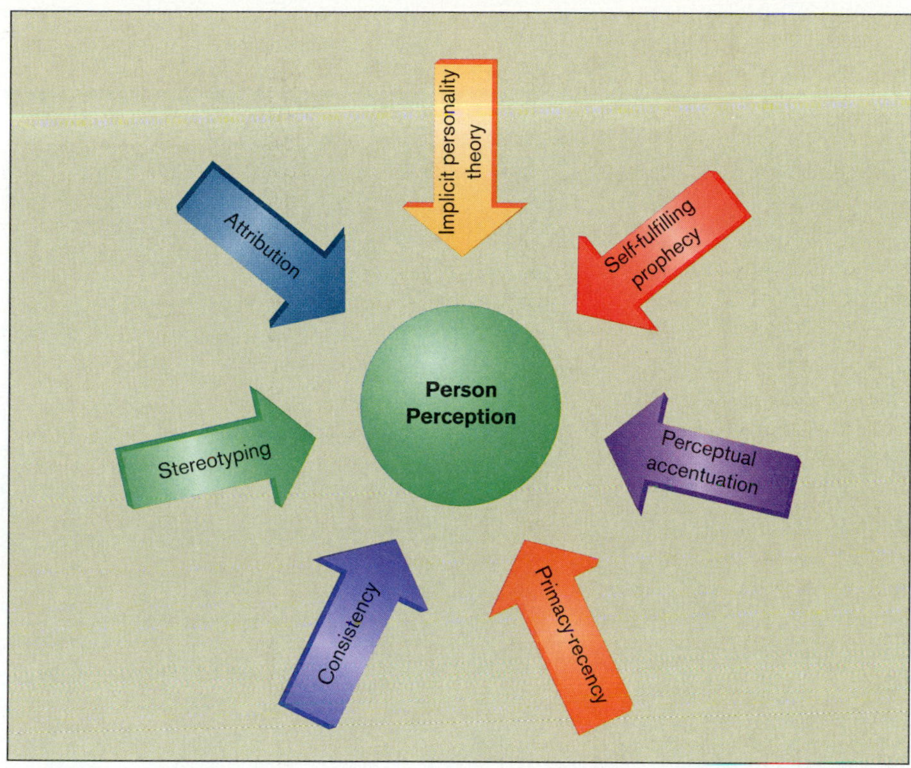

FIGURE 3.2 Processing influencing perception. Any perception is likely to be influenced by one or more of these processes. In fact, having read this unit, you will probably find it difficult to consider any significant perception that is unlikely to be influenced by at least one of these processes.

Donna has ever received in public speaking and in fact the first A she has ever received in any course.

What information contained in the brief behavior descriptions enabled you to make judgments concerning (1) consensus, (2) consistency, (3) distinctiveness, and (4) controllability? What combination of these principles would lead you to conclude that the behavior was internally motivated? What combination would lead you to conclude that the behavior was externally motivated?

Figure 3.2 summarizes the seven influences on perception and illustrates that any specific person perception may be influenced by these processes. You may find it interesting to identify your own people perceptions that have been influenced by each process.

CRITICAL PERCEPTION: MAKING PERCEPTIONS MORE ACCURATE

Communication and relational effectiveness depend in great part on your accuracy in interpersonal perception. You can improve accuracy by (1) employing strategies for reducing uncertainty, and (2) following some suggested guidelines.

General Strategies for Reducing Uncertainty

Communication is a gradual process during which people reduce uncertainty about each other. With each interaction, each person learns more about the other and gradually comes to know that person on a more meaningful level. Three major strategies help achieve this reduction in uncertainty: passive, active, and interactive strategies (Berger & Bradac 1982).

Passive Strategies

When you observe another person without their being aware of it, you are employing passive strategies. One useful strategy is to observe the person in some active task, preferably interacting with other people in informal social situations.

Active Strategies

Actively seeking information about a person in any way other than interacting with that person is to employ active strategies. For example, you can ask others about the person—"What is she like?" "Does he work

INTRODUCING RESEARCH

INTRODUCING THE RESEARCH PROCESS

Research is usually conducted on the basis of some theory and its predictions—though sometimes from a simple desire to answer a question. It is conducted so that we can learn more about how communication works, and it is these learnings and research findings that we report throughout this text. It is also on the basis of these findings that we develop the principles for more effective communication. Research, for example, often tells us what communication strategies work and what strategies don't. Understanding the research process will enable us to appreciate better how we learn about communication as well as better understand the findings, conclusions, and principles that are developed on the basis of research

Sometimes the questions are totally theoretical—How do listeners deal with ambiguous messages? Sometimes they are extremely practical, even urgent—How can children best resist drugs? Often, of course, practical implications are drawn out of "purely theoretical" research and theoretical insights are drawn out of "purely applied" research.

In some cases research is conducted simply to answer an isolated question, for example, how do people get others to like them (Bell & Daly 1984)? At other times, research is conducted to test or clarify a theory, for example, does relationship deterioration follow the reverse pattern of relationship development (Baxter 1983)?

It is the research, then, that enables us to answer questions about people's communication behavior and helps advance truth about an important aspect of human experience. Research enables us to debunk myths about communication (for example, "the more you communicate, the better your relationships will be" or "honesty is the best policy") that get in the way of understanding how communication really works.

Let us say that we discover that a democratic leader (rather than an authoritarian or laissez-faire leader) works best in raising worker morale at a particular company. How useful is that information to other companies? On the one hand, it may be very useful because all companies might respond as this one did. Or, it may be of limited usefulness if this particular company is unique and unlike all other companies in dealing with leadership. Research tries to answer these types of questions. With appropriate research designs and with the proper statistical tests research can tell us how likely it is that the superiority of the democratic leader will prevail in other companies as well.

As students we might conduct research, initially perhaps, because we're required to. Yet, there are many instances in which we probably want to conduct research because we want to answer a question we feel is important. Whatever the motivation, the advantages of conducting research are many; by conducting research, we can learn:

- the research materials and methods available, which will prove valuable throughout college and career
- the process to go through from formulating a question to developing an answer, a process that is central to all learning
- to organize a wide variety of materials into a coherent whole organized around a central and specific theme or thesis
- to improve writing skills; research reporting requires a clear and specific writing style that is essential to master
- to enhance appreciation of and skills for evaluating the research of others
- to acquire essential critical thinking skills; as illustrated throughout these research boxes, the concepts and methods of research are largely the tools of critical thinking

out?" "Does she date guys younger than she is?" You can also manipulate the environment in order to observe the individual in more specific and more revealing contexts. Employment interviews, theatrical auditions, and student teaching are examples of ways in which people manipulate situations to see how someone might act and react, hence reducing uncertainty about the person.

Interactive Strategies

When you interact with an individual, you are employing interactive strategies such as asking questions—"Do you enjoy sports?" "What did you think of that computer science course?" "What would you do if you got fired?" You also gain knowledge of another by disclosing information about yourself. Self-disclosure creates a relaxed environment that encourages disclosures from the person about whom you wish to learn more (see Unit 5).

All three general strategies are useful for reducing your uncertainty about others. Unfortunately, many people feel they know a person well enough after employing only passive strategies. Active strategies are more revealing. Interactive strategies are more revealing still. Employing all three types of strategies will give you the most information.

Specific Strategies for Increasing Accuracy in Perception

In addition to avoiding the potential barriers in the various perceptual processes noted earlier and employing all three general uncertainty-reduction strategies, here are a few more specific suggestions that will help you increase the accuracy of your interpersonal perceptions.

Look for a Variety of Cues

Try to find a variety of cues pointing in the same direction. The more perceptual cues pointing to the same conclusion, the more likely that your conclusion will be correct.

Formulate Hypotheses

On the basis of your observations of behaviors, formulate general hypotheses. Test these against additional information and evidence. Be especially alert to contradictory cues that will refute your initial hypotheses. It is easier to perceive cues that confirm your hypotheses than to perceive contradictory evidence.

Delay Conclusions

Resist the temptation to draw conclusions until you have had a chance to examine and think about a wide variety of cues. In drawing your conclusions, be sure to recognize the diversity in people. Do not assume that others are like you, that they think like you, or that they would act as you would. Beware of your own biases, for example, drawing only positive conclusions about people you like and only negative conclusions about people you do not like.

Avoid Mind Reading

Remember that regardless of how many behaviors you observe and how carefully you examine these behaviors, you can only guess what is going on in another person's mind. A person's motives, attitudes, or values are not open to outside inspection. You can only make assumptions based on overt behaviors. When you say, for example, "You forgot my birthday because you don't really love me," you are trying to mind read the other person.

Check Your Perceptions

The ability to read another person's perceptions accurately is a skill not easily perfected. There are so many factors that can get in the way of an accurate interpretation that it is almost always best to engage in **perception checking.** In its most basic form, perception checking consists of two steps.

1. Describe (in tentative terms) what you think is happening. Try to do this as descriptively (not evaluatively) as you can.
   - You seem depressed. You say you feel fine about the breakup, but you don't seem happy.
   - You don't seem to want to go out this evening.
   - You seemed disturbed when he said . . . .
   - You sound upset with my plans.
2. Ask the other person for confirmation. Be careful that your request for confirmation does not sound like you already know the answer, therefore avoid phrasing your questions defensively. Avoid saying, for example, "You really don't want to go out, do you; I knew you didn't when you turned on that lousy television." Instead, ask for confirmation in as supportive a way as possible: "Would you rather watch TV?"
   - Are you really okay about the breakup?
   - Do you feel like going out or would you rather stay home?
   - Are you disturbed?
   - Did my plans upset you?

As these examples illustrate, the goal of perception checking is not to prove that your initial perception is correct but to explore further the thoughts and feelings of the other person.

With this simple technique, you lessen your chances of misinterpreting another's feelings. At the same time, you give the other person an opportunity to elaborate on his or her thoughts and feelings.

SUMMARY

In this unit we reviewed the process of perception, the processes influencing perception, and the principles for making perception more accurate.

1. Perception refers to the process by which you become aware of the many stimuli impinging on your senses.
2. The process of perception consists of three stages: sensory stimulation occurs; sensory stimulation is organized; and sensory stimulation is interpreted-evaluated.
3. The following processes influence perception: (1) implicit personality theory, (2) self-fulfilling prophecy, (3) perceptual accentuation, (4) primacy-recency, (5) consistency, (6) stereotyping, and (7) attribution.
4. Implicit personality theory refers to the private personality theory that individuals hold and that influence how they perceive other people.
5. The self-fulfilling prophecy occurs when you make a prediction or formulate a belief that comes true because you have made the prediction and acted on it as if it were true.
6. Perceptual accentuation leads you to see what you expect and what you want to see.
7. Primacy-recency refers to the relative influence of stimuli as a result of the order in which you perceive them. If what occurs first exerts the greatest influence, you are influenced by the primacy effect. If what occurs last exerts the greatest influence, you are experiencing a recency effect
8. Consistency refers to the tendency to perceive that which enables you to achieve psychological balance or comfort among various attitude objects and the connections between and among them.
9. Stereotyping is the tendency to develop and maintain fixed, unchanging perceptions of groups of people and to use these perceptions to evaluate individual members of these groups, ignoring their individual, unique characteristics.
10. Attribution is the process by which you try to understand your own and others' behaviors and the motivations for these behaviors. In this process you utilize four types of data: consensus, consistency, distinctiveness, and controllability.
11. Accuracy in perception can be increased by using the general strategies for reducing uncertainty (passive, active, and interactive) and the more specific strategies, such as looking for a variety of cues, becoming alert to contradictory cues, and checking your perceptions.

THINKING CRITICALLY ABOUT PERCEPTION

1. What cues do you rely on most heavily in making initial judgments of people? How accurate generally are these initial judgments?
2. Can you describe a specific instance of your using the halo effect in making a judgment about another person? A reverse halo effect?
3. Thinking back to your preteen years, can you identify possible self-fulfilling prophecies that people made about you and that influenced your own behavior? Can you identify those you made about others?
4. It has been argued that the self-fulfilling prophecy may be used in organizations to stimulate higher performance (Eden 1992; Field 1989). For example, man-

agers could be made to believe that workers can perform at extremely high levels; managers would then act as if this were true and thus create this high-level behavior in the workers. How might it be used in the college classroom? How might it be used in parenting? Would you consider this technique ethical?

5. Using consistency theory, how would you explain what goes on in your head when one of your favorite people does something you evaluate negatively? How would you explain what happens when someone you dislike says good things about you?
6. In a study of stereotypes on British television it was found that gender stereotypes hadn't changed much over the last ten years and that these were comparable to those found on North American television (Furnham & Bitar 1993). Other research suggests that these stereotypes have changed and that television depictions of men and women are erasing the stereotypes (Vernon, Williams, Phillips, & Wilson 1990). Do you find gender stereotypes on television? How many can you identify? Do you find evidence to suggest that gender stereotyping is lessening?
7. Do the media perpetuate stereotypes on the basis of race, age, class, or affectional orientation? Can you give specific examples? In terms of stereotypes, how does what's on television compare to what's in a newspaper?
8. Can you describe the way in which you would use consensus, consistency, distinctiveness, and controllability in explaining why your best friend is being charged with armed robbery? In explaining why you feel depressed today?
9. How would you use perception checking in such situations as these: (a) your friend says he wants to drop out of college, (b) your cousin hasn't called you in several months though you have called her at least six times, (c) another student seems totally detached from everything that happens in class?
10. How would you go about finding answers to such questions as these:
    a. Are there gender differences in accuracy of perception? Are there age differences?
    b. Are men or women more likely to use the self-serving bias in perceiving others?
    c. Do all cultures use essentially the same perceptual processes (implicit personality theory, self-fulfilling prophecy, and so on) in making judgments about others?
    d. Does a primacy effect operate in college students' perceptions of instructors? Does a recency effect operate in college instructors' perceptions of students?

unit contents

unit goals

After completing this unit, you should be able to

1. define *listening*
2. explain the five processes involved in listening
3. explain the relevance of culture to listening
4. define and distinguish between *participatory* and *passive, empathic* and *objective, nonjudgmental* and *judgmental,* and *surface* and *deep listening*

There can be little doubt that we all listen a great deal. Upon awakening you listen to the radio. On the way to school you listen to friends, people around you, screeching brakes, singing birds, or falling rain. In school you listen to the teacher, to other students, and sometimes even to yourself. You listen to friends at lunch and return to class to listen to more teachers. You arrive home and again listen to family and friends. Perhaps you listen to CDs, radio, or television. All in all, you listen for a good part of your waking day.

Before reading about this area of human communication, examine your own listening habits and tendencies by taking the self-test, "How Good a Listener Are You?"

If we measured importance by the time we spend on an activity, then listening would be our most important communication activity. A glance at Figure 4.1, which diagrams the results of three studies, should illustrate this point. Figure 4.1(a) shows the percentage of time spent in four activities during the everyday lives of adults from a wide variety of occupations (Rankin 1929). Figure 4.1(b) reflects the results from a similar study of adults as well as high school and college students done more recently (Werner 1975). Figure 4.1(c) shows the results from a study on the communication activities of college students (Barker, Edwards, Gaines, Gladney, & Holley 1980). These studies as well as others demonstrate that listening occupies more time than any other communication activity (Steil, Barker, & Watson 1983; Wolvin & Coakley 1982).

Another way to appreciate the importance of listening is to consider its many benefits. Table 4.1 (see page 55) presents five of these benefits.

THE PROCESS OF LISTENING

The process of **listening** can be described as a series of five steps: receiving, understanding, remembering, evaluating, and responding. The process is visualized in Figure 4.2 (see page 56). Note that the listening process is a circular one. The responses of Person A serve as the stimuli for Person B, whose responses in turn serve as the stimuli for Person A, and so on. As will become clear in the discussion of the five steps that follow, listening is not a process of transferring an idea from the mind of a speaker to the mind of a listener. Rather, it is a process of speaker and listener working together to achieve a common understanding.

Receiving

Unlike listening, hearing begins and ends with this first stage of receiving. Hearing is something that just happens when you open your ears or when you get within earshot of some auditory stimuli. Listening, on the other hand, is quite different.

Listening begins (but does not end) with receiving the messages the speaker sends. The messages are both verbal and nonverbal; they consist of words as well as gestures, facial expressions, variations in volume and rate, and lots more as we will see when we discuss messages in more detail in Part Two.

At this stage you note not only what is said (verbally and nonverbally) but also what is omitted. Your friend's summary of good deeds as well as the omission of the broken promises are both received at this stage. For improved reception:

- focus attention on the speaker's verbal and nonverbal messages, on what is said and on what is not said
- look for both feedback to previous messages as well as feedforward (Unit 1), which can reveal how the speaker would like his or her message viewed

SELF TEST
how good a listener are you?

Respond to each question using the following scale:

1 = always
2 = frequently
3 = sometimes
4 = seldom
5 = never

_____ 1. I listen by participating; I interject comments throughout the conversation.
_____ 2. I listen to what the speaker is saying and feeling; I try to feel what the speaker feels.
_____ 3. I listen without judging the speaker.
_____ 4. I listen to the literal meanings that a speaker communicates; I don't look too deeply into hidden meanings.
_____ 5. I listen passively; I generally remain silent and take in what the other person is saying.
_____ 6. I listen objectively; I focus on the logic of the ideas rather than on the emotional meaning of the message.
_____ 7. I listen critically, evaluating the speaker and what the speaker is saying.
_____ 8. I look for the hidden meanings; the meanings that are revealed by subtle verbal or nonverbal cues.

Thinking Critically About Listening. These statements focus on the ways of listening discussed in this chapter. All ways are appropriate at times and all ways are inappropriate at times. It depends. The only responses that are really inappropriate, therefore, are "always" and "never." Effective listening is listening that is appropriate to the specific communication situation. Review these statements and try to identify situations in which each statement would be appropriate and situations in which each statement would be inappropriate.

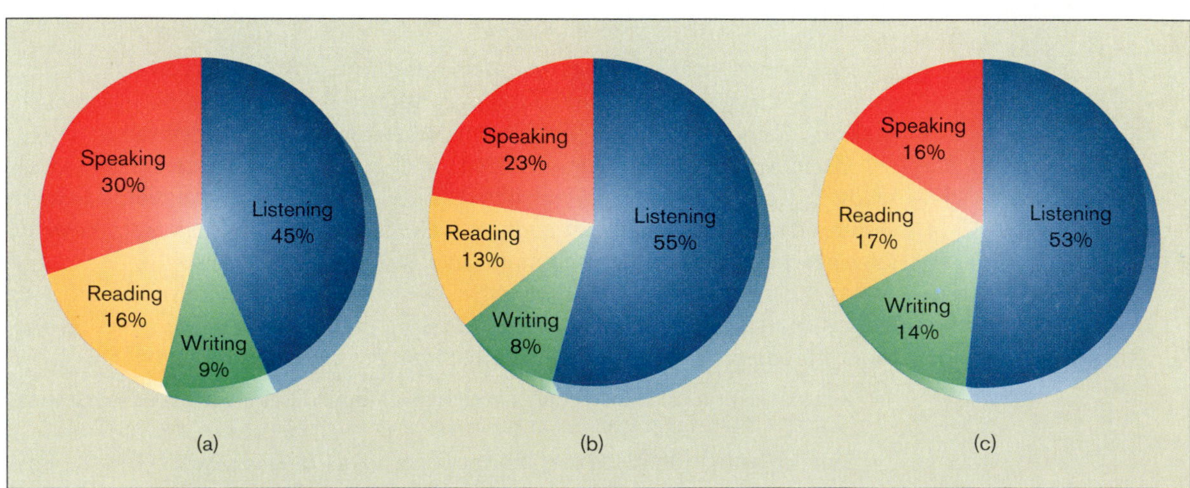

FIGURE 4.1 Amount of time spent listening. How would a pie chart of your communication activities look for a typical school day? For a typical nonschool day?

TABLE 4.1
the benefits of effective listening

This table identifies some of the benefits that can be derived from effective listening. As you read the table try to visualize the benefits as they might accrue to you from interpersonal, small group, and public communication.

Effective listening will result in increasing your ability to	Because you will	For example,
learn, to acquire knowledge of others, the world, and yourself	profit from the insights of others who have learned or seen what you have not	listening to Peter tell about his travels to Cuba will help you learn more about Peter and about life in Cuba
avoid problems and difficulties	hear and be able to respond to warnings of impending problems before they develop or escalate and become impossible to control	listening to student reactions (instead of saying "students just don't want to work hard") will help the teacher plan more relevant classes
make more reasoned and reasonable decisions	acquire more information relevant to decisions you'll be called upon to make in business or in personal life	listening to the difficulties your sales staff has (instead of saying "you're not trying hard enough") may help you offer more pertinent sales training
relate, to gain social acceptance and popularity	find that people come to like those who are attentive and supportive	others will increase their liking for you once they see your genuine concern for them, communicated through attentive and supportive listening (for example, those with effective decoding skills are less likely to experience romantic and friendship loneliness, Zakahi & Goss 1995)
influence the attitudes and behaviors of others	find that people are more likely to respect and follow those they feel have listened to and understood them	workers are more likely to follow your advice once they feel you have really listened to their insights and concerns
play	know when to suspend critical and evaluative thinking and when simply to engage in passive and accepting listening	listening to the anecdotes of co-workers will allow you to gain a more comfortable balance between the world of work and the world of play
help others	hear more, empathize more, and come to understand others more deeply	listening to your child's complaints about her teacher (instead of saying "Now what did you do wrong?") will increase your ability to help your child cope with school and her teacher

- avoid distractions in the environment and focus attention on the speaker rather than on what you will say next.
- maintain your role as listener and avoid interrupting the speaker until he or she finishes.

Understanding

Understanding is the stage at which you learn what the speaker means. This understanding must take into consideration both the thoughts that are expressed as well as the emotional tone that accompanies these thoughts—the urgency or the joy or sorrow expressed in the message. For improved understanding:

- relate new information to what is already known
- see the speaker's messages from the speaker's point of view; avoid judging the message until it is fully understood as the speaker intended it
- ask questions for clarification, if necessary; ask for additional details or examples if needed
- rephrase (paraphrase) the speaker's ideas in your own words

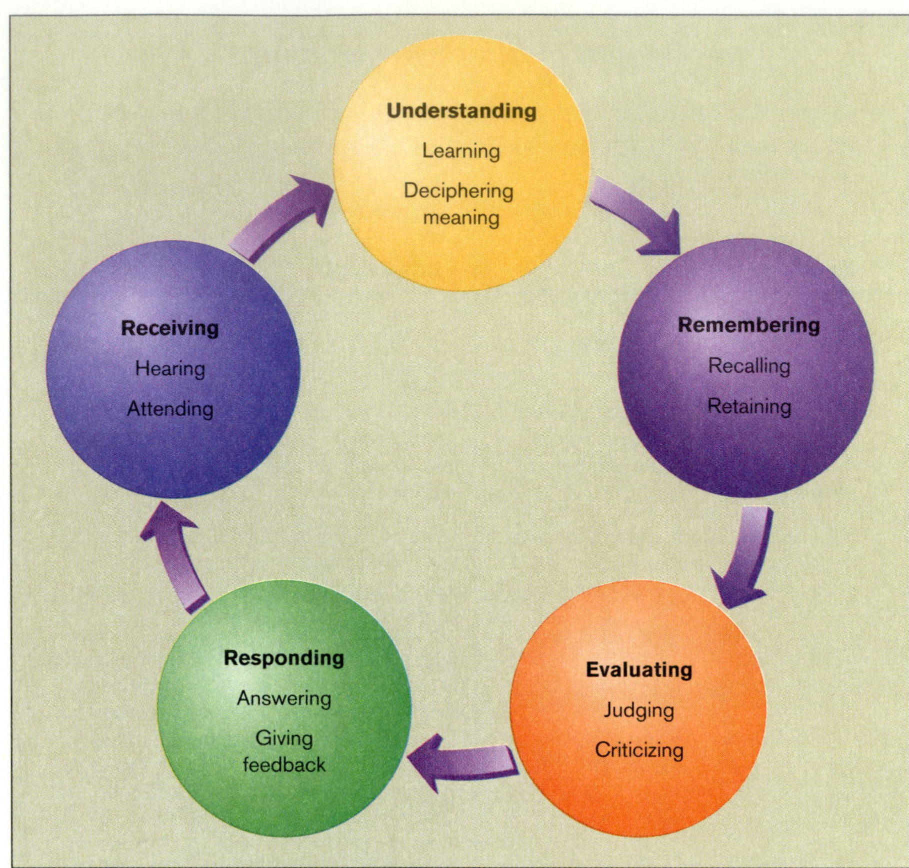

FIGURE 4.2 A five-stage model of listening. Do recognize that at each stage there will be lapses. Thus, for example, at the receiving stage, a listener receives part of the message, and because of noise and perhaps other reasons, fails to receive other parts. Similarly, at the stage of understanding, a listener understands part of the message, and because of an inability to share another's meanings exactly (see Unit 7 for more on this), fails to understand other parts. The same is true for remembering, evaluating, and responding. This model draws on a variety of previous models that listening researchers have developed (for example, Alessandra 1986; Barker 1990; Brownell 1987; Steil, Barker, & Watson 1983).

Remembering

Messages that you receive and understand need to be retained for at least some period of time. In some small group and public speaking situations you can augment your memory by taking notes or by tape recording the messages. In most interpersonal communication situations, however, such note taking would be considered inappropriate, although you often do write down a phone number, an appointment, or directions.

What you remember is actually not what was said, but what you think (or remember) was said. Memory for speech is not reproductive; you do not simply reproduce in your memory what the speaker said. Rather, memory is reconstructive; you actually reconstruct the messages you hear into a system that seems to make sense to you—a concept noted in the discussion of perception.

THINK ABOUT

Think about the way you listen and remember messages by trying to memorize the list of 12 words that follow (Glucksberg & Danks 1975). Don't worry about the order of the words; only the number remembered counts. Don't read any further until you have tried to memorize the list of words. Take about 20 seconds to memorize as many words as possible.

WORD LIST

bed	wake
rest	tired
dream	night
awake	eat
comfort	slumber
sound	snore

Now close the book and write down as many of the words from this list as you can remember. Don't read any further until you have tested your memory.

If you are like my students, you not only remembered a good number of the words on the list but you also "remembered" at least one word that was not on the list: sleep. Most people recall the word sleep being on the list—but it wasn't. What happens is that you do not simply reproduce the list but you reconstruct it. In this case you gave the list meaning, and part of that meaning included the word "sleep." You do this with all types of messages; you reconstruct the messages you hear into a meaningful whole and in the process often remember a distorted version of what was said. Memory can be improved by:

- identifying the central ideas in a message and the major support advanced for them
- summarizing the message in a more easily retained form but being careful not to ignore crucial details or qualifications
- repeating names and key concepts to yourself or, if appropriate, aloud

Evaluating

Evaluating consists of judging the messages in some way. At times you may try to evaluate the speaker's underlying intent. Often this evaluation process goes on without much conscious thought. For example, Elaine tells you that she is up for a promotion and is really excited about it. You may then try to judge her intention. Does she want you to use your influence with the company president? Is she preoccupied with her accomplishment and so tells everyone about it? Is she looking for a pat on the back? Generally, if you know the person well, you will be able to identify the intention and therefore be able to respond appropriately.

In other situations, the evaluation is more in the nature of critical analysis. For example, in listening to proposals advanced in a business meeting, you would at this stage evaluate them: Is there evidence to show that these proposals are practical and will increase productivity? Is there contradictory evidence? Are there alternative proposals that would be more practical and more productive? In evaluating, try to

- resist evaluation until you fully understand the speaker's point of view
- assume that the speaker is a person of goodwill and give the speaker the benefit of any doubt by asking for clarification on issues that you feel you must object to (are there any other reasons for accepting this new proposal?)
- distinguish facts from inferences (see Unit 9), opinions, and personal interpretations by the speaker
- identify any biases, self-interests, or prejudices that may lead the speaker to slant unfairly what is presented

Responding

Responding occurs in two phases: (1) responses you make while the speaker is talking and (2) responses you make after the speaker has stopped talking. These responses are feedback—information that you send back to the speaker and which tells the speaker how you feel and think about his or her messages. Responses made while the speaker is talking should be supportive and should acknowledge that you are listening to the speaker. These include what nonverbal researchers call **backchanneling cues**, such as "I see," "yes," "uh-huh," and similar signals that let the speaker know that you are attending to the message.

Responses made after the speaker has stopped talking are generally more elaborate and might include expressing empathy ("I know how you must feel"), asking for clarification ("Do you mean that this new health plan is to replace the old one or will just be a supplement?"), challenging ("I think your evidence is weak here"), and agreeing ("You're absolutely right on this and I'll support your proposal when it comes up for a vote"). In responding, try to:

- be supportive of the speaker throughout the speaker's talk by using and varying backchanneling cues; using only one backchanneling cue—for example, saying "uh-huh" throughout will make it appear that you are not listening but are merely on automatic pilot
- express support for the speaker in your final responses
- be honest; the speaker has a right to expect honest responses, even if these express anger or disagreement
- respond to both the disclaimer (if there is one—see Unit 1) and the content message to let the speaker know that you heard the disclaimer and

do retain a favorable impression of him or her. For example, appropriate responses might be: "I know you're not sexist, but I don't agree that . . ."

- state your thoughts and feelings as your own; use **I-messages** (for example, say "I think the new proposal will entail greater expense than you outlined" rather than "Everyone will object to the plan for costing too much.")

LISTENING AND CULTURE

Listening is difficult, in part, because of the inevitable differences in the communication systems between speaker and listener. Each person has had a unique set of experiences, therefore each person's communication and meaning system is going to be different from each other person's. When speaker and listener come from different cultures, the differences and their effects are naturally so much greater. Here are just a few points of diversity.

Language and Speech

Even when speaker and listener speak the same language, they speak it with different meanings and different accents. No two speakers speak exactly the same language. Every speaker speaks an idiolect, a unique variation of the language (King & DiMichael 1991). Speakers of the same language will, at the very least, have different meanings for the same terms because they have had different experiences.

Speakers and listeners who have different native languages and who may have learned English as a second language will have even greater differences in meaning. Translations are never precise and never fully capture the meaning in the other language. If your meaning for "house" was learned in a culture in which everyone lived in their own house with lots of land around it, then communicating with someone whose meaning was learned in a neighborhood of high-rise tenements is going to be difficult. Although you will each hear the same word, the meanings you'll each develop will be drastically different. In adjusting your listening—especially when in an intercultural setting—understand that the speaker's meanings may be very different from yours even though you each know the same language.

Still another aspect of speech is that of accents. In many classrooms throughout the country, there will be a wide range of accents. Those whose native language is a tonal one, such as Chinese (where differences in pitch signal important meaning differences), may speak English with variations in pitch that may seem puzzling to others. Those whose native language is Japanese may have trouble distinguishing "l" from "r" since Japanese does not include this distinction. The native language acts as a filter and influences the accent given to the second language.

Do you find it easier to listen to and understand members of your own culture than members of other cultures? What specific elements of communication make such listening easier or more difficult?

Nonverbal Behavioral Differences

Speakers from different cultures have different display rules, cultural rules that govern which nonverbal behaviors are appropriate and which are inappropriate in a public setting. As you listen to another person, you also "listen" to their nonverbals. If these are drastically different from what you expect on the basis of the verbal message, they may be seen as a kind of noise or interference or they may be seen as contradictory messages. Also, different cultures may give very different meanings to the same nonverbal gesture, a point well illustrated in the photo of four hand signals in Unit 2.

Direct and Indirect Styles

Some cultures—those in Western Europe and the United States, for example—favor a direct style in communication; they advise us to "say what you mean and mean what you say." Many Asian cultures, on the other hand, favor an indirect style; they emphasize politeness and maintaining a positive public image rather than absolute truth. Listen carefully to persons with different styles of directness. Consider the possibility that the meanings the speaker wishes to communicate with, say, indirectness, may be very different from the meanings you would communicate with indirectness.

Balance of Story Versus Evidence

In the United States, most people want evidence before making decisions. In fact, you are taught this cultural value for evidence throughout the critical thinking emphasis in many of your courses. You are told to seek good reasons, hard evidence, and reliable testimony before making a decision. Members of other cultures may be more influenced by a story told with complete conviction or simply by the word of a high-credibility source.

Credibility

What makes a speaker credible or believable will vary from one culture to another. In some cultures, people would claim that competence is the most important factor in, say, choosing a teacher for their preschool children. In other cultures, the most important factor might be the goodness or morality of the teacher. Similarly, members of different cultures may perceive the credibility of the various media very differently. For example, members of a repressive society in which the government controls television news may come to attribute little credibility to such broadcasts; after all, this person might reason, television news is simply what the government wants you to know. This may be hard to understand or even recognize by someone raised in the United States, where the media are free of such political control. (This issue of media credibility is explored in more detail in the Media Watch box in Unit 22.)

Feedback

Members of some cultures give very direct and very honest feedback. Speakers from these cultures—the United States is a good example—expect the feedback to be an honest reflection of what their listeners are feeling. In other cultures—Japan and Korea are good examples—it's more important to be positive than to be truthful and so they may respond with positive feedback (say, in commenting on a business colleagues proposal) even though they don't feel it. Listen to feedback, as you would all messages, with a full recognition that various cultures view feedback very differently.

LISTENING EFFECTIVELY

Because you listen for different reasons and toward different ends, the principles you follow in listening effectively should vary from one situation to another. Here we identify four dimensions of listening and illustrate the appropriateness of different listening modes for different communication situations.

Participatory and Passive Listening

The key to effective listening is to participate. Perhaps the best preparation for participatory listening is to act like one who is participating (physically and mentally) in the communication act. This may seem trivial and redundant. In practice, however, it may be the most abused rule of effective listening. Students often, for example, put their feet up on a nearby desk, nod their head to the side, and expect to listen effectively. It just will not happen this way. To see why, recall how your body reacts to important news. Almost immediately you assume an upright posture, turn toward the speaker, focus your eyes on the speaker, and remain relatively still and quiet. You do this reflexively because this is how you listen most effectively. This is not to say that you should be tense and uncomfortable when listening, but your body should reflect your active mind.

Even more important than this physical alertness is mental alertness. As a listener, participate in the communication interaction as an equal partner with the speaker, as one who is emotionally and intellectually ready to engage in the mutual sharing of meaning.

Passive listening, however, is not without merit. Passive listening—listening without talking and without directing the speaker in any nonverbal way—is a powerful means for communicating acceptance. Passive listening allows the speaker to develop his or her thoughts and ideas in the presence of another person who accepts but does not evaluate, who supports but does not intrude. By listening passively, you provide a supportive and receptive environment. Once

INTRODUCING RESEARCH

FINDING ANSWERS WITH DIFFERENT METHODS

Most communication research falls into one of three categories: *descriptive, historical/critical,* and *experimental.* An understanding of these different research approaches will further clarify the research process.

DESCRIPTIVE RESEARCH

The purpose of descriptive research is to describe what is, what exists now. It may describe behavior, attitudes, or values. Or, it may describe the relationships between or among variables. A *variable* is anything that can assume more than one value, anything that can vary, for example, height, age, religion, communication ability, persuasiveness, type of love, strength of friendship, style of leadership, fear of speaking, attitude, belief, and so on.

You might conduct descriptive research in several interesting ways (Cozby 1993). For example, you might decide to do *field work,* to go out into some natural setting and observe and describe how communication takes place in that setting. For example, what do people talk about in a single's club? You might decide to attend single's clubs and observe what people talk about, take notes unobtrusively, and summarize your findings. Or, you might use informants and interview people who do go to such clubs.

You might also engage in *systemic observation,* in which case you would identify one or two specific behaviors and describe how these operate in a specific setting. For example, you might be interested in touching behavior among kindergarten children and describe who touches whom where and when. The low cost and ease of operating videotape recorders have made these a commonly used aid in this type of research. By videotaping a variety of classes, you can then examine the tapes carefully and any number of times. And, of course, you can ask other people to examine and describe what they see on the tapes. When others, with similar training and tools, find the same things on the tapes that you did, your results are likely to be reliable, a concept explored in the Introducing Research box in Unit 17.

Or, you might want to conduct a *survey.* The familiar Harris and Gallup polls are survey research instruments. The surveys in magazines and political polls are also examples of this type of research. Surveys aim often to describe what is "average," or what the average person does or thinks (for example, how do people open conversations?). At times you might want to describe the relationships among variables. For example, do people who watch more television have stronger tendencies to commit violent acts? Are communication competence and college success related? How are the use of humor in the classroom, teacher effectiveness, and teacher likability related? Note that in a survey we are concerned with finding relationships among variables and not with claiming that one variable (say, amount of television watching) is the cause of the other (say, the tendency to commit violent acts). In conducting a survey, you need to identify your sample (the people whose communications you want to describe) and construct your questionnaire (the questions you will ask of your sample).

HISTORICAL/CRITICAL RESEARCH

Communication researchers using this method try to reconstruct the past as accurately and as completely as possible. Their aim is to gain greater insight into, for example, persuasive speakers and movements, the development of an idea throughout different societies, or the importance of a person, event, or idea.

In conducting historical/critical research, the researcher may use primary sources (original documents, transcripts, and recordings) as well as secondary sources (commentaries by third parties).

One common example of this type of research is the *literature review,* whereby you try to discover what is known about a particular communication variable, for example, What do men say about themselves? What advice do public speaking textbooks give on using humor? You might also be interested in what is known about one variable in two or more settings, for example, What are the differences between Japanese and American business meetings?

Often descriptive and experimental research have a review of the literature as an essential part of their process. Sometimes, the literature review is an end in itself.

EXPERIMENTAL RESEARCH

In experimental research two variables are studied. One variable is manipulated in some way (the independent variable) and the effect of this manipulation on the other variable (the dependent variable) is observed (measured).

For example, let's say you are interested in the effectiveness of lying with and without rehearsal. Here is one way in which you might set up an experiment to investigate this question. Ten students are presented with a brief scenario that requires them to lie without any preparation (Group A). Another ten students are presented with the same scenario but are given 20 minutes to prepare their lies (Group B). (This "preparation" variable—whether on-the-spot or with rehearsal—is the independent variable.) All 20 students present their lies to 20 different (but similar) audiences, say, college students attending different sections of the same course. All listeners are given the same questionnaire, asking their opinions about how much they believed the speaker. [The responses of the listeners on the questionnaire is the dependent variable, since it "depends upon" the independent (preparation time) variable.] Scores from Group A speakers and Group B speakers are then compared. If, say, speakers from Group B are believed significantly more than Group A speakers, then you would feel confident in concluding that lying effectiveness is greater with rehearsal.

All three of these research methods are useful. Which method you use should depend on the type of question you ask and how you want to go about answering it. What research methods would you use to answer each of the following questions?

1. Are political advertisements ethical?
2. Can listening be taught?
3. Is self-disclosure related to relationship happiness?
4. How does stereotyping influence the accuracy in receiving communication messages?
5. Is feedforward useful in conversations?
6. Does the ability to detect lying vary with the intimacy of the relationship?
7. Do eyeglasses influence perceived level of physical attractiveness?
8. What kinds of people are compulsive talkers?
9. What do we know about African American communication and how valid and reliable is that information?
10. Do men and women give different reasons in accounting for their negative behaviors?

that has been established, you may wish to participate in a more active way, verbally and nonverbally.

Another form of passive listening is just to sit back, relax, and let the auditory stimulation massage you without exerting any significant energy or effort and especially without your directing the stimuli in any way. Listening to music for pure enjoyment (rather than as a music critic) is perhaps the best example.

In regulating participatory and passive listening, keep the following guidelines in mind:

- Work at listening. Listening is hard work, so be prepared to participate actively. Avoid what James Floyd (1985) calls "the entertainment syndrome": the expectation that a speaker will entertain you. Avoid daydreaming, the natural tendency to let your mind wander.
- Combat sources of noise as much as possible. Remove distractions or other interferences (newspapers, magazines, stereos), so your listening task will have less competition.
- Because you can process information more quickly than a speaker can speak, there is often time left over. Use this time to summarize the speaker's thoughts, formulate questions, and draw connections between what you have heard and what you already know.
- Assume there is value in what the speaker is saying. Resist assuming that what you have to say is more valuable than the speaker's remarks.

Empathic and Objective Listening

If you are to understand what a person means and what a person is feeling, you need to listen with some degree of empathy (Rogers 1970; Rogers & Farson 1981). To empathize with others is to feel with them, to see the world as they see it, to feel what they feel. Only when you achieve this can you understand another person's meaning fully. Empathic listening is a means for both increasing understanding and for enhancing relationships (Barrett & Godfrey 1988; Snyder 1992).

There is no fast method for achieving empathy. Further, unlike the Empath on "Star Trek," you cannot feel what another person is feeling in any complete sense; but with hard work it is something you can approach. It is important, for example, that a student see the teacher's point of view through the eyes of the teacher; and it is equally important for the teacher to see the student's point of view from the student's perspective. Popular students might understand intellectually the reasons why an unpopular student might feel depressed, but that will not enable them to understand the feelings of depression emotionally. To accomplish that, they must put themselves in the position of the unpopular student, to role-play a bit and begin to feel that student's feelings and think that student's thoughts. Although for most communication situations, empathic listening is the preferred mode of responding, there are times when you need to go beyond it to measure the meanings and feelings against some objective reality. It is important to listen to Peter tell you how the entire world hates him and to understand how Peter feels and why he feels this way. Then you need to look a bit more objectively at Peter and perhaps see the paranoia or the self-hatred. Sometimes you have to put your empathic responses aside and listen with objectivity and detachment.

In adjusting your empathic and objective listening focus, keep the following recommendations in mind:

- Punctuate from the speaker's point of view. If you are to understand the speaker's perspective, you must see the sequence of events as the speaker does and ascertain how this can influence what the speaker says and does.
- Engage in dialogue, not monologue. View the speaker as an equal. Try to eliminate any physical or psychological barriers to equality to encourage openness and empathy (for example, step from behind the large desk separating you from your employees). Avoid interrupting the speaker—a sign that what you have to say is more important.
- Seek to understand both thoughts and feelings. Do not consider your listening task finished until you have understood what the speaker is feeling as well as thinking.
- Avoid "offensive listening," the tendency to listen to bits and pieces of information that will enable you to attack the speaker or find fault with something the speaker has said.
- Avoid focusing on yourself, for example, focusing on your own performance in interaction, on whether you are communicating the right image, or on assuming the role of speaker. During this time of self-focus, you inevitably miss what the speaker was saying.
- Strive especially to be objective when listening to friends or foes. Your attitudes may lead you to distort messages—to block out positive messages about a foe and negative messages about a friend. Guard against "expectancy hearing," when you fail to hear what the speaker is really saying and instead hear what you expect.

THINK ABOUT

Think about some typical situations. How would you respond with empathy to each of these comments? Assume that all four people are your peers.

STEPHEN: I just can't seem to get my act together. Everything just falls apart as soon as I get involved.

PAT: I never felt so alone in my life. Chris left last night and said it was all over. We were together for three years and now—after a ten-minute argument—everything is lost.

MARIA: I just got $20,000 from my aunt's estate. She left it to me! Twenty thousand! Now, I can get that car and buy some new clothes.

LIN: I just can't bear the thought of going to work today. I'm really fed up with the company. They treat us all like idiots.

Nonjudgmental and Critical Listening

Effective listening includes both nonjudgmental and critical responses. You need to listen nonjudgmentally—with an open mind with a view toward understanding. However, you also need to listen critically with a view toward making some kind of evaluation or judgment. Clearly, you should first listen for understanding and suspend judgment. Only after you have fully understood the relevant messages should you evaluate or judge. Granted, listening with an open mind is extremely difficult. It is not easy, for example, to listen to arguments against some cherished belief or to criticisms of something you value. Further, you need to listen fairly, despite the red flag of an out-of-place expression or a hostile remark. Listening often stops when such a remark is made. Admittedly, to continue listening with an open mind is difficult. Yet it is particularly important in such situations that you do continue.

If meaningful communication is to take place, however, you need to supplement open-minded listening with critical listening (see the Listen to This box in Unit 23). Listening with an open mind will help you understand the messages better. Listening with a critical mind will help you analyze that understanding and evaluate the messages. As an intelligent and educated citizen, it is your responsibility to evaluate critically what you hear. This is especially true in the college environment. It is easy simply to listen to a teacher and take down what he or she says. Yet, it is perhaps even more important to evaluate and critically analyze what you hear. Contrary to what most students believe, most teachers appreciate the responses of critical listeners. They demonstrate that someone is listening and stimulate further examination of ideas.

In adjusting your nonjudgmental and critical listening, focus on the following guidelines:

- Keep an open mind. Avoid prejudging. Delay your judgments until you fully understand the intention and the content the speaker is communicating. Avoid both positive and negative evaluation until you have a reasonably complete understanding.
- Avoid filtering out difficult messages. Avoid oversimplification—the tendency to eliminate details and to simplify complex messages so they are easier to remember. Avoid filtering out undesirable messages. None of us wants to hear that something we believe in is untrue, that people we care for are unkind, or that ideals we hold are self-destructive. Yet, it is important that educated people reexamine their beliefs by listening to these messages.
- Recognize your own biases. These may interfere with accurate listening and cause you to distort message reception through the process of assimilation—the tendency to integrate and interpret what you hear or think you hear with your own biases, prejudices, and expectations. For example, are your ethnic, national, or religious biases preventing you from appreciating a speaker's point of view?
- Judge content as delivered, not delivery as content. Although you should give attention to all aspects of the message (including delivery), do not focus on delivery to the exclusion of all else. For example, do not judge a speaker with a monotone as having nothing of interest to say, or a speaker with a foreign accent as being uninformed or uneducated.
- Avoid uncritical listening when you need to make evaluations and judgments. Recognize and combat the normal tendency to sharpen—a process in which one or two aspects of the message become highlighted, emphasized, and perhaps embellished. Often the concepts that are frequently sharpened are incidental remarks that somehow stand out from all the other messages.

Surface and Depth Listening

In Shakespeare's *Julius Caesar,* Marc Antony, in giving the funeral oration for Caesar, says: "I come to bury Caesar, not to praise him. / The evil that men do lives after them; / The good is oft interred with their bones." And later: "For Brutus is an honourable man; / So are they all, all honourable men." But Antony, as we know, did come to praise Caesar and to convince the crowd that Brutus was not an honorable man.

In most messages there is an obvious meaning that we can derive from a literal reading of the words and sentences; but there is often another level of meaning. Sometimes, as in *Julius Caesar,* it is the opposite of the literal meaning. At other times it seems totally unrelated. In reality, few messages have only one level of meaning. Most messages function on two or three levels at the same time. Consider some frequently heard messages: Carol asks you how you like her new haircut. On one level, the meaning is clear: Do you like the haircut? But there seems another level, perhaps a more important level: Carol is asking you to say something positive about her appearance. In the same way, the parent who complains about working hard at the office or in the home may in reality be asking for some expression of appreciation. The child who talks about the unfairness of the other children in the playground may be asking for affection and love, for some expression of caring. To appreciate these other meanings you need to engage in depth listening.

In listening, you have to be particularly sensitive to different levels of meaning. If you respond only to the surface-level communication (the literal meaning), you miss the opportunity to make meaningful contact with the other person's feelings and real needs. If you say to the parent, "You're always complaining. I bet you really love working so hard," you fail to respond to this call for understanding and appreciation.

In regulating your surface and depth listening, consider the following guidelines:

MEDIA WATCH

TALK RADIO

One of the most popular television shows today is "Frasier," a situation comedy based on the life of a radio talk show psychologist. And we all remember that it was through talk radio that Tom Hanks and Meg Ryan got together in *Sleepless in Seattle*. Media researchers Cameron Armstrong and Alan Rubin (1989, p. 84) note that talk radio enables listeners to "communicate with the outside world, get quick answers to questions, express opinions, and simply talk to other people. In short, talk radio allows for interpersonal communication." By placing a call, anxiety and loneliness lessen and psychological and physical security increase (Armstrong & Rubin 1989).

Armstrong and Rubin find seven motives in listening to talk radio. Generally, they find that people listen for relaxation, exciting entertainment, convenience, voyeurism or escape, useful information, passing the time, and companionship. These motives are not unlike those found for face-to-face interpersonal communication (Rubin, Perse, & Barbato 1988).

Talk radio is a kind of substitute for interpersonal, face-to-face interaction and is similar to communicating via computer. In both talk radio and computer communication, there is significantly less ego involvement and much less potential threat to self-esteem. Both systems allow for a greater amount of anonymity (and hence psychological security and protection) than does face-to-face interaction, yet they provide many of the same rewards.

Talk radio may also be an extremely persuasive medium. After the bombing of a federal building in Oklahoma City in April 1995, much criticism and defense was heard about talk radio. President Clinton criticized the extremists on talk radio for inciting and nourishing an anti-government sentiment and connected the bombing to "right-wing hate radio" (*Newsweek* May 8, 1995, p. 44). Talk radio hosts such as Rush Limbaugh and G. Gordon Liddy rushed to the defense of talk radio and the right to criticize the government, arguing that the bombing had nothing to do with talk radio (*Newsweek* May 8, 1995, p. 39). Howard Halpern, president of the American Academy of Psychotherapists, writing to *The New York Times* (May 5, 1995, p. A30), argued that extremist talk is dangerous because it cuts the empathic bond of the listener with those who are attacked; it shows the members of the attacked group to be different and deserving of hate. By doing so, it allows and may even encourage physical attacks and mass violence, argues Halpern.

Talk radio provides avenues for minority points of view in a similar way to cable television. Some would argue that this is essential because the large media—the networks, national magazines, and major newspapers—will not cover such perspectives because these major media are focused on echoing the majority point of view.

Do you listen to talk radio? If so, what purposes does it serve for you? Are you influenced by the points of view you hear expressed on talk radio? How persuasive is talk radio compared with, say, interpersonal interaction with college friends? Compared with network reporting? What type of person listens to talk radio? Is the typical listener male or female? How popular is talk radio among college students? How much time do college students spend listening to talk radio? Have you ever called in to talk radio to express an opinion? To seek advice? How often is talk radio a topic of conversation among college students?

How would you go about discovering the influence of talk radio on the attitudes, values, and beliefs of students at your college?

- Focus on both verbal and nonverbal messages. Recognize both consistent and inconsistent "packages" of messages and use these as guides for drawing inferences about the speaker's meaning. Ask questions when in doubt. Listen also to what is omitted. Remember that you communicate by what you leave out as well as by what you include. Listen, therefore, for omissions that may give you a clue to the speaker's meanings.
- Listen for both content and relational messages. The student who constantly challenges the teacher is on one level communicating disagreement over content. However, on another level—the relationship level—the student may be voicing objections to the instructor's authority or authoritarianism. To deal effectively with the student, the instructor must listen and respond to both types of messages.
- Make special note of statements that refer back to the speaker. Remember that people inevitably talk about themselves. Whatever a person says is, in part, a function of who that person is. Listening for the different levels of meaning means attending to those personal, self-reference messages.
- See the forest, then the trees. Connect the specifics to the speaker's general theme rather than merely trying to remember isolated incidents.
- Do not disregard the literal meaning of interpersonal messages in trying to uncover the more hidden meanings. Balance your listening between surface and the underlying meanings. Respond to the various levels of meaning in the messages of others as you would like others to respond to yours—sensitively but not obsessively, readily but not overambitiously.

Although these types of listening—participatory and passive, empathic and objective, nonjudgmental and judgmental, and surface and deep listening—are easy to define and distinguish in a textbook, it is not always easy to choose the appropriate listening style for any given communication situation.

THINK ABOUT

Think about the types of listening you would use in each of the following situations. What types of listening would be obviously inappropriate?

- Your steady dating partner for the last five years tells you that spells of depression are becoming more frequent and more long lasting.
- Your history instructor lectures on the contribution of the Ancient Greeks to modern civilization.
- Your five-year-old daughter says she wants to become a nurse.
- Your brother tells you he's been accepted into Harvard's MBA program.
- A salesperson tells you of the benefits of the new computer.
- A blind person asks your assistance in getting off a subway car.
- Your supervisor explains the new computerized mail system.
- A newscaster reports on a recent Arab-Israeli meeting.
- A gossip columnist details the secret lives of the stars.
- The television advertiser explains the benefits of the new Volvo.

Because of the importance of listening, the essentials of listening covered in this unit are supplemented by nine Listen to This boxes throughout this text. These boxed discussions explain how listening operates in specific contexts and how you can achieve greater listening competence. This method of presenting listening serves three main purposes: (1) it provides a foundation in listening early in the coverage of human communication, (2) it enables positioning of specific aspects of listening directly in the context to which they are most relevant, and (3) it serves to refocus attention on listening as we progress through the study of human communication. You may wish to read these now—as well as when you read the units in which they appear. The topics considered and their locations are as follows:

- Racist, Sexist, and Heterosexist Listening (Unit 6, page 98)
- Some Difficult Listeners (Unit 13, page 217)
- Listening and Gender (Unit 15, page 256)
- Active Listening (Unit 16, page 281)
- Listening to New Ideas (Unit 17, page 304)
- Listening for Groupthink (Unit 18, page 320)
- Power Listening (Unit 19, page 346)
- Ethical Listening (Unit 21, page 376)
- Critical Listening (Unit 23, page 412)

SUMMARY

In this unit we discussed the process of listening, listening and culture and the principles of effective listening.

1. Effective listening yields a wide variety of benefits in more effective learning, relating, influencing, playing, and helping.
2. Listening is a five-part process that begins with receiving and continues through understanding, remembering, evaluating, and responding.
3. Receiving consists of hearing the verbal signals and seeing the nonverbal signals.
4. Understanding involves learning what the speaker means, not merely what the words mean.
5. Remembering involves retaining the received message, a process that involves considerable reconstruction.
6. Evaluating consists of judging the messages you receive.
7. Responding involves giving feedback while the speaker is speaking and taking your turn at speaking after the speaker has finished.
8. Listening is influenced by a wide range of culture factors such as language and speech; nonverbal, direct and indirect styles; preferences for evidence versus story; credibility; and feedback differences.
9. Effective listening involves adjusting our behaviors on the basis of at least four dimensions: participatory and passive listening, empathic and objective listening, nonjudgmental and judgmental listening, and surface and deep listening.
10. Participatory and passive listening refers to the degree to which the listener actively contributes to the communication act.
11. Empathic and objective listening refers to the degree to which the listener focuses on feeling what the speaker is feeling versus understanding the objective message.
12. Nonjudgmental and judgmental listening refers to the degree to which the listener evaluates what is said.
13. Surface and deep listening refers to the extent to which the listener focuses on the obvious or literal meanings versus the less obvious or hidden meanings.

THINKING CRITICALLY ABOUT LISTENING

1. What would a pie chart of your communication activities look like? Would listening be the largest segment?
2. How satisfied are you with the level of listening that others give you? How might you make them listen more attentively?
3. What tricks do you use to help you remember people's names?
4. With which of the five stages of listening do you have the greatest difficulty?
5. Have you ever been a party to or a witness to listening problems caused by the failure to recognize cultural differences? What could have been done to prevent such listening failures?
6. Using the four dimensions of listening effectiveness, how would you describe yourself as a listener when listening in class? When listening to your best friend? When listening to a romantic partner? When listening to your parents? When listening to superiors at work?
7. Would you find it difficult to listen to friends who were complaining that the insurance premium on their Jaguars were going up? Why? Would you find it diffi-

cult to listen to friends complain that their rent was going up and that they feared becoming homeless? Why?

8. How would you describe the ideal listener? The world's worst listener?
9. Can you apply the processes of perception discussed in the previous unit to the process of listening? How can each of the perceptual processes create listening obstacles?
10. How would you go about finding answers to such questions as these:
    a. Are women and men equally effective as listeners?
    b. Can empathic listening be taught?
    c. What kinds of listening make health professional-patient communication more effective? More personally satisfying?
    d. What attitudes do business executives have toward listening and its importance in the workplace?

five

uniT

The Self in Communication

unit contents

unit goals

After completing this unit, you should be able to

1. define *self-concept* and explain how it develops
2. explain the Johari Window
3. explain self-awareness and suggestions for increasing it
4. explain self-esteem and the ways to raise it
5. define *self-disclosure* and the factors influencing it
6. explain self-disclosure's major rewards and dangers as well as the guidelines for self-disclosure and for responding to disclosures

Of all the components of the communication act, the most important is the self. Who you are and how you perceive yourself and others influence your communications and your responses to the communications of others. In this unit, we explore four aspects of the self: self-concept, self-awareness, self-esteem, and self-disclosure—the process of revealing yourself to others.

SELF-CONCEPT

Your image of who you are is your **self-concept** and is composed of your feelings and thoughts about your strengths and weaknesses, your abilities and limitations. Your self-concept develops from at least these three sources: the image that others have of you and that they reveal to you; the comparisons you make between yourself and others; and the way you interpret and evaluate your own thoughts and behaviors (Figure 5.1).

Others' Images of You

If you wanted to see how your hair looked, you would look in a mirror. What would you do if you wanted to know how friendly or how assertive you are? According to Charles Horton Cooley's (1922) concept of the **looking-glass self**, you would look at the image of yourself that others reveal to you through their behavior—especially the way they treat you and react to you.

Of course, you would not look to just anyone, but rather to those who are most significant in your life—your significant others. As a child you would look to your parents and then to your schoolteachers, for example. As an adult you might look to your friends and romantic partners.

If these significant others think highly of you, you will see this positive image of yourself reflected in their behavior; if they think little of you, you will see a more negative image. These reflected images help form the view you develop of yourself.

Social Comparisons

Another way you develop your self-concept is to compare yourself with others, a theory originally developed by Leon Festinger (1954) and referred to as **social comparison processes.** When you want to gain insight into who you are and how effective or competent you are, you look to your peers, generally to those who are distinctly similar to you (Miller, Turnbull, & McFarland 1988) or to those who have approximately the same ability as you do (Foddy & Crundall 1993). For example, after an examination you probably want to know how you performed relative to the other students in your class. This gives you a clearer idea of how effectively you performed. If you play on a baseball team, it's important to know your batting average in comparison with the batting average of others on your team or in your league. Absolute exam or batting scores may be helpful in telling you something about your performance, but you gain a different perspective when you see your score in comparison with those of your peers.

A uniqueness bias leads most of us to assume that we compare quite favorably with others. Both men and women believe that they possess desirable qualities to a greater extent than do similar others. Men evidence this uniqueness bias for both their physical characteristics and positive personality characteristics; they believe they are

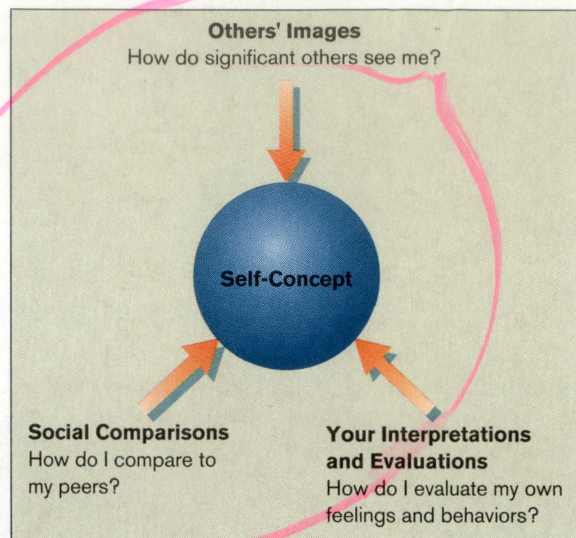

FIGURE 5.1 The Sources of Self-Concept. How do these sources influence your physical appearance self-concept? Your athletic ability self-concept? Your future success self-concept? Which source is the most influential in each case?

superior to their peers both physically and in personality. Women evidence the unique bias for personality rather than for physical characteristics; they believe they have better personalities than their peers (Furnham & Dowsett 1993).

Your Own Interpretations and Evaluations

Just as others form images of you based on what you do, you interpret and evaluate your own behavior. These interpretations and evaluations help you form your self-concept. For example, if you believe that telling lies is wrong, you are likely to react to your own lying in terms of these internalized beliefs and will react to your own lying negatively. You will probably experience some degree of guilt as a result of your behavior contradicting your beliefs. On the other hand, let's say that you pulled someone out of a burning building at great personal risk. You will probably evaluate this behavior positively; you will feel good about this behavior and, as a result, about yourself.

Understanding the way your self-concept develops increases your self-awareness. The more you understand why you view yourself as you do, the better you will understand who you are. You can gain additional insight into yourself by looking more directly at self-awareness and especially at the Johari model of the self.

SELF-AWARENESS

If you listed some of the qualities you wanted to have, self-awareness would surely rank high. **Self-awareness** is eminently practical: the more you understand yourself, the more you will be able to control your thoughts and behaviors.

The Four Selves

Figure 5.2 explains self-awareness by using the Johari Window (Luft 1969, 1984). The window is broken up into four basic areas or quadrants, each of which contains a somewhat different self. Let's assume that this window and the four selves represent you.

The Open Self

The **open self** represents all the information, behaviors, attitudes, feelings, desires, motivations, ideas, and so on, that you know about yourself and that others also know. The information included here might vary from your name, skin color, and sex to your age, political and religious affiliations, and job title. Your open self will vary in size depending on the individuals with whom you are dealing. Some people probably make you feel comfortable and support you. To them, you open yourself wide. To others you may prefer to leave most of yourself closed.

The size of the open self also varies from person to person. Some people tend to reveal their innermost desires and feelings; others prefer to remain silent about both significant and insignificant details. Most of us, however, open ourselves to some people about some things at some times.

The Blind Self

The **blind self** represents information about yourself that others know, but you do not. This may vary from relatively insignificant habits—using the expression "you know," rubbing your nose when you get angry, or having a peculiar body odor—to something as significant as defense mechanisms, fight strategies, or repressed experiences.

Communication depends in great part on both parties having the same basic information about the other. Where blind areas exist, communication will be difficult. Yet blind areas will always exist for each of us. Although we may be able to shrink our blind areas, we can never eliminate them.

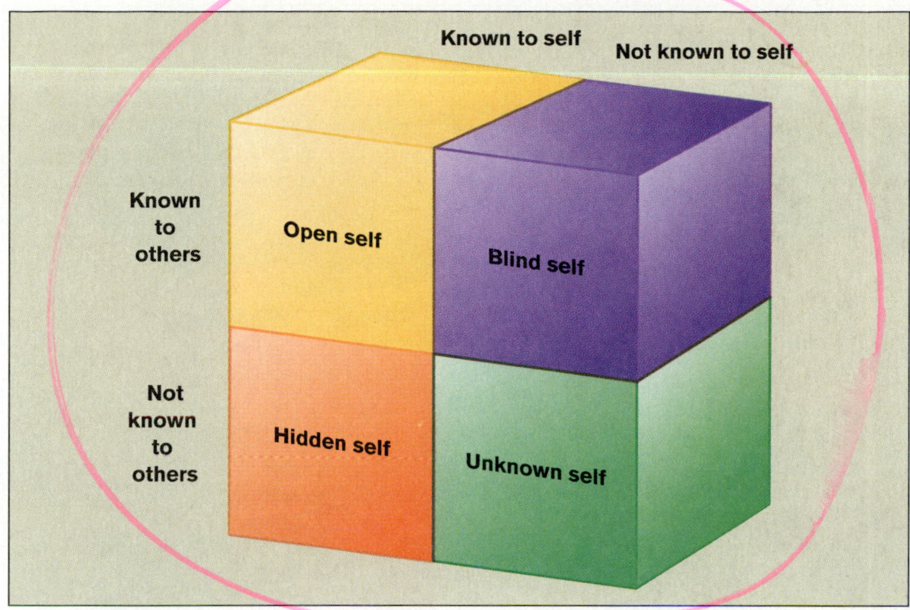

FIGURE 5.2 The Johari Window. Note that a change in any one of the quadrants produces changes in the other quadrants. Visualize the size of the entire window being constant, and the size of each quadrant being variable—sometimes small, sometimes large. As you communicate with others, information is moved from one quadrant to another. So, for example, if you reveal a secret, you shrink the hidden self and enlarge the open self. These several selves, then, are not separate and distinct from each other. Rather, each depends on the others. (*Source:* Joseph Luft, *Group Process: An Introduction to Group Dynamics*, 3rd ed. Palo Alto, CA: Mayfield, 1989, p. 11.)

The Unknown Self

The **unknown self** represents those parts of yourself about which neither you nor others know. This is the information that is buried in your unconscious or that has somehow escaped notice.

You gain insight into the unknown self from a number of different sources. Sometimes this area is revealed through temporary changes brought about by drug experiences, special experimental conditions such as hypnosis or sensory deprivation, or various projective tests or dreams. The exploration of the unknown self through open, honest, and empathic interaction with trusted and trusting others—parents, friends, counselors, children, lovers—is an effective way of gaining insight.

The Hidden Self

The **hidden self** contains all that you know of yourself but keep hidden from others. This area includes all your successfully kept secrets about yourself and others. At the extremes, there are the overdisclosers and the underdisclosers. The overdisclosers tell all, keeping nothing hidden about themselves or others. They will tell you their family history, sexual problems, financial status, goals, failures and successes, and just about everything else. The underdisclosers tell nothing. They will talk about you but not about themselves.

Most of us fall somewhere between these two extremes. We keep certain things hidden and we disclose other things. We disclose to some people and we do not disclose to others. We are, in effect, selective disclosers.

The variations in the relative sizes of the four selves can produce a variety of windows (see Figure 5.3). You may find it interesting to review these four selves as if they were your windows when interacting with different people. With whom would you be interacting in each of these four windows?

Growing in Self-Awareness

Embedded in the foregoing discussion are suggestions on how to increase your own self-awareness. Some of these may now be made explicit.

Dialogue with Yourself

No one knows you better than you do. The problem is that we seldom if ever ask ourselves about ourselves. Such a dialogue can be interesting and revealing.

THINK ABOUT

Think about what you know and think about yourself by taking the "Who Am I?" test (Bugental & Zelen 1950). Try it. Take a piece of paper, head it "Who Am I?" and write 10, 15, or 20 times, "I am . . ." Then complete the sentence each time. Try not to give only

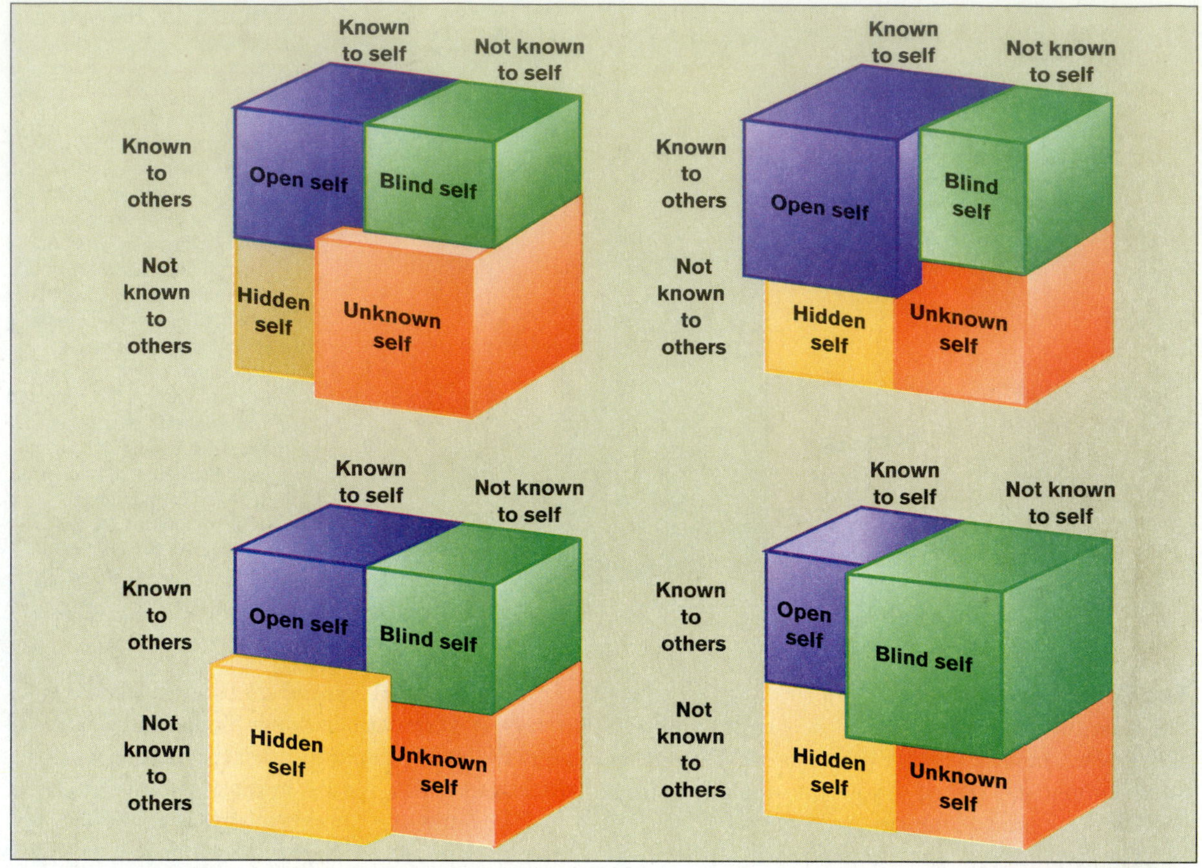

FIGURE 5.3 Johari Windows of Varied Structure. How did your windows look when you last communicated with your best friend? With a colleague at work? With a college instructor? With a family member? With a stranger on the street?

positive or socially acceptable responses; respond with what comes to mind first. Then, take another piece of paper and divide it into two columns. Head one column "Strengths" or "Virtues" and the other column "Weaknesses" or "Vices." Fill in each column as quickly as possible.

Remember too that you are constantly changing. Consequently, your self-perceptions and goals also change, often in drastic ways. Update them at regular and frequent intervals.

Listen

You can learn about yourself from seeing yourself as others do. Conveniently, others are constantly giving you the very feedback you need to increase self-awareness. In every interpersonal interaction, people comment on you in some way—on what you do, what you say, how you look. Sometimes these comments are explicit: "You really look washed-out today." Most often they are only implicit, such as a stare or averted eyes. Often they are "hidden" in the way others look, what they talk about, and the focus of their interest.

Reduce Your Blind Self

Actively seek information to reduce your blind self. People will reveal such information when you encourage them. Use some of the situations that arise every day to gain self-information: "Do you think I came down too hard on the instructor today?" "Do you think I was assertive enough when I asked for the raise?" Do not, of course, seek this information constantly—your friends would quickly find others with whom to interact. You can make use of some situations, however—perhaps those in which you are particularly unsure of what to do or how you appear—to reduce your blind self and increase self-awareness.

See Your Different Selves

To each of your friends and relatives, you are a somewhat different person. Yet you are really all of these. Try to see yourself as do the people with whom you interact. For starters, visualize how you are seen by your mother, your father, your teacher, your best friend, the stranger you sat next to on the bus, your employer, and your neighbor's child. Because you are, in fact, a composite of all of these views, it is important that you see yourself through the eyes of many people.

Increase Your Open Self

Self-awareness generally increases when you increase your open self. When you reveal yourself to others, you learn about yourself at the same time. You bring into clearer focus what you may have buried within. As you discuss yourself, you may see connections that you had previously missed. In receiving feedback from others, you gain still more insight.

Further, by increasing your open self, you increase the likelihood that a meaningful and intimate dialogue will develop. It is through such interactions that you best get to know yourself.

SELF-ESTEEM

Personal **self-esteem** refers to the way you feel about yourself. How much do you like yourself? How valuable a person do you think you are? How competent do you think you are? The answers to these questions reflect the value you place on yourself; they are a measure of your self-esteem.

There is also group self-esteem, which refers to your evaluation of your being a member of a particular racial or ethnic group (Porter & Washington 1993). Personal self-esteem is influenced by your group self-esteem. If you view your racial or ethnic group membership negatively then it's especially difficult to develop high self-esteem. Conversely, if you view your membership positively then you are more likely to have high self-esteem. Pride in one's group (racial, ethnic, religious, or gender, for example) and a supportive community contribute to group self-esteem and consequently to personal self-esteem.

The major reason that self-esteem is so important is simply that success breeds success. When you feel good about yourself—about who you are and what you are capable of doing—you perform more effectively. When you think like a success, you are more likely to act like a success. When you think you're a failure, you're more likely to act like a failure. Increasing your self-esteem will help you function more effectively in school, in your interpersonal relationships, and in your career.

Do realize, however, that there are significant cultural differences in the way we are taught to view ourselves (Gudykunst & Ting-Toomey 1988). For example, in the United States, Australia, and Western Europe people are encouraged to be independent. Members of these cultures are taught to get ahead, to compete, to win, to achieve their goals, to realize their unique potential, to stand out from the crowd. In many Asian and African cultures, on the other hand, people are taught to value an interdependent self. Members of these cultures are taught to get along, to help others, and to not disagree, stand out, or be conspicuous. Although self-esteem depends largely on achieving your goals, your culture seems to select the specific goals.

Television talk show hosts generally, but especially Oprah Winfrey, emphasize the importance of self-esteem. Why is self-esteem so important to today's afternoon television viewers? To today's college students?

Attack Your Self-Destructive Beliefs

Self-destructive beliefs are those things that you believe damage your self-esteem and prevent you from building meaningful and productive relationships. They may be about yourself ("I'm not creative," "I'm boring"), your world ("The world is an unhappy place," "People are out to get me"), and your relationships ("All the good people are already in relationships," "If I ever fall in love, I know I'll be hurt"). Identifying these beliefs will help you examine them critically and see that they are both illogical and self-defeating.

Another way of looking at self-destructive beliefs is to identify what Pamela Butler (1981) calls "drivers"—unrealistic beliefs that may motivate you to act in ways that are self-defeating. Butler identifies five such drivers: be perfect, hurry up, be strong, please others, and try hard. If you can hear yourself giving these injunctions, you may have internalized the unproductive and self-defeating drivers. Recognize instead that it is the *unrealistic* nature of these drivers that creates problems. The drive to try hard or be strong only becomes unhealthy when it becomes extreme and absolute.

The drive to *be perfect* impels you to try to perform at unrealistically high levels in just about everything you do. Whether it is work, school, athletics, or appearance, this drive tells you that anything short of perfection is unacceptable and that you are to blame for any "imperfections."

The drive to *hurry up* compels you to do things quickly, to do more than can be reasonably expected in any given amount of time. This drive is at the foundation of what has come to be called "Type A" behavior (Friedman & Rosenman 1974), the personality that is always impatient, always rushing.

The drive to *be strong* tells you that weakness and any of the more vulnerable emotions, such as sadness, compassion, or loneliness, are wrong. This driver prevents you from crying or asking for help or having unfulfilled needs.

The drive to *please others* leads you to seek approval from others. Pleasing yourself is secondary and in fact self-pleasure comes from pleasing others.

The drive to *try hard* makes you take on more responsibilities than anyone can be expected to handle, tasks that would be impossible for any normal person to handle.

Instead of helping you become successful, these drivers almost ensure your failure. Because they set unrealistically high standards, they make it impossible for you to accomplish the very things you feel are essential for approval by others and by yourself.

Recognizing that you may have internalized such drivers is a first step to eliminating them. A second step involves recognizing that these drivers are in fact unrealistic and self-defeating. Psychotherapist Albert Ellis (1988, Ellis & Harper 1975) and other cognitive therapists (for example, Beck 1988) would argue that you can accomplish this by understanding why these drivers are unrealistic and substituting more realistic ones. For example, following Ellis, you might try substituting the unrealistic belief to please others (always and in everything you do) with a more realistic belief that it would be nice if others were pleased with you, but it certainly isn't essential. A third step consists of giving yourself permission to fail, to be less than perfect, to be normal.

Engage in Self-Affirmation

Remind yourself of your successes from time to time. Focus on your good deeds, strengths, and positive qualities. Also, look carefully at the good relationships you have with friends and relatives. Concentrate on your potential, not your limitations (Brody 1991).

Seek Out Nurturing People

Seek out positive people who are optimistic and make you feel good about yourself. Avoid those who find fault with just about everything. Seek to build a network of supportive others (Brody 1991).

Work on Projects That Will Result in Success

Success builds self-esteem. Each success makes achieving the next one a little easier. Remember that the failure of a project is not the failure of you as a person; failure is something that happens, not something inside you. Everyone faces defeat somewhere along the line. The attitude that distinguishes failures from successes is that successful people know how to deal with setbacks. Further, one defeat does not mean you will fail the next time. Put failure in perspective, and don't make it an excuse for not trying again.

You Do Not Have to Be Loved by Everyone

Many people believe that everyone should love them. This belief traps you into thinking you must always please others so they will like you.

SELF-DISCLOSURE

When you reveal information from your hidden self, you are engaging in self-disclosure (Jourard 1968, 1971a, 1971b). In this section we look at self-disclosure from a number of vantage points: the nature of self-disclosure, the factors influencing self-disclosure, the rewards and dangers of self-disclosure, and some guidelines to consider before self-disclosing. But before reading about these rewards and dangers, explore your own feelings about how willing you are to self-disclose by taking the Self-Test, "How Willing to Self-Disclose Are You?" on page 76.

The Nature of Self-Disclosure

Self-disclosure is communication in which you reveal information about yourself. Because self-disclosure is a type of communication, it includes not only overt statements but also, for example, slips of the tongue and unconscious nonverbal signals. It varies from whispering a secret to a best friend to making a public confession on "Oprah Winfrey."

As the term implies, self-disclosure concerns you—your thoughts, feelings, and behaviors. It might also, however, refer to your intimates because information about them usually has some impact on yourself. Thus, self-disclosure could refer to your own actions or the actions of, say, your parents or children, since these have a direct relationship to who you are.

Although by definition self-disclosure may be any information about the self, it is most often used to refer to information that you normally keep hidden rather than simply to information that you have not previously revealed.

Factors Influencing Self-Disclosure

Self-disclosure occurs more readily under certain circumstances. Here, we identify several factors influencing self-disclosure.

Group Size. Self-disclosure occurs more in small groups than in large groups. Dyads (groups of two people) are the most hospitable setting for self-disclosure. With one listener, you can attend carefully to the person's responses. On the basis of this support or lack of it, you can monitor the disclosures, continuing if the situation is supportive and stopping if it is not.

Liking. People tend to disclose to people they like or love, and not to disclose to people they dislike (Derlega, Winstead, Wong, & Greenspan 1987). This is not surprising, since people you like (and who probably like you) will be supportive and positive. Not only do you disclose to those you like, you probably also come to like those to whom you disclose (Berg & Archer 1983). You probably also disclose more to those you trust (Wheeless & Grotz 1977; Derlega, Metts, Petronio, & Margulis 1993).

Receiver Relationship. At times self-disclosure is more likely to occur in temporary than permanent relationships—for example, between strangers on a train or plane, a kind of "in-flight intimacy" (McGill 1985). In this situation, two people establish an intimate self-disclosing relationship during some brief travel period, knowing that they will never see each other again.

When you self-disclose you generally expose some weakness or make yourself vulnerable in some way and so it is not surprising to find that intimate self-disclosures are less likely to occur in competitive rather than in noncompetitive relationships (Busse & Birk 1993).

You are also more likely to disclose to in-group members rather than to members of groups of which you are not a member. For example, people from the same race are more likely to disclose more to members of the same race than to members of another race and people with disabilities are more likely to disclose to others with disabilities than to those without disabilities (Stephan, Stephan, Wenzel, & Cornelius 1991).

Age. Self-disclosure also seems greater when we talk with those who are approximately our own age (Collins & Gould 1994). For example, young women self-disclosed more to same-aged partners than to those significantly older than them. Also, the level of intimacy seems to be more similar in similar-age dyads than in differing-age dyads. Older women disclosed more about the past than did the younger women. Further, older people are more likely to engage in painful self-disclosures (talk of illness and loneliness, for example) than are younger people (Coupland, Coupland, Giles, Henwood, et al. 1988).

Dyadic Effect. Generally, self-disclosure is reciprocal. In any interaction, it is more likely to occur if the other person has previously done so. This is the **dyadic effect**—what one person in a dyad does, the other does in response. The dyadic effect in self-disclosure takes a kind of spiral form with each self-dis-

SELF-TEST

how willing to self-disclose are you?

Respond to each of the following statements by indicating the likelihood of your disclosing such information to, for instance, other members of this class. Use the following scale:

1 = would definitely self-disclose
2 = would probably self-disclose
3 = don't know
4 = would probably not self-disclose
5 = would definitely not self-disclose

_____ 1. My religious beliefs.
_____ 2. My attitudes toward other religions, nationalities, and races.
_____ 3. My economic status.
_____ 4. My parents' attitudes toward other religions, races, and nationalities.
_____ 5. My feelings about my parents.
_____ 6. My sexual fantasies.
_____ 7. My ideal mate.
_____ 8. My drinking and/or drug-taking behavior.
_____ 9. My unfulfilled desires.
_____10. My feelings about the people in this group.

Thinking Critically About Your Willingness to Self-Disclose. Can you identify general topic areas about which you are more likely to disclose than others? Are there discrepencies between what your willingness to self-disclose as noted here indicate and your actual disclosures, say, during the past few weeks? Would the results of this questionnaire have differed if the target audience of these disclosures was your parents? A stranger you would probably never see again? A best friend or lover? A teacher or counselor? If you have the opportunity compare your responses with others: Is there much agreement among people in their willingness to self disclose? Are there gender differences? Are there cultural differences?

closure prompting an additional self-disclosure by the other person, which in turn prompts still more self-disclosure, and so on. It's interesting to note that disclosures made in response to the disclosures of others are generally more intimate than those that are not the result of the dyadic effect (Berg & Archer 1983).

This dyadic effect is not universal, however. For example, while Americans are likely to follow the dyadic effect and reciprocate with explicit, verbal self-disclosure, Koreans do not (Won-Doornink 1985).

Competence. Competent communicators self-disclose more than less competent ones. As James McCroskey and Lawrence Wheeless (1976) note:

> it may well be that people who are more competent also perceive themselves to be more competent, and thus have the self-confidence necessary to take more chances with self-disclosure. Or, even more likely, competent people may simply have more positive things about themselves to disclose than less competent people.

Personality. Highly sociable and extroverted people self-disclose more than those who are less sociable and more introverted. Sometimes, anxiety increases self-disclosing and at other times it reduces it to a minimum. People who are apprehensive about talking in general also self-disclose less than do those who are more comfortable in oral communication. People with high self-esteem are more likely to engage in self-disclosure than are those low in self-esteem (Dolgin, Meyer, & Schwartz 1991).

Topics. If you are like the people studied by researchers, you are more likely to disclose about some topics than others. For example, you are more likely to self-disclose information about your job or hobbies than about your sex life or financial situation (Jourard 1968, 1971a). You would also disclose favorable information more readily than unfavorable information. Generally, the more personal and the more negative the topic, the less likely you are to self-disclose (Nakanishi 1986). Further, you are more likely to disclose information that reflects positively on the other person than information that reflects negatively (Shimanoff 1985).

Culture. Different cultures view self-disclosure differently. People in the United States (with the exception of Puerto Rico), for example, disclose more than do those in Great Britain, Germany, and Japan (Gudykunst 1983). Among the Kabre of Togo, secrecy is a major part of their everyday interaction (Piot 1993). American students disclose more than do students from nine different Middle East countries (Jourard 1971a). Similarly, American students self-disclose more on a variety of controversial issues and also self-disclose more to different types of people than do Chinese students (Chen 1992).

However, there are also important similarities across cultures. For example, people from Great Britain, Germany, the United States (including Puerto Rico) are all more apt to disclose personal information—hobbies, interests, attitudes, and opinions on politics and religion—than information on finances, sex, personality, and interpersonal relationships (Jourard 1971a). Similarly, one study showed self-disclosure patterns between American males to be virtually identical to the patterns between Korean males (Won-Doornink 1991).

Gender. Generally, men disclose less than do women (Naifeh & Smith 1984; Rosenfeld 1979) except in initial heterosexual encounters, in which men disclose more (Derlega, Winstead, Wong, & Hunter 1985). Research shows that sex role rather than biological gender accounts for the differences in self-disclosure (Pearson 1980; Shaffer, Pegalis, & Cornell 1992). In one study, "masculine women" self-disclosed to a lesser extent than did women who scored low on masculinity scales (Pearson 1980). Further, "feminine men" self-disclosed to a greater extent than did men who scored low on femininity scales.

The major reason both men and women give for avoiding self-disclosure is the fear of projecting an unfavorable image. In addition men fear appearing inconsistent, losing control over the other person, and threatening the relationship. Women, on the other hand, fear revealing information that may be used against them, giving others the impression that they are emotionally disturbed, or hurting their relationships (Rosenfeld 1979).

Thinking Critically About Self-Disclosure

Because self-disclosure and its effects can be so significant, think critically before deciding to disclose or not disclose. Specifically, weigh the rewards and dangers carefully. Also, think about the way you will disclose and respond to the disclosures of others. In reading these topics, recall the earlier model of communication and the importance of culture (Unit 1). Not all societies and cultures view self-disclosure in the same way. In some cultures, disclosing one's inner feelings is considered a weakness. Among Anglo-Saxon Americans, for example, it would be considered "out of place" if a man cried at a happy occasion like a wedding. That same behavior would go unnoticed in some Latin cultures. Similarly, in Japan it is considered undesirable to reveal personal information, whereas in the United States it is considered desirable and is even expected (Barnlund 1989; Hall and Hall 1987).

The potential rewards and dangers of self-disclosure as well as any suggested guidelines, then, must be examined in terms of the specific culture and its rules. As with many such cultural rules, following them brings approval and violating them brings disapproval.

The Rewards of Self-Disclosure

One reason why self-disclosure is so significant is that its rewards are great. Self-disclosure may bring self-knowledge, increase your ability to cope, improve communication, and increase relationship depth.

Self-Knowledge. When you self-disclose you gain a new perspective on yourself and a deeper understanding of your own behavior. In therapy, for example, often the insight comes while the client is self-disclosing. He or she may recognize some previously unknown facet of behavior or relationship. Through self-disclosure, then, you may also come to understand yourself more thoroughly.

Coping Abilities. Self-disclosure may help you deal with your problems, especially guilt. One of the great fears many people have is that they will not be accepted because of some deep, dark secret, because of something they have done, or because of some feeling or attitude they have. By self-disclosing such feelings and receiving support rather than rejection, they may become better able to deal with any such guilt and perhaps reduce or even eliminate it (Pennebaker 1990).

Even self-acceptance is difficult without self-disclosure. If you accept yourself, in part at least through the eyes of others, then it becomes essential that you give others the opportunity to know and to respond to the "real" you. Through self-disclosure and subsequent support, you put yourself in a better position to receive positive responses to who you really are, stripped of the façade that the failure to self-disclose erects.

Communication Efficiency. Self-disclosure may help to improve communication. You understand the messages of others largely to the extent that you understand the senders of those messages. You can understand what someone says better if you know that individual well. You can tell what certain nuances mean, when the person is serious and when joking, and when the person is being sarcastic out of fear and when out of resentment. Self-disclosure is an essential condition for getting to know another individual, for the process of adjustment considered in Unit 2.

Relational Depth. Self-disclosure is often helpful for establishing a meaningful relationship between two people. Research has found, for example, that marital satisfaction is higher for couples who are middle to high self-disclosers; satisfaction is significantly less in low-disclosing relationships (Rosenfeld & Bowen 1991). Without self-disclosure, relationships of any meaningful depth seem difficult if not impossible. By self-disclosing, you tell others that you trust them, respect them, and care enough about them and your relationship to reveal yourself to them. This in turn leads the other individual to self-disclose (the dyadic effect) and forms at least the start of a meaningful relationship, one that is honest and open and goes beyond surface trivialities.

The Dangers of Self-Disclosure

In March 1995 television talk show host Jenny Jones presented a show on self-disclosing secret crushes. One panelist, Scott Amedure, disclosed his crush on another man, Jonathan Schmitz. Three days after the taping of the show—a show that was never aired—Scott Amedure was shot in his home. The police arrested Schmitz and charged him with murder (*New York Times* March 19, 1995, Section 4, p. 16). Although this is an extreme demonstration of the dangers of self-disclosure, there are many risks to self-disclosing (Bochner 1984). Here are a few general ones.

Personal and Social Rejection. Usually you self-disclose to someone whose responses you feel will be supportive of your disclosures. Of course, the person you think will be supportive may actually reject you. Parents, normally the most supportive of all interpersonal relations, have frequently rejected children who self-disclosed their homosexuality, their plans to marry someone of a different religion, their decision

How might the rewards and dangers of self-disclosure differ from one culture to another? Are there cultures that consistently reward (or punish) disclosure? How would you describe your own culture in terms of the rewards and punishments it places on self-disclosure? Does it treat disclosures by men and women in the same way?

to avoid the draft, their belief in a certain faith, or their HIV+ status. Your best friends and your closest intimates may reject you for similar self-disclosures.

Material Loss. Sometimes self-disclosures result in material losses. Politicians who disclose that they have seen a psychiatrist may later find that their own political party no longer supports them and that voters are unwilling to vote for them. Teachers who disclose former or present drug-taking behavior or cohabitation with one of their students may find themselves being denied tenure, forced to accept undesirable teaching schedules, and eventually become victims of "budget cuts." In the corporate world, self-disclosures of alcoholism or drug addiction are often met with dismissal, demotion, or transfer.

Intrapersonal Difficulties. When other people's reactions are not as predicted, intrapersonal difficulties may result. When you are rejected instead of supported, when your parents say that you disgust them instead of hugging you, and when your friends ignore you at school rather than seeking you out as before, you are in line for some intrapersonal difficulties. No one likes to be rejected, and those with fragile egos might well consider what damage such rejection could bring.

Remember that self-disclosure, like any communication, is irreversible (see Unit 2). Regardless of how many times you may try to qualify a self-disclosure or "take it back," once something is said it cannot be withdrawn. Nor can you erase the conclusions and inferences listeners have made on the basis of your disclosures.

Guidelines for Self-Disclosing

Each person has to make her or his own decisions concerning self-disclosure. Each decision will be based on numerous variables, many of which we considered in the previous discussion. The following guidelines will help you raise the right questions before making what must be your own decision.

The Motivation for Self-Disclosure. Effective self-disclosure is motivated by a concern for the relationship, for the others involved, and for yourself. Some people self-disclose out of a desire to hurt the listener. For example, a daughter who tells her parents that they hindered rather than helped her emotional development may be disclosing out of a desire to hurt and punish rather than to improve the relationship. Of course, you should not use self-disclosure to punish yourself (perhaps because of some guilt feeling or unresolved conflict).

The Appropriateness of Self-Disclosure. Effective self-disclosure should be appropriate to the context and to the relationship between speaker and listener. Before making any significant self-disclosure, ask yourself if the context is right. Could you arrange a better time and place? Is this self-disclosure appropriate to the relationship? Generally, the more intimate the disclosures, the closer the relationship should be. It is probably best to resist intimate disclosures with nonintimates and casual acquaintances, or in the early stages of a relationship. This suggestion applies especially to intimate negative disclosures, for example, financial or sexual difficulties or a history of drug dependency.

The Disclosures of the Other Person. During your disclosures, give the other person a chance to reciprocate with his or her own disclosures. If the other person does not also self-disclose, then reassess your decision to open up. The lack of reciprocity may signal that this person—at this time and in this context—does not welcome your disclosures. Disclose gradually and in small increments; when disclosures are made too rapidly and all at once, the normal reciprocity cannot operate. Further, you lose the ability to retreat if the responses are not positive enough.

The Possible Burdens Self-Disclosure Might Entail. Carefully weigh any problems you may run into as a result of a disclosure. Can you afford to lose your job if you disclose your previous prison record? Are you willing to risk losing a relationship if you disclose previous infidelities? Ask yourself whether you are making unreasonable demands on the listener. Parents often place unreasonable burdens on their children by self-disclosing marital problems, addictions, or self-doubts that children are too young or too emotionally involved in to accept. Often such disclosures do not make the relationship a better one but instead add tension and friction. Sometimes the motivation is to ease one's own guilt without considering the burden this places on the other person.

Even when you preface your disclosures with "Don't tell anyone but . . ." receivers of such private information are more likely to pass it on to others than you anticipate. Also, they are especially likely to repeat disclosures when they concern highly or moderately private information (Petronio & Bantz 1991).

MEDIA WATCH

OUTING

Self-disclosure, as already noted, is a process by which you reveal to others information about yourself. Although at times you may be forced to self-disclose, we normally think of it as a voluntary process in which you control the amount of information you reveal to others about yourself. There is, however, another side to self-disclosure and that occurs when someone else reveals your hidden self, when someone else takes information from your hidden self and makes it public. Although this third-party disclosure can concern any aspect of one's hidden self, the media have made a special case out of revealing a person's affectional orientation; the process is called *outing*.

Outing as a media process began in a relatively obscure gay magazine (*Outweek*). An article, "The Secret Gay Life of Malcolm Forbes," made public Forbes' homosexuality; it "outed" him.

In March of 1995, the *Wall Street Journal* ran a front-page story on Jann Wenner, the multimillionaire owner and publisher of *Rolling Stone, Us, Men's Journal,* and *Family Life.* The story was basically a financial one and focused on the possible effects Wenner's marital breakup would have on his media empire. The headline read: "Jann Wenner's Rift with Wife Shakes Up His Publishing Empire." Somewhat casually noted in the article—without Wenners permission and against his wishes (Rotello 1995)—was the fact that the new person in Wenner's life was a man. This article, although not the first to discuss Wenner's gay relationship—the *New York Post, Advertising Age,* and *Newsweek* (*Newsweek,* March 20, 1995, p. 58) had run similar stories—it has been singled out because of the prestige of the *Wall Street Journal* and because of the many issues this type of forced disclosure raises.

Many saw this as an invasion of privacy; Wenner's private life is his own and it is up to him if he wishes to reveal details. Others saw this as not only appropriate but the only way to deal fairly with gay relationships.

A few weeks later, across the Atlantic, the Church of England's third-highest-ranking cleric, the Bishop of London, David Hope, was pressured by gay and lesbian groups to announce his homosexuality (*New York Times* March 19, 1995, p. 10). The bishop called a news conference and condemned the tactics as "seriously intimidatory or worse."

These two cases are especially interesting in terms of self-disclosure, and raise the issue of the legitimacy of outing (Gross 1991; Signorile 1993). In the first case, if Wenner was dating a woman, the media would have mentioned it, but few would have raised the privacy issue because he is a public figure and this divorce is a relevant issue since it will likely impact on his financial empire. If the media reports on only extramarital heterosexual relationships, is it not at the same time saying that homosexual relationships are illegitimate and that they are not to be spoken of openly?

The David Hope case is different. Here, the bishop wishes not to discuss his sexuality; he says that it is "ambiguous" and that he is celibate (*New York Times* March 19, 1995, p. 10). Gay organizations in England, however, contend that he is a policymaker in the Church of England and that by "outing" him they are preventing him from taking a negative stand against homosexuality as the Church of England has done in the past. The outing serves the purpose of silencing or weakening any potential antihomosexual stand. It may be noted that at a subsequent meeting, the bishops of the Church of England, who represent 70 million members, issued a condemnation of homophobia and asked that the church reconsider its generally negative position on lesbian and gay relationships (Morales 1995).

Outing raises an interesting perspective on self-disclosure and the issues discussed here are just a small part of the subject. Further, the concept of outing might legitimately be extended to refer to revealing other hidden information—for example, an athlete's prison record or drug habit, a movie star's ill health or alcoholism, or a politician's friends or financial dealings. How do you feel about outing? If you were the editor of a newspaper, what would be your policy on outing? What guidelines should the media follow in dealing with issues that individuals wish to keep private? At what point does a person lose the right to be considered a private citizen and to privacy?

Guidelines for Responding to Self-Disclosures

When someone discloses to you, it is usually a sign of trust and affection. In serving this most important receiver function, keep the following points in mind.

Use Effective and Active Listening Skills. In Unit 4 we identify the skills of effective listening. These are especially important when listening to self-disclosures. Listen actively, listen for different levels of meaning, listen with empathy, and listen with an open mind. Paraphrase the speaker so that you can be sure you understand both the thoughts and the feelings communicated. Express understanding of the speaker's feelings to allow her or him the opportunity to see these more objectively and through the eyes of another individual. Ask questions to ensure your own understanding and to signal your interest and attention.

Support and Reinforce the Discloser. Express support for the person during and after the disclosures. Refrain from evaluation during the disclosures; don't say, "You shouldn't have done that" or "Did you really cheat?" Concentrate on understanding and empathizing with the person. Allow the speaker to set her or his own pace; don't rush the person with the too frequent "So how did it all end?" type of response. Make your supportiveness clear through your verbal and nonverbal responses: maintain eye contact, lean toward the speaker, ask relevant questions, and echo the speaker's thoughts and feelings.

Maintain Confidentiality. When a person confides in you, it is because she or he wants you to know these feelings and thoughts. If the discloser wishes others to share these details, then it is up to her or him to reveal them. If you tell others about these confidences, be prepared for all sorts of negative effects. Such indiscretion will likely inhibit future disclosures from this individual to anyone in general and to you in particular, and your relationship will probably suffer. Those to whom you reveal these disclosures will likely feel that since you have betrayed a confidence once, you will do so again, perhaps with their own personal details. A general climate of distrust is easily established. Betraying a confidence debases what should be a significant and meaningful interpersonal experience.

Don't Use the Disclosures as Weapons. Many self-disclosures expose vulnerability or weakness. If you later turn around and use these against the person, you betray that person's confidence and trust. The relationship is sure to suffer and may never fully recover.

good for class

THINK ABOUT

Think about how you would respond to each of the following situations. For each situation, indicate why you think the self-disclosure would or would not be appropriate.

1. A mother of two teen-age children (one boy, one girl) has been feeling guilty for the past year over a romantic affair she had with her brother-in-law while her husband was in prison. The mother has been divorced for the last few months. She wants to disclose this affair and her guilt to her children.
2. A student plagiarized a term paper for an anthropology class. He is sorry for having done this and especially sorry that the plagiarized paper only earned a grade C+. He wants to confess to his instructor and rewrite the paper.
3. Bob is a teacher at a state college and has recently discovered he is HIV+. He wonders—Should he reveal this to his family? To his colleagues at the college? To his students?
4. Tom is engaged to Cathy, but has recently fallen in love with another woman. He wants to call Cathy on the phone, break his engagement, and disclose his new relationship.
5. Sally is the director of marketing for a large publishing company and has been performing extremely well over the last three years. She feels guilty that she lied on her résumé and now wants to reveal this to her supervisors. Should she? If so, how should she do this? Face-to-face? Phone? Letter?
6. Mary and Jim have been married for twelve years. Mary has been honest about most things and has disclosed a great deal to Jim about her past romantic encounters, her fears, her insecurities, her ambitions, and so on. Yet Jim doesn't seem able to reciprocate. He almost never shares his feelings and has told Mary almost nothing about his life before they met. Mary wonders if she should continue to disclose or if she should begin to limit her disclosures.

SUMMARY

In this unit we looked at several aspects of the self: self-concept, self-awareness, self-esteem, and self-disclosure.

1. Self-concept refers to the image you have of yourself. It is developed from the image others have of you and reveal, the comparisons you make between yourself and others, and the way you evaluate your own thoughts and behaviors.
2. In the Johari Window model of the self, there are four major areas: the open self, the blind self, the hidden self, and the unknown self.
3. To increase self-awareness, ask yourself about yourself, listen to others to see yourself as others do, actively seek information from others about yourself, see yourself from different perspectives, and increase your open self.
4. Self-esteem refers to the way you feel about yourself, the value you place on yourself, and the positive-negative evaluation you make of yourself. It may be increased by attacking your self-destructive beliefs, engaging in self-affirmation, seeking out nurturing people, working on projects that will result in success, and recognizing that you do not have to be loved by everyone.
5. Self-disclosure refers to a form of communication in which information about the self (usually information that is normally kept hidden) is communicated to another person.
6. Self-disclosure is more likely to occur when the potential discloser is with one other person, when the discloser likes or loves the listener, when the two people are approximately the same age, when the listener also discloses, when the discloser feels competent, when the discloser is highly sociable and extroverted, and when the topic of disclosure is fairly impersonal and positive.
7. The rewards of self-disclosure include increased self-knowledge, a better ability to cope with difficult situations and guilt, more efficient communication, and a better chance for a meaningful relationship.
8. The dangers of self-disclosure include personal and social rejection, material loss, and intrapersonal difficulties.
9. Before self-disclosing, consider the motivation and appropriateness of the self-disclosure, the opportunity available for open and honest responses, the disclosures of the other person, and the possible burdens that your self-disclosure might impose on you and your listeners.
10. When listening to disclosures, practice the skills of effective and active listening, support and reinforce the discloser, keep the disclosures confidential, and do not use the disclosures as weapons against the person.

THINKING CRITICALLY ABOUT THE SELF IN COMMUNICATION

1. Do you operate with the uniqueness bias when you compare yourself to others? Do you see advantages and disadvantages to this bias?
2. Much has been written about the connection between self-esteem and bilingual education. The argument is made that bilingual education is necessary to developing a student's self-esteem. Recent research, however, does not find any such relationship (Alexander & Baker 1992). Of course, there may be a relationship that this research simply hasn't found. How do you feel about the possible connection between the use of one's native language in the classroom and self-esteem?

3. Are your self-disclosures influenced by the factors mentioned in this unit, for example, group size, degree of liking, the dyadic effect, personality, age, and topic? Can you describe how these operate? What other factors influence your self-disclosures?
4. Have you self-disclosed more in close relationships, in casual relationships, or in temporary acquaintantships? What accounts for these differences?
5. What does your culture say about self-disclosure? Does your culture encourage or discourage it? Does your culture have different expectations for men and for women? Are there certain topics that are taboo for any kind of discussion?
6. How do you see men and women in terms of their self-disclosures? Do you find, as research says, that women self-disclose more than men? Are there situations in which men disclose more? Do men and women differ in the types of disclosures? An interesting twist on the general finding that women self-disclose more than men is the finding that among married couples, both husbands and wives self-disclosed equally but wives reported that they made more emotional disclosures than did their husbands (Shimanoff 1985; also see Petronio & Martin 1986). Do you think this would also hold for dating couples?
7. As a parent would you share with your children your financial and personal worries? The answer, it seems, would depend at least in part on your socioeconomic status and on whether you are a single parent or one of two parents (McLoyd & Wilson 1992). Research finds that members of middle-class two-parent families are reluctant to share financial problems with their children, preferring to shelter them from some of life's harsher realities. Low-income single mothers, however, feel that sharing this with their children will protect them because they will know how difficult life is and what they are up against. The researchers argue that this practice of disclosing such problems actually creates problems for the child, such as aggressiveness, difficulties in concentrating on learning in school, and anxiety disorders. What would your general advice be to parents about disclosing such matters?
8. What can you do to encourage the disclosures of others? What can you do to discourage such disclosures?
9. What do you think of people self-disclosing publicly on, say, a television talk show? Would you go on such a show? What topics would you be willing to discuss? What topics would you be unwilling to discuss?
10. How would you go about finding answers to such questions as these:
    a. Under what circumstances do people compare themselves with those of less ability and under what circumstances do people compare themselves with those of greater ability?
    b. Is intelligence related to self-awareness? To self-esteem?
    c. Do men and women differ in the topics of their self-disclosures when talking with each other? When talking with same-sex others? Do same-sex and opposite-sex couples self-disclose similarly?
    d. Does the physical context influence the amount and type of self-disclosure that takes place between two people meeting for the first time?

six unit: The Culture in Communication

unit contents

unit goals

After completing this unit, you should be able to

1. define *culture, enculturation,* and *acculturation*
2. distinguish between collectivist and individualistic orientation, low- and high-context cultures, and high- and low-power distances
3. explain the theories of culture and communication discussed in this unit
4. define intercultural communication and explain the general principles for increasing effectiveness in intercultural communication

Culture (introduced briefly in Unit 1) refers to the relatively specialized life-style of a group of people—consisting of their values, beliefs, artifacts, ways of behaving, and ways of communicating. Also included in a culture are all that members of a social group have produced and developed—their language, modes of thinking, art, laws, and religion.

Culture is passed on from one generation to the next through communication, not through genes. Thus, culture does not refer to skin color or eye shape—these are passed on through genes not communication. Culture does refer to beliefs in a supreme being, to attitudes toward success and happiness, and to the values placed on friendship, love, family, or money—these are transmitted not by genes but by communication.

Culture is not synonymous with race or nationality; however, members of a particular race or country are often taught similar beliefs, attitudes, and values. This similarity makes it possible to speak of "Hispanic culture" or "African American culture." To avoid stereotyping, do recognize that within any large culture—especially a culture based on race or nationality—there will be enormous differences. The Kansas farmer and the Wall Street executive may both be, say, German American, but they may differ widely in their attitudes and beliefs and in their general life-style. In some ways the Kansas farmer may be closer in attitudes and values to the Chinese farmer than to the Wall Street executive. Further, the fact that you are born into a particular race and nationality does not mean that you necessarily have to adopt their dominant attitudes or ways of behaving.

Culture is passed from one generation to another through **enculturation**, a process by which you learn the culture into which you are born (your native culture). Parents, peer groups, schools, religious institutions, and government agencies are the main teachers of culture.

A different way of learning culture is through **acculturation**, the process by which you learn the rules and norms of a culture different from your native culture. Through acculturation, your original or native culture is modified through direct contact with or exposure to a new and different culture. For example, when immigrants settle in the United States (the host culture), their own culture becomes influenced by the host culture. Gradually, the values, ways of behaving, and beliefs of the host culture become more and more a part of the immigrants' culture. At the same time, of course, the host culture changes too as it interacts with the immigrants' culture. Generally, however, the culture of the immigrant changes more. The reasons for this are that the host country's members far outnumber the immigrant group and the media is largely dominated by and reflects the values and customs of the host culture.

The acceptance of the new culture depends on a number of factors (Kim 1988). Immigrants who come from cultures similar to the host culture will become acculturated more quickly than do the older and less well-educated. Personality factors also play a part. Persons who are risk takers and open-minded, for example, have greater acculturation potential. Also, persons who are familiar with the host culture prior to immigration—whether through interpersonal contact or media exposure—will be acculturated more readily.

Before exploring further the role of culture in communication, consider your own cultural values and beliefs by taking the self-test, "What Are Your Cultural Beliefs and Values?" on page 86. This test will help you see how you own cultural values and beliefs may influence your interpersonal, small group, and public communications in the messages you listen to and the messages you send.

SELF-TEST

what are your cultural beliefs and values?

Here the extremes of ten cultural differences are identified. For each characteristic indicate your own values:

a. if you feel your values are very similar to the extremes then select 1 or 7,
b. if you feel your values are quite similar to the extremes then select 2 or 6,
c. if you feel your values are fairly similar to the extremes then select 3 or 5, and
d. if you feel you are in the middle, then select 4.

GENDER EQUALITY

Men and women are equal and are entitled to equality in all areas.	1 2 3 4 5 6 7	Men and women are very different and should stick to the specific roles assigned to them by their culture.

GROUP AND INDIVIDUAL ORIENTATION

"Success" is measured by your contribution to the group.	1 2 3 4 5 6 7	"Success" is measured by how far you outperform others

HEDONISM

You should enjoy yourself as much as possible.	1 2 3 4 5 6 7	You should work as much as possible.

RELIGION

Religion is the final arbiter of what is right and wrong; your first obligation is to abide by the rules and customs of your religion.	1 2 3 4 5 6 7	Religion is like any other social institution; it is not inherently moral or right just because it is a religion.

FAMILY

Your first obligation is to your family; each person is responsible for the welfare of his or her family.	1 2 3 4 5 6 7	Your first obligation is to yourself; each person is responsible for himself or herself.

TIME ORIENTATION

Work hard now for a better future.	1 2 3 4 5 6 7	Live in the present; the future may never come.

RELATIONSHIP PERMANENCY

Romantic relationships, once made, are forever.	1 2 3 4 5 6 7	Romantic relationships should be maintained as long as they are more rewarding than punishing and dissolved when they are more punishing than rewarding.

EMOTIONAL EXPRESSION

People should express their emotions openly and freely.	1 2 3 4 5 6 7	People should not reveal their emotions, especially those that may reflect negatively on them or others or make others feel uncomfortable.

MONEY

Money is extremely important and should be a major consideration in just about any decision you make.	1 2 3 4 5 6 7	Money is relatively unimportant and should not enter into life's really important decisions such as what relationship to enter or what career to pursue.

BELIEF IN A JUST WORLD

The world is a just place; bad things happen to bad people and good things happen to good people; what goes around comes around.	1 2 3 4 5 6 7	The world is random; bad and good things happen to people without any reference to whether they are good or bad people.

Thinking Critically About Cultural Beliefs, Values, and Communication This test was designed to help you explore the possible influence of your cultural beliefs and values on communication. If you visualize communication as involving choices, as already noted in Unit 1, then these beliefs will influence the choices you make and thus how you communicate and how you listen and respond to the communications of others. For example, your beliefs and values about gender equality will influence the way in which you communicate with and about the opposite sex. Your group and individual orientation will influence how you perform in work teams and how you deal with your peers at school and at work. Your degree of hedonism will influence the kinds of communications you engage in, the books you read, the television programs you watch. Your religious beliefs will influence the ethical system you follow in communicating. Review the entire list of ten characteristics and try to identify one *specific* way in which each characteristic influences your communication.

HOW CULTURES DIFFER

There are at least three major ways in which cultures differ that are especially important for communication. Following Gudykunst (1991) and Hall and Hall (1987) we discuss collectivism and individualism, high and low context, and power distances.

Individual and Collective Orientation

Cultures differ in the extent to which they promote individual values (for example, power, achievement, hedonism, and stimulation) versus collectivist values (for example, benevolence, tradition, and conformity). Americans generally have a preference for the individual values (Kapoor, Wolfe, & Blue 1995) while many Asian cultures have a preference for collectivist values (Hall & Hall 1987, Bumiller 1995).

One of the major differences between these two orientations is the extent to which an individual's goals or the group's goals are given precedence. Individual and collective tendencies are, of course, not mutually exclusive; this is not an all-or-none orientation but rather one of emphasis. You probably have both tendencies. Thus, you may, for example, compete with other members of your basketball team to score the most baskets or to win the most valuable player award (and thus emphasize individual goals). At the same time, however, you will—in a game—act in a way that will benefit the entire team (and thus emphasize group goals). In actual practice both individual and collective tendencies will help you and your team each achieve your goals. Yet, most people and most cultures have a dominant orientation; they are more individually oriented or more collectively oriented in most situations, most of the time.

In some instances, however, these tendencies may come into conflict. For example, do you shoot for the basket and try to raise your own individual score or do you pass the ball to another player who is better positioned to score and thus benefit your team? You make this distinction in popular talk when you call someone a team player (**collectivist orientation**) or an individual player (**individualistic orientation**).

In an individualistic-oriented culture members are responsible for themselves and perhaps their immediate family. In a collectivist culture members are responsible for the entire group.

Success, in an individualistic culture, is measured by the extent to which you surpass other members of your group; you would take pride in standing out from the crowd. Your heroes—in the media, for example—are likely to be those who are unique and who stand apart. In a collectivist culture success is measured by your contribution to the achievements of the group as a whole; you would take pride in your similarity to other members of your group. Your heroes, in contrast, are more likely to be team players who do not stand out from the rest of the group's members.

This difference is even reflected in advertisements. For example, in the United States magazine advertisements appeal to individual benefits and preferences, personal success, and independence. In Korea, a more collectivist culture, advertisements rely on appeals that emphasize benefits to the group, harmony, and family integrity. Not surprisingly, in the United States ads emphasizing individual values were found to be more persuasive than ads emphasizing group benefits or family values (Han & Shavitt 1994).

In an individualistic culture you are responsible to your own conscience and responsibility is largely an individual matter; in a collectivistic culture you are responsible to the rules of the social group and responsibility for an accomplishment or a failure is shared by all members. Competition is fostered in individualistic cultures while cooperation is promoted in collectivist cultures.

In an individualistic culture you might compete for leadership in a small group setting and there would likely be a very clear distinction between leaders and members. In a collectivist culture leadership would be shared and rotated; there is likely to be little distinction between leader and members. These orientations will also influence the kinds of communication members consider appropriate in an organizational context. For example, individualistic members will favor clarity and directness while collectivists will favor "face-saving" and the avoidance of hurting others or arousing negative evaluations (Kim 1994, Kim & Sharkey 1995).

Distinctions between in-group members (members of the specific culture or social group) and out-group members (members of other cultures or groups) are extremely important in collectivist cultures. In individualistic cultures, where the person's individuality is prized, the distinction is likely to be less important.

High- and Low-Context Cultures

Cultures also differ in the extent to which information is made explicit, on the one hand, or is assumed to be in the context or in the persons communicating, on the other. A **high-context culture** is one in which much of the information in communication is in the context or in the person—for example, information that was shared through previous communications, through assumptions about each other, and through shared experiences. The information is thus known by all participants but it is not explicitly stated in the verbal message.

A **low-context culture** is one in which most of the information is explicitly stated in the verbal message, and in many cases it would be written down (to make it even more explicit).

To appreciate the distinction between high and low context, consider giving directions to someone who knows the neighborhood and to a newcomer to your city. To someone who knows the neighborhood (a high-context situation) who asks "Where's the voter registration center?" you can assume that she or he knows the local landmarks. So, you can give directions such as "next to the laundromat on Main Street" or "at the corner of Albany and Elm." To the newcomer (a low-context situation), you could not assume that she or he shares any information with you. You would therefore have to use only those directions that even a stranger would understand, for example, "make a left at the next stop sign" or "go two blocks and then turn right."

High-context cultures are also collectivist cultures (Gudykunst, Ting-Toomey, & Chua 1988; Gudykunst & Kim 1992). These cultures (Japanese, Arabic, Latin American, Thai, Korean, Apache, and Mexican are examples) place great emphasis on personal relationships and oral agreements (Victor 1992). Low-context cultures, then, are also individualistic cultures. These cultures (German, Swedish, Norwegian, and American are examples) place less emphasis on personal relationships and more emphasis on the verbalized, explicit explanation and on the written contracts in business transactions.

Some of the characteristics of both individual-collective and high and low context cultures are summarized in Table 6.1. The table will also serve as a useful summary of the text discussion.

It's interesting to note that as relationships become more intimate, they come to resemble high-context interactions. The more you and your partner know each other, the less verbally explicit you have to

TABLE 6.1 differences in individual (low-context) and collective (high-context) cultures

In every culture there will of course be variations in each of these characteristics. View these, therefore, as general tendencies rather than absolutes. Further, the increased mobility, changing immigration patterns, and the exposure to media from different parts of the world will gradually decrease the differences between these two orientations. [This table is based on the work of Hall (1983) and Hall and Hall (1987) and the interpretations by Gudykunst (1991) and Victor (1992).]

Individual (Low-context) Cultures	Collective (High-context) Cultures
The individual's goals are most important	The group's goals are most important
The individual is responsible for himself or herself and to his or her own conscience	The individual is responsible for the entire group and to the group's values and rules
Success depends on the individual's surpassing others	Success depends on the individual's contribution to the group
Competition is emphasized	Cooperation is emphasized
Clear distinction is made between leaders and members	Little distinction is made between leaders and members; leadership would normally be shared
In-group versus out-group distinctions are of little importance	In-group versus out-group distinctions are of great importance
Information is made explicit; little is left unsaid	Information is often left implicit and much is often omitted from explicit statement
Personal relationships are less important; hence, little time is spent getting to know each other in meetings and conferences	Personal relationships are extremely important; hence, much time is spent getting to know each other in meetings and conferences
Directness is valued; face-saving is seldom considered	Indirectness is valued and face-saving is a major consideration

be. Truman Capote once defined love as "never having to finish your sentences," which is an apt description of high-context relationships. Because you know the other person so well, you can make some pretty good guesses as to what the person will say.

Members of high-context cultures spend lots of time getting to know each other interpersonally and socially before any important transactions take place. Because of this prior personal knowledge, a great deal of information is shared by the members and therefore does not have to be explicitly stated. Members of low-context cultures spend a great deal less time getting to know each other and hence do not have that shared knowledge. As a result everything has to be stated explicitly.

This difference is partly responsible for the differences observed in Japanese and American business groups (alluded to in Unit 1). The Japanese spend lots of time getting to know each other before conducting actual business, whereas Americans get down to business very quickly. The Japanese (and other high-context cultures) want to get to know each other because important information is not made explicit. They have to know you so they can read your nonverbals, for example (Sanders, Wiseman, & Matz 1991). Americans can get right down to business because all important information will be stated explicitly.

To a member of a high-context culture, what is omitted or assumed is a vital part of the communication transaction. Silence, for example, is highly valued (Basso 1972). To a member of a low-context culture, what is omitted creates ambiguity. To this person ambiguity is simply something that will be eliminated by explicit and direct communication. For a member of a high-context culture, ambiguity is something to be avoided; it is a sign that the interpersonal and social interactions have not proved sufficient to establish a shared base of information (Gudykunst 1983).

When this difference between low- and high-context cultures is not understood, misunderstandings can easily result. For example, the directness characteristic of the low-context culture may prove insulting, insensitive, or unnecessary to a member of a high-context culture. Conversely, to a member of a low-context culture, the high-context individual may appear vague, underhanded, or dishonest in his or her reluctance to be explicit or engage in communication that a member of a low-context culture would consider open and direct.

Another frequent source of intercultural misunderstanding that can be traced to the distinction between high- and low-context cultures can be seen in face-saving (Hall & Hall 1987; Imahori & Cupach 1994). High-context cultures place a great deal more emphasis on face-saving. For example, they are more likely to avoid argument for fear of causing others to lose face whereas members of low-context cultures (with their individualistic orientation) will use argument to win a point. Similarly, in high-context cultures criticism should only take place in private. Low-context cultures, however, may not make this public-private distinction. Low-context managers who criticize high-context workers in public will find that their criticism causes interpersonal problems and does little to resolve the original difficulty that led to the criticism in the first place (Victor 1992).

Members of high-context cultures are reluctant to say no for fear of offending and causing the person to lose face. It is therefore necessary, for example, to be able to read in the Japanese executive's yes when it means yes and when it means no. The difference is not in the words used but in the way in which they are used. It is easy to see how the low-context individual may interpret this reluctance to be direct—to say no when you mean no—as a weakness or as an unwillingness to confront reality.

Power Distances

In some cultures power is concentrated in the hands of a few and there is a great difference in the power held by these people and by the ordinary citizen. These are called high power distance cultures; examples are Mexico, Brazil, India, and the Philippines (Hofstede 1982). In low power distance cultures (examples include Denmark, New Zealand, Sweden, and to a lesser extent the United States), power is more evenly distributed throughout the citizenry. These differences impact on communication in a number of ways. For example, in high power distance cultures there is a great power distance between students and teachers; students are expected to be modest, polite, and totally respectful. In low power distance cultures (and you can see this clearly in college classrooms in the United States) students are expected to demonstrate their knowledge and command of the subject matter, participate in discussions with the teacher, and even challenge the teacher, something many high power distance culture members would not even think of doing. In fact, in high power cultures such as China, specific training is given to students to encourage them to ask questions and participate in class activities (Schoenhals 1994).

Friendship and dating relationships will also be influenced by the power distance between groups (Andersen 1991). In India, for example, such relationships are expected to take place within your cultural class; in Sweden, you are expected to select friends and romantic partners on the basis not of class or culture but of individual factors such as personality, appearance, and the like.

In the workplace of low power distance cultures you are expected to confront a friend, partner, or supervisor assertively; there is in these cultures a general feeling of equality that is consistent with acting assertively (Borden 1991). In high power distance cultures, direct confrontation and assertiveness may be viewed negatively, especially if directed at a superior.

THINK ABOUT

Think about your own cultural orientations. Are you basically individualistic or collectivistic? Are you from a high- or low-context culture? A high or low power distance culture? How are your communications influenced by these orientations? Have you ever experienced communication difficulties as a result of differences in these orientations between yourself and another?

THEORIES OF CULTURE AND COMMUNICATION

A number of researchers have attempted to explain the interaction of culture and communication, to formulate a theory of culture and communication. Here are several. Although none provides a complete explanation, each gives us some understanding of how some part of culture interacts with some part of communication.

Language Relativity

The general idea that language influences thought and ultimately behavior got its strongest expression from linguistic anthropologists. In the late 1920s and throughout the 1930s, the view was formulated that the characteristics of language influence the way you think (Carroll 1956; Fishman 1960; Hoijer 1954; Miller & McNeill 1969; Sapir 1929). Since the languages of the world differ greatly in semantics and syntax, it was argued that people speaking widely different languages would also differ in how they viewed and thought about the world. This view became known as the **linguistic relativity hypothesis.**

Subsequent research and theory, however, did not support the extreme claims made by linguistic relativity researchers. A more modified hypothesis seems supported currently: the language you speak helps to highlight what you see and how you talk about it. For example, if you speak a language that is rich in color terms (English is a good example) you would find it easier to highlight and talk about nuances of color than would someone from a culture that has fewer color terms (some cultures distinguish only two or three or four parts of the color spectrum). This does not necessarily mean that people see the world differently, however, only that their language helps (or does not help) them to focus on certain variations in nature and makes it easier (or more difficult) to talk about them. Nor does it mean that people speaking differing languages are doomed to misunderstand each other. Translation enables us to understand a great deal of the meaning in a foreign language message. Of course we have our communication skills and can ask for clarification, for additional examples, for restatement. We can listen actively, give feedforward and feedback, use perception checking.

Language differences do not make for very important differences in perception, thought, or behavior. Difficulties in intercultural understanding are more often due to ineffective communication than to differences in languages.

Uncertainty Reduction

All communication interactions involve uncertainty and ambiguity. Not surprisingly, this uncertainty and ambiguity is greater when there are large cultural differences (Berger & Bradac 1982; Gudykunst 1989). Much of your communication tries to reduce this uncertainty so you can better describe, predict, and explain the behaviors of others. Because of this greater uncertainty in intercultural communication, it takes more time and effort to reduce it and to thus communicate meaningfully. In situations of great uncertainty the techniques of effective communication (for example, active listening, perception checking, being specific, and seeking feedback) take on special importance.

Active listening (Unit 12) and perception checking techniques (Unit 3), for example, help you to check on the accuracy of your perceptions and allow you the opportunity to revise and amend any incorrect perceptions. Being specific reduces ambiguity and the chances of misunderstandings. Misunderstanding is a lot more likely when talking about "neglect" (a highly abstract concept) than when talking about "forgetting your last birthday" (a specific event).

Seeking feedback helps you to correct any possible misconceptions almost immediately. Seek feedback on whether you are making yourself clear ("Does that make sense?" "Do you see where to put the widget?") as well as on whether you understand what the other person is saying ("Do you mean that you will never speak with them again? Do you mean that literally?")

Although you are always in danger of misperceiving and misevaluating another person, you are in special danger in intercultural situations. Therefore, try to resist your natural tendency to judge others quickly and permanently. Prejudices and biases complicate such communication further and when combined with high uncertainty are sure to produce judgments you'll have to revise. A judgment made early is likely to be based on too little information. This makes flexibility and a willingness to revise opinions essential intercultural skills.

Maximizing Outcomes

In intercultural communication—as in all communication—you try to maximize the outcomes of your interactions (Sunnafrank 1989). You try to gain the greatest rewards while paying the least costs. For example, you probably interact with those you predict will contribute to positive results; for example, you seek conversations that will prove satisfying, enjoyable, exciting, and so on. Because intercultural communication is difficult and positive outcomes may seem unlikely (at least at first), you may avoid it. And so, for example, you talk with the person in class who is similar to rather than different from you. However,

CULTURAL IMPERIALISM

Political imperialism is a policy of expanding the dominion of one country over that of another. **Cultural imperialism** refers to a similar process, expanding the dominion of one culture over that of another. The theory of cultural imperialism affords an interesting perspective on the influence of media, especially as they exert influence and dominate other cultures (Becker & Roberts 1992). The theory argues that the media from developed countries such as the United States and Western Europe dominate the cultures of countries importing such media.

This cultural dominance is also seen in computer communication, in which the United States and the English language dominate (also see the Media Watch box in Unit 19). "And some countries," notes one journalist, "already unhappy with the encroachment of American culture—from jeans and Mickey Mouse to movies and TV programs—are worried that their cultures will be further eroded by an American dominance of cyberspace" (Pollack 1995, p. D1).

(Although the term *cultural imperialism* is a negative one, the actual process of media influence may be viewed as either negative or positive, depending on your cultural perspective.)

Media products from the United States are likely to emphasize its dominant attitudes and values, for example, the preference for competition, the importance of individuality, the advantages of capitalism and democracy, safe sex and health consciousness, and the importance of money. In an extreme form of this theory, it could be argued that the attitudes and values of the dominant media culture will become the attitudes and values of the rest of the world.

Television programs, films, and music from the United States and Western Europe are so popular and so much in demand in developing countries that they may actually inhibit the growth of the native culture's own talent. For example, instead of creating their own vision in an original television drama or film, native writers in developing countries may find it easier and more secure to work as translators for products from more-developed countries. For the same reason native promoters may find it easier and more lucrative to sell, say, a U.S. rock groups' tapes and CDs than to cultivate and promote native talent. The fact that it is cheaper to import and translate than it is to create original works gives the developed country's products an added advantage and the native culture's productions a decided disadvantage (Becker & Roberts 1992).

The popularity of U.S. and Western Europe's media may also lead artists in developing countries to imitate rather than develop their own styles—styles more consistent with their native culture.

From another perspective, however, it may be argued that the media products from the United States are generally superior to those produced elsewhere and hence serve as a kind of benchmark for quality work throughout the world.

Finally, it might be argued that such products introduce new trends and perspectives and hence enrich the native culture. Much as people in the United States profit as new cultures exert their influence, the developing cultures profit as U.S. media introduce new perspectives on government and politics, foods, educational technologies, and health, for example.

What do you think of the influence the media from the United States and Western Europe is having on native cultures throughout the world? How do you evaluate it? Do you see advantages? Disadvantages?

extending and stretching yourself may actually result in greater satisfaction in the long run.

Also, consider that when you have positive outcomes, you continue to engage in communication and increase your communications. When you have negative outcomes, you begin to withdraw and communicate less. The implication here is obvious: Don't give up easily, especially in intercultural settings.

Since intercultural communication may be new or different from your usual communications, you will probably be more mindful about it (Gudykunst 1989; Langer 1989). This has both positive and negative consequences. On the positive side, this increased awareness probably keeps you more alert. It prevents you from saying things that might appear insensitive or inappropriate. On the negative side, it leads to guardedness, lack of spontaneity, and lack of confidence.

In your mindful state you probably make predictions about which types of communication will result in positive outcomes; you try to predict the results of, for example, the choice of topic, the positions you take, the nonverbal behaviors you display, the amount of talking versus listening that you do, and so on. You then do what you think will result in positive outcomes and avoid doing what you think will result in negative outcomes. To do this successfully, however, you will have to learn as much as you can about the other person's system of communication signals. This will help you predict the outcomes of your behavior more accurately.

Culture Shock

Culture shock refers to the psychological reaction you experience at being in a culture very different from your own (Furnham & Bochner 1986). Culture shock is normal; most people experience it when entering a new and different culture. Nevertheless, it can be unpleasant and frustrating. Part of this results from the feelings of alienation, conspicuousness, and difference from everyone else. When you do not know the rules and customs of the new society, you cannot communicate effectively. You are apt to blunder frequently and seriously. The person experiencing culture shock may not know some very basic things:

- how to ask someone for a favor or pay someone a compliment
- how to extend or accept an invitation for dinner
- how early or how late to arrive for an appointment and how long to stay
- how to distinguish seriousness from playfulness and politeness from indifference
- how to dress for an informal, formal, or business function
- how to order a meal in a restaurant or how to summon a waiter

Anthropologist Kalervo Oberg (1960), who first used the term, notes that culture shock occurs in stages. These stages are useful for examining many encounters with the new and the different. Going away to college, getting married, or joining the military, for example, can all result in culture shock.

Stage One: The Honeymoon

At first there is fascination, even enchantment, with the new culture and its people. You finally have your own apartment. You are your own boss. Finally, on your own! When you are among people who are culturally different, the early stage is characterized by cordiality and superficial friendship. Many tourists remain at this stage because their stay in foreign countries is so brief.

Stage Two: The Crisis

In this phase, the differences between your own culture and the new one create problems. No longer do you find dinner ready for you unless you do it yourself. Your clothes are not washed or ironed unless you do them yourself. Feelings of frustration and inadequacy come to the fore. This is the stage at which you experience the actual shock of the new culture. In one study of foreign students coming from over 100 different lands and studying in 11 different countries, it was found that 25 percent of the students experienced depression (Klineberg & Hull 1979).

Stage Three: The Recovery

During this period you gain the skills necessary to function effectively. You learn how to shop, cook, and plan a meal. You find a local laundry and figure you'll learn how to iron later. You learn the language and ways of the new culture. Your feelings of inadequacy subside.

Stage Four: The Adjustment

At this final stage, you adjust and come to enjoy the new culture and the new experiences. You may still experience periodic difficulties and strains, but on the whole, the experience is pleasant. Actually, you're now a pretty decent cook. You're even coming to enjoy it. You're making a good salary and you can pay someone to do your ironing for you.

Simply spending time in a foreign country is not sufficient for you to develop positive attitudes; in fact, negative attitudes are often found. Rather, it is friendships with nationals that is crucial. Contacts only with other expatriates or sojourners is not sufficient (Torbiorn 1982).

People may also experience culture shock when they return to their original culture after living in a foreign culture, a kind of reverse culture shock (Jandt 1995). Consider, for example, the Peace Corps volunteers who work in an economically deprived rural area. Upon returning to Las Vegas or Beverly Hills they too may experience culture shock. Sailors who served long periods aboard ship and then return to an isolated farming community might also experience

Another way of looking at the "interculturalization" of the United States is to look at the international visitors. For example, in 1993 over 12 million visitors came from ten countries. (That's more people than any state in the United States except for California, New York, Texas, and Florida. It's also more people than the total population of such countries as Cuba, Denmark, Ecuador, Finland, Greece, Haiti, and Israel.) Japanese visitors lead the list with over 3 million, followed closely by the United Kingdom which also sends over 3 million. Germany is next with almost 2 million, followed by (in order) France, Italy, Australia, Brazil, Venezuela, Spain, and Argentina. The ever-present visitor exerts influence on residents as residents influence them. Have you ever been a part of this influence process?

culture shock. In these cases, however, the recovery period is shorter and the sense of inadequacy and frustration is lower.

INTERCULTURAL COMMUNICATION

Understanding the role of culture in communication is an essential foundation for understanding intercultural communication as it occurs interpersonally, in small groups, in public speaking, or in the media, and for appreciating the principles for effective intercultural communication.

The Nature of Intercultural Communication

Intercultural communication refers to communication between persons who have different cultural beliefs, values, or ways of behaving. The model in Figure 6.1 illustrates this concept. The larger circles represent the culture of the individual communicator. The inner circles identify the communicators (the sources-receivers). In this model each communicator is a member of a different culture. In some instances the cultural differences are relatively slight—say, between persons from Toronto and New York. In other instances the cultural differences are great—say, between persons from Borneo and Germany, or between persons from rural Nigeria and industrialized England.

All messages originate from a specific and unique cultural context, and that context influences their content and form. You communicate as you do largely as a result of your culture. Culture (along with the processes of enculturation and acculturation) influences every aspect of your communication experience.

You receive messages through the filters imposed by your cultural context. That context influences what you receive and how you receive it. For example, some cultures rely heavily on television or newspapers and trust them implicitly. Others rely on face-to-face interpersonal interactions, distrusting many of the mass communication systems.

Intercultural communication, like so many areas of human communication, has grown rapidly. Table 6.2 on page 97 presents some of the areas or subdivisions of intercultural communication to give you a clearer idea of the area as a whole.

Principles of Intercultural Communication

Murphy's law ("If anything can go wrong, it will") is especially applicable to intercultural communication.

A commonly encountered case of culture shock occurs with international students. For example, for the 1993–1994 academic year, there were 449,749 international students. The ten countries sending the most students to the United States are China (44,381 students), Japan (43,770), Taiwan (37,581), India (34,796), South Korea (31,076), Canada (22,655), Hong Kong (13,752), Malaysia (13,718), Indonesia (11,744), and Thailand (9,537). If you are an international student, can you describe your culture shock experiences? If you are not an international student, can you visualize the culture shock you might experience if you were to study in another culture?

(*Source:* "International Students in the United States, 1993–94 Academic Year," *The New York Times,* January 4, 1995, A17. Copyright © 1995 by the New York Times Company. Reprinted by permission.)

Intercultural communication is, of course, subject to all the same barriers and problems as the other forms of communication that we discuss throughout this text. Drawing on a number of intercultural researchers, we cover here the principles designed to counteract the barriers that are unique to intercultural communication (Barna 1991; Ruben 1985; Spitzberg 1991).

Prepare Yourself

There is no better preparation for intercultural communication than learning about the other culture. Fortunately, there are numerous sources on which to draw. View a video or film that presents a realistic view of the culture. Read about the culture by persons from that culture as well as by "outsiders." Scan magazines from that culture. Talk with members of that culture. And, of course, read those works addressed to people who need to communicate with those from other cultures. Recent titles include: *Do's and Taboos of Hosting International Visitors* (Axtell 1990), *When In Rome . . . A Business Guide to Cultures and Customs in 12 European Nations* (Mole 1990). *Do's and Taboos Around the World* (Axtell 1993), *The Executive Guide to Asia-Pacific Communications* (James 1995), *How to Negotiate Anything with Anyone Anywhere Around the World* (Acuff 1993), and *Internationally Yours: Writing*

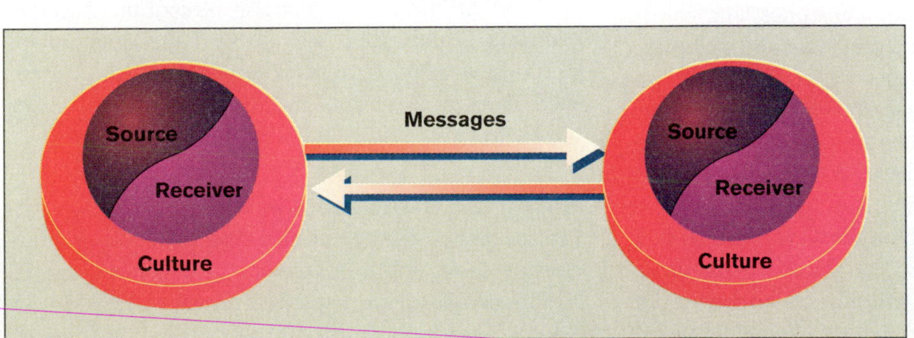

FIGURE 6.1 A Model of Intercultural Communication. This basic model of intercultural communication is designed to illustrate that culture is a part of every communication transaction.

and Communicating Successfully in Today's Global Marketplace (DeVries 1994).

Recognize and Face Fears

A major factor that stands in the way of effective intercultural communication is fear (Gudykunst 1994; Stephan & Stephan 1985). For example, you may fear for your self-esteem. You may become anxious about your ability to control the intercultural situation or you may worry about your own level of discomfort. You may fear saying something that will be considered politically incorrect or culturally insensitive and thereby lose face.

You may fear that you will be taken advantage of by the members of this other culture. Depending upon your own stereotypes, you may fear being lied to, financially duped, or made fun of.

You may fear that members of this other group will react to you negatively. You may fear, for example, that they will not like you or may disapprove of your attitudes or beliefs or they may even reject you as a person. Conversely, you may fear negative reactions from members of your own group. They might, for example, disapprove of your socializing with the culturally different.

These fears—coupled with the greater effort that intercultural communication takes and the ease with which you communicate with those who are culturally similar—can easily lead some people to give up. Some fears are in some cases reasonable. In many cases, however, they are groundless. Whatever the situation, they need to be assessed logically and their consequences weighed carefully. Then you will be able to make informed choices about your communications.

Recognize Differences Between Yourself and Those Who Are Culturally Different

Perhaps the most prevalent barrier to intercultural communication occurs when you assume that similarities exist and that differences do not. This is especially true in the area of values, attitudes, and beliefs. You might easily accept different hairstyles, clothing, and foods. In basic values and beliefs, however, you may assume that deep down everyone is really alike. They are not. When you assume similarities and ignore differences, you will fail to notice important distinctions and when communicating will convey to others that your ways are the right ways and that their ways are not important to you. Consider this example. An American invites a Filipino co-worker to dinner. The Filipino politely refuses. The American is hurt and feels that the Filipino does not want to be friendly. The Filipino is hurt when not invited a second time and concludes that the invitation was not extended sincerely. Here, it seems, both the American and the Filipino assume that their customs for inviting people to dinner are the same when, in fact, they are not. A Filipino expects to be invited several times before accepting a dinner invitation. When an invitation is given only once it is viewed as insincere.

Here's another example. An American college student hears the news that her favorite uncle has died. She bites her lip, pulls herself up, and politely excuses herself from the group of foreign students with whom she is having dinner. The Russian thinks: "How unfriendly." The Italian thinks: "How insincere." The Brazilian thinks: "How unconcerned." To many Americans, it is a sign of bravery to endure pain (physical or emotional) in silence and without any outward show of emotion. To members of other groups, such silence is often interpreted negatively to mean that the individual does not consider them friends who can share such sorrow. To members of other cultures, people are expected to reveal to friends how they feel.

Recognize Differences Among the Culturally Different Group

Within every cultural group there are wide and important differences. As all Americans are not alike, neither are all Indonesians, Greeks, Mexicans, and so on. When we ignore these differences we are guilty of stereotyping. We assume that all persons covered by the same label (in this case a national or racial label) are the same. A good example of this is seen in the use of the term *African American.* The term stresses the unity of Africa and those who are of African descent and is analogous to *Asian American* or *European American.* At the same time, it ignores the great diversity within this continent when, for example, it is used as analogous to *German American* or *Japanese American. Nigerian American* or *Ethiopian American,* on the other hand, would be analogous to, say, *German American.* Within each culture there are smaller cultures that differ greatly from each other and from the larger culture.

Recognize Differences in Meaning

Be especially sensitive to this simple principle in intercultural communication: meaning exists not in words but in people (a principle we return to in Unit 7).

TABLE 6.2
the areas of intercultural communication

This is only one view of the field of intercultural communication; theorists differ on many issues. For example, many would consider gender communication as intercultural only if the woman and man came from different races or ethnic groups. Others view male and female communication as intercultural because men and women learned different cultural values and beliefs and these influence their communications just as race influences communication. Similarly, some theorists would argue that communication between an African American and a European American born and raised in Chicago is not intercultural; others see African American and European American origins exerting different cultural influences on the individuals and hence consider such communication as intercultural.

Areas	Theories or General Theory Focus	Skills or General Skill Focus	For Further Exploration
Intercultural interaction, for example, between Chinese and Germans	Protocol communication differences, norms, customs	How intercultural communication can be made more effective	Gudykunst (1991), Samovar and Porter (1995), and Jandt (1995) provide useful introductions to theories and skills; Samovar and Porter (1994) and Gudykunst and Kim (1992) include recent research and thinking. Wiseman (1995) covers the major theoretical developments and advances. Ringer (1994) provides coverage of gay and lesbian communication. González, Houston, and Chen (1994) provide 22 personal essays on a wide variety of cultures. Wood (1994) covers gender, culture, and communication. Lustig and Koestler (1996) focuses on intercultural communication in interpersonal interactions. Popular books include those by Axtell (1990, 1992, 1993) which offer useful guides for the person in international business. Hall and Hall (1987) provide useful general principles for effective intercultural communication.
International communication, for example, business interactions between the United States and Japan	Etiquette, culture shock, business theories and strategies of different cultures, language and nonverbal differences	How the global marketplace can be made more effective	
Interreligious communication, for example, communication between Catholics and Muslims	Interfaith similarities and differences	How Irish Catholics and Irish Protestants can communicate more effectively. How interreligious tolerance can be fostered	
Interracial communication, for example, communication between Asians and Europeans	Cultural differences between the races and their influence on communication	How interracial communication can be made more effective	
Cross-cultural communication, communication variables (for example, self-disclosure) as it occurs in different cultures	Cultural similarities and differences in communication	How members of different cultures can better understand each other	
Gender communication, for example, between male and female	Obstacles to male-female communication, male and female communication differences, sexual harassment	How men and women can communicate more effectively	

Consider, for example, the differences in meaning for such words as *woman* to an American and a Muslim, *religion* to a born-again Christian and an atheist, and *lunch* to a Chinese rice farmer and a Madison Avenue advertising executive. Even though the same word is used, its meanings will vary greatly depending on the listeners' cultural definitions.

With nonverbal messages, the potential differences seem even greater. Thus, the over-the-head clasped hands gesture that signifies victory to an

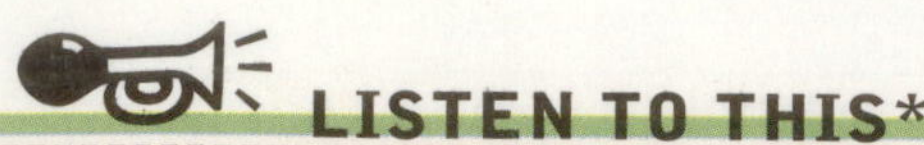

RACIST, SEXIST, AND HETEROSEXIST LISTENING

Just as racist, sexist, and heterosexist attitudes will influence your language (as we note in the discussion of verbal messages in Unit 8), they also influence your listening.

In this type of listening you only hear what the speaker is saying through your stereotypes. You assume that what the speaker is saying is unfairly influenced by the speakers sex, race, or affectional orientation.

Sexist, racist, and heterosexist listening occur in a wide variety of situations. For example, when you dismiss a valid argument or attribute validity to an invalid argument, when you refuse to give someone a fair hearing, or when you give less credibility (or more credibility) to a speaker because the speaker is of a particular sex, race, or affectional orientation, you are practicing sexist, racist, or heterosexist listening. Put differently, sexist, racist, or heterosexist listening occurs when you listen differently to a person because of his or her sex, race, or affectional orientation, when these characteristics are irrelevant to the communication.

There are, however, many instances in which these characteristics are relevant and pertinent to your evaluation of the message. For example, the sex of the speaker talking on pregnancy, fathering a child, birth control, or surrogate fatherhood is, most would agree, probably relevant to the message, therefore it is not sexist listening to hear the topic through the sex of the speaker. It is sexist listening, however, to assume that only one sex has anything to say that is worth hearing or that what one sex says can be discounted without a fair hearing. The same is true when listening through a person's race or affectional orientation.

Do you find this position reasonable? If not, how would you define sexist, racist, and heterosexist listening? Do you find this a useful concept in understanding effective communication? Do you find these types of listening operating in your classes? In your family? In your community? If you wanted to reduce this type of listening, how would you do it?

American may signify friendship to a Russian. To an American, holding up two fingers to make a V signifies victory. To certain South Americans, however, it is an obscene gesture that corresponds to the American's extended middle finger.

An American eating with the left hand may be seen by a Muslim as obscene. To the Muslim, the left hand is not used for eating or for shaking hands but to clean oneself after excretory functions. So, using the left hand to eat or to shake hands is considered insulting and obscene.

Follow Cultural Rules and Customs

Each culture has its own rules for communicating. These rules identify what is appropriate and what is inappropriate. Thus, for example, in American culture you would call a person you wish to date three or four days in advance. In certain Asian cultures, you might call the person's parents weeks or even months in advance. In American culture you say, as a general friendly gesture and not as a specific invitation, "come over and pay us a visit." To members of other cultures, this comment is sufficient for the listeners actually to come to visit at their convenience.

In some cultures, people show respect by avoiding direct eye contact with the person to whom they are speaking. In other cultures this same eye avoidance would signal disinterest. If a young American girl is talking with an older Indonesian man, for example, she is expected to avoid direct eye contact. To an Indonesian, direct eye contact in this situation would be considered disrespectful. In some southern European cultures men walk arm in arm. Other cultures (the United States, for example) consider this inappropriate.

A good example of a series of rules for an extremely large and important culture that many people do not know appears in Table 6.3.

***LEARNING AID NOTE.** Nine Listen to This boxes are distributed throughout this text. The objective of these boxes and this method of presenting the material is to integrate listening into the different forms of communication and to stress the important role that listening plays in all communication contexts. Look at this material as extensions and specific applications of the principles of listening discussed in Unit 4.

TABLE 6.3
ten commandments for communicating with people with disabilities

1. Speak directly rather than through a companion or sign language interpreter who may be present.
2. Offer to shake hands when introduced. People with limited hand use or an artificial limb can usually shake hands and offering the left hand is an acceptable greeting.
3. Always identify yourself and others who may be with you when meeting someone with a visual impairment. When conversing in a group, remember to identify the person to whom you are speaking.
4. If you offer assistance, wait until the offer is accepted. Then listen or ask for instructions.
5. Treat adults as adults. Address people who have disabilities by their first names only when extending that same familiarity to all others. Never patronize people in wheelchairs by patting them on the head or shoulder.
6. Do not lean against or hang on someone's wheelchair. Bear in mind that disabled people treat their chairs as extensions of their bodies.
7. Listen attentively when talking with people who have difficulty speaking and wait for them to finish. If necessary, ask short questions that require short answers, a nod, or shake of the head. Never pretend to understand if you are having difficulty doing so. Instead repeat what you have understood and allow the person to respond.
8. Place yourself at eye level when speaking with someone in a wheelchair or on crutches.
9. Tap a hearing-impaired person on the shoulder or wave your hand to get his or her attention. Look directly at the person and speak clearly, slowly, and expressively to establish if the person can read your lips. If so, try to face the light source and keep hands, cigarettes, and food away from your mouth when speaking.
10. Relax. Don't be embarrassed if you happen to use common expressions such as "See you later," or "Did you hear about this?" that seem to relate to a person's disability.

Source: "Ten Commandments for Communicating with People with Disabilities," *The New York Times*, June 7, 1993.

THINK ABOUT

Think about your own ability to deal with intercultural communication situations by considering how you would deal with each of the following obstacles to intercultural understanding and communication.

1. Your friend makes fun of Radha, who comes to class in her native African dress. You feel you want to object to this.
2. Craig and Louise are an interracial couple. Craig's family treat him fairly but virtually ignore Louise. They never invite Craig and Louise as a couple to dinner or to partake in any family functions. The couple decide that they should confront Craig's family and ask your advice.
3. Malcolm is a close friend and is really an open-minded person, but he has the habit of referring to members of other racial and ethnic groups with derogatory language. You decide to tell him that you object to this way of talking.
4. Tom, a good friend of yours, wants to ask Pat out for a date. Both you and Tom know that Pat is a lesbian and will refuse the date and yet Tom says he is going to have some fun and ask her anyway—just to give her a hard time. You think this is wrong and want to tell Tom you think so.
5. Your parents persist in holding stereotypes about other religious, racial, and ethnic groups. These stereotypes come up in all sorts of conversations. You are embarrassed by these attitudes and feel you must tell your parents how incorrect you think these stereotypes are.
6. Lenny, a colleague at work, recently underwent a religious conversion. He now persists in trying to get everyone else—yourself included—to undergo this same conversion. Every day he tells you why you should convert, gives you literature to read, and otherwise persists in trying to convert you. You decide to tell him that you find this behavior offensive.

SUMMARY

In this unit we introduced the study of culture and its relationship to communication and considered how cultures differ and some of the theories developed to explain how culture and communication impact on one another. In addition, we introduced the study of intercultural communication, its nature and principles.

1. Culture refers to the relatively specialized life-style of a group of people, consisting of their values, beliefs, artifacts, ways of behaving and ways of communicating, that is passed on from one generation to the next through communication rather than through genes.
2. Enculturation refers to the process by which culture is transmitted from one generation to the next.
3. Acculturation refers to the processes by which one culture is modified through contact with or exposure to another culture.
4. Cultures differ in terms of individualistic or collectivist orientations, high-context (where the information is largely in the context or in the person's nonverbals) and low-context (where most of the information is explicitly stated in the message), and in terms of high and low power distance (the degree to which power is concentrated in few or in many of its members).
5. Some theoretical approaches to intercultural communication include (1) language relativity (language helps to structure what you see and how you see it but does not impose any serious barriers to meaningful communication); (2) uncertainty reduction theory (the greater the intercultural differences, the greater the uncertainty and ambiguity, and the greater the communication difficulty); (3) maximizing outcomes (intercultural communication will be guided by the goal of maximizing the outcomes of such interactions and it often requires more effort and more time to achieve the desired outcomes); and (4) culture shock (a psychological reaction to being placed in a culture different from one's own, accompanied by a feeling of alienation and conspicuousness over being different).
6. Intercultural communication refers to communication between people who have different cultural beliefs, values, or ways of behaving.
7. Among the principles for more effective intercultural communication are: prepare yourself, recognize and face fears, recognize differences between yourself and those who are culturally different, recognize differences among those who are culturally different (avoiding stereotyping), recognize meaning differences in verbal and nonverbal messages, and follow cultural rules and customs.

THINKING CRITICALLY ABOUT CULTURE AND COMMUNICATION

1. Social Darwinism or cultural evolution holds that much as the human species evolved from lower life forms to homo sapiens, cultures also evolve. Consequently, some cultures may be considered advanced and others primitive. Most contemporary scholars reject this view because the judgments that distinguish one culture from another have no basis in science and are instead based on individual values and preferences as to what constitutes "civilized" and what con-

stitutes "primitive." Cultural relativism, on the other hand, holds that all cultures are different but that no culture is either superior or inferior to any other (Berry, Poortinga, Segall, & Dasen 1992). Today this view is generally accepted and guides the infusion of cultural materials into contemporary textbooks on all academic levels. What do you think of these positions?

2. Consider how cultural differences underlie some of the most hotly debated topics in the news today. The following, for example, is a brief list of some of these topics, here identified with specific questions. How would you answer these? How do your cultural attitudes, beliefs, and values influence your responses?
   a. Should Christian Science practitioners be prosecuted for preventing their children from receiving lifesaving treatment such as blood transfusions? Some states, such as Connecticut and Arizona, grant Christian Scientists special rights in this regard. Should this special treatment be adopted by all states? Should it be eliminated?
   b. Should immigration be expanded or limited?
   c. Should cockfighting be permitted or declared illegal in all states as "cruelty to animals"? (Some Latin Americans have argued that this is a part of their culture and should be permitted even though it is illegal in most of the United States. In five states and Puerto Rico, cockfighting is legal.)
   d. Should same-sex marriages be legalized? (A test case is currently pending in Hawaii.)
   e. Should safe-sex practices be taught in the schools? (Recall that recently President Clinton fired Joycelyn Elders from her position as United States Surgeon General for suggesting that masturbation be discussed in the schools.)
   f. Should abortion be declared illegal?
   g. Should those who commit hate or bias crimes be given harsher sentences?
   h. Should assisted suicides be legalized?
   i. Should the race of the child and that of the adopting parents be a relevant issue in adoption decisions?
   j. What should be the fate of affirmative action?
3. Recently, the U.S. Department of Education issued guidelines (recommendations that are not legally binding on school boards) covering the types of religious communications and activities public schools may permit (*New York Times* August 26, 1995, pp. 1, 8). Among the permitted activities are: student prayer, student-initiated discussions of religion, saying grace, proselytizing that would not be considered harassment, and the wearing of religious symbols and clothing. Among the forbidden activies: prayer endorsed by teachers or administrators, invitations to prayer that could constitute harassment, teaching of a particular religion (rather than about religion), encouraging (officially or through teaching) either religious or anti-religious activity, and denying school facilities to religious groups if these same facilities are provided to nonreligious groups. What do you think of these guidelines? If you were a member of a local school board, would you vote to adopt or reject these guidelines? How do your cultural beliefs influence your view of these guidelines?
4. In this age of multiculturalism, how do you feel about Article II, Section 1 of the United States Constitution? The relevant section reads: "No person except a nat-

ural born citizen, or a citizen of the United States, at the time of the adoption of this Constitution, shall be eligible to the office of President"?

5. Which of these four theories—language relativity, uncertainty reduction, maximizing outcomes, or culture shock—do you feel offers the greatest insight into the role of culture in communication?
6. Do you agree that intercultural differences are especially important in initial interactions and gradually decline as the relationship becomes more intimate? Could you make an argument for the reverse being true—that intercultural differences are least important in initial interactions and only become important after the relationship has reached a certain level of involvement or intimacy?
7. What role does intercultural communication play in your personal, social, and professional life? Has this changed in the last ten years? Is it likely to change in the next ten years? What factors have contributed to make your own social environment—school, neighborhood, workplace—more interculturally conscious?
8. Sheba has just come to your college from another galaxy. Sheba asks for your help in learning the rules of your culture, especially those rules concerning interpersonal interaction. For example, Sheba is not quite sure about the following four issues: (1) Is it considered correct to interrupt someone who is speaking, and if so when is it permissible? (2) How do you begin a conversation with someone you have never met before? (3) How long do you maintain eye contact when talking with someone? How long do you maintain eye contact when listening to someone? (4) What do you do with your hands and feet when you are sitting in a chair talking with someone? Would these rules differ depending on whether Sheba is male or female? What interpersonal communication rules can you give Sheba for dealing with these four communication situations?
9. Recently, the Emma Lazarus poem on the Statute of Liberty was changed. The words "the wretched refuse of your teeming shore" were deleted and the poem now reads:

   give me your tired, your poor,
   Your huddled masses yearning to breathe free. . . .
   Send these, the homeless, tempest-tost to me
   I lift my lamp besides the golden door.

   Harvard zoologist Stephen Jay Gould, commenting on this change, notes that with the words omitted, the poem no longer has balance or rhyme and more importantly no longer represents what Lazarus wrote (Gould 1995, p. 27). "The language police triumph," notes Gould, "and integrity bleeds." On the other hand, it can be argued that calling immigrants "wretched refuse" is insulting and degrading and that if Lazarus were writing today, she would not have used that phrase. How do you feel about this? Would you have supported the deletion of this line?
10. How would you go about finding answers to such questions as these:
    a. Are relationships between persons of similar individual-collective orientation more or less likely to experience conflicts?
    b. Are people living in high and low power distance cultures different in terms of their perceived level of happiness?

c. Do men and women differ in their preference for explicit communications, despite their high- or low-context orientation?
d. Do men and women have different rules for politeness in, say, conversation? In business dealings?
e. Do couples with similar ratings (on the cultural differences scale) stay together longer than couples with dissimilar ratings? Do couples with similar ratings have fewer and less severe conflicts than couples with dissimilar ratings?
f. Are persons with greater education more likely to enter relationships with dissimilar others than with similar others?

Part Two: Messages: Verbal and Nonverbal

In Part Two we focus on verbal and nonverbal messages. Unit 7 introduces the nature of messages and meaning and looks at the verbal and nonverbal systems as they are used together in normal communication. Units 8 and 9 consider verbal messages, their principles and barriers. Units 10 and 11 consider nonverbal messages, for example, communication by body, facial, and eye movements, paralanguage, silence, and time (Unit 10) and by space, territory, touch, smell, and artifacts (Unit 11).

In approaching verbal and nonverbal messages, keep the following in mind:

- Communication messages are combinations of verbal and nonverbal signals; understanding how they are integrated is essential to their effective encoding and decoding.
- Verbal and nonverbal message systems are a part of your culture and reflect that culture. See both verbal and nonverbal messages within their cultural context.
- Resist the temptation to draw conclusions about people on the basis of isolated bits of message behavior, whether verbal, nonverbal, or both.
- Increase your awareness of your communications and interactions and see the various verbal and nonverbal behaviors discussed here and in class in your own behavior. Learn to see in practice what you read about here in theory.

seven unit

Preliminaries to Verbal and Nonverbal Messages

unit contents

unit goals

After completing this unit, you should be able to

1. explain the major ways in which verbal and nonverbal messages interact
2. explain these principles of meaning: meanings are in people, meanings are more than words, meanings are unique, meanings are denotative and connotative, and meanings are context-based
3. explain these principles of messages: messages are rule-governed, messages vary in directness, messages vary in believability, and messages may metacommunicate

In this unit we introduce the message system, the system you use to communicate meaning to another person. The message system has both verbal and nonverbal aspects. The verbal portion is language—the words, phrases, and sentences you use. The nonverbal portion consists of a wide variety of elements—spatial relationships, time orientation, gestures, facial expressions, eye movements, touch, and variations in the rate and volume of your speech. While the verbal aspect of communication has been studied for thousands of years and has engaged the attention of both ancient and modern philosophers, scientists, and researchers from numerous fields, the study of the nonverbal aspect goes back only little more than a hundred years. Charles Darwin's 1872 volume, *The Expression of the Emotions in Man and Animals,* is usually credited as the first work on nonverbal communication.

THE INTERACTION OF VERBAL AND NONVERBAL MESSAGES

In face-to-face communication you blend verbal and nonverbal messages to best convey your meanings. Here are six ways in which nonverbal messages are used with verbal messages; these will help to highlight this important verbal-nonverbal interaction (Knapp & Hall 1992).

Accenting

Nonverbal communication is often used to emphasize some part of the verbal message. You might, for example, raise your voice to underscore a particular word or phrase, bang your fist on the desk to stress your commitment, or look longingly into someone's eyes when saying "I love you."

Complementing

Nonverbal communication may add nuances of meaning not communicated by your verbal message. Thus, you might smile when telling a story (to suggest that you find it humorous) or frown and shake your head when recounting someone's deceit (to suggest your disapproval).

Contradicting

You may deliberately contradict your verbal messages with nonverbal movements—for example, by crossing your fingers or winking to indicate that you are lying.

Regulating

Movements may be used to control, or to indicate your desire to control, the flow of verbal messages, as when you purse your lips, lean forward, or make hand gestures to indicate that you want to speak. You might also put up your hand or vocalize your pauses (for example, with "um") to indicate that you have not finished and are not ready to relinquish the floor to the next speaker.

Repeating

You can repeat or restate the verbal message nonverbally. You can, for example, follow your verbal, "Is that all right?" with raised eyebrows and a questioning look, or motion with your head or hand to repeat your verbal, "Let's go."

Substituting

You may also use nonverbal communication to take the place of verbal messages. For instance, you can signal "OK" with a hand gesture. You can nod your head to indicate yes or shake your head to indicate no.

THINK ABOUT

Think about how you integrate verbal and nonverbal messages in your own everyday communications. Try reading each of the following statements and describing (rather than acting out) the nonverbal messages that you would use in making these statements in normal conversation.

1. I couldn't agree with you more.
2. Absolutely not, I don't agree.
3. Hurry up; we're an hour late already.
4. You look really depressed. What happened?
5. I'm so depressed I can't stand it.
6. Life is great, isn't it? I just got the job of a lifetime.
7. I feel so relaxed and satisfied.
8. I'm feeling sick; I feel I have to throw up.
9. You look fantastic; what did you do to yourself?
10. Did you see that accident yesterday?

MEANINGS AND MESSAGES

Meaning is an active process created by cooperation between source and receiver—speaker and listener, writer and reader. Here are a few important corollaries concerning meaning.

Meanings Are in People

Meaning depends not only on messages (whether verbal, nonverbal, or both) but on the interaction of those messages and the receiver's own thoughts and feelings. You do not receive meaning; you create meaning. You construct meaning out of the messages you receive combined with your own social and cultural perspectives (beliefs, attitudes, and values, for example) (Berger & Luckmann 1980; Delia 1977; Delia, O'Keefe, & O'Keefe 1982). Words do not mean; people mean. Consequently, to discover meaning, you need to look into people and not merely into words.

An example of the confusion that can result when this relatively simple fact is overlooked is provided by Ronald D. Laing, H. Phillipson, and A. Russell Lee in *Interpersonal Perception* (1966) and analyzed with insight by Paul Watzlawick in *How Real Is Real?* (1977): a couple on the second night of their honeymoon are sitting at a hotel bar. The woman strikes up a conversation with the couple next to her. The husband refuses to communicate with the couple and becomes

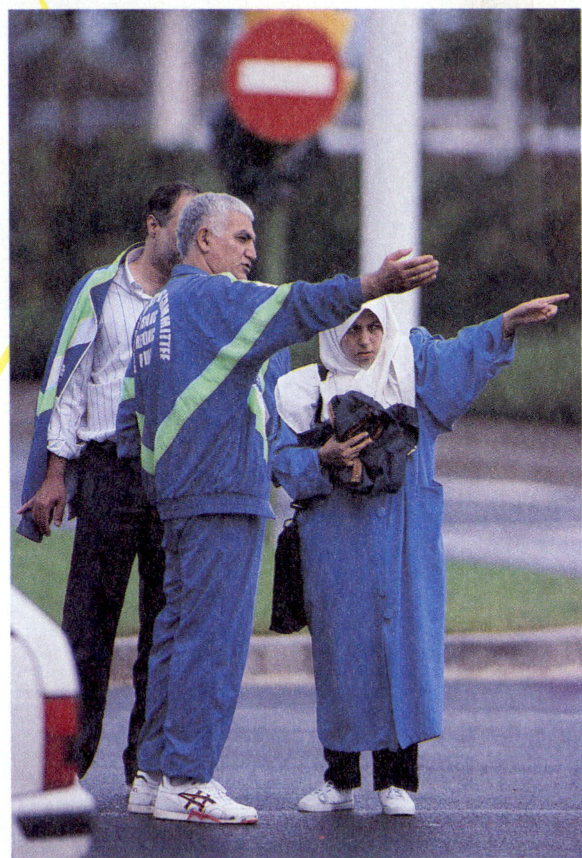

Why is it even more important to recognize that meanings are in people and not in words in intercultural communication situations than in interactions among culturally similar individuals?

antagonistic toward his wife as well as the couple. The wife then grows angry because he has created such an awkward and unpleasant situation. Each becomes increasingly disturbed, and the evening ends in a bitter conflict in which each is convinced of the other's lack of consideration. Eight years later, they analyze this argument. Apparently the idea of honeymoon had meant very different things to each of them. To the husband it had meant a "golden opportunity to ignore the rest of the world and simply explore each other." He felt his wife's interaction with the other couple implied there was something lacking in him. To the wife, honeymoon had meant an opportunity to try out her new role as wife. "I had never had a conversation with another couple as a wife before," she said. "Previous to this I had always been a 'girlfriend' or 'fiancée' or 'daughter' or 'sister.'"

One very clear implication of this principle is that meaning is always ambiguous to some extent. Each person's meaning is somewhat different from each other person's, therefore you can never know precisely what any given word or gesture means. Nonverbal gestures—with the obvious exception of emblems—are usually more ambiguous than verbal messages.

Meanings Are More Than Words and Gestures

When you want to communicate a thought or feeling to another person, you do so with relatively few symbols. These represent just a small part of what you are thinking or feeling, much of which remains unspoken. If you were to try to describe every feeling in detail, you would never get on with the job of living. The meanings you seek to communicate are much more than the sum of the words and nonverbal behaviors you use to represent them.

Because of this, you can never fully know what another person is thinking or feeling. You can only approximate it on the basis of the meanings you receive, which, as already noted, are greatly influenced by who you are and what you are feeling. Conversely, others can never fully know you; they too can only approximate what you are feeling. Failure to understand another person or to be understood are not abnormal situations. They are inevitable, although you should realize that with effort you can always understand another person a little better.

Meanings Are Unique

Because meanings are derived from both the messages communicated and the receiver's own thoughts and feelings, no two people ever derive the same meanings. Similarly, because people change constantly, no one person can derive the same meanings on two separate occasions. Who you are can never be separated from the meanings you create. As a result, you need to check your perceptions of another's meanings by asking questions, echoing what you perceive to be the other person's feelings or thoughts, and seeking elaboration and clarification—in general, practicing all the skills identified in the discussion on effective interpersonal perception and listening (Units 3 and 4).

Also recognize that as you change, you also change the meanings you created out of past messages. Thus, although the message sent may not have changed, the meanings you created from it yesterday and the meanings you create today may be quite different. Yesterday, when a special someone said, "I love you," you created certain meanings. But today, when you learn that the same "I love you" was said to three other people or when you fall in love with someone else, you drastically change the meanings you perceive from those three words.

Meanings Are Both Denotative and Connotative

To understand the nature of denotative and connotative meaning, consider a word such as *death*. To a doctor this word might mean, or denote, the point at which the heart stops beating. To a doctor, *death* is a word signifying an objective description of an event; the word is basically denotative. To a mother whose son has just died, on the other hand, the word means much more. It recalls the son's youth, his ambitions, his family, his illness, and so on. To her the word is emotional, subjective, and highly personal. These emotional, subjective, and personal reactions are the word's connotative meaning.

Nonverbal behaviors may also be viewed in terms of their denotation and connotation. Some nonverbal behaviors are largely denotative (for example, a nod signifying yes) while others are primarily connotative (for example, a smile, raised eyebrows, or a wink).

Another distinction between the two types of meaning has already been implied: the denotative meaning of a message is more general or universal; most people would agree with the denotative meanings and would give similar definitions. Connotative meanings, however, are extremely personal, and few people would agree on the precise connotative meaning of a word or nonverbal behavior. Test this idea by trying to get a group of people to agree on the connotative meanings of such words as *religion, racism, democracy, wealth,* and *freedom* or of such nonverbal behaviors as raised eyebrows, arms folded in front of one's chest, or sitting with one's legs crossed. Chances are very good that it will be impossible to reach an agreement.

Meanings Are Context-Based

Verbal and nonverbal communications exist in a context, and that context to a large extent determines the meaning of any verbal or nonverbal behavior. The same words or behaviors may have totally different meanings when they occur in different contexts. For example, the greeting, "How are you?" means "Hello" to someone you pass regularly on the street but means "Is your health improving?" when said to a friend in the hospital. A wink to an attractive person on a bus means something completely different from a wink that signifies a put-on or a lie. Similarly, the meaning of a given signal depends on the behaviors it accompanies or is close to in time. Pounding a fist on the table during a speech in support of a politician means something quite different from that same gesture in response to news of a friend's death. Divorced from the context, it is impossible to tell what meaning was intended just from examining the signals. Of course, even if you know the context in detail, you still may not be able to decipher the meaning of the verbal or nonverbal message.

THINK ABOUT

Think about how you would rate the meanings of various words on the following scales. Take a few terms—*love, college, lesbians, parents, religion, abortion, racism,* and *happiness* will work well—and rate each term by writing the initial letter of each term in the space corresponding to your meaning on each of the bipolar scales. For example, if you feel that "love" is extremely kind or extremely cruel write "L" in the space next to "kind" or next to "cruel." If you feel that love is quite kind or quite cruel write "L" in the second second or sixth space. If slightly kind or slightly cruel use the third or fifth space. If you feel it is neither kind nor cruel then use the middle (neutral) space. Compare your responses with those of others. Does this experience illustrate the five principles of meaning just considered: meanings are in people, more than words and gestures, unique, both denotative and connotative, and context-based?

kind	___:___:___:___:___:___:___	cruel
large	___:___:___:___:___:___:___	small
good	___:___:___:___:___:___:___	bad
pleasant	___:___:___:___:___:___:___	unpleasant
ugly	___:___:___:___:___:___:___	beautiful
active	___:___:___:___:___:___:___	passive
hot	___:___:___:___:___:___:___	cold
sharp	___:___:___:___:___:___:___	dull
light	___:___:___:___:___:___:___	heavy

MESSAGE CHARACTERISTICS

Communication messages are governed by cultural rules, vary in directness and believability, and may refer to objects and events in the real world as well as to other messages. Reviewing these four message characteristics will enable you to understand better how interpersonal messages are transferred and how you can better control your own messages.

Messages Are Governed by Cultural Rules

The rule-governed nature of verbal communication is well known. All languages have grammars, rules that native speakers follow in producing and understanding sentences, although they may be unable to state them explicitly.

Nonverbal communication is also regulated by a system of rules or norms that state what is and what is not meaningful, appropriate, expected, and permissible in specific social situations. Of course these rules will vary greatly from one culture to another. Rules are cultural (and relative) institutions; they are not universal laws.

In much of the United States, for example, direct eye contact signals openness and honesty. Among

MEDIA WATCH

HOW OBJECTIVE IS REPORTING?

To what extent do the media report the facts and to what extent do they interpret or mix their own attitudes and values into their reporting? The assumption that many people make is that the media will tell you when it is reporting objectively, when it is editorializing, and when it is advertising. The distinctions are not always clearly made, however. Consider these two particularly dramatic examples.

TURMOIL AT TIMES OVER JESSE JAB

Some *New York Times* staffers are furious over the way the paper covered Jesse Jackson's speech at the Democratic National Convention. The city's three other general-interest dailies had positive front-page stories on the speech, but in a largely negative page-one article, B. Drummond Ayres Jr. wrote that Jackson "is not the commanding force he once was . . . and for much of his address . . . his voice reflected it." The article was labeled NEWS ANALYSIS in late editions, but that didn't mollify staffers. "The change was a tacit admission that the story was originally misjudged," says a source. "Even if it's analysis, you have to have evidence. . . . it's not just the reporters of color who are upset. It's one of the few things around here that we're united on." Says Ayres, "No one has complained to me. The story speaks for itself."

"Our editors feel the piece accurately reflected the perception of delegates and politicians on the convention-hall floor," says a Times spokeswoman. "In retrospect, it might have included more about how the speech was received by those watching it on television. The piece continued to be edited and further reported throughout the press run, so several versions appeared in the newspaper. The news analysis [label] was appropriate in the late edition. In hindsight, it may have been appropriate in the first edition as well."

Would you prefer greater objectivity from the media or would you prefer greater editorializing? Which media and which media personalities do you find the most objective? Least objective? How objective was the media following the Oklahoma City bombing? The O.J. Simpson trial and verdict? The World Trade Center bombing?

HOW TV COVERED BUSH'S HECKLERS
Special to *The New York Times*

WASHINGTON, July 24—Was President Bush humiliated today by scores of angry hecklers or was it merely the sort of slight disruption that every politician endures now and then? It depends on which television network you watched.

All three major networks reported the incident in the first five minutes of their evening broadcasts.

On CBS and NBC, the episode came off as far more serious than on ABC. Both CBS and NBC devoted more time to Mr. Bush's angry retorts and to the pictures of furious people. NBC said there were "scores" of hecklers. CBS said that there were "about two dozen."

On the "NBC Nightly News," Mr. Bush appeared enraged as he was being shouted down, though he was shown later in the day looking relaxed as he insisted that "I didn't blow my cool."

On the "CBS Evening News," the reporter said the protest "drowned out the President's message and overshadowed his entire campaign day."

But ABC's "World News Tonight" played down the episode, mentioning it only at the end of a segment that showed Mr. Bush at a campaign rally later in the day.

(continued next page)

MEDIA WATCH *(continued)*

Using the concepts of connotation and denotation, how would you describe what happened in these two examples? How would you explain the reasons for these different interpretations of the same events? How typical do you think these examples are? Can you detect media biases in supposedly objective reporting?

Another way in which subjectivity can be seen is in the stories the media emphasizes (for example the O.J. Simpson trial) or that it does not cover or covers only superficially. For example, the *1995 Project Censored Yearbook* (*Utne*, No. 69, May-June 1995:33–36) notes that the media censored reporting on workers exposed to hazardous materials; the billions of dollars the Pentagon has given military contractors; the dangers of incineration that is presented as safe; the growth of tuberculosis which, for example, in 1993 killed almost 3 million people; and radiation experiments that were conducted on citizens without their knowledge and that were reported as early as late 1993 in the *Albuquerque Tribune*.

Can you find examples of the subjectivity of the media based on the stories it covers and those it fails to cover or gives only brief attention? What foreign countries do you feel are unfairly represented in the media (either by too much exposure or too little)? Can you identify religious or ethnic groups that are given too much or too little media attention? How would media subjectivity in the United States compare with that in other countries with which you are familiar?

How would you describe the objective-subjective presentations in such television shows as "Oprah Winfrey," "Inside Edition," "ET," "Primetime Live," "CNN News," your local area news, "Ricki Lake," and any of the many home shopping programs?

Source: "Turmoil at Times Over Jesse Jab" by Jeannette Walls, *New York Magazine*, August 3, 1992. Copyright © 1992, Los Angeles Times Syndicate. Reprinted by permission; "How TV Covered Bush's Hecklers," *The New York Times*, July 25, 1992. Copyright © 1992 by The New York Times Company. Reprinted by permission.

some Latin Americans and Native Americans, however, direct eye contact between, say, a teacher and a student is considered inappropriate, perhaps aggressive; appropriate student behavior is to avoid eye contact with the teacher. From even this simple example it is easy to see how miscommunication can take place. To a teacher in the United States, avoidance of eye contact by a Latin American or Native American could signify guilt, disinterest, or disrespect, when in fact the child was following her or his own culturally established rules.

Table 7.1, derived from Axtell (1993; also see Wilcox 1994), gives you an idea of the problems that can arise when you assume that the rules governing message behavior in one culture are the same rules used in other cultures.

You learned the ways to communicate nonverbally and the rules of meaningfulness and appropriateness from observing the behaviors of the adult community. For example, you learned how to express sympathy along with the rules that your culture has established for expressing it. You learned that touch is permissible under certain circumstances but not under others and you learned which types of touching are permissible and which are not. You learned that women may touch each other in public; for example, they may hold hands, walk arm in arm, engage in prolonged hugging, and even dance together. You also learned that men may not do this, at least not without inviting social criticism. Perhaps most obvious, you learned that there are certain parts of the body that may not be touched and others that may. The cultural rules also tell you that as a relationship changes, so do the rules for touching; as it becomes more intimate, the rules for touching become less restrictive.

Another way of looking at the role of culture in regulating verbal and nonverbal messages is to examine its maxims or general communication principles (Grice 1975). For example, in much of the United States you operate with the maxim that communication should be truthful; that is, you expect that what the other person says will be the truth. You no doubt follow that maxim by telling the truth yourself. Similarly, you operate with the maxim that what you talk

TABLE 7.1

some nonverbal taboos

Of course, these are only a small number of the nonverbal taboos that exist somewhere throughout the world. Can you add any?

Nonverbal Behavior	Taboo
Blinking your eyes	Considered impolite in Taiwan
Folding your arms over your chest	Considered disrespectful in Fiji
Waving your hand	Insulting in Nigeria and Greece
Gesturing with the thumb up	Considered rude in Australia
Tapping your two index fingers together	Means that a couple is sleeping together or, in Egypt, a request to sleep together
Pointing with the index finger	Considered impolite in many Middle-Eastern countries
Bowing to a lesser degree than your host	Implies that you are superior in Japan
With a clenched fist, inserting your thumb between your index and middle finger (called the *fig*)	Considered obscene in some southern European countries
Pointing at someone with your index and third fingers	Means you are wishing evil on the person in some African countries
Resting your feet on a table or chair	Insulting in some Middle-Eastern countries

about will be relevant to the conversation. Thus, if you are talking about A, B, and C and someone brings up D, you would assume that there is a connection between A, B, and C on the one hand and D on the other. These maxims are integrated into just about every communication textbook used in the United States. It is interesting and instructive to examine the maxims that are unlike those that are followed throughout most of the United States. Here are just three.

The Maxim of Peaceful Relations

Research on Japanese conversations and group discussions notes a maxim of keeping peaceful relationships with others (Midooka 1990). The ways in which such peaceful relationships may be maintained will vary with the person with whom you are interacting. For example, in Japan, your status or position in the hierarchy will influence the amount of self-expression you are expected to engage in. Similarly, there is a great distinction made between public and private conversations In public, this maxim is much more important than it is in private conversations, where they may be violated.

The Maxim of Self-Denigration

This maxim, observed in the conversations of Chinese speakers, may require that a speaker avoid taking credit for some accomplishment or make less of some ability or talent (Gu 1990). To put oneself down here is a form of politeness that seeks to elevate the person to whom you are speaking.

The Maxim of Politeness

It is likely that politeness is universal across all cultures (Brown & Levinson 1988). Cultures differ, however, in how they define politeness and in how important politeness is, compared with, say, openness or honesty. Cultures also differ in the rules for expressing politeness or impoliteness and in the punishments for violating the accepted rules of politeness (Mao 1994; Strecker 1993).

Asian cultures, especially Chinese and Japanese, are often singled out because they emphasize politeness more and mete out harsher social punishments for violations than would cultures in the United States and Western Europe (Steil & Hillman 1993). This has led some to propose that a maxim of politeness operates in Asian cultures (Fraser 1990). When this maxim operates, it may actually violate other maxims. For example, the maxim of politeness may require that you not tell the truth, a situation that would violate the maxim of quality.

There are also large gender differences (and some similarities) in the expression of politeness (Holmes 1995). Generally, studies from a number of different cultures show that women use more polite forms than men (Brown 1980; Wetzel 1988; Holmes 1995). For example, in informal conversation and in conflict situations women tend to seek areas of agreement more than do men. Young girls are more apt to try to modify disagreements while young boys are more apt to express more "bald disagreements" (Holmes 1995). There are also similarities. For example, both men and women in the United States and New Zealand seem to pay compliments in similar ways (Manes & Wolfson 1981; Holmes 1986, 1995).

Politeness also varies with the type of relationship. One researcher, for example, has proposed that politeness is greatest with friends and considerably less with strangers and intimates. This relationship is depicted in Figure 7.1 (Wolfson 1988).

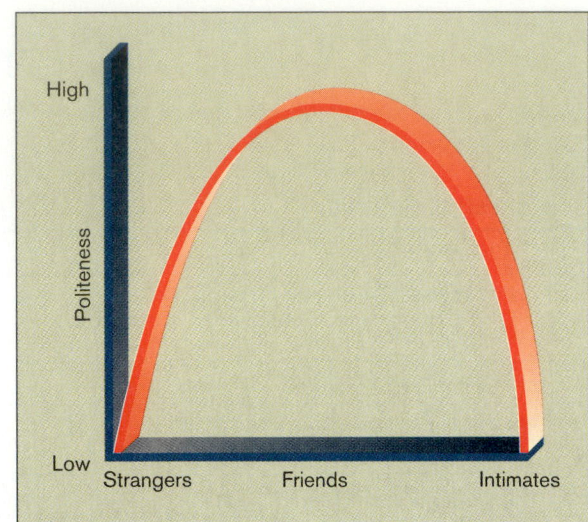

FIGURE 7.1 Wolfson's bulge model of politeness (Wolfson 1988, Holmes 1995). Do you find this model a generally accurate representation of your own level of politeness in different types of relationships? Can you build a case for an inverted U theory (where politeness would be high for both strangers and intimates and low for friends)?

Messages Vary in Directness

THINK ABOUT

Think about how you would respond to someone saying the following.:

1A: I'm so bored; I have nothing to do tonight.
2A: I'd like to go to the movies. Would you like to come?
1B: Do you feel like having hamburgers tonight?
2B: I'd like hamburgers tonight. How about you?

The statements numbered 1 are relatively indirect; they are attempts to get the listener to say or do something without committing the speaker. The statements numbered 2 are more direct—they state more clearly the speaker's preferences and then ask the listeners if they agree. A more obvious example of an indirect message occurs when you glance at your watch to communicate that it is late and that you had better be going. Before reading the text think about the potential advantages and disadvantages of indirect messages. What do you see as the greatest advantages and disadvantages of indirect messages from the speaker's point of view? From the listener's point of view?

Advantages of Indirect Messages

Indirect messages allow you to express a desire without insulting or offending anyone; they allow you to observe the rules of polite interaction. Instead of saying, "I'm bored with this group," you say, "It's getting late and I have to get up early tomorrow," or you look at your watch and pretend to be surprised by the time. Instead of saying, "This food tastes like cardboard," you say, "I just started a diet" or "I just ate." In each instance you are stating a preference but are saying it indirectly so as to avoid offending someone. Not all direct requests, however, should be considered impolite. In one study of Spanish and English speakers, for example, no evidence was found to support the assumption that politeness and directness were incompatible (Mir 1993).

Sometimes indirect messages allow you to ask for compliments in a socially acceptable manner, such as saying, "I was thinking of getting a nose job." You hope to get the desired compliment: "A nose job? You? Your nose is perfect."

INTRODUCING RESEARCH

NAVIGATING FROM QUESTION TO CONCLUSION

Research is a relatively systematic process. Most researchers would go through the seven steps that follow. These steps are presented in a very abbreviated form here—the objective is to explain how the process is pursued rather than to spell out the detailed procedures a researcher would follow in conducting a research study.

Ask a Question. Research starts with a question. As noted in previous research boxes (Units 2 and 3), it can be a purely theoretical one (How can a person's fear of communication be measured?) or one of great practical importance (What communication skills contribute most to managerial effectiveness? What motives do advertisers appeal to in selling perfume? What rhetorical strategies did the presidential candidates use in their pre-election debates?).

Sometimes the research problem remains in question form. At other times, a researcher phrases a hypothesis, a statement that predicts a certain relationship will exist between or among different variables. For example, one such hypothesis might be: People who have high self-esteem will reveal more about themselves than those with low self-esteem.

Actually, a hypothesis can also predict that there is no relationship between variables (this special hypothesis is called a null hypothesis), for example: Men and women do not differ in their level of romanticism. The researcher expects to reject this null hypothesis—the researcher hopes to find that there are differences.

Define Significant Concepts. All the key terms in the research need to be defined as specifically and as clearly as possible. The terms need to be defined so clearly that everyone who looks at the same communication behavior would classify it in the same way. For example, how would you define *fear of communication*? *Managerial effectiveness*? *Self-esteem*? *Effective teachers*?

Review Related Research. Here the previous theories and research studies bearing on the research question are examined. The researcher attempts to answer the question: What is already known that bears on my research project?

Design the Research Study. What type of study will you design (see Introducing Research box in Unit 4)? Will you design a descriptive, an historical/critical, or an experimental study? How many participants will you use? What are the major characteristics of the participants you will try to find (age, sex, educational level, political affiliation, religion, race)? For example, are 20 men and women sufficient to draw conclusions about romanticism of men and women. If you use a questionnaire, what questions will you ask? How will you order the questions?

Conduct the Study. Here you would follow through with your design. You would survey your participants, record the findings from previous research, or present your participants with the scenario.

Analyze the Data. Using appropriate methods (which vary from the most sophisticated of statistical tests to simply counting the number of times teachers used humor, to summarizing the major findings from previous research on male self-disclosure) you would analyze the data and identify the major results.

Formulate the Conclusions. What do the results mean? What can you conclude about self-disclosure on a male's self-image? What can you conclude about touching as a response to another's touching?

Disadvantages of Indirect Messages

Indirect messages, however, can also create problems. Consider the following dialogue in which an indirect request is made:

PAT: You wouldn't like to have my parents over for dinner this weekend, would you?

CHRIS: I really wanted to go to the shore and just relax.

PAT: Well, if you feel you have to go to the shore, I'll make the dinner myself. You go to the shore. I really hate having them over and doing all the work myself. It's such a drag shopping, cooking, and cleaning all by myself.

Given this situation, Chris has two basic options. One is to stick with the plans to go to the shore and relax. In this case Pat is going to be upset and Chris is going to be made to feel guilty for not helping with the dinner. A second alternative is to give in to Pat, help with the dinner, and not go to the shore. In this case Chris is going to have to give up a much-desired plan and is likely to resent Pat's manipulative tactics. Regardless of which decision is made, one person wins and one person loses. This win-lose situation creates resentment, competition, and often an "I'll get even" attitude. With direct requests, this type of situation is much less likely to develop. Consider:

PAT: I'd like to have my parents over for dinner this weekend. What do you think?

CHRIS: Well, I really wanted to go to the shore and just relax.

Regardless of what develops next, both individuals are starting out on relatively equal footing. Each has clearly and directly stated a preference. In this case, these preferences seem mutually exclusive. But it might be possible to meet both persons' needs. For example, Chris might say, "How about going to the shore this weekend and having your parents over next weekend? I'm really exhausted; I could use the rest." Here is a direct response to a direct request. Unless there is some pressing need to have Pat's parents over for dinner this weekend, this response may enable each to meet the other's needs.

With the use of indirect requests, win-win outcomes are often difficult to see because of an implied inequality and a perceived attempt to manipulate the other person. Direct requests, on the other hand, do not appear manipulative. The result is that solutions readily suggest themselves. Also, the defensiveness that makes accepting an alternative plan difficult or ego-threatening is avoided. Here both parties can get what they want; it is a win-win situation—a situation that creates supportiveness and a willingness to cooperate.

Gender and Cultural Differences in Directness

The popular stereotype in much of the United States holds that women are indirect in making requests or in giving orders. This indirectness communicates powerlessness, discomfort with their own authority. Men, the stereotype continues, are direct, sometimes to the point of being blunt or rude. This directness communicates power and comfort with one's own authority.

Deborah Tannen (1994b) provides an interesting perspective on this stereotype. Women are, it seems, more indirect in giving orders and are more likely to say, for example, "It would be great if these letters could go out today" than "Have these letters out by 3." Tannen (1994b, p. 84) argues that "issuing orders indirectly can be the prerogative of those in power" and in no way shows powerlessness. Power, to Tannen, is the ability to choose your own style of communication.

Men are also indirect, but in different situations (Rundquist 1992). According to Tannen, men are more likely to use indirectness when they express weakness, reveal a problem, or admit an error. Men are more likely to speak indirectly in expressing emotions other than anger. Men are also more indirect when they refuse expressions of increased romantic intimacy. Men are thus indirect, the theory goes, when they are saying something that goes against the masculine stereotype.

Many Asian and Latin American cultures stress the values of indirectness largely because it enables a person to avoid appearing criticized or contradicted and thereby losing face. In most of the United States, however, we are taught that directness is the preferred style. Be up front and tell it like it is are commonly heard communication guidelines. Contrast these with the following two principles of indirectness found in the Japanese language (Tannen 1994b):

> *omoiyari,* close to empathy, says that listeners need to understand the speaker without the speaker being specific or direct. This style obviously places a much greater demand on the listener than would a direct speaking style.
>
> *sassuru* advises listeners to anticipate a speaker's meanings and use subtle cues from the speaker to infer his or her total meaning.

A good example of the cultural differences in directness is seen in the differences between mothers in the United States and in Japan (Tannen 1994b). When confronted by a request from a child that they do not want to grant, the mothers respond very differently. In the United States most mothers would be very direct and simply say no. In Japan the mother will give reasons for refusing the child's request but will not say no directly. According to Tannen, mothers from the

United States might reason that giving reasons would dilute their authority. Their belief is that mothers do not have to give children reasons. Japanese mothers reason that to simply refuse would be to respond as would a child and would therefore reduce their power to the level of the child. By giving reasons they maintain and even enhance their authority.

In thinking about direct and indirect messages, it is important to realize the ease with which misunderstandings can occur. For example, a person who uses an indirect style of speech may be doing so to be polite and may have been taught this style by his or her culture. If you assume, instead, that the person is using indirectness to be manipulative, because your culture regards it as being so, then miscommunication is inevitable.

Messages Vary in Believability

For the most part, research shows that when verbal and nonverbal messages conflict, people believe the nonverbal. Nonverbal theorist Dale Leathers (1986), for example, reports that nonverbal cues are more than four times as effective as verbal cues in their impact on interpersonal impressions and ten times more important in expressing confidence. For most messages, a good guess is that approximately 60 to 65 percent of meaning is communicated nonverbally (Burgoon, Buller, & Woodall 1989).

Why do people believe the nonverbal message rather than the verbal one? It may be that verbal messages are easier to fake. Consequently, when there is a contradiction, you distrust the verbal and accept the nonverbal. Or it may be that nonverbal messages often function below the level of conscious awareness. You learned them without being aware of such learning, and you perceive them without conscious awareness. Thus, when such a conflict arises, you somehow get a "feeling" from the nonverbal messages, and because you cannot isolate its source, you assume that it is somehow correct.

Nonverbal cues help you to guess whether or not a person is lying. You also use them to help you discover the underlying truth that the lie is meant to conceal. Interestingly enough, as you become more and more intimate with a person, your ability to detect the underlying truth that your partner is trying to hide declines. Research also shows that women are better than men at discovering the underlying truth (McCormack & Parks 1990).

What nonverbal cues do you use in detecting whether or not someone is lying? Table 7.2 presents the findings from a wide variety of research studies on the cues given when someone is lying. In reviewing this material, remember to interpret communication behaviors (verbal and nonverbal) within the context in which they occur. As noted in Unit 1, all communication takes place in a context and that context greatly influences the meaning of the words and gestures.

Perhaps the most important context is the cultural one, and the failure to recognize its importance may lead you to make serious errors in judgment. For example, the Japanese use few allness terms and few gestures. Hispanics and Arabs, on the other hand, are more elaborate in their speech and use many allness terms (for example, *all, always, never*) and many gestures (Gudykunst & Ting-Toomey 1988). To use these behaviors as cues to lying—as might be done by those living in the United States—would be misleading. The differences would be due to culture and not to the fact that one or both are lying.

The examples cited in Table 7.2, then, should be used to suggest hypotheses, not firm conclusions, about possible deceit about members from your own culture or from other cultures. After reviewing the extensive literature on deception, Paul Ekman, in *Telling Lies* (1985, p. 187) cautions: "Evaluating behavioral clues to deceit is hazardous. . . . The lie catcher must always estimate the *likelihood* that a gesture or expression indicates lying or truthfulness; rarely is it absolutely certain."

Messages May Metacommunicate

Metacommunication is communication that refers to other communications. All behavior, verbal and nonverbal, can be metacommunicational. Verbally, you can say, for example, "This statement is false" or "Do you understand what I am trying to tell you?" These refer to communication and are called metacommunicational statements.

Nonverbal behavior may also be metacommunicational. Obvious examples include crossing one's fingers behind one's back or winking when telling a lie. The more subtle instances of metacommunication are more interesting: you end your blind date, but even as you say "I had a really nice time," the nonverbal messages—the lack of a smile, the failure to maintain eye contact, the extra-long pauses—contradict the verbal

TABLE 7.2
the communication behavior of liars

This table is based on the extensive research summaries of Knapp and Hall 1992; DeTurck and Miller 1985; Miller and Burgoon in DeVito and Hecht 1990; O'Hair, Cody, Goss, and Krayer 1988; Mehrabian 1978; and Leathers 1992. Note that not all studies find the same behaviors indicative of lying largely because the conditions under which lying is tested are so different. For example, some situations involved the opportunity to rehearse the lie whereas others did not. This table is intended to provide a broad overview of the cues that distinguish lying from truth-telling behavior and not to identify specific cues that should be used to distinguish a liar from a truth-teller.

Liars' Messages	Truth-tellers' Messages
Hesitate more	Hesitate less
Make more speech errors	Make fewer speech errors
Smile less	Smile more
Respond with shorter answers, often simple yes or no responses	Elaborate more in their answers
Use more allness terms, for example, *never, always, everyone*	Use fewer allness terms
Use fewer specifics, for example, references to specific people, places, and things, and more nonspecific such as "hung out" or "had fun"; use more generalizing phrases, for example, adding "stuff like that" and "you know"	Use more specifics and make more references to verifiable incidents
Blink more	Blink less
Use more adaptors (nervous type, self-touching movements)	Use fewer adaptors
Dilate their pupils	Do not dilate their pupils
Shift their posture more often	Remain more steady in posture
Have a greater response latency (pause longer before responding to another's question or statement)	Answer questions more quickly
Use excessive gestures	Use fewer gestures
Use more and longer pauses	Pause less and fewer pauses
Avert gaze more; spend more time looking away from the listener	Maintain more focused eye contact
Appear less friendly and attentive	Appear more friendly and interested

"really nice time" and tell your date that you did not enjoy the evening.

Nonverbal messages may also metacommunicate about other nonverbal messages. The individual who, upon meeting a stranger, both smiles and extends a totally lifeless hand shows how one nonverbal behavior may contradict another. Usually when nonverbal behavior is metacommunicational, it reinforces other verbal or nonverbal behavior. You may literally roll up your sleeves when talking about cleaning up the room, smile when greeting someone, run to meet the person you say you are eager to see, greet your dentist with a frown, or arrive early for a party you verbally express pleasure in attending.

Here are just a few ways to use metacommunication to check that your message is understood as you wish it to be:

- Give clear feedforward. This will help the other person get a general picture of the message that will follow. It will provide a kind of schema that makes information processing and learning easier.

- Give specific examples. Many people talk in too many and too high abstractions. Thus, if you talk of "financial security"— a relatively high-level abstraction—your listener may think "job security" when you want to emphasize the importance of "insurance." Specific examples will help make your abstractions clearer and will help your listener focus on the specifics on which you wish him or her to focus.
- Confront contradictory or inconsistent messages. At the same time, explain your messages that may appear inconsistent to your listener. Refer to the discussion of mixed messages in Unit 2.
- Explain the feelings that go with the thoughts. Often people communicate only the thinking part of their message, resulting in listeners being unable to hear the other parts of their meaning. Communicate how you feel as well as what you think.
- Paraphrase your own complex messages. It will help listeners understand you if they hear the same idea phrased differently. Similarly, to check on your own understanding of another's message, try to paraphrase what you think the other person means.
- Ask questions. If you have doubts about another's meaning, do not assume you understand; instead, ask for clarification.

SUMMARY

In this unit we introduced the message system, the ways in which verbal and nonverbal messages interact, the nature of meaning, and the general characteristics of messages.

1. Verbal and nonverbal messages interact and accent, complement, contradict, regulate, repeat, and substitute for each other.
2. Meaning is an active process created by cooperation between source and receiver; it is a function of the interaction of messages and the receiver's previous experiences, expectations, attitudes, and so on.
3. Meanings are in people, more than words and gestures, unique, both denotative (objective) and connotative (subjective), and context-based.
4. Messages are rule-governed: both verbal and nonverbal communication messages follow rules that are learned and known by native speakers of the language.
5. Messages vary in directness.
6. Messages vary in believability: when verbal and nonverbal messages contradict each other, people are more apt to believe the nonverbal.
7. Messages may refer to objects in the world or to other messages (metacommunication).

THINKING CRITICALLY ABOUT VERBAL AND NONVERBAL MESSAGES

1. What do you see as the major similarities between verbal and nonverbal communication? The major differences?
2. Can you identify a nonverbal taboo that you were taught by your culture? What would happen if someone violated this taboo?
3. One of the principles of meaning was that meanings are unique, that each person's meaning is different from each other person's meaning. Yet, it is logical that your meaning, say, and that of your best friend will be a lot more similar than would your meaning and that of someone from another culture, another gender, or another race. What factors contribute to two people's similarity or difference in meaning?
4. The National Easter Seal Society offers a number of suggestions for communicating with people with disabilities. [Also see "Ten Commandment for Communicating with People with Disabilities" in Unit 6 (page 99) and and the guidelines for respecting a blind person in Unit 9 (page 149).] Among their recommendations are:
   a. Don't use the word *handicapped;* instead, use the word *disability.*
   b. Don't emphasize the disability, emphasize the person; for example, don't label people with disabilities as *disabled, victims, epileptics;* instead, refer to the person, saying *someone who has epilepsy.*

   How would you explain these suggestions in terms of denotation and connotation?
5. Many people who communicate directly see those who communicate indirectly as being manipulative. According to Tannen (1994b, p. 92), however, "'manipulative' is often just a way of blaming others for our discomfort with their styles." Do you agree with Tannen? Or, do you think that indirectness is very often intended to be manipulative?

6. When asked what they would like to change about the communication of the opposite sex, men said they wanted women to be more direct and women said they wanted men to stop interrupting and offering advice (Noble 1994). What one change would you like to see in the communication style of the opposite sex? Of your own sex?
7. Do your experiences support the findings that women are more polite than men? Can you identify politeness forms that men use more often than women?
8. The difference between giving and not giving reasons is also seen among people of different educational backgrounds. Generally, the more education the mother has, the more likely she is to give reasons to her child. By giving the child reasons, the mother teaches the child to reason logically and to follow a logical train of thought. What does the parent who does not give reasons teach the child?
9. "Expert lie detectors" were found to be less accurate when they were suspicious of deception than when they were not suspicious. This same relationship did not hold for "novice lie detectors" (Burgoon, Buller, Ebesu, & Rockwell 1994). What reasons could you advance to explain this finding?
10. How would you go about finding answers to such questions as these:
    a. Is nonverbal communication more ambiguous than verbal communication?
    b. Do couples who talk about their talk (that is, who metacommunicate) argue less than couples who do not metacommunicate? Are teachers who metacommunicate more effective than teachers who do not?
    c. Are close relationship partners better at detecting their partners' lies than are casual acquaintances? For an interesting investigation of this question see Metts (1989).
    d. What cues does a public speaking audience use to make judgments concerning the truthfulness of the speaker?
    e. Do women prefer men who are direct or indirect? Do men prefer women who are indirect over women who are direct?
    f. In what situations is directness preferred? In what situations is indirectness preferred?

eight unit Verbal Message Principles

unit contents

unit goals

After completing this unit, you should be able to

1. define *excluding talk* and the *principle of inclusion* and provide examples of each
2. define *downward talk* and the *principle of equality* and provide examples of each
3. explain some of the ways for communicating criticism and praise
4. explain some of the disadvantages of lying from a communication point of view
5. define *gossip* and explain how the principle of confidentiality should operate
6. define *disconfirmation* and *confirmation* and provide examples of each
7. define *racism, sexism,* and *heterosexism*

The effects people have on each other come largely from the verbal messages they send and receive. In this unit, we consider seven ways in which you may create negative effects and their corresponding opposites, the principles useful in avoiding such negative reactions. These principles should enable you to create a more positive environment for communication in all its forms.

EXCLUDING AND INCLUSIVE TALK

Excluding talk is used here as a general term to refer to communication that excludes certain people, though on the surface it may appear to apply to everyone. You see this in a wide variety of forms, for example, in the use of some in-group language in the presence of some out-group member. When doctors get together and discuss medicine, there is no problem; but when they get together with someone who is not a doctor, they often fail to adjust to the presence of this new person. Instead, they simply continue with discussions of prescriptions, symptoms, medication, and all the talk that excludes others present.

Excluding talk also occurs when people of the same nationality get together within a larger, more heterogeneous group and use the language of their nationality, sometimes just isolated words, sometimes sentences, and sometimes even entire conversations. The use of these terms in the presence of nonmembers emphasizes their status as outsiders and excludes these people from full participation in the communication act.

A variation of in-group talk is self-talk, talk that revolves around the speaker and little else (Addeo & Burger 1973). It is seen perfectly in the story of the author who has been talking about his new book for the last hour. Finally, seeming to realize his own self-talk, stops himself and says: "But enough about me, what did you think of my book?" At the other extreme, there are those who never talk about themselves. These are the underdisclosers discussed in Unit 5. These are the people who want to learn everything about you but do not want to reveal anything about themselves.

Another form of excluding talk is the use of the terms of one's own cultural group as universal, as applying to everyone. In using such terms others are excluded. For example, *church* refers to the place of worship for specific religions, not all religions. Similarly, *New Testament, Quran,* and *Torah* refer to the religious scriptures unique to specific religious and not to "religious scriptures" generally. Nor does "Judeo-Christian tradition" include the religious traditions of everyone. Similarly, the use of the terms *marriage, husband,* and *wife* refer to some heterosexual relationships and exclude others; they also exclude gay and lesbian relationships.

In contrast, the principle of inclusion emphasizes the need and the general effectiveness of speaking the language of all people and including all members. Even when it is necessary to "talk shop" in the presence of a nonmember, that person can still be included in a variety of ways. Seeking a nonmember's perspective on the issue or drawing an analogy with that person's field are obvious inclusive techniques.

Satisfying interactions are characterized by the principle of balance—some self-talk, some other-talk, and rarely all of one or the other. Communication is a two-way process in which each person functions as source and receiver. Balanced communication interactions are more satisfying and result in much more interesting interactions (Hecht 1978a, 1978b). We get bored hearing too much about the other person—and others get bored with too much of us.

Alternative terms are readily available to highlight inclusion rather than exclusion. For example, the Association of American University Presses (Schwartz 1995) recommends using *place of worship* instead of *church* when you wish to include the houses of worship of all people. Similarly, *committed relationship* is more inclusive than *marriage, couples therapy* is more inclusive than *marriage counseling,* and *life partner* is more inclusive than *husband* or *wife. Religious scriptures* is more inclusive than *New Testament,* for example. Of course, if you are referring to, say, a specific Baptist church or married heterosexual couples then the terms *church* and *marriage* are perfectly appropriate.

DOWNWARD AND EQUALITY TALK

Downward talk occurs in a variety of forms. In one form it occurs when someone puts himself or herself above others by using phrases such as "You probably didn't realize this, but . . ." or "I know you don't keep up with the computer literature, but . . . ." Regardless of who is doing the talking, you get the feeling that somehow the speaker is above you for a multitude of reasons—intelligence, experience, knowledge, position, wealth, whatever. You are put into the position of learner and subordinate.

Another way some people talk down to others is by telling them how to feel. "Don't be silly, you'll pass the course." "Forget about the louse. You'll meet someone else." "Lots of people are worse off than you. Don't feel so sorry for yourself." Usually, people resent this intrusion into their private world of feelings.

Still another way to talk down is to interrupt the other person (see Unit 13). Of course, not all interruptions are negative (Murata 1994). Some interruptions are cooperative (for example, a request for more information or active listening expressions). Other interruptions (for example, taking over the speaking turn) are ways of saying that their communications are more important than yours; therefore they have a right to interrupt you.

Power Plays

A special type of talking down occurs in **power plays** (Steiner 1981), verbal maneuvers that put you down and allow the other person to get what he or she wants. Consider a few power plays analyzed by Steiner.

In "Nobody Upstairs" the other person refuses to acknowledge your request. The game takes the form of not listening to what you are saying, regardless of how you say it or how many times you say it. One common form is to refuse to take no for an answer. We see this clearly in the stereotypical man who persists in making advances to a woman despite her repeated refusals. Sometimes "Nobody Upstairs" takes the form of ignoring socially and commonly accepted (but unspoken) rules such as knocking before you enter a person's office, not opening another person's desk drawers, or not going through another person's office mailbox. The power play takes the form of expressing ignorance of the rules: "I didn't know you didn't want me to look in your mailbox" or "Do you want me to knock before I come into your office the next time?"

Another power play is "You Owe Me." Here the person does something for you and then demands something in return. The maneuver puts you in the position of owing this person something. This game is played frequently by men who take a woman on an expensive date. The objective is to make the woman owe something, usually sex. Another common example is the boss who hires you at an entry-level position and expects you to stay in that position out of gratitude for being hired. Whenever you ask for a promotion or begin looking for a new job, the boss reminds you of how much he or she has done for you: "How can you think of leaving Rawley after all we've done for you?"

In "Metaphor" the other person uses metaphors to express some negative opinion or impression. For example, say you are going out with someone your co-workers do not like. The co-workers may make such comments as "How can you go out with that dog?" or "How can you date such a pig?" Dog and pig are metaphors, figures of speech in which one word is used in the place of another. In these examples, the terms *dog* and *pig* are used in place of the names of persons referred to with the intention of identifying the most obvious characteristics of these animals (in this case ugliness and sloppiness) with the people. The object here is to deny you the chance to defend your choice—after all, it is difficult to defend dating a dog or a pig!

Management Strategy

What do you do when confronted by such power plays? Claude Steiner (1981) recommends that you follow a three-part strategy (Table 8.1 presents specific examples of these management strategies):

1. Express your feelings. Tell the person that you are angry or annoyed or disturbed by his or her behavior.
2. Describe the behavior to which you object. Tell the person—in language that describes rather than evaluates—the specific behavior that you object to, for example, reading your mail, reminding you of how much you owe him or her, or calling your date names.
3. State a cooperative response that you both can live with comfortably. Tell the person—in a cooperative tone—what you want, for example: "I want you to knock before coming into my office." "I want you to stop reminding me of how much I owe you." "I want you to stop calling my dates names."

When used unfairly to intimidate or to manipulate, downward talk creates problems for all involved. Although the three-part management strategy is useful for power plays, the most general antidote is the principle of equality. If you receive messages that talk down to you or attempt to strip you of power, remember that all parties in the communication act are equal in the sense that each person's communications are worthwhile and each person has something to contribute. You may use power plays and manipulations without being aware of them. Perhaps keeping the principle of equality in mind will lessen the likelihood of doing this in the future. As a receiver, recognize your own responsibility in these situations. When you allow people to interrupt you or somehow to treat your communications as unimportant, you are encouraging and reinforcing this behavior. Demand communication equality. The simple statement, "Excuse me, but I'd like to finish my thought," is usually effective.

TABLE 8.1
power plays and management strategies

Power Play	Management Strategy	Example
"Nobody Upstairs" *The other person refuses to acknowledge your request, as if your words are simply not received*	Statement of feeling	"I'm angry that you persist in opening my mail."
	Description of the behavior to which you object	"You have opened my mail four times this past week alone."
	Statement of cooperative response	"I want you to allow me to open my own mail. If there is anything in it that concerns you, I will let you know immediately."
"You Owe Me" *The other person demands a payback for some past favor done for you*	Statement of feeling	"I'm disturbed that you're doing this to me."
	Description of the behavior that you object to	"I'm angry that when you want me to do something, you preface it by reminding me of my obligations to you. You tell me all you did for me and then tell me that I should therefore do what you want me to do."
	Statement of cooperative response	"Please don't do things for me because you want something in return. I don't want to feel obligated. I want to do what I want because I think it is best for me and not because I would feel guilty about not paying you back for what you've done for me."
"Metaphor" *The other person expresses negative evaluations by metaphors*	Statement of feeling	"I resent your calling my dates 'dogs' and 'pigs.' I feel like a real loser when you refer to my dates in this way."
	Description of the behavior that you object to	"You've referred to the last three people I've dated with these insulting names."
	Statement of cooperative response	"If you don't like the people I'm dating, please tell me. But please don't insult them or me by using terms such as 'pig' or 'dog.'"

CRITICISM, PRAISE, AND HONEST APPRAISAL

Throughout your communication experiences you are expected to criticize, to evaluate, and otherwise render some kind of judgment. Especially in helping professions, such as teaching, nursing, or counseling, criticism is a necessary and important part of interactions and communications generally. The problem arises when criticism is used outside of its helping function and when it is inappropriate or excessive.

An especially useful skill in this connection is the ability to distinguish when a person is asking for criticism and when that person is simply asking for a compliment. For example, when a friend asks how you like a new apartment, he or she may be searching for a compliment rather than wanting you to render an objective appraisal or to itemize all the things wrong with it.

Sometimes the desire to be liked (or perhaps the need to be appreciated) is so strong that you may go to the other extreme and paint everything with praise. The most ordinary jacket, the most common thought, the most average meal are given extraordinary praise, way beyond their merits. The overly critical and the overly complimentary soon find that their comments are no longer met with concern or interest.

The ways in which praise is to be expressed and accepted vary with the culture. For example, a study conducted in the United States and South Africa, found that Americans gave lots of compliments but were reticent in their acceptance of compliments offered by others. South Africans, on the other hand, gave many fewer compliments but were more apt to accept the compliments of others (Herbert & Straight 1989).

An alternative to excessive criticism or praise is the principle of honest appraisal: telling the truth. There is, of course, an art to truth-telling, just as there is an art to other forms of effective communication. Before you respond, consider if an honest appraisal is being asked for or if the person is asking for a compliment. "How do you like my new haircut?" may simply be a request for a compliment. If it's a request for an honest appraisal (rather than for a compliment) and if your appraisal is a negative one, give some consideration to how you should phrase your criticism.

Giving Criticism

Criticism can be made more effective and less painful for both sender and receiver by following a few suggestions. For example, in giving criticism focus on the event or the behavior rather than on the person or his or her personality. Note the difference, for example, between "this paper has four errors and needs retyping" (which focuses on the behavior) and "you're a lousy typist; do this over" (which focuses on the person).

People respond more openly to criticism that is stated positively than to criticism stated negatively. Note that you can say, "You look terrible in black" or, stating it positively, "You look much better in bright colors."

Criticism owned by the speaker is generally more effective than criticism in which the speaker denies responsibility. Note the difference between these two statements: (1) "Your report was unintelligible" and (2) "I had difficulty following your ideas." Both statements communicate essentially the same information. The first statement, however, places the difficulty with the report and with the writer. In statement (2), however, the speaker assumes the responsibility for not understanding. One great advantage of assuming responsibility (of owning your own messages) is that you are less likely to create defensiveness in the other person. As soon as you say, "Your report was unintelligible" you can anticipate defensive reactions such as, "Everyone else understood it," or "It's clear; you just have to read it more carefully."

It is often helpful to state concern for the other person along with any criticism. Instead of saying, "You look terrible in that yellow plaid suit," you might say, "I want you to make a good impression. I think the dark suit would work better."

Generally, criticism is most helpful when it is specific. To say, for example, "This report is weak," provides little help in identifying what you can do to improve the report. If, on the other hand, the person says, "I think the introduction wasn't clear enough. A more specific statement of purpose might have worked better," you have a clear idea of how you can improve.

Mind reading, the tendency to infer what the other person is thinking or what the other person's motives are, almost always gets you into trouble when giving criticism. Mind reading is seen in a comment such as: "Don't you care about the impression you make? This report is terrible." The same information—in a much more usable form—can easily be communicated: "I would use a stronger introduction and a friendlier writing style."

Giving Praise

Although praise is by definition positive, not all expressions of praise are equal; some are clearly more effective than others. In expressing praise, consider the following.

Generally, I-messages are preferred. Instead of saying "that report was good," the corresponding I-message might be something like "I thought that report was good" or "I liked your report."

Positive feelings, such as praise, are best communicated both verbally and nonverbally. If you're thinking of something else or are insincere in your praise then your nonverbals may contradict your verbal expression. Often when you praise others simply because it is the socially correct response, you betray your lack of conviction with too little or inappropriate affect. To be effective, all communication channels need to work together.

Although the example, "I liked your report," is an I-message and preferred to the remote "that report was good," it is not very specific. Generally, naming the specific behavior you are praising communicates a greater genuineness and sincerity. Instead of, "I liked the report," the praise might be extended to something such as, "I liked the report; the way you integrated the charts of past performance with projected earnings made everything so clear."

LYING AND HONESTY

According to deception researcher Paul Ekman (1985, p. 28) lying occurs when "one person intends to mislead another, doing so deliberately, without prior notification of this purpose, and without having been explicitly asked to do so by the target [the person the liar intends to mislead]." As this definition makes clear, lying may be committed by omission as well as commission. When you omit something relevant, and this omission leads others to be misled, you have lied just as surely as if you had made a false statement (Bok 1978).

Similarly, although most lies are verbal, some are nonverbal and most seem to involve at least some nonverbal elements. The innocent facial expression—despite the commission of some punishable act—and the knowing nod instead of the honest expression of ignorance are common examples of nonverbal lying. Lies may range from the white lie that stretches the truth to the big lie in which one formulates falsehoods so elaborate that they seem believable.

Reasons for Lying

Most lies are told for two general reasons: (1) to gain some reward or (2) to avoid some punishment. Lying to gain a reward is motivated by such factors as these (Camden, Motley, & Wilson 1984):

- Basic needs: Lies told to gain or to retain objects that fulfill basic needs—for example, money or various material possessions.
- Affiliation: Lies told to increase desired affiliations or to decrease undesired affiliations—for example, lies told to prolong desirable social interactions, avert interpersonal conflicts, or avoid granting some request to halt undesirable interaction.
- Self-esteem: Lies told to protect or increase the self-esteem of oneself, the person one is interacting with, or some third party—for example, lies told to increase one's perceived competence, taste, or social desirability.
- Self-gratification: Lies told to achieve some personal satisfaction—for example, lies told for the sake of humor or to exaggerate for some desired effect.

Although usually people lie for their own benefit, some lies are motivated by a desire to benefit another person. An analysis of 322 lies revealed that 75.8 percent benefited the liar, 21.7 percent benefited the person who was told the lie, and 2.5 percent benefited some third party (Camden, Motley, & Wilson 1984).

THINK ABOUT

Think about your own reasons for lying and especially how your culture influences whether you lie and for what reasons. Although there is little research on lying as it is influenced by culture, some research does indicate that the individual-collective differences may influence why people lie. For example, in a study of students from the United States (an individualistic culture) and Samoa (a collectivistic culture) it was found that U.S. Americans noted that they would lie most to protect their privacy and to protect the other person. Samoan Americans, on the other hand, noted that they would be most likely to lie when that deception related to family or group issues. They were also more likely to lie to impress an authority figure (Aune & Waters 1994). Does your own individual or collective orientation influence your reasons for lying (or not lying)?

Generally, you know when you are lying and when you are not lying. No one has to tell you. Yet there are many gray areas where it is not clear when a statement is a lie. For example, sometimes, as illustrated earlier, it is difficult to tell when someone is asking for an honest opinion or merely asking for a compliment. Sometimes there is a tacit agreement between people to avoid telling the truth about certain issues. A couple, for example, may agree that extrarelational affairs are not to be disclosed and that the acceptable procedure is to make up some kind of innocent excuse—working late at the office and its variants—to cover up. In these instances, the context and the intent of the message would define whether something is or is not a lie.

Ethics and Effectiveness

Lies have both ethical and effectiveness dimensions. The ethical dimension concerns what is right and what is wrong. You may wish to examine your own beliefs about the ethics of lying by taking the Self-Test, "[When] Is Lying Unethical?"

The effectiveness dimension concerns whether the lie succeeds or fails to gain the reward or avoid the punishment. Many lies are effective; people have risen to the top of their profession and have amassed fortunes built on lies and deceit. There can be little doubt that in many instances lying works, yet lying has enough disadvantages to make you pause and reconsider any decision to involve yourself in such behavior.

As already noted, communication messages are sent and received as packages (Unit 2). Lies are no exception (Burgoon, Buller, & Woodall 1989). It is often difficult to lie nonverbally with any degree of conviction (Ekman 1985). Often lies are betrayed nonverbally, as illustrated in Unit 7. It is far easier to lie with your mouth than with your body; when the contradiction is observed, it is the nonverbal message that people believe. The result is that you have lied to no avail. Your reputation may suffer without your having achieved the reward or avoided the punishment.

Perhaps the most obvious disadvantage to lying is that there will be social disapproval if the lie is discovered. Although the vast majority of people lie—at some times and about some issues—the vast majority dislike and condemn it. Consequently, if your lie is discovered, you are likely to meet with social disapproval. It may range from mild disapproval to total ostracism from a group or organization. The upshot of all this is that the liar's communication effectiveness will be drastically impaired. A person who is known to have lied is seldom believed, even when telling the truth. You not only disbelieve the proven liar, you also give no persuasive force to his or her arguments, frequently discounting them as lies. Even a liar's relational messages and relational interactions may become less believable.

GOSSIP AND CONFIDENTIALITY

There can be no doubt that everyone spends a great deal of time gossiping. In fact, gossip seems a universal among all cultures (Laing 1993) and among some it is a commonly accepted ritual (Hall 1993). Gossip refers to third-party talk about another person; the word "now embraces both the talker and the talk, the tattler and the tattle, the newsmonger and the newsmongering" (Bremner 1980, p. 178). Gossip is an inevitable part of daily interactions; to advise anyone not to gossip would be absurd. Not gossiping would eliminate one of the most frequent and enjoyable forms of communication.

In some instances, however, gossip is unethical (Bok 1983). For example, it is unethical to reveal information that you have promised to keep secret. Although this principle may seem too obvious to even mention, it seems violated in many cases. For example, in a study of 133 school executives, board presidents, and superintendents, the majority received communications that violated an employee's right to confidentiality (Wilson & Bishard 1994). When that is impossible (Bok offers the example of the teenager who confides a suicide plan), the information should be revealed only to those who must know it, not to the world at large.

Gossip is also unethical when it invades the privacy that everyone has a right to, for example, when it concerns matters that are properly considered private and when the gossip can hurt the individuals involved. And, of course, gossip is also unethical when it is known to be false and is nevertheless passed on to others.

SELF-TEST

when is lying unethical?

Each of the following situations presents an occasion for a lie. For purposes of this exercise let's define a lie as *a deliberate misstatement intended to mislead another person.* How would you rate each in terms of its ethicality, using the scale that follows? Note that many of the situations will lead you to look for more specific information before making your decision. For example, you may want to know how old the child in No. 8 is before making your decision or you may want to know the kind of lie that will be used to get the person in No. 6 to do something good. You therefore might want to give more than one response for each statement, depending upon the specifics of the situation.

1 = definitely ethical
2 = probably ethical
3 = not sure; need to think more about this one
4 = probably unethical
5 = definitely unethical

_____ 1. to lie to a child to protect a fantasy belief, for example, to protect the child's belief in Santa Claus or the Tooth Fairy

_____ 2. to lie to achieve some greater good, for example, to lie to someone to prevent her or him from committing suicide or from getting depressed or to lie to prevent a burglary or theft

_____ 3. to lie in an employment interview in answer to a question that is overly personal (and irrelevant) or illegal

_____ 4. to lie to protect the reputation of your family, some specific family member, or some third party

_____ 5. to lie to enable the other person to save face, for example, to voice agreement with an idea you find foolish, to say you enjoyed meeting the person when you didn't, or to compliment the other person when it is totally undeserved

_____ 6. to lie to get someone to do something in his or her own best interest, for example, to diet, to stop smoking, or to study harder

_____ 7. to lie to get what you deserve but can't get any other way, for example, a well-earned promotion or raise or another chance with your relationship partner

_____ 8. to lie to protect your child from going to jail or facing charges of theft, drug dealing, or murder (though the child is guilty)

_____ 9. to lie to get out of jury duty or to the Internal Revenue Service in order to lower your tax bill

_____10. to lie to keep hidden information about yourself that you simply don't want to reveal to anyone, for example, your affectional orientation, your financial situation, or your religious beliefs

_____11. to lie to your relationship partner to avoid a fight

_____12. to lie to get yourself out of an unpleasant situation, for example, to get out of a date, an extra office chore, or a boring conversation

Thinking Critically About Lying and Ethics. Each of these situations will be responded to differently by different people, depending on the culture in which they were raised, their beliefs about lying, and their own ethical codes. Is there universal agreement among people on any one of the situations? What cultural beliefs influence the ways in which lying and ethics are looked at? Can you identify situations for which a lie is always unethical? Are there situations in which truth-telling would be unethical and lying would be ethical?

The principle of confidentiality presents a useful general guideline for dealing with gossip: keep confidential all private conversations about third parties. Messages that begin with "He said . . ." or "She thinks that you . . ." should be automatically suspect as potential violators of the principle of confidentiality. Remember too the principle of irreversibility—you cannot take messages back; once you say something, you cannot uncommunicate it.

DISCONFIRMATION AND CONFIRMATION

Before reading about these important concepts, take the self-test, "How Confirming Are You?" on page 133.

Confirmation and disconfirmation—as illustrated in the self-test—refer to the extent to which you acknowledge another person. Consider this situation. Pat arrives two hours late for work, having just missed an important meeting. Chris, a colleague, is angry and complains about Pat's missing the meeting. Consider some responses Pat might make:

1. "Don't even think of complaining. You're not my supervisor. I'm not interested in meeting your standards."
2. "What are you so angry about? Didn't you miss last week's meeting because you had to look for a new apartment? So knock it off."
3. "You have a right to be angry. I should have called when I knew I was going to be late, but I got involved in an argument at home and I couldn't leave until it was resolved."

In (1), Pat dismisses Chris's anger and even indicates a dismissal of Chris as a person. In (2), Pat rejects the validity of Chris's reasons for being angry but does not dismiss Chris's feelings of anger or Chris as a person. In (3), Pat acknowledges Chris's anger and the reasons for being angry. In addition, Pat provides some kind of explanation and in doing so shows that Chris's feelings are valid, that Chris as a person is important, and that Chris deserves to know what happened. The first response is an example of disconfirmation, the second of rejection, and the third of confirmation.

Do you find a gender difference in gossiping behavior? Do men and women both label the same behavior "gossiping"? Do men and women "gossip" about the same things? What gender differences can you identify in this general type of communication?

Psychologist William James once observed that "no more fiendish punishment could be devised, even were such a thing physically possible, than that one should be turned loose in society and remain absolutely unnoticed by all the members thereof." With this often-quoted observation James identifies the essence of disconfirmation (Veenendall & Feinstein 1996; Watzlawick, Beavin, & Jackson 1967).

Disconfirmation is a communication pattern in which you ignore someone's presence as well as his or her as communications. You say, in effect, that this person and what this person has to say are not worth serious attention or effort—that this individual and her or his contributions are so unimportant or insignificant that there is no reason to concern yourself with them.

Note that disconfirmation is not the same as rejection. To reject someone is to disagree with him or her; you indicate your unwillingness to accept something the other person says or does. In disconfirming someone, however, you deny that person's significance; you claim that what this person says or does simply does not count.

Confirmation is the opposite and the generally preferred communication pattern (Wichstrom, Holte, Husby, & Wynne 1993). In confirmation you not only acknowledge the presence of the other person but you indicate your acceptance of this person, of this person's definition of self, and of your relationship as defined or viewed by her or him.

Disconfirmation and confirmation may be communicated in a wide variety of ways. Table 8.2 shows just a few and parallels the self-test presented on page 133 so that you can see clearly not only the confirming but also the opposite, disconfirming behaviors. As you review this table, try to imagine a specific illustration for each of the ways of communicating disconfirmation and confirmation (Galvin & Brommel 1996; Pearson 1993).

THINK ABOUT

Think about these concepts and the distinctions among them by classifying the following responses as confirmation (C), rejection (R), or disconfirmation (D):

MEDIA WATCH

HUMAN COMMUNICATION IN CYBERSPACE

To paraphrase a popular advertising slogan, we have all come a long way. From the Summerians' writing system developed around 3500 B.C., to Johannes Gutenberg's invention of printing from movable type in Germany about 1440, to Alexander Graham Bell's development of the telephone in the United States in 1876, to the birth of personal computers in the early 1970s, to the Internet in the 1980s and now involving millions of users, the process of sending a message has certainly changed (Dworetsky 1994). Yet much has remained the same.

Electronic communication—no matter how sophisticated—is still very similar to ordinary face-to-face interactions. For example, electronic communication allows for the same types of communication as face-to-face interaction, whether interpersonal, small group, or public speaking. Whether you are using the Internet made available by your college or one of the commercially available services such as CompuServe, America Online, and Prodigy, you can encode your thoughts through your keyboard and send them via modem in much the same way that you encode your thoughts into words and send these through the air.

E-mail is a good example of interpersonal communication, as is traditional letter writing. Similarly, private chat rooms are available on electronic bulletin boards through which you and another party can exchange messages without anyone else participating or even seeing your messages. People engage in written conversation on-line for all the purposes already noted for communication generally: to discover, to relate, to influence, to play, and to help.

As in face-to-face communication, you can also expand your two-person group to a small group. The number of people you can have in a public chat room will vary somewhat but a limit of 40 or so participants seems common. On any system, there may be hundreds of chat rooms that you may join, just as there are hundreds of groups that you can join on campus, in your community, and so on. And, of course, you can always open your own chat room and invite those who are interested in, say, old movies, carpentry, new software, or communication to join your group.

The public speaking equivalent in cyberspace is the open forum, where you can post a message for anyone to read and then you can read their reactions to your message and so on. Bulletin boards are subject specific and you would obviously post your message on the appropriate bulletin board. If it's about politics then you would post it on the appropriate board; if it's about gardening, then you post it on another board, and so on.

When you communicate with someone face-to-face, you generally know a great deal about each other—name, sex, approximate age, general appearance, height, weight, race, and perhaps other things as well. When you communicate electronically, however, this information is only revealed if and when you want to be. If you wish, you can remain totally anonymous. Your "handle" or code name is all you need and others will simply know you by this name and no other. Should you wish to reveal who you are—your real name, sex, age, race, religion, occupation or any other information, you can certainly do so.

The electronic community may be viewed in many ways as a culture of its own (Escobar, Hess, Licha, Sibley, Strathern, & Sutz 1994) and its communications as having its own cultural norms—its own system of rules stating what is and what is not appropriate. These rules of "netiquette" include, for example:

- Before you ask a question consult the FAQs (frequently asked questions) so that you don't clog up the system with questions that have already been asked and answered.
- Generally, avoid *flaming* or participating in *flame wars*—personal attacks on other users; it results in too many messages that most people don't want to read and that uses up the system's resources.
- Don't reveal the real names of participants who may wish to be known only by their handles.

(continued next page)

MEDIA WATCH *(continued)*

Electronic communication will obviously increase tremendously in the coming years. How will electronic communication figure into your professional life? Will you be using electronic communication for social purposes, for example, to meet and eventually date someone you get to know on line? How are you preparing for this greater role that electronic communication will play in your life?

From a different point of view, consider the issue of regulation—currently a hotly debated issue (*New York Times* July 16, 1995, Section 6, p. 26). E-mail—like snail mail and telephone conversations—is generally considered as requiring no regulation. But what about pornography on the Internet? Hate speech? What about minors having access to sexually explicit material? How would you regulate (if at all) communication in cyberspace?

Enrique receives this semester's grades in the mail; they are a lot better than previous semesters' grades but are still not great. After opening the letter, Enrique says: "I really tried hard to get my grades up this semester." Enrique's parents respond:

____ Going out every night hardly seems like trying very hard.
____ What should we have for dinner?
____ Keep up the good work.
____ I can't believe you've really tried your best; how can anyone study with the stereo blasting in your ears?
____ I'm sure you've tried real hard.
____ That's great.
____ What a rotten day I had at the office.
____ I can remember when I was in school; got all B's without ever opening a book.

Peter, who has been out of work for the past several weeks, says: "I feel like such a failure; I just can't seem to find a job. I've been pounding the pavement for the last five weeks and still nothing." Peter's friend responds:

____ I know you've been trying real hard.
____ You really should get more training so you'd be able to sell yourself more effectively.
____ I told you a hundred times: you need that college degree.
____ I've got to go to the dentist on Friday. Boy, do I hate that.
____ The employment picture is real bleak this time of the year but your qualifications are really impressive. Something will come up soon.
____ You are not a failure. You just can't find a job.
____ What do you need a job for? Stay home and keep house. After all, your partner makes more than enough money to live in style.
____ What's five weeks?
____ Well, you'll just have to try harder.

Talking with the Grief-Stricken

Grief is something everyone experiences at some time. It may be experienced because of illness or death, the loss of a highly valued relationship (for example, a romantic breakup), the loss of certain physical or mental abilities, or the loss of material possessions (your house burning down or stock losses). Talking with the grief-stricken can be extremely difficult.

THINK ABOUT

Think about the ways in which the concepts of confirmation and disconfirmation are relevant when giving comfort, as when talking to a person who is experiencing grief. For example, consider the ways that disconfirmation is communicated in the following brief comment and the ways you might make it more confirming. After you read the suggestions for communicating with the grief-stricken, you may wish to return to this "expression of sympathy" and analyze it again.

I just heard that Harry died—I mean—passed away. I'm so sorry. I know exactly how you feel. But, you know, it's for the best. I mean the man was suffering. I remember seeing him last month; he could hardly stand up, he was so weak. And he looked so sad. He must have been in constant pain. It's better this way. He's at peace. You'll get over it. You'll see. Time heals all wounds. It was the same way with me and you know how close we were. I mean we were devoted to each other. Everyone said we were the closest pair they ever saw. And I got over it. So, how about we'll go to dinner tonight? We'll talk about old times. Come on. Come on. Don't be a spoil sport. I really need to get out. I've been

SELF-TEST

how confirming are you?

In your typical communications, how likely are you to display the following behaviors? Use the accompanying scale to respond to each statement:

5 = always
4 = often
3 = sometimes
2 = rarely
1 = never

_____ 1. I acknowledge the presence of another person both verbally and nonverbally.
_____ 2. I acknowledge the contributions of the other person—for example, by supporting or taking issue with what the person says.
_____ 3. During the conversation, I make nonverbal contact by maintaining direct eye contact, touching, hugging, kissing, and otherwise demonstrating acknowledgment of the other person.
_____ 4. I communicate as both speaker and listener with involvement, and with a concern and respect for the other person.
_____ 5. I signal my understanding of the other person both verbally and nonverbally.
_____ 6. I reflect the other person's feelings as a way of showing that I understand these feelings.
_____ 7. I ask questions, when appropriate, concerning the other person's thoughts and feelings.
_____ 8. I respond to the other person's requests, for example, by returning phone calls and answering letters within a reasonable time.
_____ 9. I encourage the other person to express his or her thoughts and feelings.
_____10. I respond directly and exclusively to what the other person says.

Thinking Critically About Confirmation and Disconfirmation. All ten statements are phrased so that they express confirming behaviors. Therefore, high scores (above 35) reflect a strong tendency to engage in confirmation. Low scores (below 25) reflect a strong tendency to engage in disconfirmation. Can you provide at least one specific message to illustrate how you might express confirmation in each of the ten situations identified in the self-test. For example, for the first statement, you might say: "Hi, Pat, come over and join us" or simply smile and wave Pat to join your group.

in the house all week. Come on, do it for me. After all, you have to forget; you have to get on with your own life. I won't take no for an answer. I'll pick you up at seven.

One useful way to talk with the grief-stricken is to confirm the person's feelings. "You must miss him a great deal" confirms the person's feelings, for example. Disconfirming expressions—"You can't cry now; you have to set an example"—are generally less helpful to the person experiencing grief.

Persons grieving often want permission to grieve and to express themselves. They want to know that it is okay with you if he or she grieves in the ways that feel most comfortable—for example, crying or talking about old times. This permission can be communicated in several ways. For example, you can say, quite directly, "just say what you feel." Or, you can use active listening responses (Unit 12) to encourage the other person to continue talking. Another way to communicate this permission is with nonverbal expressions of approval and attention to the grieving person's reactions. Although many people who experience grief welcome the opportunity to talk about it, not all do. Trying to force people to talk about experiences or feelings they may not be ready to share is generally as inappropriate as trying to get them to focus away from their grief.

Many people try to force the grief-stricken to focus on the bright side. Although well-intentioned, this assumes that the grief-stricken person is ready for this change in focus, which is usually not the case.

Expressions such as "You're so lucky you still have some vision left" or "It was better this way; Pat was suffering so much" are often resented because of their obvious lack of empathy.

Empathizing with the grief-stricken person and communicating this empathic understanding is often helpful. Letting the grief-stricken person know that you can understand what he or she is going through, but without assuming that your feelings (however empathic) are the same in depth or in kind, is likely to be appreciated.

Part of the art of conversation generally, and especially talking with the grief-stricken, is to develop a sensitivity to leave-taking cues. Trying to force your presence on the grief-stricken or pressing the person to stay with you or a group of people is likely to be resented.

Although these suggestions are likely to be received positively by most people, they are not likely to be received positively in all situations or by all people. Fortunately, there's an easy way to find out, and that is simply to ask. An excellent example of this occurs in the television announcement in communicating with people with AIDS. It goes something like this: "I don't know what to say. But, I want you to know that I care and that I want to help and that I love you. I want you to tell me what I can do."

We can gain insight into a wide variety of other language practices by viewing them as types of disconfirmation, as language that alienates and separates. The three obvious practices are racism, sexism, and heterosexism. You'll notice that in many cases the recommended principles or suggestions are designed to make language more inclusive, as discussed earlier in this unit.

TABLE 8.2
confirmation and disconfirmation

Confirmation	Disconfirmation
Acknowledge the presence of the other verbally or nonverbally	Ignore the presence of the other person
Acknowledge the contributions of the other by either supporting or taking issue with what the other says	Ignore what the other says: express (nonverbally and verbally) indifference to anything the other says
Make nonverbal contact by maintaining direct eye contact, touching, hugging, kissing, and otherwise demonstrating acknowledgment of the other	Make no nonverbal contact; avoid direct eye contact; avoid touching other person
Engage in dialogue—communication in which both persons are speakers and listeners, both are involved, and both are concerned with and have respect for each other	Engage in monologue—communication in which one person speaks and one person listens, there is no real interaction, and there is no real concern or respect for each other
Demonstrate understanding of what the other says and means	Jump to interpretation or evaluation rather than working at understanding what the other means
Reflect the other's feelings to demonstrate your understanding of these feelings	Express your own feelings, ignore feelings of the other, or give abstract intellectualized responses
Ask questions of the other concerning both thoughts and feelings	Make statements about yourself, ignore any lack of clarity in the other's remarks
Acknowledge the other's requests; answer the other's questions, return phone calls, and answer letters	Ignore the other's requests; fail to answer questions, return phone calls, and answer letters
Encourage the other to express thoughts and feelings	Interrupt or otherwise make it difficult for the other to express himself or herself
Respond directly and exclusively to what the other says	Respond tangentially by acknowledging the other's comment but then shifting the focus of the message in another direction

Racism

According to Andrea Rich (1974), "any language that, through a conscious or unconscious attempt by the user, places a particular racial or ethnic group in an inferior position is racist." Racist language expresses racist attitudes. It also contributes to the development of racist attitudes in those who use or hear the language.

Racist terms are used by members of one culture to disparage members of other cultures—their customs or their accomplishments. Racist language emphasizes differences rather than similarities and separates rather than unites members of different cultures. Generally, racist language is used by the dominant group to establish and maintain power over other groups. The social consequences of racist language in terms of employment, education, housing opportunities, and general community acceptance are well known.

It has often been pointed out (Bosmajian 1974; Davis 1967) that there are aspects of language that may be inherently racist. For example, in one examination of the English language there were found 134 synonyms for white. Of these, 44 have positive connotations (for example, *clean, chaste,* and *unblemished*) and only 10 have negative connotations (for example, *whitewash* and *pale*). The remaining were relatively neutral. Of the 120 synonyms for black, 60 had unfavorable connotations (*unclean, foreboding,* and *deadly*), and none had positive connotations.

THINK ABOUT

Think about such phrases as the following:

- the Korean doctor
- the Latino prodigy
- the African American mathematician
- the white nurse

What messages do these identifiers send to you? What thoughts come to your mind as you hear such phrases? Is the racial identifier relevant? Is it necessary to know the race of the person to understand the rest of the message? In some cases, of course, the racial identifier may be relevant, for instance, "The American doctor argued for hours with the French doctors over the patent." Here the aim might be to identify the nationality of the doctor or the specific doctor (as you would if you forgot her or his name).

Often, however, such identifiers are used to emphasize that the combination of race and occupation (or talent or accomplishment) is rare and unexpected. It emphasizes that this combination is out of the ordinary. It also implies that somehow racial factors are important in the context. As noted, there are times when this may be true but very often race is irrelevant.

Sexism

Consider some of the sexist language used to refer to women. A woman often loses her last name when she marries and in certain instances loses her first name as well. She may change from "Ann Smith" to "Mrs. John Jones."

You say that a woman "marries into" a man's family and that a family "dies out" if there are no male children. You do not speak of a man marrying into a woman's family (unless the family is extremely prestigious or wealthy or members of royalty), and a family can still "die out," even if there are ten female children. In the traditional marriage ceremony, you can still hear "I now pronounce you man and wife," not "man and woman" or "husband and wife." The man retains his status as man, but the woman changes hers from woman to wife. Barrie Thorne, Cheris Kramarae, and Nancy Henley, in their *Language, Gender and Society* (1983), summarize this line of research by noting that "women tend to be defined by their relation to men." "The available and 'approved' titles, pronouns, lexicons, and labels," they note, "reflect the fact that women (as well as other subordinates) have been named by others."

The National Council of Teachers of English (NCTE) has proposed guidelines for nonsexist (gender-free or gender-neutral) language. These concern the use of generic man, the use of the generic he and his, and sex-role stereotyping (Penfield 1987).

Generic Man

The word *man* refers clearly to an adult male. To use the term to refer to both men and women emphasizes maleness at the expense of femaleness. Similarly the terms *mankind* or the *common man* or even *cavemen* imply a primary focus on adult males. Gender-neutral terms can easily be substituted. Instead of *mankind,* you can say *humanity, people,* or *human beings.* Instead of the *common man,* you can say the *average person* or *ordinary people.* Instead of *cavemen,* you can say *prehistoric people* or *cave dwellers.*

Similarly, the use of such terms as policeman, fireman, salesman, chairman, mailman, and other terms that presume maleness as the norm and femaleness as a deviation are clear and common examples of sexist language. Nonsexist equivalents such as *firefighter* or *salesperson* seem now to be a part of most people's vocabulary.

Here are a few other terms that are not inclusive: *man, countryman, manmade, manpower, repairman, doorman, stewardess, waitress,* and *actress.* What alternatives can you offer for each of these terms? What advantages or disadvantages do these alternative expressions have as compared with the terms given here?

Generic He and His

The use of the masculine pronoun to refer to any individual regardless of sex further illustrates linguistic sexism. Alternating masculine and feminine pronouns or using such phrases as *he and she* or *her and him* are obvious antidotes. Alternatively, sentences can be restructured to eliminate any reference to gender. Table 8.3 provides a few examples from the NCTE Guidelines (Penfield, 1987).

Sex-Role Stereotyping

Words often reflect a sex-role bias. The assumption that some make is that certain roles or professions belong to men and others belong to women. It is seen in the tendency to make the hypothetical elementary school teacher female and the college professor male, the doctor male but the nurse female. Expressions such as "female doctor" or "male nurse" are further examples of sex-role stereotyping because they say, in effect, this doctor or this nurse is not typical so it needs to be qualified. When a specific doctor or nurse is being referred to the person's sex will become clear when the appropriate pronoun is used: Dr. Smith wrote the prescription for her new patient, or The nurse recorded the patient's temperature himself.

THINK ABOUT

Think about the following sentences, which purposely recall the popular sexist stereotypes. How would you rephrase them into more inclusive language so that they do not limit the referent to one sex and so that they punch holes in these limiting and discriminating stereotypes?

1. You really should get a second doctor's opinion. Just see what he says.
2. Johnny went to school today and met his kindergarten teacher. I wonder who she is.
3. Everyone needs to examine his own conscience.
4. No one can tell what his ultimate fortune will be.
5. The effective communicator is a selective self-discloser; he discloses to some people about some things some of the times.
6. I wonder who the new chairman will be.
7. The effective waitress knows when her customers need her.
8. Advertisers do not care what the intellectual thinks; they want to know what the man in the street thinks.
9. What do you think the ideal communicator should be like? How should he talk? How should he gesture?
10. The history of man is largely one of technology replacing his manual labor.

Heterosexism

A close relative of sexism is heterosexism. The term is a relatively new addition to our list of linguistic prejudices. As the term implies, heterosexist language is used to disparage gay men and lesbians. As with racist

TABLE 8.3
some sexist and gender-free expressions

Sexist	Gender-free
The average student is worried about his grades.	The average student is worried about grades.
Ask the student to hand in his work as soon as he is finished.	Ask students to hand in their work as soon as they are finished.
When a teacher asks his students for an evaluation, he is putting himself on the spot.	When you ask your students for an evaluation, you are putting yourself on the spot.

language, heterosexism is seen in the derogatory terms used for lesbians and gay men. As with racist language, you hear these terms on the street. Unlike racist language, however, you also hear these terms in the media and on college campuses. Heterosexist language and the intolerance it signals is, for example, a major reason why gay and lesbian students don't avail themselves of their own college health services (McKee, Hayes, & Axiotis 1994).

As with sexism, however, you also see the occurrence of heterosexism in more subtle forms of language usage. For example, when you qualify a profession—as in "gay athlete" or "lesbian doctor"—you are in effect stating that athletes and doctors are not normally gay or lesbian. Further, you are highlighting the affectional orientation of the athlete and the doctor in a context in which it may have no relevance. This practice, of course, is the same as qualifying by race or gender, which we have already noted.

Still another instance of heterosexism—and perhaps the most difficult to deal with—is the presumption of heterosexuality. Usually people assume the person they are talking to or about is heterosexual. Usually, they are correct—the majority of the population is heterosexual. At the same time, however, note that it denies the lesbian and gay male their real identity. The practice is similar to the presumption of whiteness and maleness that we have made significant inroads in eliminating. Here are a few additional ways in which communication may be heterosexist or what some call "homophobic."

Is it heterosexist to presume that an unknown athlete, senator, scientist, or performer is heterosexual (assuming that you don't know anything about the individual's affectional orientation)? Is it sexist to presume, for example, that an unknown doctor, nurse, or lawyer is of a particular sex? Is it racist to assume that a state senator, illegal alien, or college professor is of a particular race?

- Using offensive nonverbal mannerisms that parody stereotypes when talking about gays and lesbians.
- "Complimenting" gay men and lesbians because "they don't look it." To gays and lesbians, it's not a compliment. Similarly, expressing disappointment that a person is gay—often thought to be a compliment when said in such comments as "What a waste!"—is not really a compliment.
- Assuming that every gay or lesbian knows what every other gay or lesbian is thinking. It's very similar to asking a Japanese why Sony is investing heavily in the United States or, as one comic put it, asking an African American "What do you think Jesse Jackson meant by that last speech?"
- Denying individual differences. Saying things such as "lesbians are so loyal" or "gay men are so open with their feelings," which ignore the reality of wide differences within any group, is potentially insulting to all groups.
- Committing "overattribution," attributing just above everything a person does, says, and believes to being gay or lesbian. This tendency helps to recall and perpetuate stereotypes.
- Ignoring relationship milestones that are important to all people. Ignoring anniversaries or birthdays of the partners of gay or lesbian friends or relatives, for example, is often resented, though it may never be mentioned.

SUMMARY

In this unit we covered some of the basic principles for making verbal communication more effective and the messages that the violation of these principles communicate to others.

1. Excluding talk occurs when members belonging to a particular group talk about their group concerns or use their group's language in the presence of outsiders. A variation occurs when self-talk is extreme and distorts the normal give and take. It also occurs when members use terms unique to their culture as applicable to everyone.
2. Downward talk refers to the tendency to talk down to others, rather than talking as equals.
3. Lying creates communication problems by lessening credibility, by creating psychological imbalance, and by engendering social disapproval of the liar.
4. Gossip, although inevitable, creates problems when it betrays a confidence, is false and known to be so, or is used to hurt another person.
5. Disconfirmation refers to the process whereby you ignore the presence and the communications of others. Confirmation refers to the process whereby you accept, support, and acknowledge the importance of the other person.
6. Racist, sexist, and heterosexist language are specific cases of disconfirmation, of language that separates and distances rather than unites and bonds.

THINKING CRITICALLY ABOUT VERBAL MESSAGE PRINCIPLES

1. Can you find instances of excluding and inclusive talk at work? At school? What specific form does it take?
2. Have you ever had one of the power plays discussed here used on you? Have you ever used one on someone else? What short-term effects did these power plays have? What long-term effects did they have?

3. Another power play is "yougottobekidding," in which the person responds to you with disbelief that you could possibly say what you said: "You don't really mean that" or "Come on, Pat; you can't be serious." Still another power play is "thought stoppers," in which the person interrupts you, changes the topic, raises his or her voice, or uses profanity. In each case, you are literally stopped from completing your thoughts. How would you use a cooperative management strategy to deal with each of these types of power plays?
4. Can you think of instances in which lying would be preferred to truth-telling in a friendship, love, or family relationship? In a business situation? Can you think of situations in which it would be unethical to tell the truth and ethical to lie?
5. According to the notion of choice articulated in Unit 1, lying would be considered unethical simply because each person has a right to base his or her choices on the best information available. By lying you withhold at least part of that information and contribute to decisions based on incorrect assumptions and falsehoods. Does this position seem reasonable to you? If not, how would you explain why lying is unethical?
6. How would you phrase a confirmatory, rejecting, and disconfirmatory response to the following situations:

a. Your friend says: "Again, I've been passed up for promotion. What am I doing wrong? I'm getting really depressed over this."
b. Your friend tells you of relationship problems: "We just can't seem to get along anymore. Every day is a hassle. Every day, there's another conflict, another battle. I feel like walking away from the whole mess."

7. Many people feel that it is permissible for members of a culture to refer to themselves with the terms that if said by outsiders, would normally be considered racist. That is, Chinese may use the negative terms referring to Chinese, Italians may use the negative terms referring to Italians, and so on. The reasoning seems to be that groups should be able to laugh at themselves. One possible problem, though, is that these terms may just reinforce the negative stereotypes that society has already assigned this group. By using these terms, members may come to accept these labels with their negative connotations and thus contribute to their own stereotyping. Others would argue that by using such terms they are making them less negative. The use of the word *queer,* for example, by militant gay and lesbian groups is designed to give a negatively evaluated term a positive spin (see, for example, Ringer 1994). What are your feelings about this issue?
8. In one study, seventh-grade science textbooks were found to contain sexist language and failed to integrate the achievements of women scientists and to provide the necessary information on women's health (Potter & Rosser 1992). Do you find this kind of sexism in your college textbooks? Can you identify specific examples?
9. On your college campus, which would be considered the most offensive: sexist, racist, or heterosexist language? Least offensive? Are you ever in situations where this language is the approved and expected form of discourse?
10. How would you go about finding answers to questions such as these:
    a. Do men and women gossip about the same topics?
    b. Do men and women lie in the same way? Are men and women equally effective lie detectors?
    c. How important is a confirmatory communication style in contributing to a person's popularity?
    d. Does education influence the extent to which a person uses confirmation as opposed to disconfirmation? Does education influence the frequency of racist, sexist, and heterosexist language?

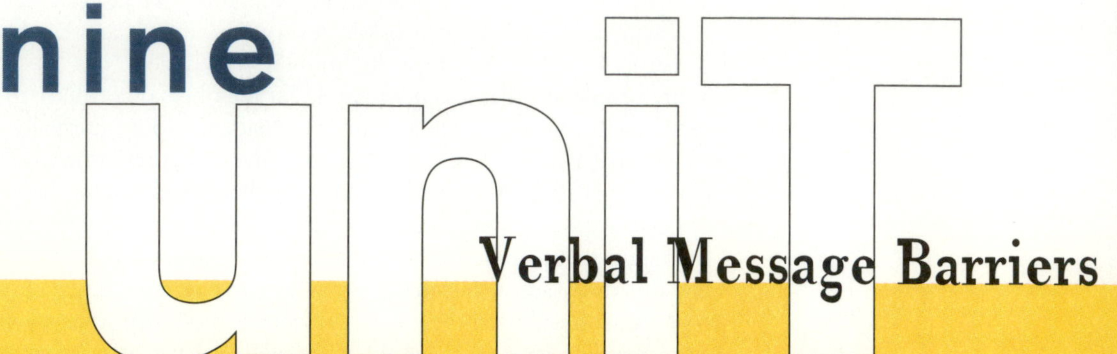

Verbal Message Barriers

unit contents

unit goals

After completing this unit, you should be able to

1. define *polarization, intensional orientation, fact-inference confusion, bypassing, allness, static evaluation,* and *indiscrimination*
2. explain how these barriers can be avoided
3. identify examples of these misevaluations in your own communications and in those of others (including the media)
4. explain the role of the et cetera, the date, and the index in reducing the barriers in language and verbal interaction

Communication may break down or encounter barriers at any point in the process from sender to receiver. Here we look at seven possible barriers in verbal messages and their correctives (DeVito 1974; Haney 1973; Rothwell 1982). These barriers may also appear in intrapersonal, interpersonal, small group, public speaking, intercultural, and mass communications. They may also be viewed as ways in which language does not reflect reality, ways in which language contradicts the scientifically known world (see Table 9.1 on page 143).

POLARIZATION

Polarization refers to the tendency to look at the world in terms of opposites and to describe it in extremes—good or bad, positive or negative, healthy or sick, intelligent or stupid. It is often referred to as the fallacy of "either-or" or "black and white." Although magnetic poles are either positive or negative and certain people are extremely rich while others are extremely poor, most people are in the middle. They exist somewhere between the extremes of good and bad, healthy and sick, intelligent and stupid, rich and poor. Yet people have a strong tendency to view only the extremes and to categorize other people, objects, and events in terms of these polar opposites.

THINK ABOUT

Think about your own tendency to polarize. Try filling in the words that would logically go where the question marks appear, the words that are the opposite of the terms on the left.

hot ______________________________ ?
high ______________________________ ?
good ______________________________ ?
popular ______________________________ ?
sad ______________________________ ?

Filling in these opposites was probably easy for you. The words you supplied were probably short. Further, if a number of people supplied opposites, you would find a high degree of agreement among them.

Now try to fill in the middle positions with words meaning, for example, "midway between hot and cold," "midway between high and low." You probably had greater difficulty here, and you probably took more time to think of these middle terms. You also probably used multiword phrases. Further, you would probably find less agreement among different people completing this same task. Although most things and people fall in between these extremes, the common tendency is to concentrate on the extremes and ignore the middle.

You create problems when you use the extreme form in inappropriate situations—for example, "The politician is either for us or against us" or when we evaluate someone as "good or bad" or "ethical or unethical." These options do not include all possibilities. The politician may be for you in some things and against you in other things, or may be neutral. A particular behavior may have both good and bad consequences.

Correcting Polarization

In correcting this tendency to polarize, beware of implying (and believing) that two extreme classes include all possible classes—that an individual must be a hawk or a dove, with no other alternatives. Although Helen Keller felt that, "Life is either a daring adventure or nothing," most people find that it is neither a daring adventure nor nothing, but something somewhere in between.

INTENSIONAL ORIENTATION

Intensional orientation (the *s* in intensional is intentional) refers to the tendency to view people, objects, and events in the way they are talked about and the way they are labeled. For example, if Sally were labeled "uninteresting" you would, responding intensionally, evaluate her as uninteresting before listening to what she has to say. Extensional orientation, on the other hand, is the tendency to look first to the actual people, objects, and events and only afterward to their labels—for example, seeing Sally without any preconceived notions. It is the tendency to be guided by what you see happening rather than by the label used for what is happening.

Intensional orientation occurs when you act as if the labels are more important than the things they represent—as if the map is more important than the territory. An extreme form of intensional orientation is seen in the person who, afraid of dogs, begins to sweat when shown a picture of a dog or when hearing people talk about dogs. Here the person is responding to the label (a picture or verbal description) as if it were the actual thing (a dog).

THINK ABOUT

Think about your tendency toward intensionalizing by visualizing yourself seated with a packet of photographs before you. Each photograph shows a person you have never seen before. You are asked to scratch out the eyes in each photograph. You are told that this is simply an experiment and that the individuals whose pictures you have will not be aware of anything that has happened here. As you progress through the pictures, scratching out the eyes, you come upon a photograph of your mother. What do you do? Are you able to scratch out the eyes as you have done with the pictures of the strangers? Or have you somehow lost your ability to scratch out eyes? If, like many others, you are unable to scratch out the eyes, you are responding intensionally. You are, in effect, responding to the map (in this case the picture) as if it were the territory (your own mother).

Cultural Identifiers

Having said that the word is not the thing does not mean that words do not have effects. They do. This is seen most clearly in the negative reactions to, for example, racist language (discussed at length in Unit 8). It is also seen in the use of labels that may be perceived as culturally insensitive or culturally unaware. Following, for example, are some of the terms that cause confusion in communicating with and about members of diverse cultural groups. As always, when in doubt, find out. The preferences and many of the specific examples identified here are drawn largely from the findings of the Task Force on Bias-Free Language of the Association of American University Presses (Schwartz 1995).

Generally: Most African Americans prefer *African American* to *black* (Hecht, Collier, & Ribeau 1993, Philogene 1994) though *black* is often used with *white* and is used in a variety of other contexts (for example, Department of Black and Puerto Rican Studies, the *Journal of Black History,* and Black History Month). The American Psychological Association recommends that both terms (Black and White) be capitalized but the *Chicago Manual of Style* (the manual used by most newspapers and publishing houses) recommends using lowercase. The terms *negro* and *colored,* although used in the names of some organizations (for example, the United Negro College Fund and the National Association for the Advancement of Colored People) are not used outside of these contexts.

White is generally used to refer to those whose roots are in European cultures and usually does not include Hispanics. Analogous to *African American* comes the phrase *European American.* Few *European Americans,* however, would want to be called that; most would prefer their national origins emphasized, for example, *German American* or *Greek American.* This preference may well change as Europe moves into a more cohesive and united entity. *People of color*—a more literary sounding term appropriate perhaps to public speaking but sounding awkward in most conversations—is preferred to *non-white,* which

TABLE 9.1
assumptions about the world and the use and misuse of language

This table presents an attempt to identify some of the assumptions about the world and the way in which these assumptions are violated in illogical language and accurately reflected in logical language. It will serve as an overview of the discussion in this unit.

Assumptions About the World	Illogical Language (Language that Distorts Reality)	Logical Language (Language that Accurately Reflects Reality)
Most of reality exists between the extremes	Divides the world into extremes, good-bad, rich-poor, success-failure (polarization)	uses middle terms, terms that reflect middle ground
Words and the things they represent are very different; words are not things	Treats words as if they were things (intensional orientation)	Treats words as abstractions of things, not the things themselves (extensional orientation)
Not all statements are factual	Treats factual and inferential statements the same (fact inference confusion)	Distinguishes between factual and inferential statements and treats them differently
People are different and give different meanings to the same words	Assumes that meaning is in words (bypassing)	Looks for meaning in people
People and events are too complex to ever be known or described completely	Assumes completeness and finality (allness)	Assumes there is always more to be known, more to be said
The world and its people are constantly changing	Holds static and unchanging notions about people and events (static evaluation)	Includes time as a variable in all messages
Everyone and everything is unique	Sees individuals through general labels and stereotypes (indiscrimination)	Distinguishes between individuals even when covered by the same general label

implies that whiteness is the norm and non-whiteness is a deviation from that norm. (The same is true of the term *non-Christian.*)

Generally: *Hispanic* is used to refer to anyone who identifies himself or herself as belonging to a Spanish-speaking culture. *Latina* (female) and *Latino* (male) refer to those whose roots are in one of the Latin American countries, for example, the Dominican Republic, Nicaragua, or Guatemala. *Hispanic American* refers to those U.S. residents whose ancestry is a Spanish culture, and includes Mexican, Caribbean, and Central and South Americans. In emphasizing a Spanish heritage the term is really inadequate in referring to those large numbers in the Caribbean and in South America whose origins are French or Portuguese. *Chicana* (female) and *Chicano* (male) refer to those with roots in Mexico, though it often connotes a nationalist attitude (Jandt 1995) and is considered offensive by many Mexican Americans. *Mexican American* is preferred.

Inuk (pl. *Inuit*), also spelled *Innuk* and *Innuit,* is preferred to *Eskimo* (a term the United States Census Bureau uses), which was applied to the indigenous peoples of Alaska by Europeans and means literally "raw meat eaters."*Indian* refers only to someone from India and is incorrectly used when applied to members of other Asian countries or to the indigenous peoples of North America. *American Indian* or *Native American* are preferred, even though many Native Americans refer to themselves as *Indians* and *Indian people.* The term *native American* (with a lower case *n*) is most often used to refer to persons born in the United States. Although the term technically could refer to anyone born in North or South America, people outside the United States generally prefer more spe-

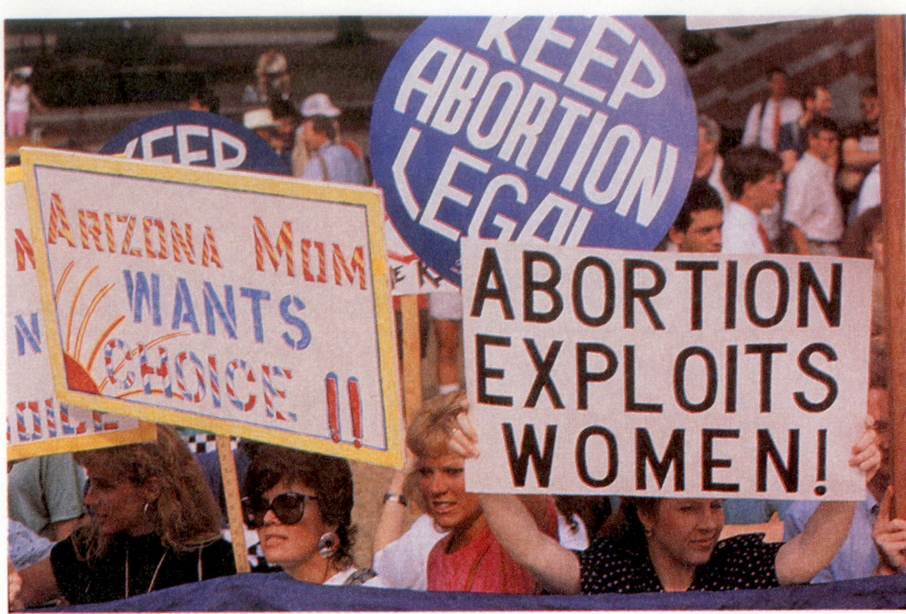

How would you describe the abortion debate in terms of polarization? In terms of a multivalued orientation?

cific designations such as *Argentinean, Cuban,* or *Canadian.* The term *native* means an indigenous inhabitant; it is not used to mean "someone having a less-developed culture."

Muslim is the preferred form (rather than the older *Moslem*) to refer to a person who adheres to the religious teachings of Islam. *Quran* (rather than *Koran*) is the preferred term for the scriptures of Islam.

When history was being written with a European perspective, it was taken as the focal point and the rest of the world was defined in terms of its location from Europe. Thus, Asia became the east or the orient and Asians became *Orientals*—a term that is today considered inappropriate or "Eurocentric." Thus, people from Asia are *Asians* just as people from Africa are *Africans* and people from Europe are *Europeans.*

Generally: *Gay* is the preferred term for a man who has an affectional preference for another man and *lesbian* is the preferred term for a woman who has an affection preference for other women. (*Lesbian* means "homosexual woman," therefore the phrase *lesbian woman* is redundant.) Agreement on the use of this term is not universal. For example, in one survey, 58 percent of these women preferred *lesbian* but 34 percent preferred *gay* (Lever 1995). *Homosexual* refers to both gays and lesbians but more often to a sexual orientation to members of one's own sex. *Gay* and *lesbian* refer to a life-style and not just to sexual orientation. *Gay* as a noun, although widely used, may prove offensive in some contexts, for example, "We have two gays on the team." *Queer,* although used within the gay community in an effort to remove the negative stigma through frequent usage, is generally resented when used by outsiders. Because most scientific thinking holds that sexuality is not a matter of choice, the term *sexual orientation* rather than *sexual preference* or *sexual status* (which is also vague) is preferred.

Generally: the term *girl* should only be used to refer to very young females and is equivalent to *boy.* Neither term should be used for people older than say 13 or 14. *Girl* is never used to refer to a grown woman, nor is *boy* used to refer to persons in blue-collar positions. *Lady* is negatively evaluated by many because it connotes the stereotype of the prim and proper woman. *Woman* or *young woman* is preferred. *Older person* is preferred to *elder, elderly, senior,* or *senior citizen* (which technically refers to someone older than 65).

Correcting Intensional Orientation

The way out of intensional orientation is to extensionalize. Give your main attention to the people, things, and events in the world as you see them and not as they are presented in words. For example, when you meet Jack and Jill, observe them, interact with them. Then form your impressions. Don't respond to them as "greedy, money-grubbing landlords" because Harry labeled them this way. Don't respond to Carmen as "lazy and inconsiderate" because Elaine told you she was.

FACT-INFERENCE CONFUSION

You can make statements about the world you observe, and you can make statements about what you cannot observe. In form or structure these statements are similar, and you cannot distinguish them by any grammatical analysis. For example, you can say, "She is wearing a blue jacket," as well as "He is harboring an illogical hatred." If you diagrammed these sentences they would yield identical structures. Yet it is clear that these are very different types of statements. You can observe the jacket and the blue color, but how do you observe "illogical hatred"? Obviously, this is not a descriptive but an inferential statement. It is a statement made on the basis not only of what you observe, but of what you infer.

There is nothing wrong with making inferential statements. You must make them to talk about much that is meaningful. The problem arises when you act as if those inferential statements are factual, a phenomenon called **fact-inference confusion.**

THINK ABOUT

Think about your own tendency to confuse facts and inferences by trying to respond to the following anecdote (Maynard 1963):

> A woman went for a walk one day and met a friend whom she had not seen, heard from, or heard of in 10 years. After an exchange of greetings, the woman said: "Is this your little boy?" and her friend replied, "Yes, I got married about six years ago." The woman then asked the child, "What is your name?" and the little boy replied, "Same as my father's." "Oh," said the woman, "then it must be Peter."

How did the woman know the boy's father's name when she had not seen, heard from, or heard of her friend in the last ten years? The answer is obvious, but only after you recognize that in reading this short passage you have made an unconscious inference that is preventing you from answering a simple question. Specifically, you have inferred that the woman's friend is a woman. Actually, the friend is a man named Peter.

You may wish to test your ability to distinguish facts from inferences by taking the self-test, "Can You Distinguish Facts from Inference?"

Correcting Fact-Inference Confusion

Table 9.2, based on Haney (1973), summarizes the differences between factual and inferential statements. Inferential statements need to be made tentatively. Recognize that such statements may prove to be wrong. Inferential statements should leave open the possibility of alternatives. If, for example, you treat the statement, "Our biology teacher was fired for poor teaching," as factual, you eliminate the possibility of any alternatives. When making inferential statements, be psychologically prepared to be proved wrong. If you are thus prepared, you will be less hurt if you are shown to be incorrect.

Pragmatic Implications

A related communication barrier is raised by what linguist philosophers call **pragmatic implication.** Consider the following: the sales manager has been re-

TABLE 9.2
differences between factual and inferential statements

Factual Statements	Inferential Statements
May be made only after observation	May be made at any time
Are limited to what has been observed	Go beyond what has been observed
May be made only by the observer	May be made by anyone
May only be about the past or the present	May be about any time—past, present, future
Approach certainty	Involve varying degrees of probability
Are subject to verifiable standards	Are not subject to verifiable standards

SELF-TEST

can you distinguish facts from inferences?

Carefully read the following report, modeled on one developed by William Haney (1973), and the list of observations based on it. Indicate whether you think the observations are true, false, or doubtful on the basis of the information presented in the report. Write T if the observation is definitely true, F if the observation is definitely false, and ? if the observation may be either true or false. Judge each observation in order. Do not reread the observations after you have indicated your judgement, and do not change any of your answers.

> *A well-liked college teacher had just completed making up the final examinations and had turned off the lights in the office. Just then a tall, broad figure appeared and demanded the examination. The professor opened the drawer. Everything in the drawer was picked up and the individual ran down the corridor. The dean was notified immediately.*

______ 1. The thief was tall and broad.
______ 2. The professor turned off the lights.
______ 3. A tall figure demanded the examination.
______ 4. The examination was picked up by the someone.
______ 5. The examination was picked up by the professor.
______ 6. A tall figure appeared after the professor turned off the lights in the office.
______ 7. The man who opened the drawer was the professor.
______ 8. The professor ran down the corridor.
______ 9. The drawer was never actually opened.
______10. Three persons are referred to in this report.

Thinking Critically About Facts and Inferences. This test was designed to trap you into making inferences and treating them as facts. Statement 3 is true (it is in the report) and statement 9 is false (the drawer was opened). All the other statements, however, are inferences and should have been marked ? Review these eight statements to see why you cannot be certain that any of them are either true or false. Try designing your own fact-inference test; it will help you highlight some of the reasons inferences are often confused with facts.

placed. You know that this manager was not doing a particularly good job and that many sales representatives complained about poor leadership. On the basis of this knowledge, you draw a pragmatic implication, an inference that is probably but not necessarily true. In this example, you infer that the sales manager was fired. There is nothing wrong with drawing such inferences, we all do it; the problem arises when we forget or disregard the fact that they are inferences and not facts.

This type of situation occurs every day. You see your supervisor in a romantic restaurant with the new sales manager. You make the pragmatic implications that they are having an affair. You might further infer that the reason the old sales manager was fired was because of the supervisor's affair with the new manager.

When inferences are made on top of inferences, it often becomes difficult to distinguish exactly where the facts stopped and the inferences began.

BYPASSING

Bypassing is a pattern of misevaluation in which people fail to communicate their intended meanings. It is "the miscommunication pattern which occurs when the sender (speaker, writer, and so on) and the receiver (listener, reader, and so forth) miss each other with their meanings" (Haney 1973).

Bypassing can take one of two forms. One type of bypassing occurs when two people use different words but give them the same meaning. On the surface there is disagreement but at the level of meaning there is agreement. Consider the following dialogue:

> **PAT:** I want a permanent relationship. I'm not interested in one-night stands. [Meaning: I want to date you exclusively and I want you to date me exclusively].

INTRODUCING RESEARCH

A SAMPLE DESCRIPTIVE STUDY

As noted in the Introducing Research box in Unit 4, descriptive research tries to describe what exists—the behaviors of happy couples, the attitudes of the effective communicator, the course of an interpersonal conflict. The sample study presented here tries to describe some of the characteristics of a "talkaholic" and will illustrate what one sample descriptive study looks like. It also provides an opportunity for discussing correlation, an essential concept in understanding research.

In this study the researchers sought to discover the correlates of compulsive communication (McCroskey & Richmond 1995). What characteristics does the compulsive talker possess? Because communication is so highly valued in this society, most research has addressed the problems of an unwillingness to communicate or of communication apprehension. This relatively new program of research focuses on persons who talk "too much" and may be considered compulsive talkers.

Some 811 college students completed a variety of tests designed to measure, for example, "talkaholism," communication apprehension, shyness, willingness to communicate, self-perception of communication competence, social style (for example, assertiveness and responsiveness), introversion and neuroticism, and affect orientation (a test designed to measure one's awareness of emotions in communication). Like you, these students were enrolled in an introductory communication course.

The researchers were primarily interested in finding correlations between talkaholism and these other characteristics (for example, apprehension, shyness, and social style). That is, they wanted to discover if a person who is high on talkaholism is also high on, say, apprehension. If so, they would be considered *positively correlated*—as one characteristic goes higher so does the other; as one goes lower so does the other. Another type of correlation—of as much interest as positive correlations—is a *negative correlation*. When characteristics are negatively related it means that as one goes up, the other goes down; as one goes down, the other goes up. The researchers discovered both types of correlations. Can you guess what they found? Look over the factors tested and try to formulate predictions before reading any further. Statistical measures applied to the results of these tests tell the researcher how great these differences are. Statistical tests also identify how much confidence you can have that the correlations found in the experiment will also be found in the rest of the world (or at least among the rest of the college population that is similar to the college population tested here).

Among the negative correlations found were those between talkaholism, on the one hand, and shyness, introversion, and communication apprehension, on the other. Shyness was clearly the most negatively correlated; the talkaholic is definitely not a shy person. Introversion and apprehension were also negatively correlated, but less so than shyness. (As test scores on talkaholism go up, scores on tests of shyness, introversion, and apprehension go down.) Among the positive correlations found were between talkaholism and assertiveness, the willingness to communicate, and self-perceived communication competence. (As test scores on talkaholism go up, scores on tests of assertiveness, willingness to communicate, and perceived communication competence also go up.)

The researchers also conducted interviews with about 21 high talkaholics and discovered, for example, that talkaholics know they are talkaholics; they know they talk a lot. Interestingly enough, none of these students felt that their compulsive communication was a problem. These students were oriented to careers that had high communication demands, for example, public relations and advertising, and a high number were majoring in journalism or communication.

On the basis of this study, what additional questions about this concept of compulsive communication might be worth researching? How might you go about seeking answers to such questions?

How would you define "cultural bypassing"? What relevance might this concept have for communication around your college campus? For communication in your professional life?

CHRIS: I'm not ready for that. [Thinking and meaning: marriage]. Let's keep things the way they are. [Meaning: let's continue dating only each other.]

This scenario illustrates a situation in which two people agree but assume, because they use different words (some of which may actually never be verbalized), that they disagree.

The second type is more common. This form of bypassing occurs when two people use the same words but give the words different meanings. On the surface it looks like the two people agree (simply because they are using the same words). But if you look more closely you see that the apparent agreement masks real disagreement. Consider this brief dialogue:

PAT: I don't really believe in religion. [Meaning: I don't really believe in God.]

CHRIS: Neither do I. [Meaning: I don't really believe in organized religions.]

Here Pat and Chris assume they agree, but actually they disagree. At some later date the implications of these differences may well become crucial.

Numerous other examples could be cited. Couples who say they are "in love" may mean very different things; one person may mean "a permanent and exclusive commitment" while the other may mean "a sexual involvement." "Come home early" may mean one thing to an anxious parent and quite another to a teenager.

The underlying assumption in bypassing is that words have intrinsic meanings. You incorrectly assume that when two people use the same word they mean the same thing, and when they use different words those words have different meanings. But words do not have meaning; meaning is in the people who use those words.

A form of bypassing often occurs when communication involves sighted and blind people. For example, examine the recommendations for communication (which follow) offered by the Lighthouse, an agency dedicated to helping partially sighted and blind people lead independent lives. Can you describe these suggestions as ways of avoiding bypassing? Consider too if you have violated any of these suggestions or seen any of them violated. Were you explicitly taught any of these principles?

Correcting Bypassing

One obvious corrective for bypassing, as Haney (1973) points out, is to look for meaning in the person and not in the words. Remember that words may be assigned a wide variety of meanings by different people and, alternatively, people may use different words to communicate the same meaning.

A second corrective is to use the active listening techniques discussed in the Listen to This box in Unit 16. By paraphrasing the speaker you can verify whether there is agreement or disagreement, not in the words but in the communicators. By reflecting back the speaker's thoughts and feelings, you can see whether you understand the speaker. You also provide the speaker with an opportunity to clarify any misun-

GIVE A BLIND PERSON THE SAME RESPECT AND CONSIDERATION YOU WOULD GIVE SOMEONE SIGHTED

On the Street
Ask if assistance would be helpful. Sometimes a blind person prefers to proceed unaided. If the person wants your help, offer your elbow. You should walk a half-step ahead so that your body movements will indicate when to change direction, stop and start, and step up or down at curbside.

Giving Directions
Verbal directions should have the blind person as the reference point. Example: "You are facing Lexington Avenue and you will have to cross it as you continue east on 59th Street."

Handling Money
When giving out bills, indicate the denomination of each so that the blind person can identify it and put it away. Coins are identified by touch.

Safety
Half-open doors are a hazard to everyone, particularly to a blind person. Keep doors closed or wide open.

Dining Out
Guide blind people to the table by offering your arm. Then place their hand on the chair back so they can seat themselves. Read the menu aloud and encourage the waiter to speak directly to the blind person rather than to you. Describe placement of food, using an imaginary clock face (e.g., vegetables are at 2 o'clock, salad plate is at 11 o'clock).

Traveling
Just as a sighted person enjoys hearing a tour guide describe unfamiliar scenery, a blind person likes to hear about indoor and outdoor sights.

Guide Dogs
These are working animals, not pets. Do not distract a guide dog by petting it or by seeking its attention.

Remember
Talk with a blind person as you would with a sighted one, in a normal tone. You may use such expressions as "See you later" and "Did you see that?"

If you enter a room in which a blind person is alone, announce your presence by speaking or introducing yourself. In a group, address blind people by name if they are expected to reply. Excuse yourself when you are leaving.

Always ask before trying to help. Grabbing an arm or pushing is dangerous and discourteous. When you accompany blind people, offer to describe the surroundings.

(*Source:* From "What Do You Do When You Meet a Blind Person," published by The Lighthouse Inc. Reprinted by permission of The Lighthouse Inc.)

derstanding or ambiguity. At the same time you can verify your own perception of the speaker's meanings.

ALLNESS

Because the world is infinitely complex, you can never know all or say all about anything. The poem by John Saxe about the six blind men and the elephant is an excellent example of an **allness** orientation and its problems. You may recall from elementary school that in Saxe's poem, six blind men come from Indostan to examine an elephant, an animal they have only heard about. From their different vantage points around the elephant's body—the side, tusk, trunk, knee, ear, and tail—the six men draw six different conclusions about what the elephant is like: a wall, a spear, a snake, a tree, a fan, and a rope, respectively. Each man reaches his own conclusion regarding what this marvelous beast is really like. Each argues that he is correct and that the others are wrong. Each, of course, is correct; but at the same time each is wrong.

Each of us is in the position of the six blind men. You never see all of anything. You never experience anything fully. You see part of an object, an event, a person. On that limited basis you then conclude what the whole is like. Of course, you have to draw conclusions on the basis of insufficient evidence (you always have insufficient evidence). Yet you must also recognize that when you make judgments based only on a part, you are actually making inferences that can later be proved wrong.

Famed British Prime Minister Benjamin Disraeli once said: "To be conscious that you are ignorant is a great step toward knowledge." That observation is an excellent example of a nonallness attitude. If you recognize that there is more to learn, more to see, and more to hear, you will leave yourself open to finding additional information.

Correcting Allness

A useful device to help you remember your nonallness orientation is to end each statement, verbally or mentally, with an et cetera (**etc.**)—a reminder that there is more to learn, more to know, and more to say, and that every statement is inevitably incomplete.

Some people overuse the et cetera. They use it not to mentally remind themselves that there is more to know and more to say but rather as a substitute for being specific. This, of course, defeats the purpose.

STATIC EVALUATION

When you form an abstraction of something or someone or you make a verbal statement about an event or person, that abstraction or statement remains static. The object or person to whom it originally referred may change enormously, however. Alfred Korzybski (1933), the founder of the study of language known as **General Semantics,** used an interesting illustration in this connection: in a tank are a large fish and many small fish, which are the natural food for the large fish. Given freedom in the tank, the large fish will eat the small fish. The tank is then partitioned, with the large fish on one side and the small fish on the other, divided only by a clear piece of glass. For a considerable time the large fish will attempt to eat the small fish but will fail each time—knocking into the glass partition in an effort to reach its "meal." After some time it learns that trying to eat the small fish is impossible and will no longer go after them. If the partition is now removed and the little fish swim all around the big fish, the big fish does not eat them and in fact will die of starvation. The large fish has learned a pattern of behavior, and even though the actual territory has changed, the map remains static.

While you would probably agree that everything is in a constant state of flux, the relevant question is whether you act as if you know this. Do you act in accordance with the notion of change instead of just accepting it intellectually? Do you treat your little sister as if she were 10 years old, or do you treat her like the 20-year-old woman she has become? Your evaluations of yourself and others must keep pace with the rapidly changing real world. Otherwise you will be left with attitudes and beliefs about a world that no longer exists—what are known as called static evaluations.

Correcting Static Evaluation

To guard against static evaluation, date your statements and especially your evaluations. Remember that Pat $Smith_{1997}$ is not Pat $Smith_{1990}$; academic $abilities_{1993}$ are not academic $abilities_{1997}$. T. S. Eliot, in *The Cocktail Party,* said that "what we know of other people is only our memory of the moments during which we knew them. And they have changed since then . . . at every meeting we are meeting a stranger."

INDISCRIMINATION

Nature seems to abhor sameness at least as much as it does a vacuum, for nowhere in the universe will you find two things that are identical. Everything is unique. Everything is unlike everything else.

Our language, however, provides you with common nouns, such as *teacher, student, friend, enemy, war, politician,* and *liberal,* which lead you to focus on similarities. Such nouns lead you to group all teachers together, all students together, and all friends together. At the same time, these terms divert attention away from the uniqueness of each person, each object, and each event. **Indiscrimination** occurs when you focus on classes of people, objects, or events and fail to see that each is unique and needs to be looked at individually. (Allness, sometimes confused with indiscrimination, refers to the assumption that we know all that needs to be known about a person or group.)

This misevaluation is at the heart of the common practice of stereotyping national, racial, and religious groups. A stereotype (Unit 3) is a fixed mental picture of some group that you apply to each individual of the group without regard to his or her unique qualities. It is important to note that although stereotypes are usually thoughts of as negative, they may also be positive. You can, for example, consider certain national groups as lazy or superstitious or mercenary or criminal, but you can also consider them as intelligent, progressive, honest, hardworking, and so on. Regardless of whether your stereotypes are positive or negative, the problem they create is the same. They provide you with shortcuts that are often inappropriate. For example, when you meet a particular person, your first reaction may be to pigeonhole him or her into some category—perhaps religious, national, or academic. Regardless of the type of category you use, you fail to give sufficient attention to the unique characteristics of the individual before you. This is indiscrimination, a denial of another person's uniqueness.

Do realize that there is nothing wrong with classifying. In fact, it is an extremely useful method of dealing with any complex matter; it puts order into thinking. The problem arises not from your classifying but from your applying an evaluation to that class and using the evaluative label as an adequate map for each and every individual in that group.

An additional perspective on indiscrimination can be gained by looking at **ethnocentrism**, the tendency to see others and their behaviors through your own cultural filters. Ethnocentrism is the tendency to evaluate the values, beliefs, and behaviors of your own culture as being more positive, logical, and natural than those of other cultures. Ideally, you would see both yourself and others as different but equal, with neither being inferior nor superior.

Ethnocentrism exists on a continuum. People are not either ethnocentric or not ethnocentric; rather, most are somewhere between these polar opposites. Of course, your degree of ethnocentrism varies depending on the group on which you focus. For example, if you are Greek American, you may have a low degree of ethnocentrism when dealing with Italian Americans but a high degree when dealing with Turkish Americans or Japanese Americans. Most important for our purposes is that your degree of ethnocentrism (and we are all ethnocentric to at least some degree) will influence your interpersonal, group, public, and mass communication behaviors.

Table 9.3, drawing from a number of studies (Gudykunst 1991; Gudykunst & Kim 1984; Lukens 1978), summarizes some of the interconnections. Five degrees of ethnocentrism are identified; in reality, of course, there are as many degrees as there are people. The "communication distances" are general terms that highlight the attitude that dominates that level of ethnocentrism. Under "communications" are some of the major ways people might interact given their particular degree of ethnocentrism.

Correcting Indiscrimination

An especially useful principle to combat indiscrimination is to recall that each person is unique (Hernandez 1994). Regardless of the number of labels (racial, religious, linguistic) two people might share, each is still unlike the other and any larger group. Using the **index,** a verbal or mental subscript that identifies each individual as an individual is a useful way to remember this principle: politician_1 is not politician_2, Hispanic police officer_1 is not Hispanic police officer_2, African American Catholic_1 is not African American Catholic_2, and so on. The index helps you discriminate among without discrimination against.

TABLE 9.3
the ethnocentrism continuum

Degree of Ethnocentrism	Communication Distance	Communications
Low	Equality	Treats others as equals; views different customs and ways of behaving as equal to one's own
	Sensitivity	Wants to decrease distance between self and others
	Indifference	Lacks concern for others; prefers to interact in a world of similar others
	Avoidance	Avoids and limits communications, especially intimate ones, with interculturally different others
High	Disparagement	Engages in hostile behavior; belittles others; views different cultures and ways of behaving as inferior to one's own

SUMMARY

In this unit we covered some of the major barriers to effective verbal communication and to effective and critical thinking.

1. Polarization occurs when you divide reality into two unrealistic extremes—for example, black and white, or good and bad.
2. Intensional orientation occurs when you respond to the way something is talked about or labeled rather than to its true nature. Extensional orientation is the tendency to respond to things as they are rather than as they are labeled or talked about.
3. Fact-inference confusion occurs when you treat inferences as if they were facts.
4. Bypassing occurs when speaker and listener miss each other with their meanings. It may occur when different words are used but are given the same meaning or when the same word is used but is given two different meanings.
5. Allness refers to the tendency to assume that one knows all that there is to know, or that what has been said is all that there is to say.
6. Static evaluation occurs when you ignore change and assume that reality is static.
7. Indiscrimination occurs when you group unlike things together and assume that because they have the same label, they are all alike.

THINKING CRITICALLY ABOUT VERBAL MESSAGE BARRIERS

1. Do you accept or reject any of the assumptions about the world as identified in Table 9.1? Can you think of other assumptions that might influence the way in which language is used?
2. One of the advantages of extreme terms is that they call greater attention to your thoughts than do middle terms or qualified phrases. Do the media, for example, give greater attention to ideas phrased in the extreme than to ideas phrased more logically as somewhere between the extremes?
3. What cultural identifiers do you prefer? Have these preferences changed over time? How can you let other people know the designations that you want and those that you do not want to be used to refer to you? An interesting exercise—especially in a large and multicultural class—is for each student to write anonymously his or her preferred cultural identification on an index card and have them all read aloud.
4. Watch a few television situation comedies. How many of the plot turns can be attributed to fact-inference confusion?
5. Do you buy brand-name items because of the name or do you examine the product and buy the one that is better or less expensive? Is your buying behavior generally intensional or extensional?
6. One of the ways in which allness statements are qualified is by reference to cultural differences. Can you identify statements in your textbooks that are phrased in terms of allness and that should be qualified in light of cultural variations?
7. Despite the obvious ever-changing nature of the universe, many of the notions in our heads remain static. Can you identify things, ideas, or people that you feel do not and will not change? Put differently, can you find exceptions to the principle of constant change?

8. How would you describe your own ethnocentrism? How similar is this to the ethnocentrism of your peers?
9. Have people ever committed indiscrimination against you because of your membership in a particular group? For example, have people ever assumed incorrectly that you believed something or behaved in a particular way because of your sex, race, nationality, religion, or affectional orientation?
10. How would you go about finding answers to such questions as these:
    a. Does a person's level of education influence his or her use of verbal message barriers?
    b. What other characteristics do highly ethnocentric people possess?
    c. Is there a sex difference in the ability to distinguish facts from inferences?
    d. Are these barriers related to a person's interpersonal popularity?

ten

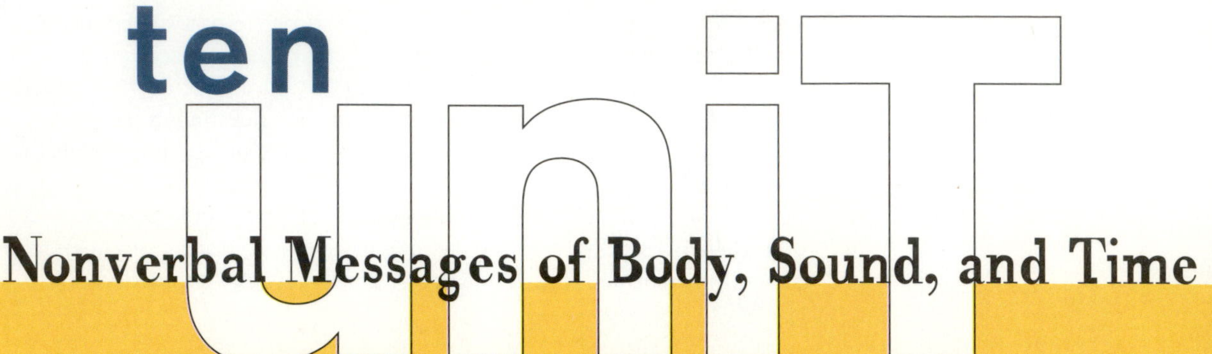

Nonverbal Messages of Body, Sound, and Time

unit contents

unit goals

After completing this unit, you should be able to

1. define and provide examples of *emblems, illustrators, affect displays, regulators,* and *adaptors*
2. identify the types of information communicated by the face and the problems in judging the meanings of facial expressions
3. identify the functions of eye movements
4. explain the types of information communicated by pupil dilation and constriction
5. define *paralanguage* and explain its role in making judgments about people and about communication
6. explain the role of silence in communication
7. explain the role of time in communication and distinguish between cultural and psychological time

In this unit we look first at body communication and examine the many ways in which body, face, and eyes communicate meaning. We also examine how vocal variation (for example, rate and volume) and silence communicate and then we look at time communication.

BODY MOVEMENTS

Five types of body movement may be identified (Ekman & Friesen 1969). Through these movements you communicate a wide variety of thoughts and feelings (see Table 10.1 on page 156).

Emblems

Emblems are nonverbal behaviors that directly translate words or phrases. Emblems include, for example, the signs for "okay," "peace," "come here," "I need a lift," "up yours," and so on. Emblems are nonverbal substitutes for specific words or phrases. You probably learn them in essentially the same way you learn words—without conscious awareness or explicit teaching and largely through a process of imitation.

Although emblems seem natural and inherently meaningful, they are as arbitrary as any word in any language. Thus our present culture's emblems are not necessarily the same as the emblems of three hundred years ago or the emblems of other cultures. For example, the nose tap (where your forefinger taps your nose several times) means "complicity" in England, "be alert" in Italy, "you're nosey" in Wales, "I'm alert" in Belgium, "he's clever" in southern Italy, and "a treat" in many cultures (Morris 1994).

Illustrators

Illustrators are nonverbal behaviors that accompany and literally "illustrate" verbal messages. They are more natural, less arbitrary, and more universal than emblems. It is likely that they include some innate component as well as some learning.

In saying, "Let's go up," for example, you may move both your head and hands in an upward direction. In describing a circle or a square you are likely to make circular or square movements with your hands. Illustrators complement the verbal message and in so doing make the message easier to understand (Rogers 1978; Bull & Frederikson 1995). So well learned are these movements that it is difficult to reverse them or to employ inappropriate ones. Most of the time you are probably only partially aware of the illustrators you use. At times they have to be brought to your attention.

Affect Displays

Affect displays are those facial movements that convey emotional meaning; they show anger and fear, happiness and surprise, eagerness and fatigue. Such facial expressions "give you away" when you try to present a false image and on occasion may lead people to say, for example, "You look angry today, what's wrong?" You can, however, consciously control affect displays, as actors do when they play a role. Affect displays may be unintentional—as when they give you away—but they may also be intentional. You may want to show anger, love, hate, or surprise and, usually, you do a credible job).

Regulators

Regulators are nonverbal behaviors that "regulate," monitor, maintain, or control an individual's speech. When you listen to another person, you are not passive; you nod your head, purse your lips, adjust your eye focus, and make various paralinguistic sounds, such as "mm-mm" or "tsk." Regulators are clearly culture-specific and are not universal.

Regulators tell speakers what you expect or want them to do as they are talking—for example, "Keep going," "What else happened? . . . I don't believe that," or "Slow down." Speakers in turn receive these nonverbal behaviors unconsciously. Depending on the speaker's degree of sensitivity, he or she will change behavior according to the directions the regulators supply.

Adaptors

Adaptors are nonverbal behaviors that when performed in private—or in public but without being seen—serve some kind of need and occur in their entirety. For example, when you are alone you might scratch your head until you put the itch to rest. In public, when people are watching you, you perform these adaptors only partially. You might, for example, put your fingers to your head and move them around a bit, but you probably would not scratch enough to eliminate the itch.

FACIAL MOVEMENTS

Facial messages communicate types of emotion as well as selected qualities or dimensions of emotion. Most researchers agree with Paul Ekman, Wallace V. Freisen, and Phoebe Ellsworth (1972) in claiming that facial messages may communicate at least the follow-

TABLE 10.1
the five body movements

	Name and Function	Examples
	Emblems directly translate words or phrases	"Okay" sign, "come here" wave, hitchhiker's "thumb"
	Illustrators accompany and literally "illustrate" verbal messages	Circular hand movements when talking of a circle; hands far apart when talking of something large
	Affect displays communicate emotional meaning	Expressions of happiness, surprise, fear, anger, sadness, disgust/contempt
	Regulators monitor, maintain, or control the speaking of another	Facial expressions and hand gestures indicating "keep going," "slow down," or "what else happened?"
	Adaptors satisfy some need	Scratching one's head

TABLE 10.2
facial management techniques

These facial management techniques are learned along with display rules, which tell you what emotions to express when; they are the rules of appropriateness. For example, when someone gets bad news in which you may secretly take pleasure, the display rule dictates that you frown and otherwise nonverbally signal your displeasure. Violators of these rules are generally judged very harshly.

Technique	Function	Example
Intensifying	To exaggerate a feeling	Exaggerating surprise when friends throw you a party, to make your friends feel good
Deintensifying	To underplay a feeling	To cover up your own joy in the presence of a friend who didn't receive such good news
Neutralizing	To hide a feeling	To cover up your sadness so as not to depress others
Masking	To replace or substitute the expression of one emotion for another	To express happiness in order to cover up your disappointment at not receiving the gift you had expected

ing "emotion categories": happiness, surprise, fear, anger, sadness, and disgust/contempt. Nonverbal researcher Dale Leathers (1986) proposes that facial movements may also communicate bewilderment and determination.

The six emotions identified by Ekman and his colleagues are generally called **primary affect displays.** These are relatively pure, single emotions. Other emotional states and other facial displays are combinations of these various primary emotions and are called affect blends. Approximately 33 affect blends have been identified. These blends are consistently recognized by trained nonverbal analysts. You can communicate these affects by different parts of your face. Thus, for example, you may show both fear and disgust at the same time: your eyes and eyelids may signal fear, and movements of your nose, cheek, and mouth area may signal disgust.

Facial Management Techniques

As you learned the nonverbal system of communication, you also learned certain facial management techniques; for example, to hide certain emotions and to emphasize others. In fact, research shows that even children in second and fourth grade use facial management techniques and that the complexity of such tactics increases as we get older (Halberstadt, Grotjohn, Johnson, Furth, et al. 1992). Table 10.2 identifies four types of facial management techniques that you will quickly recognize as being frequently and widely used (Richmond, McCroskey, & Payne 1991).

The Facial Feedback Hypothesis

According to the **facial feedback hypothesis** your facial expression influences your level of physiological arousal. People who exaggerate their facial expressions show higher physiological arousal than those who suppress them. Those who neither exaggerated nor suppressed their expressions had arousal levels between these two extremes (Lanzetta, Cartwright-Smith, & Kleck 1976; Zuckerman, Klorman, Larrance, & Spiegel 1981). In one interesting study subjects held a pen in their teeth in such a way as to simulate a sad expression. They then rated photographs. Results showed that mimicking sad expressions actually increased the degree of sadness the subjects reported feeling when viewing the photographs (Larsen, Kasimatis, & Frey 1992). Further support for this hypothesis comes from a study that compared subjects who (1) feel emotions such as happiness and anger, and (2) feel and express these emotions. In support of the facial feedback hypothesis, subjects who felt and expressed the emotions became emotionally aroused faster than did those who only felt the emotion (Hess, Kappas, McHugo, & Lanzetta 1992). Therefore, not only do your facial expressions influence the judgments and impressions that others have of you, they also influence your own level of emotional arousal (Cappella 1993).

The Influence of Context and Culture

The same facial expressions are perceived differently when associated with different contexts. For example, when a smiling face was presented looking at a glum face, the smiling face was judged to be vicious and taunting. When the same smiling face was presented looking at a frowning face, however, it was judged to be peaceful and friendly (Cline 1956).

The wide variations in facial communication that we observe in different cultures seem to reflect which reactions are permissible and which are not, rather than a difference in the way in which emotions are facially expressed. In one study, for example, Japanese and American students watched a film of an operation (Ekman 1985). The students were videotaped in both an interview situation about the film and alone while watching the film. When alone, the students showed very similar reactions; but in the interview, the American students displayed facial expressions indicating displeasure whereas the Japanese students did not show any great emotion. Keep in mind, however, that Japanese women are not supposed to reveal broad smiles and so will hide their smile, sometimes with their hands, while women in the United States have no such restrictions and so are likely to smile openly. Thus, the differences observed may not be in the way different cultures express emotions but rather in the cultural rules for displaying emotions in public.

Encoding-Decoding Accuracy

Considerable research has addressed the issue of how accurately you can encode and decode facial emotions. It is difficult to separate the ability of the encoder from the ability of the decoder, thus, a person may be quite adept at communicating emotions, but the receiver may prove insensitive. On the other hand, the receiver may be good at deciphering emotions, but the sender may be inept. For example, extroverts seem more accurate at decoding nonverbal cues than introverts (Akert & Panter 1986).

In 11 different countries, women were found to be better at encoding and decoding nonverbal cues than were men. (Rosenthal & DePaulo 1979). It may be argued that because men and women play different social roles in society they have learned different adaptive techniques and skills to help them perform these roles. Thus, in most societies women are expected to be more friendly, nurturing, and supportive and therefore learn these skills (Eagly 1987).

Accuracy also varies with the emotions themselves. Some emotions are easier to encode and decode than others. Ekman, Friesen, and Ellsworth (1972), for example, report that people judge happiness with an accuracy ranging from 55 to 100 percent, surprise from 38 to 86 percent, and sadness from 19 to 88 percent. In front of a mirror try to communicate surprise using only facial movements. Describe the specific movements of the face that make up surprise. If you signal surprise as most most people do, you probably employ raised and curved eyebrows, long horizontal forehead wrinkles, wide-open eyes, a dropped-open mouth, and lips parted with no tension.

Paul Ekman (Ekman, Friesen, & Tomkins 1971) has developed what he calls FAST—the Facial Affect Scoring Technique, which divides the face into three main parts: eyebrows and forehead, eyes and eyelids, and the lower face, from the bridge of the nose down. To use the technique, judges try to identify various emotions by observing the different parts of the face and writing descriptions (similar to the one given for surprise). Certain areas of the face seem best suited to communicating certain emotions; for example, the eyes and eyelids are best for communicating fear, and the nose, cheek, and mouth areas are best for communicating disgust.

Micromomentary Expressions

Researchers have long been interested in whether you can really hide emotions or whether they somehow reveal themselves below the level of conscious awareness. Is your contempt encoded facially without your being aware of it or even without observers being aware of it? Although we do not have a complete answer to this question, some indication that you do communicate these emotions without awareness comes from research on micromomentary expressions. Slow-motion films of people therapy show that their expressions often change dramatically during the therapy session (Haggard & Isaacs 1966). For example, a frown would change to a smile and then quickly back to a frown. If the film were played at normal speed, the smile would go unnoticed. We call these extremely brief movements, which last for less than 0.4 second, **micromomentary expressions.** These expressions, some theorists argue, indicate a person's real emotional state.

EYE MOVEMENTS

From Ben Jonson's poetic observation "Drink to me only with thine eyes, and I will pledge with mine" to the scientific observations of contemporary researchers (Hess 1975; Marshall 1983), the eyes are regarded as the most important nonverbal message system.

The messages communicated by the eyes vary depending on the duration, direction, and quality of the eye behavior. For example, in every culture there are rather strict, though unstated, rules for the proper duration for eye contact. In much of England and the United States, for example, the average length of gaze is 2.95 seconds. The average length of mutual gaze (two persons gazing at each other) is 1.18 seconds (Argyle 1988; Argyle & Ingham 1972). When eye contact falls short of this amount, you may think the person is uninterested, shy, or preoccupied. When the appropriate amount of time is exceeded, you generally perceive this as showing unusually high interest.

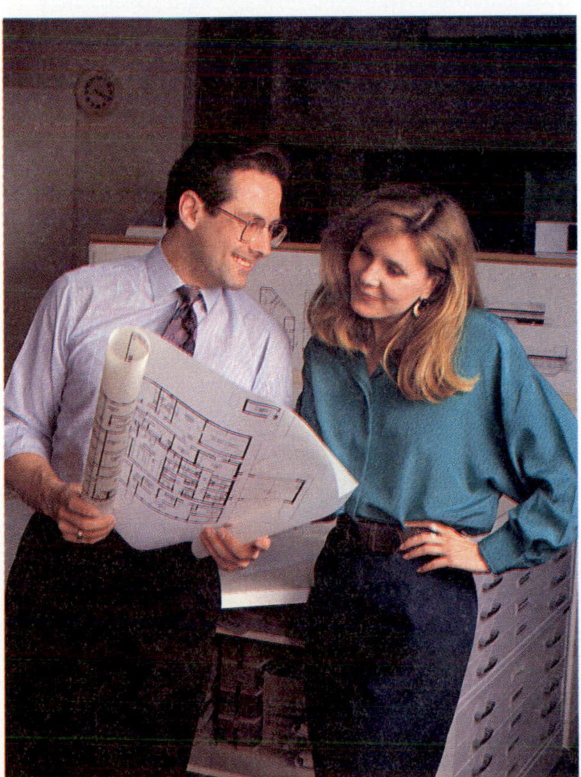

Do men and women use similar eye movements in flirting? In asserting authority? In showing anger and displeasure? In showing happiness and pleasure? How would you go about finding answers to these questions?

In much of the United States direct eye contact is considered an expression of honesty and forthrightness. The Japanese, however, often view this as a lack of respect. The Japanese will glance at the other person's face rarely and then only for very short periods (Axtell 1990a). In many Hispanic cultures direct eye contact signifies a certain equality and therefore should be avoided by, say, children when speaking to a person in authority. Try visualizing the potential misunderstandings that eye communication alone could create when people from Tokyo, San Francisco, and San Juan try to communicate.

The direction of the eye also communicates. Generally, in communicating with another person, you would glance alternatively at the other person's face, then away, then again at the face, and so on. When these directional rules are broken, different meanings are communicated—abnormally high or low interest, self-consciousness, nervousness over the interaction, and so on. The quality—how wide or how narrow your eyes get during interaction—also communicates meaning, especially interest level and such emotions as surprise, fear, and disgust.

Functions of Eye Communication

Researchers note four major functions of eye communication (Knapp & Hall 1992).

To Seek Feedback

You frequently use your eyes to seek feedback from others. In talking with someone, you look at her or him intently, as if to say, "Well, what do you think?" As you might predict, listeners gaze at speakers more than speakers gaze at listeners. Research shows that the percentage of interaction time spent gazing while listening was between 62 and 75 percent. However, the percentage of time spent gazing while talking was between 38 and 41 percent (Argyle 1988; Knapp & Hall 1992).

Women make eye contact more and maintain it longer (both in speaking and in listening) than do men. This holds true whether the woman is interacting with other women or with men. This difference in eye behavior may result from women's tendency to display their emotions more than men; eye contact is one of the most effective ways of communicating emotions. Another possible explanation, as Evan Marshall (1983) argues, is that women have been conditioned more than men to seek positive feedback from others. Women may thus use eye contact in seeking this visual feedback.

To Regulate the Conversation

A second function of eye contact is to regulate the conversation and particularly to pass the speaking turn from one person to another. You use eye contact, for example, to tell the listener that you are finished with your thought and that you would now like to assume the role of listener and hear what the other person has to say. Or, by maintaining a steady eye contact while you plan your next sentence, you tell the other person that although you are now silent, you don't want to give up your speaking turn. You also see this in the college classroom when the instructor asks a question and then locks eyes with a student—without saying anything, the instructor clearly communicates the desire for that student to say something.

To Signal the Nature of the Relationship

Eye contact is also used to signal the nature of the relationship between two people—for example, a focused attentive glance indicates a positive relationship, but avoiding eye contact shows one of negative regard. You may also signal status relationships with your eyes. This is particularly interesting because the same movements of the eyes may signal either subordination or superiority. The superior individual, for example, may stare at the subordinate or may glance away. Similarly, the subordinate may look directly at the superior or perhaps to the floor.

Eye movements may also signal whether the relationship between two people is amorous, hostile, or indifferent. Because some of the eye movements expressing these different relationships are so similar, you often use information from other areas, particularly the rest of the face, to decode the message before making any final judgments.

To Compensate for Increased Physical Distance

Last, eye movements may compensate for increased physical distance. By making eye contact you overcome psychologically the physical distance between you and the other individual. When you catch someone's eye at a party, for example, you become psychologically close even though separated by a large physical distance. Not surprisingly, eye contact and other expressions of psychological closeness, such as self-disclosure, are positively related; as one increases, so does the other.

Eye Avoidance

Sociologist Erving Goffman, in *Interaction Ritual* (1967), observed that the eyes are "great intruders." When you avoid eye contact or avert your glance, you help others maintain their privacy. You frequently do this when a couple argue in public. You turn your eyes away (though your eyes may be wide open) as if to say, "I don't mean to intrude; I respect your privacy." Goffman refers to this behavior as **civil inattention.**

Eye avoidance can signal lack of interest—in a person, a conversation, or some visual stimulus. At times, like an ostrich, you hide your eyes in an attempt to cut off unpleasant stimuli. Notice, for example, how quickly people close their eyes in the face of some extreme unpleasantness. Interestingly enough, even if the unpleasantness is auditory, you tend to shut it out by closing your eyes. Sometimes you close your eyes to block out visual stimuli and thus heighten your other senses. For example, you often listen to music with your eyes closed. Lovers often close their eyes while kissing, and many prefer to make love in a dark or dimly lit room.

Pupil Dilation

In the fifteenth and sixteenth centuries, Italian women put drops of belladonna (which literally means "beautiful woman") into their eyes to enlarge the pupils so that they would look more attractive. Contemporary research supports the intuitive logic of these women: dilated pupils are in fact judged to be more attractive than constricted ones (Hess 1975; Marshall 1983).

In one study (Hess 1975), photographs of women were retouched: in one set the pupils were enlarged, and in the other they were made smaller. Men were then asked to judge the women's personalities from the photographs. The photos of women with small pupils drew responses such as cold, hard, and selfish; those with dilated pupils drew responses such as feminine and soft. However, the male observers could not verbalize the reasons for the different perceptions. Pupil dilation and reactions to changes in the pupil size of others both seem to function below the level of awareness.

Although belladonna is no longer used, the cosmetics industry has made millions selling eye enhancers—eye shadow, eyeliner, false eyelashes, and tinted contact lenses that change eye color. These items function (ideally, at least) to draw attention to these most powerful communicators.

Pupil size also reveals your interest and level of emotional arousal. Your pupils enlarge when you are interested in something or when you are emotionally aroused. When homosexuals and heterosexuals were shown pictures of nude bodies, the homosexuals' pupils dilated more when viewing same-sex bodies, while the heterosexuals' pupils dilated more when viewing opposite-sex bodies (Hess, Seltzer, & Schlien 1965). These pupillary responses are unconscious and are even observed in persons with profound mental retardation (Chaney, Givens, Aoki, & Gombiner 1989). Perhaps we judge dilated pupils more attractive because we judge them as indicative of a person's interest in us.

PARALANGUAGE

An old exercise to increase the ability to express different emotions, feelings, and attitudes was to repeat a sentence while accenting or stressing different words. Significant differences in meaning are easily communicated depending on where the stress is placed.

THINK ABOUT

Think about, for example, the following variations and the different meanings you derive from each question.

1. *Is* this the face that launched a thousand ships?
2. Is *this* the face that launched a thousand ships?
3. Is this the *face* that launched a thousand ships?
4. Is this the face that *launched* a thousand ships?
5. Is this the face that launched a *thousand ships?*

Each rendition of the sentence communicates something different. Each, in fact, asks a totally different question, even though the words used are the same. All that distinguishes the sentences is stress, one of the aspects of paralanguage. **Paralanguage** refers to the vocal (but nonverbal) dimension of speech. It refers to the manner in which you say something rather than to what you say.

In addition to stress or **pitch**, paralanguage includes such vocal characteristics as **rate**, **volume**, and rhythm. Paralanguage also includes the vocalizations you make in crying, whispering, moaning, belching, yawning, and yelling (Argyle 1988; Trager 1958, 1961). A variation in any of these features communicates. The speaker who talks quickly, for example, communicates something different from the one who speaks slowly. Even though the words might be the same, if the speed (or volume, rhythm, or pitch) differs, the meanings you receive will also differ.

THINK ABOUT

Think about your own ability to communicate different meanings with the use of only paralinguistic cues. Read each of the ten statements below first to communicate praise and then to communicate criticism. Can others identify which meaning you are communicating? Can you identify the meanings others are communicating when they try this?

1. Now that looks good on you.
2. You lost weight.
3. You look younger than that.
4. You're going to make it.
5. That was some meal.
6. You really know yourself.
7. You're an expert.
8. You're so sensitive. I'm amazed.
9. Your parents are really something.
10. Are you ready? Already?

What paralinguistic cues did you use to communicate praise? To communicate criticism? Most people would claim that it is easier to decode praise or criticism than to encode these meanings. Was this true in your experience?

Judgments About People

People often make judgments about others on the basis of the way they speak. Sometimes these judgments turn out to be correct, and sometimes not. You may, for example, conclude that those who speak very softly do so because they feel no one wants to listen and that nothing they say is significant. Similarly, you may judge that people who speak loudly have overinflated egos and think that everyone in the world wants to hear them. Those who speak with no variation, in a complete monotone, seem uninterested in what they are saying. You might perceive such people as having a lack of interest in life in general. All these conclusions are, at best, based on little evidence. Yet, this does not stop us from making them.

One interesting research finding shows that listeners can accurately judge the socioeconomic status (whether high, middle, or low) of speakers from 60-second voice samples (Davitz 1964). In fact, many listeners reported that they made their judgments in fewer than 15 seconds. Speakers judged to be of high status were also rated as being of higher credibility than speakers rated middle and low in status.

Listeners can also judge with considerable accuracy the emotional states of speakers from vocal expression alone. In these studies, speakers recite the alphabet or numbers while expressing emotions with their voices. Some emotions, of course, are easier to identify than others. For example, it is easy to distinguish between hate and sympathy but more difficult to distinguish between fear and anxiety. Of course, listeners do vary in their ability to decode and speakers do vary in their ability to encode emotions (Scherer 1986).

Judgments About Communication

The **rate** or speed at which people speak is the aspect of paralanguage that has received the most attention (MacLachlan 1979). It is of interest to the advertiser, the politician, and in fact, anyone who tries to convey information or to influence others. It is especially important when time is limited or expensive.

Persuasiveness and Credibility

The research conducted on the rate of speech shows that in one-way communication (when one person is doing all or most of the speaking and the other person is doing all or most of the listening), those who talk fast are more persuasive and are evaluated more highly than those who talk at or below normal speeds. This finding holds true regardless of whether the speech is naturally fast or electronically speeded up.

In one experiment, for example, subjects listened to taped messages and then indicated their degree of agreement with the message and their opinion of the speaker's intelligence and objectivity (MacLachlan 1979). Experimenters used speaking rates of 111, 140 (the average speaking rate), and 191 words per minute. Subjects agreed most with the fastest speech and least with the slowest speech. Further, they rated the fastest speaker as the most intelligent and objective. They rated the slowest speaker as the least intelligent and objective. Even when the speaker was shown to have something to gain personally from persuasion (as would a used-car dealer), the fastest speaking rate was the most persuasive. Additional research finds that faster speech rates increase speaker competence and dominance (Buller, LePoire, Aune, & Eloy 1992).

Comprehension

When we look at comprehension, rapid speech shows an interesting effect. Subjects who listened to speeches at different speeds had their comprehension measured by multiple-choice tests (MacLachlan 1979). Researchers used 141 words per minute as the average and considered comprehension at this rate to be 100 percent. When they increased the rate to 201 words per minute the comprehension was 95 percent. When they further increased the rate to 282 words per minute (double the normal rate), comprehension was still 90 percent. Even though the rates increased dramatically, the comprehension rates fell only slightly. These 5 and 10 percent losses are more than offset by the increased speed and thus make the faster rates much more efficient in communicating information. If the speeds are increased more than twice normal speech, however, comprehension begins to fall dramatically.

Preferences

Most listeners prefer a somewhat faster-than-normal speed. For example, when subjects were able to adjust the speed at which they heard a message, they adjusted it to approximately 25 percent faster than normal speed. Similarly, people find commercials presented at 25 percent faster than normal more interesting than those presented at normal speeds. Further, the level of attention (indexed by the amount of electrical activity in the brain) is greater for fast speeds.

We need to be cautious, however, in applying this research to the field of communication. As John MacLachlan (1979) points out, during the time the speaker is speaking, the listener is generating and framing a reply. If the speaker talks too rapidly, there may not be enough time to compose this reply. As a result the listener may become resentful. Furthermore, the increased rate may seem so unnatural that the listener may focus on the speed of speech rather than the thought expressed. With one-way communication, especially mass communication, it is clear that increased speech rates will become more and more popular.

SILENCE

In one of the most often quoted observations on silence, Thomas Mann said, "Speech is civilization itself. The word, even the most contradictory word, preserves contact; it is silence which isolates." On the other hand, philosopher Karl Jaspers observed that "the ultimate in thinking as in communication is silence," and philosopher Max Picard noted that "silence is nothing merely negative; it is not the mere absence of speech. It is a positive, a complete world in itself." The one thing on which these contradictory observations agree is that silence communicates just as intensely as anything you verbalize (Jaworski 1993).

Functions of Silence

Like words and gestures, **silence** too serves important communication functions. Silence allows the speaker *time to think,* time to formulate and organize his or her verbal communications. Before messages of intense conflict, as well as those confessing undying love, there is often silence. Again, silence seems to prepare the receiver for the importance of these future messages.

Some people use silence as a weapon *to hurt* others. We often speak of giving someone "the silent treatment." After a conflict, for example, one or both individuals might remain silent as a kind of punishment. Silence used to hurt others may also take the form of refusing to acknowledge the presence of another person, as in disconfirmation (see Unit 8); here silence is a dramatic demonstration of the total indifference one person feels toward the other.

Sometimes silence is used as a *response to personal anxiety,* shyness, or threats. You may feel anxious or shy among new people and prefer to remain silent. By remaining silent you preclude the chance of rejection. Only when the silence is broken and you attempt to communicate with another person do you risk rejection.

Silence may be used *to prevent communication* of certain messages. In conflict situations silence is sometimes used to prevent certain topics from surfacing and to prevent one or both parties from saying things they may later regret. In such situations silence often allows us time to cool off before expressing hatred, severe criticism, or personal attacks, which, we know, are irreversible.

Like the eyes, face, or hands, silence can also be used *to communicate emotional responses* (Ehrenhaus 1988). Sometimes silence communicates a determination to be uncooperative or defiant; by refusing to engage in verbal communication, you defy the authority or the legitimacy of the other person's position. Silence is often used to communicate annoyance, usually accompanied by a pouting expression, arms crossed in front of the chest, and nostrils flared. Silence may express affection or love, especially when coupled with long and longing stares into each other's eyes.

Of course, you may also use silence when you simply have *nothing to say,* when nothing occurs to you, or when you do not want to say anything. James Russell Lowell expressed this best: "Blessed are they who have nothing to say, and who cannot be persuaded to say it."

Cultural Differences

The communicative functions of silence in the situations just cited are not universal. In the United States, for example, silence is often taken as negative. At a business meeting or even in informal social groups, silence may often be interpreted negatively—perhaps the silent member wasn't listening, has nothing interesting to add, doesn't understand the issues, is insensitive, is too self-absorbed to focus on the messages of others, or isn't interested in or isn't paying attention to the conversation. Other cultures, however, view silence more positively. In many situations in Japan, for example, silence is preferred to speech (Haga 1988). Among the Navajo, school children are silent because they do not wish to put themselves above their peers and because they have been taught that silence is the appropriate behavior for a student (Plank 1994).

The traditional Apache also regard silence very differently (Basso 1972). Among the Apache, mutual friends do not feel the need to introduce strangers who may be working in the same area or on the same project. The strangers may remain silent for several days. During this time they are looking each other over, trying to determine if the other person is all right. Only after this period do the individuals talk. When courting, especially during the initial stages, the Apache remain silent for hours; if they do talk, they generally talk very little. Only after a couple has been dating for several months will they have lengthy conversations. These periods of silence are generally attributed to shyness or self-consciousness. The use of silence is explicitly taught to Apache women, who are especially discouraged from engaging in long discussions with their dates. Silence during courtship is a sign of modesty to many Apache.

TEMPORAL COMMUNICATION

Temporal communication (**chronemics**) concerns the use of time—how you organize it, how you react to it, and the messages it communicates (Bruneau 1985, 1990). Cultural and psychological time are two aspects of particular interest in human communication.

Cultural Time

We can distinguish three types of **cultural time** (Bruneau 1985, 1990). Technical time is precise, scientific time. Milliseconds and atomic years are examples of technical or scientific time. This time system is used only in the laboratory, and has little relevance in our daily lives.

Formal time refers to how a culture defines and teaches time. In our culture time is divided into seconds, minutes, hours, days, weeks, months, and years. Other cultures may use phases of the moon or the seasons to delineate time periods. We divide college courses into 50- or 75-minute periods that meet two or three times a week for 14-week periods called semesters. Eight semesters of 15 or 16 periods per week equal a college education. As these examples illustrate, formal time units are arbitrary. The culture establishes them for convenience.

Informal time refers to a rather loose use of time terms—for example, *forever, immediately, soon, right away, as soon as possible.* This is the area of time that creates the most communication problems because the terms have different meanings for different people.

Displaced and Diffused Time Orientations

An important distinction is between displaced and diffused time orientations. In a displaced time orientation, time is viewed exactly. Persons with this orientation will be exactly on time. In a diffused time orientation, people see time as approximate rather than exact. People with this orientation are often late for appointments because they understand, for example, a scheduled time of 8 P.M. as meaning anywhere from 7:45 to 8:15 or 8:30.

In one study, researchers examined the accuracy of the clocks in different cultures and found considerable variation (LeVine & Bartlett 1984). Clocks in Japan were the most accurate, while clocks in Indonesia were the least accurate. Clocks in England, Italy, Taiwan, and the United States fell between these two extremes. Not surprisingly, when the speed of pedestrians in these cultures was measured, the researchers found that the Japanese walked the fastest and the Indonesians the slowest. Such differences reflect the different ways in which cultures treat time and their general attitude toward the importance of time in their everyday lives.

Monochronism and Polychronism

Another interesting distinction is that between **monochronic** and **polychronic time orientations** (Hall 1959, 1983; Hall and Hall, 1987). Monochronic people or cultures (the United States, Germany, Scandinavia, and Switzerland are good examples) schedule one thing at a time. Time is compartmentalized; there is a time for everything, and everything has its own time. Polychronic people or cultures (Latin Americans, Mediterranean people, and Arabs are good examples), on the other hand, schedule a number of things at the same

MEDIA WATCH

THE SPIRAL OF SILENCE

Consider your own tendency to discuss your attitudes and beliefs with others. Are you equally likely to voice opinions that agree with others as those that disagree? The **spiral of silence theory** would argue that you are more likely to voice agreement positions than disagreement ones (Noelle-Neumann 1973, 1980, 1991; Becker & Roberts 1992; Windahl, Signitzer, & Olson 1992).

The spiral of silence theory claims that when a controversial issue arises, people estimate the opinions of others; they try to estimate public opinion on the issue. They estimate which views are popular and which are not and they estimate *how* popular these positions are. At the same time, they also judge the likelihood of being punished for expressing minority opinions and the severity of that punishment. They do this largely by attending to the media. Once these assumptions about the popularity of an issue are formed, people use these to regulate their willingness to express their own opinions on that issue.

When people feel their opinions are in agreement with the majority, they are more likely to voice them than if they feel they are in disagreement. Of course there are many reasons people might be reluctant to voice minority opinions. After all, we want to be one of the crowd and resist any possible isolation. Another reason is that disagreement often means confrontation with the possibility of being proven wrong. Both are unpleasant results. And, many people assume that the majority, because they are a majority, must be right; and we want to be right, not wrong.

Not all people seem affected by this spiral equally (Noelle-Neumann 1991). For example, younger people and men are more likely to express minority opinions than are older people and women. Educated people are more likely to express minority opinions than are those who are less educated. This is not surprising—the expression of a minority opinion often requires some defense, which the educated feel competent to present but the uneducated do not.

As these people remain silent, the media position gets stronger (because those who agree with it are the only ones who are speaking). As the media's position grows stronger, the silence of the opposition also grows. The silence becomes an ever-widening spiral.

One of the problems this situation creates is that the media are likely to express the same general opinions, values, and beliefs and thus present a false picture of the extent to which people are in agreement. Those who take their cues from the media are therefore likely to misestimate the real degree of agreement and disagreement.

Consider your own part in the spiral of silence. How much, if any, do you contribute to this spiral of silence? How much do your peers contribute? To what degree does your college provide for the presentation of minority values, opinions, and beliefs? How does this theory relate to interpersonal communication generally? Can you apply this theory to the way in which small groups within organizations operate? To contemporary political speaking?

Consider too how you would go about testing this theory. According to Elisabeth Noelle-Neumann (1991), who developed this theory, four assumptions about this theory must be investigated to test the theory. Stated as questions, these are:

1. Does society threaten deviant individuals?
2. Do individuals continuously experience fear of isolation?
3. Does the fear of isolation lead individuals to assess the climate of public opinion?
4. Do these assessments affect an individual's openness to express or conceal opinions?

How would you go about testing these assumptions?

Here is a photo of the Mud Men of the Solomon islands in a ceremonial dance. If you knew nothing about this culture, what guesses would you make about their concept of time? Would it differ from your own? Is your own view of time consistent with your achieving your personal and professional goals?

time. Eating, conducting business with several different people, and taking care of family matters may all be conducted at the same time. No culture is entirely monochronic or polychronic; rather these are general tendencies that are found across a large part of the culture. Some cultures combine both time orientations; Japanese and parts of American culture are examples in which both orientations are found. Table 10.3, based on Hall (1987), identifies some of the distinctions between these two time orientations.

The Social Clock

Another interesting aspect of cultural time is your "social clock" (Neugarten 1979). Your culture and your

TABLE 10.3
monochronic and polychronic time

As you read down this table note the potential for miscommunication that these differences might create when monochronic-time and polychronic-time people interact.

The Monochronic Person	The Polychronic Person
Does one thing at a time	Does several things at one time
Treats time schedules and plans very seriously; they may only be broken for the most serious of reasons	Treats time schedules and plans as useful (not sacred); they may be broken for a variety of causes
Considers the job the most important part of ones life, ahead of even family	Considers the family and interpersonal relationships more important than the job
Considers privacy extremely important, seldom borrows or lends to others, works independently	Is actively involved with others, works in the presence of and with lots of people at the same time

more specific society maintains a time schedule for the right time to do a variety of important things, for example, the right time to start dating, to finish college, to buy your own home, to have a child. You no doubt learned about this clock as you were growing up. On the basis of this social clock you then evaluate your own social and professional development. If you are on schedule with your peers—for example, you all started dating at around the same age or you are all finishing college at around the same age—then you will feel well adjusted, competent, and a part of the group. If you are late, you will probably experience feelings of dissatisfaction.

Psychological Time

Psychological time refers primarily to the importance you place on the past, present, and future. If you have a past orientation, you relive old times and regard the old methods as the best. You see events as circular and recurring, so the wisdom of yesterday is applicable also to today and tomorrow. Having a present orientation means you live in the present; for now, not tomorrow. If you have a future orientation you look toward and live for the future. You save today, work hard in college, and deny yourself luxuries because you are preparing for the future.

Recent research has provided some interesting conclusions about ourselves on the basis of the way we view time (Gonzalez & Zimbardo 1985). Before reading these conclusions take the self-test, "What Time Do You Have?"

Consider some of the findings relevant to psychological time orientation found by Gonzalez and Zimbardo (1985). Future income is positively related to future orientation. The more future-oriented a person is, the greater that person's income is likely to be. Present orientation is strongest among lowest-income males.

The time orientation that people develop depends a great deal on their socioeconomic class and their personal experiences. Gonzalez and Zimbardo (1985) observe: "A child with parents in unskilled and semiskilled occupations is usually socialized in a way that promotes a present-oriented fatalism and hedonism. A child of parents who are managers, teachers, or other professionals learns future-oriented values and strategies designed to promote achievement."

Different time perspectives also account for much intercultural misunderstanding because different cultures will often teach their members drastically different time orientations. The future-oriented person who works for tomorrow's goals will frequently look down on the present-oriented person who avoids planning and focuses on enjoying today as being lazy and poorly motivated. In turn the present-oriented person may see those with strong future orientations as obsessed with accumulating wealth or rising in status.

Time and Status

Time is especially linked to status considerations. For example, the importance of being on time varies directly with the status of the individual you are visiting. If the person is extremely important, you had better be there on time. In fact, you had better be there early just in case he or she is able to see you ahead of schedule. As the individual's status decreases, it is less important for you to be on time. Students, for example, must be on time for conferences with teachers, but it is more important to be on time for deans and still more important to be on time for the president of the college. Teachers, on the other hand, may be late for conferences with students but not for conferences with deans or the president. Deans, in turn, may be late for teachers but not for the president. Business organizations and other hierarchies have similar rules.

Even the time of dinner and the time from the arrival of guests to eating varies on the basis of status. Among lower-status individuals, dinner is served relatively early. If there are guests, they eat soon after they arrive. For higher-status people, dinner is relatively late, and a longer time elapses between arrival and eating.

Time and Appropriateness

Promptness or lateness in responding to letters, returning telephone calls, acknowledging gifts, and returning invitations all communicate significant messages to others. We can analyze these messages on such scales as interest-disinterest, organized-disorganized, considerate-inconsiderate, sociable-unsociable, and so on.

Also, there are times when certain activities are considered appropriate and other times when they are

SELF-TEST

what time do you have?

For each statement, indicate whether the statement is true (T) of your general attitude and behavior, or false (F) of your general attitude and behavior. (A few statements are purposely repeated to facilitate scoring and analyzing your responses.)

_____ 1. Meeting tomorrow's deadlines and doing other necessary work comes before tonight's partying.
_____ 2. I meet my obligations to friends and authorities on time.
_____ 3. I complete projects on time by making steady progress.
_____ 4. I am able to resist temptations when I know there is work to be done.
_____ 5. I keep working at a difficult, uninteresting task if it will help me get ahead.
_____ 6. If things don't get done on time, I don't worry about it.
_____ 7. I think that it's useless to plan too far ahead because things hardly ever come out the way you planned anyway.
_____ 8. I try to live one day at a time.
_____ 9. I live to make better what is rather than to be concerned about what will be.
_____10. It seems to me that it doesn't make sense to worry about the future, since fate determines that whatever will be, will be.
_____11. I believe that getting together with friends to party is one of life's important pleasures.
_____12. I do things impulsively, making decisions on the spur of the moment.
_____13. I take risks to put excitement in my life.
_____14. I get drunk at parties.
_____15. It's fun to gamble.
_____16. Thinking about the future is pleasant to me.
_____17. When I want to achieve something, I set subgoals and consider specific means for reaching these goals.
_____18. It seems to me that my career path is pretty well laid out.
_____19. It upsets me to be late for appointments.
_____20. I meet my obligations to friends and authorities on time.
_____21. I get irritated at people who keep me waiting when we've agreed to meet at a given time.
_____22. It makes sense to invest a substantial part of my income in insurance premiums.
_____23. I believe that "a stitch in time saves nine."
_____24. I believe that "a bird in the hand is worth two in the bush."
_____25. I believe it is important to save for a rainy day.
_____26. I believe a person's day should be planned each morning.
_____27. I make lists of things I must do.
_____28. When I want to achieve something, I set subgoals and consider specific means for reaching those goals.
_____29. I believe that "a stitch in time saves nine."

Thinking Critically About Time Communication. This time test measures seven different factors. If you scored True for all or most of the questions within any given factor, then you are probably high on that factor. If you scored False for all or most of the questions within any given factor, then you are probably low on that factor's scale.

The first factor, measured by questions 1 through 5, is a future, work motivation, perseverance orientation. People with this orientation have a strong work ethic and are committed to completing a task despite difficulties and temptations.

The second factor, measured by questions 6 through 10, is a present, fatalistic, worry free orientation. People who score high on this factor live one day at a time, not necessarily to enjoy the day but to avoid planning for the next day and to avoid the anxiety about a future that seems determined by fate rather than by anything they can do themselves.

The third factor, measured by questions 11 through 15, is a present, hedonistic, pleasure-seeking, partying orientation. These people seek to enjoy the present, take risks and engage in a variety of impulsive actions. Teenagers score particularly high on this factor.

The fourth factor, measured by questions 16 through 18, is a future, goal-seeking, and planning orientation. These people derive special pleasure from planning and achieving a variety of goals.

The fifth factor, measured by questions 19 through 21, is a time sensitivity orientation. People who score high on this factor are especially sensitive to time and its role in social obligations.

The sixth factor, measured by questions 22 through 25, is a future, pragmatic action orientation. These people do what they have to do to achieve the future they want. They take practical actions for future gain.

The seventh factor, measured by questions 26 through 29, is a future, somewhat obsessive daily planning orientation. People who score high on this factor make daily "to do" lists, devoting great attention to specific details and subordinate goals.

Source: From "Time in Perspective" by Alexander Gonzalez and Philip G. Zimbardo, *Psychology Today* 19, March 1985. Reprinted with permission from Psychology Today Magazine, Copyright © 1985 Sussex Publishers, Inc.

considered inappropriate. Thus, it is permissible to make a social phone call during the late morning, afternoon, and early evening, but not before 8 or 9 o'clock in the morning, during dinnertime, or after 11 o'clock at night. Similarly, in making dates, an appropriate amount of notice is customary. When you give that acceptable amount of notice, you communicate a recognition of the accepted standards, respect for the individual, and perhaps a certain social grace. Should you violate any of these time conventions, however, you would communicate other meanings. For example, a phone call at an abnormal hour will almost surely communicate urgency of some sort. You begin to worry as you race toward the phone.

SUMMARY

In this unit we began exploring nonverbal communication and looked at the movements of the body, face, and eyes and at paralanguage and silence and the meanings communicated by these movements.

1. Emblems are nonverbal behaviors that rather directly translate words or phrases.
2. Illustrators are nonverbal behaviors that accompany and literally illustrate the verbal messages.
3. Affect displays are nonverbal movements that communicate emotional meaning.
4. Regulators are nonverbal movements that coordinate, monitor, maintain, or control the speaking of another individual.
5. Adaptors are nonverbal behaviors that are emitted without conscious awareness and that usually serve some kind of need, as in scratching an itch.
6. Facial movements may communicate a wide variety of emotions. The most frequently studied are happiness, surprise, fear, anger, sadness, and disgust/contempt. Communications of these six emotions are referred to as primary affect displays.
7. Micromomentary expressions are extremely brief movements that are not consciously perceived and that are thought to reveal a person's real emotional state.
8. Eye movements may serve to seek feedback, to inform others to speak, to signal the nature of a relationship, and to compensate for increased physical distance.
9. Pupil size seems indicative of interest and level of emotional arousal. Pupils enlarge when you are interested in something or when you are emotionally aroused in a positive way.
10. Paralanguage (variations in sound) provides cues for impression formation, for identifying emotional states, for judgments about people, and for judgments about communication (credibility, comprehension, and preferences).
11. Silence communicates just as surely as do words and gestures and can provide thinking time, hurt another person, hide anxiety, prevent communication, and communicate feelings.
12. Time may be viewed from at least two perspectives: cultural and psychological. Cultural time is concerned with how our culture defines and teaches time, and with the difficulties created by the different meanings people have for informal time terms, differences between displaced and diffused time orientations, and monochronic and polychronic orientation. Psychological time is concerned with people's time orientations, whether past, present, or future.
13. The messages that time communicates are greatly influenced by status considerations and by the social rules for appropriateness and inappropriateness.

THINKING CRITICALLY ABOUT NONVERBAL MESSAGES OF BODY, SOUND, AND TIME

1. Do you find that adaptors give the impression of discomfort and being ill at ease? If so, why do you suppose this is true?
2. Try to test the facial feedback hypothesis by smiling. Hold the smile for a minute or so. Did smiling increase your sense of well-being and happiness?
3. Research shows that women smile more than men, even when making negative comments or expressing negative feelings (see Shannon 1987). What implications

does this have for male-female communication? What implications might this have for child rearing? For teaching? For success in a multinational corporation?

4. What nonverbal cues do you use in judging whether someone likes you or not? How accurate have your judgments been?
5. How do you interpret eye avoidance? What impressions do you develop about a person who avoids maintaining eye contact while talking with you?
6. Have you ever given someone "the silent treatment"? Has someone ever done this to you? What effects did it have?
7. How would you describe the meanings a member's silence communicates in, say, a corporate meeting? A student's silence in a classroom?
8. Another type of time often mentioned is that of biological time, which refers to our body clocks, the ways our bodies function differently at different times. Our intellectual, physical, and emotional lives, according to theories of biorhythms, are lived in cycles. During the up cycle, we function at our best; during the down cycle we function less effectively; and during the changes from an up to a down cycle, we are especially vulnerable to, for example, writer's block, catching cold, or feeling depressed. What do you think of this theory? Detailed explanations and instructions for calculating your biorhythms (your own intellectual, physical, and emotional cycles) can be found in Luce (1971), O'Neil and Phillips (1975), and Mallardi (1978).
9. What time orientation operates in your family? Your school? Your workplace? If these differ, do the differences create any difficulties for you?
10. How would you go about finding answers to such questions as these:
    a. What meanings do adaptors communicate in business meetings?
    b. Are there situations in which men are more facially expressive than women?
    c. Is the facial feedback hypothesis applicable to both positive and negative emotions? Can it explain changes from one emotion to another as well as the strengthening or lessening of an emotional feeling?
    d. Do men and women differ in their sensitivity to the pupil dilations of others?
    e. Do different religions promote different time orientations?

eleven unit

Nonverbal Messages of Space, Touch, Smell, and Artifact

unit contents

unit goals

After completing this unit, you should be able to

1. explain the four spatial distances and give examples of the kinds of communication that take place at each distance
2. define *territoriality*
3. explain the types of territorial encroachment and possible reactions to it
4. define *marker* and distinguish among central, boundary, and earmarkers
5. explain the meanings communicated by touch
6. explain the factors that influence whom one touches and where
7. explain the nature of touch avoidance and its relationship to apprehension, self-disclosure, age, and sex
8. explain the nature of artifactual communication and how such messages are communicated

In addition to communicating with words and with our hands, face, and eyes, we communicate with space, territoriality, touch, smell, and artifact. These forms of nonverbal communication figure in almost every communication transaction. In this unit, we focus on how these systems operate in human communication.

PROXEMICS

The use of space speaks as surely and as loudly as words and sentences. A speaker who stands close to her listener, with her hands on the listener's shoulders and her eyes focused directly on those of the listener, communicates something very different from the speaker who sits crouched in a corner with his arms folded and his eyes on the floor. Similarly, the penthouse executive suite with huge windows, private bar, and plush carpeting communicates something very different from the 6-foot-square cubicle occupied by the rest of the workers.

This study of the communicative function of space is called **proxemics,** a term coined by anthropologist Edward T. Hall (1963). In our discussion we focus first on the four major spatial distances that people maintain when they communicate. Second, we look at public space. Third, we examine some of the influences on these spatial distances. Fourth, we look at some of the theories of space communication.

Spatial Distances

Edward Hall (1959, 1966) distinguishes four distances that define the type of relationship permitted (see Figure 11.1).

Intimate Distance

Intimate distance ranges from a close phase of actual touching to a far phase of 6 to 18 inches; from this distance, the presence of the other individual is unmistakable. Each person experiences the sound, smell, and feel of the other's breath. You use the close phase for lovemaking and wrestling, for comforting and protecting. In the close phase the muscles and the skin communicate, while actual verbalizations play a minor role. In this close phase, even whispering has the effect of increasing the psychological distance between the two individuals.

The far phase allows you to touch another person by extending your hands. This distance is still so short that it is not considered proper in public. Because this distance feels inappropriate and uncomfortable with nonintimates (at least for Americans), the eyes seldom meet. They remain fixed on some remote object.

Personal Distance

Each of us, says Hall, carries around a protective bubble defining our **personal distance.** This bubble keeps you protected and untouched by others. In the close phase of personal distance ($1\frac{1}{2}$ to $2\frac{1}{2}$ feet), you can still hold or grasp another person but only by extending your arms. You take into your protective bubble only certain individuals, for example, loved ones. In the far phase ($2\frac{1}{2}$ to 4 feet), two people can touch each other only if they both extend their arms. This far phase represents the extent to which you can physically get your hands on people. As a result, it defines, in one sense, the limits of our physical control over others.

Even at this distance you can see many details of an individual—the gray hairs, tooth stains, clothing lint, and so on. However, you can no longer detect body heat.

FIGURE 11.1 Proxemic distances. Most people would agree that our relationships determine our proxemic distances; intimate relationships create intimate distances and public relationships create public distances, for example. Could you make a case for the reverse assumption, namely that our proxemic distances influence (even determine) our relationships?

At times you may detect breath odor, but at this distance etiquette demands that you direct your breath to some neutral corner so as not to offend (as television commercials warn that you might do).

When personal space is invaded, you often become uncomfortable and tense. Your speech may become disrupted, unsteady, jerky, and staccato. You may have difficulty maintaining eye contact and may frequently look away from the person. This discomfort may also reveal itself in excessive body movement. At other times you do not mind the invasion of personal space—for example, when others enter your personal space bubble at a crowded party. Similarly, when people you like come close to you, you perceive the situation as being less crowded than when less-liked people enter the same space. People you like crowd you psychologically less than people you do not like.

Social Distance

At **social distance** you lose the visual detail you have in personal distance. The close phase (4 to 7 feet) is the distance at which you conduct impersonal business and interact at social gatherings. The far phase (7 to 12 feet) is the distance at which you stand when someone says, "Stand back so I can look at you." At this distance, business transactions have a more formal tone. In offices of high officials desks are positioned so that the official is assured of at least this distance when dealing with clients. Unlike intimate distance, where eye contact is awkward, the far phase of social distance makes eye contact essential. Otherwise, communication would be lost. The voice is generally 1ouder than normal at this distance. Shouting or raising the voice, however, has the effect of reducing the social distance to a personal distance.

Public Distance

In the close phase of **public distance** (12 to 15 feet), a person is protected by space. At this distance a person could take defensive action when threatened. On a public bus or train, for example, you might keep at least this distance from a drunkard. Although at this distance you lose fine details of the face and eyes, you are still close enough to see what is happening.

At the far phase (more than 25 feet), you see people not as separate individuals but as part of the whole setting. You automatically allow about 30 feet of space around important public figures, and, it seems, you do this whether or not there are guards preventing you from entering this space. This far phase is of course the distance from which actors perform on stage. At this distance, actions and voices have to be somewhat exaggerated to convey detail.

Influences on Space Communication

Several factors influence the way you treat space in communication, and a number of generalizations are especially important to communication (Burgoon, Buller, & Woodall 1989).

Culture

Americans stand fairly far apart when conversing, at least compared with people in certain European and Middle Eastern cultures. Arabs, for example, stand much closer to each other than do Americans. Italians and Spaniards likewise maintain less distance in their interactions than many northern Europeans.

In the United States, if you live next door to someone, then you are almost automatically expected to be friendly and to interact with that person. This cultural expectation is not shared by all cultures. In Japan, for example, the fact that your house is next to another person's house does not imply that you should become close or that you should visit each other. Consider, therefore, the situation in which a Japanese buys a house next to an American. The Japanese may well see the American as overly familiar and as taking friendship for granted. The American may see the Japanese as distant, unfriendly, and unneighborly. Yet each person is merely fulfilling the expectations of his or her own culture (Hall & Hall 1987).

Status

People of equal status maintain a shorter distance between themselves than do people of unequal status. When the status is unequal, the higher-status person may approach the lower-status person more closely than the lower-status person may approach the higher-status person.

Context

Generally, the larger the physical space you are in, the smaller the interpersonal space. Thus, for example, the space between two people conversing will be smaller in the street than in an apartment. The larger the space, the more you seem to need to close it off to make the immediate communication context manageable.

Subject Matter

If you talk about personal matters or share secrets, you maintain a short distance. When you talk about impersonal, general matters, the space is generally larger. Psychologically, it seems you are trying to exclude others from hearing even though physically there may be no one within earshot. You maintain a shorter distance if you are being praised than if you are being blamed. Perhaps you want to move in closer to the praise lest it fall on someone else, and perhaps you try to remove yourself (physically) from blame.

Sex and Age

Women stand closer to one another than men do. Opposite-sex pairs stand the farthest apart. Similarly, in most of the United States women are "allowed" to touch each other more than men and more than unacquainted opposite-sex pairs. Children stand closer to each other than do adults, showing that maintained distance is a learned behavior.

In a study of space violations, two people were positioned across from each other in a busy hallway; they were arranged so that there was enough space for another person to either go around them or between them. Most often, people do not violate the dyad and prefer to go around a couple in conversation. When this dyadic space was violated, however, it was found that both men and women were more likely to invade the space of two women rather than that between a man and a woman or between two men (Lomax 1994).

Positive and Negative Evaluation

You stand farther from enemies, authority figures, and higher-status individuals than from friends and peers. You maintain a greater distance from people you see as different from yourself, for example, in race or in physical condition. Typically, you maintain more distance between yourself and people you may unconsciously evaluate negatively.

How culturally universal do you think these four spatial distances and their corresponding relationships are? Can you think of a culture that does not make these same connections between space and its appropriate type of interaction? Do men and women generally follow the same rules concerning spatial distances?

Theories About Space

A number of researchers of nonverbal communication have offered explanations as to why people maintain the distances they do. Prominent among these theories are protection theory, equilibrium theory, and expectancy violation theory—rather complex names for simple and interesting explanations.

Protection Theory

Protection theory holds that you establish a body buffer zone around yourself as protection against unwanted touching or attack (Dosey & Meisels 1976). When you feel that you may be attacked, your body buffer zone increases, you want more space around you. For example, if you found yourself in a dangerous neighborhood at night, your body buffer zone would probably expand well beyond what it would be if you were in familiar and safe surroundings. If someone entered this buffer zone, you would probably feel threatened and seek to expand that distance by walking faster or crossing the street.

On the other hand, when you are feeling secure and protected, your buffer zone becomes much smaller. For example, if you are with a group of close friends and feel secure, your buffer zone would shrink and you may welcome the close distances and mutual touching.

Equilibrium Theory

Equilibrium theory holds that intimacy and distance vary together. The greater the intimacy, the closer the distance; the lower the intimacy, the greater the distance. This theory says that you maintain close distances with those with whom you have close interpersonal relationships and that you maintain greater distances with those with whom you do not have close relationships (Argyle & Dean 1965).

At times, of course, your interpersonal distance does not accurately reflect your level of intimacy. When this happens you make adjustments. For example, let us say that you have an intimate relationship with someone but for some reason you are separated—perhaps because you could not get concert seats next to each other or you are at a party and have each been led to different parts of a large banquet hall. When this happens you would probably try to preserve your psychological closeness by maintaining frequent eye contact or perhaps by facing each other.

At other times, however, you are forced into close distances with someone with whom you are not intimate (or may even dislike), for example, on a crowded bus or perhaps in the dentist's chair. In these situations, you also compensate, but this time you seek to make the psychological distance greater. You therefore might avoid eye contact and turn in an opposite direction. In the dentist's chair you probably close your eyes to decrease this normally intimate distance. If seated to the right of a stranger, you might cross your legs and turn your torso to the left.

Expectancy Violations Theory

Expectancy violations theory explains what happens when you increase or decrease the distance between yourself and another in an interpersonal interaction (Burgoon 1978; Burgoon, Buller, & Woodall 1989). Each culture has certain expectancies for the distance that people are expected to maintain in their conversations. Of course, each person has certain idiosyncrasies. Together these determine "expected distance." What happens when these expectations are violated?

If you violate the expected distance to a great extent—small violations most often go unnoticed—then the relationship itself comes into focus. Then the other person begins to turn attention away from the topic of conversation to you and to your relationship with him or her.

If this other person perceives you positively—for example, you are a high-status person or you are particularly attractive—then you will be perceived even more positively if you violate the norm. If, on the other hand, you are perceived negatively and you violate the norm, you will be perceived even more negatively. Thus, the positively evaluated person will be perceived more positively if he or she violates the norm, while the negatively evaluated person will be more positively perceived if the distance norm is not violated.

TERRITORIALITY

One of the most interesting concepts in ethology (the study of animals in their natural surroundings) is **territoriality.** For example, male animals will stake out a particular territory and consider it their own. They will allow prospective mates to enter but will defend it against entrance by others, especially other males of the same species. Among deer, the size of the territory signifies the power of the buck, which in turn determines how many females he will mate with. Less powerful bucks will be able to control only small parcels of land and so will mate with only one or two females. This is a particularly adaptive measure, since it ensures that the stronger members will produce most of the offspring. When the "landowner" takes possession of an area—either because it is vacant or because he gains it through battle—he marks it, for example, by urinating around the boundaries. The size of the animal's territory indicates the status of the animal within the herd.

The size and location of human territory also say something about status (Mehrabian 1976; Sommer 1969). An apartment or office in midtown Manhattan or downtown Tokyo, for example, indicates extremely high status. The cost of the territory restricts it to those who have lots of money.

Status is also signaled by the unwritten law granting the right of invasion. Higher-status individuals have more of a right to invade the territory of others than vice versa. The boss of a large company, for example, can invade the territory of a junior executive by barging into her or his office, but the reverse would be unthinkable.

Some researchers claim that territoriality is innate and demonstrates the innate aggressiveness of humans. Others claim that territoriality is learned behavior and is culturally based. Most, however, agree that a great deal of human behavior can be understood and described as territorial, regardless of its origin.

Types of Territories

THINK ABOUT

Think about how you would act in these three different types of territories: primary, secondary, and public (Altman 1975).

Primary Territory

Primary territories are your exclusive preserve; your desk, room, house, or backyard, for example. In these areas you are in control. It's similar to the home field advantage that a sports team has when playing in its own ballpark. When you are in these primary areas, you generally have greater influence over others than you would in someone else's territory. For example, when in their own home or office people take on a kind of leadership role; they initiate conversations, fill in silences, assume relaxed and comfortable postures, and maintain their positions with greater conviction. Because the territorial owner is dominant, you stand a better chance of getting your raise, your point accepted, and the contract resolved in your favor if you are in your own primary territory (Marsh 1988).

Secondary Territory

Secondary territories, although they do not belong to you, are associated with you perhaps because you have occupied them for a long period of time or they have been assigned to you. For example, your desk in a classroom may be a secondary territory if it was assigned to you or if you have regularly occupied it and others treat it as yours. Your neighborhood turf, a cafeteria table that you regularly occupy, or a favorite corner of a local coffee shop may be secondary territories. You feel a certain "ownership-like" attachment to the place although it is really not yours in any legal sense.

Public Territory

Public territories are those areas that are open to all people: a park, movie house, restaurant, or beach, for example. The European café, the food court in a suburban mall, and the public spaces in large city office buildings are public spaces that, although established for eating, also serve to bring people together and to stimulate communication. The electronic revolution, however, may well change the role of public space in stimulating communication (Drucker & Gumpert 1991, Gumpert & Drucker 1995). For example, home shopping clubs make it less necessary for people to go shopping "downtown" or to the mall, and consequently they have less opportunity to run into other people and to talk and to exchange news. Similarly, electronic mail permits communication without talking and without even going out of one's home to mail a letter. Perhaps the greatest change is telecommuting (Giordano 1989) which allows people to work without even leaving their homes. The face-to-face communication that normally takes place in an office is replaced by communication via computer.

Territorial Encroachment

Look around your home. You probably see certain territories that different people have staked out and where invasions are cause for at least mildly defensive action. This is perhaps seen most clearly with siblings who each have (or "own") a specific chair, room, radio, and so on. Father has his chair and Mother has her chair.

In classrooms where seats are not assigned, territoriality can also be observed. When a student sits in a seat that has normally been occupied by another student, the regular occupant will often become disturbed and resentful.

Following Lyman and Scott (1967; DeVito & Hecht 1990), Table 11.1 identifies the three major types of territorial encroachment: violation, invasion, and contamination.

You can react to encroachment in several ways (Lyman & Scott 1967; DeVito & Hecht 1990). The most extreme form is **turf defense.** When you cannot tolerate the intruders, you may choose to defend the territory against them and try to expel them. This is the method of gangs that defend "their" streets and neighborhoods by fighting off members of rival gangs (intruders) who enter the territory.

A less extreme defense is **insulation,** a tactic in which you erect some sort of barrier between yourself and the invaders. Some people do this by wearing sunglasses to avoid eye contact. Others erect fences to let others know that they do not welcome interpersonal interaction.

Linguistic collusion, another method of separating yourself from unwanted invaders, involves speaking in a language unknown to these outsiders. Or you might use professional jargon to which they are not privy. Linguistic collusion groups together those who speak that language and excludes those who do not know the linguistic code. Still another type of response is withdrawal; you leave the territory altogether.

Markers

Much as animals mark their territory, humans mark theirs with three types of markers: central, boundary, and earmarkers (Hickson & Stacks 1993). **Central markers** are items you place in a territory to reserve it. For example, you place a drink at the bar, books on your desk, and a sweater over the chair to let others know that this territory belongs to you.

Boundary markers set boundaries that divide your territory from "theirs." In the supermarket checkout line, the bar placed between your groceries and those of the person behind you is a boundary marker. Similarly, the armrests separating seats in movie theaters and the rises on each side of the molded plastic seats on a bus or train are boundary markers.

Earmarkers—a term taken from the practice of branding animals on their ears—are those identifying marks that indicate your possession of a territory or

TABLE 11.1
three types of territorial encroachment

Name	Definition	Example
Violation	Unwarranted use of another's territory and thereby changing the meaning of that territory	Entering another's office or home without permission
Invasion	Entering the territory of another and thereby changing the meaning of that territory	Parents entering a teen's social group
Contamination	Rendering a territory impure	Smoking a cigar in a kitchen

object. Trademarks, nameplates, and initials on a shirt or attache case are all examples of earmarkers.

TOUCH COMMUNICATION

Touch communication, also referred to as **haptics,** is perhaps the most primitive form of communication (Montagu 1971). Developmentally, touch is probably the first sense to be used. Even in the womb the fetus is stimulated by touch. Soon after birth the infant is fondled, caressed, patted, and stroked. In turn, the baby explores its world through touch. In a short time, the child learns to communicate a wide variety of meanings through touch.

The Meanings of Touch

Touch communicates a wide variety of messages (Jones & Yarbrough 1985). Here are five major ones that will illustrate this great variety.

Positive Affect

Touch often communicates positive emotions. This occurs mainly between intimates or others who have a relatively close relationship. "Touch is such a powerful signalling system," notes Desmond Morris (1972), "and it's so closely related to emotional feelings we have for one another that in casual encounters it's kept to a minimum. When the relationship develops, the touching follows along with it." Among the most important of these positive emotions are support, appreciation, inclusion, sexual interest or intent, and affection (Jones & Yarbrough 1985). Additional research found that touch communicated such positive feelings as composure, immediacy, affection, trust, similarity and quality, and informality (Burgoon 1991). Touch has also been found to facilitate self-disclosure (Rabinowitz 1991).

Playfulness

Touch often communicates our intention to play, either affectionately or aggressively. When you communicate affection or aggression in a playful manner, the playfulness lessens the emotion and tells the other person not to take it seriously. Playful touch lightens an interaction.

Control

Touch may also direct the behaviors, attitudes, or feelings of the other person. Such control may communicate a number of messages. In compliance, for example, you touch the other person to communicate "move over," "hurry," "stay here," and "do it." You might also touch a person to gain his or her attention, as if to say "look at me" or "look over here."

Touching to control sometimes communicates dominance as well (Burgoon 1991). Consider, as Nancy Henley suggests in her *Body Politics* (1977), who would touch whom—say, by putting an arm on the other person's shoulder or by putting a hand on the other person's back—in the following dyads: teacher and student, doctor and patient, master and servant, manager and worker, minister and parishioner, police officer and accused, business executive and secretary. Most people brought up in American culture would say that the first-named person in each dyad would more likely touch the second-named person than the other way around. In other words, the higher-status person is permitted to touch the lower-status person. It would be a breach of etiquette for the lower-status person to touch the person of higher status.

Henley further argues that in addition to indicating relative status, touching demonstrates the assertion of male power and dominance over women. Men may, says Henley, touch women in the course of their daily routine. In the restaurant, office, and school, for example, men touch women and thus indicate their "superior status." When women touch men, on the other hand, the interpretation that it designates a female-dominant relationship is not acceptable (to men). Men may therefore explain and interpret this touching as a sexual invitation.

Ritual

Ritualistic touching centers on greetings and departures. Shaking hands to say "hello" or "good-bye" is a clear example of ritualistic touching. Ritualistic touching also includes hugging, kissing, or putting your arm around another's shoulder when greeting someone or saying farewell. Ritualistic touching is of course greatly influenced by culture. In Mediterranean cultures, for example, men hug each other in their greeting ritual; men in the United States, on the other hand, shake hands and would usually hug only if they are close relatives or under extraordinary circumstances.

Task-Relatedness

Task-related touching is associated with the performance of some function. This ranges from removing a speck of dust from another person's face to helping someone out of a car or checking someone's forehead for fever.

Who Touches Whom Where

A great deal of research has been directed at the question of who touches whom where. Most of it has addressed two basic questions: First, are there gender differences? Do men and women communicate through touch in the same way? Are men and women touched in the same way? Second, are there cultural differences? Do people in widely different cultures communicate through touch in the same way?

Gender Differences and Touch

Early research reported that touching and being touched differ little between men and women (Jourard 1968). Men touch and are touched as often and in the same places as women. The major exception to this finding is the touching behavior of mothers and fathers. Mothers touch children of both sexes and of all ages more than do fathers. In fact, many fathers go no further than touching the hands of their children. More recent research has found differences.

Contrary to popular stereotype, research shows that females initiate more opposite-sex touching (especially more opposite-sex touching designed to control) than do men (Jones 1986). In another study, women were found to initiate touch more in married relationships and less in casual romantic relationships than did men (Guerrero & Andersen 1994).

Opposite-sex friends report more touching than do same-sex friends. Both male and female college students report that they touch and are touched more by their opposite-sex friends than by their same-sex friends. No doubt the strong societal bias against same-sex touching accounts for these generalizations.

Culture Differences and Touch

Students from the United States reported being touched twice as much as did students from Japan (Barnlund 1975). In Japan there is a strong taboo against touching between strangers. The Japanese are therefore especially careful to maintain sufficient distance.

Another obvious cross-cultural contrast is displayed in the Middle East, where same-sex touching in public is extremely common. Men, for example, walk with their arms around each other's shoulders—a practice that would cause many raised eyebrows in the United States. Middle Easterners, Latin Americans, and southern Europeans touch each other while talking a great deal more than do people from "noncontact cultures"—Asia and northern Europe, for example.

Even such seemingly minor nonverbal differences as these can create difficulties when members of different cultures interact. Southern Europeans may perceive northern Europeans and Japanese as cold, distant, and uninvolved. Southern Europeans in turn may be perceived as pushy, aggressive, and inappropriately intimate.

Touch Avoidance

Much as you have a need and desire to touch and be touched, you also have a tendency to avoid touch from certain people or in certain circumstances (Andersen & Leibowitz 1978). You may wish to examine your own tendency by taking the self-test, "Do You Avoid Touch?"

Based on the self-test presented here, a number of interesting connections between touch avoidance and other factors were found (Andersen & Liebowitz 1978). For example, touch avoidance is positively related to communication apprehension. If you have a strong fear of oral communication then you probably also have strong touch-avoidance tendencies. Touch avoidance is also high with those who self-disclose less.

Both touch and self-disclosure are intimate forms of communication. People who are reluctant to get close to another person by self-disclosing also seem reluctant to get close by touching.

Older people avoid touch with opposite-sex persons more than do younger people. As people get older they are touched less by members of the opposite sex; this decreased frequency of touching may lead them to avoid touching.

Males avoid same-sex touch more than do females. This accords well with current stereotypes. Men avoid touching other men, but women may and do touch other women. Andersen and Liebowitz (1978) also found that women say they avoid touching opposite-sex members more than do men. This male-female difference is contrary to that found by Jones (1986) who reports that women initiate more opposite-sex touching than do men. Women also report feeling less positively about opposite-sex touching than do men (Guerrero & Andersen 1994).

SELF-TEST

do you avoid touch?

This instrument is composed of 18 statements concerning how you feel about touching other people and being touched. Please indicate the degree to which each statement applies to you by indicating whether you

1 = strongly agree
2 = agree
3 = are undecided
4 = disagree
5 = strongly disagree

______ 1. A hug from a same-sex friend is a true sign of friendship.
______ 2. Opposite-sex friends enjoy it when I touch them.
______ 3. I often put my arm around friends of the same sex.
______ 4. When I see two friends of the same sex hugging, it revolts me.
______ 5. I like it when members of the opposite sex touch me.
______ 6. People shouldn't be so uptight about touching persons of the same sex.
______ 7. I think it is vulgar when members of the opposite sex touch me.
______ 8. When a member of the opposite sex touches me, I find it unpleasant.
______ 9. I wish I were free to show emotions by touching members of same sex.
______10. I'd enjoy giving a massage to an opposite-sex friend.
______11. I enjoy kissing a person of the same sex.
______12. I like to touch friends that are the same sex as I am.
______13. Touching a friend of the same sex does not make me uncomfortable.
______14. I find it enjoyable when my date and I embrace.
______15. I enjoy getting a back rub from a member of the opposite sex.
______16. I dislike kissing relatives of the same sex.
______17. Intimate touching with members of the opposite sex is pleasurable.
______18. I find it difficult to be touched by a member of my own sex.

Thinking Critically About Touch Avoidance. To score your Touch Avoidance Questionnaire:

1. Reverse your scores for items 4, 7, 8, 16, and 18. For example, if you scored 1, reverse it to 5; if you scored 2, reverse it to 4; if you scored 3, it remains 3; if you scored 4, reverse it to 2, and if you scored 5, reverse it to 1. Use these reversed scores in all future calculations.
2. To obtain your same-sex touch avoidance score (the extent to which you avoid touching members of your sex), total the scores for items 1, 3, 4, 6, 9, 11, 12, 13, 16, and 18.
3. To obtain your opposite-sex touch avoidance score (the extent to which you avoid touching members of the opposite sex), total the scores for items 2, 5, 7, 8, 10, 14, 15, and 17.
4. To obtain your total touch avoidance score, add the subtotals from steps 2 and 3.

The higher the score, the higher the touch avoidance—that is, the greater your tendency to avoid touch. In studies by Andersen and Leibowitz (1978), who constructed this test, average opposite-sex touch avoidance scores for males was 12.9 and for females 14.85. Average same sex touch avoidance scores were 26.43 for males and 21.70 for females. How do your scores compare with those college students in Andersen and Leibowitz's study? Is your touch avoidance likely to be higher when interacting with persons who are culturally different from you? Can you identify types of people and types of situations in which your touch avoidance would be especially high? Especially low?

SMELL COMMUNICATION

Smell communication, or **olfactics,** is extremely important in a wide variety of situations and is now "big business" (Kleinfeld 1992). Odor can communicate a wide variety of messages. Here are some of the most important.

Attraction Messages

In many animal species the female gives off a scent that draws males, often from afar, and thus ensures the continuation of the species. Humans use perfumes, colognes, after-shave lotions, powders, and the like to enhance attractiveness. Sophia Loren, Elizabeth Taylor, Cher, and, more recently, Billy Dee Williams, all sell perfumes by associating their own attractiveness with the fragrance. The implication is that others can smell likewise and can therefore be equally attractive.

You also use odors to make yourself feel better; after all, you also smell yourself. When the smells are pleasant, you feel better about yourself; when the smells are unpleasant, you feel less good about yourself and probably shower and perhaps put on some cologne.

Taste Messages

Without smell, taste would be severely impaired. For example, it would be extremely difficult to taste the difference between a raw potato and an apple without the sense of smell. Street vendors selling hot dogs, sausages, and similar foods are aided greatly by the smells that stimulate the appetites of passersby.

Memory Messages

Smell is a powerful memory aid; you can often recall situations from months and even years ago when you happen upon a similar smell. One reason why smell can so effectively recall a previous situation is that it is often associated with significant emotional experiences (Rubin, Groth, & Goldsmith 1984; Malandro, Barker, & Barker 1989).

Identification Messages

Smell is often used to create an image or an identity for a product. Advertisers and manufacturers spend millions of dollars each year creating scents for cleaning products and toothpastes, for example, which have nothing to do with their cleaning power. Instead, they function solely to help create an image for the product. There is also evidence that we can identify specific significant others by smell. For example, young children were able to identify the t-shirts of their brothers and sisters solely on the basis of smell (Porter & Moore 1981).

ARTIFACTUAL COMMUNICATION

Artifactual messages are those made by human hands. Thus, color, clothing, jewelry, and the decoration of space would be considered artifactual. We look at each of these here briefly.

Color Communication

THINK ABOUT

Think about the wide variety of meanings that colors can communicate. Before looking at Table 11.3, think about the meanings your own culture(s) gives to such colors as red, green, black, white, blue, yellow, and purple.

There is some evidence that colors affect you physiologically. For example, when subjects are exposed to red light, respiratory movements increase; exposure to blue light decreases respiratory movements. Similarly, eye blinks increase in frequency when eyes are exposed to red light and decrease when exposed to blue. This seems consistent with intuitive feelings about blue being more soothing and red being more arousing. After changing a school's walls from orange and white to blue, the blood pressure of the students decreased while their academic performance improved (Mella 1988).

Colors also influence perceptions and behaviors (Kanner 1989). Consumer acceptance of a product, advertisers find, is largely determined by packaging. For example, the very same coffee taken from a yellow can was described by subjects as weak, from a dark brown can too strong, from a red can rich, and from a blue can mild. Even acceptance of a person may depend on the colors worn. Consider, for example, the comments of one color expert (Kanner 1989): "If you have to pick the wardrobe for your defense lawyer heading into court and choose anything but blue, you deserve to lose the case." Black is so powerful it could work against the lawyer with the jury. Brown lacks sufficient authority. Green would probably elicit a negative response.

Clothing and Body Adornment

In addition to any legible messages, as discussed in the Media Watch box, clothing serves a variety of additional functions. It protects you from the weather and, in sports like football, from injury. It helps you conceal parts of your body and thus serves a modesty function. Clothing also serves as a cultural display by communicating your cultural affiliations (Morris 1977). In the United States, where there are so many different ethnic groups, you regularly see examples of dress that tell you the wearer's country of origin.

People make inferences about who you are in part by the way you dress. Whether these inferences prove to be accurate or inaccurate, they will nevertheless influence what people think of you and how they react to you. Your social class, your seriousness, your attitudes (for example, whether you are conservative or liberal), your concern for convention, your sense of style, and perhaps even your creativity will all be judged partly from the way you dress. In fact, the very popular *Dress for Success, The Woman's Dress for Success Book,* and *Molloys Live for Success* (Molloy 1975, 1977, 1981) all instruct men and women in how to dress so that they can communicate a number of desirable images—for example, efficiency, reliability, power, or authoritativeness. Similarly, college students will perceive an instructor dressed informally as friendly, fair, enthusiastic, and flexible, and the same instructor dressed formally as prepared, knowledgeable, and organized (Malandro, Barker, & Barker 1989). In another study, male and female fourth-, seventh-, and ninth-grade students evaluated a female teacher dressed in three different ways (Phillips & Smith 1992). In casual clothing this teacher was perceived as friendly, fair, and interesting. Moderate attire communicated friendliness, organization, interestingness, understanding, and discipline. Conversative dress communicated organization, knowledge, and disciplinary skills.

Your jewelry likewise communicates messages about you. Wedding and engagement rings are obvious examples of jewelry that communicates very specific messages. College rings and political buttons also send specific messages. If you wear a Rolex watch or

TABLE 11.3

some cultural meanings of color

This table, constructed from the research reported by Henry Dreyfuss (1971) and Nancy Hoft (1995), illustrates only some of the different meanings that colors may communicate and especially how they are viewed in different cultures.

Color	Cultural Meanings and Comments
Red	In China red signifies prosperity and rebirth and is used for festive and joyous occasions; in France and the United Kingdom, masculinity; in many African countries, blasphemy or death; and in Japan it signifies anger and danger
Green	In the United States green signifies capitalism, go ahead, and envy; in Ireland, patriotism; among some Native Americans, femininity; to the Egyptians, fertility and strength; and to the Japanese, youth and energy
Black	In Thailand black signifies old age; in parts of Malaysia, courage; and in much of Europe, death
White	In Thailand white signifies purity; in many Muslim and Hindu cultures, purity and peace; and in Japan and other Asian countries, death and mourning
Blue	In Iran blue signifies something negative; in Egypt, truth; in Ghana joy; among the Cherokee, defeat; for the Egyptian, virtue and truth
Yellow	In China yellow signifies wealth and authority; in the United States, caution and cowardice; in Egypt, happiness and prosperity; and in many countries throughout the world, femininity
Purple	In Latin America purple signifies death; in Europe, royalty; in Egypt, virtue and faith; in Japan, grace and nobility; and in China, barbarism

MEDIA WATCH

LEGIBLE CLOTHING

Legible clothing is anything that you wear which contains some verbal message; such clothing can literally be read. In some instances it says status; it tells others that you are, for example, rich or stylish or youthful. The Gucci or Louis Vuitton logos on your luggage communicate your status and financial position. In a similar way your sweatshirt saying Bulls or Pirates communicates your interest in sports and perhaps your favorite team.

John Molloy (1981), in *Molloy's Live for Success,* advises you to avoid legible clothing except the kind that says rich. Legible clothing, argues Molloy, communicates lower status and lack of power. Humorist Fran Lebowitz says that legible clothes "are an unpleasant indication of the general state of things. I mean, be realistic. If people don't want to listen to you, what makes you think they want to hear from your sweater?"

Yet legible clothing is being bought and worn in record numbers. Many designers and manufacturers have their names integrated into the design of the clothing: DKNY, Calvin Klein, L.L. Bean, and Levi's are just a few examples. At the same time that you are paying extra to buy the brand name, you also provide free advertising for the designer and manufacturer. To paraphrase Vidal Sassoon, "As long as you look good, so does the advertiser. And, when you look bad, the advertiser looks bad." Imitators—the cheap knock-offs you see on the street—are resisted by the original manufacturers not only because these impact on their own sales. In fact, the impact is probably minimal since the person who would pay $6,000 for a Rolex would not buy a $10 imitation on the street. Rather, such knock-offs are resisted because they are perceived to be worn by the wrong people—people who would destroy the image the manufacturer wishes to communicate.

How do you feel about the legible clothing you see on your campus? On the street and generally in public places? What do these clothing messages tell you about the people wearing them? How would you go about studying the relationship between the meanings the wearer wants to communicate and the meanings derived by different viewers/readers?

T-shirts and sweatshirts are especially popular as message senders. In one study, the types of t-shirt messages were classified into four main categories (Sayre 1992). The order in which these are presented reflects the shirts the subjects (600 male and female college students) considered their favorites. Thirty-three percent, for example, considered affiliation message shirts their favorites while 17 percent considered those with personal messages their favorites. The order from most favorite down, was:

- Affiliation messages, for example, a club or school name. It communicates that you are a part of a larger group.
- Trophy, for example, a shirt from a high-status event such as a concert or perhaps a ski lodge. This is a way of saying that the wearer was in the right place.
- Metaphorical expressions, for example, pictures of rock groups or famous athletes.
- Personal messages, for example, "beliefs, philosophies and causes as well as satirizing current events" (Sayre 1992, p. 77).

Another important dimension of clothing, currently being debated in educational and legal circles, is the use of gang clothing (Burke 1993). Some argue that gang clothing and gang colors contribute to violence in the schools and should therefore be prohibited. Others argue that gang clothing—or any clothing—is covered by the first amendment to the Constitution. Consider a specific case. In Harvard, Illinois, you can be arrested for wearing a Star of David in public—not because it's a religious symbol, but because certain gangs use it as a gang symbol (*New York Times,* February 7, 1995, A12). In 1993, Harvard passed a law that make it illegal "for any person within the city to knowingly use, display or wear colors, emblems, or insignia" that would communicate their membership in (or sympathy for) gangs.

Consider your own use of legible clothing. Do you wear legible clothing? What messages do you wish to communicate? Are you successful in communicating the messages you want? Do labels influence your perceptions of others? How do you feel about the law in Harvard, Illinois? Would you support such a law in your own community?

large precious stones, others are likely to infer that you are rich. Men with earrings will be judged differently from men without earrings.

The way you wear your hair says something about who you are. Your hair may communicate a concern for being up-to-date, a desire to shock, or perhaps a lack of concern for appearances. Men with long hair will generally be judged as less conservative than will men with shorter hair.

In a study on interpersonal attraction, slides of male and female models with and without glasses were shown and were evaluated by both men and women. Results indicated that persons with glasses were rated more negatively than the very same persons without glasses (Hasart & Hutchinson 1993).

Clothing also seems to influence your own behavior and the behavior of groups. For example, it has been argued by organizational theorist David Morand [cited in *Psychology Today* 28 (March/April 1995), p. 16] that people who dress casually act more informally. Therefore, meetings with such casually dressed people are more likely to involve a freer exchange of thoughts and ideas, which stimulates creativity. This casual attire seems to work well in companies that must rely heavily on creative developments, such as a computer software company. It is interesting to note in this connection that it was only very recently that I.B.M. relaxed its conversative dress code and allowed some measure of informal dress among its workers (*New York Times,* February 7, 1995, p. B1). Banks and insurance companies, which traditionally have resisted change, tend to prefer a more formal attire that creates distance between workers as well as between employees and customers.

Space Decoration

The way you decorate your private spaces also communicates who you are. The office with mahogany desk and bookcases and oriental rugs communicates the occupant's importance and status within the organization, just as the metal desk and bare floors distinguishes a worker who is much further down in the hierarchy. Similarly, people will make inferences about you on the basis of the way you decorate your home. The luxuriousness of the furnishings may communicate your status and wealth; their coordination may communicate your sense of style. The magazines display your interests. The arrangement of chairs around a television set show how important watching television is to you. Bookcases lining the walls reveal the importance of reading. In fact, there is probably little in your home that does not send messages to others and that others do not use for making inferences about you. Computers, wide-screen televisions, well-equipped kitchens, and oil paintings of great grandparents, for example, all say something about the people who display them.

The lack of certain items will communicate something else about you. Consider, for example, what messages you would get from a home without a television, or one without a telephone or books.

THINK ABOUT

Think about the meanings that even animal images communicate. As sentinels in front of homes and businesses, these animals communicate meaning just as they might when worn as jewelry or when part of a corporate logo. Here are a few animals and their meanings in many diverse cultures (*New York Times* February 19, 1995, p. 4). Do they have additional or different meanings in your particular culture?

Dog = protection
Dove = peace
Eagle = power
Frog = reincarnation
Lion = supremacy

SUMMARY

In this unit we covered the nonverbal messages communicated by space, territory, touch, smell, and artifact, and we looked at some of the factors that influence these messages and some of the meanings these messages communicate.

1. Proxemics refers to the communicative function of space and spatial relationships.
2. Four major proxemic distances are: (1) intimate distance, ranging from actual touching to 18 inches; (2) personal distance, ranging from $1\frac{1}{2}$ to 4 feet; (3) social distance, ranging from 4 to 12 feet; and (4) public distance, ranging from 12 to more than 25 feet.
3. Our treatment of space is influenced by such factors as status, culture, context, subject matter, sex, age, and positive or negative evaluation of the other person.
4. Among the theories of space are protection theory (people establish a buffer zone for self-protection), equilibrium theory (intimacy and distance vary together), and expectancy violations theory (each culture has its own expectations concerning space and when that is violated the relationship between the parties comes into focus).
5. Territoriality refers to one's possessive reaction to an area of space or to particular objects.
6. Territorial encroachment may take any of three major forms: violation, invasion, and contamination.
7. You may react to territorial encroachment by turf defense, insulation, linguistic collusion, and withdrawal.
8. Markers are devices that identify a territory as yours; these include central markers, boundary markers, and earmarkers.
9. Touch communication (haptics) may communicate a variety of meanings, the most important being positive affect, playfulness, control, ritual, and task-relatedness.
10. Touch avoidance refers to our desire to avoid touching and being touched by others; it has been found to be related to apprehension, self-disclosure, age, and sex.
11. Generally, women touch each other more than do men and initiate opposite-sex touching more than do men. This seems especially pronounced in messages of control and in married relationships. Touching patterns vary greatly from one culture to another. Both gender and culture differences in touch behavior are learned rather than innate.
12. Smell can communicate a wide variety of messages, such as messages to enhance attractiveness, taste, memory, and identification.
13. Artifactual communication concerns the use of objects and human-made materials to communication meaning. Colors, clothing, jewelry, and the ways in which space may be decorated are examples.

THINKING CRITICALLY ABOUT NONVERBAL MESSAGES OF SPACE, TOUCH, SMELL, AND ARTIFACT

1. Can you find examples of the correlation between amount and desirability of space, on the one hand, and status, on the other, on your college campus?
2. How does your home communicate? What specific meanings might a first-time guest to your home derive from the physical space and the way it's decorated?

3. Which of the three theories of space do you find most interesting? Can you give examples of how you have acted in accordance with or in contradiction to any of the predictions of these theories?
4. Writing in their introduction to readings on public space, Diana George and John Trimbur (1995, p. 279) state: "Whether you live in the city, the suburbs, or the country, if you have visited historical monuments, spent time in New York or Los Angeles, attended a ball game, watched a parade, shopped in a mall, eaten in a fast food restaurant, played for a day in an amusement park, or simply attended a church bazaar or school dance, you already know a good deal about how public space is organized in contemporary America, and you probably make more judgments about public spaces than you think." What do you know about public space? What judgments about public spaces do you make?
5. Women, it seems, are permitted to touch children more than are men. For example, a female elementary school teacher seems to be granted greater latitude in touching children than would a male teacher. Do you agree that this is generally the case? If so, why do you think this attitudinal difference exists?
6. Do you use smell to communicate? How important is it for you to smell right? How much are you willing to spend—say, per month—on products whose primary function is to make you smell better?
7. The "Pygmalion gift" is one that is designed to change the person into what the donor wants that person to become. The parent who gives a child books or science equipment may be asking the child to be a scholar. What messages have you recently communicated in your gift-giving behavior? What messages do you think others communicated to you by the gifts they gave you?
8. How do you feel about gang clothing being worn in elementary, high school, or college? Do you think it contributes to violence in the schools? If so, should students be prevented from wearing gang clothing? Or, do you think gang clothing should be covered by the right to freedom of expression? If you were given the authority to make a decision concerning the wearing of gang colors and clothing in the schools in your community, what would you decide? What arguments would you use to defend your decision?
9. A popular defense tactic in sex crimes is to blame the victim by referring to the way the victim was dressed and to imply that the victim, by virtue of the clothing worn, provoked the attack. Currently, New York and Florida are the only states that prohibit defense attorneys from referring to the way a sex-crime victim was dressed at the time of the attack (*New York Times* July 30, 1994, p. 22). Do you agree with the rulings in New York and Florida or do you think that the clothing of the victim is a legitimate issue? If you do not live in New York or Florida, have there been similar proposals in your state to limit this popular defense tactic?
10. How would you go about finding answers to such questions as these:
    a. How does touch communicate power?
    b. What types of touching do you observe in the college classroom? In group meetings?
    c. Are college students more future-oriented than, say, high school students?
    d. Are educated people less susceptible to the influence of smell than the less educated?
    e. What types of uniforms command the greatest respect among college students? Which uniforms are accorded the highest credibility by college students?

three parT

Interpersonal Communication and Relationships

In this third part, consisting of Units 12 through 16, we look at interpersonal communication and interpersonal relationships. Unit 12 explores the preliminaries to both interpersonal communication and interpersonal relationships and defines interpersonal communication and explains the stages of interpersonal relationships. Unit 13 focuses on interpersonal communication, on the seemingly simple process of conversation. Units 14 and 15 focus on interpersonal relationships, their development, deterioration, maintenance, and repair (Unit 14), and on the major forms of interpersonal relationships, friendship, love, and family (Unit 15). The last unit in this part (Unit 16) looks at interpersonal conflict and the ways in which interpersonal conflict can be most effectively managed.

In approaching the area of interpersonal communication and relationships, keep the following in mind:

- Each person and each relationship is unique. What is true of the majority of people or of some large group is not necessarily true of you.
- Interpersonal relationships are dynamic, living things. They are always in the process of becoming. Although we artificially stop the process to discuss specific issues, remember that relationships and the people who are part of the relationship are never static. They are always changing.
- Culture influences not only the way you communicate but also the way you think about communication and especially about the way you are expected to communicate in developing and maintaining relationships and in managing conflict. Violating even arbitrary customs may have important consequences.

twelve unit

Preliminaries to Interpersonal Communication and Relationships

unit contents

unit goals

After completing this unit, you should be able to

1. define the three approaches to interpersonal communication
2. describe the six-stage model of interpersonal relationships and the movement between the stages
3. describe attraction theory and the factors that increase interpersonal attractiveness
4. describe social penetration theory
5. describe social exchange theory
6. describe equity theory
7. describe the relationship rules approach

In this unit we look at some preliminaries to interpersonal communication and relationships. First, we consider the nature of interpersonal communication. Second, we consider the nature and growth of interpersonal relationships. Finally, we look at several theories that try to explain how and why relationships develop. The area of interpersonal communication and relationships is a large one, and we only scratch the surface of it here. Some of the more important areas are noted in Table 12.1.

INTERPERSONAL COMMUNICATION

Communication theorists define interpersonal communication in different ways (Bochner 1978; Cappella 1987). Each of the three following main approaches adds a different perspective to understanding interpersonal communication.

A Componential Definition

A componential definition explains interpersonal communication by noting its major components—here, the sending of messages by one person and the receiving of messages by another person or small group of persons, with some effect and with some opportunity for immediate feedback. (These components were discussed in Unit 1.) The model of the universals of human communication is essentially a model of the interpersonal communication process.

A Relational (Dyadic) Definition

In a relational definition, interpersonal communication is viewed as communication that takes place between two persons who have a clearly established relationship. A "dyadic consciousness" must be present to some degree; each person is aware of his or her connection with the other person. There is some degree of interdependence; what one person does has implications for the other person. Thus, for example, interpersonal communication would include what takes place between a waiter and a customer, a son and his father, two people in an interview, and so on. Under this definition it is almost impossible to have dyadic (two-person) communication that is not interpersonal. Not surprisingly, this definition is also referred to as the dyadic definition. Almost inevitably, there is some relationship between two persons. Even the stranger in the city who asks directions from a resident has a clearly defined relationship with the resident as soon as the first message is sent. Sometimes this relational definition is extended to include small groups of persons, such as family members or groups of three or four friends.

A Developmental Definition

In the developmental approach, interpersonal communication is seen as the end of a progression from impersonal communication at one extreme to highly personal or intimate communication at the other end. This progression signals or defines the development of interpersonal communication. According to communicologist Gerald Miller's (1978) analysis, interpersonal communication is characterized by and distinguished from impersonal communication on the basis of at least three factors: psychologically based predictions, explanatory knowledge, and personally established rules.

TABLE 12.1 the areas of interpersonal communication and relationships

The related academic areas identified here are not exhaustive and are presented to suggest just some of the close academic ties among different areas of study. Intercultural communication, although it can occur in any type of communication, is often grouped with the area of interpersonal communication. An overview of the intercultural communication area is provided in Table 6.2 in Unit 6.

General Area	Some Topics	Related Academic Areas	For Further Exploration
Interpersonal interaction; two-person communication	Characteristics of effectiveness Conversational processes Interviewing Self-disclosure Listening actively Nonverbal messages in conversation	Psychology Education Linguistics	Knapp and Vangelisti (1992) and Weber and Harvey (1995) provide useful overviews of interpersonal relationships. Petronio, Alberts, Hecht, and Buley (1993) and Redmond (1995) both provide excellent collections of research articles covering this broad field. Knapp and Miller (1995) offer an authoritative review of research and theory in interpersonal communication and relationships. Blieszner and Adams (1992) and Rawlins (1992) review research and theory on adult friendships; Aron and Aron (1986, 1995), Hendrick and Hendrick (1992), and Sternberg (1988) cover love; Galvin and Brommel (1996) and Pearson (1993) cover family communication. Donohue and Kolt (1992) and Folger, Poole, and Stutman (1993) cover the field of interpersonal conflict.
Health Communication: communication between health professional and patient	Talking about AIDS Increasing doctor-patient effectiveness Communication and aging Therapeutic communication	Medicine Psychology Counseling	
Family communication: communication within the family system	Power in the family Dysfunctional families Family conflict Heterosexual and homosexual families Parent-child communication	Sociology Psychology Family studies	
Social and personal relationships: communication in close relationships such as friendship and love	Relationship development Relationship breakdown Repairing relationships Gender differences in relationships Increasing intimacy Verbal abuse	Psychology Sociology Anthropology	

Psychologically Based Predictions

In impersonal encounters you respond to another person on the basis of sociological data—the classes or groups to which the person belongs. For example, you respond to a particular college professor the way you respond to college professors in general. Similarly, the college professor responds to a particular student in the way professors respond to students generally. As the relationship becomes more personal, however, both the professor and the student begin to respond to each other not as members of their groups but as individuals. You respond to another person on the basis of psychological data, on the ways this person differs from the members of his or her group.

Explanatory Knowledge

In interpersonal interactions you base your communications on explanatory knowledge of each other. When you know a particular person, you can predict how that person will act in a variety of situations. As you get to know that person better, however, you can predict not only how a person will act but also why the person behaves as he or she does. The college professor may, in an impersonal relationship, know that

Pat will be five minutes late to class each Friday. That is, the professor is able to predict Pat's behavior. In an interpersonal situation, however, the professor can also offer explanations for the behavior (giving reasons for Pat's lateness).

Personally Established Rules

Society sets up rules for interaction in impersonal situations. As noted in the previous example of the student and professor, the social rules of interaction set up by the culture lose importance as the relationship becomes more personal. In the place of these social rules, the individuals set up rules of their own. When individuals establish their own rules for interacting with each other rather than using the rules set down by the society, the situation is interpersonal.

These three factors vary in degree. You respond to another on the basis of psychological data to some degree. You can explain another's behavior to some degree. And you interact on the basis of mutually established rules rather than on socially established norms to some degree. A developmental approach to communication implies a continuum ranging from highly impersonal to highly intimate. "Interpersonal communication" occupies a part of this continuum, though each person might draw its boundaries a bit differently.

Communication theorists are divided among these three definitions. For our purposes interpersonal communication is best defined, in its broadest sense, to include any interaction in which there is a relationship established between or among the participants. At the same time, recognize that interpersonal communication changes as it becomes more intimate—a progression clearly explained in the developmental definition. And, of course, the componential definition helps highlight the essential ingredients that need to be considered in understanding and analyzing interpersonal communication. Thus, all three definitions are helpful in explaining what interpersonal communication is and how it develops.

THE STAGES OF INTERPERSONAL RELATIONSHIPS

Interpersonal relationships are established in stages. You do not become intimate friends with someone immediately upon meeting. Rather, you grow into an intimate relationship gradually, through a series of steps from the initial contact, through intimacy, and perhaps on to dissolution. The same is probably true with most other relationships as well. In all, six major stages are identifiable (see Figure 12.1): contact, involvement, intimacy, deterioration, repair, and dissolution. Each stage can be divided into an early and a late phase, as noted in the diagram. For each specific relationship, you might wish to modify and revise the basic model in various ways. As a general description of relationship development, however, the stages seem fairly standard.

These stages are not static; rather, within each there are dynamic tensions between various opposites. Within each relationship and within each relationship stage, there are dynamic tensions between several opposites. For example, research has found three such opposites (Baxter 1988, 1990; Baxter & Simon 1993). The tension between *autonomy and connection* expresses your desire to remain an individual but also to be intimately connected to another person and to a relationship. This theme is also seen in womens magazines and seems to teach readers to want both autonomy and connection (Prusank, Duran, & DeLillo 1993). The tension between *novelty and predictability* focuses on the dual desires for newness and adventure on the one hand and sameness and comfortableness on the other. The tension between *closedness and openness* relates to the desires to be in an exclusive relationship and one that is open to different people. Therefore, view each of the stages as dynamic transactions rather than as static events.

Contact

At the first stage you make contact. At first, the contact is perceptual; you see what the person looks like, you hear what the person sounds like. You get a physical picture of the person—sex, approximate age, height, and so on. After this perception, there is usually interactional contact. According to some researchers (Zunin & Zunin 1972), it is during this stage—within the first four minutes of initial interaction—that you decide whether you want to pursue the relationship. It is at this stage that physical appearance is so important, because the physical dimensions are most open to easy inspection. Yet qualities such as friendliness, warmth, openness, and dynamism are also revealed at this stage. If you like the individual and want to pursue the relationship, you proceed to the second stage.

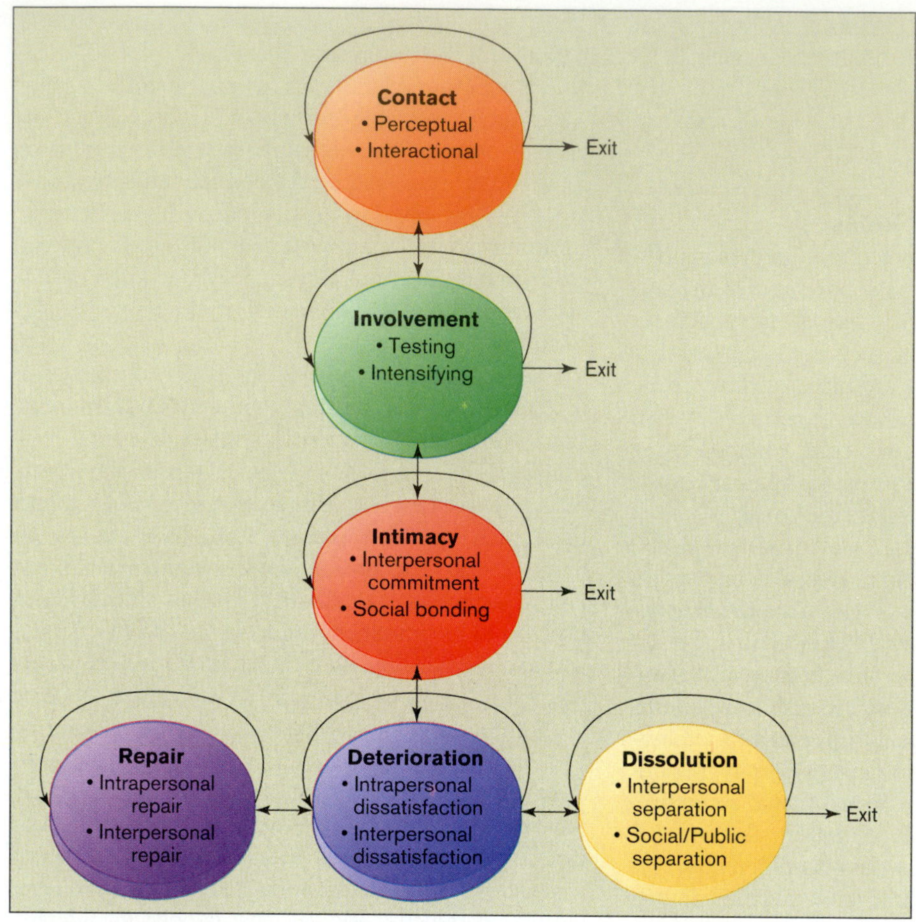

FIGURE 12.1 A six-stage relationship model. Because relationships differ so widely, models of relationships are perhaps best thought of as tools for talking about relationships rather than as specific maps that indicate how you move from one relationship position to another.

Involvement

The involvement stage is the stage of acquaintance, during which you commit yourself to getting to know the other person better and also to revealing yourself. At first, this involvement takes the form of testing the other person and the relationship. In the later phase, you may intensify your involvement. If this is to be a romantic relationship, then you might date at this stage. If it is to be a friendship, you might share your mutual interests—go to the movies or to some sports event together.

Dating couples use a variety of strategies, identified in Table 12.2, to intensify their relationship and to move close to intimacy (Tolhuizen 1989). In reviewing this list do realize that these strategies are culturally influenced. For example, in a study of African, Asian, and Caucasian Americans it was found that African American men spent a longer time on managing their personal appearance than either Asian or Caucasian men. But, African American women spent less time than either Asian or Caucasian women (Aune & Aune 1994). Further research is likely to discover that many of these strategies will prove to be heavily influenced by culture.

Intimacy

During the **intimacy** stage, you commit yourself still further to the other person. Usually the intimacy stage divides itself neatly into two phases: an interpersonal commitment phase, during which you commit yourselves to each other in a kind of private way, and a social bonding phase, during which the commitment is made public—perhaps to family and friends, perhaps to the public at large through, say, a legal or religious ceremony. This stage is reserved for very few people—sometimes just one and sometimes two, three,

TABLE 12.2
dating strategies:
fifteen ways to intensify relationships

Dating Strategies		Examples
Social Rewards and Attraction Strategies	Increase rewards	Increase giving partner rewards
	Tokens of affection	Give partner gifts
	Behavioral adaptation	Do things to impress or increase partner's favorable impression
	Personal appearance	Increase personal attractiveness
	Social enmeshment	Interact with partner's network of friends or family
Implicitly Expressed Intimacy Strategies	Suggestive actions	Declare interest indirectly through suggestions
	Nonverbal expressions of affection	Use nonverbal communication to convey the desire for increased intimacy
	Sexual intimacy	Become more intimate sexually
Passive and Indirect Strategies	Accept definitional bid	Say yes to partner's invitation to increase intimacy
	Social support and assistance	Ask others for relationship advice
Verbal Directness and Intimacy Strategies	Relationship negotiation	Talk about the relationship and desires for the future
	Direct definitional bid	Directly request a more intimate relationship
	Personalized communication	Disclose personal information, use terms to reflect the intimacy of the relationship
	Verbal expression of affection	Declare love or caring
	Increased contact	Increase interaction with partner

or perhaps four. Rarely do people have more than four intimates, except in a family situation.

When the intimacy stage involves marriage, people are faced with three main premarital anxieties (Zimmer 1986):

- the security anxiety: Will my mate leave me for someone else? Will my mate be sexually unfaithful?
- the fulfillment anxiety: Will we be able to achieve a close, warm, and special rapport? Will we be able to have an equal relationship?
- the excitement anxiety: Will boredom and routine set in? Will I lose my freedom and become trapped?

Of course, not everyone strives for intimacy (Bartholomew 1990). Some may consciously desire intimacy, but are so fearful of its consequences that they avoid it. Others dismiss intimacy and defensively deny their need for more and deeper interpersonal contact. To some people relational intimacy is extremely risky. To others, it involves only low risk.

THINK ABOUT

Think about your own attitudes toward relationship risks. How true of your attitudes are the following statements?

- It is dangerous to get really close to people.
- I'm afraid to get really close to someone because I might get hurt.
- I find it difficult to trust other people.
- The most important thing to consider in a relationship is whether I might get hurt.

People who agree with these statements (and similar statements), which come from research on risk in

What reasons might you give in support of the proposition that intimacy is easier to achieve between members of the same culture? That intimacy is easier to achieve when members come from different cultures? How might you go about testing which of those propositions has greater validity?

intimacy (Pilkington & Richardson 1988), perceive intimacy to involve great risk. Such people, it has been found, have fewer close friends, are less likely to be involved in a romantic relationship, have less trust in others, have a low level of dating assertiveness, and are generally less sociable than those who see intimacy as involving little risk.

Deterioration

Although many relationships become stabilized at one of the previous stages, some relationships experience **deterioration.** The first phase of deterioration is usually intrapersonal dissatisfaction. You begin to feel that this relationship may not be as important as you had previously thought. You grow further and further apart. You share less of your free time, and when you are together there are awkward silences, fewer self-disclosures, and a self-consciousness in your exchanges. If this dissatisfaction continues or grows, you may pass to the second phase, interpersonal dissatisfaction, when you discuss these dissatisfactions with your partner. During this stage, some people may seek to repair their relationship.

Repair

The **repair** stage is optional, and so is indicated in the model as a broken circle (see Figure 12.1). Some relational partners may pause during deterioration (or at any one of the previous stages that may not be as productive or as happy as one would want) and try to repair their relationship. Others, however, may progress—without stopping or thinking—to dissolution. Repair usually occurs in at least two stages: intrapersonal and interpersonal. At the intrapersonal level, you analyze what went wrong and consider ways to straighten out your difficulties. At this stage you might consider changing your behaviors or perhaps your expectations of your partner. You might also evaluate the rewards of continuing your relationship as it is now and those of ending it. At the interpersonal level, you might discuss with your partner the problems that you see in the relationship, the corrections you want to see, and perhaps what you are willing to do and what you want the other person to do. You and your partner might try to solve your problems yourselves, seek the advice of friends or family, or perhaps undergo professional counseling. (A wide variety of repair strategies are considered in Unit 14.)

Dissolution

If repair is not successful, you might enter the stage of **dissolution.** The early phase of dissolution takes the form of interpersonal separation; you might move into separate apartments and begin to lead lives apart from each other. If the relationship is a marriage, you might seek a legal separation. If the separation period

MEDIA WATCH

PARASOCIAL RELATIONSHIPS

Many television viewers develop **parasocial relationships;** these are relationships that the viewer perceives himself or herself to have with a media personality (Rubin & McHugh 1987). At times viewers develop these relationships with real media personalities—O. J. Simpson, Regis Philbin or Kathy Lee Gifford, or Geraldo Rivera, for example. As a result they may watch these shows faithfully and communicate with the individual in their own imaginations. At other times, the relationship is with the fictional character—a doctor on "E.R." or Roseanne or Dan from "Roseanne." In fact those who play doctors frequently get mail asking their medical advice. Soap opera stars who are about to be "killed" frequently get warning letters from their parasocial relationship partners. Most people obviously don't go quite this far. Yet, many viewers consider the role real enough to make that actor in that role a bankable spokesperson for a product. For example, actor Susan Sullivan, who played a nurse on television some ten years ago, is still a spokesperson for a particular medication.

Parasocial relationships develop from an initial attraction with the character's social and task roles, to a perceived relationship, and finally to a sense that this relationship is an important one (Rubin & McHugh 1987). A viewer's ability to predict the behavior of a character seems to contribute to the development of parasocial relationships (Perse & Rubin 1989). As can be expected, these parasocial relationships are most important to those who spend a great deal of time with the media and who have few interpersonal relationships (Rubin, Perse, & Powell 1985).

Even the relationship between talk show host and guest is a parasocial one, media researcher Janice Peck (1995) argues. The reason is that such relationships are basically one-sided and the roles are not interchangeable. The interaction is not one of dialogue but rather one in which the host controls the interaction and the guests essentially answer the questions the host asks.

In many instances, relationships are not that easy to classify as real or parasocial. For example, most of us can probably recall at least one real relationship we have had in which the talk was basically one-sided, the roles were not interchangeable, and the interaction was largely controlled by one person.

Some talk shows invite viewers to write in to meet the guests from the show. Relationships begun this way start as parasocial but quickly move to real. For example, a "Sally Jesse Raphael" show in early 1995 was devoted to viewers who had crushes on former guests and who the show's producers got together for another show. Viewers can now see the characters on television—and in some ways talk show panelists are very much like dramatic characters in a play—as potential relationship partners. Even though such occurrences are infrequent, they seem to happen often enough for people to write in with the possibility of meeting a guest. On home shopping programs, you can often talk with the host or with a product's spokesperson. You can, for example, talk to Suzanne Somers, Frankie Avalon, and Connie Stevens about their products. As the ability to interact with the television programs increases, the distinction between real and parasocial relationships will become increasingly blurred.

Do you maintain parasocial relationships with media personalities? If so, what functions do these relationships serve? Are the substitutes for or are they supplementary to real relationships?

proves workable and if the original relationship is not repaired, you may enter the social or public separation phase; the dissolution is symbolized by a divorce. Sometimes there is relief and relaxation. At other times there is intense anxiety and frustration. There may be recriminations and hostility and resentment over time ill-spent and now lost.

Movement Among the Stages

Figure 12.1 contains three types of arrows. The exit arrows indicate that each stage offers the opportunity to exit the relationship. After saying "hello," you can say "good-bye" and exit. The vertical or movement arrows going to the next stage and back again (including the horizontal arrow from dissolution to repair) represent the ability to move to another stage. You can move to a stage that is more intense (from involvement to intimacy) or less intense (from intimacy to deterioration). You can also go back to a previously established stage. For example, you may have established an intimate relationship but no longer want to maintain it at that level. At the same time, you are relatively pleased with the relationship, so it is not really deteriorating, you just want it to be less intense. You might go back to the involvement stage and reestablish the relationship at that more comfortable level.

The self-reflexive arrows return to the same level or stage. These signify that any relationship may become stabilized at any point. You may, for example, maintain a relationship at the intimate level without the relationship deteriorating or going back to the less intense stage of involvement. Or you might remain at the, "Hello, how are you" stage—the contact stage—without getting involved any further.

THEORIES OF INTERPERSONAL RELATIONSHIPS

You can gain considerable insight into interpersonal relationships by looking at the theories that try to explain what happens when you enter relationships, and your reasons for entering or exiting such relationships. Here we look at five general theories: social penetration, attraction, social exchange, equity, and relationship rules. Each offers a different perspective; each provides different insight.

Social Penetration Theory

Social penetration theories describe relationships in terms of the number of topics that people talk about and their degree of "personalness" (Altman & Taylor 1973; Taylor & Altman 1987). This theory is not so much concerned with why relationships develop but with what happens when they do; it provides an additional step in the six-stage model just discussed.

Breadth and Depth of Relationships

In social penetration theory, relationships are described by the number of topics the two people talk about and the degree of "personalness" with which they pursue these topics. The number of topics about which you communicate is referred to as **breadth.** The degree to which the inner personality—the core of an individual—is penetrated is referred to as **depth.**

Let us represent an individual as a circle and divide that circle into parts, as in Figure 12.2 (Altman & Taylor 1973). These parts represent the topics or areas that people talk about (breadth). Further, let's visualize the circle and its parts as consisting of concentric inner circles. These represent the different levels of communication, or the depth. Note that in circle (a) only three of the topic areas are penetrated. Two are penetrated only to the first level and one is penetrated to the second level. In this type of interaction, three topic areas are talked about and they are discussed at a rather superficial level. This is the type of relationship you might have with an acquaintance.

Circle (b) represents a more intense relationship, both broader (here four topics are discussed) and deeper. This is the type of relationship you might have with a friend. Circle (c) shows a still more intense relationship. Here seven of the eight areas are penetrated and most of the areas are penetrated to the deepest levels. This is the type of relationship you might have with a lover, a parent, or a sibling.

We can describe relationships—friendships, loves, families—in terms of breadth and depth. In its initial stage, a relationship is normally characterized by narrowness (few topics are discussed) and shallowness (the topics discussed are discussed only superficially). If early in a relationship topics are dis-

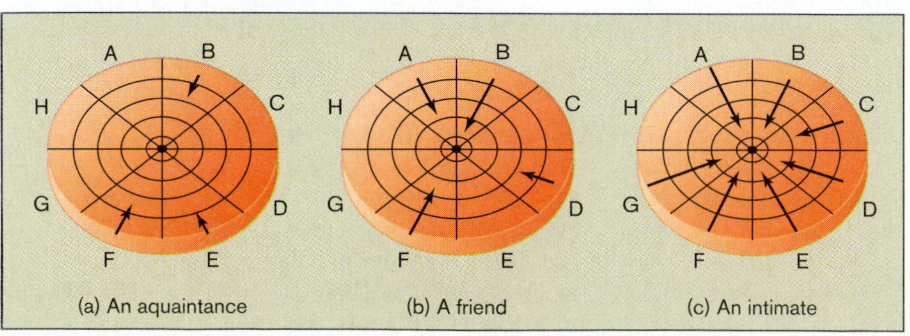

FIGURE 12.2 Social penetration with (a) acquaintance, (b) friend, and (c) intimate. How accurately do these concepts of breadth and depth express your communication in relationships of different intensities? Can you identify other dimensions of messages that change as you go from talking with an acquaintance, a friend, or an intimate?

INTRODUCING RESEARCH

A SAMPLE HISTORICAL/CRITICAL STUDY

As noted in the Introducing Research box in Unit 4, one type of historical/critical research is the literature review. The study presented here is an example of a literature review; it reviews and critically analyzes the research literature on African American communication in an effort to evaluate previous research and posit new directions (Orbe 1995). To this end the researcher examined almost a hundred research studies and on this basis identifies problems with previous research and issues challenges for future research.

One problem is that the literature has obscured the differences among the African American population (a problem that confronts much intercultural communication, as noted in Unit 6). You cannot generalize from, say, "a group of African American students at a midwestern university" to all African Americans. Another problem is that researchers often seem to polarize the situation, with African American communication on one side and European American communication on the other.

Among the researcher's recommendations for the future is the use of a greater variety of research methods and theories. Especially singled out are Hecht, Collier, and Ribeau's (1993) ethnic identity theory and Asante's (1987) Afrocentricity theory. Research needs to become more sensitive to the diversity within the African American population. Other factors that help explore the influence of ethnicity on communication need to be studied, for example, age, gender, religion, affectional orientation, and socioeconomic status. The researcher also calls for work that will have practical applications, that will be of significant social use, that will help improve lives.

These suggestions—ideally ones that will result in improved research—were derived, then, from a critical examination of previously conducted research. Through this critical analysis, the researcher was able to identify the strengths and weaknesses of previous efforts as well as the gaps in present knowledge.

Many researchers feel that research should never be judged by its practical applications and yet researcher Orbe in this study calls for investigators that have very clear practical applications for improving interethnic communication. How do you feel about the purposes of research? Should it be judged on the basis of its practical usefulness?

cussed to a depth that is normally reserved for intimates, you would probably experience considerable discomfort. As already noted (Unit 5), when intimate disclosures are made early in a relationship, you may feel something is wrong with the disclosing individual. As the relationship grows in intensity and intimacy, both the breadth and the depth increase and these increases are seen as comfortable, normal, and natural.

When you perceive someone to have attitudes similar to yours, you are more likely to engage in conversation that is more personal than you would with those you perceive as having dissimilar attitudes. Interestingly enough, this similarity-dissimilarity in attitudes may be more important than even ethnic similarity (Hammer 1989). This does not mean that dissimilarity cannot enhance communication. In fact, it has been argued that some degree of dissimilarity may actually facilitate effective communication (Rogers & Shoemaker 1971; Hammer 1989).

Depenetration

When a relationship begins to deteriorate, the breadth and depth often (but not always) reverse themselves—a process of **depenetration** (Baxter 1983). For example, while terminating a relationship, you might stop talking about certain topics. At the same time you might discuss the remaining topics in less depth. You would reduce the level of your self-disclosures and reveal less of your innermost feelings.

Attraction Theory

You are no doubt attracted to some people and not attracted to others. In a similar way, some people are attracted to you and some are not. If you were to examine the people to whom you are attracted and those to whom you are not attracted, you would probably see that your judgments were largely based around three main factors: attractiveness (physical appearance and personality), proximity, and similarity.

Attractiveness: Physical Appearance and Personality

When you say, "I find that person attractive," you probably mean either that (1) you find that person physically attractive, or that (2) you find that person's personality or behavior attractive. For the most part you probably like physically attractive rather than physically unattractive people, and you probably like people who possess a pleasant rather than an unpleasant personality. Generally, you attribute positive characteristics to people you find attractive and negative characteristics to people you find unattractive.

Numerous studies have supported the importance of attraction (Aronson 1980). When photographs of men and women varying in attractiveness were viewed by both men and women who were asked to assess these persons, the more attractive persons were judged to be sexually warmer and more responsive, more sensitive, kinder, more interesting, stronger, more poised, more modest, more sociable, more outgoing, more competent spouses, to have happier marriages, and to secure more prestigious jobs.

Research—in Bulgaria, Nigeria, Indonesia, Germany, and the United States—finds that men consider physical attractiveness in their partner more important than do women (Buss & Schmitt 1993). Similarly, in a study of gay male dating behavior the physical attractiveness of the partner was the most important factor in influencing how much the person enjoyed his date and how much he wished to date this person again (Sergios & Cody 1985).

Those who are perceived as attractive are also perceived as more competent. Interestingly enough, those who are perceived as more competent in communication—as a partner working on a joint task, socially, and physically—are also perceived as more attractive (Duran & Kelly 1988).

Proximity

If you look around at people you find attractive, you will probably find that they are the ones who live or work close to you. For example, in a study of friendships in a student housing development researchers found that the closer the students' rooms were to each other, the better the chances that they would become friends (Festinger, Schachter, & Back 1950). Also, the students who lived in units facing the courtyard had more friends than those who lived in units facing the street. The people who became friends were those who had the greatest opportunity to interact. Not surprisingly, physical closeness is most important in the early stages of interaction, for example, during the first days of school or the first days on a new job. It decreases (but always remains significant) as the opportunity to interact with more distant others increases.

One reason that proximity influences attraction is that you probably have positive expectations of people who are near you and consequently fulfill these expectations by liking or being attracted to them. Proximity also allows you to get to know the other person. You come to like people you know because you can better predict their behavior, and perhaps because of this they seem less frightening than complete strangers (Berger & Bradac 1982).

Another approach argues that *mere exposure* to others leads us to develop positive feelings for them (Zajonc 1968). In one study (Saegert, Swap, & Zajonc 1973), women who were supposedly participating in a taste experiment were exposed throughout to other people, some ten times, others five times, others two times, others one time, and some not at all. The results showed that the subjects rated highest the persons they had seen ten times, next highest those they had seen five times, and so on down the line. How can we account for these results except by mere exposure? Mere exposure seems to increase attraction when the initial interaction is favorable or neutral. When the initial interaction is negative, repeated exposure may actually decrease attraction.

Similarity

If you could construct your mate, he or she would probably look, act, and think very much like you. By being attracted to people like yourself, you validate yourself; you tell yourself that you are worthy of being liked. Although there are exceptions, you probably are attracted to your own mirror image, to people who are similar to you in nationality, race, ability, physical characteristics, intelligence, and especially attitudes. Even young children have this preference for **similarity.** For example, third- and fourth-grade children's friendships were heavily influenced by their similarity in gender, race, income level, aggressiveness, and academic achievement; the greater the similarity the greater the likelihood that they would be friends (Kupersmidt, DeRosier, & Patterson 1995).

If you were to ask a group of friends, "To whom are you attracted?" they would probably name very attractive people; in fact, the most attractive people they know. If you were to observe these friends, however, you would find that they go out with and establish relationships with people who are quite similar to themselves in physical attractiveness. This tendency, known as the **matching hypothesis,** predicts that although you may be attracted to the most physically attractive people, you will date and mate with people who are similar to yourself in physical attractiveness (Walster et al. 1978). Intuitively this seems satisfying. In some cases, however, you notice discrepancies; for example, an attractive person dating someone much less attractive. In a case such as this, you would probably look for compensating factors, for qualities that compensate for the lack of physical attractiveness: prestige, money, power, intelligence, and various personality characteristics are obvious examples.

Similarity in attitudes is especially important in attraction. Not surprisingly, people who are similar in attitudes will grow in attraction for each other over time, whereas people who are dissimilar in attitudes grow less attracted to each other (Neimeyer & Mitchell 1988). Perceived attitudinal similarity seems related to marital happiness (Honeycutt 1986). We are particularly attracted to people who have attitudes similar to our own, who like what we like and dislike what we dislike. The more significant the attitude, the more important the similarity. Marriages between people with great and salient dissimilarities are more likely to end in divorce than marriages between people who are very much alike (Blumstein & Schwartz 1983).

Attitude similarity is especially significant in initial attraction. It also seems to predict relationship success: People who are similar in attitude become more attracted to each other over time, whereas people who are dissimilar in attitude become less attracted to each other over time (Neimeyer & Mitchell 1988). Also, the more intellectually similar—the more similar people are in the way they perceive the world—the greater the interpersonal attraction (Neimeyer & Neimeyer 1983).

Much new research emphasizes the importance of similarity in communication in increasing attraction. For example, research finds that similarities in communication values for "seriously involved" dating couples (for example, the ability to give comfort to a depressed or sad partner, to make the other person feel good about himself or herself, or to reach mutually satisfying solutions to conflicts) was positively correlated with their degree of satisfaction with the relationship and their attraction for the other person (Burleson, Kunkel, & Birch 1994). Friends are also found to be more similar in their communication values than are nonfriends (Burleson, Samter, & Luccetti 1992). Further evidence for the importance of similarity in communication comes from research on communication accommodation theory (discussed in Unit 2). Recall that research found that similarity of communication style in speech rate (Buller, LePoire, Aune, & Eloy 1992) and in language intensity (Buller & Aune 1992) increases liking and attraction.

Although many people would argue that "birds of a feather flock together," others would argue that "opposites attract." This latter concept is the principle of complementarity. People are attracted to dissimilar others only in certain situations. For example, the submissive student may get along especially well with an aggressive teacher but may not get along with an aggressive spouse. In *A Psychologist Looks at Love* (1944), Theodore Reik argues that we fall in love with people who possess characteristics that we do not possess and actually envy. The introvert, for example, if displeased with being shy, might be attracted to an extrovert. Although there seems to be intuitive support for both complementarity and similarity, the research evidence favors similarity.

Affinity-Seeking Strategies

In addition to the three factors already noted, attractiveness also depends on a broad class of behaviors known as **affinity-seeking strategies** (Bell & Daly 1984). For example, it has been found that when teachers use these affinity-seeking strategies, students evaluate the teachers as being more competent than those who do not use them (Prisbell 1994). Students also come to like the instructors who use affinity-seeking strategies (offering evidence that they work) and feel they are learning more (Roach 1991). Several of these strategies are presented in Table 12.3.

THINK ABOUT

Think about such issues as the following as you read through Table 12.3 on page 202:

- Are there other strategies that you would add to this list?
- Do you find some of these strategies ineffective?
- Which strategies work best for you? Which strategies work best *on* you?

- What are the ethical implications of these strategies? When is the use of a given strategy unethical?

Social Exchange Theory

Social exchange theory claims that you develop relationships that will enable you to maximize your profits (Chadwick-Jones 1976; Gergen, Greenberg, & Willis 1980; Thibaut & Kelley 1986), a theory based on an economic model of profits and losses. The theory begins with the following equation:

Profits = Rewards – Costs

Rewards are anything that you would incur costs to obtain. For example, in order to acquire the reward of financial gain, you might have to work rather than play. To earn an A in interpersonal communication, you might have to write a term paper or study more than you might want to. Love, affection, status, money, gifts, security, social acceptance, companionship, friendship, and intimacy are just a few examples of the rewards for which you might be willing to work.

Costs are those things that you normally try to avoid, the things you consider unpleasant or difficult. Working overtime, washing dishes and ironing clothes, watching your partner's favorite television show (which you find boring), and doing favors for those you dislike might all be considered costs.

Using this basic economic model, social exchange theory claims that you seek to develop relationships (friendship and romantic) that will give you the great-

TABLE 12.3

affinity-seeking strategies: how to get people to like and feel positively toward us

These strategies were derived from studies in which people were asked to "produce a list of things people can say or do to get others to like them"; other participants were asked to identify those things that lead others to dislike them. Thus, these strategies represent what people *think* makes us attractive to others, what people *think* makes people like us, what people *think* makes others feel positively toward us. In the definitions, the term Other is used as shorthand for "other person or persons."

Affinity-Seeking Strategy	Examples
Altruism	Be of help to Other
Assume control	Appear "in control," as a leader, as one who takes charge
Assume equality	Present yourself as socially equal to Other
Comfortable self	Present yourself as comfortable and relaxed when with Other
Dynamism	Appear active, enthusiastic, and dynamic
Elicit Other's disclosures	Stimulate and encourage Other to talk about himself or herself; reinforce disclosures and contributions of Other
Inclusion of Other	Include Other in your social activities and groupings
Listening	Listen to Other attentively and actively
Openness	Engage in self-disclosure with Other
Optimism	Appear optimistic and positive rather than pessimistic and negative
Self-concept confirmation	Show respect for Other and help Other to feel positively about himself or herself
Self-inclusion	Arrange circumstances so that you and Other come into frequent contact
Sensitivity	Communicate warmth and empathy to Other
Similarity	Demonstrate that you share significant attitudes and values with Other
Trustworthiness	Appear to Other as honest and reliable

How would you apply social exchange and equity theories to explain the development, maintenance, and deterioration of relationships in the culture of professional sports?

est profits; that is, relationships in which the rewards are greater than the costs. The most preferred relationships, according to this theory, are those that give you the greatest rewards with the least costs.

THINK ABOUT

Think about your current or past relationships. Did you pursue and maintain relationships that provided you with profits, with rewards that were greater than costs? Equally important, did you not pursue or did you end relationships that were not profitable, where costs exceeded the rewards?

Comparison Levels

When you enter a relationship, you bring a certain comparison level—a general idea of the kinds of rewards and profits that you feel you ought to get out of such a relationship. It is your realistic expectations concerning what you feel you deserve from a relationship. For example, in a study of married couples it was found that most people expect reasonably high levels of trust, mutual respect, love, and commitment. Their expectations are significantly lower for time spent together, privacy, sexual activity, and communication (Sabatelli & Pearce 1986). When the rewards that you get equal or surpass this comparison level, you feel satisfied with your relationship.

You also have a comparison level for alternatives; that is, you compare the profits that you get from your current relationships with the profits you think you can get from alternative relationships. Thus, if you see that the profits from your present relationship are below the profits that you could get from an alternative relationship, you might decide to leave your current relationship and enter this new, more profitable relationship.

Social Exchange and Relationship Power

Social exchange affords us an interesting perspective on relationship power. Relationship power may be viewed as the control of the more significant rewards and costs in the relationship. The person who controls the rewards and punishments controls the relationship. The person who needs to receive the rewards and to avoid the costs or punishments controlled by the other person is less powerful. Alternatively, the person who can effectively ignore both the rewards and the costs is the less interested party and therefore possesses the controlling power in the relationship.

In any interpersonal relationship, the person who holds the power is the one less interested in and less dependent on the rewards and punishments controlled by the other person. If, for example, Pat can walk away from the rewards that Chris controls or can suffer the punishments that Chris can mete out, Pat controls the relationship. If, on the other hand, Pat needs the rewards that Chris controls or is unable or unwilling to suffer the punishments that Chris can administer, Chris maintains the power and controls the relationship. Put differently, Chris holds the relationship power to the degree that Chris is not dependent upon the rewards and punishments under Pat's control.

The more a person needs a relationship, the less power that person has in it. The less a person needs a relationship, the greater the power possessed. In a love relationship, for example, the person who maintains greater power is the one who would find it easier to break up the relationship. The person who is unwilling (or unable) to break up has little power, precisely because he or she is dependent on the relationship and on the rewards provided by the other person.

Equity Theory

Equity theory uses the concepts of social exchange but goes a step further and claims that you develop and maintain relationships in which the ratio of your rewards compared to costs is approximately equal to your partner's (Messick & Cook 1983; Walster, Walster & Berscheid 1978). An equitable relationship, then, would be one in which each of you derives rewards that are proportional to your costs. If you work harder for the relationship than your partner, then equity demands that you should get greater rewards. If you each work equally hard, then equity demands that you should each get approximately equal rewards. Conversely, inequity exists in a relationship if you pay more of the costs (for example, you do more of the unpleasant tasks) but your partner enjoys more of the rewards, or if you and your partner work equally hard, but your partner gets more of the rewards. Not surprisingly, research in the United States finds that people want equity and feel that relationships should be characterized by equity (Ueleke et al. 1983).

Equity theory puts into clear focus the sources of relational dissatisfaction seen every day. For example, in a relationship both partners may have full-time jobs but one may also be expected to do the major share of the household chores. Thus, although both may be deriving equal rewards—they have equally good cars, they live in the same three-bedroom house, and so on—one partner is paying more of the costs. According to equity theory, this partner will be dissatisfied because of this lack of equity.

Equity theory claims that you will develop and maintain relationships and will be satisfied with relationships that are equitable. You will not develop, will terminate, and will be dissatisfied with relationships that are inequitable. The greater the inequity, the greater the dissatisfaction.

Equity in Cultural Perspective

THINK ABOUT

Think about equity as a reflection of culture values. Equity, as you probably surmised, is consistent with the capitalistic orientation of Western culture, where each person is paid according to his or her contributions. The more you contribute to the organization or the relationship, the more rewards you should get out of it. In other cultures, a principle of equality or need might operate. Under equality, each person would get equal rewards, regardless of their own individual contribution. Under need, each person would get rewards according to his or her individual need (Moghaddam, Taylor, & Wright 1993). Thus, in the United States equity is found to be highly correlated with relationship satisfaction and with relationship endurance (Schafer & Keith 1980); but in Europe, equity seems to be unrelated to satisfaction or endurance (Lujansky & Mikula 1983).

In one study, for example, subjects in the United States and India were asked to study situations in which a bonus was to be distributed between a worker who contributed a great deal but who was economically well-off and a worker who contributed much less but who was economically needy. Their choices were to distribute the bonus equitably (on the basis of contribution), equally, or in terms of need (Berman, Murphy-Berman, & Singh 1985; Moghaddam, Taylor, & Wright 1993). Subjects from the United States distributed the bonus on the basis of equity (49 percent) while only 16 percent of the subjects from India did this. Only 16 percent of the subjects from the United States said they would distribute the bonus on the basis of need compared to 51 percent of the subjects from India.

Other findings include, for example, that Chinese subjects were more likely than U.S. subjects to sacrifice self-gain to benefit other members of the group (Leung & Bond 1984; Leung & Iwawaki 1988). Equity seems to fit persons from the United States more than those from the Netherlands (Van-Yperen & Buunk 1991). In another study, persons from the United States and Japan were found to prefer equity more than South Koreans (Kim, Park, & Suzuki 1990). When Austrialians and Japanese were compared it was found that Australians were more positive toward equity than the Japanese (Kashima, Siegal, Tanaka, & Isaka 1988). Some studies find similarities. For example, Indonesian and U.S. students both distributed rewards on the basis of equity (Marin 1985). These research efforts are merely beginning attempts to understand equity and distributive justice generally. They are presented here merely to illustrate that different people see things very differently.

Relationship Rules Approach

You can gain an interesting perspective on interpersonal relationships by looking at them in terms of the rules that govern them. The general assumption of

TABLE 12.4
keeping and breaking up a friendship

To Keep a Friendship	To Break Up a Friendship
Stand up for Friend in his or her absence	Be intolerant of Friend's friends
Share information and feelings about successes	Discuss confidences between yourself and Friend with others
Demonstrate emotional support	Don't display any positive regard for Friend
Trust each other; confide in each other	Don't demonstrate any positive support for Friend
Offer to help Friend when in need	Nag friend
Try to make Friend happy when you are together	Don't trust or confide in Friend

this view is that relationships—friendship and love in particular—are held together by mutual adherence to certain rules. When those rules are broken, the relationships may deteriorate and even dissolve.

Discovering relationship rules serves several functions. Ideally, these rules help identify successful versus destructive relationship behavior. In addition, these rules help pinpoint more specifically why relationships break up and how they may be repaired. Further, if we know what the rules are we will be better able to teach the social skills involved in relationship development and maintenance.

Since these rules vary from one culture to another, it will be necessary to identify those unique to each culture so that intercultural relationships may be more effectively developed and maintained. For example, in Japan the rules for obedience include avoiding the loss of face, maintaining peaceful relationships with others, and holding back emotional expression. In Hong Kong, rules concerning respect for parents and in Italy rules about maintaining intimacy in intimate relationships were particularly important (Argyle 1986).

Friendship Rules

The left-hand column of Table 12.4 presents some of the most important rules of friendship (Argyle & Henderson 1984). When these rules are followed, the friendship is strong and mutually satisfying. When these rules are broken, the friendship suffers and may die. The right-hand column presents the abuses that are most significant in breaking up a friendship (Argyle & Henderson 1984). Note that some of the rules for maintaining a friendship directly correspond to the abuses that break up friendships. For example, it is important to "demonstrate emotional support" to maintain a friendship, but when emotional support is not shown, the friendship will prove less satisfying and may well break up. The strategy for maintaining a friendship would then depend on your knowing the rules and having the ability to apply the appropriate interpersonal skills (Trower 1981; Blieszner & Adams 1992).

Romantic Rules

Other research has identified the rules that romantic relationships establish and follow. Leslie Baxter (1986), for example, has identified eight major rules and argues that these rules both keep the relationship together and when broken lead to deterioration and eventually dissolution. The general form for each rule, as Baxter phrases it, is "If parties are in a close relationship they should . . .

1. acknowledge one another's individual identities and lives beyond the relationship"
2. express similar attitudes, beliefs, values, and interests"
3. enhance one another's self-worth and self-esteem"
4. be open, genuine and authentic with one another"
5. remain loyal and faithful to one another"
6. have substantial shared time together"
7. reap rewards commensurate with their investments relative to the other party"
8. experience a mysterious and inexplicable 'magic' in one another's presence"

None of these theories fully explain interpersonal relationships. Yet, they do highlight important concepts and processes and help explain what happens as you progress from contact through involvement to intimacy and perhaps to deterioration, repair, and dissolution—topics pursued in more detail in Unit 14.

SUMMARY

In this unit we reviewed the stages of relationships, from initial contact through possible dissolution and five theories that try to explain the how and why of interpersonal relationships.

1. A componential definition of interpersonal communication identifies the components or elements in the interpersonal communication act.
2. A relational or dyadic definition defines interpersonal communication as that which takes place between two persons who have a clearly established relationship.
3. A developmental definition defines interpersonal communication as a development or progression from impersonal communication at one extreme to personal communication at the other. Interpersonal communication is distinguished from other types in that (1) predictions are based on psychological rather than sociological data; (2) predictions are based on explanatory knowledge of each other; and (3) behaviors are based on personally established rules.
4. Relationships are established in stages. At least the following six stages should be recognized: contact, involvement, intimacy, deterioration, repair, and dissolution.
5. Social penetration theory describes relationships in terms of breadth (the number of topics talked about) and depth (the degree of "personalness" to which the topics are pursued). As relationships develop, the breadth and depth increase. When a relationship deteriorates, the breadth and depth will often (but not always) decrease, a process referred to as depenetration.
6. Interpersonal attraction depends on such factors as physical appearance and personality, proximity, similarity, and the use of affinity-seeking strategies.
7. The matching hypothesis holds that you would probably date and mate with those who are about equivalent to yourself in physical attractiveness.
8. Social exchange theory claims that you seek and maintain relationships in which the rewards exceed the costs. Conversely, relationships deteriorate and dissolve when the costs exceed the rewards.
9. Equity theory builds on social exchange theory and asserts that people also want an equitable distribution of the rewards based on the costs paid by each person.
10. Relationship rules theory views relationships as bound by a mutually agreed-upon set of rules; when these rules are broken the relationship suffers.

THINKING CRITICALLY ABOUT INTERPERSONAL COMMUNICATIONAND RELATIONSHIPS

1. Can you identify specific examples for each of the strategies to intensify a relationship (Table 12.2)?
2. How effectively does the six-stage model explain your own relationships? How would you modify or adapt the model to suit your own experiences better?
3. Recall the tensions that were noted as existing at the different stages of a relationship. Research shows that the closedness-openness tension is more in evidence during the early stages of development and that autonomy-connection and novelty-predictability were more frequent as the relationship progressed (Baxter 1988, 1990; Baxter & Simon 1993). Why do you suppose this is true?

4. Which of the factors involved in attraction theory (physical appearance and personality, proximity, or similarity) do you feel is most important for you in developing romantic relationships?
5. Can you provide a specific example to illustrate the difference in the way you use affinity-seeking strategies depending on the person you hope to influence and the purpose you hope to achieve?
6. In addition to attraction, proximity, and similarity you are probably also attracted to people who give you rewards or reinforcements. These may be social, as in the form of compliments or praise, or they may be material, as in the case of the suitor whose gifts eventually win the hand of the beloved. How important is reinforcement in your own friendship and romantic relationships? Interestingly enough, you are probably also attracted to people you reward (Aronson 1980; Jecker & Landy 1969). Has your liking for another person increased after buying them an expensive present or going out of your way to do them a special favor? Why do you think this happens?
7. Can you identify who has the power in the relationships you have been in or are currently in? Does power follow the principle of less interest?
8. Are all your current relationships equitable? If not, are you satisfied with the equitable ones and dissatisfied with the inequitable ones? What form does your dissatisfaction take? For example, do you consider dissolving the inequitable relationships? Is equity more important to you in your friendship or in your romantic relationships?
9. One of the currently debated issues concerning social security payments revolves largely around equity versus need. Some argue that payments should be made on the basis of the person's contributions (equity). That is, the millionaire and the person living at the poverty line should each get out what they put in; payments should be made without regard to need. Others argue that payments should be based on need and that the millionaire, for example, should not receive payments and that the poor person should—regardless of how much they each contributed. How do you feel about equity versus need in social security payments? How valid do you think the principle of need would be if applied to relationships? This principle would claim that the partner in a relationship who has the greater need for reward should be given greater rewards and the partner needing fewer rewards should get fewer.
10. How would you go about finding answers to such questions as these:
    a. Which affinity-seeking strategies are used more by women and which are used more by men?
    b. Do the functions of interpersonal relationships change with age?
    c. Do the tensions in interpersonal relationships (for example, autonomy versus connection, novelty versus predictability, and closedness versus openness) vary from one culture to another?

thirteen unit
Interpersonal Communication: Conversation

unit contents

unit goals

Upon completion of this unit, you should be able to

1. explain the five-step model of conversation
2. explain the processes involved in managing conversations: opening, maintaining, and closing them
3. explain the skills for conversational competence
4. explain the nature and functions of the disclaimer and the excuse

Looking at conversation will give you an opportunity to look at the verbal and nonverbal messages you use in your day-to-day communications as interconnected signaling systems. In this unit, then, we look at the conversational process—what it is, how we manage a conversation, and how we can be most effective. This unit will also serve as an introduction to the process of interpersonal communication, to which we devote the next four units.

Before reading about the process of **conversation**, think of your own conversations, the ones that were satisfactory and the ones that were not. Think of a specific recent conversation as you respond to the self-test, "How Satisfying Is Your Conversation?" on page 211. This test will highlight the characteristics of conversational behavior and what makes some conversations satisfying and others unsatisfying.

THE PROCESS OF CONVERSATION

The process of conversation takes place in five steps: opening, feedforward, business, feedback, and closing (see Figure 13.1).

The Opening

The first step is to open the conversation, usually with some kind of greeting: "Hi," "How are you?" "Hello, this is Joe." Greetings can be verbal or nonverbal and are usually both (Krivonos & Knapp 1975; Knapp & Vangelisti 1992). Verbal greetings include, for example, verbal salutes ("Hi," "Hello"), initiation of the topic ("The reason I called . . ."), making reference to the other ("Hey, Joe, what's up?"), and personal inquiries ("What's new?" "How are you doing?"). Nonverbal greetings include waving, smiling, shaking hands, and winking. Usually, you greet another person both verbally and nonverbally: you smile when you say "Hello."

Greeting can serve three major functions (Knapp & Vangelisti 1992; Krivonos & Knapp 1975). First, the greeting signals a stage of access; it opens up the channels of communication for more meaningful interaction and is a good example of phatic communion. Phatic communion opens the channels of communication; it's the "small talk" that paves the way for the "big talk." Phatic communion, a clear example of feedforward, tells you that the normal, expected, and accepted rules of interaction will be in effect. It tells you that there is a willingness to communicate, an openness, and a receptivity.

Second, the greeting reveals important information about the relationship between the two persons. For example, a big smile and a warm, "Hi, it's been a long time," signals that the relationship is still a friendly one.

Third, the greeting helps maintain the relationship. You see this function served between workers who pass each other frequently. This greeting-in-passing assures you both that even though you do not stop and talk for an extended period, you still have access to each other.

In normal conversation, your greeting is reciprocated with a greeting from the other person that is similar in degree of formality or informality and in intensity. When it isn't—when the other person turns away or responds coldly to your friendly "good morning"—you know that something is wrong. Openings are also generally consistent in tone with the main part of the conversation; a cheery "How're you doing today, big guy?" is not normally followed by news of a family death.

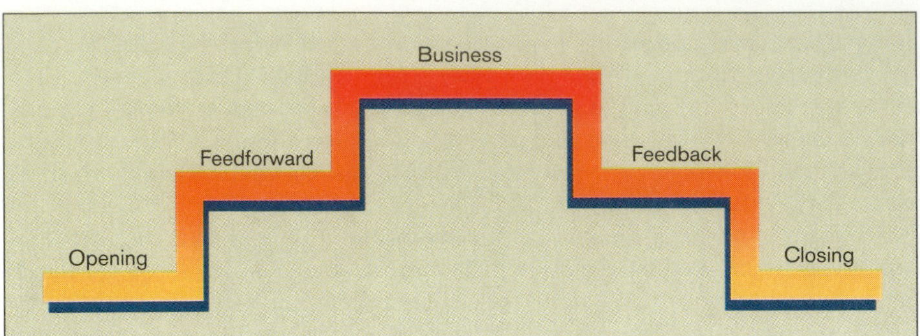

FIGURE 13.1 The process of conversation. As with the model of interpersonal relationships, this model of the stages of conversation is best seen as a way of talking about conversation and not as the unvarying stages all conversations follow. How accurately do you think this model reflects the normal progression of a conversation?

Initiating Conversations

Opening a conversation is especially difficult. At times you may not be sure of what to say or how to say it. You may fear being rejected or having someone not understand your meaning.

One way to develop opening approaches is to focus on some of the elements of the communication process discussed in Unit 1. From these we can derive several avenues for opening a conversation:

- *Self-references.* Say something about yourself. Such references may be of the name, rank, and serial number type of statement, for example: "My name is Joe; I'm from Omaha." On the first day of class students might say, "I'm worried about this class," or, "I took a course taught by this instructor last semester; she was excellent."
- *Other references.* Say something about the other person or ask a question: "I like that sweater," "Didn't we meet at Charlie's?"
- *Relational references.* Say something about the two of you, for example, "May I buy you a drink?" "Would you like to dance?" or simply, "May I join you?"
- *Context references.* Say something about the physical, social-psychological, or temporal context. The familiar, "Do you have the time?" is of this type. But, you can be more creative, for example, "This place seems real friendly" or "That painting is just great."

Keep in mind two general rules. First, be positive. Lead off with something positive rather than something negative. Say, for example, "I really enjoy coming here," instead of, "Don't you just hate this place?" Second, do not be too revealing; don't self-disclose too early in an interaction. If you do, you risk making the other person feel uncomfortable.

The Opening Line

Another way of looking at the process of initiating conversations is to examine the infamous "opening line," of which there are three basic types (Kleinke 1986).

Cute-flippant openers are humorous, indirect, and ambiguous as to whether or not the one opening the conversation really wants an extended encounter. Examples include: "Is that really your hair?" "Bet I can out drink you." "I bet the cherries jubilee isn't as sweet as you are."

Innocuous openers are highly ambiguous as to whether they are simple comments that might be made to just anyone or whether they are in fact openers designed to initiate an extended encounter. Examples include: "What do you think of the band?" "I haven't been here before. What's good on the menu?" "Could you show me how to work this machine?"

Direct openers clearly demonstrate the speaker's interest in meeting the other person. Examples include: "I feel a little embarrassed about this, but I'd like to meet you." "Would you like to have a drink after dinner?" "Since we're both eating alone, would you like to join me?"

According to Kleinke (1986), the most preferred opening lines by both men and women are generally those that are direct or innocuous. The least preferred lines by both men and women are those that are cute-flippant; women, however, dislike these openers more than men.

Men generally underestimate how much women dislike the cute-flippant openers and probably continue to use them because they are indirect enough to cushion any rejection. Men also underestimate how much women actually like innocuous openers.

Women prefer men to use openers that are relatively modest and to avoid coming on too strong.

SELF TEST

how satisfying is your conversation?

Respond to each of the following statements by recording the number best representing your feelings, using this scale:

1 = Strongly agree
2 = Moderately agree
3 = Slightly agree
4 = Neutral
5 = Slightly disagree
6 = Moderately disagree
7 = Strongly disagree

_____ 1. The other person let me know that I was communicating effectively.
_____ 2. Nothing was accomplished.
_____ 3. I would like to have another conversation like this one.
_____ 4. The other person genuinely wanted to get to know me.
_____ 5. I was very *dis*satisfied with the conversation.
_____ 6. I felt that during the conversation I was able to present myself as I wanted the other person to view me.
_____ 7. I was very satisfied with the conversation.
_____ 8. The other person expressed a lot of interest in what I had to say.
_____ 9. I did NOT enjoy the conversation.
_____10. The other person did NOT provide support for what he/she was saying.
_____11. I felt I could talk about anything with the other person.
_____12. We each got to say what we wanted.
_____13. I felt that we could laugh easily together.
_____14. The conversation flowed smoothly.
_____15. The other person frequently said things which added little to the conversation.
_____16. We talked about something I was NOT interested in.

Thinking Critically About Conversational Satisfaction You can compute your score as follows:

1. Add the scores for items 1, 3, 4, 6, 7, 8, 11, 12, 13, and 14
2. Reverse the scores for items 2, 5, 9, 10, 15, and 16 such that 7 becomes 1, 6 becomes 2, 5 becomes 3, 4 remains 4, 3 becomes 5, 2 becomes 6, and 1 becomes 7
3. Add the reversed scores for items 2, 5, 9, 10, 15, and 16
4. Add the totals from Steps 1 and 3 to yield your communication satisfaction score

You may interpret your score along the following scale:

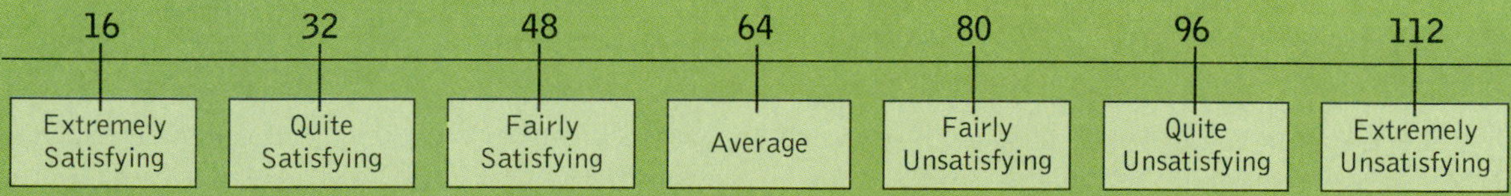

Are there additional dimensions of satisfying conversation that are not included in this scale? What is the single most important factor in determining your conversational satisfaction?

Source: From Michael Hecht, "The Conceptualization and Measurement of Interpersonal Communication Satisfaction," *Human Communication Research* 4, 1978:253–264. Reprinted by permission of the author.

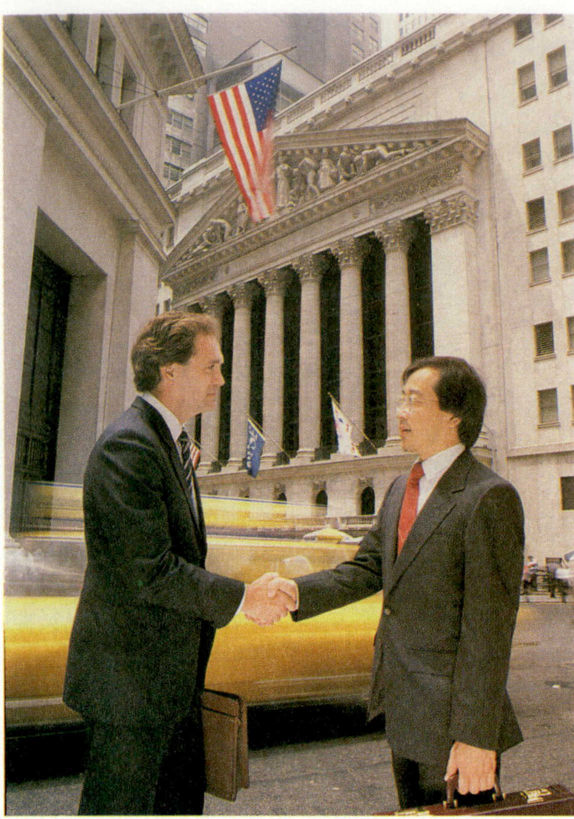

How universal do you think these five steps are in describing conversation in other cultures? Can you identify a culture that views conversation very differently?

Women generally underestimate how much men like direct openers. Most men prefer openers that are very clear in meaning, which may be because men are not used to having a women initiate a meeting. Women also overestimate how much men like innocuous lines.

THINK ABOUT

Think about how you might open a conversation with the persons described in each of these situations. What general approaches would meet with a favorable response? What would be the most inappropriate opener you can think of?

1. On the first day of class, you and another student are the first to come into the classroom and are seated in the room alone.
2. You are a guest at a friend's party. You are one of the first guests to arrive and are now there with several other people to whom you have only just been introduced. Your friend, the host, is busy with other matters.
3. You have just started a new job in a large office in which you are one of several computer operators. It seems as if most of the other people know each other.
4. You are in the college cafeteria eating alone. You see another student who is also eating alone and who you have seen in your English lit class. You're not sure if this person has noticed you in class.

Feedforward

At the second step, there is usually some kind of feedforward. Here you give the other person a general idea of what the conversation will focus on: "I've got to tell you about Jack," "Did you hear what happened in class yesterday?" or, "We need to talk about our vacation plans." Feedforward may also identify the tone of the conversation ("I'm really depressed and need to talk with you") or the time required ("This will just take a minute") (Frentz 1976; Reardon 1987) or preface the conversation to ensure that your message will be understood and will not reflect negatively on you (see Unit 1).

Business

The third step is the "business," the substance or focus of the conversation. Business is a good term to use for this stage because it emphasizes that most conversations are goal-directed. You converse to fulfill one or several of the general purposes of interpersonal communication: to learn, relate, influence, play, or help (see Unit 1). The term is also sufficiently general to incorporate all kinds of interactions.

The business is conducted through an exchange of speaker and listener roles. Usually, brief (rather than long) speaking turns characterize most satisfying conversations. Here you talk about Jack, what happened in class, or your vacation plans. This is obviously the longest part of the conversation and the reason for both the opening and the feedforward.

Maintaining Conversations

The defining feature of conversation is that the roles of speaker and listener are exchanged throughout the interaction. You accomplish this by using a wide variety of verbal and nonverbal cues to signal **conversational turns**—the changing (or maintaining) of the speaker or listener role during the conversation. Combining the insights of a variety of communication researchers (Burgoon, Buller, & Woodall 1989; Duncan 1972; Pearson & Spitzberg 1990), we can look at conversational turns in terms of speaker cues and listener cues.

Speakers regulate the conversation through two major types of cues: turn-maintaining cues and turn-yielding cues. Their effective use not only ensures communication efficiency but also increases likability (Place & Becker 1991, Heap 1992). The ways of using conversational turns identified here have been derived largely from studies conducted in the United States. Each culture appears to define the types and appropriateness of turns differently (for example, Iizuka 1993). Polychronic people, for example, will often disregard the turn-taking principles used by monochronic people. The effect is that to monochronic people—who carefully follow these rules—polychronic people will often appear rude, as they interrupt and overlap conversations, for example (Lee 1984; Grossin 1987).

Turn-maintaining Cues. These are designed to enable the speaker to maintain the role of speaker and may be communicated in a variety of ways (Burgoon, Buller, & Woodall 1989; Duncan 1972):

- audibly inhaling breath to show that the speaker has more to say
- continuing a gesture or series of gestures to show that the thought is not yet complete
- avoiding eye contact with the listener so there is no indication that the speaker is passing the speaking turn on to the listener
- sustaining the intonation pattern to indicate that more will be said
- vocalizing pauses (*er, umm*) to prevent the listener from speaking and to show that the speaker is still talking

In most cases you expect the speaker to maintain relatively brief speaking turns and to turn over the speaking role to the listener willingly (when so signaled by the listener). Those who don't are likely to be evaluated negatively.

Turn-yielding Cues. These cues tell the listener that the speaker is finished and wishes to exchange the role of speaker for the role of listener. They tell the listener (and sometimes they are addressed to a specific listener rather than to just any listener) to take over the role of speaker. For example, you may at the end of a statement add some paralinguistic cue such as "oh?" which asks one of the listeners to assume the role of speaker. You can also indicate that you have finished speaking by dropping your intonation, by a prolonged silence, by making direct eye contact with a listener, by asking some general question, or by nodding in the direction of a particular listener.

In much the same way that you expect a speaker to yield the role of speaker, you also expect the listener to willingly assume the speaking role. Those who don't may be regarded as reticent or unwilling to involve themselves and take equal responsibility for the conversation. For example, in an analysis of turn-taking violations in the conversations of married couples, the most common violation found was that of no response (DeFrancisco 1991). Forty-five percent of the 540 violations identified involved a lack of response to an invitation to take on the role of speaker. Of these "no response" violations, 68 percent were committed by men and 32 percent by women. Other turn-taking violations include interruptions, delayed responses, and inappropriately brief responses. DeFrancisco argues that with these violations, all of which are committed more frequently by men, men silence women in marital interactions.

As a listener you can regulate the conversation by using three types of cues: turn-requesting cues, turn-denying cues, and backchanneling cues.

Turn-requesting Cues. These cues let the speaker know that you would like to say something, that you would like to take a turn as speaker. Sometimes you can do this by simply saying, "I'd like to say something," but often it is done more subtly through some vocalized *er* or *um* that tells the speaker that you would now like to speak. This request to speak is also often made with facial and mouth gestures. Frequently a listener will indicate a desire to speak by opening his or her eyes and mouth wide as if to say something, by beginning to gesture with a hand, or by leaning forward.

Turn-denying Cues. You would use turn-denying cues to indicate your reluctance to assume the role of speaker, for example, intoning a slurred, "I don't know," or by giving some brief grunt that signals you have nothing to say. You can often turn-deny by avoiding eye contact with the speaker who wishes you to take on the role of speaker, or by engaging in some behavior that is incompatible with speaking—for example, coughing or blowing your nose.

Backchanneling Cues. You would use backchanneling cues to communicate various types of information back to the speaker without assuming the role of the speaker. You can send a variety of messages with such cues (Burgoon, Buller, & Woodall 1989; Pearson & Spitzberg 1990). You can indicate your agreement or disagreement with the speaker through smiles or frowns, gestures of approval or disapproval, brief comments such as "right" or "never," or a vocalization such as *uh-huh*.

You can also indicate your degree of involvement or boredom with the speaker. Attentive posture, forward leaning, and focused eye contact will tell the speaker that you are involved in the conversation just as inattentive posture, backward leaning, and avoidance of eye contact will communicate your lack of involvement.

Giving the speaker pacing cues helps regulate the speed of speech. You can, for example, ask the speaker to slow down by raising your hand near your ear and leaning forward and to speed up by continuously nodding your head. You can also do this verbally by simply asking the speaker to slow down ("Slow down, I want to make sure I'm getting all this"). Similarly, you can tell the speaker to speed up by saying something like "and . . ." or "go on, go on . . . ."

A request for clarification is still another function of backchanneling cues. A puzzled facial expression, perhaps coupled with a forward lean, will probably tell most speakers that you want some clarification. Similarly, you can ask for clarification by interjecting some interrogative: "Who?" "When?" "Where?"

Some of these backchanneling cues are actually interruptions. These interruptions, however, are generally confirming rather than disconfirming. They tell the speaker that you are listening and are involved (Kennedy & Camden 1988).

Figure 13.2 provides an illustration of the various turn-taking cues and how they correspond to the conversational wants of speaker and listener.

Feedback

The fourth step is the reverse of the second. Here you reflect back on the conversation to signal that as far as you're concerned, the business is completed: "So, you may want to send Jack a get well card," "Wasn't that the craziest class you ever heard of?" or "I'll call for reservations while you shop for what we need" (see Unit 1).

Of course, the other person may not agree that the business is completed and may therefore counter with, for example, "But what hospital is he in?" When this happens, you normally go back a step and continue the business.

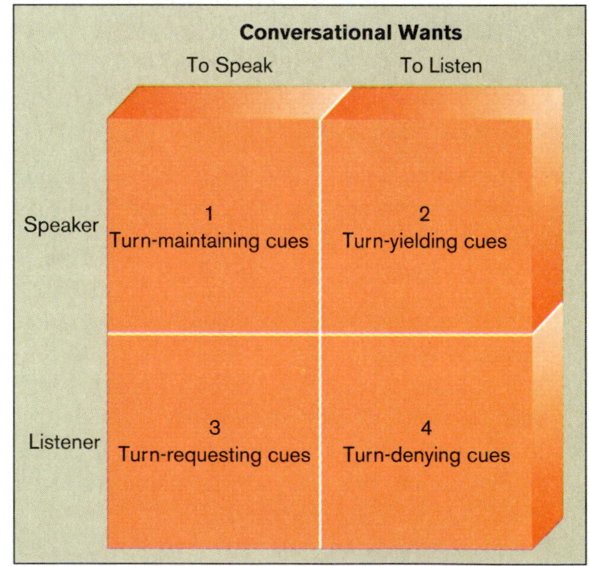

FIGURE 13.2 Turn-taking and conversational wants. Quadrant 1 represents the speaker who wants to speak (continue to speak) and uses turn-maintaining cues; Quadrant 2, the speaker who wants to listen and uses turn-yielding cues; Quadrant 3, the listener who wants to speak and uses turn-requesting cues; and Quadrant 4, the listener who wants to listen (continue listening) and uses turn-denying cues. Backchanneling cues would appear in Quadrant 4, as they are cues that listeners use while they continue to listen.

Closing

The fifth and last step, the opposite of the first step, is the closing, the good-bye (Knapp, Hart, Friedrich, & Shulman 1973; Knapp & Vangelisti 1992). Like the opening, the closing may be verbal or nonverbal but is usually a combination of the two. Most obviously, the closing signals the end of accessibility. Just as the opening signaled access, the closing signals the end of access. The closing usually also signals some degree of supportiveness, for example, you express your pleasure in interacting: "Well, it was good talking with you." The closing may also summarize the interaction.

Closing Conversations

Closing a conversation is almost as difficult as opening a conversation. It is frequently an awkward and uncomfortable part of interpersonal interaction. Following are a few ways you might consider for closing a conversation.

- Reflect back on the conversation and briefly summarize it so as to bring it to a close. For example, "I'm glad I ran into you and found out what happened at that union meeting. I'll probably be seeing you at the next meeting."
- State the desire to end the conversation directly and to get on with other things. For example, "I'd like to continue talking but I really have to run. I'll see you around."
- Refer to future interaction. For example, "Why don't we get together next week sometime and continue this discussion?"
- Ask for closure. For example, "Have I explained what you wanted to know?"
- State that you enjoyed the interaction. For example, "I really enjoyed talking with you."

With any of these closings, it should be clear to the other person that you are attempting to end the conversation. Obviously, you will have to use more direct methods with those who don't take these subtle hints—those who don't realize that both persons are responsible for bringing the conversation to a satisfying close.

THINK ABOUT

Think about how you might go about closing each of the following conversations. What types of closings seem most effective? Which seem least effective?

1. You and a friend have been talking on the phone for the last hour but not much new is being said. You have a great deal of work to get to and would like to close the conversation. Your friend just doesn't seem to hear your subtle cues.
2. You are at a party and are anxious to meet a person with whom you have exchanged eye contact for the last ten minutes. The problem is that a friendly, and talkative, former teacher of yours is demanding all your attention. You don't want to insult the instructor but at the same time want to make contact with this other person.
3. You have had a conference with a teacher and have learned what you needed to know. This teacher, however, doesn't seem to know how to end the conversation, seems very ill at ease, and just continues to go over what has already been said. You have to get to your next class and must close the conversation.
4. You are at a party and notice a person you would like to get to know. You initiate the conversation but after a few minutes realize that this person is not the kind of person with whom you would care to spend any more time. You want to close this conversation as soon as possible.

Reflections on the Model

Not all conversations will be easily divided into these five steps. Often the opening and the feedforward are combined, as when you see someone on campus and say, "Hey, listen to this," or when in a work situation, someone says, "Well, folks, let's get the meeting going." In a similar way, the feedback and the closing might be combined: "Look, I've got to think more about this commitment, okay?"

As already noted, the business is the longest part of the conversation. The opening and the closing are usually about the same length and the feedforward and feedback are usually about equal in length. When these relative lengths are severely distorted, you may feel that something is wrong. For example, when someone uses a long feedforward or a too-short opening, you might suspect that what is to follow is extremely serious.

It is also important to note that effectiveness or competence in conversation and following the appropriate conversational rules will contribute to your own interpersonal attractiveness. For example, in a study of 10-year-old girls, four conversational skills were studied: making an appropriate request, turn-taking, responding without excessive delay when spoken to, and following the logic of the conversation. The girls who demonstrated these skills were liked more and were described in more positive terms than those who lacked these conversational skills (Place & Becker 1991).

THINK ABOUT

Think about applying this model to identify skill deficiencies and distinguish effective and satisfying from ineffective and unsatisfying conversations. Consider, for example, the following violations and some meanings each might communicate? What other meanings might these violations, noted in italics, communicate?

- *using openings that are insensitive,* for example, "Wow, you've gained a few pounds"
- *using overly long feedforwards* that make you wonder if the other person will ever get to the business
- *omitting feedforward before a truly shocking message* (for example, the death or illness of a friend or relative), that leads you to see the other person as insensitive or uncaring
- *doing business without the normally expected greeting,* as when you go to a doctor who begins the conversation by saying, "Well, what's wrong?"
- *omitting feedback,* which leads you to wonder if the other heard what you said or cared about it
- *omitting an appropriate closing,* which makes you wonder if the other person is disturbed or angry with you

Of course, each culture will alter these basic steps in different ways. In some cultures, the openings are especially short, whereas in others the openings are elaborate, lengthy, and, in some cases, highly ritualized. It is easy in intercultural communication situations to violate another culture's conversational rules. Being overly friendly, too formal, or too forward may easily hinder the remainder of the conversation.

The reasons such violations may have significant consequences is that you may not be aware of these rules and hence may not see violations as cultural differences but rather as aggressiveness, stuffiness, or pushiness—and almost immediately dislike the person and put a negative cast on the future conversation.

THE MANAGEMENT OF CONVERSATION

In developing conversational competence or effectiveness we need to look at interpersonal skills on two levels. On one level there are the skills of effectiveness such as openness and supportiveness. On another level, however, are skills that guide us in regulating our openness and our supportiveness. They are skills about skills, or **metaskills.** These qualities will provide a good foundation for communicating interpersonally, in small groups, in public speaking, and especially in intercultural communication.

Metaskills

Because each conversation is unique, the qualities of interpersonal competence cannot be applied indiscriminately. You need to know how the skills themselves should be applied. You should be mindful, flexible, and culturally sensitive.

Mindfulness

After you have learned a skill or a rule you often apply it without thinking; you apply it **mindlessly,** without considering the novel aspects of this unique situation. Instead, conversational skills need to be applied **mindfully,** a concept that was introduced briefly in Unit 6 (Langer 1989). For example, after learning the skills of active listening, many will respond to all situations with active listening responses. Some of these responses will be appropriate but others will prove inappropriate and ineffective. Before responding, think about the unique communication situation you face and consider your alternatives. Be alert and responsive to small changes in the situation that may cue which behaviors will be effective and which ineffective. Be especially mindful of the cultural differences among people, as outlined in the section "Cultural Sensitivity."

Langer (1989) offers several suggestions for increasing mindfulness that will prove useful in most conversations, and in fact in most communications

LISTEN TO THIS

SOME DIFFICULT LISTENERS

The poet Walt Whitman once said, "To have great poets, there must be great audiences too." The same is true of conversation; to have great conversation, there must be great listeners as well as great talkers. In terms of our earlier discussion of sources-receivers (see Unit 1), we need great speakers-listeners. Listening is as crucial to effective conversation as talking. Here, in brief, are a few types of listeners that make conversation difficult. It's easy to see others in these roles; it's harder but more important to see ourselves as listeners who make conversation difficult.

Is there any way that you (as a speaker) can help your listeners become less difficult? That is, how can you prevent your listeners from giving monotonous feedback? From avoiding eye contact? As a listener what can you do to prevent yourself from falling into one of these difficult modes?

Listening Type	Listening Behavior	(Mis)interpreting Thoughts
The static listener	Gives no feedback, remains relatively motionless, reveals no expression	"Why isn't she reacting? Am I not producing sound?"
The monotonous feedback giver	Seems responsive but the responses never vary; regardless of what you say, the response is the same	"Am I making sense? Why is he still smiling? I'm being dead serious."
The overly expressive listener	Reacts to just about everything with extreme responses	"Why is she so expressive? I didn't say anything that provocative. She'll have a heart attack when I get to the punchline."
The reader/writer	Reads or writes, while "listening" and only occasionally glances up	"Am I that boring? Is last week's student newspaper more interesting than me?"
The eye avoider	Looks all around the room and at others but never at you	"Why isn't he looking at me? Do I have spinach on my teeth?"
The preoccupied listener	Listens to other things at the same time, often with headphones with the sound so loud that it interferes with your own thinking	"When is she going to shut that music off and really listen? Am I so boring that my talk needs background music?"
The waiting listener	Listens for a cue to take over the speaking turn	"Is he listening to me or rehearsing his next interruption?"
The thought-completing listener	Listens a little and then finishes your thought	"Am I that predictable? Why do I bother saying anything? He already knows what I'm going to say."

generally. As you read through these suggestions, try to provide a specific example or application for each.

- Create and re-create categories. See an object, event, or person as belonging to a wide variety of categories. Avoid storing in memory an image of a person, for example, with only one specific label; it will be difficult to recategorize it later.
- Be open to new information even if it contradicts your most firmly held stereotypes.

- Be open to different points of view. This will help you avoid the tendency to blame outside forces for your negative behaviors ("that test was unfair") and internal forces for the negative behaviors of others ("Pat didn't study," "Pat isn't very bright"). Be willing to see your own and others' behaviors from a variety of perspectives.
- Be careful not to rely too heavily on first impressions, what psychologists call "premature cognitive commitment" (Chanowitz & Langer 1981; Langer 1989). Treat your first impressions as tentative, as hypotheses.

Flexibility

Before reading about **flexibility,** take the self-test, "How Flexible Are You in Communication?"

Although here we provide general principles for conversational effectiveness, be flexible and sensitive to the unique factors present in every situation. You may need to be frank and spontaneous when talking with a close friend about your feelings but you may not want to be so open when talking with your grandmother about the dinner she prepared that you disliked.

Cultural Sensitivity

In applying the skills for interpersonal effectiveness be sensitive to the cultural differences among people (see Unit 6; also, Guo-Ming & Starosta 1995). What may prove effective for upper-income people working in the IBM subculture of Boston or New York may prove ineffective for lower-income people working as fruit pickers in Florida or California. What works in Germany may not work in Mexico. The direct eye contact that signals immediacy in most of the United States may be considered rude or too intrusive in other cultures. The specific skills discussed in the next section are considered to be generally effective in the United States and among most people living in the United States; but do be aware that these skills and the ways you communicate them may not apply to other cultures (Kim 1991).

Effectiveness in intercultural settings, according to Kim, requires that you be

- open to new ideas and to differences among people
- flexible in ways of communicating and in adapting to the communications of the culturally different
- tolerant of other attitudes, values, and ways of doing things
- creative in seeking varied ways to communicate

From another perspective, the successful sojourner—one who enters another culture for a relatively short period of time, such as a traveler or one who spends a year or so working in this other culture—is one who is self-confident, interested in others, open, flexible, and competent professionally (Kealy & Ruben 1983; Berry, Poortinga, Segall, & Dasen 1992).

Another study found that persons were more likely to be competent in intercultural communication when they had a high positive self-concept and when they were appropriate self-disclosives, high self-monitors, behaviorally flexible, highly involving (attentive and responsive, for example), adaptable, and culturally aware (Chen 1990).

These qualities—along with some knowledge of the other culture and the general skills of effectiveness—"should enable a person to approach each intercultural encounter with the psychological posture of an interested learner . . . and to strive for the communication outcomes that are as effective as possible under a given set of relational and situational constraints" (Kim, 1991, p. 271).

Skills in Conversational Competence

The skills of conversational competence discussed here are (1) openness, (2) empathy, (3) positiveness, (4) immediacy, (5) interaction management, (6) expressiveness, and (7) other-orientation. As you read the discussions of these concepts, keep in mind that the most effective communicator is one who is flexible and who adapts to the individual situation. To be always open or empathic, for example, will probably prove ineffective. Although these qualities are generally appropriate to most interpersonal interactions, do remember that the ability to control these qualities—rather than exhibiting them reflexively—should be your aim.

These qualities would not be effective in all cultures, nor would the specific verbal and nonverbal behaviors carry the same meanings in all cultures. For example, assertiveness is evaluated differently by African Americans and Hispanics (Rodriguez 1988). Similarly, whites, African Americans, and Hispanics

SELF-TEST

how flexible are you in communication?

Instructions: Here are some situations that illustrate how people sometimes act when communicating with others. The first part of each situation asks you to imagine that you are in the situation. Then, a course of action is identified and you are asked to determine how much your own behavior would be like the action described in the scenario. If it is EXACTLY like you, circle a **5**; if it is A LOT like you, circle a **4**; if it is SOMEWHAT like you, circle a **3**; if it is NOT MUCH like you, circle a **2**; and it is NOT AT ALL like you, circle a **1**.

IMAGINE:

1. Last week, as you were discussing your strained finances with your family, family members came up with several possible solutions. Even though you already decided on one solution, you decided to spend more time considering all the possibilities before making a final decision.
2. You were invited to a Halloween Party and assuming it was a costume party, you dressed as a pumpkin. When you arrived at the party and found everyone else dressed in formal attire, you laughed and joked about the misunderstanding, and decided to stay and enjoy the party.
3. You have always enjoyed being with your friend Chris, but do not enjoy Chris's habit of always interrupting you. The last time you met, every time Chris interrupted you, you then interrupted Chris to teach Chris a lesson.
4. Your daily schedule is very structured and your calendar is full of appointments and commitments. When asked to make a change in your schedule, you replied that changes are impossible before even considering the change.
5. You went to a party where over 50 people attended. You have a good time, but spent most of the evening talking to one close friend rather than meeting new people.
6. When discussing a personal problem with a group of friends, you notice that many different solutions were offered. Although several of the solutions seemed feasible, you already had your opinion and did not listen to any of the alternative solutions.
7. You and a friend are planning a fun evening and you're dressed and ready ahead of time. You find that you are unable to do anything else until your friend arrives.
8. When you found your seat at the ball game, you realized you did not know anyone sitting nearby. However, you introduced yourself to the people sitting next to you attempted to strike up a conversation.
9. You had lunch with your friend Chris, and Chris told you about a too-personal family problem. You quickly finished your lunch and stated that you had to leave because you had a lot to do that afternoon.
10. You were involved in a discussion about international politics with a group of acquaintances and you assumed that the members of the group were as knowledgeable as you on the topic; but, as the discussion progressed, you learned that most of the group knew little about the subject. Instead of explaining your point of view, you decided to withdraw from the discussion.
11. You and a group of friends got into a discussion about gun control and, after a while, it became obvious that your opinions differed greatly from the rest of the group. You explained your position once again, but you agreed to respect the group's opinion also.
12. You were asked to speak to a group you belong to, so you worked hard preparing a 30-minute presentation; but at the meeting, the organizer asked you to lead a question and answer session instead of giving your presentation. You agreed, and answered the group's questions as candidly and fully as possible.
13. You were offered a managerial position where every day you would face new tasks and challenges and a changing day-to-day routine. You decided to accept this position instead of one that has a stable daily routine.

(*continued on next page*)

35

(continued)

14. You were asked to give a speech at a Chamber of Commerce breakfast. Because you did not know anyone at the breakfast and would feel uncomfortable not knowing anyone in the audience, you declined the invitation.

Thinking Critically About Flexibility To compute your score:

1. Reverse the scoring for items 4, 5, 6, 7, 9, 10, and 14. That is, for each of these questions, substitute as follows:

 If you answered 5, reverse it to 1
 If you answered 4, reverse it to 2
 If you answered 3, it remains 3
 If you answered 2, reverse it to 4
 If you answered 1, reverse it to 5

2. Add the scores for all 14 items. Be sure that you use the reversed scores for items 4, 5, 6, 7, 9, 10, and 14 instead of your original responses. Use your original scores for items 1, 2, 3, 8, 11, 12, and 13.

In general, you can interpret your score as follows:

65–70 = much more flexible than average
57–64 = more flexible than average
44–56 = about average
37–43 = less flexible than average
14–36 = much less flexible than average.

Do you agree with the assumption made that flexibility is an essential ingredient in communication competence? Are you satisfied with your level of flexibility? What might you do to cultivate flexibility in general and communication flexibility in particular.

Source: From "Development of a Communication Flexibility Measure," by Matthew M. Martin and Rebecca B. Rubin, *The Southern Communication Journal* Volume 59, Winter 1994, pp. 171–178. Reprinted by permission of the Southern States Communication Association.

define what is satisfying communication in different ways. What follows then are general suggestions that should prove useful most of the time. Always go to the specific culture for specific recommendations.

Openness

Openness refers to three aspects of interpersonal communication. First, you should be willing to self-disclose—to reveal information about yourself. Of course, these disclosures need to be appropriate to the entire communication act (see Unit 3). There must also be an openness in regard to listening to the other person; you should be open to the thoughts and feelings of the person with whom you're communicating.

A second aspect of openness refers to your willingness to listen and react honestly to the messages and situations that confront you. You demonstrate openness by responding spontaneously and honestly to the communications and the feedback of others.

Third, openness calls for the "owning" of feelings and thoughts. To be open in this sense is to acknowledge that the feelings and thoughts you express are yours and that you bear the responsibility for them; you do not try to shift the responsibility for your feelings to others. For example, consider these comments:

1. Your behavior was grossly inconsiderate.
2. Everyone thought your behavior was grossly inconsiderate.
3. I was really disturbed when you told my father he was an old man.

Comments 1 and 2 do not evidence ownership of feelings. In 1, the speaker accuses the listener of being inconsiderate without assuming any of the responsibility for the judgment. In 2, the speaker assigns responsibility to the convenient but elusive "everyone" and again assumes none of the responsibility. In comment 3, however, a drastic difference appears. Note that here the speaker is taking responsibility for his or her own feelings ("I was really disturbed").

When you own your own messages you use I-messages instead of you-messages. Instead of saying, "You make me feel so stupid when you ask what everyone else thinks but don't ask my opinion," the person who owns his or her feelings says, "I feel stupid when you ask everyone else what they think but don't ask me." When you own your feelings and thoughts, when you use I-messages, you say in effect, "This is how I feel," "This is how I see the situation," "This is what I think," with the "I" always paramount. Instead of saying, "This discussion is useless," one would say, "I'm bored by this discussion," or "I want to talk more about myself," or any other such statement that includes a reference to the fact that "I" am making an evaluation and not describing objective reality. By doing so, you make it explicit that your feelings are the result of the interaction between what is going on in the world outside your skin (what others say, for example) and what is going on inside your skin (your preconceptions, attitudes, and prejudices, for example).

Empathy

When you empathize with someone, you are able to experience what the other is experiencing from that person's point of view. Empathy does not mean that you agree with what the other person says or does. You never lose your own identity or your own attitudes and beliefs. To sympathize, on the other hand, is to feel for the individual—to feel sorry for the person. To empathize is to feel the same feelings in the same way as the other person does. **Empathy,** then, enables you to understand, emotionally and intellectually, what another person is experiencing.

Most people find it easier to communicate empathy in response to a person's positive statements (Heiskell & Rychiak 1986). Similarly, empathy will be more difficult to achieve with persons who are culturally different from you than for persons who are culturally similar. Perhaps you will have to exert special effort to communicate empathy for negative statements and in intercultural situations.

Of course, empathy will mean little if you are not able to communicate this empathic understanding back to the other person. Here are a few suggestions for communicating empathy both verbally and nonverbally:

- Confront mixed messages. Confront messages that seem to be communicating conflicting feelings to show you are trying to understand the other person's feelings. For example, "You say that it doesn't bother you but I seem to hear a lot of anger coming through."
- Avoid judgmental and evaluative (nonempathic) responses. Avoid "should" and "ought" statements that try to tell the other person how he or she should feel. For example, avoid expressions such as "Don't feel so bad," "Cheer up," "In time you'll forget all about this," and "You should start looking for another job; by next month you won't even remember this place."
- Use reinforcing comments. Let the speaker know that you understand what the speaker is saying and encourage the speaker to continue talking about this issue. For example, use comments such as "I see," "I get it," "I understand," "Yes," and "Right."
- Demonstrate interest by maintaining eye contact (avoid scanning the room or focusing on objects or persons other than the person with whom you are interacting), maintaining physical closeness, leaning toward (not away from) the other person, and showing your interest and agreement with your facial expressions, nods, and eye movements.

Although empathy is almost universally considered positive, there is some evidence to show that even it has a negative side. For example, people are most empathic with those who are similar—racially and ethnically as well as in appearance and social status. The more empathy one feels towards one's own group, the less empathy—possibly even hostility—one feels toward other groups. The same empathy that increases your understanding of your own group, decreases your understanding of other groups. Therefore, while empathy may encourage group cohesiveness and identification, it can also create dividing lines between one's own group and "them" (Angier 1995).

Positiveness

You can communicate **positiveness** in interpersonal communication in at least two ways. First, you can state positive attitudes. Second, you can "stroke" the person with whom you interact.

People who feel negatively about themselves invariably communicate these feelings to others, who in turn probably develop similar negative feelings. On the other hand, people who feel positively about themselves convey this feeling to others, who then return the positive regard.

Positiveness in attitudes also refers to a positive feeling for the general communication situation. A negative response to a communication makes you feel almost as if you are intruding, and communication is sure to break down. Positiveness is most clearly evident in the way you phrase statements. Consider these two sentences:

1. You look horrible in stripes.
2. You look your best, I think, in solid colors.

The first sentence is critical and will almost surely encourage an argument. The second sentence, on the other hand, expresses the speaker's thought clearly and positively and should encourage responses that are cooperative.

You also communicate positiveness through stroking, which acknowledges the importance of the other person. It is the opposite of indifference. When you stroke someone, whether positively or negatively, you acknowledge him or her as a person, as a significant human being.

Stroking may be verbal, as in "I like you," "I enjoy being with you," or "You're a pig." Stroking may also be nonverbal. A smile, a hug, or a slap in the face are also examples of stroking. Positive stroking generally takes the form of compliments or rewards. Positive strokes bolster your self-image and make you feel a little bit better than you did before you received them. Negative strokes, on the other hand, are punishing; sometimes, like cruel remarks, they hurt you emotionally; sometimes, like a punch in the mouth, they hurt you physically.

Immediacy

Immediacy refers to the joining of the speaker and listener, the creation of a sense of togetherness. The communicator who demonstrates immediacy conveys a sense of interest and attention, a liking for and an attraction to the other person. Here are a few ways immediacy may be communicated nonverbally and verbally:

- Maintain appropriate eye contact and limit looking around at others.
- Maintain a physical closeness which suggests a psychological closeness.
- Use a direct and open body posture, for example, by arranging your body to keep others out.
- Smile and otherwise express that you are interested in and care about the other person.
- Use the other person's name; for example, say "Joe, what do you think?" instead of "What do you think?" Say, "I like that, Mary" instead of "I like that."
- Focus on the other person's remarks. Make the speaker know that you heard and understood what was said and will base your feedback on it. For example, use questions that ask for clarification or elaboration, such as, "Do you think the same thing is true of baseball?" or, "How would your argument apply to the Midwest?" Also, refer to the speaker's previous remarks, as in, "I never thought of that being true of all religions," or, "Colorado does sound like a great vacation spot."
- Reinforce, reward, or compliment the other person. Make use of such expressions as, "I like your new outfit," or, "Your comments were really to the point."
- Incorporate self-references into evaluative statements rather than depersonalizing them. Say, for example, "I think your report is great," rather than, "Your report is great," or, "Everyone likes your report."

Do realize that these immediacy behaviors will be evaluated differently in different cultures. For example, in the United States these immediacy behaviors are generally seen as friendly and appropriate. In other cultures, however, the same immediacy behaviors may be viewed as overly familiar, as presuming that a close relationship exists when it is only one of acquaintanceship. In the United States, to take one specific example, we move rather quickly from Mr. LastName and Ms. LastName to Fred and Ginger. In more formal countries (Japan and German are two examples) a much longer period of acquaintanceship would be necessary before first names would be considered appropriate (Axtell 1993).

SELF-TEST

are you a high self-monitor?

These statements concern personal reactions to a number of different situations. No two statements are exactly alike, so consider each statement carefully before answering. If a statement is true, or mostly true, as applied to you, mark it T. If a statement is false, or not usually true, as applied to you, mark it F.

______ 1. I find it hard to imitate the behavior of other people.
______ 2. At parties and social gatherings, I do not attempt to do or say things that others will like.
______ 3. I can only argue for ideas which I already believe.
______ 4. I can make impromptu speeches even on topics about which I have almost no information.
______ 5. I guess I put on a show to impress or entertain people.
______ 6. I would probably make a good actor.
______ 7. In a group of people I am rarely the center of attention.
______ 8. In different situations and with different people, I often act like very different persons.
______ 9. I am not particularly good at making other people like me.
______10. I'm not always the person I appear to be.
______11. I would not change my opinions (or the way I do things) in order to please someone or win their favor.
______12. I have considered being an entertainer.
______13. I have never been good at games like charades or improvisational acting.
______14. I have trouble changing my behavior to suit different people and different situations.
______15. At a party I let others keep the jokes and stories going.
______16. I feel a bit awkward in company and do not show up quite as well as I should.
______17. I can look anyone in the eye and tell a lie with a straight face (if for a right end).
______18. I may deceive people by being friendly when I really dislike them.

Thinking Critically About Self-Monitoring. Give yourself one point for each T response you gave to questions 4, 5, 6, 8, 10, 12, 17, and 18 and give yourself one point for each F response you gave to questions 1, 2, 3, 7, 9, 11, 13, 14, 15, and 16. According to Snyder (1987), scores may be interpreted roughly as follows: 13 or higher = very high self-monitoring; 11–12 = high self-monitoring; 8–10 = low self-monitoring; 0–7 = very low self-monitoring.

Although there seem to be two clear-cut types of persons—high and low self-monitors—we all engage more or less in selective monitoring, depending on the situation. If you go to a job interview, you are likely to monitor your behaviors very carefully. On the other hand, you are less likely to monitor your performance with a group of friends. In what situations and with what people are you most likely to self-monitor? Least likely to self-monitor? How do these situations and people differ?

Source: From Mark Snyder, *Public Appearances/Private Realities* (New York: W. H. Freeman and Company, 1987), p. 179.

Interaction Management

The effective communicator controls the interaction to the satisfaction of both parties. In effective **interaction management**, neither person feels ignored or on stage. Each contributes to the total communication interchange. Maintaining your role as speaker or listener and passing back and forth the opportunity to speak are interaction management skills. If one person speaks all the time and the other listens all the time, effective conversation becomes difficult if not impossible. Depending on the situation, one person may speak more than the other person. This imbalance, however, should be a function of the situation and not that one person is a "talker" and another a "listener."

Generally, effective interaction managers also avoid interrupting the other person. Interruptions often signal that what you have to say is more important than what the other person is saying and puts the other person in an inferior position. The result is dissatisfaction with the conversation. In the United States some interruptions may be seen as signs of involvement and interest in the conversation. In other cultures, however, these same interruptions may be seen as rude and insulting. Similarly, keeping the conversation flowing and fluent without long and awkward pauses that make everyone uncomfortable are signs of effective interaction management.

One of the best ways to look at interaction management is to take the self-test, "Are You a High Self-Monitor?" This test will help you to identify the qualities that make for the effective management of interpersonal communication situations.

Self-monitoring, the manipulation of the image that you present to others in your interpersonal interactions, is integrally related to interpersonal interaction management. High self-monitors carefully adjust their behaviors on the basis of feedback from others so that they produce the most desirable effect. Low self-monitors are not concerned with the image they present to others. Rather, they communicate their thoughts and feelings with no attempt to manipulate the impressions they create. Most of us lie somewhere between the two extremes.

When you compare high and low self-monitors, you find several interesting differences. For example, high self-monitors are more apt to take charge of a situation, are more sensitive to the deceptive techniques of others, and are better able to detect self-monitoring or impression management techniques when used by others. High self-monitors prefer to interact with low self-monitors, over whom they are able to assume positions of influence and power.

How has technology changed the way in which you carry on a conversation? Are there some conversations that you would feel more comfortable holding via phone (or e-mail) rather than face-to-face?

Expressiveness

The speaker displaying **expressiveness** communicates genuine involvement in the interpersonal interaction. He or she plays the game instead of just being a spectator. Expressiveness is similar to openness in its emphasis on involvement. It includes taking responsibility for thoughts and feelings, encouraging expressiveness or openness in others, and providing appropriate feedback. Do recognize that here too there are wide cultural differences. For example, in the United States women are expected to participate fully in business discussions, to smile, laugh, and initiate interactions. These behaviors are so expected and seemingly so natural that it seems strange even mentioning them. In many other countries (Arab countries and many Asian countries), however, this expressiveness would be considered inappropriate (Lustig & Koester 1996; Axtell 1993, Hall & Hall 1987).

Expressiveness also includes taking responsibility for both talking and listening and in this way is similar to equality. In conflict situations, expressiveness involves fighting actively and stating disagreement directly. Expressiveness means using I-messages in which you accept responsibility for your thoughts and feelings, for example, "I'm bored when I don't get to talk," or, "I want to talk more," rather than you-messages ("you ignore me," "you don't ask my opinion").

It is the opposite of fighting passively, withdrawing from the encounter, or attributing responsibility to others.

More specifically, expressiveness may be communicated in a wide variety of ways. Here are a few guidelines:

- Practice active listening by paraphrasing, expressing understanding of the thoughts and feelings of the other person, and asking relevant questions (as explained in Unit 5).
- Avoid clichés and trite expressions that signal a lack of personal involvement and originality.
- Address mixed messages—messages (verbal or nonverbal) that are communicated simultaneously but that contradict each other.
- Address messages that somehow seem unrealistic to you (for example, statements claiming that the breakup of a long-term relationship is completely forgotten or that failing a course doesn't mean anything).
- Use I-messages to signal personal involvement and a willingness to share your feelings. Instead of saying "You never give me a chance to make any decisions," say "I'd like to contribute to the decisions that affect both of us."
- Communicate expressiveness nonverbally by using appropriate variations in vocal rate, pitch, volume, and rhythm to convey involvement and interest, and by allowing facial muscles to reflect and echo this inner involvement.
- Similarly, use gestures appropriately: too few gestures signal disinterest, while too many may communicate discomfort, uneasiness, and awkwardness.

Other-Orientation

Some people are primarily self-oriented and talk mainly about themselves, their experiences, their interests, and their desires. They do most of the talking, and pay little attention to verbal and nonverbal feedback from the other person. **Other-orientation** is the opposite of self-orientation; it involves the ability to communicate attentiveness and interest in the other person and in what is being said. Without other-orientation each person pursues his or her own goal instead of cooperating and working together to achieve a common goal.

Other-orientation is especially important (and especially difficult) when you are interacting with people who are very different from you, as in, for example, talking with people from other cultures. Try the following methods to improve your other-orientation:

- Use focused eye contact, smiles, and head nods.
- Lean toward the other person.
- Display feelings and emotions through appropriate facial expression.
- Avoid focusing on yourself (as in preening, for example) or on anyone other than the person to whom you're speaking (through frequent or prolonged eye contact or body orientation).
- Ask the other person for suggestions, opinions, and clarification as appropriate. Statements such as, "How do you feel about it?" or, "What do you think?" will go a long way toward focusing the communication on the other person.
- Express agreement when appropriate. Comments such as, "You're right," or, "That's interesting," help to focus the interaction on the other person, which encourages greater openness.
- Use minimal responses to encourage the other person to express himself or herself. Minimal responses are those brief expressions that encourage another to continue talking without intruding on her or his thoughts and feelings or directing her or him to go in any particular direction. For example, "yes," "I see," or even, "aha," are minimal responses that tell the other person that you are interested in his or her continued comments.
- Use positive affect statements to refer to the other person and to his or her contributions to the interaction; for example, "I really enjoyed your presentation at the department meeting today," or, "That was a clever way of looking at things," are positive affect statements that are often felt but rarely expressed.

Other-orientation demonstrates consideration and respect—for example, asking if it's all right to dump your troubles on someone before doing so, or asking if your phone call comes at an inopportune time before launching into your conversation. Other-orientation involves acknowledging others' feelings as legitimate: "I can understand why you're so angry; I would be too."

PROBLEMS IN CONVERSATION: PREVENTION AND REPAIR

In conversation, you may anticipate a problem and seek to prevent it. Or you may discover that you said or did something that will lead to disapproval, and you may seek to excuse yourself. Following is just one example of a device to prevent potential conversational problems (the disclaimer) and one example of a device to repair conversational problems (the excuse). They are given simply to illustrate the complexity of these processes and not to present an exhaustive listing of the ways in which conversational problems may be prevented or repaired.

Preventing Conversational Problems: The Disclaimer

Let us say, for example, that you fear your listeners will think your comment is inappropriate in the present context, or that they may rush to judge you without hearing your full account, or that you are not in full possession of your faculties. In these cases, you may use some form of disclaimer, a statement that aims to ensure that your message will be understood and will not reflect negatively on you.

THINK ABOUT

Think about your own use of disclaimers as you read about these five types (Hewitt & Stokes 1975; McLaughlin 1984). What types have you used? In what situations? Did they help you achieve your purpose?

A **hedge** helps you to separate yourself from the message so that if your listeners reject your message, they need not reject you (for example, "I may be wrong here, but . . ."). Hedges decrease the attractiveness of both women and men (Wright & Hosman 1983) if they are seen as indicating a lack of certainty or conviction because of some inadequacy. On the other hand, if the hedges are seen as indicating a belief in "nonallness" (that no one can know all about any subject) and a belief that tentative statements are all one can reasonably make (Hosman 1989; Pearson, West, & Turner, 1995), they will be more positively received.

Credentialing helps you to establish your special qualifications for saying what you are about to say (for example, "Don't get me wrong, I'm not homophobic . . ."). **Sin licenses** ask listeners for permission to deviate in some way from some normally accepted convention (for example, "I know this may not be the place to discuss business, but . . ."). **Cognitive disclaimers** help you to make the case that you are in full possession of your faculties (for example, "I know you'll think I'm crazy, but let me explain the logic of the case"). **Appeals for the suspension of judgment** ask listeners to hear you out before making a judgment (for example, "Don't hang up on me until you hear my side of the story"). These disclaimers, along with their definitions and additional examples, are summarized in Table 13. 1.

Generally, disclaimers are effective when, for example, you think you might offend listeners in telling a joke ("I don't usually like these types of jokes, but . . ."). In one study, for example, 11-year-old children were read a story about someone whose actions created negative effects. Some children heard the story with a disclaimer and others hear the same story without the disclaimer. When the children were asked to indicate how the person should be punished, those who heard the story with the disclaimer recommended significantly less severe punishments (Bennett 1990).

Disclaimers can also get you into trouble, however. For example, to preface remarks inappropriately with "I'm no liar" may well lead listeners to think that perhaps the speaker is a liar. Also, if you use too many disclaimers you may be perceived as someone who doesn't have any strong convictions or as one who wants to avoid responsibility for just about everything. This seems especially true of hedges.

In responding to statements containing disclaimers, it is often necessary to respond to both the disclaimer and to the statement. By doing so, you let the speaker know that you heard the disclaimer and that you aren't going to view this communication negatively. Appropriate responses might be: "I know you're no sexist but I don't agree that . . . ," or, "Well, perhaps we should discuss the money now even if it doesn't seem right."

Repairing Conversational Problems: The Excuse

Earlier we examined the concept of irreversibility, the idea that once something is said, it cannot be *un*com-

TABLE 13.1
disclaimers

Disclaimer	Definition/Function	Examples
Hedging	Speaker disclaims the importance of the message to his or her own identity; speaker makes it clear that listeners may reject the message without rejecting the speaker.	"I didn't read the entire report, but . . . ." "I'm no physiologist, but that irregularity seems . . . ."
Credentialing	Speaker tries to avoid undesirable inferences that may be drawn by listeners; speaker seeks to establish special qualifications.	"Don't get the wrong idea; I'm not sexist, but . . . ." "Some of my best friends are . . . ." "I've lived with Martians all my life so I know what they're like."
Sin licenses	Speaker announces that he or she will violate some social or cultural rule but should be "forgiven" in advance (a "license to sin").	"I realize that this may not be the time to talk about money, but . . . . "I know you'll think this suggestion is out of order, but do consider . . . ."
Cognitive disclaimers	Speaker seeks to reaffirm his or her cognitive abilities in anticipation of listener doubts.	"I know you think I'm drunk, but I'm as sober and as lucid as . . . ."
Appeals for the suspension of judgment	Speaker asks the listeners to delay making judgments until a more complete account is presented.	"Don't say anything until I explain the real story." "If you promise not to laugh, I'll tell you exactly what happened."

municated (Unit 2). In part because of this fact, we need at times to defend or justify messages that may be perceived negatively. Perhaps the most common method for doing so is the excuse. Excuses pervade all forms of communication and behavior. Although we emphasize their role in conversation, recognize that the excuse is applicable to all human behaviors, not just conversational ones.

You learn early in life that when you do something that will be perceived negatively, an excuse is in order to justify your poor performance. The excuse, as C. R. Snyder (1984) notes, "plays a central role in how we get along in life, both with yourself and with other people."

The excuse usually follows from three conditions:

1. You say something.
2. Your statement is viewed negatively; you desire to disassociate yourself from it.
3. Someone hears the message or the results of the message. (The "witness" may be an outsider, for example, a boss, a friend, a colleague, but also could be yourself—you are a witness to your own messages.)

More formally, Snyder (1984; Snyder, Higgins, & Stucky 1983) defines **excuses** as "explanations or actions that lessen the negative implications of an actor's performance, thereby maintaining a positive image for oneself and others."

Excuses seem especially in order when we say or are accused of saying something that runs counter to what is expected, sanctioned, or considered "right" by the people involved or by society in general. The excuse, ideally, lessens the negative impact of the message.

Some Motives for Excuse-Making

The major motive for excuse-making seems to be to maintain self-esteem, to project a positive image to ourselves and to others. Excuses are also offered to reduce the stress that may be created by a bad performance. If you can offer an excuse—especially a good one that is accepted by those around you—it will lessen the negative reaction and the subsequent stress that accompanies a poor performance.

Excuses enable you to take risks and engage in behavior that may be unsuccessful; you may offer an anticipatory excuse: "My throat's a bit sore but I'll give

INTRODUCING RESEARCH

A SAMPLE EXPERIMENTAL STUDY

In this study (actually a small part of a much larger and more complex study), the researchers investigated whether men and women differed when they gave accounts of their negative behaviors (Mongeau, Hale, & Alles 1994). In this experimental study, scenarios were given to men and women. These scenarios described a heterosexual dating relationship in which one partner (the infidel) goes to a bar and winds up having a sexual relationship with another person. Some scenarios (the no-revenge condition) described the infidel as being alone for the weekend and going to the bar for a drink. Other scenarios (the revenge condition) described the infidel as one who discovers that his or her partner has been having a sexual relationship with another person and goes to the bar after a heated argument.

The 239 students who read these scenarios were asked to place themselves in the role of the infidel and give an account of their behavior. The accounts were then categorized (by coders who did not know the purposes of the experiment) into one of five categories: (1) concessions, (2) excuses, (3) justifications, (4) refusals, and (5) silence. The accounts were also coded for their degree of aggravation (defined by such terms as aggravating, worsening, intensifying, exasperating, and provoking) or mitigation (defined by such terms as soothing, alleviating, subduing, relieving, and easing).

There were no statistically significant differences in the types of accounts men and women gave. There was a tendency for women to give more excuses than men and for men to give more refusals and justifications than women. There was a sex difference found in the no-revenge condition. In these cases, women presented more excuses and men presented more refusals and silences. Accounts by men were judged to be more aggravating than accounts by women.

Are these results intuitively satisfying? Do they seem logical to you on the basis of your own experience? Do you think the same results would be found if, instead of college students, the informants were middle-aged blue-collar workers?

the speech a try." The excuse is designed to lessen the criticism should you fail to deliver, in this case an acceptable speech.

Excuses also enable you to maintain effective interpersonal relationships even after some negative behavior. For example, after criticizing a friend's behavior and observing the negative reaction to your criticism, you might offer an excuse such as, "Please forgive me; I'm really exhausted. I'm just not thinking straight." Excuses enable you to place your messages—even your possible failures—in a more favorable light.

Three Types of Excuses

There are three kinds of identifiable excuses (Snyder 1984; Snyder, Higgins, & Stucky 1983). In the "I Didn't Do It" type, the excuse-maker claims not to have done the behavior of which he or she is accused: "I didn't say that," "I wasn't even near the place when it happened." In the "It Wasn't So Bad" type, the excuse-maker claims that the behavior was not really so bad, certainly not as bad as others may at first think: "I only copied one answer," "The fire was smoking and your mink coat was the only thing I could find," "Sure, I punched him out; he asked for it." In the "Yes, But" type, the excuse-maker claims that extenuating circumstances accounted for the behavior: "It was the liquor talking," "I really tried to help him; I didn't mean to hurt his feelings," "It was just my jealousy making those accusations."

Good and Bad Excuses

The most important question to most people is what makes a good excuse and what makes a bad excuse (Snyder 1984, Slade 1995). How can you make good excuses and thus get out of problems, and how can you avoid bad excuses and thus only make matters worse? Good excuse-makers use excuses in moderation; bad excuse-makers rely on excuses too often. Good excuse-makers avoid using excuses in the presence of those who know what really happened; bad excuse-makers will make excuses even in these inappropriate situations. Good excuse-makers avoid blaming others, especially those they work with; bad excuse-makers blame even their work colleagues. In a similar way, good excuse-makers do not attribute their failure to others or to the company; bad excuse-makers do. Good excuse-makers acknowledge their own responsibility for the failure by noting that they did something wrong (not that they lack competence); bad excuse-makers refuse to accept any responsibility for their failure.

The best excuses are apologies because they contain three essential elements for a good excuse (Slade 1995):

- acknowledge some of the responsibility
- ask forgiveness
- suggest that things will be done better in the future

The worst excuses are the "I didn't do it" type, because they fail to acknowledge responsibility and also because they offer no assurance that this failure will not happen again.

SUMMARY

In this unit we covered the conversation process, from opening to closing; the principles of conversational effectiveness; and conversational problems, their prevention and repair.

1. Conversation consists of five general stages: opening, feedforward, business, feedback, and closing.
2. Initiating conversations can be accomplished in various ways, for example, with self, other, relational, and context references.
3. The business of conversation is maintained by the passing of speaking and listening turns; turn-maintaining and turn-yielding cues are used by the speaker, and turn-requesting, turn-denying, and backchanneling cues are used by the listener.
4. Closing a conversation may be achieved through a variety of methods; for example: reflect back on the conversation by summarizing, directly state your desire to end the conversation, refer to future interaction, ask for closure, and state your pleasure with the interaction.
5. The skills of conversational effectiveness need to be applied with mindfulness, flexibility, and cultural sensitivity (as appropriate).
6. Among the skills of conversational effectiveness are openness, empathy, positiveness, immediacy, interaction management, expressiveness, and other-orientation.
7. One way potential conversational problems may be averted is through the disclaimer, a statement that helps to ensure that your message will be understood and will not reflect negatively on the speaker.
8. One way to repair a conversational problem is with the excuse, a statement designed to lessen the negative impact of a speaker's messages.

THINKING CRITICALLY ABOUT CONVERSATION

1. How generally satisfying are most of your conversations? With whom are they most satisfying? With whom are they least satisfying? What one rule of conversation do you wish more people would follow?
2. What type of opening line would you want people to use to meet you? What type of opening line would you react to negatively?
3. How sensitive are you to the conversational turns of others? How sensitive are you to leave-taking cues? How sensitive are others to your conversational turns and leave-taking cues? If you feel you are the more sensitive, could you be operating with the uniqueness bias discussed in Unit 4?
4. Do you give backchanneling cues? If so, what kind do you give most often? Are these generally effective?
5. How mindful, flexible, and culturally sensitive are you in most of your conversations?
6. After reviewing the research on the empathic and listening abilities of men and women, Pearson, West, and Turner (1995) conclude: "Men and women do not differ as much as conventional wisdom would have us believe. In many instances, she thinks like a man, and he thinks like a woman because they both think alike." Does your experience support or contradict this observation?
7. What conversational skills do you feel you use most effectively? Least effectively?

8. Animal researchers have argued that some animals show empathy. For example, consider the male gorilla who watched a female try in vain to get water that collected in an automobile tire and who then secured the tire and brought it to the female. This gorilla, it has been argued, demonstrated empathy; he felt the other gorilla's thirst (Angier 1995). Similarly, the animal that cringes when another of its species gets hurt seems also to be showing empathy. What evidence would you demand before believing that animals possess empathic abilities? What evidence would you want before believing that a relationship partner or a friend feels empathy for you?
9. Try collecting examples of disclaimers from your interpersonal interactions as well as from the media. Consider: What type of disclaimer is being used? Why is it being used? Is the disclaimer appropriate? What other kinds of disclaimers could have been used more effectively?
10. How would you go about answering such questions as these:
    a. Are same-sex or opposite-sex conversations generally more satisfying? Does this level of satisfaction vary with the age of the participants?
    b. Are conversational satisfaction and speaker flexibility related?
    c. Are high self-monitors generally more successful in interpersonal relationships than low self-monitors? In business relationships?
    d. Do happy and unhappy couples use disclaimers in the same way? Do effective and ineffective managers use disclaimers in the same way?

fourteen unit

Relationship Development, Deterioration, Maintenance, and Repair

unit contents

unit goals

After completing this unit, you should be able to

1. explain the reasons for and the process of relationship development
2. explain the reasons for relationship deterioration and the changes in communication that take place during this stage
3. explain the nature of relationship maintenance
4. explain the suggestions for relationship repair
5. explain the suggestions for self-repair

In this unit the relationship process, introduced in Unit 12, is examined in more detail. First, we examine the process of relationship development—why we seek relationships and how we initiate them. Second, we consider relationship deterioration: its nature and causes, and the changes in communication that take place when relationships deteriorate. Third, we look at relationship maintenance, how people seek to keep their relationship together. Last, we look at how a relationship might be repaired and offer some suggestions for dealing with relationships that do end.

Relationships in a Cultural Context

The model of interpersonal relationships presented in Unit 12 and the explanations offered in this unit derive in great part from research conducted in the United States. This research and the corresponding theory reflect the way most relationships are viewed in the United States. Seldom do we pause to consider how extensively culture influences relationship attitudes and behaviors. For example, we assume in the model and in the discussion of relationship development that follows that we voluntarily choose our relationship partners. We choose to pursue certain relationships and not others. In many cultures throughout the world and in some cultures within the United States, however, a romantic partner is chosen by the parents (Jaleshgari 1995). In some cases, a husband or wife is chosen to solidify two families or to bring some financial advantage to the family or village.

In the United States researchers study and textbook authors write about dissolving relationships and how to manage after a relationship breaks up. We assume that the individual has the right to exit an undesirable relationship. But that is not always true. In some cultures, you simply cannot dissolve a relationship once it is formed or once there are children. In the practice of Roman Catholicism, once people are validly married, they are always married and cannot dissolve that relationship.

A similar assumption of choice is seen in the research and theory on friendships. In most of the United States, interpersonal friendships are drawn from a relatively large pool. Out of all the people you come into regular contact with, you choose relatively few of these as friends. Now with on-line chat groups, the number of friends people can have has increased enormously as has the range from which these friends can be chosen. In rural areas and in small villages throughout the world, however, you would have very few choices for face-to-face friends. The two or three other children your age become your friends; there is no real choice because these are the only possible friends you could make.

A cultural bias is also seen in the research on maintenance; it is assumed that relationships should be permanent or at least long lasting. Consequently, it is assumed that people want to keep relationships together and will exert considerable energy to maintain relationships. There is little research that studies how to move effortlessly from one intimate relationship to another or that advises how to do this more effectively and efficiently.

Keep in mind that the way you view relationships and the way you conduct your own relationships are heavily influenced by your culture. With these considerations as a preface, we can explore how relationships develop and deteriorate, how they are maintained, and how they may be repaired.

RELATIONSHIP DEVELOPMENT

There is probably nothing as important to most people than contact with others. So important is this contact that when it is absent for prolonged periods, depression sets in, self-doubt surfaces, and people find it difficult to carry out even the basics of daily living.

Reasons for Relationship Development

Of course, each person pursues a relationship for unique reasons. Yet there are also some general reasons for developing relationships: to lessen loneliness, to secure stimulation, to acquire self-knowledge, and to maximize pleasures and minimize pain.

THINK ABOUT

Think about the development of your own relationships as you read through these reasons. Are these reasons adequate to explain why you have developed the relationships you did? Are there other reasons that motivated your relationships that are not noted here?

Lessening Loneliness

One reason we enter relationships is because contact with another human being helps lessen loneliness. It doesn't always, of course. At times, for example, you may experience loneliness even though you are with other people. And at other times you don't feel lonely even when physically alone (Perlman & Peplau 1981). Yet, generally, contact with other people helps lessen the uncomfortable feelings of loneliness (Peplau & Perlman 1982; Rubenstein & Shaver 1982).

Securing Stimulation

Human beings need stimulation, and interpersonal relationships provide one of the best ways to get this stimulation. Because you are, in part, an intellectual creature and need intellectual stimulation, you talk about ideas, attend classes, and argue about different interpretations of a film or novel. Because you are also a physical creature who needs physical stimulation, you touch and are touched, hold and are held. Because you are an emotional creature who needs emotional stimulation, you laugh and cry, feel hope and surprise, and experience warmth and affection. Such stimulation comes most easily within an interpersonal relationship—whether it is one of friendship, love, or family.

Acquiring Self-Knowledge

It is largely through contact with other human beings that you learn about yourself. As noted in the discussion of self-awareness (see Unit 5) you see yourself in part through the eyes of others—and those with the best eyesight are usually your friends, lovers, and family members.

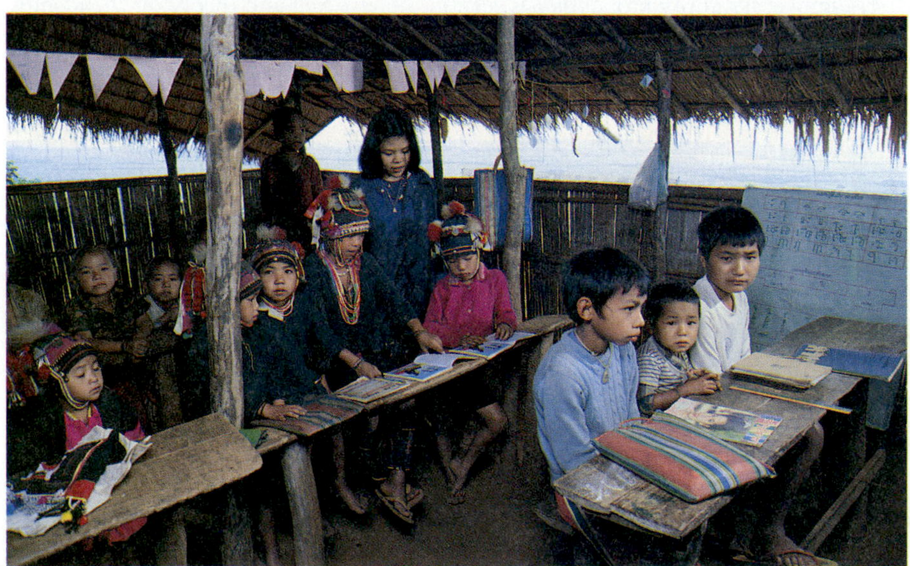

What values did your culture teach you about friendship, romantic, and family relationships? Has your college experience strengthened or weakened (or left unchanged) these values?

Maximizing Pleasures, Minimizing Pains

The most general reason to establish relationships, and one that could include all the others, is that you seek human contact to maximize your pleasures and minimize your pains. Most people want to share with others both their good fortune and their emotional or physical pain. The first impulse upon having something extreme happen (positive or negative) is often to tell it to a relationship partner.

Initiating Relationships: The First Encounter

Perhaps the most difficult and yet the most important aspect of relationship development is the beginning. Meeting the person, presenting yourself, and somehow moving to another stage is a difficult process. Three major phases can be identified in the first encounter: examining the qualifiers, determining clearance, and communicating your desire for contact. Before reading about this first encounter you may wish to take the self-test, "How Apprehensive Are You in Interpersonal Conversations?"

Examining Qualifiers

Qualifiers are those qualities that make the individual you wish to meet an appropriate choice (Davis 1973). Some qualifiers are obvious, such as beauty, style of clothes, jewelry, and the like. Others are hidden, such as personality, health, wealth, talent, and intelligence.

MEDIA WATCH

USES AND GRATIFICATION THEORY

In much the same way that you enter relationships to serve some specific purpose, you also use the media to serve specific purposes. Wilbur Schramm, in *Men, Women, Messages, and Media* (Schramm & Porter 1982) proposes this formula:

$$\frac{\text{promise of reward}}{\text{effort required}} = \text{probability of selection}$$

Under the promise of reward, Schramm includes both immediate and delayed rewards. Rewards satisfy the needs of the audience; that is, you watch a particular television program because it satisfies your need for information or entertainment. The effort required for attending to mass communications depends on the availability of the media and the ease with which we may use them. Effort also includes the expense involved. For example, there is less effort required—less expense, less time lost—in watching television than in going to a movie. There is less effort in going to a movie than in going to a play. When we divide the effort required into the promise of reward, we obtain the probability of selection of a particular mass communication medium.

This approach to media has come to be referred to as the **uses and gratifications** approach. We can understand people's interaction with the media by the uses they put the media to and the gratifications they derive.

Four general gratifications are identified in the research (Dominick 1994): (1) learning something—finding out what the new tax laws will involve or how Siskel and Ebert rate the new film you want to see; (2) diversion—allowing you to escape your worries, to stimulate you, or perhaps to allow you to release emotional energy; (3) affiliation—going to the movies together, talking about the developments on "Days of Our Lives," or developing parasocial relationships (see Media Watch box in Unit 12); and (4) withdrawal—from worries, responsibilities, and from other people.

According to uses and gratifications theory, the audience members actively and consciously link themselves to certain media to gain gratification. The media are seen in this approach as competing with other sources (largely interpersonal) to serve the needs of the audience.

Can you use this theory of uses and gratifications to explain your conversational behavior? What uses does conversation serve for you? What gratifications do you derive from your conversations? Do you gravitate toward those conversations that will give you immediate gratification? Delayed gratification?

SELF-TEST
how apprehensive are you in interpersonal conversations?

Although we often think of apprehension or fear of speaking in connection with public speaking, each of us has a certain degree of apprehension in all forms of communication. The following brief test is designed to measure your apprehension in interpersonal conversations (the subject of Unit 13) and is especially appropriate for exploring your communication patterns in initiating relationships (one of the subjects of this unit).

This questionnaire consists of six statements concerning your feelings about interpersonal conversations. Indicate in the space provided the degree to which each statement applies to you by marking whether you (1) Strongly Agree, (2) Agree, (3) Are Undecided, (4) Disagree, or (5) Strongly Disagree with each statement. There are no right or wrong answers. Some of the statements are similar to other statements. Do not be concerned about this. Work quickly; just record your first impression.

______ 1. While participating in a conversation with a new acquaintance, I feel very nervous.
______ 2. I have no fear of speaking up in conversations.
______ 3. Ordinarily I am very tense and nervous in conversations.
______ 4. Ordinarily I am very calm and relaxed in conversations.
______ 5. While conversing with a new acquaintance, I feel very relaxed.
______ 6. I'm afraid to speak up in conversations.

Thinking Critically About Apprehension in Conversations. To obtain your apprehension score, use the following formula: Add 18 to your score for items 2, 4, and 5; then subtract your scores for items 1, 3, and 6. A score above 18 shows some degree of apprehension.

This self-test is the first of five that deal with communication apprehension, one of the most important obstacles to effective communication interaction. Future apprehension tests deal with group discussions (Unit 17), meetings (Unit 19), interviews (Unit 20), and public speaking (Unit 21). Apprehension, as explained throughout this text, is especially strong in intercultural situations in which there is greater uncertainty and ambiguity. As you take these tests, think about the reasons for your apprehension and the ways in which you might be able to more effectively manage apprehension. Together with the presentation of the last apprehension self-test (in Unit 21) specific suggestions for managing apprehension are provided.

Source: From James C. McCroskey, *An Introduction to Rhetorical Communication*, 6th ed. (Upper Saddle River, N.J.: Prentice-Hall, 1993).

These qualifiers tell you something about who the person is and help you to decide if you wish to pursue this initial encounter.

Determining Clearance

Your second step is to determine if the person is available for the type of meeting you are interested in (Davis 1973). If you are interested in a date, then you might look to see if the person is wearing a wedding ring. Does the person seem to be waiting for someone else?

Communicating Contact

The next stage is making *contact*. You need to open the encounter nonverbally and verbally. Nonverbally you might signal this desire for contact in a variety of ways. Here are just a few things you might do:

- Establish eye contact. The eyes communicate awareness of and interest in the other person.
- While maintaining eye contact, smile and further signal your interest in and positive response to this other person.
- Concentrate your focus. Nonverbally shut off from your awareness the rest of the room. Be careful, however, that you do not focus so directly that you make the person uncomfortable.
- Establish physical closeness or at least lessen the physical distance between the two of you. Approach the other person, but not to the point of

discomfort, so your interest in making contact is obvious.

- Maintain an open posture. Throughout the encounter, maintain a posture that communicates a willingness to enter into interaction with the other person. Hands crossed over the chest or clutched around your stomach communicate a closedness, an unwillingness to let others enter your space.
- Reinforce the positive behaviors of the other person to signal continued interest and a further willingness to make contact. Again, nod, smile, or somehow communicate your favorable reaction.

Although nonverbal contact is signaled first, much of the subsequent nonverbal contact takes place at the same time that you are communicating verbally. Here are some methods for making verbal contact:

- Introduce yourself. Try to avoid trite opening lines, such as, "Haven't I seen you here before?" It is best simply to say, "Hi, my name is Pat."
- Focus the conversation on the other person. Get the other person talking about himself or herself. No one enjoys talking about any topic more. Also, you will gain an opportunity to learn something about the person you want to get to know. For example, the hidden qualifiers or disqualifiers such as intelligence or the lack of it will begin to emerge here.
- Exchange favors and rewards. Compliment the other person. If you cannot find anything to compliment, then you might want to reassess your interest in this person.
- Stress the positives. Positiveness contributes to a good first impression simply because people are more attracted to positive than to negative people.
- Avoid negative or too intimate self-disclosures. Enter a relationship gradually and gracefully. Disclosures should come slowly and should be reciprocal (see Unit 5). Anything too intimate or too negative, when revealed too early in the relationship, will create a negative image. If you cannot resist self-disclosing, try to stick to the positives and to issues that are not overly intimate.
- Establish commonalities. Seek to discover in your interaction those things you have in common with the other person—attitudes, interests, personal qualities, third parties, places—anything that will stress a connection.

RELATIONSHIP DETERIORATION

The opposite end of relationship development is deterioration and possible dissolution. **Relational deterioration,** the weakening of the bonds that hold people together, may be gradual or sudden, slight or extreme. Murray Davis (1973), in his *Intimate Relations,* uses the terms *passing away* to designate gradual deterioration and *sudden death* to designate immediate or sudden deterioration. An example of passing away occurs when one of the parties develops close ties with a new intimate and this new relationship gradually pushes out the old. An example of sudden death occurs when one or both of the parties break a rule that was essential to the relationship (for example, the rule of fidelity). As a result, both realize that the relationship must be terminated.

Although you may be accustomed to thinking of relationship breakup as negative, this is not necessarily so. At times a relationship may be unproductive for one or both parties, and a breakup is often the best thing that could happen. Ending a relationship may provide a period for the individuals to regain their independence and self-reliance. Some relationships are so absorbing that there is little time available for re-

Do men and women communicate similarly in relationship deterioration? If not, what are some of the major differences? Can you identify racial or national differences in the ways people communicate during relationship deterioration? How would you go about finding answers to these questions?

flection about oneself, others, and the relationship itself. In these cases, distance often helps. For the most part, it is up to you to draw out of any decaying relationship some positive characteristics and some learning that can be used later on.

Causes of Relationship Deterioration

The causes of relationship deterioration are as numerous as the individuals involved. All these causes may also be seen as effects of relational deterioration. For example, when things start to go sour, the individuals may remove themselves physically from one another in response to the deterioration. This physical separation may in turn cause further deterioration by driving the individuals farther apart emotionally and psychologically. Or it may encourage them to seek other partners.

THINK ABOUT

Think about your own relationships that may have deteriorated. Consider the following as you read through this discussion. Do the reasons given here adequately explain why your own relationships deteriorated? Can you identify reasons in addition to those covered here that explain why relationships deteriorate?

Reasons for Establishing the Relationship Have Diminished

When the reasons you developed the relationship change drastically, your relationship may deteriorate. For example, when loneliness is no longer lessened, the relationship may be on the road to decay. When the stimulation is weak, one or both may begin to look elsewhere. If self-knowledge and self-growth prove insufficient, you may become dissatisfied with yourself, your partner, and your relationship. When the pains (costs) begin to exceed the pleasures (rewards), you begin to look for ways to exit the relationship or in some cases ways to improve or repair it.

Relational Changes

Relational changes in one or both parties may encourage relational deterioration. Psychological changes such as the development of different intellectual interests or incompatible attitudes may create relational problems. Behavioral changes such as preoccupation with business or schooling may strain the relationship and create problems. Status changes may also create difficulties for a couple.

Undefined Expectations

Sometimes each person's expectations of the other are unrealistic. This often occurs early in a relationship when, for example, the individuals think that they will want to spend all their time together. When they discover that neither one does, each resents this "lessening" of feeling in the other. The resolution of such conflicts lies not so much in meeting these unrealistic expectations as in discovering why they were unrealistic and substituting more attainable expectations.

Sex

Few sexual relationships are free of sexual problems. In fact, sexual problems rank among the top three problems in almost all studies of newlyweds (Blumstein & Schwartz 1983). Although sexual frequency is not related to relational breakdown, sexual satisfaction is. It is the quality and not the quantity of a sexual relationship that is crucial. When the quality is poor, the partners may seek sexual satisfaction outside the primary relationship. Extrarelational affairs contribute significantly to breakups for all couples, whether married or cohabiting, whether heterosexual or homosexual. Even "open relationships"—ones that are based on sexual freedom outside the primary relationship—experience these problems and are more likely to break up than the traditional "closed" relationship.

Work

Unhappiness with work often leads to difficulties in relationships. Most people cannot separate problems with work from their relationships (Blumstein & Schwartz 1983). This is true for all types of couples. With heterosexual couples (both married and cohabiting), if the man is disturbed over the woman's job—for example, if she earns a great deal more than he does or devotes a great deal of time to the job—the relationship is in for considerable trouble.

This is true whether the relationship is in its early stages or is a well-established one. One research study, for example, found that husbands whose wives worked were less satisfied with their own jobs and lives than were men whose wives did not work

(Staines, Pottick, & Fudge 1986). Often the man expects the woman to work but does not reduce his expectations concerning her household responsibilities. The man may become resentful if the woman does not fulfill these expectations, and the woman may become resentful if she takes on both outside work and full household duties.

Financial Difficulties

In surveys of problems among couples, financial difficulties loom large. Money is seldom discussed by couples beginning a relationship, yet it proves to be one of the major problems faced by all couples as they settle into their relationship. Dissatisfaction with money usually leads to dissatisfaction with the relationship. This is true for married and cohabiting heterosexual couples and gay male couples. It is not true for lesbian couples, who seem to care a great deal less about financial matters. This difference has led some researchers to speculate that concern over money and its equation with power and relational satisfaction are largely male attitudes (Blumstein & Schwartz 1983).

The unequal earnings of men and women create further problems, regardless of who earns more. In most relationships, the man earns more money than the woman, and because of this he controls a disproportionate share of power. When the woman earns more than the man, the problems are different. Although our society has finally allowed women to achieve success in business and the professions, it has not taught men to accept this very well. As a result, the higher-earning woman is often resented by the lower-earning man. This is true for both married and cohabiting couples.

Money also creates problems in heterosexual relationships because men and women view it differently. To men, money is power. To women, it is security and independence. Conflicts over how the couple's money is to be spent or invested can easily result from such different perceptions (Blumstein & Schwartz 1983).

Inequitable Distribution of Rewards and Costs

Generally, and as predicted by social exchange and equity theories (see Unit 12), you stay in relationships that are rewarding, and leave relationships that are punishing. Further, you expect and desire equity in your relationships (Berscheid & Walster 1978; Hatfield & Traupman 1981). When partners see their relationship as equitable, they will continue building it. When the relationship is not equitable, it may deteriorate.

Equity is culturally defined, as noted in Unit 12. Therefore it is not possible to tell when relationships are perceived as equitable and when as inequitable. These differences in what constitutes equity can easily cause intercultural difficulties. For example, consider the American woman, used to an American man's average of 108 minutes a day spent on household work, who encounters the Japanese man whose time spent on household work averages 11 minutes (Crohn 1995).

Communication in Relationship Deterioration

Like relational development, relational deterioration involves unique and specialized communication. These communication patterns are in part a response to the deterioration itself. However, these patterns are also causative. The way you communicate influences the course of a relationship.

Withdrawal

Nonverbally, **withdrawal** is seen in the greater space each person seems to require and the ease with which tempers are aroused when that space is encroached on. When people are close emotionally, they can comfortably occupy close physical quarters, but when they are growing apart, they need wider spaces. Withdrawal of another kind may be seen in the decrease in similarities in clothing and in the display of "intimate trophies" such as bracelets, photographs, and rings (Knapp & Vangelisti 1992). Other nonverbal signs include the failure to engage in eye contact, to look at each other generally, and to touch each other (Miller & Parks 1982).

Verbally, withdrawal is seen in a number of ways. Where once there was a great desire to talk and listen, there is now less desire—perhaps none. At times small talk is engaged in as an end in itself. Whereas small talk is usually a preliminary to serious conversation (as in phatic communion) here it is used as an alternative to or a means of forestalling serious talk. Thus people in the throes of dissolution may talk a great deal about insignificant events—the weather, a movie on television, a neighbor down the hall. By focusing on these topics, they avoid confronting serious issues.

Self-Disclosure

Self-disclosing communications decline significantly when a relationship deteriorates. Self-disclosure may not be thought worth the effort if the relationship is dying. Or, you may also limit self-disclosures because you feel that the other person may not be supportive or may use the disclosures against you. Probably the most general reason is that you no longer have a desire to share intimate thoughts and feelings with someone for whom your positive feelings are decreasing.

Deception

Deception generally increases as relationships break down. Lies may be seen as a way to avoid arguments over staying out all night, not calling, or being seen in the wrong place with the wrong person. At other times lies are used because of some feeling of shame. Perhaps you want to save the relationship and do not want to add another obstacle or you may not want to appear to be the cause of any further problems and so you lie. Sometimes deception takes the form of avoidance—the lie of omission. You talk about everything except the crux of the difficulty. Whether by omission or commission, deception has a way of escalating and creating a climate of distrust and disbelief.

Evaluative Responses

Relational deterioration often brings an increase in negative evaluations and a decrease in positive evaluations. Where once you praised the other's behaviors, talents, or ideas, you now criticize them. Often the behaviors have not changed significantly: what has changed is your way of looking at them. Negative evaluation frequently leads to outright fighting and conflict. And although conflict is not necessarily bad (see Unit 16), in relationships that are deteriorating, the conflict (often coupled with withdrawal) is often not resolved.

Exchange of Favors

During relational deterioration there is little favor exchange. Compliments, once given frequently and sincerely, are now rare. Positive stroking is minimal. Nonverbally, eye contact, smiling, touching, caressing, and holding each other occur less frequently.

RELATIONSHIP MAINTENANCE

Relationship maintenance concerns that part of the relationship process in which you act to continue (maintain, retain) the relationship. Of course, maintenance behaviors can serve a variety of functions, for example:

- to keep the relationship intact, to retain the semblance of a relationship, to prevent completely dissolving the relationship
- to keep the relationship at its present stage, to prevent it from moving too far either toward less or toward greater intimacy
- to keep the relationship satisfying, to maintain a favorable balance between rewards and penalties

Some people, after entering a relationship, assume that the relationship will continue unless something catastrophic happens. Therefore, while they may seek to prevent any major mishaps, they are unlikely to engage in much maintenance behavior. Others will be ever on the lookout for something wrong and will seek to patch it up as quickly and as effectively as possible. In between lie most people, who will engage in maintenance behaviors when things are going wrong and when there is the possibility that the relationship can be improved. Behaviors directed at improving badly damaged or even broken relationships are considered under "Relationship Repair," later in this unit.

Reasons for Maintaining Relationships

THINK ABOUT

Think about the relationships you are in now. What maintains these relationships? Put differently, why have they survived rather than deteriorated or dissolved? What keeps your relationships together? Can you identify the reasons other than those given here that might account for relationship maintenance? Following are some of the more popular and frequently cited reasons.

Emotional Attachment

The most obvious reason for maintaining a relationship is that the individuals like or love each other and want to preserve their relationship. They do not find alternative couplings as inviting or as potentially enjoyable—the individuals' needs are being satisfied and so the relationship is maintained. In some cases, these needs are predominantly for love and mutual caring, but in other cases, the needs being met may not be quite so positive. For example, one individual may maintain a relationship because it provides a means of exercising control over another. Another might continue the relationship because it provides ego gratification. Each acts according to his or her specific need.

Convenience

Often the relationship involves neither great love nor great need satisfaction but is maintained for reasons of convenience. Perhaps both partners may jointly own a business or have mutual friends who are important to them. In these cases it may be more convenient to stay together than to break up and go through the difficulties involved in finding another person to live with or another business partner or another social escort.

Children

Relationships are often maintained because there are children involved. Children are sometimes brought into the world to save a relationship. In some cases they do. The parents stay together because they feel, rightly or wrongly, that it is in the best interests of the children. In other cases, the children provide a socially acceptable excuse to mask the real reason—convenience, financial advantage, a fear of being alone, and so on. In childless relationships, both parties can be more independent and can make life choices based more on individual needs and wants. These individuals, therefore, are less likely to remain in relationships they find unpleasant or uncomfortable.

Fear

Fear motivates many couples to stay together. The individuals may fear the outside world; they may fear being alone and of facing others as "singles." They may remember the horrors of the singles bars, the one-night stands, and the lonely weekends. As a result they may elect to preserve their current relationship as the better alternative. Sometimes the fear may be of social criticism: "What will our friends say? They'll think I'm a failure because I can't hold on to another person." Sometimes the fear concerns the consequences of violating some religious or parental tenet that tells you to stay together, no matter what happens.

Financial Considerations

Financial advantages motivate many couples to stick it out. Divorces and separations are both emotionally and financially expensive. Some people fear a breakup that may cost them half their wealth or even more. Also, depending on where the individuals live and their preferred life-style, being single can be expensive. The cost of living in Boston, Tokyo, Paris, and many other cities is almost prohibitive for single people. Many couples stay together to avoid facing additional economic problems.

Inertia

A major reason for the preservation of many relationships is inertia, the tendency for a body at rest to remain at rest and a body in motion to remain in motion. Many people just go along with the program, and it hardly occurs to them to consider changing their status; change seems to be too much trouble. Inertia is greatly aided by the media. It is easier for many individuals to remain in their present relationship and to seek vicarious satisfactions from situation comedies, dramas, and especially soap operas, wherein the actors do all the things the viewer would do if he or she were not so resistant to change.

Commitment

An important factor influencing the course of relationship deterioration (as well as relationship maintenance) is the degree of commitment the individuals have toward each other and toward the relationship (Knapp & Taylor 1994; Kurdek 1995). Before reading any further examine your own commitment by taking the self-test, "How Committed Are You?" on page 242.

Interpersonal researchers Mark Knapp and Eric Taylor (1994), building on the work of Johnson (1973, 1982, 1991), divide commitment into three types, but note that in real life these types of commitments are often combined and blend into each other.

"Want to" commitment is based on your positive feelings for the other person or the relationship; for example, you love your partner and therefore are committed to him or her and to the relationship. "Ought to" commitment is based on your sense of moral obligation; for example, you made a promise to stay together or you would feel guilty if you broke up the relationship. "Have to" commitment is based on your belief that you have no acceptable alternative, for example, your friends would disapprove or you would incur too many problems in breaking up.

All relationships are held together, in part, by one or some combination of these types of commitments. The strength of the relationship, including its resistance to possible deterioration, is also related to this degree of commitment. When a relationship shows signs of deterioration and yet there is a strong commitment to preserving it, the individuals may well

SELF-TEST
how committed are you?

Think about a current romantic relationship—long time and serious or short time and casual—and respond to each of the following questions according to the following scale: 1 = the statement is "absolutely" true, 7 = the statement is "absolutely not" true, and numbers 2–6 for statements that are sometimes true and sometimes not true.

______ 1. I am likely to pursue another relationship or a single lifestyle.
______ 2. I believe there will be a lot of future rewards associated with the relationship.
______ 3. I feel a strong sense of "we" when thinking of my partner and me.
______ 4. I am willing to exert a great deal of effort on behalf of this relationship.
______ 5. I have a lot invested in this relationship.
______ 6. I can imagine having an affair with another person and not having it affect my relationship with __________.
______ 7. I expect to be with __________ for the rest of my life.
______ 8. There is nothing holding me in this relationship expect my own free choice.

Thinking Critically About Commitment To compute your score follow these steps:

1. add your scores from questions 2, 3, 4, 5, 7, and 8,
2. add your score from items 1 and 6 and subtract this sum from 16 (chosen simply to eliminate negative numbers), and
3. add the totals from steps 1 and 2.

Your score should range somewhere between 8 and 56. Low scores indicate great commitment and high scores indicate less commitment. One of the purposes of including this self-test here is that it encourages you to look at your own commitment in very specific terms; it stimulates you to ask yourself the reasons for your own relationship commitment. Did it achieve this purpose or did you already have a good idea of the extent and reasons for your commitment in a relationship? Are there other items that you would add to this test? That is, are there other aspects of commitment that this test does not tap?

Source: "Commitment and It's Communication in Romantic Relationships," by Mark L. Knapp and Eric H. Taylor from *Perspectives on Close Relationships*, edited by Ann L. Weber and John H. Harvey (Boston, MA: Allyn & Bacon, 1994, pp. 153–175). Reprinted by permission of the author.

surmount the obstacles and reverse the process. When commitment is weak and the individuals doubt that there are good reasons for staying together, the relationship deteriorates faster and more intensely.

THINK ABOUT

Think about both the type of commitment that exists in one of your relationships and also about the strength of the relationship. A good way of doing this is to consider such questions as the following (drawn from the research of Knapp & Taylor 1994):

- What kind of future do you see for the relationship? If you believe that the relationship will provide important rewards in the future, you will be more committed to preserving it. If you see few rewards or even punishments or costs, then you are likely to feel little commitment and perhaps will allow the relationship to dissolve. (Statement 2 in the self-test taps this dimension.)
- To what extent do you identify with the relationship? To what extent do you see yourself as a part of a pair? If your relationship identity is a strong one, then your commitment is also strong and you would be likely to try to preserve the relationship. (Statements 3 and 7 in the self-test get at this dimension.)
- Are you considering alternatives to the relationship? If you have a strong commitment to your relationship, then you are less likely to look for alternative relationships. If you are still on the lookout for alternatives, then your commitment is

weak. (Statements 1 and 6 in the self-test refer to this dimension.)

- How willing are you to spend effort (energy and time, for example) on the relationship? The more willing you are to exert effort, the more committed you are to the relationship. (Statement 4 focuses on this factor.)
- How invested in the relationship are you? Increasing your investments in the relationship (for example, the more time you spend with a person or the more money you put into a relationship), usually means an increase in commitment. (Statement 5 taps this dimension.)
- Do you take personal responsibility for being in the relationship or do you feel you *have* to be in it? If you feel that your relationship involvement is due to your own free choice, then your commitment is likely to be stronger than if you feel you were forced or had to be in the relationship. (Statement 8 in the self-test reflects this dimension.)

Communication Patterns

Obviously, the way in which people communicate also contributes to the maintenance of the relationship. In one research study, four communication patterns were identified (Gao 1991):

Openness. The willingness to maintain open and honest communication.

Involvement. A strong sense of being a pair, a couple; lots of time put into the relationship.

Shared meanings. Mutual understanding of each other's nonverbal communication messages.

Relationship assessment. Both individuals see the relationship and its future in similar and mutually compatible ways.

More generally we might say that the communication patterns that help maintain a relationship are those singled out for effective conversation, such as openness, empathy, positiveness, immediacy, interaction management, expressiveness, and other orientation—performed mindfully, flexibly, and with cultural sensitivity. Add to these appropriate self-disclosure, active listening, and confirmation—and in fact all the skills considered throughout this text—and you have a pretty comprehensive list of potentially useful communication tools for maintaining a relationship.

Few couples stay together for a single reason. Rather, there are usually a multiplicity of reasons that vary in intensity and from one relationship to another. Obviously, the more urgent the reason, the more likely it is that the relationship will be preserved. So many of the reasons for relational preservation are unconscious, however, therefore, it is difficult to discover why a particular couple stays together or breaks up, or to predict which relationships will last and which will not.

Maintenance Behaviors

Another reason relationships last is that people try to make them work. A number of researchers have focused on the maintenance strategies that people use in their various relationships (Ayres 1983; Canary & Stafford 1994; Dindia & Baxter 1987; Dainton & Stafford 1993; Guerrero, Eloy, & Wabnik 1993). Here are four general types of strategies (Dindia & Baxter 1987).

- *Prosocial behaviors* include being polite, cheerful, and friendly; avoiding criticism; and compromising even when it involves self-sacrifice. Prosocial behaviors also include talking about a shared future, for example, talking about a future vacation or buying a house together.
- *Ceremonial behaviors* include celebrating birthdays and anniversaries, discussing past pleasurable times, and eating at a favorite restaurant.
- *Communication behaviors* include calling just to say, "How are you?" talking about the honesty and openness in the relationship, and talking about shared feelings. Responding constructively in a conflict (even when your partner may act in ways harmful to the relationship) is another type of communicative maintenance strategy (Rusbult & Buunk 1993).
- *Togetherness behaviors* include spending time together visiting mutual friends, doing specific things as a couple, and sometimes just being together with no concern for what is done. Controlling extrarelational activities would be another type of togetherness behavior (Rusbult & Buunk 1993).

Following are examples of specific maintenance strategies identified in recent studies (Canary,

Stafford, Hause, & Wallace 1993; Dainton & Stafford 1993):

- *Openness.* Person engages in direct discussion and listens to other, for example, self-disclosing, talking about what the person wants from the relationship, gives advice, expressing empathy (rather than judgment).
- *Assurances.* Person assures the other of the significance of the relationship, for example, comforting the other, putting the partner first, expressing love for the person.
- *Sharing joint activities.* Person spends time with the other, for example, playing ball together, going to events together, or simply talking.
- *Positivity.* Person tries to make interactions pleasant and upbeat, for example, holding hands, giving in to make the other person happy, doing favors for the other person.
- *Cards, letters, and calls.* Person sends cards or letters or calls the other.
- *Avoidance.* Person stays away from the other or from certain issues, for example, doing some things with third parties or not talking about potentially sensitive issues.
- *Sharing tasks.* Person performs various tasks with the other, for example, cleaning the house.
- *Social networks.* Person relies on friends and relatives for support and to help with various problems.

Also found were such strategies as *humor* (making jokes or teasing the other); *talk* (engaging in small talk and establishing specific times for talking); *affection, including sexual intimacy* (acts affectionately and romantically); and *focus on self* (making oneself look good)(Canary, Stafford, Hause, & Wallace 1993; Dainton & Stafford 1993).

RELATIONSHIP REPAIR

If you wish to salvage a relationship, you may try to do so by changing your communication patterns and, in effect, putting into practice the insights and skills learned in this course. You can look at the strategies for repairing a relationship in terms of the following six suggestions, which conveniently spell out the word REPAIR (see Figure 14.1), a useful reminder that **relationship repair** is not a one-step but a multistep process:

Recognize the problem
Engage in productive conflict resolution
Propose possible solutions
Affirm each other
Integrate solutions into normal behavior
Risk

Recognize the Problem

Your first step is to identify the problem and to recognize it both intellectually and emotionally. Specify what is wrong with your present relationship (in concrete, specific terms) and what changes would be needed to make it better (again, in specific terms). Without this first step there is little hope for improving any interpersonal relationship. It sometimes helps to create a picture of your relationship as you would want it to be and compare that picture to the way the relationship looks now. You can then specify the changes that would have to take place to have the present picture become the idealized picture.

Try to see the problem from your partner's point of view and to have your partner see the problem from yours. Exchange these perspectives, empathically and with open minds. Try to be descriptive when discussing grievances, being especially careful to avoid such troublesome terms as *always* and *never.* Also, own your own feelings and thoughts; use I-messages and take responsibility for your feelings instead of blaming your partner.

Engage in Productive Conflict Resolution

Interpersonal conflict is an inevitable part of relationship life. It is not so much the conflict that causes relationship difficulties but rather the way in which you pursue the conflict. If you confront it with productive strategies, the conflict may be resolved and the relationship may actually emerge stronger and healthier. If, on the other hand, you use unproductive and destructive strategies, the relationship may well deteriorate further. (Because this topic is so crucial, Unit 16 is devoted exclusively to the process of conflict and especially to the ways to engage in productive interpersonal conflict.)

Propose Possible Solutions

After the problem is identified, you need to discuss ways to lessen or eliminate the difficulty. Look for solu-

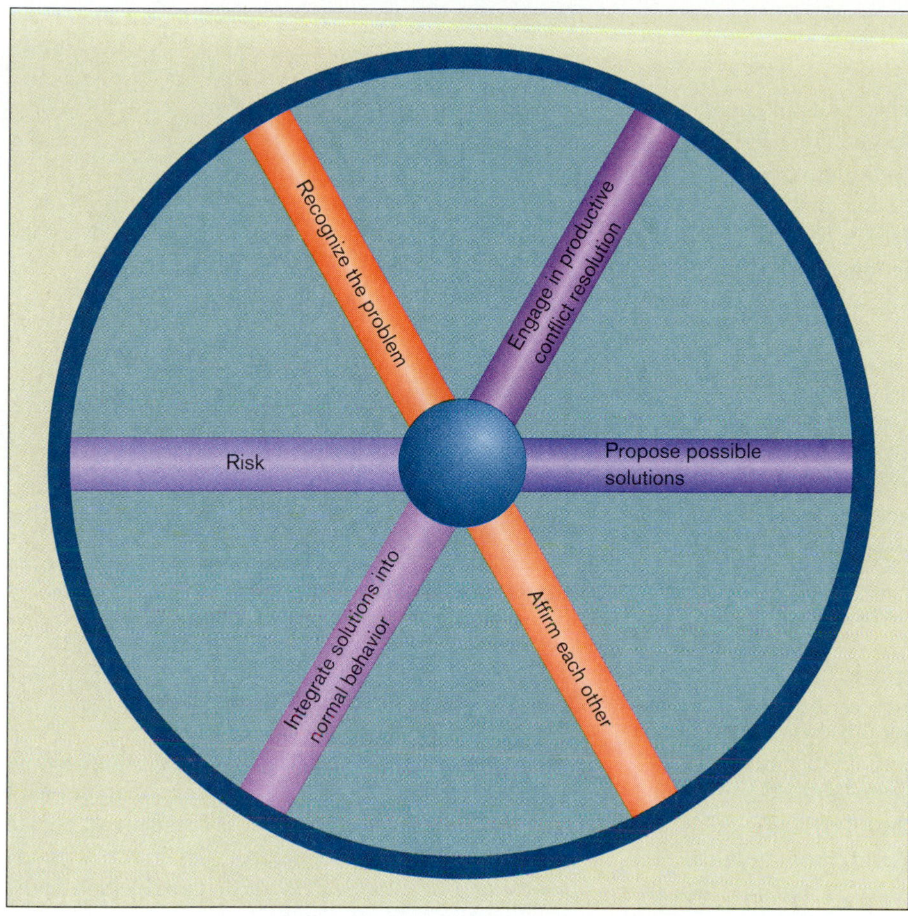

FIGURE 14.1 The relationship repair wheel. This metaphorical wheel is designed to suggest that relationship repair consists of several processes, working together, enabling the relationship to move from one place to another, and works best when another wheel (propelled by the other person) is moving in the same direction. You may find it interesting to create your own metaphor for relationship repair and for how the process of repair works.

tions that will enable both of you to win. Try to avoid "solutions" by which one person wins and the other person loses, in which case resentment and hostility are likely to fester. The suggestions offered in the discussion of the problem-solving group (see Unit 17) are especially applicable to this phase of relationship repair.

Affirm Each Other

It should come as no surprise to find that happily married couples engage in greater positive behavior exchange; they communicate more agreement, approval, and positive affect than do unhappily married couples (Dindia & Fitzpatrick 1985). Clearly, these behaviors result from the positive feelings these spouses have for each other. It can also be argued that these expressions help to increase the positive regard that each person has for his or her partner. Other affirming messages are also needed, such as the exchange of favors, compliments, positive stroking, and all the nonverbals that say "I care."

One especially insightful way to increase favor exchange is to use **cherishing behaviors** (Lederer, 1984), those small gestures that you enjoy receiving from your relational partner (a smile, a wink, a squeeze, a kiss). Cherishing behaviors should be (1) specific and positive, (2) focused on the present and future rather than related to issues about which the partners have argued in the past, (3) capable of being performed daily, and (4) easily executed. People can make a list of cherishing behaviors that they each wish to receive and then exchange lists. Each person then performs the cherishing behaviors desired by the partner. At first these behaviors may seem self-conscious and awkward. In time, however, they will become a normal part of interaction.

Integrate Solutions into Normal Behavior

Often solutions that are reached after an argument are followed for only a very short time; then the couple go back to their previous unproductive behavior patterns. Instead, they need to integrate solutions into normal behavior; they need to become integral to everyday relationship interactions. Exchanging favors, compliments, and cherishing behaviors need to become a part of everyday communication.

Risk

Take risks in trying to improve your relationship. Risk giving favors without any certainty of reciprocity. Risk rejection; make the first move to make up or say you are sorry. Be willing to change, to adapt, and to take on new tasks and responsibilities. Also, be willing to try new and different communication strategies.

Solo Relationship Repair

The six repair strategies noted are traditionally considered as a joint undertaking. Both parties mutually engage in relationship repair. Relationship repair may also be undertaken by just one of the individuals. This important implication for repair comes from the principle of punctuation (see Unit 2) and the idea that communication is circular rather than linear (see Unit 1; Duncan & Rock 1991). Consider the example of Pat and Chris: Pat is highly critical of Chris; Chris is defensive and attacks Pat for being insensitive, overly negative, and unsupportive. If you view the communication process as beginning with Pat's being critical as the stimulus and with Chris's attacks as the response, you have a pattern such as the one depicted in Figure 14.2.

With this view, the only way to stop this unproductive pattern is for Pat to stop criticizing. But, what if you are Chris and cannot get Pat to stop being critical? What if Pat doesn't want to stop being critical?

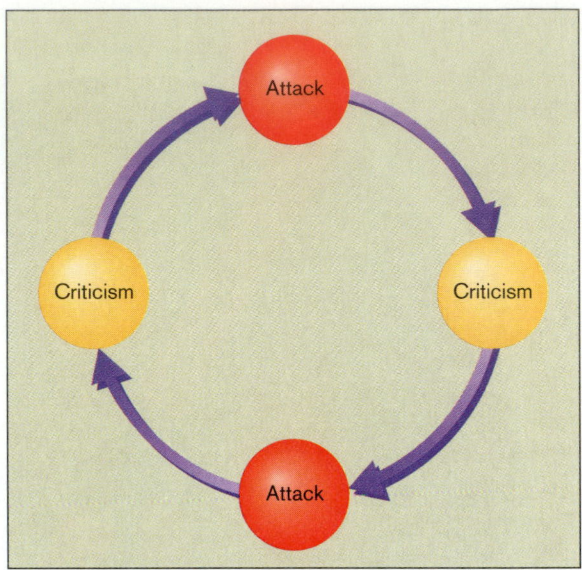

FIGURE 14.3 A circular view of relationship problems. This view of relationship problems implies that the problem is a pattern of behavior participated in by both parties. Unlike the view depicted in Figure 14.2, this view makes no assumptions about what caused the problem.

You get a different view of this same problem when you view communication as circular and invoke the principle of punctuation. Viewing this same process as a circular one, you get a pattern such as the one depicted in Figure 14.3.

The only assumption made here is that each response triggers another response, each response depends in part on the previous response. Therefore, the pattern can be broken at any point: Pat's criticism, for example, may be stopped by Chris's not responding to criticism with attacks. Similarly, Pat can stop Chris's attacks by not responding to attacks with criticism.

In this view, either person can break an unproductive and damaging circle. Clearly, relationship communication can be most effectively improved when both parties change their unproductive patterns. However, communication can still be improved

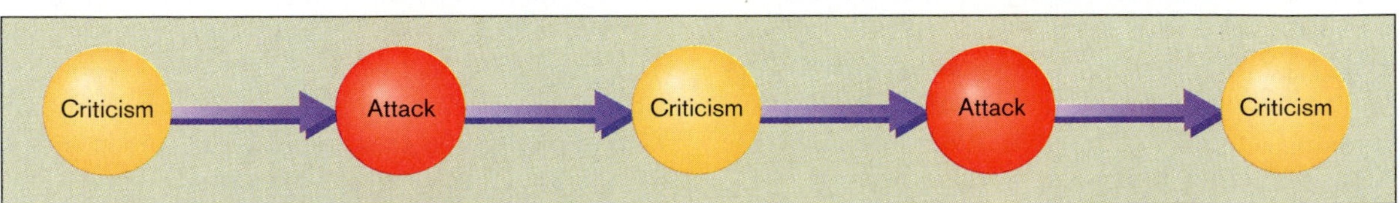

FIGURE 14.2 A stimulus-response view of relationship problems. This view of relationship problems implies that there is a *cause* of the problem and an *effect* of that problem. With this view you can only eliminate the problem by eliminating its cause. This view also assumes that you can identify what the cause of a particular relationship problem is.

even if only one person changes and begins to use a more productive pattern. This is true to the extent that Pat's criticism depends on Chris's attacks and to the extent that Chris's attacks depend on Pat's criticism.

SELF-REPAIR

Of course, some relationships end. Sometimes there is simply not enough to hold the couple together or there are problems that cannot be resolved. Sometimes the costs are too high and the rewards too few, or the relationship is recognized as destructive and escape seems the only alternative. Given the inevitability that some relationships will break up, here are some suggestions to ease the difficulty that is sure to follow. These suggestions can apply to the termination of any type of relationship, between friends or lovers, through death, separation, or breakup. The language of romantic breakups is used here because these are the ones we deal with most frequently.

Break the Loneliness-Depression Cycle

Loneliness and depression, the two most experienced feelings following the ending of a relationship, are serious. Depression, for example, may lead to physical illness. Ulcers, high blood pressure, insomnia, stomach pains, and sexual difficulties frequently accompany or are seriously aggravated by depression. In most cases loneliness and depression are temporary. Your task then is to eliminate or lessen these uncomfortable and potentially dangerous feelings by changing the situation. When depression does last or proves particularly upsetting, it is time to seek professional help.

Take Time Out

Take time out for yourself. Renew your relationship with yourself. If you were in a long-term relationship, you probably saw yourself as part of a team, as part of a couple. Now get to know yourself as a unique individual, standing alone now but fully capable of entering a meaningful relationship in the near future.

Bolster Self-Esteem

When relationships fail, self-esteem often falls. You may feel guilty for having been the cause of the breakup or inadequate for not holding on to a permanent relationship. You may feel unwanted and unloved. All of these feelings contribute to lowering self-esteem. Your task here is to regain the positive self-image that is needed to function effectively as an individual and as a member of another relationship.

Take positive action to raise your self-esteem. Oddly enough, helping others is one of the best ways to do this (Rubenstein & Shaver 1982). When you do things for others, either informally for people you know or by volunteer work in some community agency, you get the positive stroking from others that helps you feel better about yourself. Positive and successful experiences are extremely helpful in building self-esteem, so engage in activities that you enjoy, that you do well, and that are likely to result in success.

Seek Support

Although many people feel they should bear their burdens alone (men, in particular, have been taught that this is the only "manly" way to handle things), seeking the support of others is one of the best antidotes to the unhappiness caused when a relationship ends. Avail yourself of your friends and family for support. Tell your friends of your situation—in only general terms, if you prefer—and make it clear that you need support now. Seek out people who are positive and nurturing. Make the distinction between seeking support and seeking advice. If you feel you need advice, seek out a professional. For support, friends are best.

Avoid Repeating Negative Patterns

Many people enter second and third relationships with the same blinders, faulty preconceptions, and unrealistic expectations with which they entered earlier relationships. It is possible, however, to learn from failed relationships and not repeat the same patterns. Ask yourself at the start of a new relationship if you are entering a relationship modeled on the previous one. If the answer is yes, be especially careful not to repeat the same pattern.

At the same time, do not become a prophet of doom. Do not see in every new relationship vestiges of the old. Treat the new relationship as the unique relationship it is and do not evaluate it through past experiences. Past relationships and experiences should be guides, not filters.

SUMMARY

In this unit we looked at relationship development, deterioration, maintenance, and repair and at some of the ways communication operates during these relationship stages.

1. Relationships develop for a variety of reasons; some of the most important are: to lessen loneliness, secure stimulation, gain self-knowledge, and maximize pleasures and minimize pain.
2. Three main phases in initiating relationships may be noted: examining the qualifiers, determining clearance, and communicating your desire for contact.
3. The following nonverbal behaviors are useful in initiating relationships: establish eye contact, signal positive response, concentrate your focus, establish proximity, maintain an open posture, respond visibly, use positive behaviors, and avoid overexposure.
4. The following verbal behaviors are helpful in initiating relationships: introduce yourself, focus the conversation on the other person, exchange favors and rewards, be energetic, stress the positives, avoid negative or too intimate self-disclosures, and establish commonalities.
5. Relationship deterioration—the weakening of the bonds holding people together—may be gradual or sudden and may have positive as well as negative effects.
6. Among the causes for relationship deterioration are diminution of the reasons for establishing the relationship, relational changes, undefined expectations, sex conflicts, work problems, financial difficulties, and the inequitable distribution of rewards and costs.
7. Among the communication changes that take place during relationship deterioration are general withdrawal, a decrease in self-disclosure, an increase in deception, a decrease in positive and an increase in negative evaluative responses, and a decrease in the exchange of favors.
8. Relationship maintenance focuses on behaviors designed to continue the relationship, to keep it intact, keep it confined to one stage, or keep it from deteriorating.
9. Relationships may stay together because of emotional attachments, convenience, children, fear, financial considerations, inertia, and commitment.
10. Among the maintenance behaviors observed are prosocial, ceremonial, communication, and togetherness behaviors.
11. A useful approach to relationship repair is first to recognize the problem, engage in productive conflict resolution, pose possible solutions, affirm each other, integrate solutions into relationship behaviors, and take risks.
12. Generally, relationship repair is most effectively undertaken by mutual intervention of both parties, but the process may also be undertaken by only one person.
13. If the relationship does end, engage in self-repair. Break the loneliness-depression cycle, take time out, bolster self-esteem, seek emotional support, and avoid repeating negative patterns.

THINKING CRITICALLY ABOUT RELATIONSHIP DEVELOPMENT, DETERIORATION, MAINTENANCE, AND REPAIR

1. Can you identify the specific reasons why you developed a particular friendship or love relationship?
2. How would you describe the process of initiating an interpersonal relationship?
3. Research finds that when relationships break up it is usually the more attractive partner who leaves (Blumstein & Schwartz 1983). Why do you think this is found? What other factors might account for who leaves a relationship first?
4. What other behaviors seem to characterize relationship deterioration? Can these be viewed as the reverse of those behaviors used to develop and maintain a relationship?
5. It was only as recently as 1967—after nine years of trials and appeals—that the United States Supreme Court forbade any state laws against interracial marriage (Crohn 1995). How would you describe the state of interracial marriage (and romantic relationships generally) today? What obstacles do such relationships face? What advantages do they offer?
6. Can you identify any maintenance behaviors that you engage in on a regular basis? Can you identify the maintenance behaviors of a friend or romantic partner?
7. How important is money to your relationship? If you had considerably more money than your potential partner, would you insist on a prenuptial agreement? If you were to form a relationship with another person who wanted a prenuptial agreement, would you sign it?
8. How important is public opinion in relationship deterioration and dissolution? For example, do the opinions of your friends influence you in deciding whether or not to end a relationship?
9. The discussion of relationship repair focused on repairing close relationships such as a friendship or love relationship. How applicable are the suggestions for repair to, say, the business context, for example, restoring a relationship between a disenchanted customer and small retail store or between an employee and employer?
10. How would you go about finding answers to such questions as these:
    a. Are the reasons for developing relationships similar for female-male, female-female, and male-male relationships?
    b. Do the reasons for developing relationships change with age? How do the reasons differ between, say, 20-year-olds, on the one hand, and 50–60-year-olds, on the other?
    c. Do men and women use the same maintenance strategies?
    d. How do the maintenance strategies differ for friends and for romantic partners?
    e. Under what conditions is solo repair likely to improve a relationship?

fifteen unit

Friendship, Love, and Family Communication

unit contents

unit goals

After completing this unit, you should be able to:

1. define *friendship,* its three stages, and the communications that occur at each stage
2. define *ludus, storge, mania, pragma, eros,* and *agape*
3. define *family* and identify its major characteristics and types
4. explain the four communication patterns that characterize family communication
5. describe the suggestions for improving friendship, love, and family communication

Of all your interpersonal relationships, no doubt the most important are those with your friends, lovers, and family. In this unit we cover these important relationships with special attention to the role of communication.

THINK ABOUT

Think about your own relationships as you read this unit. What is the role of communication in establishing and maintaining your friendships, love, and family relationships? How did communication figure into relationships that deteriorated and dissolved? Think about, too, the way in which this communication will differ depending on the general context in which the relationship is developed, maintained, and perhaps dissolved. For example, most of the research conducted on friendships have involved those developed by choice and maintained largely through face-to-face interaction. Online friendships and even love relationships are just beginning to be researched. For now, however, you might want to speculate on how communication would be different in face-to-face and computer-mediated relationships.

FRIENDSHIP COMMUNICATION

Friendship has engaged the attention and imagination of poets, novelists, and artists of all kinds. In television, the most influential mass medium, friendships have become almost as important as romantic pairings; "Seinfeld," "Ellen," and "Friends" are current examples. Friendship now engages the attention of a range of interpersonal communication researchers. Here are a selection of findings—from the extensive literature review by Blieszner and Adams (1992)—to illustrate the range of topics addressed. In reviewing this list, consider why these results were obtained and what implications they may have for developing, maintaining, and repairing friendship relationships:

- Young single men see their friends more often than young married men (Farrell & Rosenberg 1989).
- Women are more expressive in their friendships than are men. Men talk about business, politics, and sports whereas women talk about feelings and relationship issues (Fox, Gibbs, & Auerbach 1989).
- When women were asked about the most important benefit they derive from their friendships, conversation was highlighted and included supportive listening, enhancing feelings of self-esteem, and validating their experiences (Johnson & Aries 1983).
- Men and women did not differ in their rankings of the characteristics of personal relationships with friends (Albert & Moss 1990).
- Similarity in personality was not a strong basis for selecting friends but similarity of needs and beliefs was (Henderson & Furnhman 1982). Friends with dissimilar attitudes were preferred in recent friendships while in established friendships similar attitudes were preferred (McCarthy & Duck 1976).
- The average number of friends of college students varies from 2.88 to 9.1 (Blieszner & Adams 1992); for older persons the average varies between 1 and 12.2 (Adams 1987).

Throughout your life you will meet many people, but out of this wide array you'll develop relatively few relationships you would call friendships. Yet, despite the low number, the importance of friendship is great.

The Nature of Friendship

Friendship is an interpersonal relationship between two persons that is mutually productive and characterized by mutual positive regard. The friendship relationship involves a "personalistic focus" (Wright 1978, 1984); friends react to each other as complete persons, as unique, genuine, and irreplaceable individuals. Liking these other people is essential if you are to call them friends. Trusting them, emotionally supporting them, and sharing interests (three major characteristics of friends, Blieszner & Adams 1992) testify to this positive regard.

Friendship can be further defined by identifying the essential characteristics in any friendship relationship (Davis 1985):

- *Enjoyment.* Friends enjoy each other's company.
- *Acceptance.* Friends accept each other as each is now; a friend does not attempt to change a friend into another person.
- *Mutual assistance.* Friends can count on each other for assistance and support.
- *Confiding.* Friends share feelings and experiences with each other.
- *Understanding.* Friends understand what is important and why friends behave as they do. Friends are good predictors of their friends' behaviors and feelings.
- *Trust.* Friends trust each other to act in the other's best interest.
- *Respect.* Friends respect each other; each assumes that the other will demonstrate good judgment in making choices.
- *Spontaneity.* Friends do not have to engage in self-monitoring; friends can express their feelings spontaneously, without worrying that these expressions will create difficulties for the friendship.

The nature of friendship can be further appreciated by looking at the responses of people who were asked to identify the qualities they felt most important in a friend. The responses, presented in Table 15.1, are derived from a *Psychology Today* survey of 40,000 respondents (Parlee 1979). As you examine the list, think about whether a list compiled today would look different from this one.

TABLE 15.1
the most frequently mentioned qualities of a friend

Friendship Qualities	Percentage of Respondents
Keep confidence	89
Loyalty	88
Warmth, affection	82
Supportiveness	76
Frankness	75
Sense of humor	74
Willingness to make time for me	62
Independence	61
Good conversationalist	59
Intelligence	57

Stages and Communication in Friendship Development

Friendships develop over time in stages. At one end are "strangers" or two persons who have just met, and at the other end are "intimate friends." What happens between these two extremes? As you progress from the initial contact stage to the intimate friendship, the depth and breadth of communications increase, a progression noted in the discussion of the theory of social penetration in Unit 12. You talk about issues that are closer and closer to your inner core. Similarly, the number of communication topics increases as your friendship becomes closer. As depth and breadth increase, so does the satisfaction you derive from the friendship.

Earlier (see Unit 12) the concept of dynamic tension in relationships was discussed. It was pointed out that there is a tension between, for example, autonomy and connection—the desire to be an individual but also to be connected to another person. Interpersonal communication researcher William Rawlins (1983, 1989) argues that friendships are also defined by dynamic tensions. One tension is between, for example, the impulse to be open and to reveal personal thoughts and feelings on the one hand and the impulse to protect oneself by not revealing personal information to others. Also, there is the tension between being open and candid with a friend and being discreet. These contradictory impulses make it clear that friendships do not follow a straight path of, say, ever-increasing openness or candor. This is not to say that openness and candor do not increase as you progress from initial to casual to close friendships, they do. But, the pattern does not follow a straight line; throughout the friendship development process there are tensions that periodically restrict openness and candor.

Three stages of friendship development (Figure 15.1) are discussed along with the characteristics of effective conversation identified earlier (see Unit 13). The assumption made here is that as the friendship progresses from initial contact and acquaintanceship, through casual friendship, to close and intimate friendship, the qualities of effective interpersonal communication increase. We do not assume, however, that close relationships are necessarily the preferred types of relationships or that they are better than casual or temporary relationships. Indeed, we need all types.

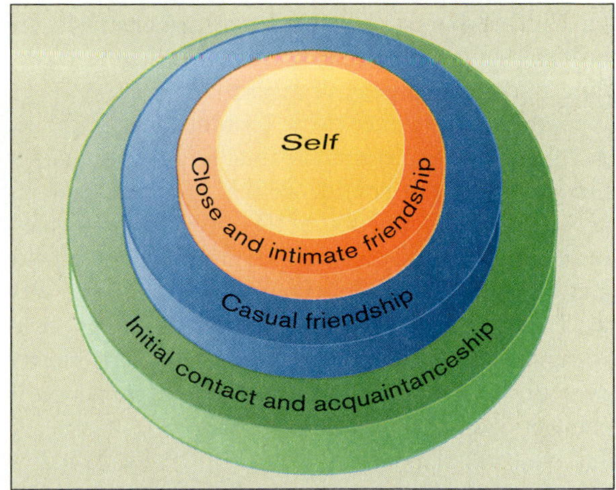

FIGURE 15.1 The stages of friendship. One of the assumptions made in this unit is that as the friendship becomes more intimate the communication becomes more effective. Effective communication is likely to be both the cause and the effect of increased intimacy (in all relationships). Do you agree with this basic assumption?

Initial Contact and Acquaintanceship

The first stage of friendship development is obviously an initial meeting of some kind. This does not mean that what has happened prior to the encounter is unimportant—quite the contrary. In fact, your prior history of friendships, your personal needs, and your readiness for friendship development are extremely important in determining whether the relationship will develop.

At the initial stage, the characteristics of effective interpersonal communication are usually present to only a weak degree. You are guarded, rather than open or expressive, lest you reveal aspects of yourself that might be viewed too negatively. Because you do not really know the other person, your ability to empathize or to orient yourself significantly to the other is limited, and the "relationship"—at this stage at least—is probably viewed as too temporary to be worth the effort. Because you really do not know the other person, supportiveness, positiveness, and equality would all be difficult to manifest in any meaningful sense. The characteristics that are demonstrated are probably more the result of politeness than any genuine expression of positive regard.

At this stage there is little genuine immediacy; the people see themselves as separate and distinct rather than as a unit. The confidence that is demonstrated is probably more a function of the individual personalities than of the relationship. The relationship is new, and because the people do not know each other very well, the interaction is often characterized by awkwardness—for example, overlong pauses, uncertainty over the topics to be discussed, and ineffective exchanges of speaker and listener roles.

Casual Friendship

In this second stage there is a dyadic consciousness, a clear sense of "we-ness," of togetherness; communication demonstrates a sense of immediacy. At this stage you participate in activities as a unit rather than as separate individuals. A casual friend is one you would call to go to the movies, sit with in the cafeteria or in class, or ride home from school with.

At this casual friendship stage you begin to see the qualities of effective interpersonal interaction more clearly. You start to express yourself openly, and become interested in the other person's disclosures. You begin to own your feelings and thoughts and respond openly to his or her communications. You are beginning to understand this person and therefore you empathize and demonstrate significant other-orientation. You also demonstrate supportiveness and develop a genuinely positive attitude toward the other person and toward mutual communication situations. As you learn this person's needs and wants you can stroke more effectively.

At this stage there is an ease, a coordination in the interaction between the two persons. You communicate with confidence, maintain appropriate eye contact and flexibility in body posture and gesturing, and use few adaptors signaling discomfort.

Close and Intimate Friendship

At the close and intimate friendship stage there is an intensification of the casual friendship; you see yourselves more as an exclusive unit and each derives greater benefits (for example, emotional support) from the friendship of intimacy than from the casual friendship (Hays 1989).

You know each other so well (for example, values, opinions, attitudes)—your uncertainty about each other has been significantly reduced—that you are able to predict each other's behaviors with considerable accuracy. This knowledge makes significant interaction management possible. Similarly, you can read the other's nonverbal signals more accurately, and use these signals as guides to your interactions—avoiding certain topics at certain times or offering consolation on the basis of facial expressions.

At this stage you exchange significant messages of affection, messages that express fondness, liking, loving, caring for the other person. Openness and expressiveness are more clearly in evidence.

You become more other-oriented, willing to make significant sacrifices for the other person. You will go far out of your way for the benefit of this friend, and the friend in turn does the same for you.

You empathize and exchange perspectives a great deal more, and you expect in return that your friend will empathize with you. With a genuinely positive feeling for this individual, your supportiveness and positive stroking become spontaneous. You see yourselves as an exclusive unit, therefore both equality and immediacy are clearly evident. You view this friend as one who is important in your life; as a result, conflicts—inevitable in all close relationships—become important to work out and resolve through compromise and empathic understanding rather than, for example, a refusal to negotiate or a show of force.

You are willing to respond openly, confidently, and expressively to this person and to own your feelings and thoughts. Your supportiveness and positiveness are genuine expressions of the closeness you feel for this person. Finally, each person in an intimate friendship is truly equal; each can initiate and each can respond; each can be active and each can be passive; each speaks and each listens.

Gender Differences in Friendship

Perhaps the best documented finding—already noted in the discussion of self-disclosure—is that women self-disclose more than do men. This difference holds throughout male and female friendships: male friends self-disclose less often and with less intimate details than female friends.

Women engage in significantly more affectional behaviors with their friends than do males (Hays 1989). This difference, Hays notes, may account for the greater difficulty men experience in beginning and in maintaining close friendships. Women engage in more casual communication and also share greater intimacy and more confidences with their friends than do men. Communication, in all its forms and functions, seems a much more important dimension of women's friendships.

When women and men were asked to evaluate their friendships, women rated their same-sex friendships higher in general quality, intimacy, enjoyment, and nurturance than did men (Sapadin 1988). Men, on the other hand, rated their opposite-sex friendships higher in quality, enjoyment, and nurturance than did women. These differences may be due, in part, because our society looks with suspicion on male friendships; as a result a man may be reluctant to admit to having close relationship bonds with another man. Men and women rate their opposite-sex friendships similarly in intimacy.

Men's friendships are often built around shared activities—attending a ball game, playing cards, working on a project at the office. Women's friendships, on the other hand, are built more around a sharing of feelings, support, and "personalism." Similarity in status, in willingness to protect one's friend in uncomfortable situations, in academic major, and even in proficiency in playing Password were significantly related to the relationship closeness of male-male friends but not of female-female or female-male friends (Griffin & Sparks 1990). Perhaps similarity is a criterion for male friendships but not for female or mixed-sex friendships.

The ways in which men and women develop and maintain their friendships will undoubtedly change considerably—as will all sex-related variables—in the next several years. Perhaps there will be a further differentiation or perhaps an increase in similarities. In the meantime, given the present state of research in gender differences, we need to be careful not to exaggerate and to treat small differences as if they were highly significant. "Let us," in the warning of friendship researcher Paul Wright (1988), "avoid stereotypes or, worse yet, caricatures."

Further, friendship researchers warn that even when we find differences, the reasons for them are not always clear (Blieszner & Adams 1992). They provide an interesting example, noting middle-aged men have more friends than middle-aged women and women have more intimate friendships (Firscher & Oliker 1983). Why is this so? Do men have more friends because they are friendlier than women, or because they have more opportunities to develop such friendships? Do women have more intimate friends because they have more opportunities to pursue such friendships or because they have a greater psychological capacity for intimacy?

LOVE COMMUNICATION

Of all the qualities of interpersonal relationships, none seems as important as love. "We are all born for love," noted famed British Prime Minister Benjamin Disraeli; "It is the principle of existence and its only end." It is also an interpersonal relationship developed, maintained, and sometimes destroyed through communication.

Much research is currently devoted to identifying the ingredients of love. What makes up the love experience? What are its major parts? Here are two well-reasoned explanations.

Passion and Caring

Keith Davis (1985) identifies two clusters of behaviors that characterize love—the passion cluster and the caring cluster:

- The *passion cluster* consists of fascination (seen in the lovers' preoccupations with each other), exclusiveness (seen in their mutual commitment), and sexual desire (seen in the desire to touch).
- The *caring cluster* consists of giving the utmost (seen in sacrificing for the lover) and serving as the lover's champion or advocate (seen in supporting the lover's interest and success).

Intimacy, Passion, and Commitment

Robert Sternberg (1986, 1988, 1991; Beall & Sternberg 1995) proposes three ingredients of love—intimacy, passion, and commitment:

LISTENING AND GENDER

A major difficulty in opposite-sex friendship, love, and family communication occurs because one sex fails to understand the listening patterns of the other. According to Deborah Tannen (1990) in her best-selling book, *You Just Don't Understand: Women and Men in Conversation,* women seek to build rapport and establish a closer relationship and use listening to achieve these ends. Men, on the other hand, will play up their expertise, emphasize it, and use it in dominating the interaction. Women play down their expertise and are more interested in communicating supportiveness. Tannen argues that the goal of a man in conversation is to be accorded respect and therefore he seeks to show his knowledge and expertise. A woman, on the other hand, seeks to be liked and so she expresses agreement.

Men and women also show that they are listening in different ways. In conversation, a woman is more apt to give lots of listening cues such as interjecting "*yeah,*" *uh-huh,*" nodding in agreement, and smiling. A man is more likely to listen quietly, without giving lots of listening cues as feedback. Subsequent research seems to confirm Tannen's position. For example, in an analysis of calls to a crisis center in Finland, it was found that the calls received by a female counselor were significantly longer for both men and women callers (Salminen & Glad 1992). It is likely that the greater number of listening cues given by the women encouraged the callers to keep talking. This same study also found that male callers were helped by "just listening," whereas women callers were helped by "empathic understanding."

Tannen argues, however, that men do listen less to women than women listen to men. The reason, says Tannen, is that listening places the person in an inferior position whereas speaking places the person in a superior position.

We can try to apply these gender differences to listening in friendship, love, and family relationships. Men may seem to assume a more argumentative posture while listening. They may also appear to ask questions that are more argumentative or that are designed to puncture holes in your position as a way to play up their expertise. Women are more likely to ask supportive questions and perhaps offer criticism that is more positive. Women also use more cues in listening. They let the speaker see that they are listening. Men, on the other hand, use fewer listening cues. Men and women act this way to both men and women; their customary ways of listening do not seem to change depending on whether the communicator is male or female.

There is no evidence to show that these differences represent any negative motives on the part of men to prove themselves superior or of women to ingratiate themselves. Rather, these differences in listening are largely the result of the way in which men and women have been socialized. Of course, the absence of evidence can never be taken to mean the absence of a connection or relationship; it merely means that researchers haven't found any evidence. It doesn't mean that evidence cannot or will not be found. Do you think it would be worthwhile looking for evidence to show that men or women may have ulterior motives in listening as they do? If so, how might you go about seeking answers to this question?

- *Intimacy* (corresponding to part of the caring cluster) is the emotional aspect of love and includes sharing, communicating, and mutual support; a sense of closeness and connection.
- *Passion* is the motivational aspect (corresponding to the passion cluster) and consists of physical attraction and romantic passion.
- *Commitment* (corresponding to part of the caring cluster) is the cognitive aspect and consists of the decisions you make concerning your lover.

In Sternberg's three factor theory, when you have a relationship with only intimacy, then you have essentially a *liking* relationship. When you have only passion, you have a relationship of *infatuation.* When you have only commitment, you have *empty love.* When you have all three components to about equal degrees, you have *complete* or *consummate love.*

The Types of Love

Loving, of course, means very different things to different people. To illustrate this important concept, take the self-test, "What Kind of Lover Are You?" on page 258.

Eros: Beauty and Sensuality

Erotic love focuses on beauty and physical attractiveness, sometimes to the exclusion of qualities you might consider more important and more lasting. The erotic lover has an idealized image of beauty that is unattainable in reality. Consequently, the erotic lover often feels unfulfilled. In defense of eros, however, it should be noted that both male and female eros lovers have the highest levels of reward and satisfaction when compared with all other types of lovers (Morrow, Clark, & Brock 1995).

Ludus: Entertainment and Excitement

Ludus love is seen as fun, a game to be played. To the ludic lover, love is not to be taken too seriously; emotions are to be held in check lest they get out of hand and make trouble. Passions never rise to the point at which they get out of control. A ludic lover is self-controlled and consciously aware of the need to manage love rather than to allow it to control him or her. The ludic lover is manipulative and the extent of one's ludic tendencies has been found to correlate with the use of verbal sexual coercion (Sarwer, Kalichman, Johnson, Early, et al. 1993). Ludic-oriented sexually coercive men also experience less happiness, friendship, and trust in their relationships than do noncoercive men (Kalichman, Sarwer, Johnson, & Ali 1993). Ludic lover tendencies in women are likewise related to a dissatisfaction with life (Yancey & Berglass 1991).

Storge Love: Peaceful and Slow

Like ludus love, **storge love** lacks passion and intensity. Storgic lovers do not set out to find lovers but to establish a companion-like relationship with someone they know and with whom they can share interests and activities. Storgic love develops over a period of time rather than in one mad burst of passion. Sex in storgic relationships comes late, and when it comes it assumes no great importance. Storgic love is sometimes difficult to separate from friendship; it is often characterized by the same qualities that characterize friendship: mutual caring, compassion, respect, and concern for the other person.

Pragma: Practical and Traditional

The **pragma lover** is practical and wants compatibility and a relationship in which important needs and desires will be satisfied. In its extreme, pragma may be seen in the person who writes down the qualities wanted in a mate and actively goes about seeking someone who matches up. The pragma lover is concerned with the social qualifications of a potential mate even more than personal qualities; family and background are extremely important to the pragma lover, who relies not so much on feelings as on logic. The pragma lover views love as a necessity—or as a useful relationship—that makes the rest of life easier. The pragma lover therefore asks such questions about a potential mate as, "Will this person earn a good living?" "Can this person cook?" and "Will this person help me advance in my career?"

Manic Love: Elation and Depression

The quality of mania that separates it from other types of love is the extremes of its highs and lows, its ups and downs. The **manic lover** loves intensely and at the same time worries intensely about and fears the loss of the love. With little provocation, for example, the manic lover may experience extreme jealousy. Manic love is obsessive; the manic lover has to possess the beloved completely—in all ways, at all times. In return, the manic lover wishes to be possessed, to be loved intensely. It seems almost as if the manic lover is driven to these extremes by some outside force or perhaps by some inner obsession that cannot be controlled.

Agape: Compassionate and Selfless

Agape (uh-GAH-pay) is a compassionate, egoless, self-giving love. Agape is nonrational and nondiscriminative. Agape creates value and virtue through love rather than bestowing love only on that which is valuable and virtuous. The agapic lover loves even people with whom he or she has no close ties. This lover loves the stranger on the road, and the fact that they

SELF-TEST

what kind of lover are you?

Respond to each of the following statements with T (if you believe the statement to be a generally accurate representation of your attitudes about love) or F (if you believe the statement does not adequately represent your attitudes about love).

______ 1. My lover and I have the right physical "chemistry" between us.
______ 2. I feel that my lover and I were meant for each other.
______ 3. My lover and I really understand each other.
______ 4. My lover fits my ideal standards of physical beauty/handsomeness.
______ 5. I try to keep my lover a little uncertain about my commitment to him/her.
______ 6. I believe that what my lover doesn't know about me won't hurt him/her.
______ 7. My lover would get upset if he/she knew of some of the things I've done with other people.
______ 8. When my lover gets too dependent on me, I want to back off a little.
______ 9. To be genuine, our love first required caring for a while.
______10. I expect to always be friends with my lover.
______11. Our love is really a deep friendship, not a mysterious, mystical emotion.
______12. Our love relationship is the most satisfying because it developed from a good friendship.
______13. In choosing my lover, I believed it was best to love someone with a similar background.
______14. A main consideration in choosing my lover was how he/she would reflect on my family.
______15. An important factor in choosing a partner is whether or not he/she would be a good parent.
______16. One consideration in choosing my lover was how he/she would reflect on my career.
______17. When things aren't right with my lover and me, my stomach gets upset.
______18. Sometimes I get so excited about being in love with my lover that I can't sleep.
______19. When my lover doesn't pay attention to me, I feel sick all over.
______20. I cannot relax if I suspect that my lover is with someone else.
______21. I try to always help my lover through difficult times.
______22. I would rather suffer myself than let my lover suffer.
______23. When my lover gets angry with me, I still love him/her fully and unconditionally.
______24. I would endure all things for the sake of my lover.

Thinking Critically About Love Styles. This scale is designed to enable you to identify those styles that best reflect your own beliefs about love. The statements refer to the six types of love discussed on pages 257 and 259: eros, ludus, storge, pragma, mania, and agape. "True" answers represent your agreement and "false" answers represent your disagreement with the type of love to which the statements refer. Statements 1 through 4 are characteristic of the eros lover. If you answered "true" to these statements, you have a strong eros component to your love style. If you answered "false" you have a weak eros component. Statements 5 through 8 refer to ludus love; 9 through 12 to storge love, 13 through 16 to pragma love, 17 through 20 to manic love, and 21 through 24 to agapic love.

How accurately do you think this scale measures your love style? Does your style of love (as indicated by your score on the love scale) correspond to (or contradict) your self-image? Are you satisfied with your love style or is it something that you would like to change? If so, how might you go about changing it? Which type of love relationship (ludus, storge, mania, pragma, eros, or agape) do you think stands the best chance for survival?

Source: Adapted from "What Kind of Lover Are You?" from "A Relationship: Specific Version of the Love Attitudes Scale" by C. Hendrick and S. Hendrick, from *Journal of Social Behavior and Personality*, 1990, Volume 5. Reprinted by permission of Select Press, Inc. (This scale is based on the work of Lee (1976); our discussion of the six types of love is based on Lee, Hendrick and Hendrick, and other studies cited in the text discussion.)

will probably never meet again has nothing to do with it. Jesus, Buddha, and Gandhi practiced and preached this unqualified love. Agape is a spiritual love, offered without concern for personal reward or gain. The agapic lover loves without expecting that the love will be returned or reciprocated. For women, agape is the only love style positively related to their own life satisfaction (Yancy & Berglass 1991).

THINK ABOUT

Think about these love styles in relation to the personality traits you think these lovers might have. Following are personality traits that recent research finds people assign to each love style. Try identifying which personality traits people perceive to go with each love style. The six styles are Ludus, eros, pragma, storge, agape, and mania.

1. inconsiderate, secretive, dishonest, selfish, and dangerous
2. honest, loyal, mature, caring, loving, and understanding
3. jealous, possessive, obsessed, emotional, and dependent
4. sexual, exciting, loving, happy, optimistic
5. committed, giving, caring, self-sacrificing, and loving
6. family-oriented, planning, careful, hard-working, and concerned

Very likely you perceived these personality factors in the same way as did the participants in research from which these traits were drawn (Taraban & Hendrick 1995): 1 = ludus, 2 = storge, 3 = mania, 4 = eros, 5 = agape, and 6 = pragma.

Recent research shows that concepts of beauty may not be as culturally influenced as formerly thought; beauty may not be in the eye of the beholder. As science writer Jane E. Brody puts it, "an accumulating body of evidence indicates that concepts of attractiveness may be universal and hard-wired into the human brain, whether that brain serves a Briton or a Japanese" (*New York Times* March 21, 1994, A14). How would you go about testing the validity of this position?

Communicating Love

THINK ABOUT

Think about how you communicate love. How do you let the other person know that you love him or her? What do you say? What do you do? Some research evidence is available to help us answer this often asked question.

Verbally, you tend to exaggerate your beloved's virtues and minimize his or her faults. You share emotions and experiences and speak tenderly, with an extra degree of courtesy; "please," "thank you," and similar politenesses abound. You frequently use "personalized communication." This type of communication includes telling secrets you keep from other people and messages that have meaning only within this specific relationship (Knapp, Ellis, & Williams 1980). Researchers have examined examples of the latter category, calling these *personal idioms*—those words, phrases, and gestures that carry meaning only for the particular relationship (Hopper, Knapp, & Scott 1981). When outsiders try to use personal idioms—as they sometimes do—they seem inappropriate, at times an invasion of privacy.

Lovers engage in greater self-disclosure (see Unit 8). There is greater confirmation and less disconfirmation among lovers than among nonlovers or those who are going through romantic breakups. Lovers are also more aware of what is and is not appropriate to the loved one. They know how to reward but also how to punish each other. In short, lovers know what to do to obtain the desired response.

Love may also be communicated nonverbally. We have all seen moonstruck lovers staring into each other's eyes. This prolonged and focused eye contact is perhaps the clearest nonverbal indicator of love. Lovers lean toward each other in an attempt, it would seem, to minimize physical distance and keep any possible intruders outside the privacy of the relationship. The physical closeness (even a spatial overlap) echoes the emotional closeness.

Lovers grow more aware not only of their loved one but also of their own physical selves. Muscle tone is heightened; people in love tend to engage in preening gestures, especially immediately prior to meeting the loved one, and to set the body (to the extent possible) into its most attractive position—stomach pulled in, shoulders square, legs arranged in the appropriate masculine or feminine positions.

Lovers' speech may even have a somewhat different vocal quality. There is some evidence to show that sexual excitement enlarges the nasal membranes, which introduces a certain nasal quality into the voice (Davis 1973).

Perhaps the most obvious nonverbal behavior of all is the elimination of socially taboo adaptors (see Unit 10), at least in the presence of the loved one: scratching one's head, picking one's teeth, cleaning one's ears, and passing wind are avoided. Interestingly enough, these adaptors often return after the lovers have achieved a permanent relationship.

Lovers touch more frequently and more intimately. There is also greater use of *tie signs*, nonverbal gestures that indicate that people are together, such as holding hands, walking with arms entwined, and kissing. Lovers also dress alike. The styles of clothes and even the colors selected by lovers are more similar than those worn by nonlovers.

When college students were asked how they communicate love, they gave the following responses (Marston, Hecht, & Robers 1987):

- Tell the person face-to-face or by telephone, "I love you"
- Do special (or traditional) things for the other person; for example, send a card or flowers
- Be supportive, understanding, and attentive to loved one
- Touch the loved one; for example, hold hands or hug
- Be together
- Negotiate, talk things out, cooperate

Cultural and Gender Differences in Loving

Relatively little cross cultural research has been done on this topic. The love test included in this unit and others like it and the love styles derived from such tests have been found to have validity among Germans (Bierhoff & Klein 1991). Asians have been found to be more friendship-oriented in their love style than are Europeans (Dion & Dion 1993). One study finds a love style among Mexicans characterized as calm, compassionate, and deliberate (Leon, Philbrick, Parra, Escobedo et al. 1994). In comparisons between loves styles in the United States and France, it was found that subjects from the United States scored higher on storge and mania than the French; in contrast, the French scored higher on agape (Murstein, Merighi, & Vyse 1991). Caucasian women, compared to African American women, scored higher on mania whereas African American women scored higher on agape. Caucasian and African American men, however, scored very similarly; no statistically significant differences have been found (Morrow, Clark, & Brock 1995).

Men and women differ in the types of love they prefer, though research results are not always consistent. In one study, for example, men were found to score higher on erotic and ludic love whereas women scored higher on manic, pragmatic, and storgic love. No difference has been found for agapic love (Hendrick, Hendrick, Foote & Slapion-Foote 1984, Dion & Dion 1993). In another study men scored higher than women on ludus and agape; women scored higher on storge and pragma. No significant differences were found for mania (though women had "marginally higher" scores) or for eros (Morrow, Clark, & Brock 1995).

Contrary to popular myth, men were found to place more emphasis on romance than women. For example, college students were asked the following question: "If a boy (girl) had all the other qualities you desired, would you marry this person if you were not in love with him (her)?" Approximately two-thirds of the men responded no, which seems to indicate that a high percentage were concerned with love and romance. However, less than one-third of the women responded no (Kirkpatrick & Caplow 1945; Hendrick, Hendrick, Foote & Slapion-Foote 1984). Further, when men and women were surveyed concerning their views on love—whether it is basically realistic or basically romantic—it was found that married women had a more realistic (less romantic) conception of love than did married men (Knapp 1984).

Additional research confirms this view that men are more romantic. For example, "Men are more likely than women to believe in love at first sight, in love as the basis for marriage and for overcoming obstacles, and to believe that their partner and relationship will be perfect" (Sprecher & Metts 1989, p. 408). This difference seems to increase as the romantic relationship develops; men become more romantic and women less so (Fengler 1974).

FAMILY COMMUNICATION

All of us are now or were at one time part of a family. Some of our experiences have been pleasant and positive and are recalled with considerable pleasure. Other experiences have been unpleasant and negative and are recalled only with considerable pain. Part of the reason for this lies with the interpersonal communication patterns that operate within the family.

Using the concepts from this unit, how would you describe the characteristics of your family, the type of primary relationship(s) in the family, and the communication patterns most often in evidence? How typical is the family depicted in this photo of families throughout the United States? Of families throughout the world? How typical is this family of families portrayed in television sitcoms and dramas?

The Nature of Family

If you had to define *family,* you would probably note that a family consists of a husband, a wife, and one or more children. When pressed you might add that some of these families also consist of other relatives—in-laws, brothers and sisters, grandparents, aunts and uncles, and so on. There are, however, other types of relationships that are, to their own members, "families."

One obvious example is the family with one parent. Statistics from 1992 indicate that there are over 10 million single-parent households (Wright 1995). If current trends continue, notes *American Demographic* magazine (July 1992), 61 percent of all children (up to age 18) will spend part of their time in a single-parent family (Wright 1995).

Another obvious example is that of people living together in an exclusive relationship but who are not, in fact, married. For the most part, these cohabitants live as if they were married: there is an exclusive sexual commitment, there may be children, there are shared financial responsibilities, shared time and space, and so on. These relationships mirror traditional marriage unions except that in one case the union is recognized by church or state and in the other it is not. In their comprehensive *American Couples* (1983), sociologists Philip Blumstein and Pepper Schwartz report that although cohabiting couples represent only around 2.0 to 3.8 percent of all couples, their number is increasing. One bit of evidence supporting the theory of continuing increase is that among couples in which the male is under 25, the percentage of cohabiting couples is 7.4 percent. In Sweden, a country that often leads in sexual trends, 12 percent of all couples are cohabitants.

Another example is the gay male or lesbian couple who live together as *domestic partners*—a relatively new term used to designate nonmarrieds (heterosexual or homosexual) living together—with all the other characteristics of a family. Research estimates the number of gay or lesbian couples at 70 to over 80 percent of the homosexual population (itself estimated variously at between 4 and 16 percent of the total population, depending on the definitions used and the studies cited). In summarizing these previous studies and their own research, Blumstein and Schwartz (1983) conclude, "'Couplehood' either as a reality or as an aspiration, is as strong among gay people as it is among heterosexuals."

The communication principles that apply to the traditional nuclear family (the mother-father-child family) also apply to these "nontraditional" families. In the following discussion the term *primary relationship* is used to designate the relationship between the two principal parties—for example the husband and wife, the lovers, or the domestic partners—and the term **family** to designate the broader constellation that includes children, relatives, and assorted significant others. A variety of definitions of "family" by the authors of works in family communication are presented on page 265. All primary relationships and families have several characteristics that will further define this relationship type: defined roles, recognition of responsibilities, shared history and future, and shared living space.

Defined Roles

Family members have a relatively clear perception of the roles each person is expected to play in relation to the other members and to the family as a whole. Each acquired the rules of the culture and social group; each knows approximately what his or her obligations, duties, privileges, and responsibilities are. Such roles might include wage earner, cook, house cleaner, child-care giver, social secretary, home decorator, plumber, carpenter, food shopper, money manager, and so on. At times the roles may be shared, but even then it is generally assumed that one person has primary responsibility for certain tasks and the other person for others. In cases in which the family includes children or aunts and uncles or grandparents, they too may have their assigned roles.

Most heterosexual couples divide the roles rather traditionally, with the man as primary wage earner and maintenance person, and the woman as primary cook, child-rearer, and housekeeper. This is less true among the more highly educated and those in the higher socioeconomic classes, where changes in these traditional role assignments are first seen. Among gay male and lesbian couples, however, the popular stereotypes of clear-cut male and female roles are not found. In her review of the research literature, psychologist Letitia Anne Peplau (1988) notes that scientific studies "have consistently debunked this myth. Most contemporary gay relationships do not conform to traditional 'masculine' and 'feminine' roles; instead, role flexibility and turn-taking are more common patterns. . . . In this sense, traditional heterosexual mar-

MEDIA WATCH

FROM MOM AND POP TO THE MEDIA: GATEKEEPERS

As you were growing up, your parents gave you certain information and withheld other information. For example, depending on the culture in which you were raised, you may have been told about Santa Claus and the tooth fairy but not about cancer or mutual funds. That is, your parents served as gatekeepers—they regulated the information to which you were exposed. When you went to school, your teachers served a similar function. They taught you about certain historical events, for example, but not others. Gatekeepers are all around us; the most important of these are the media, including the numerous internet providers (Lewis 1995).

In the passage of a message from the source of mass media to the viewer, a gatekeeper intervenes. The term **gatekeeping** was originally used by Kurt Lewin in *Human Relations* (1947). It refers to (1) the process by which a message passes through various gates, as well as to (2) the people or groups that allow the message to pass (gatekeepers).

A gatekeeper's main function is to filter the messages an individual receives. Teachers are perfect examples of gatekeepers. Teachers read the various books in an area of study. They read journal articles and listen to papers presented at conventions. They share information among themselves and conduct their own research in the field. From all this information, they pass some of it on to their students. Textbook authors are also gatekeepers. For example, in a thorough review of the research used in history textbooks, one researcher concluded that the content included was designed "to preserve political and economic power" rather than truth (Robinson 1993). Editors of newspapers, magazines, and publishing houses are also gatekeepers. They allow only certain information to get through. For example, in a study of news coverage in Great Britain (focusing on global warming and the Sudan famine), media owners, editors, and reporters served the gatekeeping function and in effect regulated the flow of news and public discourse about such issues (Lacey & Longman 1993).

The media, usually on the basis of their own codes and sometimes because of legal regulations, censor what gets through to viewers. For example, MTV serves as a gatekeeper and rejects a variety of video clips because they violate some standard. Thus, for example, Madonna's "Justify My Love" was rejected because of its depiction of group sex, while David Bowie's "China Girl" was rejected because of a nude beach scene. Neil Young's "This Note's for You"

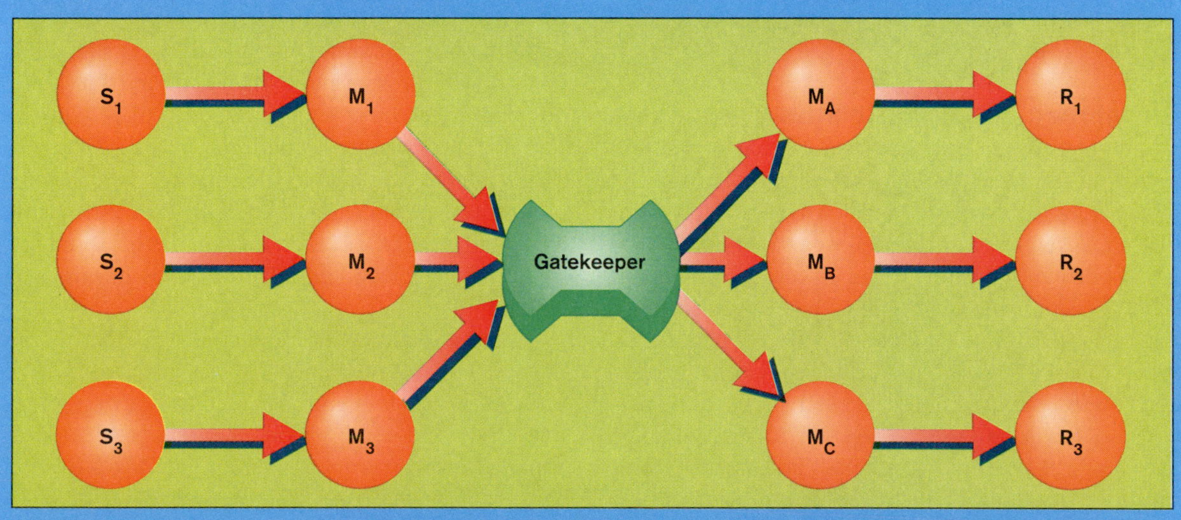

(continued on next page)

(continued)

and Seaweed's "Kid Candy" were rejected because they showed brand-name products (Banks 1995). Newspapers and magazines regularly reject stories they consider too sexual and photos they consider too graphic. Currently, commercial on-line vendors, political groups, and civil liberties groups are debating restrictions on pornography on the Internet. Fines of up to $100,000 and even prison sentences are being proposed for people who transmit material considered "lewd" or "indecent" (*New York Times* December 2, 1995, pp. 1, 9).

The gatekeeper, then, limits the messages we receive. Note also, however, that the gatekeeper also helps us learn a great deal more by distilling, organizing, and analyzing the information that is passed on to the student, newspaper reader, or television viewer. That is, without gatekeepers we would not get half the information we now receive.

We might diagram the gatekeeping process as in the figure on page 263.

Note that the messages (M_1, M_2, M_3) received by the gatekeeper come from different sources (S_1, S_2, S_3). Therefore the gatekeeper must select the messages to be communicated. The gatekeeper selectively transmits numerous messages (M_a, M_b, M_c) to different receivers (R_1 R_2, R_3). Liberal and conservative talk show hosts, for example, do not pass on the same information—although they may both receive the same news releases. Perhaps the most important aspect to note about this process is that messages received by the gatekeeper (M_1, M_2, M_3) are not the same as the messages the gatekeeper sends (M_a, M_b, M_c).

You may find it interesting to translate this relatively abstract discussion into concrete reality by asking yourself how the following people function as gatekeepers:

- your communication course instructor
- the editor of your local or college newspaper
- Ricki Lake and Oprah Winfrey
- your romantic partner (past or present)
- the president of the United States
- network news shows
- General Motors' advertising department
- a corporate CEO

riage is not the predominant model or script for current homosexual couples."

Recognition of Responsibilities

Family members see themselves as having certain obligations and responsibilities to each other. A single person does not have the same kinds of obligations to another as someone in a close love or family relationship. For example, family members have an obligation to help each other financially. There are also emotional responsibilities: to offer comfort when family members are distressed, to take pleasure in their pleasures, to feel their pain, to raise their spirits. Each person also has a temporal obligation to reserve some large block of time for the others. Time sharing seems important to all relationships, although each couple will define this differently.

Shared History and Future

Members of a primary relationship have a shared history and the prospect of a shared future. For a relationship to become a primary one, there must be some history, some significant past interactions. These interactions enable the members get to know each other, to understand each other a little better, and ideally to like and even love each other. Similarly, the individuals view the relationship as having a potential future.

Despite researchers' predictions that 50 percent of those couples now entering first marriages will divorce (the rate is higher for second marriages), and that 41 percent of all persons of marriageable age will experience divorce, most couples entering a relationship such as marriage view it—ideally at least—as permanent.

Shared Living Space

In American culture, persons in primary interpersonal relationships usually share the same living space. When living space is not shared, it is generally seen as an "abnormal" or temporary situation both by the culture as a whole and by the individuals involved in the relationship. Even those who live apart for a good part of the time probably perceive a shared space as the ideal and, in fact, usually do share some special space at least part of the time. In some cultures, men and women do not share the same living space; the women may live with the children while the men live together in a communal arrangement.

THINK ABOUT

Think about your own definition of family. What constitutes a family to you? What relationships does your definition include that these definitions exclude? What relationships does your definition exclude that these definitions include? Following are several definitions of family that researchers in family communication use. How do these definitions compare with yours?

- ". . . networks of people who share their lives over long periods of time, bound by ties of marriage, blood, or commitment, legal or otherwise, who consider themselves as family, and who share a significant history and anticipated future of functioning in a family relationship" (Galvin & Brommel 1996 p. 4).
- "A group of intimates, who generate a sense of home and group identity, complete with strong ties of loyalty and emotion, and an experience of a history and a future" (Noller & Fitzpatrick 1993, p. 6).
- ". . . an organized, relational transaction group, usually occupying a common living space over an extended time period, and possessing a confluence of interpersonal images that evolve through the exchange of meaning over time" (Pearson 1993, p. 14).
- ". . . a multigenerational social system consisting of at least two interdependent people bound together by a common living space (at one time or another) and a common history, and who share some degree of emotional attachment to or involvement with one another" (Yerby, Buerkel-Rothfuss, & Bochner 1990, p. 9)

Did your definition differ significantly from those presented here? Would you modify your definition in light of these views?

Types of Family Relationships

Although each relationship is unique, a few basic types of primary relationships can be identified (Fitzpatrick 1983, 1988; Noller & Fitzpatrick 1993). This typology was derived from a series of studies conducted largely in the United States but also including a few cross-cultural ones (for example, Noller & Hiscock 1989). Eight significant aspects of relational life were investigated in developing this scale (see accompanying self-test) and this typology:

- *ideology of traditionalism,* the extent to which the individuals believe in the traditional sex roles for couples
- *ideology of uncertainty and change,* the extent to which unpredictability and change are tolerated or welcomed
- *sharing,* the extent to which the individuals share their feelings for each other and engage in significant self-disclosure
- *autonomy,* the extent to which each retains his or her own identity and autonomy
- *undifferentiated space,* the extent to which the individuals have their own space and privacy
- *temporal regularity,* the extent to which the individuals spend time together
- *conflict avoidance,* the extent to which the individuals seek to avoid conflict and confrontation
- *assertiveness,* the extent to which each asserts his or her own rights

At this point you may wish to examine your own relational attitudes and style by taking the self-test, "Perceptions of Relationships." If you have a relational partner, you might wish to have him or her also complete the test and then compare your results.

Based on responses to questions covering these eight dimensions from over a thousand couples, three major types of relationships were identified: traditionals, separates, and independents.

SELF TEST

perceptions of relationships

Respond to the following 24 statements by indicating the degree to which you agree with each. Encircle *high* if you agree strongly, *med* if you agree moderately (medium), and *low* if you feel little agreement. For now, do not be concerned with the fact that these terms appear in different positions in the columns to the right. Note that in some cases there are only two alternatives. When you agree with an alternative that appears twice, circle it both times.

IDEOLOGY OF TRADITIONALISM

high low med 1. A woman should take her husband's name when she marries.
high low med 2. Our wedding ceremony was (will be) very important to us.
high low med 3. Our society, as we see it, needs to regain faith in the law and in our institutions.

IDEOLOGY OF UNCERTAINTY AND CHANGE

low high med 4. In marriage/close relationships, there should be no constraints or restrictions on individual freedom.
low high med 5. The ideal relationship is one marked by novelty, humor, and spontaneity.
low high med 6. In a relationship, each individual should be permitted to establish the daily rhythm and time schedule that suits him/her best.

SHARING

high med low 7. We tell each other how much we love or care about each other.
high med low 8. My spouse/mate reassures and comforts me when I am feeling low.
high med low 9. I think that we joke around and have more fun than most couples.

AUTONOMY

low high high 10. I have my own private work space (study, workshop, utility room, etc.).
low high high 11. My spouse has his/her own private work space (study, workshop, utility room, etc.).
low high high 12. Ithink that it important for one to have some private space which is all his/her own and separate.

UNDIFFERENTIATED SPACE

low high high 13. I feel free to interrupt my spouse/mate when he/she is concentrating on something if he/she is in my presence.
high med low 14. I open my spouse/mate's personal mail without asking permission.
high high low 15. I feel free to invite guests home without informing my spouse/mate.

TEMPORAL REGULARITY

high low high 16. We eat our meals (i.e., the ones at home) at the same time every day.
high low high 17. In our house, we keep a fairly regular daily time schedule.
high low high 18. We serve the main meal at the same time every day.

CONFLICT AVOIDANCE

med low high 19. If I can avoid arguing about some problems, they will disappear.
med low high 20. In our relationships, we feel it is better to engage in conflicts than to avoid them.
med low high 21. It is better to hide one's true feelings in order to avoid hurting your spouse/mate.

ASSERTIVENESS

low med med 22. My spouse/mate forces me to do things I do not want to do.
low med med 23. We are likely to argue in front of friends or in public places.
low med med 24. My spouse/mate tries to persuade me to do something I do not want to do.

Thinking Critically About Relationships The responses noted in the left most column (column 1) are characteristic of traditionals. The number of circled items in this column, then, indicates your agreement with and similarity to those considered "traditionals." Responses noted in column 2 are characteristic of "independents"; those noted in column 3 are characteristic of "separates." How accurately do you think this test measures your general relationship orientation? Can you identify relationships portrayed in the media with this three-part system? For example, what orientation would Roseanne and Dan Conner (from "Roseanne") have?

Source: These statements are from Mary Anne Fitzpatrick's *Relational Dimensions Instrument* and are reprinted by permission of Mary Anne Fitzpatrick.

Traditionals

Traditional couples are, as the term implies, traditional in several ways. For example, they share a basic belief system and philosophy of life. They see themselves as a blending of two persons into a single couple rather than as two separate individuals. They are *inter*dependent and believe that an individual's independence must be sacrificed for the good of the relationship.

Traditionals believe in mutual sharing and do little separately. For example, they spend a lot of time together, eat their meals together, place considerable emphasis on the home, and, perhaps most importantly, present themselves to others as a unified couple. This couple holds to the traditional sex roles and there are seldom any role conflicts. There are few power struggles and few conflicts because each person knows and follows a specified role within the relationship. Perhaps as a result of the relative serenity of their lives, traditionals view their relationship as well-adjusted and permanent. Traditionals rarely even think of separation or divorce.

In their communications, traditionals are highly responsive to each other. Traditionals lean toward each other, smile, talk a lot, interrupt each other, and finish each other's sentences. Although they claim to be open with each other and free to express their vulnerabilities and weaknesses, in actual fact their self-disclosures involve relatively low-risk rather than high-risk items and positive rather than negative disclosures.

Independents

In contrast to traditionals, independents stress their individuality. The relationship is important but never more important than each person's individual identity—identities that they frequently discuss. A strong sense of self is essential to independents. The relationship exists to provide satisfaction for each individual. Although independents spend a great deal of time together, they do not ritualize it, for example, with time schedules. Each individual spends time with outside friends.

Independents see themselves as relatively androgynous, as individuals who combine the traditionally feminine and the traditionally masculine roles and qualities. The communication between independents is responsive. Although they do not finish each other's sentences, they do interrupt with questions. They engage in conflict openly and without fear. Their disclosures are quite extensive and include high-risk and negative disclosures that are absent from the disclosures of traditionals. This couple sees their relationship as relatively well-adjusted.

Separates

Separates live together but view their relationship as more a matter of convenience than a result of their mutual love or closeness. They seem to have little desire to be together and, in fact, usually are so only at ritual functions, for example, mealtime or holiday get-togethers. It is important to these separates that each has his or her own physical as well as psychological space. Separates share little; each seems to prefer to go his or her own way. They try to avoid conflict and the expression of negative feelings but when conflict does emerge it frequently takes the form of personal attack.

Separates hold relatively traditional values and beliefs about sex roles, and each person tries to follow the behaviors normally assigned to each role. They see their relationship as a part of normal life rather than as one created out of a strong emotional attachment or love. What best characterizes this type, however, is that each person sees himself or herself as a separate individual and not as a part of a "we."

In addition to these three pure types, there are also combinations; for example, the separate/traditional couple, in which one individual is a separate and one a traditional. Another common pattern is the traditional/independent, where one individual believes in the traditional view of relationships and one in autonomy and independence.

Communication Patterns in Primary Relationships and Families

Another way to gain insight into primary relationships is to focus on relationships in terms of their communication patterns rather than on attitudes and beliefs as in the previous discussion. Four general communication patterns are identified here; each interpersonal relationship may then be viewed as a variation on one of these basic patterns.

The Equality Pattern

The equality pattern probably exists more in theory than in practice, but it is a good starting point for examining communication in primary relationships. In the *equality pattern* each person shares equally in the communication transactions; the roles played by each are equal. Thus each person is accorded a similar degree of credibility by the other; each is equally open to the ideas, opinions, and beliefs of the other; each engages in self-disclosure on a more or less equal basis. The communication is open, honest, direct, and free of the power plays that characterize so many other interpersonal relationships. There is no leader or follower, opinion giver or opinion seeker; rather, both parties play these roles equally. This basic equality means that the communication exchanges themselves, over a substantial period of time, are equal. For example, the number of questions asked, the depth and frequency of self-disclosures, the nonverbal behavior of touching and eye gaze would all be about the same for both people.

Both parties share equally in the decision-making processes—the insignificant ones such as which movie to see, as well as the significant ones, such as where to send a child to school, whether to attend church, what house to buy, and so on. Conflicts in equality relationships may occur with some frequency, but they are not seen as threatening to the individuals or to the relationship. They are viewed, rather, as exchanges of ideas, opinions, and values. Their conflicts are content rather than relational in nature (see Unit 2). This couple has few power struggles within the relationship domain.

If a communication model of this relationship were drawn in which arrows were used to signify individual messages, there would be an equal number of arrows emanating from each person. Further, if the arrows were classified into different types, they would likewise be similar. A representation of this is given in part A of Figure 15.2.

The Balanced Split Pattern

In the *balanced split pattern,* Figure 15.2 (B), an equality relationship is maintained, but here each person has authority over different domains. Each person is seen as an expert in different areas. For example, in the traditional nuclear family, the husband maintains high credibility in business matters and perhaps in politics. The wife maintains high credibility in such matters as child care and cooking. Although these patterns are changing, they can still be seen clearly in numerous traditional families.

Conflict is generally viewed as nonthreatening by these individuals since each has specified areas of expertise and so the win-lose patterns are more or less determined before the conflict begins.

The Unbalanced Split Pattern

In the *unbalanced split relationship,* Figure 15.2 (C), one person dominates; one person is seen as an expert in more than half the areas of mutual communication. In many unions this expertise takes the form of control. Thus, in the unbalanced split, one person is more or less regularly in control of the relation-

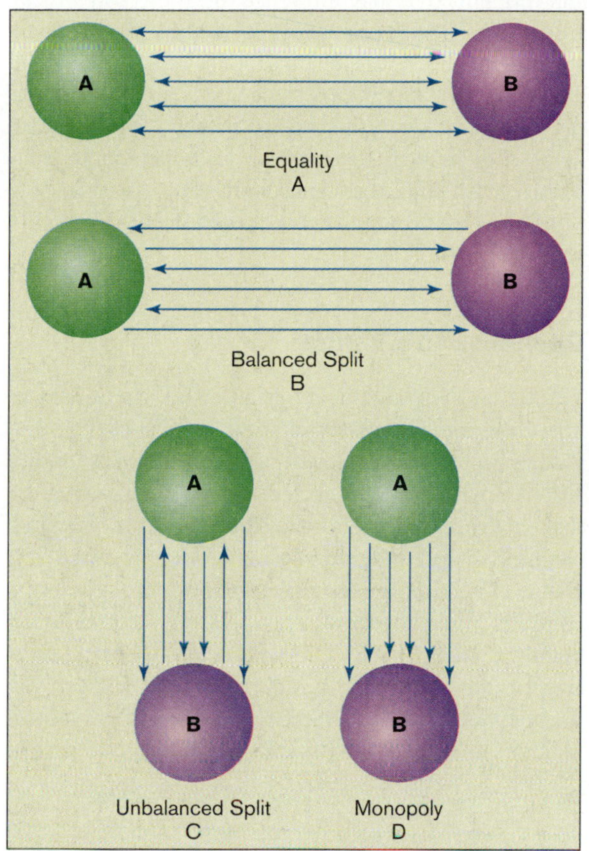

FIGURE 15.2 Communication patterns in primary relationships. These four general patterns try to capture some broad differences in relationship communication generally and in family communication in particular. Can you identify the general pattern that best describes your own family communication? What specific differences do you observe that are not captured by these general types?

ship. In some cases this person is the more intelligent or more knowledgeable, but in many cases it is the more physically attractive or the higher wage earner. The less attractive or lower-income partner compensates by giving in, allowing the other person to win the arguments or to have his or her way in decision making.

The person in control makes more assertions, tells the other person what should or will be done, gives opinions freely, plays power games to maintain control, and seldom asks for opinions in return. The noncontrolling person, conversely, asks questions, seeks opinions, and looks to the other person for decision-making leadership.

The Monopoly Pattern

In a *monopoly relationship,* Figure 15.1 (D), one person is seen as the authority. This person lectures rather than communicates. Rarely does this person ask questions to seek advice, and he or she always reserves the right to have the final say. In this type of couple, the arguments are few because both individuals already know who is boss and who will win the argument should one arise. When the authority is challenged, there are arguments and bitter conflicts. One reason the conflicts are so bitter is that these individuals have had no rehearsal for adequate conflict resolution. They do not know how to argue or how to disagree agreeably, so their arguments frequently take the form of hurting the other person.

The controlling person tells the partner what is and what is not to be. The controlling person talks more and talks more about matters independent of the other person's remarks than does the noncontrolling partner (Palmer 1989). The noncontrolling person looks to the other to give permission, to voice opinion leadership, to make decisions, almost as a child looks to an all-knowing, all-powerful parent.

Reflections on Types and Patterns of Primary and Family Relationships

In thinking about the three types and four patterns of primary and family relationships, it is easy to identify with, say, those who are independents or those in the equality pattern. Many decisions are based on subconscious factors, however, and therefore motivations are not always "logical" and "mature." What makes for happiness, satisfaction, and productivity in a relationship varies with the individuals involved. For example, an equality pattern that might give satisfaction in one relationship may lead to dissatisfaction among individuals who need either to control another person or to be controlled. The type and pattern of relationship that makes you happy might make your father and mother or your son and daughter unhappy. A clear recognition of this factor of relativity is essential to understanding and appreciating your own and other people's relationships.

IMPROVING COMMUNICATION IN FRIENDSHIP, LOVE, AND FAMILY RELATIONSHIPS

Communication in these close relationships can be improved by applying the same principles that improve communication in any other context, but to be most effective, these principles need to be adapted to the unique context of the primary relationship. The purpose of this section is to suggest how the general principles of effective communication may be best applied to friendship, love, and family relationships.

Empathic Understanding

Unless you are like the empaths in science fiction where you automatically and completely feel the pain or joy of another, your empathy is likely to be only partial. Your empathy can only approach what the other person is feeling, never reproduce it. But even this partial empathy is necessary if meaningful communication is to be established. We have to learn to see (even partially) the world from the other person's point of view, to feel that person's pain and insecurity, to experience the other person's love and fear. Empathy is an essential ingredient if a friendship, love, or family relationship is to survive as a meaningful and productive union. It is essential, for example, that the individuals be allowed—and, in fact, encouraged—to explain how and why they see the world, their relationship, and their problems as they do.

Self-Disclosures

The importance of self-disclosure in the development and maintenance of a meaningful interpersonal relationship has been noted repeatedly. Recall that total self-disclosure may not always be effective (Noller & Fitzpatrick 1993). In fact, at times it may be expedient to omit, for example, past indiscretions, certain fears, and perceived personal inadequacies, if these disclosures may lead to negative perceptions or damage the relationship in some way. In any decision as to whether or not to self-disclose, the possible effects on the relationship should be considered. It is also necessary to consider the ethical issues involved, specifically the other person's right to know about behaviors and thoughts that may influence the choices he or she will make. Most relationships would profit from greater self-disclosure of present feelings rather than details of past sexual experiences or past psychological problems. The sharing of present feelings also helps a great deal in enabling each person to empathize with the other; each comes to better understand the other's point of view when these self-disclosures are made.

Openness to Change

Throughout any significant relationship there will be numerous and significant changes in each of the individuals and in the relationship. Because persons in relationships are interconnected with each impacting on the other, changes in one person may demand changes in the other person. Frequently asked for changes include, for example, giving more attention, complimenting more often, expressing feelings more openly (Noller 1982). The willingness to be responsive to such changes, to be adaptable and flexible, will likely enhance relationship satisfaction and is, in fact, included in the major theories of family functioning (Noller & Fitzpatrick 1993).

Fair Fighting

Conflict, we know, is inevitable; it is an essential part of every meaningful interpersonal relationship. Perhaps the most general rule to follow is to *fight fair,* a topic explored in detail in Unit 16. Winning at all costs, beating down the other person, getting one's own way, being verbally aggressive, and the like have little use in a primary relationship or family. Instead, cooperation, compromise, and mutual understanding must be substituted. If we enter into conflict with a person we love with the idea that we must win and the other must lose, the conflict has to hurt at least one partner, very often both. In these situations the loser gets hurt and frequently retaliates so that no one really wins in any meaningful sense. On the other hand, if we enter a conflict with the aim of resolving it by reaching some kind of mutual understanding, neither party need be hurt, and in fact both parties may benefit from the clash of ideas or desires and from the airing of differences.

Reasonableness

Some people expect their relationship to be perfect. Whether from the media, from the self-commitment to have a relationship better than that of one's parents, or from the mistaken belief that other relationships are a lot better than one's own, many people expect and look for perfection. This, of course, is likely to result in disappointment and dissatisfaction with any existing relationship. Psychologist John DeCecco (1988) argues that relationships should be characterized by reasonableness: "*reasonableness* of need and expectation, avoiding the wasteful pursuit of the extravagant fantasy that *every* desire will be fulfilled, so that the relationship does not consume its partners or leave them chronically dissatisfied."

SUMMARY

In this unit we looked at friendship, love, and family relationships and especially at the role of communication in these relationships.

1. Friendship is an interpersonal relationship between two persons that is mutually productive and characterized by mutual positive regard.
2. Enjoyment, acceptance, mutual assistance, confiding, understanding, trust, respect, and spontaneity are among the essential characteristics of friendship.
3. Friendships can be described as progressing from initial contact and acquaintanceship, through casual, to close and intimate. As friendships progress in intimacy, so does interpersonal communication effectiveness.
4. Love may focus on beauty and sensuality (eros love), entertainment and excitement (ludus love), peace and calm (storge love), the practical and traditional (pragma love), elation and depression (manic love), and compassion and selflessness (agape). It may also involve some combination of these six primary types.
5. A family may be defined as an interpersonal relationship between two people (often with children or with other biologically related members) who have defined roles, relationship responsibilities, a shared history and a prospect for a shared future, and who share a living space.
6. Couples may be classified as traditional (they are interdependent and believe that an individual's independence must be sacrificed for the good of the relationship), independents (they stress their own individuality above the relationship), and separates (they live together but go about much of their lives separately).
7. Equality, balanced split, unbalanced split, and monopoly communication patterns provide a useful way to talk about communication among couples.
8. Communication in friendship, love, and family may be enhanced by empathic understanding, self-disclosure, openness to change, fair fighting, and the willingness to be reasonable and to expect what is reasonable.

THINKING CRITICALLY ABOUT FRIENDSHIP, LOVE, AND FAMILY COMMUNICATION

1. What are the five most important qualities of your best friend? How would your best friend answer this question about you? Which of these qualities is the most important in maintaining your friendship?
2. After meeting someone for the first time, how long (on average) does it take you to decide if this person will become a friend? What specific qualities do you look for? How would you describe the progression from acquaintance to intimate friend?
3. Do you find significant sex differences in your own friendships with men and women? In what ways are men and women different in their friendship behaviors?
4. Some researchers have proposed that ludic love tendencies may reveal tendencies to sexual aggression (Sarwer, Kalichman, Johnson, Early et al. 1993). Do you find this to be true?
5. Lord Byron, in *Don Juan*, said: "Man's love is of man's life a thing apart, / Tis woman's whole existence." Do you agree with this? If you do, what are some specific implications of this difference for the ways in which men and women ap-

proach love? Do you think that the love in a man and in a woman develop in essentially the same way in heterosexual and in homosexual relationships? How would you go about finding evidence to help answer these question?

6. The researchers who investigated idioms, discussed on page 260, offer some interesting predictions on the basis of their analysis of these personal idioms (Hopper, Knapp, and Scott 1981). They predict that personal idioms will occur more frequently during the time the couple wishes to emphasize relational commitment and create a bond between themselves. After the relationship has existed for a time, the use of personal idioms will probably decrease. Lastly, the researchers note that these idioms may appear deceitful when used during times of relationship difficulty. Do you agree with these predictions?
7. Psychotherapist Albert Ellis (1988, Ellis & Harper 1975) has argued that love and infatuation are really the same emotion and that we use the term *infatuation* to describe relationships that did not work out and we use the term *love* to describe our current romantic relationships. Do you agree that infatuation and love are essentially the same basic emotion? If you disagree, in what specific ways are they different?
8. Recently, a number of court decisions have allowed gay male and lesbian domestic partners to legally adopt the biological children of their partners. Similarly, in some cases, courts have allowed gay male and lesbian couples to adopt children who are biologically unrelated to either party (Goleman 1992; *New York Times,* November 5, 1995, 41–42). Do you see affectional or sexual orientation as relevant in adoption decisons?
9. Can you describe couples you know as being traditionals, independents, or separates? With what type of relationship (traditional, independent, and separate) do you most identify? Can you describe couples who have clearly identified equality, balanced split, unbalanced split, or monopoly communication patterns?
10. How would you go about finding answers to the following questions:
    a. Why are women's friendships considered more intimate than men's?
    b. Why do men's friendships seem to revolve around doing something while women's friendships revolve around talking and relating?
    c. How is friendship related to loneliness? To self-esteem? To having successful romantic relationships?
    d. What types of lovers (eros, ludus, storge, pragma, mania, agape) were the great lovers of history and literature?
    e. Do persons who are high self-disclosers make better relationship partners than low self-disclosers? Do high disclosers make better parents?
    f. Are couples with children happier than couples without children?

Interpersonal Conflict

unit contents

unit goals

After completing this unit, you should be able to

1. define *interpersonal conflict* and distinguish between content and relationship conflict
2. explain the strategies of conflict management
3. describe the suggestions for preparing for and following up an interpersonal conflict.

In this unit we consider interpersonal conflict, what it is, how it can go wrong, and how it can be used to improve relationships.

THE NATURE OF INTERPERSONAL CONFLICT

Pat wants to go to the movies with Chris; Chris wants to stay home. Pat's insisting on going to the movies interferes with Chris's staying home and Chris's determination to stay home interferes with Pat's going to the movies.

Jim and Bernard own a small business. Jim wants to expand the business and open a branch in California. Bernard wants to sell the business and retire. Each has opposing goals and each interferes with each other's attaining these goals.

As experience shows, **interpersonal conflicts** can be of various types:

- goals to be pursued ("We want you to go to college and become a teacher or a doctor, not a disco dancer")
- allocation of resources such as money or time ("I want to spend the tax refund on a car, not on new furniture")
- decisions to be made ("I refuse to have the Jeffersons over for dinner")
- behaviors that are considered appropriate or desirable by one person and inappropriate or undesirable by the other ("I hate it when you get drunk/pinch me/ridicule me in front of others/flirt with others/dress provocatively")

THINK ABOUT

One of the problems in studying and in dealing with interpersonal conflict is that you may be operating with false assumptions about what **conflict** is and what it means. Think about your own assumptions about conflict, which were probably derived from the communications you witnessed in your family and in your social interactions. For example, do you think the following are true or false?

- If two people who are in a relationship fight, it means their relationship is a bad one.
- Fighting damages an interpersonal relationship.
- Fighting is bad because it reveals our negative selves—our pettiness, our need to be in control, our unreasonable expectations.

Simple answers are usually wrong. These three assumptions may all be true or may all be false; it depends. In and of itself, conflict is neither good nor bad. Conflict is a part of every interpersonal relationship, between parents and children, brothers and sisters, friends, lovers, co-workers. If it isn't, then the relationship is probably dull, irrelevant, or insignificant. Conflict is inevitable in any meaningful relationship.

It is not so much the conflict that creates the problem as the way in which you approach and deal with the conflict. Some ways of approaching conflict can resolve difficulties and actually improve the relationship. Other ways can hurt the relationship; they can destroy self-esteem, create bitterness, and foster suspicion. Your task, therefore, is not to try to create relationships that will be free of conflict but rather to learn appropriate and productive ways of managing conflict.

Similarly, it is not the conflict that will reveal your negative side but the fight strategies you use. Thus if you personally attack the other person, use force, or use

What myths about conflict do you think are most prevalent among members of your culture? Do men and women entertain the same myths? Do teenagers and, say, persons in their 50s, view relationship conflict in the same general way? If not, how do those groups differ from each other?

personal rejection or manipulation you will reveal your negative side. In fighting you can also reveal your positive self—your willingness to listen to opposing points of view, your readiness to change unpleasant behaviors, and your willingness to accept imperfection in others.

Content or Relationship Aspects of Conflict

Using concepts developed earlier (Unit 2), we may distinguish between content conflict and relationship conflict. Content conflict centers on objects, events, and persons in the world that are usually, but not always, external to the parties involved in the conflict. These include the millions of issues that you argue and fight about every day—the value of a particular movie, what to watch on television, the fairness of the last examination or job promotion, and the way to spend your savings.

Relationship conflicts are equally numerous and include such conflict situations as a younger sibling who does not obey an older sibling, two partners who each want an equal say in making vacation plans, and the parent and child who each want to have the final word concerning the child's life-style. Here the conflicts are concerned not so much with some external object as with the relationships between the individuals, with such issues as who is in charge, the equality of a primary relationship, and who has the right to set down rules of behavior.

Content conflicts are usually manifest; they are clearly observable and identifiable. Relationship conflicts are often latent; they are often hidden and much more difficult to identify. Thus, a conflict over where you should vacation may on the surface or manifest level center on the advantages and disadvantages of Mexico versus Hawaii. On a relationship and often latent level, however, it may center on who has the greater right to select the place to vacation, who should win the argument, who is the decision maker in the relationship, and so on.

THINK ABOUT

Think about the issues you argue about. Make a list of the five or six issues that most frequently create conflict before looking at Table 16.1 or at the bulleted list that follows. In the first study (see Table 16.1) gay, lesbian, and heterosexual couples were surveyed on the issues they argued about most (Kurdek 1994).

In another study four conditions led up to a couple's "first big fight" (Siegert & Stamp 1994):

- uncertainty over commitment
- jealousy
- violation of expectations
- personality differences

Rarely are conflicts all content- or all relationship-oriented. In fact, the vast majority of conflicts contain elements of both content and relationship. Try identifying the possible relationship aspects and the possible content aspects in each of the causes of conflict just listed as well as the causes of your own conflicts. Distinguishing the content from the relationship dimensions of any given conflict is one of the first steps toward conflict resolution.

The Context of Conflict

Conflict, like any form of communication, takes place in a context that is physical, sociopsychological, temporal, and cultural.

Physical Context

Whether you engage in conflict privately or publicly, alone or in front of children or other relatives, for example, will influence the way the conflict is conducted as well as the effects that this conflict will have.

Sociopsychological Context

The sociopsychological context will also influence the conflict. If the atmosphere is one of equality, for example, the conflict is likely to progress very differently than if in an atmosphere of inequality. A friendly and a hostile context will exert different influences on the conflict.

Temporal Context

The temporal context will likewise prove important to understand. A conflict after a series of similar conflicts will be seen differently than a conflict after a series of enjoyable experiences and an absence of conflict. A conflict immediately after a hard day at work will engender feelings different from a conflict after an enjoyable dinner.

TABLE 16.1
relationship conflict issues

This table presents the rank order of the six most frequently argued about issues (1 = the most argued about). Note that these issues involve both content and relationship dimensions. Note also the striking similarity among all couples. It seems that affectional orientation and gender have little to do with the topics people argue about.

Issue	Gay ($N = 75$)	Lesbian ($N = 51$)	Heterosexual ($N = 108$)
Intimacy issues, such as affection and sex	1	1	1
Power issues, such as excessive demands or possessiveness, lack of equality in the relationship, friends, and leisure time	2	2	2
Personal flaws issues, such as drinking or smoking, personal grooming, and driving style	3	3	4
Personal distance issues, such as frequent absenteeism and school or job commitments	4	4	5
Social issues, such as politics and social issues, parents, and personal values	5	5	3
Distrust issues, such as previous lovers and lying	6	6	6

Cultural Context

The cultural context is as influential in conflict as it is with all other topics of human communication. Culture will influence the issues that people fight about as well as what are considered appropriate and inappropriate ways of dealing with conflict. For example, cohabitating 18-year-olds are more likely to have conflict with their parents about their living style if they lived in the United States than if they lived in Sweden, where cohabitation is much more accepted. Similarly, male infidelity is more likely to cause conflict among American couples than among Southern European couples. Students from the United States are more likely to pursue a conflict with another student from the same culture than with someone from another culture. On the other hand, Chinese students, consistent with a collectivist orientation and an emphasis on preserving in-group harmony, are more likely to pursue a conflict with a non-Chinese than with a Chinese student (Leung 1988).

The types of conflicts that arise will depend on the cultural orientation of the individuals. For example, it is likely that in high-context cultures conflicts are more likely to center on violating collective or group norms and values. Conversely, it is likely that in low-context cultures conflicts are more likely to come up when individual norms are violated (Ting-Toomey 1985).

In Japan it is especially important that you not embarrass the person with whom you are in conflict, especially if that conflict occurs in public. This **face-saving** principle prohibits the use of such strategies as personal rejection or verbal aggressiveness. In the United States, men and women, ideally at least, are both expected to express their desires and complaints openly and directly. Many Middle Eastern and Pacific Rim cultures would discourage women from such expressions; rather, a more agreeable and permissive posture would be expected.

African Americans and European Americans engage in conflict in very different ways (Kochman 1981). The issues that cause conflict and that aggravate conflict, the conflict strategies that are expected and accepted, and the entire attitude toward conflict vary from one group to the other.

Different cultures also view conflict management techniques differently. For example, in one study (Collier 1991) it was found that African American men preferred clear arguments and a focus on problem solving. African American women, however, preferred assertiveness and respect. In another study, African American females were found to use more direct controlling strategies (for example, assuming control over the conflict and arguing persistently for their point of view) than did white females. White females, on the other hand, used more problem-solution-oriented conflict styles than did African American females. African American and white men were very similar in their conflict strategies; both tended to avoid or withdraw from relationship conflict. They preferred to keep quiet about their differences or make them seem insignificant (Ting-Toomey 1986).

Mexican American men emphasized mutual understanding achieved through discussing the reasons for the conflict while women focused on support for the relationship. Anglo-American men preferred direct and rational argument while women preferred flexibility. These, of course, are merely examples, but the underlying principle is that techniques for dealing with interpersonal conflict will be viewed differently by different cultures.

The following brief dialogue (from an idea by Crohn 1995) is designed to illustrate the issue of cultural differences in conflict and some of the problems these may create. As you read it try to explain what is possibly going on interculturally.

PAT: Why did you tell her I was home? I told you an hour ago that I didn't want to speak with her. You just don't listen.

CHRIS: I'm sorry. I completely forgot. But, you seemed to have had a nice talk. So, no harm done—right?

PAT: Wrong. You just don't understand. I didn't want to talk with her.

CHRIS: O.K. Sorry. *[Withdraws to next room and remains silent. To Pat's repeated comments and criticisms, he says nothing. After about two hours the dialogue continues.]*

PAT: I can't stand your silent treatment; you're making me the villain. You're the one who screwed up.

CHRIS: I'm sorry. *[Walks away]*

Communication continued in this way for the rest of the evening—with Pat ranting and raving every few minutes and with Chris saying hardly anything and always trying to walk away. Pat comes from a culture in which anger is regularly and expectedly expressed. Yelling and screaming are customary ways of dealing with conflict. Chris comes from a culture in which anger is expressed by silence. The extent to which you remain silent is a clear measure of your anger.

From Chris's silence it is easy for Pat to conclude that Chris doesn't care about what happened and is indifferent to Pat's anger. From Pat's outburst Chris may easily conclude that Pat is unhappy in their relationship.

If Pat and Chris came from the same culture—with the same rules for expressing anger—or had sufficient intercultural awareness, their argument would have been no less real. Don't fool yourself into thinking that cultural awareness will resolve all conflicts or that culture is the only factor that can cause such differences: it will not and it is not. It would, however, have prevented a large part of the conflict—for example, the anger over the way the other person expressed anger—and would have prevented each from making inaccurate assumptions about the other. The problem is made even more difficult to resolve because these cultural rules are so deeply ingrained that you assume everyone has the same rules, and you never get to explore the problem from the point of view of intercultural communication differences because you assume this underlying similarity.

The Negatives and Positives of Conflict

The kind of conflict focused on here is conflict among or between "connected" individuals. Interpersonal conflict occurs frequently between lovers, best friends, siblings, and parent and child. Interpersonal conflict is made all the more difficult because, unlike many other conflict situations, you often care for, like, even love the individual with whom you are in disagreement. There are both negative and positive aspects or dimensions to interpersonal conflict, and each of these should be noted.

Negative Aspects

Conflict often leads to increased negative regard for the opponent, and when this opponent is someone you love or care for very deeply, it can create serious problems for the relationship. One problem is that many conflicts involve unfair fighting methods that aim largely to hurt the other person. When one person hurts the other, increased negative feelings are inevitable; even the strongest relationship has limits.

Conflict frequently leads to a depletion of energy better spent on other areas. This is especially true when unproductive conflict strategies are used, as examined later in this unit.

At times conflict leads you to close yourself off from the other individual. Though it would not be to your advantage to reveal your weaknesses to your "enemy," when you hide your true self from an intimate, you prevent meaningful communication from taking place. One possible consequence is that one or both parties may seek intimacy elsewhere. This often leads to further conflict, mutual hurt, and resentment—qualities that add heavily to the costs carried by the relationship. As these costs increase, exchanging rewards may become difficult—perhaps impossible. The result is a situation in which the costs increase and the rewards decrease—a situation that often results in relationship deterioration and eventual dissolution.

Positive Aspects

The major value of interpersonal conflict is that it forces you to examine a problem and work toward a potential solution. If productive conflict strategies are used, the relationship may well emerge from the encounter stronger, healthier, and more satisfying than before.

Conflict enables you to state what you each want and—if the conflict is resolved effectively—perhaps to get it. In fact, a better understanding of each other's feelings has been found to be one of the main results of the "first big fight" (Siegert & Stamp 1994). For example, say that you want to spend your money on a new car (your old one is unreliable) and your partner wants to spend it on a vacation (your partner feels the need for a change of pace). Through your conflict and its resolution, you learn, it is hoped, what each really wants—in this case, a reliable car and a break from routine. You may then be able to figure out a way for each to get what each wants. You might accept a good used car or a less expensive new car and your partner might accept a shorter or less expensive vacation. Or you might buy a used car and take an inexpensive motor trip. Each of these solutions would satisfy both of you—they are win-win solutions.

Conflict also prevents hostilities and resentments from festering. Suppose you're annoyed at your partner for talking with colleagues from work for two hours on the phone instead of giving that time to you. If you say nothing, your annoyance and resentment are likely to grow. Further, by saying nothing you implicitly approve of such behavior and so it is likely that such phone calls will be repeated.

Through discussing your conflict and working on its resolution you stop resentment from increasing. In the process you also let your own needs be known—that you need lots of attention when you come home from work and that your partner needs to review and get closure on his or her day's work. If you both can appreciate the legitimacy of these needs, then solutions may be easily identified. Perhaps the phone call can be made after your attention needs are met or perhaps you can delay your need for attention until your partner gets closure about work. Or perhaps you can learn to provide for your partner's closure needs and in so doing also get the attention you need.

Consider too that when you try to resolve conflict within an interpersonal relationship, you are saying in effect that the relationship is worth the effort; otherwise you would walk away from such a conflict. Although there may be exceptions—as when you confront conflict to save face or to gratify some ego need—usually confronting a conflict indicates concern, commitment, and a desire to preserve the relationship.

CONFLICT MANAGEMENT

The conflict management strategies that you choose will be influenced by a variety of considerations. Understanding these factors may help you select more appropriate and more effective strategies.

For example, the goals, (both short-term and long-term) you wish to achieve will influence what strategies seem appropriate to you. If you just want to save tonight's date, you might want to simply "give in" and basically ignore the difficulty. On the other hand, if you want to build a long-term relationship, you might want to analyze the cause of the problem fully and look for strategies that will enable both parties to win.

Your emotional state will influence your strategies. You are unlikely to select the same strategies when you are sad as when you are angry. Different strategies will be used if you are seeking to apologize or looking for revenge.

Your cognitive assessment of the situation will exert a powerful influence. For example, your attitudes and beliefs about what is fair and equitable will influence your readiness to acknowledge the fairness in the other person's position. Your own assessment of who (if anyone) is the cause of the problem will also influence your conflict style. You might also assess the likely effects of your various strategies. For example, what do you risk if you fight with your boss by using blame or personal rejection? Do you risk alienating your teenager when you use force?

Your personality and level of communication competence will influence the way you engage in conflict. For example, if you are shy and unassertive, you may be more likely to want to avoid a conflict rather than fight actively. If you are extroverted and have a strong desire to state your position, then you may be more likely to fight actively and to argue forcefully.

Your cultural background will influence your strategies. As noted earlier, many Asian cultures emphasize the importance of saving face, of not embarrassing another person, especially in public. Consequently, Asians are probably less likely to use conflict strategies such as blame and personal rejection since these are likely to result in a loss of face. Of course many Asians are more likely to use a variety of strategies to preserve and enhance their public image. Those from cultures that look more favorably upon the open discussion of conflict might be more apt to use argumentativeness and to fight actively. Students from collective cultures preferred mediation and bargaining as conflict resolution strategies whereas students from individual cultures preferred a conflict style that was more adversarial and confrontational (Leung 1987; Berry, Poortinga, Segall, & Dasen 1992).

Also, many cultures have different rules for men and women engaging in conflict. Asian cultures are more strongly prohibitive of women's conflict strategies. Asian women are expected to be exceptionally polite; this is even more important when women are in conflict with men and when the conflict is public (Tannen 1994b). In the United States, there is a verbalized equality; men and women have equal rights when it comes to permissible conflict strategies. In reality, there are many who expect women to be more polite,

LISTEN TO THIS

ACTIVE LISTENING

Active listening is a special kind of listening and one of the essential techniques for improving relationship communication in general and conflict communication in particular. Active listening owes its development to Thomas Gordon (1975), who made it a cornerstone of his P-E-T (Parent-Effectiveness-Training) technique. (This box is positioned before the discussion of conflict management because active listening is an effective principle to follow in your conflict talk, in talking through your conflict.) Active listening as a technique, however, is not limited to interpersonal conflict but will prove useful in all forms of communication—in relationship communication, in small group interaction, in organizational communication, and in interviewing.

Consider the following brief exchange. Which person most closely represents what you would probably say?

SPEAKER: That creep gave me a C on the paper. I really worked on that project and I get a lousy C.

LISTENER 1: hat's not too bad; most people got around the same grade. I got a C too.

LISTENER 2: So what? This is your last semester. Who cares about grades anyway?

LISTENER 3: You should be pleased with a C. Peggy and Michael both failed and John and Judy got D's.

LISTENER 4: You got a C on that paper you were working on for the last three weeks? You sound really angry and hurt.

All four listeners are probably anxious to make the speaker feel better, but they go about it in very different ways and, we can be sure, with very different results. The first three listeners give rather typical responses. Listeners 1 and 2 both try to lessen the significance of a C grade but do little to promote meaningful communication and understanding. Listener 3 tries to give the C grade a more positive meaning. Note, however, that all three listeners are also saying that the speaker should not be feeling as he or she does. They are saying the speaker's feelings are not legitimate and should be replaced with feelings that are more logical.

Listener 4, however, uses active listening, a process of sending back to the speaker what you as a listener think the speaker meant—both in content and in feelings. Active listening is not a process of merely repeating the speaker's exact words, but rather of putting together into some meaningful whole your understanding of the speaker's total message.

THE FUNCTIONS OF ACTIVE LISTENING

Active listening serves several important functions. First, it enables the listener to check on his or her understanding of what the speaker said and, more important, what the speaker meant. When the listener reflects back to the speaker what he or she perceived to be the speaker's meaning, the listener gives the speaker an opportunity to clarify whatever may need it. In this way, future messages will have a better chance of being relevant and purposeful. As you can appreciate, this function is especially important in conflict communication, in which misunderstandings often underlie and aggravate the conflict.

Second, through active listening the listener expresses acceptance of the speaker's feelings. Note that in the sample responses given earlier, the first three listeners challenged the speaker's feelings. The active listener, who reflected back to the speaker what he or she thought was said, gave the speaker acceptance. The speaker's feelings were not challenged but instead were echoed in a sympathetic and empathic manner. Note too that in the first three responses the speaker's feelings are denied. Listener 4, however, not only accepts the speaker's feelings but identifies them explicitly—"You sound really angry and hurt"—again allowing an opportunity for correction. Any attempt at conflict resolution will be vastly improved when it is based on acceptance of each other's feelings.

Third, and perhaps most important, active listening stimulates the speaker to explore feelings and thoughts. With the response of Listener 4, the speaker has an opportunity to elaborate on his or

(*continued on next page*)

(continued)

her feelings. Active listening encourages the speaker to explore and express thoughts and feelings and facilitates meaningful dialogue. In stimulating this further exploration, active listening also encourages the speaker to solve his or her own problems by providing the opportunity to talk them through. This often helps makes the sources of conflict concrete and makes their eventual solution easier.

THE TECHNIQUES OF ACTIVE LISTENING

Three simple techniques may prove useful in learning active listening.

Paraphrase the Speaker's Thoughts

State in your own words what you think the speaker meant. This will help ensure understanding, since the speaker will be able to correct your restatement if necessary. It will show the speaker that you are interested in what is being said. Everyone wants to feel attended to, especially when angry or depressed. The paraphrase also gives the speaker a chance to elaborate on or extend what was originally said. Thus, when Listener 4 echoes the speaker's thoughts, the speaker may next elaborate on why that paper was an important one. Perhaps the speaker fears that the next paper will receive a similar grade.

In your paraphrase, be especially careful that you do not lead the speaker in the direction you think he or she should go. Paraphrases should be objective descriptions.

Express Understanding of the Speaker's Feelings

In addition to paraphrasing the content, echo the feelings you felt the speaker expressed or implied. ("I can imagine how you must have felt. You must have felt really horrible.") Just as the paraphrase enables you to check on your perception of the content, the expression of feelings enables you to check on your perception of the speaker's feelings. This expression of feelings will also provide the speaker with the opportunity to see his or her feelings more objectively. It is especially helpful when the speaker feels angry, hurt, or depressed. We all need that objectivity; we need to see our feelings from a somewhat less impassioned perspective if we are to deal with them effectively.

When you echo the speaker's feelings, you also give the speaker permission to elaborate on these feelings. In echoing these feelings be careful that you do not over- or understate the speaker's feelings. Just try to restate the feelings as accurately as you can.

Ask Questions

Ask questions to ensure your own understanding of the speaker's thoughts and feelings and to secure additional information ("How did you feel when you saw that grade?"). The questions should be designed to provide just enough stimulation and support for the speaker to express the thoughts and feelings he or she wants to express. Questions should not pry into unrelated areas or challenge the speaker in any way. These questions will further confirm your interest and concern for the speaker.

to pursue conflict is a nonargumentative way, while men are expected to argue forcefully and logically.

You might wish to pause at this point and ask yourself what your own culture teaches about conflict and its management. What strategies does it prohibit? Are some strategies prohibited when in conflict with certain people (say, your parents) but not with others (say, your friends)? Does your culture prescribe certain ways of dealing with conflict? Does it have different expectations for men and for women? To what degree have you internalized these teachings? What effect do these teachings have on your actual conflict behaviors?

Avoidance and Active Fighting

Avoidance may involve actual physical flight. You may leave the scene of the conflict (walk out of the apartment or go to another part of the office), fall asleep, or blast the stereo to drown out all conversation. It may also take the form of emotional or intellectual avoidance. Here you may leave the conflict psychologically by not dealing with any of the arguments or problems raised. In the United States men are more likely to use avoidance than women (Markman, Silvern, Clements, & Kraft-Hanak 1993; Oggins, Veroff, & Leber 1993), often coupled with denials that anything is wrong (Haferkamp 1991–92).

Nonnegotiation is a special type of avoidance, by which you refuse to discuss the conflict or to listen to the other person's argument. At times nonnegotiation takes the form of hammering away at one's own point of view until the other person gives in, a method referred to as steamrolling.

Instead of avoiding the issues, take an active role in your interpersonal conflicts. Don't close your ears (or mind), blast the stereo, or walk out of the house during an argument. This is not to say that a cooling-off period is not at times desirable, but if you wish to resolve conflicts, you need to confront them actively.

Involve yourself on both sides of the communication exchange. Participate actively as a speaker-listener; voice your own feelings and listen carefully to the voicing of your opponent's feelings. Although periodic moratoriums are sometimes helpful, be willing to communicate as both sender and receiver—to say what is on your mind and to listen to what the other person is saying.

Another part of active fighting involves taking responsibility for your thoughts and feelings. For example, when you disagree with your partner or find fault with her or his behavior, take responsibility for these feelings. Say, for example, "I disagree with . . ." or "I don't like it when you . . . ." Avoid statements that deny your responsibility, as in, "Everybody thinks you're wrong about . . ." or "Even Chris thinks you shouldn't . . . ."

Force and Talk

When confronted with conflict, many people prefer not to deal with the issues but rather to force their position physically on the other person. The force may be emotional or physical. In either case, the issues are avoided and the person who "wins" is the one who exerts the most force. This is the technique of warring nations, children, and even some normally sensible and mature adults. This is surely one of the most serious problems confronting relationships today, but many approach it as if it were of only minor importance or even something humorous.

Over 50 percent of both single and married couples reported that they had experienced physical violence in their relationship. If we add symbolic violence (for example, threatening to hit the other person or throwing something), the percentages are above 60 percent for singles and above 70 percent for marrieds (Marshall & Rose 1987).

In a study of divorced couples, 70 percent reported at least one episode of violence in their premarital, marital, or postmarital relationship. Violence during marriage was higher than for pre- or postmarital relationships (Olday & Wesley 1990). In another study, 47 percent of a sample of 410 college students reported some experience with violence in a dating relationship (Deal & Wampler 1986). In most cases the violence was reciprocal—each person in the relationship used violence. In cases in which only one person was violent, the research results are conflicting. For example, Deal and Wampler (1986) found that in cases in which one partner was violent, the aggressor was significantly more often the female partner. Earlier research found similar sex differences (for example, Care et al. 1982). Other research, however, has found that the popular conception of men being more likely to use force than women is indeed true (DeTurck 1987): men are more apt than women to use violent methods to achieve compliance.

One of the most puzzling findings is that many victims of violence interpret it as a sign of love. For some reason, they see being beaten, verbally abused, or raped as a sign that their partner is fully in love with them. Many victims, in fact, accept the blame for contributing to the violence instead of blaming their partners (Gelles & Cornell 1985).

Findings such as these point to problems well beyond the prevalence of unproductive conflict strategies that you want to identify and avoid. They demonstrate the existence of underlying pathologies that we are discovering are a lot more common than were thought previously, when issues such as these were never mentioned in college textbooks or lectures. Awareness, of course, is only a first step in understanding and eventually combating such problems.

The only real alternative to force is talk. Instead of using force, you need to talk and listen. The qualities of empathy, openness, and positiveness (see Unit 13), for example, are suitable starting points.

Blame and Empathy

Conflict is rarely caused by a single, clearly identifiable problem or by only one of the parties. Usually, conflict is caused by a wide variety of factors, in which both individuals play a role. Any attempt to single out one person for blame is sure to fail. Yet, a frequently used fight strategy is to blame the other person. Consider, for example, the couple who fight over their child's getting into trouble with the police. The parents may—instead of dealing with the conflict itself—blame each other for the child's troubles. Such blaming, of course, does nothing to resolve the problem or to help the child.

Often when you blame someone you attribute motives to the person, a process often referred to as mind-reading. Thus, if the person spoke against you at a department meeting and this disturbs you, fight about what was said at the meeting (the actual behavior). Try not to presuppose motives: "Well, it's obvious you want to make me look bad in front of the entire office. If you were a friend you never would have done that."

Empathy is an excellent alternative to blame. Try to feel what the other person is feeling and to see the situation as the other person does. Try to see the situation as punctuated by the other person and how this differs from your own punctuation.

Demonstrate empathic understanding (see Unit 11). Once you have empathically understood your opponent's feelings, validate those feelings where appropriate. If your partner is hurt or angry, and you feel that such feelings are legitimate and justified (from the other person's point of view), say so; say, "You have a right to be angry; I shouldn't have spoken against you at the meeting. I'm sorry. But I still think you were wrong to do what you did . . . ." In expressing validation you are not necessarily expressing agreement on the issue in conflict, you are merely stating that your partner has feelings that are legitimate and that you recognize them as such.

Silencers and Facilitating Open Expression

Silencers cover a wide variety of fighting techniques that literally silence the other individual. One frequently used silencer is crying. When a person is unable to deal with a conflict or when winning seems unlikely, he or she may begin to cry and thus silence the other person.

Another silencer is to feign extreme emotionalism—to yell and scream and pretend to be losing control of yourself. Still another is to develop some "physical" reaction—headaches and shortness of breath are probably the most popular. One of the major problems with silencers is that you can never be certain that they are strategies to win the argument or real physical reactions that demand attention. Regardless of what you do, the conflict remains unexamined and unresolved.

To facilitate open expression, grant the other person permission to express himself or herself freely and openly, to be himself or herself. Avoid power tactics that suppress or inhibit freedom of expression. Avoid, for example, the tactics such as "Nobody Upstairs" or "You Owe Me" (identified in Unit 8). Such tactics are designed to put the other person down and to subvert real interpersonal equality.

Gunnysacking and Present Focus

A gunnysack is a large bag usually made of burlap. As a conflict strategy, **gunnysacking** refers to the practice of storing up grievances so you may unload them at another time. The immediate occasion may be relatively simple (or so it might seem at first), such as someone's coming home late without calling. Instead of arguing about this, the gunnysacker empties the whole bag of past grievances. The birthday you forgot, the time you arrived late for dinner, the hotel reservations you forgot to make are all noted. As you probably know from experience, gunnysacking begets gunnysacking. When one person gunnysacks, the other person gunnysacks. The result is two people dumping their stored-up grievances on one another. Frequently the original problem never gets addressed: instead, resentment and hostility escalate.

Focus your conflict on the here and now rather than on issues that occurred two months ago. Similarly, focus your conflict on the person with whom you are fighting, and not on the person's mother, child, or friends.

Manipulation and Spontaneity

Manipulation involves an avoidance of open conflict. The individual attempts to divert the conflict by being especially charming (disarming, actually). The manipulator gets the other individual into a receptive and noncombative frame of mind, and then presents his or her demands to a weakened opponent. The manipulator relies on the tendency to give in to people who are especially nice to you.

Instead of manipulating, try expressing your feelings with spontaneity, with honesty. Remember that in interpersonal conflict situations there is no need to plan a strategy to win a war. The objective is not to win but to increase mutual understanding and to reach a decision that both parties can accept.

Personal Rejection and Acceptance

A person practicing personal **rejection** withholds love and affection from his or her opponent in conflict. He or she seeks to win the argument by getting the other person to break down in the face of this withdrawal. The "rejector" acts cold and uncaring in an effort to demoralize the other person. In withdrawing affection, the individual hopes to make the other person question his or her own self-worth. Once the other is demoralized and feels less than worthy, it is relatively easy for the rejector to get his or her way. The renewal of love and affection is held out as a reward for resolving the conflict in the manipulator's favor.

Instead of rejection, express positive feelings for the other person and for the relationship between the two of you. Throughout any conflict, many harsh words will probably be exchanged, later to be regretted. The words cannot be unsaid or uncommunicated, but they can be partially offset by the expression of positive statements. If you are engaged in combat with someone you love, remember that you are fighting with a loved one and express that feeling. "I love you very much, but I still don't want your mother on vacation with us. I want to be alone with you."

Fighting Below and Above the Belt

Much like boxers in a ring, each of us has a "beltline." When you hit someone below it, a tactic called **beltlining**, you can inflict serious injury. When you hit above the belt, however, the person is able to absorb the blow. With most interpersonal relationships, especially those of long standing, we know where the belt line is. You know, for example, that to hit Pat with the inability to maintain a productive relationship is to hit below the belt. You know that to hit Chris with the failure to get a permanent job is to hit below the belt. Hitting below the beltline causes everyone involved added problems. Keep blows to areas your opponent can absorb and handle.

Remember that the aim of a relationship conflict is not to win and have your opponent lose. Rather, it is to resolve a problem and strengthen the relationship. Keep this ultimate goal always in clear focus, especially when you are angry or hurt.

Face-detracting and Face-enhancing Strategies

Another dimension of conflict strategies is that of face orientation. Face-detracting or face-attacking orientation involves treating the other person as incompetent or untrustworthy, as unable or bad (Donahue & Kolt 1992). Such attacks can vary from mildly embarrassing the other person to severely damaging his or her ego or reputation. When such attacks become extreme they may be similar to verbal aggressiveness—a tactic explained in the next section.

Face-enhancing techniques involve helping the other person to maintain a positive image, an image as competent and trustworthy, able and good. There is some evidence to show that even when you get what you want, say at bargaining, it is wise to help the other person retain positive face. This makes it less likely that future conflicts will arise (Donahue & Kolt 1992). Not surprisingly, people are more likely to make a greater effort to support the listener's "face" if they like the listener than if they didn't (Meyer 1994).

Confirming the other person's definition of self (see Unit 8), avoiding attack and blame, and using excuses and apologies as appropriate are some generally useful face-positive strategies.

Aggressiveness and Argumentativeness

An especially interesting perspective on conflict is emerging from the work on verbal aggressiveness and argumentativeness (Infante 1988; Infante & Rancer 1982, 1995; Infante & Wigley 1986). Understanding these two concepts will help you understand some of the reasons why things go wrong and some of the ways in which you can use conflict to actually improve your relationships.

What gender differences, if any, do you observe in verbal aggressiveness? In argumentativeness? Do you notice any cultural differences?

Verbal Aggressiveness

Verbal aggressiveness is a method of winning an argument by inflicting psychological pain, by attacking the other person's self-concept. The technique relies on many of the unproductive conflict strategies just considered. It is a type of disconfirmation in that it seeks to discredit the individual's view of self (see Unit 8). To explore this tendency further, take the self-test, "How Verbally Aggressive Are You?"

THINK ABOUT

Think about your own tendency toward aggressiveness. In reviewing your score, for example, make special note of the characteristics identified in the 20 statements that refer to the tendency to act verbally aggressive. Note those inappropriate behaviors that you are especially prone to commit. Review previous encounters when you acted verbally aggressive. What effect did such actions have on your subsequent interaction? What effect did they have on your relationship with the other person? What alternative ways of getting your point across might you have used? Might these have proved more effective?

Argumentativeness

Contrary to popular belief, argumentativeness is a quality to be cultivated rather than avoided. **Argumentativeness** refers to your willingness to argue for a point of view, your tendency to speak your mind on significant issues. It is the mode of dealing with disagreements that is the preferred alternative to verbal aggressiveness. Before reading about ways to increase your argumentativeness, take the heavily researched self-test, "How Argumentative Are You? on page 289.

Generally, those who score high in argumentativeness have a strong tendency to state their position on controversial issues and argue against the positions of others. A high scorer sees arguing as exciting, intellectually challenging, and as an opportunity to win a kind of contest.

The moderately argumentative person possesses some of the qualities of the high argumentative and some of the qualities of the low argumentative. The person who scores low in argumentativeness tries to prevent arguments. This person experiences satisfaction not from arguing, but from avoiding arguments. The low argumentative sees arguing as unpleasant and unsatisfying. Not surprisingly, this person has little confidence in his or her ability to argue effectively.

SELF-TEST

how verbally aggressive are you?

This scale is designed to measure how people try to obtain compliance from others. For each statement, indicate the extent to which you feel it is true for you in your attempts to influence others. Use the following scale:

1 = almost never true
2 = rarely true
3 = occasionally true
4 = often true
5 = almost always true

_____ 1. I am extremely careful to avoid attacking individuals' intelligence when I attack their ideas.
_____ 2. When individuals are very stubborn, I use insults to soften the stubbornness.
_____ 3. I try very hard to avoid having other people feel bad about themselves when I try to influence them.
_____ 4. When people refuse to do a task I know is important, without good reason, I tell them they are unreasonable.
_____ 5. When others do things I regard as stupid, I try to be extremely gentle with them.
_____ 6. If individuals I am trying to influence really deserve it, I attack their character.
_____ 7. When people behave in ways that are really in very poor taste, I insult them in order to shock them into proper behavior.
_____ 8. I try to make people feel good about themselves even when their ideas are stupid.
_____ 9. When people simply will not budge on a matter of importance, I lose my temper and say rather strong things to them.
_____ 10. When people criticize my shortcomings, I take it in good humor and do not try to get back at them.
_____ 11. When individuals insult me, I get a lot of pleasure out of really telling them off.
_____ 12. When I dislike individuals greatly, I try not to show it in what I say or how I say it.
_____ 13. I like poking fun at people who do things which are very stupid in order to stimulate their intelligence.
_____ 14. When I attack a person's ideas, I try not to damage their self-concepts.
_____ 15. When I try to influence people, I make a great effort not to offend them.
_____ 16. When people do things which are mean or cruel, I attack their character in order to help correct their behavior.
_____ 17. I refuse to participate in arguments when they involve personal attacks.
_____ 18. When nothing seems to work in trying to influence others, I yell and scream in order to get some movement from them.
_____ 19. When I am not able to refute others' positions, I try to make them feel defensive in order to weaken their positions.
_____ 20. When an argument shifts to personal attacks, I try very hard to change the subject.

Thinking Critically About Verbal Aggressiveness. In order to compute your verbal aggressiveness score, follow these steps:

1. Add your scores on items 2, 4, 6, 7, 9, 11, 13, 16, 18, 19.
2. Add your scores on items 1, 3, 5, 8, 10, 12, 14, 15, 17, 20.
3. Subtract the sum obtained in step 2 from 60.
4. To compute your verbal aggressiveness score, add the total obtained in step 1 to the result obtained in step 3.

(*continued next page*)

(continued)

If you scored between 59 and 100, you are high in verbal aggressiveness; if you scored between 39 and 58, you are moderate in verbal aggressiveness; and if you scored between 20 and 38, you are low in verbal aggressiveness. Can you identify relationships in which verbal aggressiveness is the customary way of dealing with conflict? What do you see as the primary disadvantage of verbal aggressiveness as a conflict strategy? Can you identify any advantages of verbal aggressiveness?

Source: From "Verbal Aggressiveness" by Dominic Infante and C. J. Wigley, *Communication Monographs, 53,* pp. 61–69, 1986. Used by permission of the Speech Communication Association and the authors.

Men generally score higher in argumentativeness (and in verbal aggressiveness) than women. Men are also more apt to be perceived (by both men and women) as more argumentative and verbally aggressive than women (Nicotera & Rancer 1994). High and low argumentatives also differ in the way in which they view argument (Rancer, Kosberg, & Baukus 1992). High argumentatives see arguing as enjoyable and its outcomes as pragmatic. They see arguing as having a positive impact on their self-concept, having functional outcomes, and being highly ego-involving. Low argumentatives, on the other hand, believe that arguing has a negative impact on their self-concept, that it has dysfunctional outcomes, and that it is not very ego-involving. They see arguing as having little enjoyment or pragmatic outcomes.

The researchers who developed this test note that both high and low argumentatives may experience communication difficulties. The high argumentative, for example, may argue needlessly, too often, and too forcefully. The low argumentative, on the other hand, may avoid taking a stand even when it seems necessary. Persons scoring somewhere in the middle are probably the most interpersonally skilled and adaptable, arguing when it is necessary but avoiding the many arguments that are needless and repetitive.

Here are some suggestions for cultivating argumentativeness and for preventing it from degenerating into aggressiveness (Infante 1988):

- Treat disagreements as objectively as possible; avoid assuming that because someone takes issue with your position or your interpretation that they are attacking you as a person.
- Avoid attacking the other person (rather than the person's arguments) even if this would give you a tactical advantage—it will probably backfire at some later time and make your relationship more difficult. Center your arguments on issues rather than personalities.
- Reaffirm the other person's sense of competence; compliment the other person as appropriate.
- Avoid interrupting; allow the other person to state her or his position fully before you respond.
- Stress equality (see Unit 11) and the similarities that you have with the other person; stress your areas of agreement before attacking the disagreements.
- Express interest in the other person's position, attitude, and point of view.
- Avoid presenting your arguments too emotionally; using an overly loud voice or interjecting vulgar expressions will prove offensive and eventually ineffective.
- Allow the other person to save face; never humiliate the other person.

THINK ABOUT

Think about the major productive and unproductive conflict strategies just discussed, and summarized in Table 16.2, (on page 290) as they might apply to the specific situations that follow. Assume that these statements are addressed to you and are made by someone close to you. Try developing an unproductive and an alternative productive strategy for each situation.

1. "You're late again. You're always late. Your lateness is so inconsiderate of my time and my interests. What is wrong with you?"
2. "I just can't bear another weekend of sitting home watching television. You never want to do anything. I'm just not going to do that again and that's final."
3. "Guess who forgot to phone for reservations again? Don't you remember anything?"

SELF-TEST

how argumentative are you?

This questionnaire contains statements about controversial issues. Indicate how often each statement is true for you personally according to the following scale:

1 = almost never true
2 = rarely true
3 = occasionally true
4 = often true
5 = almost never true

______ 1. While in an argument, I worry that the person I am arguing with will form a negative impression of me.
______ 2. Arguing over controversial issues improves my intelligence.
______ 3. I enjoy avoiding arguments.
______ 4. I am energetic and enthusiastic when I argue.
______ 5. Once I finish an argument, I promise myself that I will not get into another.
______ 6. Arguing with a person creates more problems for me than it solves.
______ 7. I have a pleasant, good feeling when I win a point in an argument,
______ 8. When I finish arguing with anyone, I feel nervous and upset.
______ 9. I enjoy a good argument over a controversial issue.
______10. I get an unpleasant feeling when I realize I am about to get into an argument.
______11. I enjoy defending my point of view on an issue.
______12. I am happy when I keep an argument from happening.
______13. I do not like to miss the opportunity to argue a controversial issue.
______14. I prefer being with people who rarely disagree with me.
______15. I consider an argument an exciting intellectual challenge.
______16. I find myself unable to think of effective points during an argument.
______17. I feel refreshed and satisfied after an argument on a controversial issue.
______18. I have the ability to do well in an argument.
______19. I try to avoid getting into arguments.
______20. I feel excitement when I expect that a conversation I am in is leading to an argument.

Thinking Critically About Argumentativeness. To compute your argumentativeness score follow these steps:

1. Add your scores on items 2, 4, 7, 9, 11, 13, 15, 17, 18, and 20.
2. Add 60 to the sum obtained in step 1.
3. Add your scores on items 1, 3, 5, 6, 8, 10, 12, 14, 16, 19.
4. To compute your argumentativeness score, subtract the total obtained in step 3 from the total obtained in step 2.

Interpreting Your Score

Scores between 73 and 100 indicate high argumentativeness.
Scores between 56 and 72 indicate moderate argumentativeness.
Scores between 20 and 55 indicate low argumentativeness.

Can you identify relationships in which argumentativeness is the customary way of dealing with conflicts? What is the primary advantage of argumentativeness? Can you identify any disadvantages?

Source: Reprinted by permission of Waveland Press, Inc. from *Arguing Constructively* by Dominic Infante. (Prospect Heights, IL.: Waveland Press, Inc., 1988).

TABLE 16.2
conflict management strategies

Unproductive Strategies	Productive Strategies
Avoid the conflict	Fight actively
Use force	Talk
Blame the other person	Empathize with the other person
Use silencers	Facilitate open expression
Gunnysack	Focus on the present
Strategically manipulate the other person	Act spontaneously and honestly
Stress personal rejection	Stress acceptance
Hit below the belt	Hit only above the belt
Use face-detracting techniques	Use face-enhancing techniques
Fight with verbal aggressiveness	Fight with argumentativeness

4. "You can't possibly go out with Pat. We're your parents and we simply won't allow it. And we don't want to hear any more about it. It's over."
5. "Why don't you stay out of the neighbors' business. You're always butting in and telling people what to do. Why don't you mind your own business and take care of your own family instead of trying to run everybody else's?"

BEFORE AND AFTER THE CONFLICT

If you are to make conflict truly productive you will need to consider a few suggestions for preparing for the conflict and for using the conflict as a method for relational growth.

Before the Conflict

Try to fight in private. When you air your conflicts in front of others you create a wide variety of other problems. You may not be willing to be totally honest when third parties are present; you may feel you have to save face and therefore must win the fight at all costs. This may lead you to use strategies to win the argument rather than strategies to resolve the conflict. You also run the risk of embarrassing your partner in front of others, which will incur resentment and hostility.

Be sure you are both ready to fight. Although conflicts arise at the most inopportune times, you can choose the time when you will try to resolve them. Confronting your partner when she or he comes home after a hard day at work may not be the right time for resolving a conflict. Make sure you are both relatively free of other problems and ready to deal with the conflict at hand.

Know what you're fighting about. Sometimes people in a relationship become so hurt and angry that they lash out at the other person just to vent their own frustration. The "content" of the conflict is merely an excuse to express anger. Any attempt at resolving this "problem" will of course be doomed to failure because the problem addressed is not what gave rise to the conflict. Instead, you may need to deal with the underlying hostility, anger, and frustration.

At other times, people argue about general and abstract issues that are poorly specified, for example, the person's lack of consideration or failure to accept responsibility. Only when you define your differences in specific terms can you begin to understand them and hence resolve them.

Fight about problems that can be solved. Fighting about past behaviors or about family members or situations over which you have no control solves nothing; instead, it creates additional difficulties. Any attempt at resolution is naturally doomed to failure because the problems cannot be solved. Often such conflicts are concealed attempts at expressing one's frustration or dissatisfaction.

After the Conflict

After the conflict is resolved, there is still work to be done. Often after one conflict is supposedly settled, another conflict will emerge because, for example, one person feels that harm was done to her or him and she or he needs to retaliate and take revenge in order to restore her or his own self-worth (Kim & Smith 1993). It is especially important, therefore, that the conflict be resolved and not allowed to generate other, perhaps more significant, conflicts.

Learn from the conflict and from the process you went through in trying to resolve the conflict. For example, can you identify the fight strategies that aggravated the situation? Does the other person need a cooling off period? Do you need extra space when upset? Can you identify when minor issues are going to escalate into major arguments? Does avoidance make matters worse? What issues are particularly disturbing and likely to cause difficulties? Can these be avoided?

Keep the conflict in perspective. Be careful not to blow it out of proportion, defining your relationship in terms of conflict. Avoid the tendency to see disagreement as inevitably leading to major blowups. Conflicts in most relationships actually occupy a very small percentage of real time, and yet in recollection they often loom extremely large. Also, don't allow the conflict to undermine your own or your partner's self-esteem. Don't view yourself, your partner, or your relationships as failures just because you had an argument or even lots of arguments.

Negative feelings frequently arise after an interpersonal conflict, most often because unfair fight strategies were used to undermine the other person—for example, personal rejection, manipulation, or force.

Resolve to avoid such unfair tactics in the future, but at the same time let go of guilt and blame for yourself and your partner. If you think it would help, discuss these feelings with your partner or even a therapist.

Increase the exchange of rewards and cherishing behaviors to demonstrate your positive feelings and that you are over the conflict. It's a good way of saying you want the relationship to survive and to flourish.

SUMMARY

In this unit we explored interpersonal conflict, the types of conflicts that occur, the don'ts and do's of conflict management, and what to do before and after the conflict.

1. Relationship conflict refers to a situation in which two persons have opposing goals and interfere with each other's attaining these goals.
2. Content conflict centers on objects, events, and persons in the world that are usually, but not always, external to the parties involved in the conflict.
3. Relationship conflicts are concerned not so much with some external object as with the relationships between the individuals, with such issues as who is in charge, the equality of a primary relationship, and who has the right to set down rules of behavior.
4. Unproductive and productive conflict strategies include: avoidance and fighting actively, force and talk, blame and empathy, silencers and facilitating open expression, gunnysacking and present focus, manipulation and spontaneity, personal rejection and acceptance, fighting below and above the belt, and fighting aggressively and argumentatively.
5. To cultivate argumentativeness, treat disagreements objectively and avoid attacking the other person; reaffirm the other's sense of competence; avoid interrupting; stress equality and similarities; express interest in the other's position; avoid presenting your arguments too emotionally; and allow the other to save face.
6. Prepare for the conflict and try to fight in private and when you are both ready to fight. Have a clear idea of what you want to fight about and be specific, and fight about things that can be solved.
7. After the conflict, assess what you've learned, keep the conflict in perspective, let go of negative feelings, and increase the positiveness in the relationship.

THINKING CRITICALLY ABOUT INTERPERSONAL CONFLICT

1. What assumptions has your culture taught you about interpersonal conflict? Did it, for example, teach you that men and women should deal differently with conflict? That certain strategies were appropriate or inappropriate?
2. Are the myths about conflict similar in, say, business relationships and in friendship or love relationships?
3. Can you identify an interpersonal conflict that had no relationship aspects to it? Can you identify both positive and negative aspects of a specific conflict in which you engaged?
4. Why are men more likely to withdraw from a conflict than are women? What arguments can you present for or against any of these reasons (Noller 1993): Because men have difficulty dealing with conflict? Because the culture has taught men to avoid it? Because withdrawal is an expression of power?
5. Are you more likely to pursue a conflict with someone from your own culture or someone from a different culture? If there is a difference, did you learn this difference from your culture?
6. One of the most puzzling findings on violence is that many victims interpret it as a sign of love. For some reason, they see being beaten or verbally abused as a sign that their partner is fully in love with them. Also, many victims blame themselves for the violence instead of blaming their partners (Gelles & Cornell 1985). Why

do you think this is so? What part does force or violence play in your own interpersonal relationship conflicts?

7. Can you identify examples of face-negative or face-positive strategies that were used during your last interpersonal conflict? Are you more likely to use one rather than the other type of strategy?
8. What character in a television sitcom, drama, or feature film resembles the verbally aggressive personality? What character would you consider argumentative? What are some of the other distinctions that the writers have drawn between these characters?
9. How does the person you are in conflict with and the nature of the particular conflict influence the types of strategies that you would use? For example, are you more likely to use some strategies with colleagues at work and other strategies with close friends or romantic partners?
10. How would you go about finding answers to such questions as these:
    a. Are more-educated people less likely to use verbal aggressiveness and more likely to use argumentativeness than less-educated people?
    b. Do men and women differ in the satisfaction or dissatisfaction they derive from a conflict experience?
    c. What types of strategies are more likely to be used by happy couples than by unhappy couples?
    d. How do man-man, woman-woman, and woman-man interpersonal conflicts differ from each other?

four parT

Group and Public Communication

This last part, consisting of Units 17 through 23, focuses on communication in a broader context, that of small group and public speaking situations. Unit 17 identifies the nature and types of small groups and of small group communication. Unit 18 focuses on group membership and leadership. Unit 19 expands this focus to organizations, where we explore communication within the organizational setting. Unit 20 focuses on interviewing, an area that traditionally is considered with the study of small groups and organizations (though it can just as logically be grouped with interpersonal communication), largely because so many kinds of interviews are a major part of organizational communication.

The last three units focus on public speaking, the form of communication in which a speaker addresses a relatively large audience with a relatively continuous speech. Unit 21 introduces the nature of public speaking, the audience, and speaker apprehension. Unit 22 focuses on the principles of informative and persuasive speaking and on the criticism of public discourse. The last unit, Unit 23, provides a brief guide to preparing and delivering public speeches, the nuts and bolts of public speaking. A separate booklet, "The Public Speaking Guide," which accompanies this text, covers these more practical aspects of public speaking preparation and delivery in greater detail.

In approaching the study of small group and public speaking communication, keep the following in mind:

- The skills of small group and public communication are largely the skills of leadership generally. Look at this section as a guide to improving your own leadership skills.
- Small groups are much like cultures. Each develops its own code of behavior—what a member should and should not do—and each fixes the price that a member pays for violating these rules.
- Small groups are usually more effective in solving problems than are individuals working alone. Creative solutions emerge from a combination of thoughts. Therefore, approach small group situations with flexibility.
- The principles for communicating information and persuading are not limited to public speaking but are applicable to all forms of communication—to interpersonal conversation as well as to small groups.

seventeen unit

Preliminaries to Small Group Communication

unit contents

unit goals

After completing this unit, you should be able to

1. describe the nature of a small group
2. explain the four principles of brainstorming
3. describe the types and nature of personal growth groups
4. explain the functions of the learning group and the focus group
5. identify the steps that should be followed in problem-solving discussions
6. distinguish among the roundtable, panel, symposium, and symposium-forum

Everyone is a member of a wide variety of small groups. The family is the most obvious example, but you also function as a member of a team, a class, a collection of friends, and so on. Some of your most important and most personally satisfying communications take place within small groups.

In this unit we look into the nature of the small group and identify its characteristics. With this as a foundation, we examine four major types of small groups (brainstorming, personal growth, information-sharing, and problem-solving), and the procedures to follow in participating in these groups. Last, we examine four popular small group formats.

The area of small group communication is a huge one, and only a sample of topics are discussed here. Table 17.1 gives an idea of some of the major subareas.

THE SMALL GROUP

A small group is a relatively small collection of individuals who are related to each other by some common purpose and have some degree of organization among them. Each of these characteristics needs to be explained a bit further.

A small group is, first, a collection of individuals, few enough in number that all members may communicate with relative ease as both senders and receivers. Generally, a small group consists of approximately 5 to 12 people. The important point to keep in mind is that each member should be able to function as both source and receiver with relative ease. If the group gets much larger than 12 this becomes difficult.

Second, the members of a group must be connected to one another in some way. People on a bus would not constitute a group, since they are not working at some common purpose, unless, of course, the bus get stuck in a ditch, then the riders may quickly become a group and work together to get the bus back on the road. In a small group the behavior of one member is significant for all other members. This does not mean that all members must have exactly the same purpose in being members of the group, but generally there must be some similarity in the individuals' reasons for interacting.

Third, the members must be connected by some organizing rules or structure. At times the structure is rigid—as in groups operating under parliamentary procedure, in which case each comment must follow prescribed rules. At other times, as in a social gathering, the structure is very loose. Yet in both groups there is some organization and some structure: two people do not speak at the same time, comments or questions by one member are responded to by others rather than ignored, and so on.

Before beginning your study of small group communication, examine how apprehensive you are in group discussions by taking the self-test, "How Apprehensive Are You in Group Discussion?"

Small Group Culture

Many groups—especially those of long standing, such as work groups—develop into a kind of small culture with its own **norms.** Norms are the rules or standards of behavior identifying which behaviors are considered appropriate (for example, willingness to take on added tasks or directing conflict toward issues rather than toward people) and which are considered inappropriate (for example, coming late or not contributing actively). Sometimes these rules for appropriate behavior are explicitly stated in a company contract or policy: all members must attend department meetings. Sometimes the rules are implicit: members should be well-groomed. Regardless of whether norms are spelled out or not, they are powerful regulators of members' behaviors.

Norms may apply to individual members as well as to the group as a whole and, of course, will differ from one group to another (Axtell 1990a, 1993). For example, in Japan it is customary to begin meetings with what Americans would think is unnecessary socializing. While Americans prefer to get right down to business, the Japanese prefer rather elaborate socializing before getting to the business at hand. In the United States men and women in business are expected to interact when making business decisions as well as when socializing. In Muslim and Buddhist societies, however, there are religious restrictions that prevent mixing the sexes. In the United States, Bangladesh, Australia, Germany, Finland, and Hong Kong, for example, punctuality for business meetings is very important. In such countries as Morocco, Italy, Brazil, Zambia, Ireland, and Panama, for example, time is less highly regarded and being late is no great insult and is even expected. In

TABLE 17.1 the areas of small group and organizational communication

The area of health communication, considered in the interpersonal area, might just as logically be placed here; similarly, there are good reasons for including interviewing in the interpersonal area instead of here.

Areas	A Few Theoretical Concerns	A Few Skills Concerns	For Further Exploration
Discussion groups and meetings	How problem solving works, solving patterns, group climates, training, decision-making groups, idea-generation groups	Solving problems systematically, creating effective climates for group interaction, principles for decision making, ideas for increasing creativity	Beebe and Masterson (1994), Schultz (1996), Rothwell (1995), and Lumsden and Lumsden (1993) offer excellent overviews of the principles and skills of small group communication. Cathcart, Samovar, and Henman (1996) provide a wide range of research articles. Barge (1994) and Hackman and Johnson (1996) offer insightful approaches to leadership. Jablin (1990), Goldhaber (1990), Hutchinson (1992), Shockley-Zalabak (1991), and Miller (1995) cover the major approaches to organizational communication.
Organizational communication	Communication through the corporate hierarchy, improving internal corporate communications, improving external corporate communications, corporate image making, communication networks, network productivity and morale	How to get ahead in the organization, how to make corporate communication more effective, enhancing the corporate image, increasing worker productivity and morale	
Leadership	Opinion leadership, leadership in groups, leadership training	How to develop leadership qualities, ways to lead a group effectively, how to build leadership qualities in others	
Interviewing	Interview types, structures, and functions; research interviews and survey construction; counseling	How to use interview more effectively, ways to use interviewing to achieve organizational goals	
Negotiation	Conflict resolution, mediation, arbitration	How to identify and resolve conflicts, how third parties can help resolve conflicts	
Therapeutic groups	Theories of therapeutic groups, styles of family therapy	How can therapy groups be used in education, how therapy groups can be made more effective	
Informal social groups	How groups form, interpersonal attraction and influence	How to influence social groups, resolving inter-and intragroup conflicts	

the United States, and in much of Asia and Europe, meetings are held between two groups. In many Persian Gulf states, however, the business executive is likely to conduct meetings with several different people—sometimes dealing with totally different issues—at the same time. In this situation, you have to expect to share what in the United States would be "your time" with these other parties. In the United States very little interpersonal touching goes on during business meetings; in Arab countries, however, touching (for example, hand holding) is common and is a gesture of friendship.

Norms that regulate a particular member's behavior, called role expectations, identify what each person in an organization is expected to do, for example, Pat has a great computer setup and therefore should play the role of secretary.

THINK ABOUT

Think about the situations in which you would be most likely to accept the norms of your group. When are you more likely to violate these norms? According to research on group norms, you are more likely to accept the norms of your group's culture when you answer "yes" to the following questions (Napier & Gershenfeld 1989).

- Do you want to continue your membership in the group?
- Do you feel that your group membership is important?
- Is your group cohesive? Are you and the other members closely connected? Are you attracted to each other? Do you depend on each other to meet individual needs?

SELF-TEST
how apprehensive are you in group discussions?

Just as you have apprehension in interpersonal interactions (see Unit 14), you have some degree of apprehension in group discussions. This brief test is designed to measure your apprehension in the small group situation.

This questionnaire consists of six statements concerning your feelings about communication in group discussions. Please indicate in the spaces provided the degree to which each statement applies to you by marking whether you (1) Strongly Agree, (2) Agree, (3) Are Undecided, (4) Disagree, or (5) Strongly Disagree. There are no right or wrong answers. Some of the statements are similar to other statements. Do not be concerned about this. Work quickly; just record your first impression.

_____ 1. I dislike participating in group discussions.
_____ 2. Generally, I am comfortable while participating in group discussions.
_____ 3. I am tense and nervous while participating in group discussions.
_____ 4. I like to get involved in group discussions.
_____ 5. Engaging in a group discussion with new people makes me tense and nervous.
_____ 6. I am calm and relaxed while participating in group discussions.

Thinking Critically About Apprehension in Group Discussions This test will enable you to obtain your apprehension score for group discussions. To obtain your score use the following formula:

18 plus scores for items 2, 4, and 6

minus scores for items 1, 3, and 5

A score above 18 shows some degree of apprehension.

Apprehension in group discussion is usually considerably lower than apprehension in employment interviews (see Unit 20) or public speaking (see Unit 21). Why do you suppose this is so? In what type of group discussions would your apprehension be highest? Lowest?

Source: From James C. McCroskey, *An Introduction to Rhetorical Communication*, 6th ed. (Upper Saddle River, NJ: Prentice-Hall, 1993).

In what ways are cultural norms similar to (or different from) small group norms? Can you identify two or three cultural norms that influence your communication behavior in your social groups? In the classroom?

- Would you be punished by negative reactions or exclusion from the group for violating the group norms?

Small Group Phases

The small group develops in much the same way that a conversation develops. As in conversation, there are five stages: opening, feedforward, business, feedback, closing. The *opening* period is usually a getting-acquainted time during which members introduce themselves and engage in phatic communion. After this preliminary get-together, there is usually some *feedforward,* some attempt to identify what needs to be done, who will do it, and so on. In a formal group, the agenda (which is a perfect example of feedforward) might be reviewed and the tasks of the group identified. In more informal social groups, the feedforward might consist simply of introducing a topic of conversation or talking about what the groups members should do. The *business* portion is the actual discussion of the tasks—the problem solving, the sharing of information, or whatever else the group needs to do. During the *feedback* stage, the group might reflect on what it has done and perhaps what remains to be done. Some groups may even evaluate their performance at this stage. In the *closing* stage the group members again return to their focus on individuals and will perhaps exchange closing comments—"good seeing you again," and so forth. A typical pattern is presented in Figure 17.1.

These stages are rarely separate from one another. Rather, like the colors of the rainbow, they seem to blend into one another. For example, the opening stage is not completely finished before the feedforward begins. Instead, as the opening comments are completed, the group begins to introduce feedforward and as the feedforward begins to end the business starts.

Power in the Small Group

Power permeates all small groups and in fact all relationships. It influences what you do, and when and with whom you do it. It influences the employment you seek and the employment you get. It influences the friends you choose and do not choose and those who choose you and those who do not. It influences your romantic and family relationships—their success, failure, and level of satisfaction or dissatisfaction.

Power is what enables one person (the one with power) to control the behaviors of the others. Thus, if A has power over B and C, then A, by virtue of this power and through the exercise of this power (or the

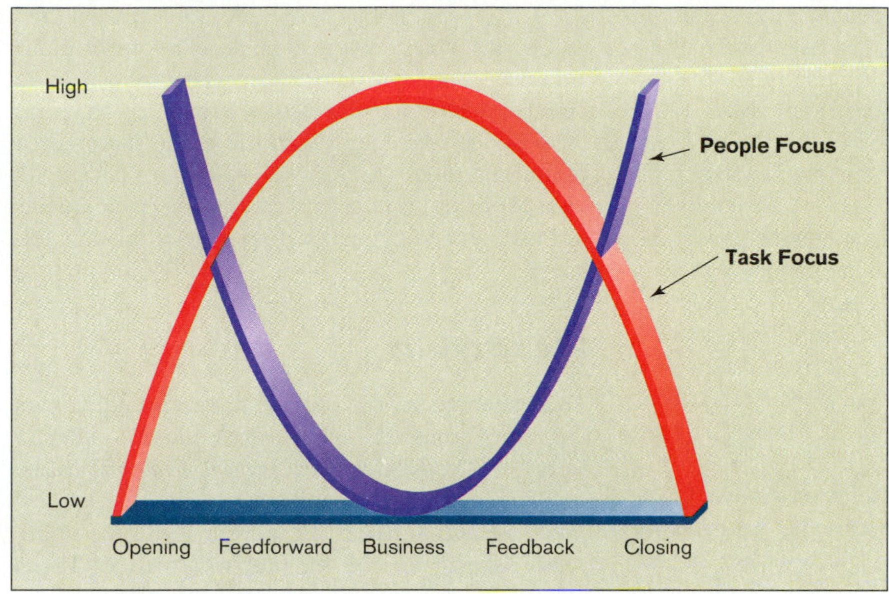

FIGURE 17.1 Small group stages and the focus on task and people. Of course, different types of groups will evidence different patterns. For example, a problem-solving group is likely to spend a great deal more time focused on the task whereas an informal social group, say two or three couples who get together for dinner, will spend more time focused on people concerns. Similarly, the amount of time spent on the opening or business or closing, for example, will vary with the type of group and with the purposes that the group wishes to accomplish.

threat of its being exercised), can control the behaviors of B and C. Differences in the amount and type of power influence who makes important decisions, who will prevail in an argument, and who will control the finances.

Although all relationships are the same in that they all involve power, they differ in the types of power that the people use and to which they respond. It is useful to distinguish among six types of power (French & Raven 1968; Raven, Centers, & Rodrigues 1975): referent, legitimate, reward, coercive, expert, and information or persuasion power.

THINK ABOUT

Think about your own power as you read through these six types of power. Try to answer the following questions:

- Do you hold this kind of power over anyone? What is the specific basis of the power?
- Does anyone hold this kind of power over you? What are the specific reasons for this power relationship?
- How satisfied are you with your own levels of power? For example, are you satisfied with those situations in which others hold power over you? Are you satisfied with the power that you hold over others? How might you go about changing your levels of power?

The *referent power* holder wields power over "Other" because Other wishes to be like the power holder. Often the referent power holder is attractive, has considerable prestige, is well-liked, and well-respected; as these qualities increase, so does power. For example, a more experienced member may have power over another because the less experienced member wants to be like the more experienced member.

The *legitimate power* holder wields power because Other believes that the power holder has a right—by virtue of his or her position—to influence or control Other's behavior. Usually legitimate power derives from the roles people occupy and from the belief that because they occupy these roles, they have a right to influence others. For example, employers, judges, managers, and police officers are usually seen to hold legitimate power. In a small group, legitimate power may be ascribed to the designated leader or chairperson. You give these people power because you believe they have the right to regulate your behaviors.

The *reward power* holder controls the rewards that Other wishes to receive. Rewards may be material (for example, money, promotion, jewelry) or social (love, friendship, respect). The degree of power wielded is directly related to the desirability of the reward as seen by Other. For example, teachers have reward power over students because they control grades, letters of recommendation, and social approval.

The *coercive power* holder has the ability to administer punishments to or remove rewards from Other if Other does not do as the power holder wishes. Usually, people who have reward power also have coercive power. For example, parents may deny extended privileges concerning time or recreation or withhold money. Group leaders often have both reward and coercive power because they can reward group members (recognizing and praising their contributions) or punish them (not recognizing or even criticizing their contributions).

The *expert power* holder wields power over Other because Other believes the power holder has expertise or knowledge. Expert power increases when the expert is seen as unbiased with nothing personally to gain from exerting this power. Expert power decreases if the expert is seen as biased and as having something to gain from securing Other's compliance. For example, lawyers have expert power in legal matters and doctors have expert power in medical matters. In any group, certain members are likely to be seen as possessing expert power and while the topic of their expertise is being considered, they are likely to wield disproportionate power.

The *information or persuasion power* holder wields power over Other because Other attributes to the power holder the ability to communicate logically and persuasively. For example, researchers and scientists may be given information power because of the perception that they are informed, critical thinkers. In a small group, members who can articulate clearly and argue convincingly for a position are normally accorded greater power than are the less articulate and persuasive members.

IDEA-GENERATION GROUPS

Many small groups exist solely to generate ideas and often follow a formula called brainstorming (Beebe & Masterson 1994; Osborn 1957; DeVito 1996). **Brainstorming** is a technique for bombarding a problem and generating as many ideas as possible. In this system the process occurs in two phases. The first is the brainstorming period proper; the second is the evaluation period.

The procedures are simple. A problem is selected that is amenable to many possible solutions or ideas. Group members are informed of the problem to be brainstormed before the actual session, so they can think about the topic. When the group meets, each person contributes as many ideas as he or she can. All ideas are recorded either in writing or on tape. During this idea-generating session, four general rules are followed.

Don't Criticize

All ideas are recorded. They are not evaluated, nor are they even discussed. Any negative criticism—whether verbal or nonverbal—is itself criticized by the leader or the members. This is a good general rule to follow in all creative thinking. Allow your idea time to develop before you look for problems with it. At the same time, don't praise the ideas either. All evaluations should be suspended during the brainstorming session.

THINK ABOUT

Think about how you can be on guard against negative criticism and how you can respond to such "idea killers" or "killer messages" as the following. These phrases are directed at stopping an idea from being developed, to kill it in its tracks, before it can even get off the ground. As you read down the list of these commonly heard killer messages, try to think of responses you might use if someone used one of these on you. Also consider responses you might make on occasions when you use these terms to censor your own creative thinking.

We tried it before and it didn't work.
It'll never work.
No one would vote for it.
It's too complex.
It's too simple.
It would take too long.
It's too expensive.
It doesn't sound right.
It's not logical.
We don't have the facilities.
It's a waste of time and money.
What we have is good enough.
It won't fly.

It just doesn't fit us.
It's impossible.

Be careful when you hear others say these phrases to you, when you say them to others, and especially when you say them to yourself.

Strive for Quantity

Linus Pauling, winner of the Nobel Prize in chemistry in 1954 and the Noble Peace Prize in 1962, once said, "The best way to have a good idea is to have lots of ideas." This second rule of brainstorming uses this concept. If you need an idea, you are more likely to find it in a group of many than in a group of few. Thus, in brainstorming, the more ideas the better.

Combine and Extend Ideas

While you may not criticize a particular idea, you may extend it or combine it in some way. The value of a particular idea may be the way it stimulates someone to combine or extend it. Even if your modification seems minor or obvious, say it. Don't censor yourself.

Develop the Wildest Ideas Possible

The wilder the idea, the better. It is easier to tone an idea down than to build it up. A wild idea can easily be tempered, but it is not so easy to elaborate on a simple or conservative idea.

At times, the brainstorming session may break down with members failing to contribute new ideas. At this point, the moderator may prod the members with statements such as the following:

- Let's try to get a few more ideas before we close this session.
- Can we piggyback any other ideas or add extensions on the suggestion to . . . .
- Here's what we have so far. As I read the list of contributed suggestions, additional ideas may come to mind.
- Here's an aspect we haven't focused on. . . . Does this stimulate any ideas?

After all the ideas are generated—a period lasting no longer than 15 or 20 minutes—the entire list of ideas is evaluated, using the critical thinking skills covered throughout this textbook. The ones that are unworkable are thrown out; the ones that show promise are retained and evaluated. During this phase negative criticism is allowed.

Although brainstorming was designed as a group experience, there is some evidence to show that individual brainstorming can work even more effectively than group brainstorming (Peters 1987). As with group brainstorming, individuals brainstorming alone need to follow the same rules as the group. Be especially careful that you do not censor yourself and that you record (on paper or tape) every idea that comes to you. Remember that these are ideas, not necessarily solutions; do not be afraid to record even the seemingly most absurd ideas.

PERSONAL GROWTH GROUPS

Some **personal growth groups,** sometimes referred to as support groups, aim to help members cope with particular difficulties, such as drug addiction, having an alcoholic parent, being an ex-convict, or having hyperactive child or a promiscuous spouse. Other groups are more clearly therapeutic and are designed to change significant aspects of one's personality or behavior.

Some Popular Personal Growth Groups

There are many varieties of support or personal growth groups. The encounter group, for example, tries to facilitate personal growth and the ability to deal effectively with other people (Rogers 1970). One of its assumptions is that the members will be more effective psychologically and socially if they get to know and like themselves better. Consequently, the atmosphere of the encounter group is one of acceptance and support. Freedom to express one's inner thoughts, fears, and doubts is stressed. The assertiveness training group aims to increase the willingness of its members to stand up for their rights and to act more assertively in a wide variety of situations (Adler 1977).

The **consciousness-raising group** aims to help people cope with the problems with which society confronts them. The members of a consciousness-raising group all have one characteristic in common (for example, they are all women, all unwed mothers,

LISTENING TO NEW IDEAS

Generating new ideas—whether through brainstorming or some other process (see DeVito 1996)—needs to be complemented by giving these new ideas a fair hearing, by listening openly and honestly. Be careful not to be unduly swayed by what others think. Appropriate responses to creativity will often run counter to the majority opinion, if only because there seems to be a natural tendency to resist change and innovation. Focus first on the idea; make sure you understand it and its implications. Then, consider what others are saying.

A useful technique in listening to new ideas is PIP'N, a technique that derives from the insights of Carl Rogers' (1956) emphasis on paraphrase as a means for ensuring understanding and Edward deBono's (1976) PMI (plus, minus, interesting) technique. Pip'n involves four steps:

P = *Paraphrase.* State in your own words what you think the other person is saying. This will ensure that you and the person proposing the idea are talking about the same thing. Your paraphrase will also provide the other person with the opportunity to elaborate or clarify his or her ideas.

I = *Interesting.* State something interesting that you find in the idea. Say why you think this idea might be interesting to you, to others, to the organization.

P = *Positive.* Say something positive about the idea. What is good about it? How might it solve a problem or make a situation better?

N = *Negative.* State any negatives that you think the idea might entail. Might it prove expensive? Difficult to implement? Is it directed at insignificant issues?

You may want to try using Pip'n the next time you hear about a new idea, say, in conversation or in a small group. For practice, you may want to try Pip'n on the Pip'n technique itself: (1) paraphrase the Pip'n technique, (2) say why the technique is interesting, (3) say something positive about it, and (4) say something negative about it.

all gay fathers, or all recently unemployed executives). It is this commonality that leads the members to join together and assist one another. In the consciousness-raising group the assumption is that similar people are best equipped to assist each other's personal growth. Structurally, the consciousness-raising group is leaderless. All members (usually ranging from 6 to 12) are equal in their control of the group and in their presumed knowledge.

Although all personal growth groups will function somewhat differently, we can illustrate at least one possible pattern by looking at the steps and procedures that a sample consciousness-raising group might follow. These procedures are generally much more flexible than those followed in a problem-solving group, for example.

Some Rules and Procedures

In a personal growth group, a topic is selected, usually by majority vote of the group. This topic may be drawn from a prepared list or suggested by one of the group members. Regardless of the topic selected, it is always discussed from the point of view of the larger topic that brings these particular people together—let's say, sexual harassment. Whether the topic is men, employment, or family, it is pursued in light of the issues and problems of sexual harassment.

After a topic is selected, a starting point is established through some random procedure. That member speaks for about ten minutes on his or her feelings, experiences, and thoughts. The focus is always on oneself. No interruptions are allowed. After the member has finished, the other group members may ask questions of clarification. The feedback from other members is to be totally supportive.

After questions of clarification have been answered, the next member speaks. The same procedure is followed until all members have spoken. Then, general discussion follows. During this time members may relate different aspects of their experience to what the others have said. Or they may tell the group how they feel about some of the issues raised by others.

The personal growth group grew out of 1960s culture—in large part the feminist movement—that valued openness and honesty and believed that the average person can (and wants to) help another average person. Could this type of group have grown out of 1990s culture? What types of groups are emerging today? What kinds of personal growth groups (if any) would you be likely to join?

With this procedure your consciousness is raised by formulating and verbalizing your thoughts on a particular topic, hearing how others feel and think about the same topic, and formulating and answering questions of clarification.

INFORMATION-SHARING GROUPS

The purpose of **information-sharing groups** is to acquire new information or skills through a sharing of knowledge. In most information-sharing groups, all members have something to teach and something to learn. In others, the interaction takes place because some have information and some do not.

Learning Groups

In learning groups, the members pool their knowledge for the benefit of all. Members may follow a variety of discussion patterns. For example, a historical topic might be developed chronologically, with the discussion progressing from the past into the present and perhaps predicting the future. Issues in developmental psychology such as language development in the child or physical maturity might also be discussed chronologically. Some topics lend themselves to spatial development. For example, the development of the United States might take a spatial pattern going from east to west or a chronological pattern going from 1776 to the present. Other suitable patterns, depending on the nature of the topic and the needs of the discussants, might be developed in terms of causes and effects, problems and solutions, or structures and functions.

Perhaps the most popular is the topical pattern. A group might discuss the problems of raising a hyperactive child by itemizing and discussing each of the major problems. The structure of a corporation might also be considered in terms of its major divisions. As can be appreciated, each of these topics may be further systematized, for instance, by ordering the problems of hyperactivity in terms of their importance or complexity and ordering the major structures of the corporation in terms of decision-making power.

Focus Groups

A different type of learning group is the **focus group**, a kind of in-depth interview of a small group. The aim here is to discover what people think about an issue or product; for example, What do men between 18 and 25 think of the new aftershave lotion and its packaging? What do young executives earning over $70,000 a year think of buying a foreign luxury car?

In the focus group the leader tries to discover members' beliefs, attitudes, thoughts, and feelings in order to guide decisions on changing a scent or redesigning the packaging or constructing advertisements for luxury cars. It is the leader's task to prod members to analyze their thoughts and feelings on a deeper level and to use the thoughts of one member to stimulate the thoughts of others.

For example, in one study the researcher tried "to collect supplementary data on the perceptions graduates have of the Department of Communication at ABC University" (Lederman 1990). Two major research questions, taken directly from Lederman's study, motivated this focus group: "(1) What do graduates of the program perceive the educational effectiveness of their major to be at ABC? and (2) What would they want implemented in the program as it exists today?" Group participants then discussed their perceptions, organized around such questions as these (Lederman 1990, p. 123):

- The first issue to discuss is what the program was like when you were a major in the department. Let's begin by going around the table and making introductions. Will you tell me your name, when you graduated from ABC, what you are doing now, and what the program was like when you were here, as you remember it?"
- "Based on what you remember of the program and what you have used from your major since graduating, what kinds of changes, if any, would you suggest?"

PROBLEM-SOLVING GROUPS

A problem-solving group is a collection of individuals who meet to solve a problem or to reach a decision. In one sense this is the most exacting kind of group in which to participate. It requires not only a knowledge of small group communication techniques, but also a thorough knowledge of the particular problem, and it usually demands faithful adherence to a somewhat rigid set of rules. We look at this group first in terms of the classic and still popular problem-solving approach, whereby we identify the steps to go through in solving a problem. Next we look at several types of groups that are popular in organizations today: the nominal group, the Delphi method, quality circles, improvement groups, and task groups. Lastly, we consider the major decision-making methods.

The Problem-Solving Sequence

The approach developed by philosopher John Dewey is probably the most often used **problem-solving sequence.** Six steps are identified (see Figure 17.2) and are designed to make problem solving more efficient and effective.

Define and Analyze the Problem

In many instances the nature of the problem is clearly specified. For example, a group of designers might discuss how to package a new soap product. In other instances, however, the problem may be vague, and it remains for the group to define it in concrete terms. Thus, for example, the general problem may be poor campus communications. Such a vague and general topic is difficult to tackle in a problem-solving discussion, therefore it is helpful to specify the problem clearly. For purposes of discussion, a group might specify the problem as, "How can we improve the student newspaper?"

Generally, it is best to define the problem as an open-ended question ("How can we improve the student newspaper?") rather than as a statement ("The student newspaper needs to be improved") or a yes/no question ("Does the student newspaper need improvement?"). The open-ended question allows for greater freedom of exploration. It does not restrict the ways in which the group may approach the problem.

The problem should also be limited in some way so that it identifies a manageable area for discussion. A question such as, "How can we improve the university?" is too broad and general. Rather, it would be more effective to limit the problem and to identify one subdivision of the university on which the group might focus. You might choose one of the following categories for discussion: the student newspaper, student-faculty relationships, registration, examination scheduling, or student advisory services.

In defining the problem, the group seeks to identify its dimensions. Appropriate questions (for most problems) revolve around the following issues: (1) Duration—How long has the problem existed? Is it likely to continue in the future? What is the predicted course of the problem? For example, will it grow or lessen in influence? (2) Causes—What are the major causes of the problem? How certain can we be that these are the actual causes? (3) Effects—What are the effects of the problem? How significant are they? Who

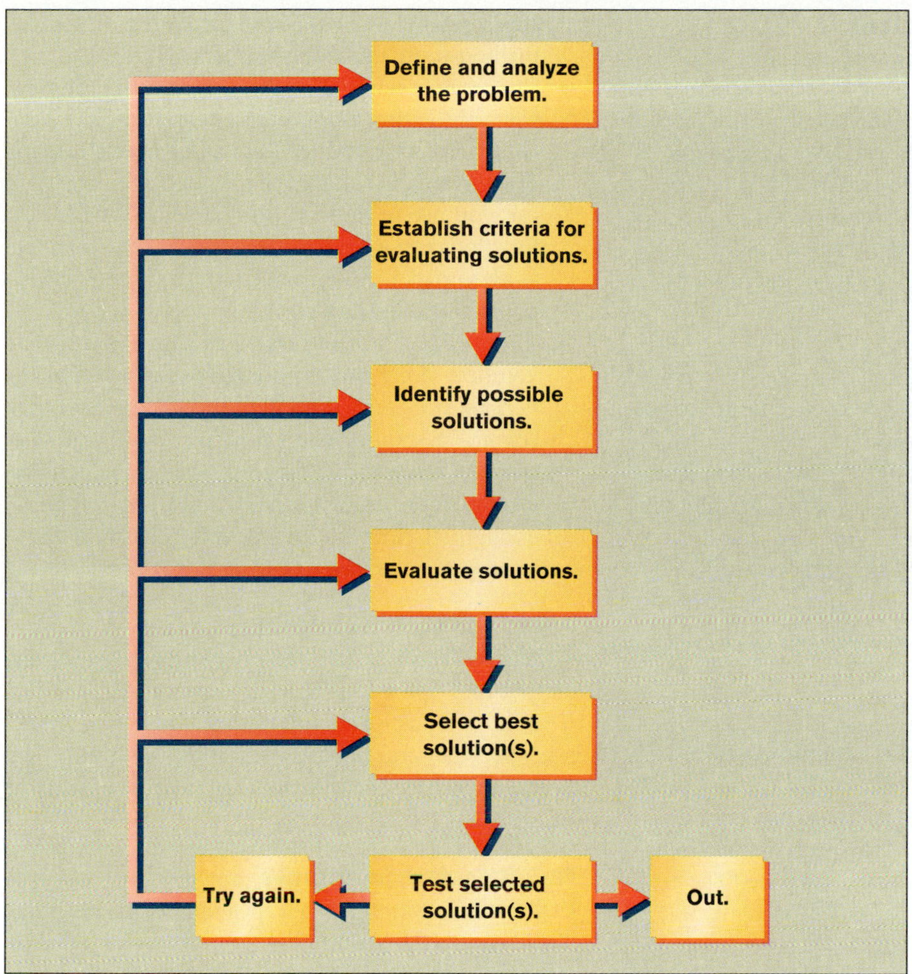

FIGURE 17.2 Steps in problem-solving discussion. While most small group theorists would advise you to follow the problem-solving pattern as presented here, others would alter it somewhat. For example, the pattern here advises you to define the problem first and then establish criteria for identifying possible solutions. You would then keep these criteria in mind as you generate possible solutions (Step 3). Another school of thought, however, would advise you to generate solutions first and only consider how they will be evaluated after these solutions are proposed (Brilhart & Galanes 1992). The advantage of this second approach is that you are likely to generate more creative solutions since you will not be restricted by standards of evaluation. The disadvantage is that you might spend a great deal of time generating very impractical solutions that would never meet the standards you will eventually propose.

is affected by this problem? How significantly are they affected? Is this problem causing other problems? How important are these other problems? Applied to our student newspaper example, the specific questions might look something like this:

1. Duration: How long has there been a problem with securing advertising? Does it look as though it will grow or lessen in importance?
2. Causes: What seems to be causing the newspaper problem? Are there specific policies (editorial, advertising, or design) that might be causing the problem?
3. Effects: What effects is this problem producing? How significant are these effects? Who is affected? Students? Alumni? Faculty? People in the community?

Establish Criteria for Evaluating Solutions

Before any solutions are proposed, you need to decide how to evaluate them. At this stage you identify the standards or criteria that you will use in evaluating the solutions or in selecting one solution over another. Generally, two types of criteria need to be considered. First, there are the practical criteria. For example, you might decide that the solutions must not increase the budget, must lead to a higher number of advertisers, must increase the readership by at least 10 percent, and so on.

Second, there are the value criteria. These are more difficult to identify. These might include, for example, that the newspaper must be a learning experience for all those who work on it, that it must reflect the attitudes of the board of trustees, the faculty, or the students.

Identify Possible Solutions

At this stage identify as many solutions as possible. Focus on quantity rather than quality. Brainstorming may be particularly useful at this point (see discussion of idea-generation groups). Solutions to the student newspaper problem might include incorporating reviews of faculty publications, student evaluations of specific courses, reviews of restaurants in the campus area, outlines for new courses, and employment information.

Evaluate Solutions

After all the solutions have been proposed, you would go back and evaluate each according to the criteria established for evaluating solutions. For example, to what extent does incorporating reviews of area restaurants meet the criteria for evaluating solutions? Would it increase the budget? Would it lead to an increase in advertising revenue? Each potential solution should be matched against the criteria for evaluating solutions.

THINK ABOUT

Think about how you might evaluate possible solutions to a specific problem with the six **critical thinking hats technique.** Critical thinking pioneer Edward deBono (1987) suggests that with each hat you look at the problem from a different perspective. The technique provides a convenient and interesting way to explore a problem from a variety of different angles. As you read about each hat, ask yourself what unique perspective you gain on your problem from looking at it with that particular hat.

- The *fact hat* focuses attention on the data, the facts and figures that bear on the problem. For example, What are the relevant data on the newspaper? How can you get more information on the paper's history? How much does it cost to print? How much advertising revenue can you get?
- The *feeling hat* focuses attention on your feelings, emotions, and intuitions concerning the problem. How do you feel about the newspaper and about making major changes?
- The *negative argument hat* asks that you become the devil's advocate. Why might this proposal fail? What are the problems with publishing reviews of courses? What is the worst-case scenario?
- The *positive benefits hat* asks that you look at the upside. What are the opportunities that this new format will open up? What benefits will reviewing courses provide for the students? What would be the best thing that could happen?
- The *creative new idea hat* focuses attention on new ways of looking at the problem and can be easily combined with the techniques of brainstorming discussed earlier in this chapter. What other ways can you use to look at this problem? What other functions can a student newspaper serve? Can the student paper provide a service to the nonacademic community as well?
- The *control of thinking hat* helps you analyze what you have done and are doing. It asks that you reflect on your own thinking processes and synthesize the results of your thinking. Have you adequately defined the problem? Are you focusing too much on insignificant issues? Have you given enough attention to the possible negative effects?

Select the Best Solution(s)

At this stage the best solution or solutions are selected and put into operation. Thus, for example, if "reviews of faculty publications" and "outlines for new courses" best met the criteria for evaluating solutions, the group might then incorporate these two new items in the next issue of the newspaper.

Test Selected Solution(s)

After the solution(s) are put into operation, test their effectiveness. The group might, for example, poll students about the new newspaper or examine the number of copies purchased. Or you might analyze the advertising revenue or see if readership did increase 10 percent.

If these solutions prove ineffective, you would go back to one of the previous stages and repeat part of the process. Often this takes the form of selecting other solutions to test, but, it may also involve going further back to, for example, a reanalysis of the problem, an identification of other solutions, or a restatement of criteria.

Problem Solving at Work

Here are a few types of groups currently used widely in businesses that rely largely on the problem-solving techniques just discussed.

The Nominal Group

In a typical **nominal group** a problem is proposed and members submit solutions in writing (Huseman

INTRODUCING RESEARCH

EVALUATING METHODS AND CONCLUSIONS

Just as you need to evaluate the proposed solutions to a problem, you also need to evaluate research—its methods and its conclusions. After all, not all research is good research. In reading "the literature," evaluate the research by asking, for example, the following questions:

ARE THE RESULTS RELIABLE?

Reliability is a measure of the extent to which research findings are consistent and is always important to consider in evaluating research findings. In investigating reliability, you would ask if another researcher, using the same essential tools, would find the same results with similar populations. Will the same people respond in the same way at other times? If the answer to such questions is yes, then the results are reliable. If the answer is no, then the results are unreliable. Generally, we are more interested in conclusions that are consistent over time and across a wide spectrum of people. Conclusions that are more limited, are usually (but not always), less valuable.

ARE THE RESULTS VALID?

Validity is a measure of the extent to which a measuring instrument measures what it claims to measure and, like reliability, is important to consider in evaluating any research study. Do the instruments measure what they claim to measure? For example, does a score on an intelligence test really measure what most people think of as intelligence? Does a score on a test of communication apprehension measure what most people think of as constituting apprehension? This is referred to as *internal validity*.

You might also ask: To what extent do the results obtained in the laboratory (or classroom) represent what people do in real life? Are the results valid outside of the text or laboratory situation? For example, are responses to a "How do you express love?" questionnaire accurate recollections and descriptions of what really happens? This is referred to as *external validity*. If these responses are accurate descriptions then there is high external validity; if they are not then there is low external validity.

DO THE RESULTS JUSTIFY THE CONCLUSION?

Remember that results and conclusions are two different things. Results are objective findings, such as "men scored higher than women on this test of romanticism" or "college students have the greatest number of friends of any age group." Conclusions are the researcher's (or reader's) interpretation of the results and might include, for example, "Men are more romantic than women," or, "Few college students are lonely." Ideally, conclusions extend the research findings in reasonable and justifiable ways.

WHAT DO THE RESULTS AND CONCLUSIONS MEAN?

How do the results and conclusions enlarge upon, contradict, or modify a principle of communication covered in a lecture or textbook chapter? How do they relate to a particular theory or proposed research study? Although even isolated findings are useful, findings and conclusions related to a general theory or principle are usually more valuable.

You may find it interesting to read one of the studies referred to in this text and evaluate the methods used and the conclusions drawn with the aid of these four questions.

1977). The solutions are written down on a board for members to see. Members may ask for clarification but do not discuss the solutions, instead, they work individually to rank the solutions in order of merit. Their rank orders are collected and recorded, again for all to see. If there is agreement, the work of the nominal group is completed. If there is insufficient agreement, then the members again consider the solutions individually and again rank them. The process is continued until the group reaches some agreement.

The Delphi Method

The **Delphi method**, originally developed by the RAND Corporation, brings together a pool of experts but there is no interaction among them (Tersine & Riggs 1980). Members may, in fact, be scattered throughout the world. A Delphi questionnaire is distributed to all members asking them to respond to what they feel are, for example, the communication problems the organization will have to face in the next 25 years. Members record their predictions, and the questionnaires are sent back anonymously. Responses are tabulated, recorded, and distributed to the experts, who then revise their predictions in light of the composite list. They then submit their revised predictions. These are again tabulated, recorded, and returned. The process continues until the responses no longer change significantly. The composite or final list represents the predictions or forecast of this group of experts.

Quality Circles

Quality circles consist of workers whose task it is to improve some aspect of the work environment, for example, morale, productivity, or communication. The basic idea is that people who work on similar tasks will be able to devise better ways of doing things by pooling their insights and working through common problems. The group then reports its findings—for example, ways to increase worker-management communication—to those who can do something about it.

Quality circles are especially effective when used as a way of improving communication and raising worker consciousness concerning productivity and quality. They are also effective when organizations need to address certain critical issues such as retooling its members or introducing a new technology. Quality circles also help provide a smooth transition toward greater worker participation in managerial decisions (Marks 1986) and have been found to stimulate creative change in an organization (Stohl 1987). Research shows that workers who participate in quality circle groups become more effectively integrated into the organization (Stohl 1986), increased their productivity, and reduced absenteeism (Marks 1986).

Improvement Groups

A somewhat different type of group is the improvement group, or what is often called *kaizen,* Japanese for "continual improvement" (Beebe & Masterson 1994). These groups are based on the assumption that every process or product in any organization can be improved. Such groups may be set up for a certain amount of time or may be permanent.

Task Groups

Often groups are formed for specific tasks—how to deal with the new administration, how to get plan XYZ accepted by the membership, or how to phase in the new computer technology. Often these task groups are formed for this one specific task and are then disbanded.

Decision-making Methods

Groups may use different decision-making methods in deciding, for example, which criterion to use or which solution to accept. Generally, groups use one of three methods.

Authority

In decision making by authority, members voice their feelings and opinions but the leader, boss, or CEO makes the final decision. This is surely an efficient method; it gets things done quickly and the amount of discussion can be limited as desired. Another advantage is that experienced and informed members (for example, those who have been with the company longest) will probably exert a greater influence on the decision maker.

The great disadvantage is that members may not feel the need to contribute their insights and may become distanced from the power within the group or organization. Another disadvantage is that it may lead members to give the decision maker what they feel she or he wants to receive, a condition that can easily lead to groupthink (see the Listen to This box in Unit 18).

Majority Rule

With this method the group agrees to abide by the majority decision and may vote on various issues as the group progresses to solve its problem. Majority rule is efficient since there is usually an option to call for a vote when the majority are in agreement. This is a useful method for issues that are relatively unimportant (What company should service the water cooler?) and where member satisfaction and commitment is not needed.

One disadvantage is that it can lead to factioning, whereby various minorities align against the majority. The method may also lead to limiting discussion once a majority has agreed and a vote is called.

Consensus

The group operating under consensus reaches a decision only when all group members agree, as in the criminal jury system. This method is especially important when the group wants the satisfaction and commitment of each member to the decision and to the decision-making process as a whole (DeStephen & Hirokawa 1988; Rothwell 1992).

Consensus obviously takes longest and can lead to a great deal of wasted time if members wish to prolong the discussion process needlessly or selfishly. This method may also put great pressure on the person who honestly disagrees but who doesn't want to prevent the group from making a decision.

SMALL GROUP FORMATS

Small groups serve their functions in a variety of formats. Among the most popular formats for relatively formal groups are the roundtable, the panel, the symposium, and the symposium-forum (see Figure 17.3).

The Roundtable

In the **roundtable** format, group members arrange themselves in a circular or semicircular pattern. They share the information or solve the problem without any set pattern of who speaks when. Group interaction is informal and members contribute as they see fit. A leader or moderator may be present who may, for example, try to keep the discussion on the topic or encourage more reticent members to speak up.

The Panel

In the **panel**, group members are "experts" and participate informally and without any set pattern of who speaks when. The difference is that there is an audience whose members may interject comments or ask questions. Many television talk shows use this format.

A variation is the two-panel format, with an expert panel and a lay panel. The lay panel discusses the topic but when in need of technical information, additional data, or direction, they may turn to the expert panel members to provide the needed information.

The Symposium

In the **symposium**, each member delivers a prepared presentation, much like a public speech. All speeches are addressed to different aspects of a single topic. In the symposium, the leader introduces the speakers, provides transitions from one speaker to another, and may provide periodic summaries.

The Symposium-Forum

The **symposium-forum** consists of two parts: a symposium, with prepared speeches, and a forum, with questions from the audience and responses by the speakers. The leader introduces the speakers and moderates the question-and-answer session.

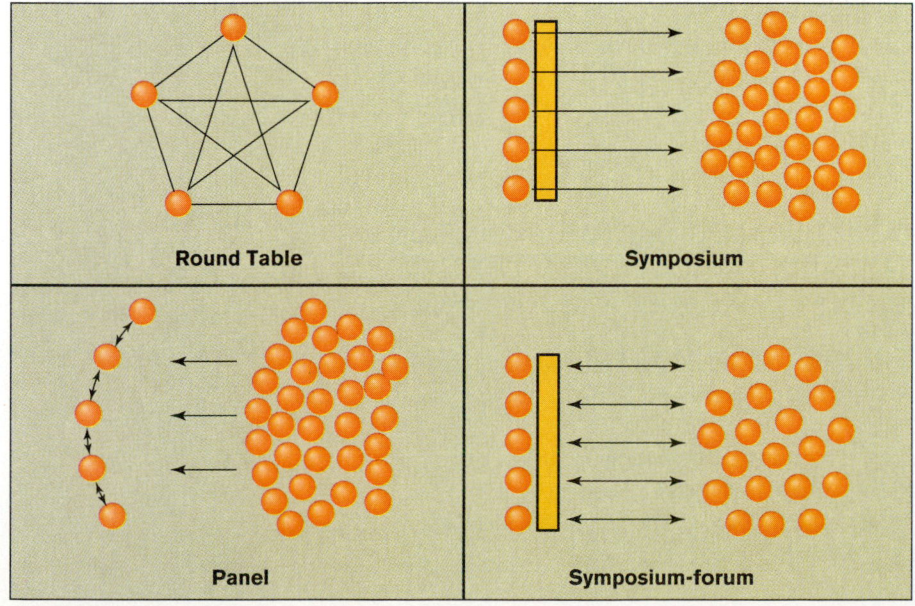

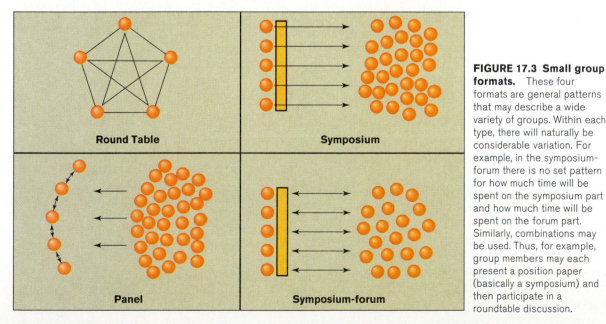

FIGURE 17.3 Small group formats. These four formats are general patterns that may describe a wide variety of groups. Within each type, there will naturally be considerable variation. For example, in the symposium-forum there is no set pattern for how much time will be spent on the symposium part and how much time will be spent on the forum part. Similarly, combinations may be used. Thus, for example, group members may each present a position paper (basically a symposium) and then participate in a roundtable discussion.

SUMMARY

In this unit we introduced the nature of the small group, the major types of groups and their functions, and some of the small group formats.

1. A small group is a collection of individuals that is small enough for all members to communicate with relative ease as both senders and receivers. The members are related to each other by some common purpose and have some degree of organization or structure among them.
2. Most small groups develop norms or rules, which operate much like a culture's norms, identifying what is considered appropriate behavior for its members.
3. Power operates in all groups. Six types of power may be identified: referent, legitimate, reward, coercive, expert, and information or persuasion.
4. The idea-generation or brainstorming group attempts to generate as many ideas as possible.
5. The personal growth group helps members deal with personal problems and function more effectively. Popular types of personal growth groups are the encounter group, the assertiveness training group, and the consciousness-raising group.
6. The educational or learning group attempts to acquire new information or skill through a mutual sharing of knowledge or insight.
7. The focus group aims to discover what people think about an issue or product through a kind of in-depth group interview.
8. The problem-solving group attempts to solve a particular problem or at least to reach a decision that may be a preface to the problem solving itself.
9. The six steps in the problem-solving approach are: define and analyze the problem, establish criteria for evaluating solutions, identify possible solutions, evaluate solutions, select best solution(s), and test solution(s).
10. The six hats technique is especially useful in analyzing problems and consists of focusing on different aspects of the problem: facts, feelings, negative arguments, positive benefits, creative or new ways of viewing problems, and your thinking processes.
11. Decision-making methods include authority, majority rule, and consensus.
12. Small groups that are widely used in business today include the nominal group, the Delphi method, quality circles, improvement groups, and task groups.
13. Small groups make use of four major formats: the roundtable, the panel, the symposium, and the symposium-forum.

THINKING CRITICALLY ABOUT SMALL GROUP COMMUNICATION

1. Of what types of small groups are you a member? What functions do the various groups serve?
2. How do your group relationships compare to your interpersonal ones? For example, which are the more personally rewarding? The more time-consuming? The more profitable?
3. Can you identify some of the norms that operate in your interpersonal relationships? In your family? In the groups to which you belong?
4. Do you find evidence that groups go through the five stages identified here? How else might the stages of a group be defined?

5. What types of power do you hold over others? What types of power do others hold over you?
6. How many types of power can you identify operating in this class?
7. How can you use brainstorming in your academic, professional, and/or personal life?
8. Studies find that persons high in communication apprehension are generally less effective in idea-generation groups than are those low in apprehension (Jablin 1981; Comadena 1984; Cragan & Wright 1990). Why do you think this is so?
9. With which type of decision-making method do you usually feel most comfortable? Least comfortable?
10. How might you go about finding answers to such questions as these:
    a. Are group memberships more important to men or to women?
    b. How effective is peer group instruction compared to instruction by lecture?
    c. What personality or cultural factors are correlated with one's tendency to abide by the rules or norms of the group?
    d. Is communication apprehension related to one's effectiveness in personal growth groups? In information-sharing groups? In problem-solving groups?

eighteen unit

Members and Leaders in Small Group Communication

unit contents

unit goals

After completing this unit, you should be able to

1. identify the three major types of member roles and give examples of each type
2. define *groupthink* and identify its major symptoms
3. explain the traits, functional, and situational theories of leadership
4. define the three leadership styles and the occasions when each would be most appropriate
5. explain at least four functions of leaders in small group communication
6. explain the influence of culture on group membership and leadership

In this unit we consider the roles or functions of small group members and leaders. By gaining insight into the roles of both members and leaders, you will be in a better position to analyze your own small group behavior (as member and leader) and to modify it as you wish.

MEMBERS IN SMALL GROUP COMMUNICATION

Membership in small group communication situations can be viewed from a variety of perspectives—the roles that members serve, the types of contributions they make, and the principles for more effective participation.

Member Roles

Member roles fall into three general classes: group task roles, group building and maintenance roles, and individual roles, a classification introduced in early research (Benne & Sheats 1948) and still widely used today (Lumsden & Lumsden 1993; Beebe & Masterson 1994). These roles are, of course, frequently served by leaders as well.

THINK ABOUT

Think about your own behavior, your own membership style, as you read these discussions of roles. Which of these do you regularly serve? Are there productive roles that you never or rarely serve? Are there destructive roles that you often serve?

Group Task Roles

Group task roles are those that help the group focus more specifically on achieving its goals. In serving any of these roles, you do not act as an isolated individual, but rather as a part of the larger whole. The needs and goals of the group influence the roles you serve. As an effective group member you would serve several of these functions.

Some people, however, lock into a few specific roles. For example, one person may almost always seek the opinions of others, another may concentrate on elaborating details, still another on evaluating suggestions. Usually, this single focus is counterproductive. It is usually better for the roles to be spread more evenly among the members so that each may serve many group task roles. The 12 specific group task roles are identified in Table 18.1.

Group Building and Maintenance Roles

Most groups focus not only on the task to be performed but on interpersonal relationships among members. If the group is to function effectively, and if members are to be both satisfied and productive, these relationships must be nourished. When these needs are not met, group members may become irritable when the group process gets bogged down, engage in frequent conflicts, or find the small group process unsatisfying. The group and its members need the same kind of support that individuals need. The group building and maintenance roles serve this general function. Group building and maintenance are broken down into seven specific roles (see Table 18.2).

TABLE 18.1
group task roles

Group Roles	Examples
Initiator-contributor	Presents new ideas or new perspectives on old ideas; suggests new goals, or new procedures or organizational strategies
Information seeker	Asks for facts and opinions; seeks clarification of the issues being discussed
Opinion seeker	Tries to discover the values underlying the group's task
Information giver	Presents facts and opinions to the group members
Opinion giver	Presents values and opinions and tries to spell out what the values of the group should be
Elaborator	Gives examples and tries to work out possible solutions, trying to build on what others have said
Coordinator	Spells out relationships among ideas and suggested solutions; coordinates the activities of the different members
Orienter	Summarizes what has been said and addresses the direction the group is taking
Evaluator-critic	Evaluates the group's decisions; questions the logic or practicality of the suggestions and thus provides the group with both positive and negative feedback
Energizer	Stimulates the group to greater activity
Procedural technician	Takes care of the various mechanical duties such as distributing group materials and arranging the seating
Recorder	Writes down the group's activities, suggestions, and decisions; serves as the memory of the group

Individual Roles

The group task and the group building and maintenance roles are productive roles; they aid the group in achieving its goals. The roles are group-oriented. Individual roles, on the other hand, are counterproductive. These roles, often termed dysfunctional, hinder the group's productivity and member satisfaction largely because they focus on serving individual rather than group needs. Eight specific types are identified in Table 18.3.

Interaction Process Analysis

Another way of looking at the contributions group members make is through **interaction process analysis,** developed by Robert Bales (1950). In this system you analyze the contributions of members in four general categories: (1) social-emotional positive contributions, (2) social-emotional negative contributions, (3) attempted answers, and (4) questions. Each of these 4 areas contains 3 subdivisions, yielding a total of 12 categories into which you can classify group members' contributions (see Table 18.4). Note that the categories under social-emotional positive are the natural opposites of those under social-emotional negative, and those under attempted answers are the natural opposites of those under questions.

Try out Bales' system by listening to a small group discussion and recording the interactions using Table 18.4. In the spaces at the top write in the participants names. In the column under each participant's name, place a slash mark for each contribution in one of the 12 categories. You can also try this out when watching a videotape of a film or a television sitcom such as "Seinfeld," "Frazier," or "Friends" and classify the contributions of the characters. After completing such an analysis—even for say 10 or 20 minutes of a discussion—you should find that the interaction process analysis enables you to identify the different types of contribution individual members make during a discussion and enables you to identify problems with the participants' contributions. You should also be in a better position to offer

TABLE 18.2
group building and maintenance roles

Group Roles	Examples
Encourager	Supplies members with positive reinforcement in the form of social approval or praise for their ideas
Harmonizer	Mediates the various differences between group members
Compromiser	Tries to resolve conflict between his or her ideas and those of others; offers compromises
Gatekeeper-expediter	Keeps the channels of communication open by reinforcing the efforts of others
Standard setter	Proposes standards for the functioning of the group or for its solutions
Group observer and commentator	Keeps a record of the proceedings and uses this in the group's evaluation of itself
Follower	Goes along with the members of the group; passively accepts the ideas of others and functions more as an audience than as an active member

TABLE 18.3
individual roles

Group Roles	Examples
Aggressor	Expresses negative evaluation of the actions or feelings of the group members; attacks the group or the problem being considered
Blocker	Provides negative feedback, is disagreeable, and opposes other members or suggestions regardless of their merit
Recognition seeker	Tries to focus attention on oneself rather than the task at hand, boasts about own accomplishments
Self-confessor	Expresses his or her own feelings and personal perspectives rather than focusing on the group
Playboy/playgirl	Jokes around without any regard for the group process
Dominator	Tries to run the group or the group members by pulling rank, flattering members of the group, or acting the role of the boss
Help seeker	Expresses insecurity or confusion or deprecates oneself and thus tries to gain sympathy from the other members
Special-interest pleader	Disregards the goals of the group and pleads the case of some special group

improvement suggestions for individual members based on this interaction process analysis.

Both the three-part member role classification and the categories of interaction process analysis are useful in viewing the contributions that members make in small group situations. When you look at member contributions through these systems, you can see, for example, if one member is locked into a particular role or if the group process breaks down because too many people are serving individual rather than group goals or because social-emotional negative comments dominate the discussion. These systems are designed to help you see more clearly what is go-

TABLE 18.4
interaction process analysis form

Social-Emotional Positive	Shows solidarity							
	Shows tension release							
	Shows agreement							
Social-Emotional Negative	Shows disagreement							
	Shows tension							
	Shows antagonism							
Attempted Answers	Gives suggestions							
	Gives opinions							
	Gives information							
Questions	Asks for suggestions							
	Asks for opinions							
	Asks for information							

ing on in a group and what specific contributions may mean to the entire group process.

Member Participation

Another perspective on group membership may be gained from studying the following recommendations for effective participation in small group communication. Look at these suggestions as an elaboration and extension of the characteristics of effective conversation (see Unit 13).

Be Group-Oriented

In the small group you are a member of a team, a larger whole. Your participation is of value to the extent that it advances the goals of the group and promotes member satisfaction. Your task is to pool your talents, knowledge, and insights so that the group may arrive at a better solution than any one person could have developed alone. Solo performances hinder the group.

This call for group orientation is not to be taken as a suggestion that members abandon their individuality or give up their personal values or beliefs for the sake of the group. Individuality with a group orientation is what is advocated here.

Center Conflict on Issues

Conflict in small group situations is inevitable and its management should follow the general rules for dealing with conflict already covered in Unit 16. As in interpersonal communication, conflict is a natural part of the small group process.

It is particularly important in the small group to center conflict on issues rather than on personalities. When you disagree, make it clear that your disagreement is with the solution suggested or the ideas expressed, and not with the person who expressed

What member roles would your culture reward most? Punish most? Can you identify any general cultural principles that govern what is positively valued and what is negatively valued in group membership?

them. Similarly, when someone disagrees with what you say, do not take this as a personal attack. Rather, view this as an opportunity to discuss issues from an alternative point of view.

Be Critically Open-Minded

One common but unproductive development occurs when members come to the group with their minds already made up. When this happens, the small group process degenerates into a series of individual debates in which each person argues for his or her own position. Instead, members should come to the group equipped with relevant information that will be useful to the discussion. They should not have decided on the solution or conclusion they will accept. Any solutions or conclusions should be advanced tentatively rather than with certainty. Members should be willing to alter their suggestions and revise them in light of the discussion.

Listen openly but critically to the comments of all other members (see the Listen to This box in Unit 23). Do not accept or reject any member's suggestions without critically evaluating them. Be judiciously open-minded. Be critical of your own contributions as well as those of others.

Ensure Understanding

Make sure that your ideas and information are understood by all participants. If something is worth saying, it is worth saying clearly. When in doubt, ask: "Is that clear?" "Did I explain that clearly?"

Make sure, too, that you understand fully the contributions of the other members, especially before you take issue with them. In fact, it is often wise to preface any extended disagreement with some kind of paraphrase. For example, you might say, "As I understand it, you want to exclude freshmen from playing on the football team. Is that correct? I disagree with that idea and I'd like to explain why I think that would be a mistake." Then you would go on to state your objections. In this way you give the other person the opportunity to clarify, deny, or otherwise alter what was said.

Take a moment to study the Group Membership Evaluation Form I use in my course in small group communication (see page 321). It provides a convenient summary of the member's roles and responsibilities as discussed here. This form seems especially suited to problem-solving or decision-making groups and less appropriate for other types. How would you construct an evaluation form for an idea-generation group? For a personal growth group?

LEADERS IN SMALL GROUP COMMUNICATION

A leader is one who influences the thoughts and behaviors of others; a leader is one who establishes the direction that others follow. In many small groups, one person serves as leader. In others, leadership may be shared by several persons. In some groups, a person may be appointed as leader or may serve as leader because of her or his position within the company or hierarchy.

LISTENING FOR GROUPTHINK

Groupthink is a way of thinking that people use when agreement among members becomes extremely important in a cohesive ingroup. So important is agreement among members that it tends to shut out realistic and logical analysis of a problem or of possible alternatives (Janis 1983, Mullen, Tara, Salas, & Driskell 1994). The term itself is meant to signal a "deterioration of mental efficiency, reality testing, and moral judgment that results from in-group pressures" (Janis 1983, p. 9). Both members and leaders need to be able to listen to the symptoms of groupthink and combat its negative effects.

Many specific behaviors of group members can lead to groupthink. One of the most significant occurs when the group limits its discussion to only a small number of alternative solutions, overlooking other possibilities. Another occurs when the group does not reexamine its decisions even when there are indications of possible dangers. A third happens when the group spends little time discussing why certain initial alternatives were rejected. For example, if the group rejected a certain alternative because it was too costly, members will devote little time, if any, to the ways in which the cost may be reduced.

In groupthink, the group members are extremely selective in the information they consider seriously. Facts and opinions contrary to the position of the group are generally ignored. Facts and opinions that support the position of the group, however, are easily and uncritically accepted.

The following list of symptoms should help you listen critically for the possible existence of groupthink in the groups you observe or in which you participate (Janis 1983):

- Group members think the group and its members are invulnerable to dangers.
- Members create rationalizations to avoid dealing directly with warnings or threats.
- Group members believe their group is moral.
- Those opposed to the group are perceived in simplistic, stereotyped ways.
- Group pressure is put on any member who expresses doubts or who questions the group's arguments or proposals.
- Group members censor their own doubts.
- Group members believe all members are in unanimous agreement, whether such agreement is stated or not.
- Group members emerge whose function it is to guard the information that gets to other members of the group, especially when such information may create diversity of opinion.

Have you ever been in a group when groupthink was operating? If so, what were its symptoms? What effect did groupthink have on the process and conclusions of the group?

In still other groups, the leader may emerge as the group proceeds in fulfilling its functions or may be voted as leader by the group members. The single most important factor in determining who emerges as the group leader is the extent of active participation; the one who talks the most emerges as leader (Shaw & Gouran 1990). The "emergent leader" performs the duties of leadership, though not asked or expected to and gradually becomes recognized by the members as the group's leader. Since this person has now proven herself or himself to be an effective leader, it is not surprising that this emergent leader often becomes the designated leader for future groups. Generally, the emergent leader serves as leader as long as the group members are satisfied. When they are not, they may encourage another member to emerge as leader. As long as the emergent leader serves effectively, however, the group will probably not look to others.

In any case the role of the leader or leaders is vital to the well-being and effectiveness of the group. Even in leaderless groups, in which all members are equal, leadership functions must still be served.

Approaches to Leadership

Not surprisingly, leadership has been the focus of considerable attention from theorists and researchers who have used a number of approaches to understand this particular communication behavior. Three of these are are discussed here and summarized in

GROUP MEMBERSHIP EVALUATION FORM

Circle those roles played by the group member and indicate the specific behaviors that led to these judgments.

Group task roles: initiator-contributor, information seeker, opinion seeker, information giver, opinion giver, elaborator, coordinator, orienter, evaluator-critic, energizer, procedural technician, recorder

Group building and maintenance roles: encourager, harmonizer, compromiser, gatekeeper-expediter, standard setter or ego ideal, group observer and commentator, follower

Individual roles: aggressor, blocker, recognition seeker, self-confessor, playboy/playgirl, dominator, help seeker, special-interest pleader

Interaction process analysis: shows solidarity, shows tension release, shows agreement, shows disagreement, shows tension, shows antagonism, gives suggestions, gives opinions, gives information, asks for suggestions, asks for opinions, asks for information

GROUP PARTICIPATION

Is group-oriented	YES!	YES	yes	?	no	NO	NO!
Centers conflict on issues	YES!	YES	yes	?	no	NO	NO!
Is critically open-minded	YES!	YES	yes	?	no	NO	NO!
Ensures understanding	YES!	YES	yes	?	no	NO	NO!

IMPROVEMENT SUGGESTIONS

Do you have different leadership styles for your interpersonal relationships (friends, lovers, and family, for example) and your business relationships (acquaintances, colleagues, and supervisors, for example)? How would you characterize each style? What are the major strengths of each style? The major weaknesses?

Table 18.5. Although contemporary theorists favor the situational approach, the traits and the functional approach continue to have merit.

The Traits Approach

The **traits approach** merits consideration because it emphasizes that leaders must possess certain qualities if they are to function effectively. Some of the traits found to be associated with leadership are intelligence, dominance, honesty, foresight, altruism, popularity, sociability, cooperativeness, knowledge, and dependability (Hackman & Johnson 1991). The problem with the traits approach is that these qualities will vary with the situation, with the members, and with the culture in which the leader functions. Thus, for example, the leaders' knowledge or personality are generally significant factors. But, for some groups a knowledge of financial issues and a serious personality might be effective, whereas for other groups a knowledge of design and a good sense of humor might be effective.

The Functional Approach

The **functional approach** is significant because it helps identify what the leader should do in a given situation. Some of these functions have already been examined in the discussion of group membership in which group roles were identified (see Tables 18.1 and 18.2). Other functions found to be associated with leadership are setting group goals, giving the group member direction, and summarizing the group's progress (Schultz 1996). Additional functions are identified in the discussion, Functions of Leadership, later in this unit.

The Situational Approach

The **situational approach** deserves attention because it focuses on the two major tasks of the leader—accomplishing the task at hand and ensuring the satisfaction of the members—and because it recognizes that the leader's style must vary on the basis of the specific situation. Just as you adjust your interpersonal style in conversation or your motivational appeals in public speaking on the basis of the uniqueness of the situation, so you must adjust your leadership style.

Leaders must be concerned with getting the task accomplished (the task dimension) and with ensuring

TABLE 18.5
what is a leader?

Approach	Definition	Qualities Identified
Traits approach	A leader is one who possesses those characteristics (or traits) that contribute to leadership	Achievement, popularity, higher status, intelligence
Functional approach	A leader is one who behaves (or functions) as a leader	Serves task roles, ensures member satisfaction, energizes group members
Situational approach	A leader is one who balances task accomplishment and member satisfaction on the basis of the unique situation	Delegates, participates, sells, and tells, depending on the members and the situation

that members are satisfied (the people dimension). Leadership effectiveness, then, depends on combining the concerns for task and people according to the specifics of the situation—hence, the "situational theory of leadership." Some situations, for example, will call for high concentration on task issues but will need little in the way of people encouragement. For example, a group of AIDS researchers would probably need a leader who provides them with the needed information to accomplish their task. They would be self-motivating and would probably need little in the way of social and emotional encouragement. On the other hand, a group of recovering alcoholics might require leadership that stresses the social and emotional needs of the members.

The situational theory of leadership visualizes these two dimensions as in the diagram in the self-test, "What kind of Leader Are You?" (Hersey & Blanchard 1988), which you may wish to take at this point. It will help you visualize more specifically the task and people dimensions included in this theory.

Styles of Leadership

In addition to looking at the concerns of leadership for both task and function, as we did with the situational theory of leadership, we can also look at leadership in terms of its three major styles: laissez-faire, democratic, and authoritarian (Bennis & Nanus 1985; Hackman & Johnson 1991).

THINK ABOUT

Think about your own leadership style and the leadership styles of those you've worked with as you read these descriptions. Which of these styles are you likely to feel most comfortable using? Most comfortable working with as a group member?

Laissez-Faire Leader

As a **laissez-faire leader** you would take no initiative in directing or suggesting alternative courses of action. Rather, you would allow the group to develop and progress on its own, even allowing it to make its own mistakes. You would in effect give up or deny any real authority. As a laissez-faire leader you would answer questions or provide relevant information, but only when specifically asked. You would give little if any reinforcement to the group members. At the same time you would not punish members either. As a result you would be seen as nonthreatening. Generally this type of leadership results in a satisfied but inefficient group.

Democratic Leader

As a **democratic leader** you would provide direction but allow the group to develop and progress the way its members wish. You would encourage group members to determine their own goals and procedures. You would stimulate self-direction and self-actualization of the group members. Unlike the laissez-faire leader, a democratic leader would give members reinforcement and contribute suggestions for direction and alternative courses of action. Always, however, you would allow the group to make its own decisions. Generally, this form of leadership results in both satisfaction and efficiency.

Authoritarian Leader

As an **authoritarian leader** you would be the opposite of the laissez-faire leader. You would determine the group policies or makes decisions without consulting or securing agreement from the members. You would be impersonal and would encourage communication that goes to you and from you but not from member to member; you would seek to minimize intragroup communication. In this way, you would enhance your own importance and control (see Figure 18.1).

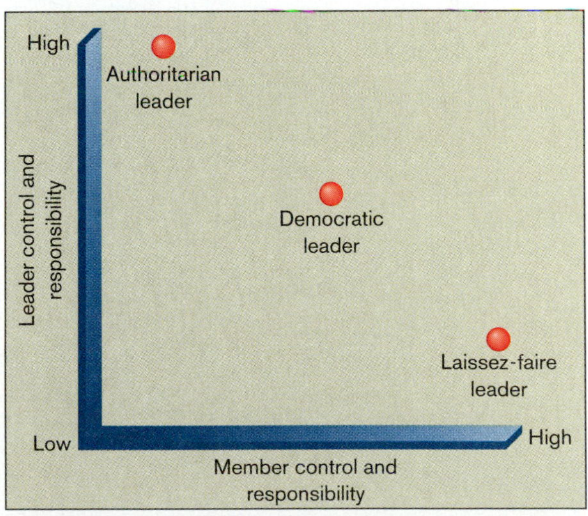

FIGURE 18.1 Leadership style and control. This figure visualizes the major differences among the three styles of leadership in terms of control. Note that the authoritarian leader takes greater control and great responsibility and gives little to the members. The laissez-faire leader, at the other extreme, assumes little personal control while members have much. The democratic leader is in the middle and takes some control and responsibility but also gives some to the membrs.

SELF-TEST

what kind of leader are you?

The following items describe aspects of group member behavior. Respond to each item according to the way you would be most likely to act if you were in a problem-solving group. Circle whether you would be likely to behave in the described way: always (A), frequently (F), occasionally (O), seldom (S), or never (N).

IF I WERE A MEMBER OF A PROBLEM-SOLVING GROUP:

A F O S N 1. I would be very likely to act as the spokesperson of the group.
A F O S N 2. I would encourage overtime work.
A F O S N 3. I would allow members complete freedom in their work.
A F O S N 4. I would encourage the use of uniform procedures.
A F O S N 5. I would permit the others to use their own judgment in solving problems.
A F O S N 6. I would stress being ahead of competitive groups.
A F O S N 7. I would speak as a representative of the group.
A F O S N 8. I would encourage members toward greater effort.
A F O S N 9. I would try out my ideas in the group.
A F O S N 10. I would let the others do their work the way they think best.
A F O S N 11. I would be working hard for personal recognition.
A F O S N 12. I would be able to tolerate postponement and uncertainty.
A F O S N 13. I would speak for the group when visitors were present.
A F O S N 14. I would keep the work moving at a rapid pace.
A F O S N 15. I would help to identify a task and let the others do it.
A F O S N 16. I would settle conflicts when they occur in the group.
A F O S N 17. I would be likely to get swamped by details.
A F O S N 18. I would represent the group at outside meetings.
A F O S N 19. I would be reluctant to allow the others freedom of action.
A F O S N 20. I would decide what should be done and how it should be done.
A F O S N 21. I would push for better results.
A F O S N 22. I would let other members have some authority.
A F O S N 23. Things would usually turn out as I predicted.
A F O S N 24. I would allow the others a high degree of initiative.
A F O S N 25. I would try to assign group members to particular tasks.
A F O S N 26. I would be willing to make changes.
A F O S N 27. I would ask the others to work harder.
A F O S N 28. I would trust the group members to exercise good judgment.
A F O S N 29. I would try to schedule work to be done.
A F O S N 30. I would refuse to explain my actions when questioned.
A F O S N 31. I would persuade others that my ideas are to their advantage.
A F O S N 32. I would permit the group to set its own pace.
A F O S N 33. I would urge the group to beat its previous record.
A F O S N 34. I would act without consulting the group.
A F O S N 35. I would ask that group members follow standard rules and regulations.

Thinking Critically About Leadership To compute your score follow these detailed but simple directions.

a. Circle the item letter for 1, 4, 7, 13, 16, 17, 18, 19, 20, 23, 29, 30, 31, 34, and 35.
b. Put an X in front of only those circled item numbers for items to which you responded S (seldom) or N (never).
c. Put an X in front of those items whose numbers were not circled only when you responded to such items with A (always) or F (frequently).
d. Circle any X that you have put in front of any of the following item numbers: 3, 5, 8, 10, 12, 15, 17, 19, 22, 24, 26, 28, 30, 32, and 34.
e. Count the circled Xs. This is your Person Orientation (P) Score.
f. Count the uncircled Xs. This is your Task Orientation (T) Score.

An individual's T and P scores are then plotted on the grid and are interpreted in terms of the descriptive elements given in the appropriate cell. To locate yourself on the grid below, find your score on the Person dimension (P) on the horizontal axis of the graph. Next, start up the column above your P score to the cell that corresponds to your Task score (T). Place an X in the cell that represents your two scores.

The horizontal axis is the people dimension. The farther you go to the right on this axis, the greater your concern for the members' social and emotional satisfaction (high P). The vertical axis is the task dimension. The more you move toward the top, the greater your concern for accomplishing the task (high T).

Leaders in the upper left area of the chart have little concern for people but great concern for accomplishing the task (high T, low P). Those in the lower left have little concern for either people or task (low T, low P). Those in the upper right have great concern for both task and people (high T, high P). Those in the lower right have little concern for task but high concern for people (low T, high P). Those in the middle has average concern for both task and people.

Does your score coincide with your image of your leadership focus? Can you identify specific people who would fit into each of the five major cells of this grid?

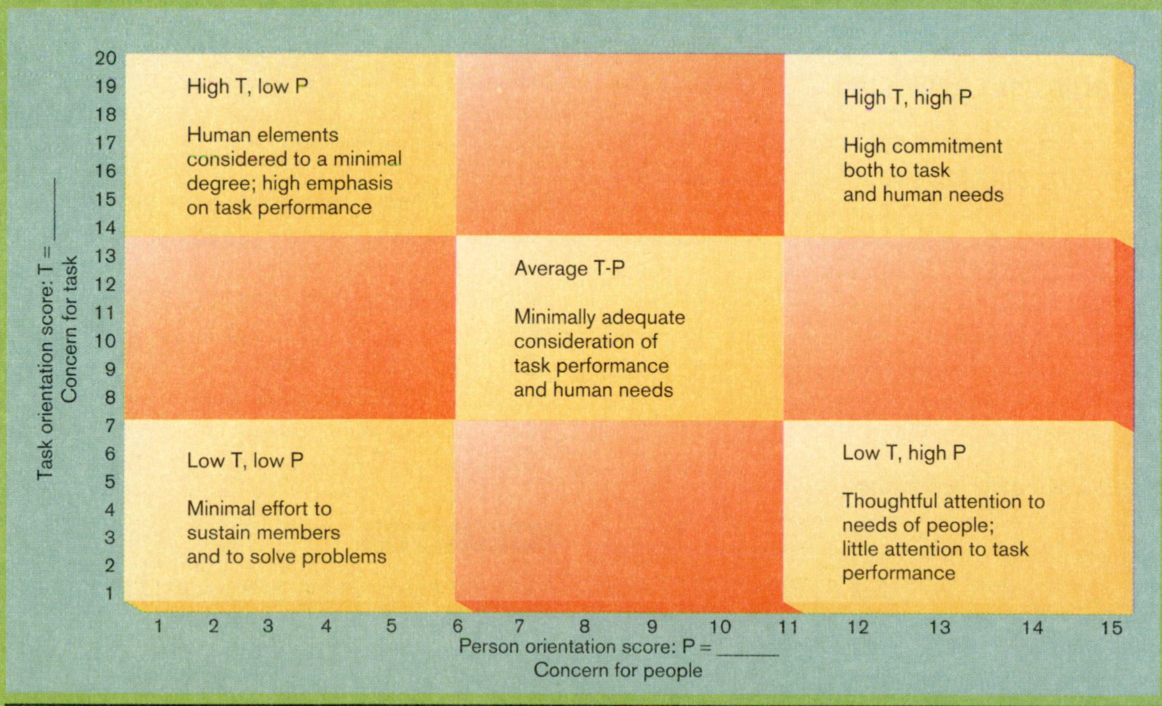

Source: Adapted from *A Handbook of Structured Experiences for Human Relations Training*, Vol. 1, by J. W. Pfeiffer & J. E. Jones (eds.). Copyright © 1974 by Pfeiffer & Company, San Diego, CA. Used with permission. The T. P. Leadership Questionnaire was adapted from Sergiovonni, Metzcus, and Burden's revision of the Leadership Behavior Description Questionnaire, T*he American Educational Research Journal 6,* pages 62–79.

As an authoritarian leader you assume the greatest responsibility for the progress of the group and would not want interference from members. You would be concerned with getting the group to accept your decisions rather than making its own decisions. You might satisfy the group's psychological needs. You would reward and punish the group much as a parent does. If the authoritarian leader is a competent one, the group members may be highly efficient but are likely to be less personally satisfied.

Each of these leadership styles has its place; one style should not be considered superior to the others. Each is appropriate for a different purpose and for a different situation. In a social group at a friend's house, any leadership other than laissez-faire would be difficult to tolerate; but, when speed and efficiency are paramount, authoritarian leadership may be more appropriate.

Authoritarian leadership may also be more appropriate when group members continue to show lack of motivation toward the task despite democratic efforts to move them. When all members are about equal in their knowledge of the topic or when the members are very concerned with their individual rights, the democratic leadership style seems more appropriate.

Functions of Leadership

With the situational view of leadership and the three general styles of leadership in mind, we can look at some of the major functions leaders serve. In relatively formal small group situations, as when politicians plan a strategy, advertisers discuss a campaign, or teachers consider educational methods, the leader has several specific functions. Keep in mind that these functions are not the exclusive property of the leader. Nevertheless, when there is a specific leader, he or she is expected to perform them.

Prediscussion Functions

It often falls to the leader to provide members with necessary materials prior to the meeting. It may involve, for example, arranging a convenient meeting time and place, informing members of the purposes and goals of the meeting, providing them with materials they should read or view, and recommending that they come to the meeting with, for example, general ideas or specific proposals.

Similarly, groups form gradually and need to be eased into meaningful discussion. Diverse members should not be expected to sit down and discuss a problem without becoming familiar with each other. Put more generally, the leader is responsible for any preparations and preliminaries necessary to ensure an orderly and productive group experience.

Activate the Group Agenda

Most groups have an agenda. An agenda is simply a list of the tasks the group wishes to complete. It is an itemized listing of that to which the group should devote its attention. At times, the agenda is prepared by the supervisor or consultant or CEO and is simply presented to the group. The group is then expected to follow the agenda item by item. At other times, the group will develop its own agenda, usually as its first or second order of business.

Generally, the more formal the group, the more important this agenda becomes. In informal groups, the agenda may simply be general ideas in the minds of the members (for example, review the class assignment and then make plans for the weekend). In formal business groups the agenda will be much more detailed and explicit. Some agendas specify not only the items that must be covered, but the order in which they should be covered, and even the amount of time that should be devoted to each item.

The agenda must be agreed upon by the group members. At times, the leader might initiate a brief discussion on the agenda and secure a commitment from all members to follow it.

Activate Group Interaction

Many groups need some prodding and stimulation to interact. Perhaps the group is newly formed and the members feel a bit uneasy with one another. As the group leader you would stimulate the members to interact. You would also serve this function when members act as individuals rather than as a group. In this case you would want to focus the members on their group task.

THINK ABOUT

Think about the types of cues you use to get members to do certain things. Do you think you would get greater power from emphasizing your ability to do a task (task cues) or from threats (dominance cues)? Consider the results from one interesting study (Driskell, Olmstead, & Salas 1993). In this study, task cues included, for example, maintaining eye contact, sitting at the head of the table, using a relatively rapid

MEDIA WATCH

AGENDA-SETTING THEORY

In much the same way that a small group has an agenda, so do the media. In fact, the media establish the agenda for viewers by focusing attention on certain people and events (McCombs & Shaw 1972). The media tell us—by virtue of what they cover—who is important and what events are significant. They tell us, in effect, that these are the people and the events to which we should give our attention.

Agenda-setting theory, as Agee, Ault, and Emery (1994) put it, refers to the "ability of the media to select and call to the public's attention both ideas and events." The media tell us what is and what is not important. The media "do not tell people 'what to think' but 'what to think about'" (Edelstein 1993). The things you think are important and the things you discuss are very probably the very things on which the media concentrate. In fact, it may be argued that nothing important can happen without media coverage. If the media don't cover it, then it isn't important. The question remains—Does the media concentrate on events because they are important, or does media concentration make them important?

Surely the media lead you to focus attention on certain subjects. Although there is clearly no one-to-one relationship between media attention and popular perception of importance (interpersonal factors are also operating), the media do probably set your agendas to some significant degree.

Recognize too that most media are controlled by persons of enormous wealth and power (network owners and executives, advertisers, or directors of multimillion-dollar corporations). These people want to retain and increase such wealth and power. What gets attention from the media and influences what the media present is dictated largely by this small but extremely influential group. The media exist to make profit for this group. Of course, there are public service media that do not focus on financial gain, but they too have agendas. All communicators have agendas, and the messages from any person or organization establish agendas for the receiver.

To what extent does the media establish your agenda? To what extent do you establish the media's agenda?

---

speech rate, speaking fluently, and gesturing appropriately. Dominance cues, included, for example, speaking in a loud and angry voice, pointing fingers, maintaining rigid posture, using forceful gestures, and lowering of the eyebrows. Which leader would you be more apt to follow? Results showed that most people will be more influenced by speakers using task cues. They will also see such speakers as more competent and more likable. Persons using dominance cues, on the other hand, are perceived as less competent, less influential, less likable, and more self-oriented. The implication, from at least this one study, is that if you wish to gain influence in a group (and be liked) use task cues and avoid dominance cues.

Maintain Effective Interaction

Even after the group is stimulated to group interaction, you would strive to see that members maintain effective interaction. When the discussion begins to drag, you would prod the group to effective interaction: "Do we have any additional comments on the proposal to eliminate required courses?" "What do those of you who are members of the college curriculum committee think about the English Department's proposal to restructure required courses?" "Does anyone want to make any additional comments on eliminating the minor area of concentration?" As the leader you would want to ensure that all members have an opportunity to express themselves.

Identify and Counteract Major Group Problems

Three major problems seem to get in the way of small group effectiveness (Patton, Giffin, & Patton 1989). Understanding these problems will help the leader see these as they arise but before they can become major obstacles.

Procedural problems include role conflicts (where members might compete for leadership positions or members are unclear as to their functions), problem analysis (where members short-circuit the process of analyzing the problem), and evaluating proposals (where members evaluate proposals without agreement on the criteria for judging proposals and solutions).

Process problems include too little cohesion (when members lack affiliation with each other and may leave the group) and too much cohesion (when members may ignore problems in the interest of maintaining group interpersonal relationships). Another process problem is the pressure to conform (when members seek to conform and may not voice legitimate differences of opinion and disagreements). Still another process problem centers on logic and occurs, for example, when members might misunderstand the nature of the problem or reject accurate information.

Personality problems involve members who are reticent to express themselves or disagreements that are taken personally.

Keep Members on Track

Many individuals are egocentric and will pursue only their own interests and concerns. As the leader it is your task to keep all members reasonably on track. You might accomplish this by asking questions, by interjecting internal summaries, or by providing transitions so that the relationship of an issue just discussed to one about to be considered is clear. If there is a formal agenda, it may assist you in serving this function.

Ensure Member Satisfaction

Members have different psychological needs and wants, and many people enter groups to satisfy these personal concerns. Even though a group may, for example, deal with political issues, the members may have come together for reasons that are more psychological than political. If a group is to be effective, it must meet not only the surface purposes of the group, but also the underlying or interpersonal purposes that motivated many of the members to come together in the first place.

Encourage Ongoing Evaluation and Improvement

Most groups encounter obstacles as they try to solve a problem, reach a decision, or generate ideas. Therefore, most could use some improvement. If the group is to improve, it must focus on itself. Along with trying to solve some external problem, it must try to solve its own internal problems as well, for example, personal conflicts, failure of members to meet on time, or members who come unprepared. As the leader, try to identify any such difficulties and encourage and help the group to analyze and resolve them.

Carry Out Postdiscussion Functions

Just as the leader is responsible for prediscussion functions, so is the leader responsible for postdiscussion functions. Such functions might include summarizing the group's discussion, organizing future meetings, or presenting the group's decisions to some other group. Again, the leader is responsible for whatever needs to be done to ensure that the group's experience proves to be a productive one.

Qualities of Leadership

In addition to the leader's functions, a mixture of task and people functions, an effective leader needs two major qualities: knowledge and communication competence.

Knowledge

The leader needs knowledge of both the substance of the discussion and the ways of effectively leading a group. The leader needs to understand the problem facing the group and be able to identify alternatives for viewing and solving the problem and to assess both the positive and the negative consequences of each alternative (Hirokawa 1985, 1988).

Communication Competence

The effective leader needs also to be an effective communicator as both listener and speaker. The qualities noted in the discussion of effective conversation (see Unit 13) are obvious qualities that an effective leader needs: mindfulness, flexibility, and cultural sensitivity plus the more specific skills of openness, empathy, positiveness, immediacy, interaction management, expressiveness, and other-orientation.

Some researchers have proposed that small groups have a natural tendency to take detours and divert their attention from the task at hand. As a result, they view the effective leader as one whose communications prevent the group from these natural but unproductive diversions (Gouran & Hirokawa 1986).

A useful summary of the general qualities of the effective leader is presented in Table 18.6 (Qubein 1986). These qualities, together with the functions already considered, should further clarify what makes an effective leader.

THINK ABOUT

Think about your own leadership style and manner as you read through this table and the bulleted list that follows. Are there qualities on these lists that you wish to strengthen? What can you say or do to communicate your possession of these qualities?

From a somewhat different perspective, consider these leadership qualities, paraphrased from Wes Roberts' *The Leadership Secrets of Attila the Hun* (1987).

- *Empathy*. Leaders must develop an appreciation for and an understanding of other cultures and the values of their members.
- *Courage*. Leaders should be fearless and have the courage to complete their assignments; they must not complain about obstacles nor be discouraged by adversity.
- *Accountability*. Leaders must hold themselves responsible for their own actions and for those of their members.
- *Dependability*. Leaders must be dependable in carrying out their responsibilities; leaders must also depend upon their members to accomplish matters they themselves cannot oversee.
- *Credibility*. Leaders must be believable to both friends and enemies; they must possess the integrity and intelligence needed to secure and communicate accurate information.
- *Stewardship*. Leaders must be caretakers of their members' interests and well-being; they must guide and reward subordinates.

In addition to these six, Roberts also identifies loyalty, desire, emotional stamina, physical stamina, decisiveness, anticipation, timing, competitiveness, self-confidence, responsibility, and tenacity. You might find it profitable to review these 11 additional qualities and explain how you think they can contribute to effective organizational leadership.

I use the Leadership Evaluation Form on page 330 in small group communication courses to evaluate the effectiveness of the group leader. As with the Group Member Evaluation Form on page 321, this leadership form should serve to summarize the wide variety of functions a group leader is expected to serve. Like that form, this leadership form is more appropriate to problem-solving groups than to others. How would a leadership evaluation form look for an idea-generation group leader? For a personal growth group leader?

MEMBERSHIP AND LEADERSHIP IN CULTURAL PERSPECTIVE

Most of the research and theory of small group communication, membership, and leadership has been conducted in universities in the United States and reflects American culture. For example, in the United States—and in individualistic cultures generally—the individual group member is extremely important. In collectivist cultures, the individual is less important; it is the group that is the significant entity. In Japan, for example, note group researchers Dolores and Robert Cathcart (1985, p. 191), "individual fulfillment of self is attained through finding and maintaining one's place within the group." In the United States, individ-

TABLE 18.6
qualities of the effective leader

An Effective Leader:	
Values people	Acknowledges the importance of and the contributions of others
Listens actively	Works hard at understanding the wants and concerns of others
Is tactful	Criticizes sparingly, constructively, and courteously
Gives credit	Praises others and their contributions publicly
Is consistent	Controls personal moods, treats others similarly, does not play favorites
Admits mistakes	Willingly admits errors
Has a sense of humor	Maintains a pleasant disposition and an approachable manner
Sets a good example	Does what others are expected to do

LEADERSHIP EVALUATION FORM

INTRODUCTORY REMARKS

Opens discussion	YES!	YES	yes	?	no	NO	NO!
Explains procedures	YES!	YES	yes	?	no	NO	NO!
Gets group going	YES!	YES	yes	?	no	NO	NO!

MAINTENANCE OF INTERACTION

Keeps members on schedule	YES!	YES	yes	?	no	NO	NO!
Keeps to agenda	YES!	YES	yes	?	no	NO	NO!

COMMUNICATION GUIDANCE

Encourages conflict resolution	YES!	YES	yes	?	no	NO	NO!
Ensures members understanding	YES!	YES	yes	?	no	NO	NO!
Involves all members	YES!	YES	yes	?	no	NO	NO!
Encourages expression of differences	YES!	YES	yes	?	no	NO	NO!
Uses transitions	YES!	YES	yes	?	no	NO	NO!

DEVELOPMENT OF EFFECTIVE INTERPERSONAL CLIMATE

Works for member satisfaction	YES!	YES	yes	?	no	NO	NO!
Builds open atmosphere	YES!	YES	yes	?	no	NO	NO!
Encourages supportiveness	YES!	YES	yes	?	no	NO	NO!

ONGOING EVALUATION AND IMPROVEMENT

Encourages process suggestions	YES!	YES	yes	?	no	NO	NO!
Accepts disagreements	YES!	YES	yes	?	no	NO	NO!
Directs group self-evaluation	YES!	YES	yes	?	no	NO	NO!
Encourages improvement	YES!	YES	yes	?	no	NO	NO!

CONCLUDING REMARKS

Summarizes	YES!	YES	yes	?	no	NO	NO!
[Involves audience]	YES!	YES	yes	?	no	NO	NO!
Closes discussion	YES!	YES	yes	?	no	NO	NO!

IMPROVEMENT SUGGESTIONS

ual fulfillment of self is attained by the individual and through his or her own efforts, not by the group.

It is often thought that because group membership and group identity are so important in collectivist cultures that it is the group that makes important decisions. Actually this does not seem to be the case. In fact, in a study of 48 Japanese organizations (highly collectivistic) participating in decision-making groups did not give the members decision-making power. Members are encouraged to contribute ideas but the decision-making power is reserved for the CEO and for managers higher up the organizational ladder (Brennan 1991).

In the discussion of member roles earlier in this unit, an entire category was devoted to individual roles, roles that individuals played to satisfy individual rather than group goals. In some cultures (notably collectivist cultures), these roles would probably not even be mentioned simply because they would not be acted out often enough to deserve such extended discussion. In many collectivist cultures, the group orientation is too pervasive for individuals to violate it by acting as the blocker, the recognition seeker, or the dominator, for example.

One obvious consequence of this difference can be seen when a group member commits a serious error, for example, when a team member submits the wrong advertising copy to the media. In a group governed by individualistic norms, that member is likely to be singled out, reprimanded, and perhaps fired. Further, the leader or supervisor, say, is likely to distance himself or herself from this member for fear that this error will rub off. In a more collectivist culture, this error is more likely to be seen as a group mistake. The individual is unlikely to be singled out—especially not in public—and the leader is likely to bear part of the blame. The same is true when one member comes up with a great idea. In individualistic cultures, that person is likely to be rewarded and only indirectly does this person's work group benefit. In a collectivistic culture, it is the group that is recognized and rewarded for the idea.

In a similar way, each culture maintains its own belief system which influences group members' behavior (Jandt 1995). For example, members of many Asian cultures, influenced by Confucian principles, believe that "the protruding nail gets pounded down" and are therefore not likely to voice disagreement with the majority of the group. Americans, on the other hand, influenced by the belief that "the squeaky wheel gets the grease," are more likely to voice disagreement or to act in ways different from other group members in order to get what they want.

Also, each culture has its own rules of preferred and expected leadership style (Victor 1992). In the United States the general and expected style for a group leader is democratic. Our political leaders are elected by a democratic process; similarly, CEOs are elected by the shareholders of a corporation. In other situations, of course, leaders are chosen by those in authority. The president of the company will normally decide who will supervise and who will be supervised. Even in this situation, however, we expect the supervisor to behave democratically—to listen to the ideas of the members, to take their views into consideration when decisions are to be made, to keep them informed of corporate developments, and to generally respect their interests. Also, we expect that leaders will be changed fairly regularly. We elect a president every four years and company elections are normally held each year.

In other cultures, leaders are chosen by right of birth. They are not elected, nor are they expected to behave democratically. Similarly, their tenure as leaders is usually extremely long and may in fact last their entire lives and then be passed on to their children. In other cases, leaders in a wide variety of situations may be chosen by a military dictator.

The important point to realize is that your membership and leadership styles are influenced by the culture in which you were raised. Consequently, when in a group with members of different cultures, consider the differences in both membership and leadership styles that individuals bring with them. For example, a member who plays individual roles may be tolerated in many groups in the United States and in some may even be thought amusing and different. That same member playing the same roles in a group with a more collectivist orientation is likely to be much more negatively evaluated. Multicultural groups may find it helpful to discuss the views they have of group membership and leadership and what constitutes comfortable interaction for them.

SUMMARY

In this unit we examined the role of members and leaders and the principles that govern effective group interaction.

1. A popular classification of small group member roles divides them into group task roles, group building and maintenance roles, and individual roles.
2. Twelve group task roles are: initiator-contributor, information seeker, opinion seeker, information giver, opinion giver, elaborator, coordinator, orienter, evaluator-critic, energizer, procedural technician, and recorder.
3. Seven group building and maintenance roles are: encourager, harmonizer, compromiser, gatekeeper-expediter, standard setter or ego ideal, group observer and commentator, and follower.
4. Eight individual roles are: aggressor, blocker, recognition seeker, self-confessor, playboy or playgirl, dominator, help seeker, and special-interest pleader.
5. Interaction process analysis categorizes contributions into four areas: social-emotional positive, social-emotional negative, attempted answers, and questions.
6. Member participation should be group-oriented, should center conflict on issues, should be critically open-minded, and should ensure understanding.
7. Groupthink is defined as a way of thinking that people use when agreement among members becomes so important that it overrides realistic and logical analysis.
8. In the traits approach, leaders are viewed in terms of traits or qualities, such as knowledge and sociability. People are often perceived and selected as leaders when they possiss these traits.
9. In the functional approach, leaders are viewed in terms of the functions they serve, such as setting goals and giving directions. People are often perceived as leaders when they perform these functions.
10. In the situational theory of leadership, leadership is seen as concerned with accomplishing the task and serving the interpersonal needs of the members. The degree to which either concern is emphasized should depend on the specific group, the unique situation.
11. Three major leadership styles are: laissez-faire, democratic, and authoritarian.
12. Among the leader's functions are: to activate the group interaction, maintain effective interaction, keep members on track, ensure member satisfaction, encourage ongoing evaluation and improvement, and prepare members for the discussion.
13. The effective leader values people, listens actively, is tactful, gives credit, is consistent, admits mistakes, has a sense of humor, and sets a good example.
14. The culture in which one is raised will greatly influence the ways in which members and leaders interact in small groups.

THINKING CRITICALLY ABOUT MEMBERS AND LEADERS IN SMALL GROUP COMMUNICATION

1. Can you identify roles that you habitually serve in certain groups (review Tables 18.1, 18.2, and 18.3 for some possibilities). Do you serve these roles in your friendship, love, and family relationships as well?

2. Do you see groupthink on campus? In your class discussions? In family discussions?
3. How would you characterize the leadership style of one of your local politicians, religious leaders, or college instructors? How would you analyze the leadership style of one of the popular talk show hosts? For example, how does Geraldo Rivera differ from Ricki Lake or Jenny Jones? How does Sally Jessy Raphael differ from Montel Williams or Richard Bey?
4. Would you find the Membership Evaluation Form presented here a useful guide for evaluating the contributions of group members? What changes might you make?
5. What approach to leadership do you find provides the greatest insight into what leadership is? Did the leadership test score confirm or contradict what you saw as your leadership style?
6. Would you find the Leadership Evaluation Form presented here a useful guide for evaluating leadership in a group meeting? How might you improve it?
7. What leadership style do you feel most comfortable exercising? Most comfortable working under?
8. What qualities of the effective leader do you possess? How might you go about strengthening these qualities?
9. How would you describe your own culture's perspective on the effective group member? The effective leader?
10. How would you go about finding answers to such questions as these:
    a. Does serving individual functions in a group make a member unpopular with other group members?
    b. Can leadership styles be used to describe approaches to teaching? To parenting? To managing?
    c. Do women and men respond similarly to the different leadership styles? Do women and men exercise the different leadership styles with equal facility?
    d. Are members of collectivistic cultures more likely to experience groupthink than are members of individualistic cultures?

nineteen unit

Organizational Communication

unit contents

unit goals

After completing this unit, you should be able to

1. define *organization* and *organizational communication*
2. describe the scientific, behavioral, systems, and cultural approaches to organizations
3. define and describe five communication network structures and describe the ways in which these structures influence communication
4. define *upward, downward, lateral,* and *grapevine communication* and *information overload,* and identify the major problems and effectiveness guidelines for dealing with each
5. define *sexual harassment* and explain the suggestions for avoiding such messages

In his landmark book, *The Functions of the Executive* (1938), Chester Barnard observed: "In an exhaustive theory of organization, communication would occupy a central place, because the structure, extensiveness, and scope of organizations are almost entirely determined by communication techniques." In this unit we explain this central position of communication in organizations, an area now called *organizational communication.* First, we define organizations and organizational communication. Second, we explore four approaches to organizations, looking specifically at the role communication plays in each. Third, we examine communication patterns (networks) and their influence on productivity and morale. Fourth, we consider the issue of communication flow: upward, downward, lateral, and grapevine communication, information overload, and finally sexual harassment.

ORGANIZATIONS AND ORGANIZATIONAL COMMUNICATION

To understand organizational communication, we need to define what an organization is and what characterizes the communication within organizations.

The Organization

An **organization** may be defined as a group of individuals brought together to achieve specific goals. The number of individuals varies greatly from one organization to another: some have three or four members working in close contact; others have thousands of workers scattered throughout the world. What is important is that these individuals operate within a defined structure.

The level of structure also varies greatly from one organization to another. In rigidly structured organizations, each person's role and position within the hierarchy is clearly defined. In more loosely structured organizations, roles may be interchanged, and hierarchical status may be unclear and relatively unimportant. Figure 19.1 depicts a representative organizational chart of a publishing company, which clearly shows the hierarchical structure of an organization and how the varied functions of the organization are related and coordinated. The organizational chart is a kind of road map for message travel; it visualizes the routes that messages—at least the formal ones—generally take. It also, of course, visualizes the power structure and identifies who is in charge of whom and where the decision-making power lies.

Within any organization, there are both formal and informal structures. For example, in a college there is the formal academic structure, with the president at the top, the provost at the next level, deans at the next, department chairpersons at the next, and faculty at the next. Through this structure the work of the university is accomplished; the president communicates to the provost who communicates to the deans, and so on. There are also informal structures throughout the university, and in many cases these cross hierarchical lines. These might include, for example, the four math professors who bowl together, the sociology instructor and the dean of arts who attend AA meetings together, and the graduate assistants and junior faculty members who study together. These informal structures serve the human needs of the individuals and keep the workers together as a unit.

The goal of most organizations is to make money. A variety of subordinate goals, however, must be achieved if this ultimate goal is to be reached. Thus, for example, in

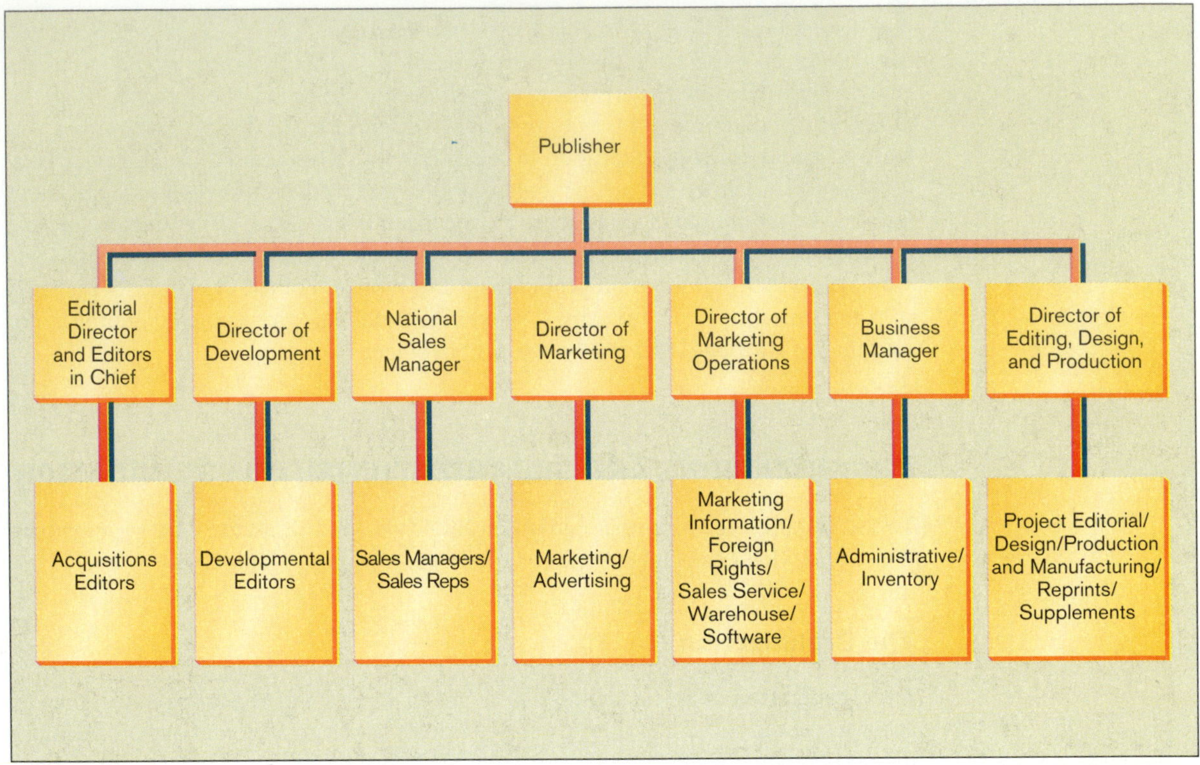

FIGURE 19.1 Hierachy of an organization. Organizations differ widely in the number of hierarchical levels they maintain. *Tall organizations* are those with many levels between the CEO and the trainee; *flat organizations* are those with few hierarchical levels. How would you describe the organization of your college? The U.S. government? The organization you work for?

order to make money, the organization must maintain an effective workforce. To do this, it is necessary to have satisfied workers. To have satisfied workers, it may be necessary to have adequate parking facilities, merit bonuses, clean and safe working conditions, and so on.

A nonprofit organization, on the other hand, would have as its ultimate goal something other than making money. For example, the goal may be to disseminate information, offer legal counsel to the poor, or defend animal rights. In these cases, the goal of obtaining funds would probably be a subordinate one, necessary to achieve if these other goals are to be realized.

Each worker in each organization will naturally have different goals. The ultimate goal for most people is make money. Like organizations, workers, too, have subordinate goals that are usually consistent with this general goal. Workers may therefore have such goals as to perform a job well, to get a promotion, to interact with others in pleasant surroundings, or to develop a network of friends.

The goals of the organization and the worker are often compatible. For example, performing a job well and thus earning a promotion is consistent with the organization's goal of increasing productivity and earning more money. Sometimes, however, these goals are incompatible. For example, workers may want raises, which means less profit for the organization. These goals of both the organization as a whole and the individual workers—and their frequent reconciliation—are achieved largely through the formal and informal communication that takes place within the organization.

Organizational Communication

Organizational communication refers to the messages sent and received within the organization's formal and informal groups. As the organization becomes larger and more complex, so do the communications. In a three-person organization, communication is relatively simple, but in an organization of thousands it becomes highly complex. Organizational communication includes such varied activities as giving directions, counseling workers, interviewing prospective employees, evaluating personnel, motivating people, analyzing problems, resolving conflicts, and establishing and monitoring work groups. Organizational communication relies upon the skills of interpersonal, small group, and public communication discussed throughout this text.

Organizational communication may be both formal and informal. The formal communications are those that are sanctioned by the organization itself and are organizationally oriented. They deal with the workings of the organization, with productivity, and with the various jobs done throughout the organization. Such communications are made through memos, policy statements, press releases, and employee newsletters. The informal communications are socially sanctioned. They are oriented not to the organization itself, but to the individual members and might include birthday celebrations and discussion of family problems as well as feelings about the organization and the job and plans for the future.

Although we have defined organizational communication as occurring within the organization, organizations also spend considerable time, energy, and money on securing information from outside and on disseminating information to other organizations and to the general public. Although these outgoing messages are organizationally motivated, they are probably best treated as examples of public, mass, or even interpersonal communication, depending on the situation.

APPROACHES TO ORGANIZATIONS

We can approach organizations from at least four perspectives: the scientific management or classical approach, the behavioral or human relations approach, the systems approach, and the cultural approach (Goldhaber 1990).

The Scientific Approach

The **scientific approach** holds that organizations should make use of scientific methods to increase productivity. Scientifically controlled studies help management identify the ways and means for increasing productivity, and ultimately, profit.

In this approach productivity is viewed in terms of the physical demands of the job and the physiological capabilities of the workers. Time-and-motion studies are perhaps the most characteristic type of research. These studies are designed to enable the organization to reduce the time it takes to complete a specific task—to cut down the motion and best fit the person to the task. Frederick Taylor (1911), to whom the scientific management approach owes much of its development and from which industrial engineering grew, conducted time-and-motion studies of coal shoveling. He analyzed and compared different sizes of shovels and the various tasks to be accomplished. As a result, he was able to reduce the number of workers needed to do the same work from between 400 and 600 to 140.

In this approach, communication is viewed as the giving of orders and the planning of procedures and operations. Only the formal structure of the organization and the formal communication system are recognized.

Today the scientific management approach is held in disfavor, largely because it emphasizes productivity over the needs of the workers and also because it was an approach better suited to manufacturing than to present information technologies. As one management expert puts it: "The acquisition, storage, handling, and retrieval of information has become the main industry in the United States, with well over 65 percent of the workforce employed in information-related jobs" (Montana 1991, p. 113).

The Behavioral Approach

The **behavioral approach** (also referred to as the humanistic, organic, or human relations approach) **to organizations** was developed as a reaction against the exclusive concern with physical factors in measuring organizational success. One of the principal assumptions of this approach is that increases in worker satisfaction lead to increases in productivity: a happy worker is a productive worker. Management's function, therefore, is to keep the workers happy.

Because leaders establish the norms that group members follow, control of leadership is considered one of the best ways to increase satisfaction and production. Management tries to influence the leaders, who then influence the workers to be happy and hence productive. The behavioral approach strongly favors the democratic leader. This leader encourages members to participate in the running of the organization by offering suggestions, giving feedback, and sharing their problems and complaints. What is desired is "participatory management" (Likert 1961), in which all members of the organization are to participate in the decisions that ultimately affect them. Communication is one of the main tools in this endeavor.

Another reason for the importance of communication was advanced by Chester Barnard's (1938) "acceptance theory of authority"—a principle that held that workers will perform effectively and accept management's directives if they feel these are acceptable to their personal needs and goals. Hence, a prime task of management was to communicate this acceptability to its workers, to persuade them to see that the company's goals would advance their personal goals. The behavioral approach acknowledges the importance of the social, informal groups within the organization and gives special consideration to the interpersonal communications within the subgroups of these organizations.

But even in this seemingly best of all possible worlds, in which the communication is free and the leadership democratic, the human relations school encountered difficulties. The major problem was that the approach was based on an invalid assumption—namely, that satisfaction and productivity were positively related. They are in some cases, but certainly not in all. As you know from your own courses, there are some classes in which you are very productive, learn a great deal, and do well, but that you simply do not enjoy; and there are others you enjoy, but from which you gain little. Another problem with the human relations approach is that it gives too much attention to agreement. It fails to recognize the very important contribution played by conflict and competition. Some authorities go so far as to claim that there is no relationship between productivity and satisfaction (Strauss & Sayles 1980).

At this point you may wish to take the self-test, "X or Y? What Kind of Manager Are You?" It will provide an additional perspective on some of the issues just discussed.

The Systems Approach

The **systems approach to organizations** combines the best elements of the scientific and behavioral approaches. It views an organization as a system in which all parts interact and in which each part influences every other part. This view is the same view we take of communication (see Unit 1). The organization is viewed as an open system—open to new information, responsive to the environment, dynamic and ever changing.

The systems approach argues that both the physical and physiological factors of the scientific management approach and the social and psychological factors of the behavioral approach are important. Each influences the others. All must be taken into consideration if a fully functioning organization is to be achieved.

In this approach, communication keeps the system vital and alive. If a system is to survive, its parts to be coordinated, and its activities synchronized, communication is essential. Communication relates the various parts to each other and brings in the new ideas.

The Cultural Approach

The **cultural approach to organizations** holds that a corporation should be viewed as a society or a culture (Pilotta, Widman, & Jasko 1988; Putnam & Pacanowsky 1983; Zamanov & Glaser 1994). Much as a social group or culture has rules of behaviors rituals, heroes, and values, for example, so does an organization. In this approach, then, an organization is studied to identify the type of culture it is and its specific norms or values. The aim of such an analysis is to enable you to understand the ways the organization functions and how it influences and is influenced by the members (workers) of that organizational culture.

You can make educated guesses about what makes a successful corporation by examining those qualities that make for a successful social group or society. For example, heroes are important to a social group and successful corporations can sometimes create their own. If an organization can create a hero—perhaps like Thomas Edison to General Electric, Henry Ford to Ford Motor Company, and Lee Iacocca to Chrysler—it may succeed in developing a dominant culture (or corporation).

The cultural perspective views both the organization and the workers as having a similar set of values and goals. Much like citizens of a country, workers contribute to the growth and prosperity of the organi-

SELF-TEST

x or y? what kind of manager are you?

Respond to each of the following statements with T (true) if you believe the statement is generally or usually true and F (false) if you believe the statement is generally or usually false.

The average worker:

_______ 1. will avoid work if possible.
_______ 2. will accept and even seek responsibility.
_______ 3. must be persuaded, even motivated by fear, to do work.
_______ 4. feels that physical and mental effort exerted in work is as natural as play.
_______ 5. has little real ambition.
_______ 6. will direct herself or himself to achieve objectives she or he accepts.
_______ 7. wants to be directed as a way of avoiding responsibility.
_______ 8. is creative and imaginative.
_______ 9. dislikes work.
_______10. is capable (and willing) to learn new tasks.

Thinking Critically About Management Styles. These statements refer to the theories labeled theory X and theory Y by Douglas McGregor (1960). Theory X holds that the worker is unmotivated and really does not want to work; theory Y holds that the worker is motivated and responsible and is represented by the behavioral or humanistic view of management. The odd-numbered statements (1, 3, 5, 7, 9) all refer to a belief in theory X and the even-numbered statements (2, 4, 6, 8, 10) to a belief in theory Y. To which statements did you give more true responses? If to odd-numbered statements, then you have a strong belief in theory X; if to even-numbered statements, then you have a strong belief in theory Y.

There is also a theory Z, identified most clearly by William Ouchi (1981), which characterizes a Japanese management style. Some of the major features of theory Z is a focus on the entire organization rather than on just one's own department, group rather than individual decision making and responsibility, and the expansion of career opportunities (rather than specialization) within the organization.

With which style of management would you be most comfortable as a worker? As a manager?

zation. Workers also, however, reap the benefits of this growth and prosperity. Worker morale and productivity, therefore, go hand in hand. They are not separate and isolated goals but integrally related ones.

In this view, communication is not simply messages that are sent from one member to another through one or more channels (as conceived in some network analyses). Rather, communication is seen as integral to the very definition of an organization. Communication, in fact, defines and constructs the organization, its divisions, and its functions. The organization is not something apart from its workers and its communications. Rather, the organization is created and takes its form from its workers and their communication interactions.

The characteristics of an effective organizational culture include, for example, teamwork, pride in work and in accomplishment, commitment to high standards and to the organization, honesty, and a willingness to change in order to grow despite difficulties from competition or regulations (Uris 1986).

In one of the most popular books on the topic of organizations, *In Search of Excellence: Lessons from America's Best-Run Companies,* Thomas Peters and Robert Waterman (1982) make great use of this view of corporations as cultures—though they use other approaches and perspectives as well—and propose that excellent corporations are characterized by eight qualities. A review of these qualities should effectively round out the discussion of approaches to organizations. In reviewing these qualities, you will see the organizational approach that each derives from or supports and the pivotal role of communications.

THINK ABOUT

Think about the organizations with which you are familiar as you read through this list. Do they possess these qualities? Excellent companies, according to Peters and Waterman (1982) do the following:

1. They have a bias for action. These companies prefer action to lengthy surveys, reports, and committee meetings.
2. They stay close to the customer. These companies listen to their customers and try to provide the quality and service that customers want.
3. They encourage leaders who are autonomous and entrepreneurial. These companies encourage practical risk taking and creativity in their workers.
4. They achieve productivity through people. These companies regard the rank-and-file members as the major source of productivity; sharp divisions between management and labor are discouraged.
5. They encourage hands-on management. In these companies management knows what is going on because management stays close to the main operations of the company, for example, visiting the stores and inspecting the plants.
6. They stick to what they know. These companies know the business the company is in and do not attempt to involve themselves in operations about which they are not expert.
7. They have simple organizational structures and are lean at the top. These companies are structured very simply, without a complicated organizational structure to create problems, and with a relatively small staff at the top of the hierarchy.
8. They are both decentralized (loose) and centralized (tight). These companies are generally decentralized in that the workers are relatively autonomous but highly centralized in terms of their goals and their values.

COMMUNICATION NETWORKS

Because of their rigidly structured hierarchies, the large physical distances between people, the great differences in competence, and the specialized tasks that must be accomplished, organizations have evolved a number of different **communication networks** (Baird 1977; Kreps 1990). A network refers to the channels through which messages pass from one person to another. Five major networks are examined briefly here, first in terms of structure and second in terms of their actual operation within an organization. These networks are among the most commonly used organizational communication patterns.

The Network Structures

The five network structures are presented in Figure 19.2. Each diagram shows five individuals, although each network may include any number of people. The arrows indicate the direction in which the messages travel.

The *circle* has no leader. There is total equality. All members of the circle have exactly the same authority or power to influence the group. Each member may communicate with the two members on either side.

The *wheel* has a clear leader (central position). This person is the only one who can send and receive messages to all members. Therefore, if one member wishes to communicate with another member, the message must go through the leader.

The Y pattern is less centralized than the wheel but more centralized than some of the other patterns. In the Y there is also a clear leader (the third person from the bottom in Figure 18.2), but one other member plays a type of secondary leadership role (the second person from the bottom). This member can send and receive messages from two others. The remaining three members are restricted to communicating with only one other person.

The *chain* is similar to the circle except that the members on the ends may communicate with only one person each. There is some centrality here. The middle position is more leaderlike than any of the other positions.

The *all-channel* or *star* pattern is similar to the circle in that all members are equal and all have exactly the same amount of power to influence others. In the all-channel, however, each member may communicate with any other member. This pattern allows for the greatest member participation.

Network Productivity and Morale

No network is good or bad in or of itself. They are all better viewed as useful or useless for specific tasks.

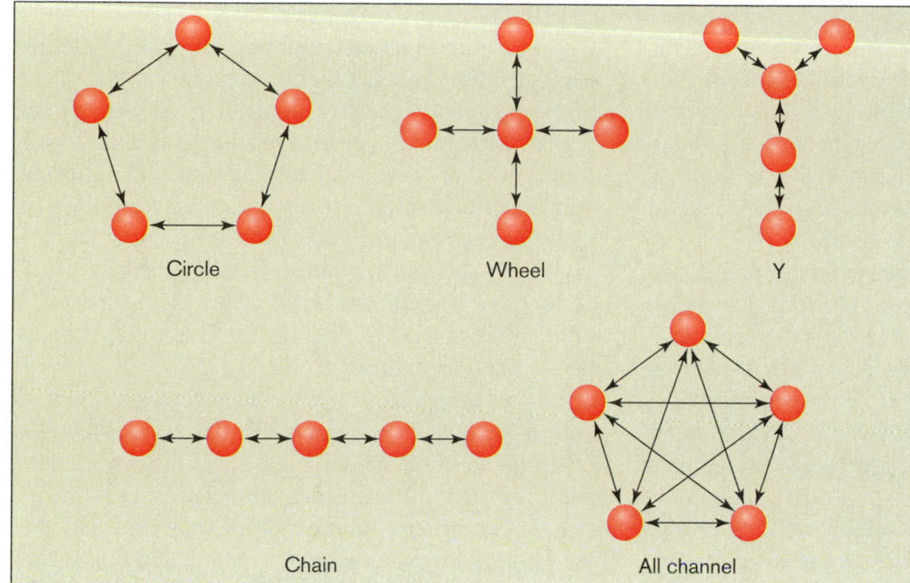

FIGURE 19.2 Five network structures. These networks are defined and sustained by the exchange of messages. Such messages may be transmitted face-to-face, by telephone or by e-mail, or written in informal memos or in formal reports. Groups may also communicate in a teleconference, wherein several members are simultaneously connected by telephone or computer, or in a video teleconference, wherein each member can both see and hear the other members although they may be in separate offices, buildings, or cities.

For example, the highly centralized patterns—the wheel and the Y—are most efficient for dealing with relatively simple and repetitive tasks, such as those in which information must be collected in one place and disseminated to others. Information overload, to be discussed later, is most likely to occur in the highly centralized groups, since all information is coming to one person. These central individuals often become gatekeepers and prevent information from getting to the various members. Sometimes this may be due simply to information overload. At other times the leader may decide not to pass information along to the group.

Those in the central positions seem to have relatively high morale. They do a lot of work, have the most power, and are the most satisfied. The others in these centralized groups, however, develop low morale since they do little and have little or no influence on the group. Members of an all-channel group, in contrast, usually have high morale.

How does your college culture view productivity versus morale? How does your family culture view these concepts? Are you comfortable with these relative emphases, or would you like them to be different?

All highly centralized groups depend on the effectiveness of the person in the central position. If that person is an effective leader-communicator, the success of the group as a whole is almost ensured. Conversely, if that person is ineffective, the entire group will suffer. In the all-channel pattern, however, the effectiveness or ineffectiveness of any one individual will not make or break the group.

Even the relationship between morale and participation or power may be oversimplified. For example, although morale is high when participation is high, as in the all-channel group, this group is inefficient in dealing with relatively simple and repetitive tasks. This inefficiency may well lead to a decline in morale, since few people want to be associated with an inefficient organization.

Some groups seem to adapt well to change, whereas others do not. Groups in the wheel pattern, for example, have difficulty adapting to changing tasks and changing conditions. But in the circle, where everyone is equal, the group adapts well. It accepts new ideas readily.

COMMUNICATION FLOW IN ORGANIZATIONS

It is useful to discuss communication in organizations in terms of the direction in which it flows. Upward and downward (also called vertical) communication and lateral communication are the formal channels, those that can be found in an organizational chart, for example, and which are officially sanctioned by the organization. In addition, we also need to look at the grapevine—the informal channel that no organization seems to be without, information overload, a problem that is becoming more and more prevalent, and sexual harassment, a form of communication that is not limited to the organizational setting but certainly is most relevant within this organizational context.

In most organizations, management controls the communication system. The managers have the time, the expertise, and the facilities to improve the communication that takes places in an organization, therefore it seems logical to assign the responsibility for an effective communication system to them. This is not to say that the workers are absolved of their responsibility; effective communication is a two-way process. Nevertheless, management bears the larger responsibility for establishing and maintaining an effective and efficient internal communication system.

Do realize, as with all issues raised in this text, that the culture you are communicating in will influence the effectiveness of your communications; messages that prove effective in the United States may prove ineffective in Japan or Saudi Arabia or South Africa. Further, your own native culture will influence your communications in organizations regardless of where the communications take place (Jang & Barnett 1994). For example, Japanese businesspersons, operating in the United States, still reflect the perspectives of their native culture. And the same seems true of all persons and all cultures.

Effective organizational communication, then—and in fact effective communication of any kind—is based on an understanding not only of the other person's culture but of your own and especially how this culture (its beliefs, values, norms, and expectations, for example) influences your communication behavior (Knodt 1994). So, as you read about these forms of organizational communication, keep the influence of culture in mind. Ask yourself how these forms of communication and our suggestions for greater effectiveness might have to be modified in light of the specific culture.

Another factor that influences communication in an organization—as it does with communication in other forms—is communication apprehension. So, before looking at communication flow in organizations, consider your communication apprehension by taking the self-test, "How Apprehensive Are You in Meetings?" on page 344.

Upward Communication

Upward communication refers to messages sent from the lower levels of the hierarchy to the upper levels—for example, line worker to manager, faculty member to dean. This type of communication is usually concerned with (1) job-related activities—that is, what is going on at the job, what was accomplished, what remains to be done, and similar issues; (2) job-related problems and unresolved questions; (3) ideas for change and suggestions for improvement; and (4) job-related feelings about the organization, about the work, about other workers, and similar issues.

Upward communication is vital to the maintenance and growth of the organization. It gives management the necessary feedback on worker morale and possible sources of dissatisfaction; it gives subordinates a sense of belonging to and being a part of the

MEDIA WATCH

THE KNOWLEDGE GAP

The **knowledge gap** refers to the difference in knowledge between one group and another and is particularly interesting to examine in the context of a discussion of organizational communication. There is often a major division between those who have a great deal of knowledge and those who have significantly less. In mass communication (for which the theory was developed), the knowledge gap hypothesis refers to the influence of the media in widening this knowledge gap (Tichenor, Donohue, & Olien 1970; Severin & Tankard 1988, Viswanath & Finnegan 1995).

Information is, of course, valuable. It brings wealth and gives power. It even gives you the means you need to live a healthy life (Viswanath et al. 1993). More generally, information enables you to do more things more effectively.

Information is expensive, however, and not everyone has equal access to it. This is especially true as we live more of our lives in cyberspace. The new communication technologies—computers, CD ROMs, the Internet, satellite and cable television, for example—are major ways for gaining information and in the very near future will be the primary means. But, these technologies are expensive and require skills that uneducated people do not have. (In fact, it may be argued that our society as a whole is increasingly coming to define *educated* as the ability to use the technologies of communication.) Thus, the better educated have the skills and the money to own and master the new technologies and thus grow in information. The less educated do not have the skills or the money to own and master the new technologies and thus cannot grow in information. For example, in a 1995 survey 53 percent of children in families with incomes under $20,000 had access to computers in elementary and high school but 68 percent of those in families with incomes over $75,000 had this access. This difference of 15 percent is small when we compare it with at-home computer access. Only 15 percent of the children in families with incomes under $20,000 had a computer in the home. But 74 percent of those children in families with incomes over $75,000 had home computers. Commenting on these statistics, *Newsweek* (February 27, 1995, p. 50) notes: "The United States is dividing into two societies—one that's comfortable with PCs, the other that doesn't have access." The magazine estimates that "techno-savvy kids" are likely to earn 10 to 15 percent more than those without this technological background.

The knowledge gap hypothesis may be applied to other cultures as well. Developed countries, for example, have the new technologies in their schools and offices and many individuals can afford to buy their own computers and satellite systems. Access to the new technologies help these countries develop further. Undeveloped countries, with little or no access to such technologies, cannot experience the same gain in knowledge and information as those with technological access.

Even the language of a culture may influence the extent of the knowledge gap. For example, English dominates the Internet and it will therefore be more easily accessible to people in the United States and other English-speaking countries. As well, the Internet will be accessible to the educated in non-English-speaking countries many of whom learn English as a second language. As one South Korean computer user put it, "It's not only English you have to understand but American culture, even slang. All in all, there are many people who just give up" (Pollack 1995, p. D4).

The knowledge gap can also be applied to organizations. As you go up in the hierarchy, organizational members have more knowledge generally and more knowledge that is specific to the organization. Some organizations actively try to reduce the knowledge gap by offering training courses and making company information freely available. Other organizations do little to reduce the gap and may actually encourage it by making it difficult for workers to attend classes or to find out information about the company. In fact, it might be argued that the likelihood of your moving up in an organization is inversely related to the size of the knowledge gap between you and those on higher hierarchical levels. As you narrow the gap you increase your chances for advancement in the organization.

SELF-TEST

how apprehensive are you in meetings?

Just as you have apprehension in interpersonal interactions (see Unit 14), in group discussions (Unit 16), and public speaking (see Unit 19), you have some degree of apprehension in meetings. This brief test is designed to measure your apprehension in this small group situation.

This questionnaire consists of six statements concerning your feelings about communication in meetings. Please indicate in the space provided the degree to which each statement applies to you by marking whether you (1) Strongly Agree, (2) Agree, (3) Are Undecided, (4) Disagree, or (5) Strongly Disagree. There are no right or wrong answers. Some of the statements are similar to other statements. Do not be concerned about this. Work quickly; just record your first impression.

______ 1. Generally, I am nervous when I have to participate in a meeting.
______ 2. Usually, I am calm and relaxed while participating in meetings.
______ 3. I am very calm and relaxed when I am called upon to express an opinion at a meeting.
______ 4. I am afraid to express myself at meetings.
______ 5. Communicating at meetings usually makes me uncomfortable.
______ 6. I am very relaxed when answering questions at a meeting.

Thinking Critically About Apprehension in Meetings To obtain your apprehension for meetings score, use the following formula:

18 plus scores for items 2, 3, and 6
minus scores for items 1, 4, and 5

Scores above 18 show some degree of apprehension. As you read this unit, consider the reasons for your apprehension and especially try to identify the specific communication situations in which you would be most apprehensive. What features do these situations have in common? Can you identify the communication skills that would enable you to reduce the apprehension?

Source: From James C. McCroskey, *An Introduction to Rhetorical Communication*, 6th ed. (Upper Saddle River, NJ: Prentice-Hall, 1993).

organization; and it provides management with the opportunity to acquire new ideas from workers.

Problems with Upward Communication

Despite its importance to the organization, upward communication is difficult to handle. One problem is that messages that travel up the ladder are often messages that higher-ups want to hear. Workers are often reluctant to send up a negative message for fear that they will be viewed as troublemakers.

Often the messages that do get sent up, especially those concerning worker dissatisfaction, are not heard or responded to by management because of its preoccupation with productivity. When these messages are ignored, workers feel there is no point to sending them. Dissatisfactions then fester and become major problems.

Sometimes the messages never get through. Gatekeepers (those who regulate the messages that get through) may be so rigid that certain types of messages are automatically rerouted. When the issues concern clarification of job assignments, many workers prefer to go to other workers rather than to management for fear that they will be thought incompetent. Students often do the same thing. Rather than ask the teacher to clarify something, they ask other students, who probably do not understand any better.

Still another problem is that management, preoccupied with sending messages down the ladder, may have lost some capacity for receiving messages. Managers are so used to serving as sources for messages that they become poor listeners. Workers easily sense this and, quite logically, don't waste their time on upward communication.

One further barrier is the purely physical one. Management is often physically separated from the workers. Usually management offices are on separate floors of the building; not infrequently, they are in other cities. It becomes difficult in such situations to go to management with a work-related problem that needs immediate attention.

Guidelines for Upward Communication

Important guidelines for improving upward communication can be easily derived from an analysis of the problems already identified. Here are the major ones:

- Some nonthreatening system for upward communication should be established. Many organizations, for example, have suggestion boxes in which workers can submit their opinions and complaints anonymously. Another system is to seek out and reward workers' comments actively and to respond to these comments to show that they are received and are considered.
- Management must be open to hearing worker comments and must eliminate unnecessary gatekeepers that prevent important messages from traveling up the organizational hierarchy. Like most people, managers think they communicate more often and with greater recognition than their subordinates think (Callan 1993).
- Management must listen; management must receive, understand, remember, evaluate, and respond to worker messages.
- Convenient channels must be established for workers to communicate to management. It is especially important to design these channels with the cultural attitudes and beliefs of the members of the organization clearly in mind. For example, asking for suggestions in a public forum from Asian workers would probably prove ineffective, since Asians generally prefer not to offer any form of criticism in public.

Downward Communication

Downward communication refers to messages sent from the higher levels of the hierarchy to the lower levels. For example, messages sent by managers to workers, or from deans to faculty members are examples of downward communication. Orders are the most obvious example of downward communication: "Type this in duplicate," "Send these crates out by noon," "Write the advertisement copy," and so on. Along with these order-giving messages are the accompanying explanations of procedures, goals, and the like. Managers are also responsible for giving appraisals of workers and for motivating them, all in the name of productivity and for the good of the organization as a whole. It's interesting to note that subordinates who were more satisfied with their job reported better quality communication with their superiors (Callan 1993).

Problems with Downward Communication

Management and labor often speak different languages. Many managers simply do not know how to make their messages understandable to workers. Most managers, for example, have more education and a greater command of the technical language of the business than their workers do. Another problem is that many managers do not distinguish between information that workers need and do not need. Providing too little information will prevent the worker from functioning effectively. Providing too much information will bog the worker down and contribute to information overload.

Guidelines for Downward Communication

Downward communication can be made more effective by heeding the following suggestions:

- Management needs to use a vocabulary known to the workers. Technical jargon, for example, must be kept to a minimum. At the same time, many workers throughout the industrialized world are not native speakers of the managers' language and this needs to be taken into consideration.
- Provide workers with sufficient information for them to function effectively. At the same time, avoid contributing to information overload.

When communications are negative, management needs to be especially careful not to violate deeply held cultural beliefs in making this criticism. For example, members of some cultures (participants and bystanders) will be greatly offended by even mild criticism being given in public. Face-saving is so important that management risks offending an entire workforce with the public criticism of one worker.

Lateral Communication

Lateral communication refers to messages between equals—manager to manager, worker to worker. Such

POWER LISTENING

In much the same way that you can communicate power and authority with words and nonverbal expression (see Units 8 and 17), you also communicate power through listening, a topic with obvious relevance to the organizational setting. After all, throughout your listening, you are communicating messages to others and these messages comment in some way on your power. The ways in which power is communicated through listening can be seen in looking at powerful and powerless listeners.

Powerful listeners listen actively; they focus and concentrate (with no real effort) on what is being said. Powerless listeners, on the other hand, listen passively; they appear to be thinking about something else and only pretend to be listening.

Powerful listeners respond visibly but in moderation; an occasional nod of agreement or a facial expression that says "that's interesting" are usually sufficient. Responding with too little or too much reaction is likely to be perceived as powerlessness. Too little response says you aren't listening and too much response says you aren't listening critically. Powerful listeners also use backchanneling cues—head nods and brief oral responses that say "I'm listening," "I'm following you"—when appropriate. When no backchanneling cues are given, the speaker comes to wonder if the other person is really listening.

Powerful listeners generally maintain more focused eye contact than do those perceived to have less power. In conversation, normal eye contact is intermittent—you glance at the speaker's face, then away, then back again, and so on. In a small group or public speaking situation, eye contact with the speaker is normally greater.

Adaptors—playing with one's hair or a pencil or drawing pictures on a styrofoam cup—give the appearance of discomfort and thus adaptors communicate a lack of power. These body movements show the listener to be more concerned with himself or herself than with the speaker. The lack of adaptors, on the other hand, make the listener appear in control of the situation and comfortable in the role of listener.

Powerful listeners are more likely to maintain an open posture. When around a table or in an audience they resist covering their stomach or face with their hands. Persons who maintain a defensive posture with, for example, arms crossed around their stomach, may communicate a feeling of vulnerability and hence powerlessness.

Powerful listeners avoid interrupting the speaker in conversations or in small group situations. The reason is simple: not interrupting is one of the rules of business communication that powerful people follow and powerless people don't. Completing the speaker's thought (or what the listener thinks is the speaker's thought) has a similar powerless effect.

Powerful listeners take modest notes when appropriate in small group or public speaking situations. Taking too many notes may communicate a lack of ability to distinguish between what is and what is not important. Taking too few notes may communicate a lack of interest or unwillingness to deal with the material.

Powerful listeners also signal power through visual dominance behavior (Exline, Ellyson, & Long 1975). For example, the average speaker maintains a high level of eye contact while listening and a lower level while speaking. When powerful individuals want to signal dominance, they may reverse this pattern. They may, for example, maintain a high level of eye contact while talking but a much lower level while listening.

messages may move within the same subdivision or department of the organization or across divisions. Lateral communication refers to the communication that takes place between two history professors at Arizona State University. It also refers to communication between the psychologist at the University of Akron and the communicologist at Kent State.

Lateral communication facilitates the sharing of insights, methods, and problems. It helps the organization to avoid some problems and to solve others.

Lateral communication also builds morale and worker satisfaction. Good relationships and meaningful communication between workers are among the main sources of worker satisfaction. More generally, lateral communication serves to coordinate the various activities of the organization and enable the various divisions to pool insights and expertise.

Problems with Lateral Communication

One obvious problem with lateral communication is the specialized languages that divisions of an organization may develop. Such languages are often unintelligible to receivers. To communicate with the psychologist, for example, it is essential to speak the language of psychology—to know the meaning of such terms as *reinforcement schedules, egoism, catharsis, STM,* and *free association.* Not everyone does. And as knowledge becomes increasingly specialized, it becomes increasingly difficult for the behavioral psychologist to understand the clinical psychologist and, even within clinical psychology, for the Freudian to understand the Jungian.

Another problem is the tendency of workers in a specialized organization to view their area as the one that is most important to the health and success of the company. This is often the case within a university. Each faculty member sees her or his department as the most important for the education of the student. This attitude prevents them from seeing the value in the work of others and often precludes a meaningful exchange of ideas.

Another barrier is the competitiveness that exists in many organizations which prevents lateral communication from being an honest sharing and pooling of insights and resources. If there is only one promotion available and that promotion is to be made on the basis of quality of work accomplished, it really does not benefit workers to share their best insights.

Guidelines for Lateral Communication

To improve lateral communication, the following suggestions should prove helpful:

- Recognize that your own specialty has a technical jargon that others outside your specialty might not know. Clarify when and as needed.
- See the entire organizational picture and recognize the importance of all areas. Seeing one's own area as important and all others as unimportant does little to foster meaningful communication.
- Balance the needs of an organization that relies on cooperation and a system that rewards competition. In most cases it seems that cooperation can be increased without doing any individual damage.

Informal Communication: The Grapevine

The types of communication discussed to this point follow the formal structure of the organization. **Grapevine** messages do not follow such formal lines. Rather, they seem to have a life of their own and are concerned primarily with personal and social matters rather than with the organization itself. Grapevine communication, however, can be and often is used to enhance a feeling of stability and to establish the credibility of the organization (Mishra 1990).

Grapevine communications grow along with the formal communications; the more active the formal communication system, the more active the informal system. Not surprisingly, the grapevine also grows as the size of the organization increases.

The term *grapevine* seems to have originated during the Civil War, when telegraph wires were hung from tree to tree and resembled grapevines. Messages that travel through no organized structure also resemble the physical grapevine, with its unpredictable pattern of branches.

According to organizational theorist Keith Davis (1977, 1980), the grapevine seems most likely to be used when (1) there is great upheaval or change within the organization; (2) the information is new—no one likes to spread old and well-known information; (3) face-to-face communication is physically easy; and (4) workers "cluster in clique-groups along the vine." The grapevine is most active immediately after the happening that is to be communicated and is most likely to be activated when the news concerns one's intimates, friends, and associates. Although the grapevine is part of every large organization's informal communications, it is not used as frequently as folklore would have us believe (Baird 1977). It is unlikely to grow in climates that are stable and comfortable. Change, ambiguity, and organizational secrecy nourish the grapevine.

Even more surprising than its relative infrequency of use, however, is its reported accuracy. Approximately 75 to 95 percent of grapevine information is correct (Davis 1980; Hellweg 1992). Even though many details are omitted, the stories are basically true.

Problems with Grapevine Communication

One obvious problem with the grapevine is that it is difficult to discover the source of the original message because the message's route is so circuitous and cannot be easily traced. For this reason it is also often difficult to determine the truth or falsity of grapevine information. Grapevine information is often incomplete (Hellweg 1992) and may easily be distorted as it passes through its many users. The distortions we discussed earlier (see Unit 4) can all damage the fidelity of the information as it passes from one receiver to another.

Grapevine information can often lead to morale problems because it may be leaked before the necessary groundwork has been laid or explanation offered. For example, the grapevine might report that a department will be reduced by five workers. The assumption that may be made is that five people will be fired, which logically enough could cause severe morale problems. It could be, however, that five workers are taking early retirement.

In what ways might the grapevine be used to improve morale? To improve productivity?

Guidelines for Grapevine Communication

Among the useful suggestions for dealing with the inevitable grapevine are the following:

- Understand the role of the grapevine in the organization. For example, many managers view the grapevine as a great inconvenience. Actually, it serves useful purposes. "A lively grapevine," notes Davis (1980), "reflects the deep psychological need of people to talk about their jobs and their company as a central life interest. Without it, the company would literally be sick." Its speed and general accuracy make it an ideal medium to carry a great deal of the social communications that so effectively bind workers together in an organization.
- Although grapevine information is generally accurate, it is usually incomplete and may contain crucial distortions. Therefore, treat grapevine information as tentative—as possibly true, not necessarily true.
- Tap into the grapevine. Whether worker or management, it is important that you hear grapevine information. It may clue you in to events that will figure into your future with the organization. It will also help you bond and network with others in the organization.

Information Overload

Today, with the explosion of technology, **information overload** is one of our greatest problems. Information is generated at such a rapid rate that it is impossible to keep up with all that is relevant to one's job. Invariably, each person must select certain information to attend to and other information to omit.

Information is so easily and quickly generated and disseminated throughout an organization that we often forget that it still takes time to digest the information and make use of it in a meaningful way. The junk mail that seems to grow every day is a perfect example. Technological advances make it easy, quick, and inexpensive to send information. Now what we need is the corresponding technology to enable us to read and use the information just as quickly.

Another major cause of overload is that many managers disseminate information about a problem instead of solving it. A department head confronted with a problem may write a memo or set up a study group. The manager has thus bought time, but has also added to the information overload.

Information overload has probably crept into all organizations, and is the major reason why so many organizations have computerized their operations. Putting everything on computer is a relatively easy and efficient way to deal with vast amounts of information, but it doesn't solve the entire problem. Some individual must still do something about the information—at least usually. And under conditions of information overload, errors are more likely simply because the person cannot devote the needed time to any one item. The more rushed you are, the more likely you are to make mistakes. There are also likely to be great delays between sending a message and taking a required action. Such delays are inefficient and costly to an organization.

Problems with Information Overload

Information overload, by definition, is a problem for any organization. For one thing, it absorbs an enormous amount of work time at all levels of the hierarchy. The more messages you have to deal with, the less time you have for those messages or tasks that are central to your organizational functions.

Another problem is that the overabundance of messages may make it difficult for a worker to determine efficiently which messages need immediate attention and which do not, which messages may be discarded and which must be retained.

Guidelines for Dealing with Information Overload

Several suggestions should prove useful in dealing with information overload:

- Think before passing on messages. Not all messages must be passed on; not everyone needs to know everything.
- Consider the suggestions for "wastebasketry" offered by Auren Uris (1986):
  1. Use the messages as they come to you and then throw them out; for example, write the relevant dates for a meeting on your calendar and then throw out the announcement.
  2. Get rid of extra copies. When you receive multiple copies get rid of all but the one you need, if you need it.
  3. Summarize the material you need from lengthy reports and retain the summary and file or throw out the rest.
  4. Distinguish between material that you should save and material that is only cluttering up your space.
  5. Throw out materials that can be easily located elsewhere. Data posted on nearby bulletin boards usually do not have to be on your desk as well.

Sexual Harassment

A special type of message—often a type of downward communication—is sexual harassment. **Sexual harassment** is not a single act but rather a series of communicative acts that come to characterize a work relationship (see Keyton 1995).

One research team defines sexual harassment as "conduct, typically experienced as offensive in nature, in which unwanted sexual advances are made in the context of a relationship of unequal power or authority. The victims are subjected to verbal comments of a sexual nature, unconsented touching and requests for sexual favors" (Friedman, Boumil, & Taylor 1992). Attorneys note that legally "sexual harassment is any unwelcome sexual advance or conduct on the job that creates an intimidating, hostile or offensive working environment" (Petrocelli & Repa 1992).

The Equal Employment Opportunity Commission (EEOC) has defined sexual harassment as follows (Friedman, Boulmi, & Taylor 1992, p. 114):

> Unwelcome sexual advances, requests for sexual favors and other verbal or physical conduct of a sexual nature constitute sexual harassment when (1) submission to such conduct is made either explicitly or implicitly a term or condition of an individual's employment, (2) submission to or rejection of such conduct by an individual is used as the basis for employment decisions affecting such individual, or (3) such conduct has the purpose or effect of unreasonably interfering with an individual's work performance or creating an intimidating, hostile, or offensive working environment.

Although most sexual harassment behaviors are directed against women, sexual harassment can and does occur against men (see Claire 1994). In one Harris Poll (*New York Times,* June 2, 1993) of sexual harassment in junior and senior high school 56 per-

TABLE 19.1
major sexual harassment behaviors

Behavior	Boys	Girls
Sexual comments or looks	56%	76%
Touched, grabbed, or pinched	42	65
Intentionally brushed up against	36	57
Sexual rumors spread about them	34	42
Clothing pulled at	28	38
Shown, given, or left sexual materials	34	31
Had sexual messages written about them in public areas	16	20

Source: "Major Sexual Harassment Behaviors," *The New York Times*, June 2, 1993.

cent of the boys and 75 percent of the girls said that they were the target of some form of sexual harassment consisting of sexually explicit comments, jokes, or gestures. Forty-two percent of the boys and 66 percent of the girls said they were the victims of sexual touching, grabbing, or pinching.

Table 19.1 presents the major behaviors and the percentage of students reporting that they were the victims of such behaviors. All such behaviors were sexual in nature.

The students noted that among the effects of such sexual harassment were not wanting to go to school, reluctance to talk in class, finding it difficult to pay attention or to study, getting lower grades, and even considering changing schools.

THINK ABOUT

Think about how you would go about discovering whether behavior is sexually harassing. Memory VanHyning (1993) suggests that you ask:

1. Is this really sexually harassing? Does this behavior have the meaning it seems to have?
2. Is it job-related? Does it have something to do with or will it influence the way you do your job?
3. Did you reject this behavior? Did you make your rejection of these messages clear to the other person?
4. Have these types of messages persisted? Is there a pattern, a consistency to these messages?

Avoiding Sexual Harassment Messages

Three suggestions for avoiding behaviors that might be considered as sexual harassment will help to clarify the concept further and to prevent its occurrence (Bravo & Cassedy 1992):

- Begin with the assumption that others at work are not interested in your sexual advances, sexual stories and jokes, or sexual gestures.
- Listen and watch for negative reactions to any sexually related discussion. Use the suggestions and techniques discussed throughout this book to discover any such reactions (for example, Unit 6). Of course, when in doubt, ask questions. Use your perception-checking skills (Unit 3).
- Avoid saying or doing what you think would/might prove offensive to your parent, partner, or child should they be working with someone who engages in such behavior.

To these we need add that these judgments you will make will be all the more difficult when you are in a multicultural environment. When people differ widely in their cultural beliefs, there is a much greater chance of misunderstanding and misinterpretation. Be careful of using the standards of your own culture when predicting how those from different cultures will react.

What to Do about Sexual Harassment

What should you do if you feel you are being sexually harassed and you feel you should do something about it? Here are a few suggestions recommended by workers in the field (Petrocelli & Repa 1992; Bravo & Cassedy 1992; Rubenstein 1993):

1. Talk to the harasser. Tell this person, assertively, that you do not welcome this behavior and that you find it offensive. Simply informing Fred that his sexual jokes are not appreciated and are seen as offensive may be sufficient to make him stop this joke-telling. Unfortunately, in some instances such criticism goes unheeded and the offensive behavior continues.
2. Collect some evidence, perhaps corroboration from others who have experienced similar harassment at the hands of the same individual, perhaps put together a log of such offensive behaviors.
3. Use appropriate channels within the organization. Most organizations have established channels to deal with such grievances. This step will in most cases eliminate any further harassment. In the event that it doesn't, you may consider going further.
4. File a complaint with some organization or government agency or perhaps take legal action.
5. Don't blame yourself. Like many who are abused, there is a tendency to blame yourself, to feel that you are somehow responsible for being harassed. You aren't, but you may need to secure emotional support from friends or perhaps from trained professionals.

SUMMARY

In this unit we looked at the communications taking place within an organizational setting, the main approaches to organizations, and suggested some ways in which organizational communications may be made more effective.

1. An organization is a group of individuals organized for the achievement of specific goals.
2. Organizational communication refers to the messages sent and received within the organization, within both its formally structured and informally established groups.
3. Four major approaches to organizations have been identified: the scientific management or classical approach, the behavioral or human relations approach, the systems approach, and the cultural approach.
4. Communication networks refer to the channels that messages pass through from one person to another.
5. Upward communication refers to messages sent from the lower levels of the hierarchy to the upper levels.
6. Downward communication refers to messages sent from the higher levels of the hierarchy to the lower levels.
7. Lateral communication refers to messages sent by equals to equals.
8. The grapevine refers to the informal channels that messages pass through in an organization.
9. Information overload refers to the situation in which the information sent to any person exceeds that person's capacity to process it effectively.
10. Sexual harassment occurs frequently in the organizational setting and may be defined, broadly, as unwelcome sexual communication.

THINKING CRITICALLY ABOUT ORGANIZATIONAL COMMUNICATION

1. Construct an organizational chart of your college, your place of employment, the United Nations, a particular country's government, your state or local government, or any organization in which you're interested. Is the organization a relatively flat one in which there are few hierarchical levels? Or, is it tall with many hierarchical levels? What are the advantages and disadvantages of flat and tall organizations?
2. What approach to organizations (scientific, behavioral, systems, or cultural) do you find provides the greatest insight into the nature of contemporary organizations?
3. What type of communication networks exist on your job? In your family? In your class? How are these similar or different from the five formal networks described in this unit?
4. Are your productivity and morale positively correlated? As one goes up, does the other also go up? Is one the cause and one the effect?
5. With which type of communication (upward, downward, or lateral) are you most comfortable? With which are you most effective? Can you identify skills that would be useful in all three types of communication?
6. How active are you in grapevine communication on your job? Are you as often a source as you are a receiver? What accounts for your status?

7. Has information overload entered your life? In what way? What are you doing about it?
8. How is sexual harassment defined on your campus? At your job? What policy does your college have on sexual harassment? What policy prevails on the job?
9. In 1994 a Federal court in Massachusetts barred enforcement of a high school's sexual harassment policy that banned T-shirts with slogans that demeaned women. Similarly, speech codes designed to ban sexual harassment at the University of Michigan and the University of Wisconsin were struck down by the courts (Bader 1995). At what point (if any) do bans against sexual harassment infringe on free speech? If you were the president of your college, how would you deal with the right to free speech on the one hand and the right to be free from sexual harassment on the other?
10. How would you go about finding answers to such questions as these:
    a. What kind of managers (X or Y) are you most likely to find in college administration? At McDonald's? At a Fortune 500 company?
    b. What communication problems do managers and workers identify as most significant in hindering productivity? In reducing morale?
    c. Do popular workers receive more grapevine messages than less-popular workers? Do they send more grapevine messages? If so, is it a person's popularity that leads others to send them more messages? Or, do people become popular because they are readily available and receptive grapevine channels?
    d. What effects does information overload have on the typical college student?
    e. What personality factors are associated with sexual harassment?

Interviewing

unit contents

unit goals

After completing this unit, you should be able to

1. define *interviewing*
2. describe the major types of interviews
3. describe the four dimensions of questions
4. describe the sequence of steps recommended for an information interview
5. explain the principles suggested for the employment interview
6. distinguish between lawful and unlawful questions

Interviewing includes a wide range of communication situations. Here are just a few examples:

1. A salesperson tries to sell a shopper a new car.
2. A teacher talks with a student about the reasons the student failed the course.
3. A counselor talks with a family about their communication problems.
4. A recent graduate applies to IBM for a job in the product development division.
5. A building owner talks with a potential apartment renter.
6. A minister talks with a church member about relationship problems.
7. A lawyer examines a witness during a trial.
8. A theatrical agent talks with a potential client.
9. A client discusses with a dating service employee some of the qualities desired in a potential mate.
10. An employer talks with an employee about the reasons for terminating his or her employment.

THINK ABOUT

Think about the role that interviewing will play in your own life—not only as an interviewee but as an interviewer. How will you use interviewing on your job? Do you use it interpersonally with friends, romantic partners, or family members?

INTERVIEWING DEFINED

Interviewing is a particular form of communication in which you interact largely through a question-and-answer format to achieve specific goals. These goals guide and structure the interview in both content and format. In an employment interview, for example, the goal for the interviewer is to find an applicant who can fulfill the tasks of the position. The interviewee's goal is to get the job, if it seems desirable. These goals guide the behaviors of both parties, are relatively specific, and are usually clear to both parties.

The interview is distinctly different from other forms of communication because it proceeds through questions and answers. Both parties in the interview ask and answer questions, but most often the interviewer asks the questions and the interviewee answers them.

Two-Person and Team Interviews

Most interviews follow a two-person structure but team interviews are becoming more popular. In the media, on "Nightline," for example, several journalists might interview a political candidate or one journalist might interview several candidates. On the ubiquitous television talk show (see Media Watch box in this unit), a moderator interviews several people at the same time.

In employment situations team interviews are extremely important, especially as you go higher up in the organizational hierarchy. It is not uncommon, for example, for an entire academic department to interview a candidate for a teaching position, often followed by a similar team interview with members of the administration. In business organizations, three or four vice presidents might interview a candidate for a middle management position.

The main advantage of the team interview is that it gives the audience or the organization different viewpoints and perspectives on the person being interviewed. With several interviewers all ready with their questions, the interview is more likely to follow a productively rapid pace.

Team interviews, however, are expensive (in an organization, time *is* money), may degenerate into what may appear to be an interrogation (which may be desirable on television but inappropriate in an employment setting), and may result in focusing too much time on those conducting the interview and not enough on the person being interviewed (see Kanter 1995).

General Interview Structures

Interviews vary from relatively informal talks that resemble everyday conversations to those that ask rigidly prescribed questions in a set order. Table 20.1 presents the major types of general interview structures identified by Ralph Hambrick (1991). Depending on your specific purpose, you would select the interview structure that best fits your needs.

Types of Interviews

We can distinguish the different types of interviews on the basis of the goals of interviewer and interviewee. Here we identify briefly the persuasive, appraisal, disciplinary, exit, and counseling interview (Stewart & Cash 1988; Zima 1983). The information and employment interviews are probably the most important for most college students, therefore these are covered at length later in the unit.

The Persuasive Interview

In the **persuasive interview** the goal is to change an individual's attitudes, beliefs, or behaviors. The interviewer may either ask questions that will lead the interviewee to the desired conclusion or answer questions in a persuasive way. For example, if you go into a showroom to buy a new car, you interview the salesperson. The salesperson's goal is to get you to buy a particular car. He or she attempts to accomplish this by answering your questions persuasively. You ask about mileage, safety features, and finance terms. The salesperson discourses eloquently on the superiority of this car above all others.

All interviews contain elements of both information and persuasion. When, for example, a guest appears on "The Tonight Show" and talks about a new movie, information is communicated. The performer, however, is also trying to persuade the audience to see the movie. Informing and persuading usually go together in actual practice.

The Appraisal Interview

In the **appraisal** or evaluation **interview**, the interviewee's performance is assessed by management or more experienced colleagues. The general aim is to discover what the interviewee is doing well (and to praise this), and not doing well and why (and to correct this). These interviews are important because they help new members of an organization see how their performance matches up with the expectations of those making promotion and firing decisions.

The Disciplinary Interview

Similar in some ways to the appraisal interview, the disciplinary interview focuses on ways to correct an employee's inadequate job performance. Generally, inadequate performance involves some violation of company policy or standards or a consistently inadequate job performance, despite assistance from managers or supervisors (Goodale 1992). In an effort to prevent lawsuits for "wrongful dismissal" many companies have established formal guidelines for handling an employee's inadequate performance. The disciplinary interview is best viewed as a series of interviews, beginning with a simple warning and, if corrections are not made, followed by increasingly specific and lengthy interviews. This is an especially difficult interview because an employee is likely to be highly ego-involved and defensive about his or her job performance and also because most managers lack the necessary skills for this form of communication.

The Exit Interview

The **exit interview** is used widely by organizations throughout the world. All organizations compete in one way or another for superior workers. When an employee leaves a company voluntarily, it is important to know why, to prevent other valuable workers from leaving as well. Another function of this interview is to provide a way of making the exit as pleasant and as efficient as possible for both employee and employer.

The Counseling Interview

Counseling interviews are given to provide guidance. The goal here is to help the person deal more effectively with problems, to work more effectively, to get along better with friends or lovers, or to cope more effectively with day-to-day living. For the interview to be of any value, the interviewer must learn a considerable amount about the person—habits, problems, self-

TABLE 20.1
general interview structures

You can, of course, combine the various types and create an interview structure that will best suit your specific needs.

Interview Structure	Characteristics and Uses
Informal interview, for example, two friends finding out what happened on their respective dates or employment interviews	Resembles conversation; general theme for interview is chosen in advance but the specific questions arise from the context; useful for obtaining information informally
Guided interview, for example, a guest on "The Tonight Show" is interviewed about a new television series	Topics are chosen in advance but specific questions and wordings are guided by the ongoing interaction; useful in assuring maximum flexibility and responsiveness to the dynamics of the situation
Standard open interview, for example, interviewing several candidates for a job	Open-ended questions and their order are selected in advance; useful when standardization is needed
Quantitative interview, for example, a researcher surveys students' political opinions	Questions and their order are selected in advance as are the possible response categories, for example, A, B, C, D; agree-disagree; check from 1 to 10. Useful when statistical analyses are to be performed and when large amounts of information are to be collected.

perceptions, goals, and so on. With this information, the counselor then tries to persuade the person to alter certain aspects of his or her thinking or behaving. The counselor may try to persuade you, for example, to listen more attentively when your spouse disagrees with you or to devote more time to your classwork.

QUESTIONS AND ANSWERS

Understanding the different types of questions may help you respond to questions more effectively—as in an employment interview—and ask questions more effectively—as in an information-gathering interview. Questions may be analyzed in terms of at least the following dimensions: open-closed, neutral-biased, primary-follow up, and direct-indirect.

open ___:___:___:___:___:___:___ closed
neutral ___:___:___:___:___:___:___ biased
primary ___:___:___:___:___:___:___ follow-up
direct ___:___:___:___:___:___:___ indirect

This diagram is designed to reflect some of the ways in which questions may vary. You can visualize each question as existing at some specific position on each of these scales. In thinking about and formulating your questions you would make choices along these dimensions, for example, to use a relatively open-ended question, phrased in a neutral and direct manner, and designed to follow up a previous response. The specific way in which you ask your questions would, ideally, be based on a thorough analysis of the specific interview situation and on what you hope to achieve in the interview.

Open-Closed

Openness refers to the degree of freedom you have to respond, both in content and format. At times there is almost unlimited latitude in what may constitute an answer, for example to such questions as, "What are you goals?" "Why do you want to work at Peabody and Peabody?" At the opposite extreme are closed questions, which require only a yes or no, for example, "Are you willing to relocate to San Francisco?" "Can you use Lotus 1-2-3?" Between these extremes of openness are short-answer questions, those that are relatively closed and to which you have only limited freedom in responding, for example, "What would you do as manager here?" "What computer skills do you have?" Part of the art of successful interviewing is to respond with answers that are appropriate to the question's level of openness. Thus, if you are asked a question such as "Why do you want to work at Peabody and Peabody?" you are expected to speak at some length. If you are asked, "Are you willing to relocate to San Francisco?" then a simple yes or no with or without a qualification, for example, "Absolutely, though it would take me a few months to close my affairs here in Boston" will suffice.

Neutral-Biased

Neutrality and its opposite, *bias,* refer to the extent to which the question provides the answer the interviewer wants from the interviewee. Some questions are neutral and do not specify any answer as more appropriate than any other. At the other extreme are questions that are biased, or loaded. These indicate quite clearly the particular answer the interviewer expects or wants. Compare the following questions:

- How did you feel about managing your own desktop publishing company?
- You must really enjoy managing your own desktop publishing company, don't you?

The first question is neutral and allows you to respond in any way; it asks for no particular answer. The second question is biased; it specifies that the interviewer expects a yes. Between the neutrality of "How did you feel about your previous job?" and the bias of "You must have loved your previous job, didn't you?" there are questions that specify with varying degrees of strength the answer the interviewer expects or prefers. For example:

- Did you like your previous job?
- Did you dislike your previous job very much?
- It seems like it would be an interesting job, no?

An interviewer who asks too many biased questions will not learn about the interviewee's talents or experiences, but only about the interviewee's ability to give the desired answer. As an interviewee, pay special attention to any biases in the question. Do not give the responses your interviewer expects if they are not what you believe to be correct or know to be the truth. This would be unethical. However, when your responses are not what the interviewer expects, consider explaining why you are responding as you are. For example, to the biased question, "It seems like it would be an interesting job, no?" you might respond: "It was interesting most of the time, but it didn't allow for enough creativity."

Primary–Follow-up

Primary questions introduce a topic and follow-up questions ask for elaboration on what was just said. Too many primary questions and not enough follow-up questions will often communicate a lack of interest and perhaps a failure to listen as effectively as possible. When we introduce a topic we expect people to ask follow-up questions. When they don't, we feel that they are not interested in what we are saying or aren't really listening.

The stereotypical psychiatric interviewer would ask a lot of follow-up questions, probing each and every thought the patient expresses. The stereotypical unresponsive partner would ask no follow-up questions. A balance between primary and follow-up questions, determined in large part by the situation and by your own communication goals, is the desired balance.

One way to judge whether you are balancing these appropriately is to pause mentally and ask yourself how you and your listener are enjoying the conversation or interview. If your listener seems not to be enjoying the interaction, try increasing your follow-up responses. Use the active listening responses discussed in Unit 12. If you are not finding it satisfactory, then probably your listener is not asking enough follow-up questions, not giving your statements enough attention. One helpful guide is to talk in specifics about yourself. Instead of "life is difficult," say "I'm going through a bad time." Also, clue your listener in a more obvious way to your desire to pursue this topic. Instead of just saying "I'm going through a bad time," continue with "and I'm not sure what I should do." To be even more direct add, "and I need advice."

Direct-Indirect

This aspect of questions will vary greatly from one culture to another. In the United States, be prepared for rather direct questions, whether you are being interviewed for information or for a job. In Japan, on the other hand, the interviewee is expected to reveal himself or herself despite the indirectness of the questions.

Similarly, cultures vary in what they consider appropriate directness in speaking of one's accomplishments, say in a job interview. In many Asian cultures, the interviewee is expected to appear modest and unassuming and should allow his or her competencies to emerge indirectly during the interview. In the United States, on the other hand, you are expected to state your competencies without any significant modesty. In fact, many interviewers expect a certain amount of hyperbole and exaggeration.

THE INFORMATION INTERVIEW

In the information interview, the interviewer tries to learn something about the interviewee. In the information interview—unlike the employment interview—the person interviewed is usually a person of some reputation and accomplishment. The interviewer asks a series of questions designed to elicit the interviewee's views, beliefs, insights, perspectives, predictions, life history, and so on. Examples of the information interview include those published in popular magazines, the TV interviews conducted by Jay Leno, Ted Koppel, and Barbara Walters, for example, as well as those conducted by a lawyer during a trial. All aim to elicit specific information from someone who supposedly knows something others do not know. In this discussion, we concentrate on your role as the interviewer, since that is the role you are likely to find yourself serving now and in the near future.

Let's say that your interview is designed to get information about a particular field, for example, desktop publishing. You want to know about the available job opportunities and the preparation you would need to get into this field. Here are a few guidelines for conducting such information-gathering interviews.

How might you use interviewing to research the question, "How does the business community view the importance of communication skills to professional success?"

Select the Person You Wish to Interview

You might, for example, look through your college catalogue for a course in desktop publishing and interview the instructor. Or you might call a local publishing company and ask if there is someone in charge of desktop publishing. This is the first step; you've selected one of the people you hope to interview. But don't stop there. Before you pursue the interview, try to learn something about the people you will interview. Look through your library catalogue or through one of the computerized databases that might be related to this person's area of interest to see if he or she has written anything on the topic. Also, look through some of the biographical dictionaries to see if your interviewee is listed.

Secure an Appointment

Phone the person or send a letter requesting an interview. In your call or letter, identify the purpose of your request and that you would like a brief interview. For example, you might say: "I'm preparing for a career in desktop publishing and I would appreciate it if I could interview you to learn more about the subject. The interview would take about 15 minutes." (It is helpful to let the person know it will not take overly long; he or she is more likely to agree to being interviewed.) Generally, it is best to be available at the interviewee's convenience, therefore indicate flexibility on your part, for example, "I can interview you any afternoon this week."

You may find it necessary to conduct the interview by phone. In this case, call to set up a time for a future call. For example, you might say: "I'm interested in a career in desktop publishing and I would like to interview you on the job opportunities in this field. If you agree, I can call you back at a time that's convenient for you." In this way, you don't run the risk of asking the person to hold still for an interview while eating lunch, talking with colleagues, or running to class.

Prepare Your Questions

Preparing questions ahead of time will ensure that you use the time available to your best advantage. Of course, as the interview progresses other questions will come to mind and should be asked. Having a prepared list of questions, however, will help you obtain the information you need most easily.

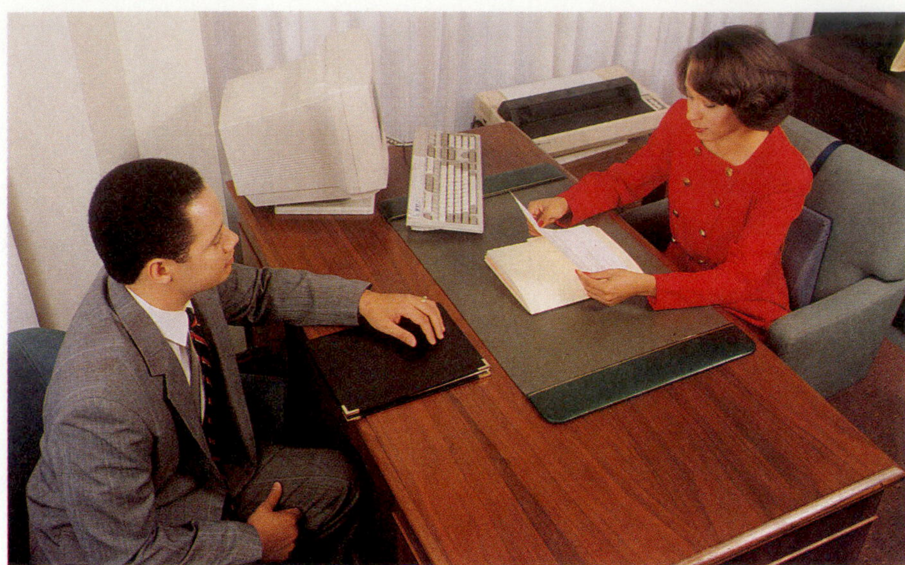

Would you find it easier to interview for a job with a same-sex or an opposite-sex interviewer or would there be no difference? Why? What factors other than sex will influence your level of interviewing comfort?

Establish Rapport with the Interviewee

Open the interview with an expression of thanks for making the time available to you. Many people receive lots of requests and it helps if you also remind the person of your specific purpose. You might say something like this: "I really appreciate your making time for this interview. As I mentioned, I'm interesting in learning about the job opportunities in desktop publishing and your expertise and experience in this area will help a great deal."

Ask Permission to Tape the Interview

Generally, it is a good idea to tape the interview. It will enable you to secure a more complete record of the interview which you'll be able to review as you need to. It will also free you to concentrate on the interview rather than on trying to write down the person's responses. Remember to ask permission first; some people prefer not to have informal interviews taped. If you intend to tape a phone interview, get permission first. In some cases you might even run into legal difficulties if you tape without permission.

Ask Open-ended Questions

Use questions that provide the interviewee with room to discuss the issues you want to raise. Thus, instead of asking, "Do you have formal training in desktop publishing?" (a question that requires a simple yes or no response and will not be very informative), you might ask, "Can you tell me something of your training in this field?" (a question that is open-ended and allows the person greater freedom). You can then ask follow-up questions.

Close the Interview with an Expression of Appreciation

Thank the person for making the time available for the interview, for being informative, cooperative, helpful, or whatever. Showing your appreciation will make it a great deal easier if you want to return for a second interview.

Follow Up the Interview

Follow up the interview with a brief note of thanks in which you might express your appreciation for the time given you, your enjoyment in speaking with the person, and your accomplishing your goal of getting the information you needed.

These general principles will also prove useful in the other types of interviews, especially in the employment interview, which we consider next.

THE EMPLOYMENT INTERVIEW

Perhaps of most concern to college students is the **employment** or selection **interview.** In this type of interview, a great deal of information and persuasion

MEDIA WATCH

THOSE TELEVISION TALK SHOWS

Interviewing is a form of communication used widely in the media—in newspapers and magazines as well as on talk radio and on television. It is the television talk show, however, that has most captured the attention of the media consumer, and it is a media phenomenon that needs to be examined.

In an article entitled, "Talk Shows Are Good for You," frequent talk show psychologist Gilda Carle (1995) identifies some of the benefits of talk shows. Among these are that they show us new communication techniques, teach us about new topics, break down myths, show us celebrities as real people, and make us laugh. And, media critic A. J. Jacobs (1995) notes additional values:

- Talk shows are "models of diversity." All cultures are represented on talk shows.
- Talk shows also "break new ground" and discuss issues that are too often neglected by the mainstream shows; cross dressing, interracial relationships, and child abuse, for example, are frequent topics of talk shows.
- Talk shows are in the American tradition. Television viewers are interested in people like themselves and enjoy seeing a person's private life exposed.
- Talk shows make the viewers' problems seem minor.

Mass communication researcher Janice Peck (1995) notes, from an analysis of shows hosted by Oprah Winfrey and Sally Jessy Raphael that the talk shows have made public issues that were once hidden and give a public platform to groups that have generally not had media exposure (for example, women).

Consider some of the disadvantages, however. For example, talk shows dispense advice on a variety of issues—especially in the monologue that closes many of the shows—from someone with little to no professional training in the field. Do you really want to take relationship advice from Ricki Lake or Montel Williams or Richard Bey? They regularly give communication advice with no basis in scientific research and generally foster myths about communication. Perhaps the most prevalent myth about communication is that communication will solve all problems and that the more communication a couple has the better the relationship will be.

Talk shows are entertaining but they often present themselves as educational, as therapy for the masses, and as arbiters of how you and your family and your friends should live their lives. Talk shows also create an impression that the world is divided into two extremes. Polarizing guests—the gay activist and the fundamentalist preacher, the pro- and anti-abortionist, the liberal and the conservative—makes for interesting debate and generally holds viewer attention, but, the extremes do not represent the world. They are extreme precisely because they do not represent the vast majority of the world.

Talk shows also give the impression that therapy takes one hour—the problem is introduced, the therapy is given, the catharsis takes place, and the cure emerges. Of course, we know that it doesn't happen like that and yet it is difficult to dismiss examples shown repeatedly and with generally good production values. Some shows make continued therapy available for their guests and this is certainly one gesture in the right direction. Most shows, however, seem to imply that the problem is over when the show is over and that the problem is resolved. Janice Peck (1995, p. 76) argues: "the programs discourage critical engagement with and reflection on those problems in favor of immediate identification and catharsis, and undermine the ability to take these problems seriously in the service of making them entertaining."

Still another effect seems to be the sanctioning or approval of violating societal or cultural rules. Talk shows present what is to many "unthinkable" and make it thinkable. It ultimately positions these behaviors within the range of normalcy (Abt 1995). For example, by giving a platform to pregnant teenagers who continue to smoke, drink, and use drugs and who refuse to alter their behavior (as on a 1995 Sally Jessy Raphael show), the talk show may be saying in effect that this really cannot be that bad. The same is true for shows devoted to gangs that rob

(continued on next page)

(continued)

for pleasure, children who abuse their parents, or spouses who deceive their mates. Depending on your own political and social values, you can add a lot more examples. The more you come into contact with a pattern of behavior, the more normal it will appear to you. If this effect is real—and if talk shows can only thrive based on the degree to which their guests can shock the audience—then the standards for acceptable (socially sanctioned) behavior are likely to change in the direction of these extremes.

Do you watch talk shows? If so, why? What do you get out of them? Do talk shows provide a popular conversational topic for you and your peers? What is to you the main advantage of television talk shows? The main disadvantage?

will be exchanged. The interviewer will learn about you, your interests, your talents—and, if clever enough, some of your weaknesses and liabilities. You will be informed about the nature of the company, its benefits, its advantages—and, if you are clever enough, some of its disadvantages and problems. For the purpose of this discussion, assume you are the interviewee.

As with the other forms of communication considered throughout this text, each culture has its own rules for employment interviewing. In the United States you would be advised to express confidence in your ability and to "blow your own horn." In Japan and China, on the other hand, you would be expected to demonstrate modesty and a willingness to learn from those who know more. This would be doubly true if you are a woman.

In some cultures, a job is seen as a lifetime deal. Once you are hired, you are expected to stay with that firm throughout your entire professional life. Consequently, your prospective employer will want to know a great deal about you and your family. In other cultures, jobs are seen as more temporary and you are expected to move from one job to another several times during your professional career.

In China, Japan, Korea, and other Asian cultures, your family is looked at just as carefully as you are. In other cultures (the United States, for example), it would be illegal to ask a job candidate if she or he is married.

Prepare Yourself

Preparation is perhaps the most difficult aspect of the entire interview process. It is also the step that is most often overlooked. At the most obvious level, prepare yourself intellectually. Educate yourself as much as possible about relevant topics. Learn something about the company and its specific product or products. Call the company and ask them to send you any company brochures or newsletters or perhaps a quarterly report. If it's a publishing company, familiarize yourself with their books. If it's an advertising agency, familiarize yourself with their major clients and their major advertising campaigns.

Also, recognize that employment interviews are anxiety provoking and that you are likely to experience some communication apprehension. You may wish to take the self-test, "How Apprehensive Are You in Employment Interviews?" to assess your job interviewing apprehension before reading about this interview type.

If you are applying for a job, both you and the company want something. You want a job that will meet your needs. The company wants an employee who will meet its needs. In short, you each want something that perhaps the other has. View the interview as an opportunity to engage in a joint effort to gain something beneficial to both. If you go into the interview in this cooperative frame of mind, you are much less likely to become defensive in your communications, which in turn will make you a more appealing potential colleague.

A great number of jobs are won or lost on the basis of physical appearance alone, so also give attention to physical preparation. Dress in a manner that shows that you care enough about the interview to make a good impression. At the same time, dress comfortably. To avoid extremes is perhaps the most specific advice to give you. When in doubt, it is probably best to err on the side of formality: wear the tie, high heels, or dress.

Bring with you the appropriate materials, whatever they may be. At the very least bring a pen and paper, an extra copy or two of your résumé and, if appropriate, a business card. If you are applying for a

SELF TEST

how apprehensive are you in employment interviews?

This questionnaire is composed of five questions concerning your feelings about communicating in the job interview setting. Indicate in the spaces provided the degree to which each statement adequately describes your feelings about the employment interview. Use the following scale: (1) strongly agree, (2) agree, (3) undecided, (4) disagree, or (5) strongly disagree.

______ 1. While participating in a job interview with a potential employer, I am not nervous.
______ 2. Ordinarily, I am very tense and nervous in job interviews.
______ 3. I have no fear of speaking up in job interviews.
______ 4. I'm afraid to speak up in job interviews.
______ 5. Ordinarily, I am very calm and relaxed in job interviews.

Thinking Critically About Apprehension in Employment Interviews In computing your score, follow these steps:

1. Reverse your scores for items 2 and 4 as follows:

If you said . . .	reverse it to . . .
1	5
2	4
3	3
4	2
5	1

2. Add the scores from all five items; be sure to use the reverse scores for items 2 and 4 and the original scores for 1, 3, and 5.

The higher your score, the greater your apprehension. Since this test is still under development, specific meanings for specific scores are not possible. A score of 25 (the highest possible score) would indicate an extremely apprehension individual while a score of 5 (the lowest possible score) would indicate an extremely unapprehensive individual. How does your score compare with those of your peers? What score do you think would ensure optimum performance at the job interview?

Your apprehension will probably differ somewhat depending on the type of job interview, your responsibilities, the need and desire you have for the job, and so on. What factors would make you especially apprehensive? Do these answers give you clues as to how to lessen your apprehension?

It seems clear that persons demonstrating apprehension during a job interview will be perceived less positively than would someone demonstrating confidence and composure. How might you learn to display confidence better?

Source. "How Apprehensive Are You in Employment Interviews" from "A Progress Report on the Development of an Instrument to Measure Communication Apprehension in Employment Interviews" by Joe Ayres, Debbie M. Ayres, and Diane Sharp, *Communication Research Reports 10*, 1993. Reprinted by permission of the Eastern Communication Association.

job in a field in which you have worked before, you might bring samples of your previous work.

The importance of your résumé cannot be stressed too much. The résumé is a summary of essential information about your experience, goals, and abilities, and it is often the first contact a potential employer has with you. If the employer finds it interesting, the candidate is asked in for an interview. The résumé's importance in communicating an impression of who you are cannot be overstated, therefore give special care to its form. Typographical errors, incorrect spelling, poorly spaced headings and entries, and generally sloppy work will not produce the effect you want. Because of the importance of the résumé and its close association with the interview, a sample is provided on page xxx, along with some guidelines to assist you in preparing your own.

❷ For most people just graduating college, career goals are tentative. Although this career goal description may seem a bit general, it is probably realistic. Of course, if you do have more precise career goals, put them down. In setting your career goals, do not imply that you will take just anything. At the other extreme, do not be too specific or demanding.

❶ Your name, address, and phone number generally appear at the top of the résumé.

❸ It will be helpful to potential employers if you give a bit more information than simply your educational degree. Even the major department in which you earned your degree might be too vague. For example, in a communication arts and sciences department you could have concentrated on speech pathology, speech science, audiology, public communication, journalism, interpersonal communication, mass media theory, media production, film criticism, and so on. The same is true for many other departments as well, therefore identify your emphasis. If you earned honors or awards, list these if they are relevant to your educational experience or to your job experience. Note, for example, that you were on the Dean's List, debate team, received departmental honors, or won awards for working in your field. If the awards are primarily educational (for example, Dean's List), put them under the Education heading. If they are job-related, them put them under the Work Experience heading.

❹ List your work experience in reverse chronological order, beginning with the most recent position and working backward. Depending on your work experience, you may have little or nothing to write and therefore you will want to search through your history for some relevant experience. The example given here focuses on work experience during college that relates specifically to the position. Don't include what is not clearly related to your career goals.

❶ **PAT JEFFERSON**
166 Josen Road
Accord, New York 12404
(914) 555-1221

❷ **OBJECTIVE**	To secure a position with a college textbook publisher as a sales representative
❸ **EDUCATION**	A.A., Nassau Community College, 1988 B.A., Hofstra University, 1998 [expected] Major: Communications, with emphasis in interpersonal and public communication Minor: Psychology *Courses included: Interpersonal Communication, Public Speaking, Small Group Communication, Interviewing, Organizational Communication, Public Relations, Persuasion: Theory and Practice, Psychology of Attitude Change* *Extracurricular Activities: Debate team (2 years), reporter on student newspaper (1 year)*
❹ **WORK EXPERIENCE**	Two years, salesclerk in college bookstore (part-time) Six years in retail sales at Macy's; managed luggage department for last three years
❺ **SPECIAL COMPETENCIES**	Working knowledge of major word processing and spreadsheet programs Basic knowledge of college bookstore operation Spoken and written knowledge of Spanish
❻ **PERSONAL**	Enjoy working with computers and people; willing to relocate and travel
❼ **REFERENCES**	References from the following people are on file in the Office of Student Personnel, Hofstra University (Hempstead, New York 11550) Dr. Martha Hubbard (Hofstra University), major advisor and instructor for three courses Mr. Jack Sprat (Hofstra University) manager, bookstore Professor Mary Contrary (Hofstra) debate coach Dr. Robert Hood (Nassau Community College), communication instructor

❺ The section on special competencies is an often overlooked area, but one in which college students and recent graduates actually have a great deal to say. Do you have some foreign language ability? Do you know how to perform statistical analyses? Do you know how to write a computer program? Do you know how to keep profit-and-loss statements? If you do, put it down. Such competencies are relevant to a wide variety of jobs.

❻ Include any personal information that is relevant to the position you seek.

❼ References may be handled in a number of different ways. Here, the specific names of people the potential employer may contact are listed. Sometimes phone numbers are included. If your school maintains personnel files for its students, you may simply note that references may be obtained by writing to the relevant department. (Be sure you keep your file up to date.) It is sometimes helpful to identify briefly the relationship between you and the person named as reference. Three references are generally considered enough. Note that the people listed should have special knowledge about you that is relevant to the job.

Establish Goals

All interviews have specific objectives. As part of your preparation, fix these goals firmly in mind. Use them as guides to the remainder of your preparation and also to your behavior during and even after the interview. After establishing your objectives clearly in your own mind, relate your preparation to these goals. For example, in considering how to dress, what to learn about the specific company, and what questions to ask during the interview, ask yourself how your goals might help you answer these questions.

Prepare Answers and Questions

If the interview is at all important to you, you will probably think about it for some time. Use this time productively by rehearsing the predicted course of the interview. Try also to predict the questions that will be asked and the answers you will most likely give.

THINK ABOUT

Think about the questions that are likely to be asked and how you will answer them. Table 20.2 presents a list of questions, organized around the major topics on the résumé, commonly asked in employment interviews. The questions are drawn from a variety of interviewing experts (Seidman 1991; Sincoff & Goyer 1984; Skopec 1986; Stewart & Cash 1988; Zima 1983). As you read down this list, visualize yourself at a job interview and try responding to the questions in the middle column. After you have formulated a specific response, look at the suggestions opposite each set of questions. Did you follow the suggestions? Can you rephrase your responses for greater effectiveness? You may also find it helpful to rehearse with this list before going into the interview. Although not all of these questions would be asked in any one interview, be prepared to answer all of them.

Even though the interviewer will ask most of the questions, you too will want to ask questions. In addition to rehearsing some answers to predicted questions, fix firmly in mind the questions you want to ask the interviewer.

After the preparations, you are ready for the interview proper. Several suggestions may guide you through this sometimes difficult procedure.

Make an Effective Presentation of Self

This is probably the most important part of the entire procedure. If you fail here and make a bad initial impression, it will be difficult to salvage the rest of the interview, therefore devote special care to the way in which you present yourself.

Arrive on Time

In interview situations this means five to ten minutes early. This will allow you time to relax, to get accustomed to the general surroundings, and perhaps to fill out any forms that may be required. It also gives you a cushion should something delay you on the way.

Be sure you know the name of the company and the interviewer's name and job title. Although you will have much on your mind when you go into the interview, the interviewer's name is not one of the things you can afford to forget (or mispronounce).

In presenting yourself, be sure that you do not err on the side of too much casualness or too much formality. When there is doubt, act on the side of increased formality. Slouching back in the chair, smoking, and chewing gum or candy are obvious behaviors to avoid when you are trying to impress an interviewer.

Demonstrate Effective Interpersonal Communication

Throughout the interview, be certain that you demonstrate the skills of interpersonal communication that are spelled out in this book. The interview is the ideal place to put into practice all the skills you have learned. Here, for example, are the seven characteristics of conversational effectiveness considered in Unit 13, with special reference to the interview situation.

- *Openness.* Answer questions fully. Avoid one-word answers that may signal a lack of interest or knowledge.
- *Empathy.* See the questions from the asker's point of view. Focus your eye contact and orient your body toward the interviewer. Lean forward as appropriate.
- *Positiveness.* Emphasize your positive qualities. Express positive interest in the position. Avoid statements critical of yourself and others.
- *Immediacy.* Connect yourself with the interviewer throughout the interview, for example, by using the interviewer's name, focusing clearly on the in-

TABLE 20.2
common interview questions

Question Areas	Examples	Suggestions
Objectives and career goals	What made you apply to Datacomm? Do you know much about Datacomm? What did you like most about Datacomm? If you took a job with us, where would you like to be in five years? What benefits do you want to get out of this job?	Be positive (and as specific as you can be) about the company. Demonstrate your knowledge of the company. Take a long-range view; no firm wants to hire someone who will be looking for another job in six months.
Education	What do you think of the education you got at Hofstra University? Why did you major in communication? What was majoring in communication at Hofstra like? What kinds of courses did you take? Did you do an internship? What were your responsibilities?	Be positive about your educational experience. Try to relate your educational experience to the specific job. Demonstrate competence but at the same time the willingness to continue your education (either formally or informally).
Previous work experience	Tell me about your previous work experience. What did you do exactly? Did you enjoy working at Happy Publications? Why did you leave? How does this previous experience relate to the work you'd be doing here at Datacomm? What kinds of problems did you encounter at your last position?	Again, be positive; never knock a previous job. If you do the interviewer will think you may be criticizing them in the near future. Especially avoid criticizing specific people with whom you worked.
Special competencies	I see here you have a speaking and writing knowledge of Spanish. Could you talk with someone on the phone in Spanish or write letters in Spanish to our customers? Do you know any other languages? How much do you know about computers? Accessing databases?	Before going into the interview, review your competencies. Explain your skills in as much detail as needed to establish their relevance to the job and your own specific competencies.
Personal	Tell me. Who is Chris Williams? What do you like? What do you dislike? Are you willing to relocate? Are there places you would not consider relocating to? Do you think you'd have any trouble giving orders to others? Do you have difficulty working under deadlines?	Place yourself in the position of the interviewer and ask yourself what kind of person you would hire. Stress your ability to work independently but also as a member of a team. Stress your flexibility in adapting to new work situations.
References	Do the people you listed here know you personally or academically? Which of these people know you the best? Who would give you the best reference? Who else might know about your abilities that we might contact?	Be sure the people you list know you well and especially that they have special knowledge about you that is relevant to the job at hand.

terviewer's remarks, and expressing responsibility for your thoughts and feelings.

- *Interaction Management.* Ensure the interviewer's satisfaction by being positive, complimentary, and generally cooperative.
- *Expressiveness.* Let your nonverbal behaviors (especially facial expression and vocal variety) reflect your verbal messages and your general enthusiasm. Avoid fidgeting and excessive moving about.
- *Other-orientation.* Focus on the interviewer and on the company. Express agreement and ask for clarification as appropriate.

In addition to demonstrating these qualities of effectiveness, avoid those behaviors that create negative impressions during employment interviews (see Table 20.3).

Demonstrate Confidence

A special type of communication skill is that of communicating confidence. Make the interviewer see you as someone who can get the job done, who is confident. Here are some suggestions for communicating confidence that are not limited in their application to interviewing but have relevance to all forms of communication.

- Control your emotions. Once your emotions get the best of you, you will have lost your power and influence and will appear to lack the confidence necessary to deal with the relevant issues.
- Admit mistakes. Attempting to cover up obvious mistakes communicates a lack of confidence. Only a confident person can openly admit her or his mistakes and not worry about what others will think.
- Take an active role in the interview. Initiate topics or questions when appropriate. Avoid appearing as a passive participant, waiting for some stimulus.
- Don't ask for agreement from the interviewer by using tag questions, for example, "That was appropriate, don't you think?" or by saying normally declarative sentences with a rising intonation and thereby turning them into questions, for example, "I'll arrive at nine?" By asking for agreement you communicate a lack of confidence in making decisions and in expressing opinions.
- Avoid excessive movements, especially self-touching movements. Tapping a pencil on a desk, crossing and uncrossing your legs in rapid succession, or touching your face or hair all communicate an uneasiness, a lack of social confidence.
- Maintain eye contact with the interviewer. People who avoid eye contact are often judged to be ill-at-ease, as if they are afraid to engage in meaningful interaction.
- Avoid vocalized pauses—the *ers* and *ahs*—that frequently punctuate conversations and that communicate that you lack certainty and are hesitating, not quite sure what to say.

Mentally Review the Interview

By reviewing the interview, you will fix it firmly in your mind. What questions were asked? How did you answer them? Review and write down any important information the interviewer gave. Ask yourself what you could have done more effectively. Consider what you did effectively that you could repeat in other interviews. Ask yourself how you might correct your weaknesses and capitalize on your strengths.

Follow Up

In most cases, follow up an interview with a thank-you note to the interviewer. In this brief, professional letter, thank the interviewer for his or her time and consideration. Iterate your interest in the company and perhaps add that you hope to hear from him or her soon. Even if you did not get the job, you might in a follow-up letter ask to be kept in mind for future openings.

TABLE 20.3

why people fail at interviews

Trait	Examples
Unprepared	They forget to bring their résumé, don't show that they know anything about the company
Poor communication skills	They avoid looking at the interviewer, slouch, slur their words, speak in an overly low or rapid voice, give one-word answers, fidget, dress inappropriately
Unpleasant personality	They appear defensive, cocky, lacking in assertiveness, extremely introverted, overly aggressive
Lack of initiative	They fail to pick up on ramifications of interviewer's questions, give one-word answers, don't ask questions as would be appropriate
Poor listening skills	They are easily distracted, need to have questions repeated, fail to maintain appropriate eye contact

This letter provides you with an opportunity to resell yourself—to mention again those qualities you possess and wish to emphasize, but may have been too modest to discuss at the time. It will make you stand out in the mind of the interviewer, since not many interviewees write thank-you letters. It will help to remind the interviewer of your interview. It will also tell the interviewer that you are still interested in the position. It is a kind of pat on the back to the interviewer that says, in effect, that the interview was an effective one.

THE LAWFULNESS OF QUESTIONS

Through the Equal Employment Opportunity Commission, the federal government has classified some interview questions as unlawful. These are federal guidelines and therefore apply in all 50 states; individual states, however, may have added further restrictions. You may find it interesting to take the self-test, "Can You Identify Unlawful Questions?" (constructed with the good help of Stewart and Cash 1988, and Zincoff and Goyer 1984) to see if you can identify which questions are lawful and which are unlawful (see Pullum 1991).

Unlawful Information Requests

Some of the more important areas about which unlawful questions are frequently asked concern age, marital status, race, religion, nationality, citizenship, physical condition, and arrest and criminal records. For example, it is legal to ask applicants whether they meet the legal age requirements for the job and could provide proof of it, but it is unlawful to ask their exact age, even in indirect ways as illustrated in question 2 in the self-test. It is unlawful to ask about a person's marital status (question 1) or about family matters that are unrelated to the job (question 7). An interviewer may ask you, however, to identify a close relative or guardian if you are a minor, or any relative who currently works for the company.

Questions concerning your race (questions 3 and 6), religion (question 4), national origin (question 9), affectional orientation (question 5), age (question 2), handicaps unrelated to job performance (question 8), or even arrest record (question 10) are unlawful, as

SELF-TEST
can you identify unlawful questions?

For each question write L (Lawful) if you think the question is legal for an interviewer to ask in an employment interview and U (Unlawful) if you think the question is unlawful. For each question you consider unlawful, indicate why you think it is so classified.

_____ 1. Are you married, Tom?
_____ 2. When did you graduate from high school, Mary?
_____ 3. Do you have a picture so I can attach it to your resume?
_____ 4. Will you need to be near a mosque (church, synagogue)?
_____ 5. I see you taught courses in "gay and lesbian studies." Are you gay?
_____ 6. Is Chinese your native language?
_____ 7. Will you have difficulty getting a babysitter?
_____ 8. I notice that you walk with a limp. Is this a permanent injury?
_____ 9. Where were you born?
_____10. Have you ever been arrested for a crime?

Thinking Critically About the Legality of Interview Questions. All ten questions are unlawful. The remaining unit discussion illustrates why each of these and similar questions are unlawful. Before reading the text discussion try to develop general principles of what is and what is not legal based on the questions given earlier. Put differently, can you predict the generalizations about illegal questions that will be presented on the basis of knowing that these ten questions are illegal?

are questions that get at this same information in oblique ways. (Note, for example, that requiring a picture may be a way of discriminating against an applicant on the basis of sex, race, and age.)

Thus, for example, the interviewer may ask you what languages you are fluent in but may not ask what your native language is (question 6), what language you speak at home, or what language your parents speak. The interviewer may ask you if you if are in this country legally but may not ask if you were born in this country (question 9).

The interviewer may inquire into your physical condition only insofar as the job is concerned. For example, the interviewer may ask, "Do you have any physical problems that might prevent you from fulfilling your responsibilities at this job?" but the interviewer may not ask about any physical disabilities (question 8). The interviewer may ask you if you have been convicted of a felony but not if you've been arrested (question 10).

These are merely examples of some of the lawful and unlawful questions that may be asked during an interview. Note that even the questions used as examples here might be lawful in specific situations. The test to apply is simple: Is the information related to your ability to perform the job? Such questions are referred to as BFOQ—Bona Fide Occupational Qualification—questions.

Once you have discovered what questions are unlawful, consider how to deal with them if they come up during an interview.

Strategies for Dealing with Unlawful Questions

Your first strategy should be to deal with such questions by answering the part you do not object to and omitting any information you do not want to give. For example, if you are asked the unlawful question concerning what language is spoken at home, you may respond with a statement such as, "I have some language facility in German and Italian," without specifying a direct answer to the question. If you are asked to list all the organizations of which you are a member (an unlawful question in many states, since it is often a way of getting at political affiliation, religion, nationality, and various other areas), you might respond by saying something like: "The only organizations I belong to that are relevant to this job are the International Communication Association and the Speech Communication Association."

This type of response is preferable to the one that immediately tells the interviewer he or she is asking an unlawful question. In many cases, the interviewer may not even be aware of the legality of various questions and may have no intention of trying to get at information you are not obliged to give. For example, the interviewer may recognize the nationality of your last name and simply want to mention that he or she is also of that nationality. If you immediately take issue with the question, you will be creating problems when none really exist.

On the other hand, do recognize that in many employment interviews, the unwritten intention is to keep certain people out, whether it is people who are older or those of a particular marital status, affectional orientation, nationality, religion, or whatever. If you are confronted by questions that are unlawful and that you do not want to answer, and if the gentle method described previously does not work and your interviewer persists—saying, for example, "Is German the language spoken at home?" or, "What other organizations have you belonged to?"—you might counter by saying that such information is irrelevant to the interview and to the position you are seeking. Again, be courteous but firm. Say something such as, "This position does not call for any particular language skill and so it does not matter what language is spoken in my home." Or you might say, "The organizations I mentioned are the only relevant ones; whatever other organizations I belong to will certainly not interfere with my ability to perform in this company at this job."

If the interviewer still persists—and it is doubtful that many would after these rather clear and direct responses—you might note that these questions are unlawful and that you are not going to answer them.

SUMMARY

In this unit we introduced the process of interviewing, explored the nature of questions and answers, and identified the major forms of interviewing (focusing on the information gathering and the employment interviews).

1. Interviewing is a form of communication in which two persons interact largely through a question-and-answer format to achieve specific goals.
2. Seven types of interviews and their goals are: (1) the persuasive interview: the goal is to change a person's attitudes or behaviors; (2) the appraisal interview: the goal is to assess a worker's performance; (3) the disciplinary interview: the goal is to correct an employee's inadequate performance; (4) the exit interview: the goal is to discover why a worker is leaving or, if the leaving is not voluntary, to make the termination of a worker's employment as pleasant as possible; (5) the counseling interview: the goal is to help a person deal more effectively with problems or work more effectively; (6) the information interview: the goal is to secure information; and (7) the employment interview: the goal is to get a job or hire the best person for the job.
3. Questions may be viewed as varying in their degree of openness, neutrality, primacy (or follow up), and directness.
4. In the information interview the following guidelines should prove useful: select the person you wish to interview, secure an appointment, prepare your questions, establish rapport with the interviewer, ask permission to tape the interview, ask open-ended questions, and follow up the interview.
5. In employment interviews the following guidelines should prove useful: prepare yourself intellectually and physically for the interview, establish your objectives, prepare answers to predicted questions, make an effective presentation of yourself, mentally review the interview, and follow up the interview with a brief letter.
6. Review one of the résumé writing software programs. (Your college is likely to have several of these available to you.) What advice do they offer? What different types of organization for the résumé do they suggest? Try producing a résumé with this software.
7. Interviewees should familiarize themselves with possible unlawful questions and develop strategies for dealing with these questions.

THINKING CRITICALLY ABOUT INTERVIEWING

1. How will interviewing figure into your professional life?
2. How would you analyze the interviewing style of one of the popular radio or television talk show hosts?
3. It has been argued that teaching is an art of assisting students to ask appropriate questions and to help them discover how to find answers. For example, "what" questions help students think more specifically and concretely whereas "why" questions restrict the listener's freedom to respond and imply that there is a correct answer that needs to be found (Yoshida 1992). How do "what" and "why" questions function in interviews?
4. What would be your three greatest strengths as a job applicant in your chosen profession? How would you go about communicating these to the interviewer during your first interview?

5. How is a blind date like an interview? How is the first day of class like an interview?
6. If you could interview anyone in the world, who would it be? What questions would you ask?
7. How might you tailor the résumé presented in this unit to your own needs and job aspirations?
8. How would you prepare a short interview guide to study one of the following questions:
   a. Why do students select the elective courses they do?
   b. Why do people become teachers (or lawyers, law enforcement officers, athletes, and so on)?
   c. Why do people watch the television shows they watch?
9. How do you feel about the illegality of various interview questions? As a potential employer do you think you have a right to certain information that is currently judged as unlawful to demand of a prospective employee?
10. How would you go about finding answers to such questions as these:
    a. Are men and women equally effective in interviewing for information? Are men and women equally effective in job interview situations?
    b. What questions do people ask about prospective blind dates? Do these questions change as people get older?
    c. Who are the most credible television interviewers?
    d. What characteristics do television talk show hosts have in common? How do they differ?
    e. Do television talk shows influence viewer's attitudes and opinions? What type of person is likely to be influenced the most.

twenty-one unit

Preliminaries to Public Communication

unit contents

unit goals

After completing this unit, you should be able to

1. define and diagram the *public communication process*
2. define the components of public communication: *speaker, listeners, noise, effect, context, messages* and *channels, language* and *style, delivery, and ehthics*
3. define *speaker apprehension* and explain the theories of speaker apprehension
4. explain the sociological and the psychological characteristics of an audience that a speaker needs to consider

In this unit we introduce public communication and consider the nature of public communication, apprehension in public communication situations, and the audience of public communication. Table 21.1 outlines some of the major subdivisions of this area of public communication.

THE NATURE OF PUBLIC COMMUNICATION

In **public communication** a speaker addresses a relatively large audience with a relatively continuous discourse, usually in a face-to-face situation. You deliver an oral report in your economics class, you give a talk to your co-workers in an election campaign for shop steward, you address a community meeting to convince your neighbors to clean up the streets, or you speak to the students in your class to persuade them to donate blood. These are all public communication situations.

Unlike conversation, where the "audience" is one listener, the public communication audience is relatively large, ranging from groups of 10 or 12 to audiences of hundreds of thousands. During conversation, the role of speaker shifts repeatedly from one person to another. In public communication, the speaker gives a relatively continuous talk. This does not mean that only the speaker communicates. Both speaker and audience communicate throughout the public communication situation. The speaker communicates by delivering the speech and the audience by responding to the speech with feedback.

Figure 21.1 shows the public communication process and how it works. Its major elements are: speaker, listeners, noise, effect, context, messages and channels, language and style, delivery, and ethics.

Speaker

As a public speaker you bring to the communication situation all that you are and all that you know. Further, you bring with you all that the audience thinks you are and thinks you know. Everything about you becomes significant and contributes to the total effect of your speech. Your knowledge, your speech purpose, your speaking ability, your attitudes toward your audience, and other factors tell the audience who you are. These factors interact both during and after the public speaking event. As the public speaker you are the center of the transaction. The audience members look to you as the speaker; you and your speech are the reason for the gathering.

Listeners

Listeners are separate individuals and are symbolized as such in Figure 21.1 to emphasize that each is unique. Although we often speak of "the audience" as a collective body, it actually consists of separate and often very different individuals. Each of these listeners comes to the public speaking situation with different purposes, motives, expectations, attitudes, beliefs, and values. Each listener is going to respond differently to you and to the entire public speaking act.

Noise

Noise is interference—whether audible or not—that interferes with your listeners' receiving the messages you wish them to receive. The "noise band" around the speaker

TABLE 21.1
the areas of public communication

Areas	Some Theoretical Concerns	Some Skills Concerns	For Further Exploration
Public speaking, the study of the principles and skills for informing and persuading	Audience analysis, organizational strategies, principles of information transfer and for persuasion, style and language delivery	How can the speaker analyze and adapt to a public audience? How can the speaker be a more effective spokesperson? How can the speaker communicate credibility to an audience?	Sprague and Stuart (1996) present the principles of public speaking in handbook form. Larson (1995), Bettinghaus and Cody (1994), and Woodward and Denton (1996) educate the consumer of persuasion. Axtell (1992), Walters (1993), and Linver (1994) are representative of the many popular works on the practical skills and strategies of public communication. Golden, Berquist, & Coleman (1993) survey rhetorical theories and Foss (1996) covers rhetorical criticism.
Public address, the study of the transaction of public communication and society	The role of public speaking in the American revolution, public speaking as a democratic force	How can speakers persuade an audience more effectively? How do they inform an electorate?	
Rhetoric, the study of the theory of communication	Metaphor, theories of communication, feminist rhetoric and criticism	How can language be used to more effectively move an audience? How can misunderstandings be avoided?	
Homiletics, the study of religious speaking	Pulpit speaking, interreligious communication, conversion, cultism	How can the minister strengthen the beliefs of the congregation? How can religions be more effective at conversion? How can cults better indoctrinate their members?	
Public relations, the study of protecting and preserving and creating a positive image	Speech writing, credibility building, corrective advertising	How can the speechwriter be more effective? How can one's credibility be enhanced?	
Persuasion, the study of influencing attitudes and behaviors	Theories of persuasion, attitude change, opinion formation	How can listeners be more easily persuaded? How can listeners inoculate themselves against being persuaded?	
Ethics, the study of moral values	Theories of communication ethics, free speech, hate speech, emotional and logical discourse, plagiarism	How can a person recognize unethical communications? How can a person communicate ethically? How can a person avoid plagiarism?	
Political communication (a subdivision of public address), the study of the role of public speaking in politics and of politics in public speaking	Presidential rhetoric, campaign speaking, advertising, credibility, speech writing	How can a positive spin be put on a negative incident? How can campaign speaking be made more effective? How can competitors be smeared most effectively? How can you sell more cereal? How can you make the public love your product?	

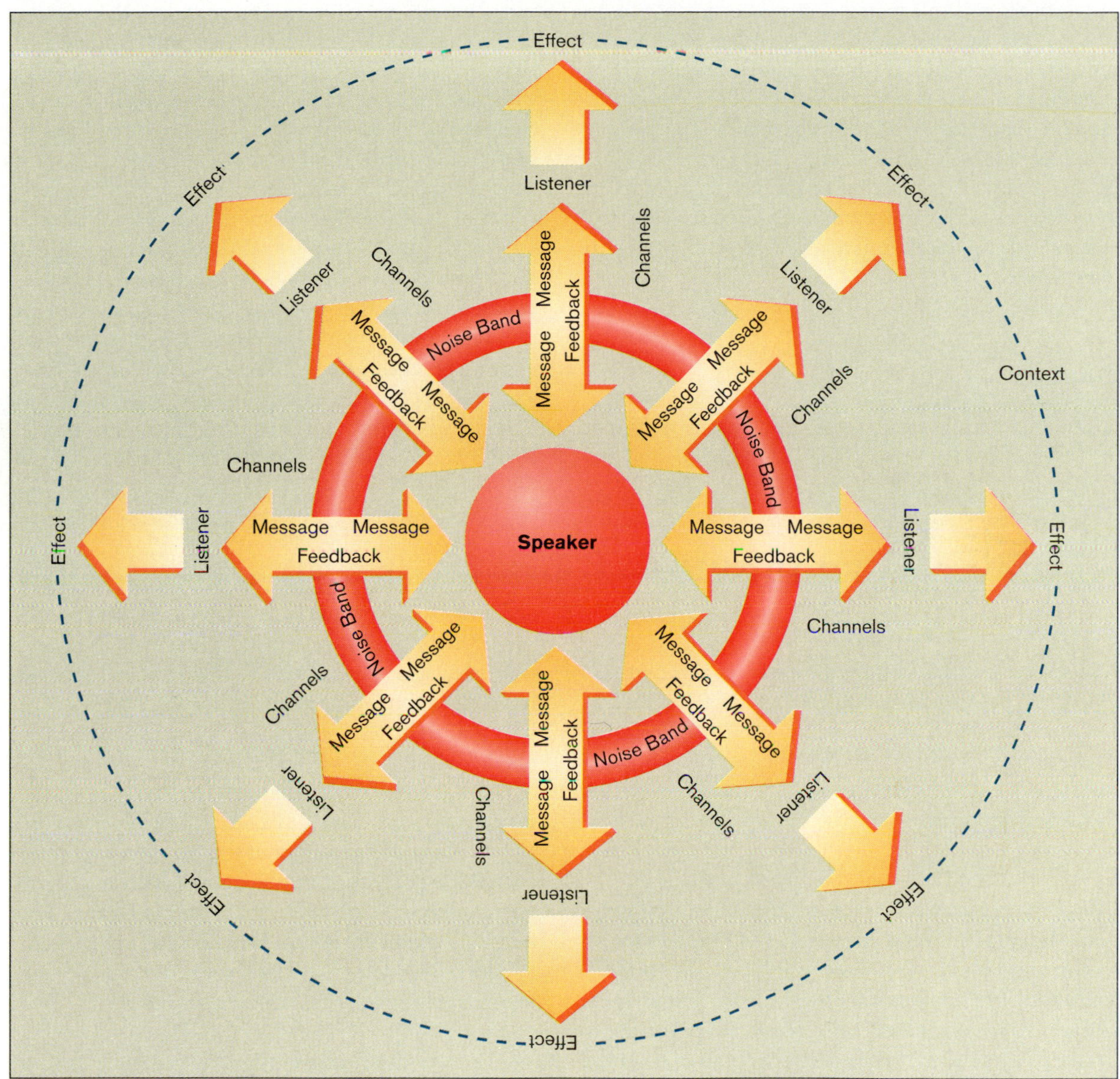

FIGURE 21.1 The public communication transaction. The specifics of this model are explained in the accompanying discussion. Note, however, that like all forms of communication, public speaking is a transactional process; speaker and audience members simultaneously exchange messages.

(see Figure 21.1) shows how noise interferes with your messages. As discussed in Unit 1, noise may be physical, psychological, or semantic.

As a speaker you may cut out some noise sources or lessen their effects, but you cannot cut out all noise. Therefore, learn to combat its effects by speaking louder, repeating important assertions, organizing your ideas so they are easy to follow, gesturing to reinforce your spoken messages, or defining technical or complex terms.

Effect

As a public speaker, you design and deliver your speeches to influence your listeners. Politicians give campaign speeches in an effort to secure your vote.

Advertisers and salespersons give sales pitches to get you to buy their products. Teachers give lectures to influence your thinking about history, psychology, or communication. The model of public communication in Figure 21.1 shows each effect separately to emphasize that, as each listener is unique, each effect is also unique. In reacting to the very same speech, one listener may agree completely, another may disagree, and still another may misunderstand the entire message.

Context

Like all communicators, speaker and listeners operate in a physical, social-psychological, temporal, and cultural context (see Unit 1). The context influences you as the speaker, the audience, the speech, and the effects of the speech. Therefore, analyze the context with care and prepare your speech with this specific context in mind. For example, you cannot treat a speech in a small intimate room and one in a sports arena in the same way (physical context). Similarly, you could not address a supportive and a hostile audience in the same way (social-psychological context). Your speech at a protest rally will have to differ depending on whether you are the first speaker or the twentieth; the previous speeches—and even the anticipated speeches—will influence how the audience sees your speech (temporal context). Appealing to the "competitive spirit" and "financial gain" may prove effective with Wall Street executives but may insult

ETHICAL LISTENING

Because public communication is a two-way process, both speaker and listener share in the success or failure of the interaction. Both share in the moral implications of the public communication exchange as well. Two major principles govern the ethics of listening.

HONEST HEARING

Give the speaker an honest hearing. Avoid prejudging the speaker before hearing her or him. Try to put aside prejudices and preconceptions so you can evaluate the speaker's message fairly. At the same time, try to empathize with the speaker. You don't have to agree with the speaker but try to understand emotionally as well as intellectually what the speaker means. Then, accept or reject the speaker's ideas on the basis of the information offered, not on the basis of some bias or incomplete understanding.

HONEST RESPONDING

Just as the speaker should be honest with the listener, the listener should be honest with the speaker. This means giving open and honest feedback to the speaker. In a learning environment such as a public speaking class, it means giving honest and constructive criticism to help the speaker improve. It also means reflecting honestly on the questions that the speaker raises. Much as the listener has a right to expect an active speaker, the speaker has the right to expect an active listener. The speaker has a right to expect a listener who will actively deal with, rather than just passively hear, the message.

As illustrated throughout this text, culture influences all aspects of communication; listening is not an exception. Consider, for example, these few questions involving ethical listening and cultural differences. To what extent are your answers a statement of culture-specific ethical principles?

- Do you listen differently (for example, less or more openly) to a speech by a culturally different person than by a culturally similar person?
- Would you listen fairly to a speaker explaining religious beliefs and practices that are very different from your own?
- Would you assign similar credibility rankings (all other things being equal) to speakers from culturally different groups and culturally similar groups? Put differently, would you ascribe a person a credibility rating based solely or partially on the person's cultural identification?

Buddhist missionaries (cultural context). This cultural context will influence the ways in which you need to prepare your speech (see discussions of culture in this and the next two units) and in the ways in which listeners will receive your message (see Unit 4).

Messages and Channels

Messages are the signals sent by the speaker and received by the listener. These signals pass through one or more channels (the medium that carries the message signals) on their way from speaker to listener and from listener to speaker. Both the auditory and the visual channels are significant in public communication. Through the auditory channel you send your spoken messages—your words and your sentences. At the same time, you also send messages through the visual channel, through eye contact (and the lack of it), body movement, hand and facial gestures, and clothing, for example.

Language and Style

In conversation you vary your language on the basis of the person with whom you are speaking. When speaking with friends, for example, you would use your normal, everyday language. You would speak to them in much the same language you would use when you talk to yourself. When talking with children, you might use easier words and shorter sentences. If you were trying to impress someone, you might use a different style.

In public communication situations it is especially important that language be adjusted to the audience. In public communication, however, your listeners cannot interrupt to ask, for example, what a particular word means. Therefore you need to make sure that your language is free of any terms that might not be instantly clear to your listeners. You don't want your listeners to stop listening to what you are saying while they try to figure out to what "maximize the latter" or "unauthorized bribery" refers. In public communication, your language must be instantly intelligible.

Effective speakers generally speak with **oral style**, a quality of spoken language that clearly separates it from written language. Researchers who have examined a great body of speech and writings have found several important differences (Akinnaso 1982; DeVito 1965, 1970). Generally, spoken language consists of shorter, simpler, and more familiar words than does

How would you describe the language and style of some specific person you admire? How would you contrast this style with that of a person you find boring and difficult to listen to?

written language. Spoken language also contains a greater number of self-reference terms (references to the speaker) and terms that incorporate the speaker as part of the observation (for example, "It seems to me that . . ." or "As I see it . . ."). Spoken language also contains a greater number of allness terms (for example, all, none, every, always, never) as well as more pseudo-quantifying terms (for example, many, much, very, and lots).

Delivery

In conversation you usually don't even think of delivery. You don't ask yourself how you should sit or stand or gesture. If public speaking is a relatively new experience, you will probably feel uncomfortable at first. You may find yourself wondering what to do with your hands or whether or not you should move about. With time and experience, you will find that your delivery will follow naturally from what you are saying, just as it does in conversation.

Ethics

Ethics is a crucial consideration in all communications. In public communication, ethics is especially important because there are so many listeners and the potential effects of unethical messages are so wide-ranging (Bok 1978; Jaksa & Pritchard 1988; Johannesen 1991). Communications can vary from highly ethical to highly unethical. Speakers may, for example, argue for a position because they believe it is right, even if it means they will be censured and criticized. Whistleblowers, critics of the rich and powerful, and social reformers are generally good examples of people who risk considerable losses to say what they feel has to be said. At the other extreme are speakers who will use the audience for their own gain—the advertising hucksters, con artists, and liars.

Between these extremes are the vast majority—those who exaggerate or slant the findings of a study to support their own position, emphasize their positive and hide their negative qualities, or lead others to think their motives are altruistic when they are actually selfish.

The questions that need to be asked regarding all communication are, "To what extent is this message ethical?" "To what extent is the message morally responsible?" For some messages, the answers are easy. Thus, most would probably agree that to take someone else's work and pass it off as one's own is plagiarism and that this is unethical. For other situations, however, the answers are not so easy; not everyone agrees on what is ethical and what is unethical.

THINK ABOUT

Think about, for example, some of the questions that raise ethical issues. These are similar to those raised in Unit 1 but are especially applicable to public communication.

- Is it ethical to exaggerate the merits of your proposal to secure acceptance?
- Is it ethical to take phrases or ideas from others without acknowledging their source?
- Is it ethical to leave out negative aspects of your proposal and just reveal the positive aspects?
- Is it ethical to spread negative gossip about your opposition if you know it's true?
- Is it ethical to persuade audience members to do something by scaring them? By threatening them? By making them feel guilty?

APPREHENSION IN PUBLIC COMMUNICATION

As explained throughout this text, apprehension is a normal part of most communication interactions (see Units 14, 17, 19, and 20), but it is in public communication that it is usually most prominent. Apprehension is experienced not only by the beginning public speaker; it is also felt by even the most experienced. People do not seem to get rid of apprehension but rather learn to deal with it and control it (Richmond & McCroskey 1996).

Speaker apprehension affects the way people feel and the way they act. Some people develop negative feelings about their ability to communicate orally. They predict that their communication efforts will fail. They feel that whatever gain they would make as a result of speaking is not worth the fear they would experience. As a result, apprehensive speakers avoid communication situations and, when forced to partic-

INTRODUCING RESEARCH

ETHICS IN RESEARCH

Ethical considerations must govern the way in which scholarship is used and the way in which human subjects are treated.

SCHOLARSHIP

According to Stacks and Hocking (1992) ethical scholarship involves such issues as these:

1. giving appropriate credit to others for their ideas and statements or for their contribution to the actual research project (for example, did others help you collect your data or make suggestions that you incorporated into your study?)
2. reporting conflicting findings (even when these upset your pet theory)
3. explaining the limitations or flaws of your research
4. using primary sources whenever possible

DEALING WITH HUMAN SUBJECTS

The American Psychological Association (APA) has proposed a list of ethical guidelines for using humans in research studies which many other organizations have adopted (reprinted in Stacks and Hocking 1992, pp. 52–53). Among the guides are these:

1. Do not put human subjects at risk of harming themselves psychologically or physically.
2. Don't force people to participate in a research study; they should have the right to participate or not and to terminate their participation at any time.
3. Debrief subjects; after data are collected, subjects should be told about the research study; any misconceptions that may have arisen should be clarified.
4. Keep confidential any information learned about a subject during the course of the research study.

Do you agree with these guidelines? Are there other guidelines that you think should be a part of the code of ethics for a researcher? Consider, for example, in reference to item No. 2: are students "forced" to participate in research when instructors/researchers give students extra credit for participating in their research studies?

Consider too the ethics of deception. The APA code of research ethics notes that the use of concealment or deception may be necessary. The code cautions, however, that the researcher should (1) determine if deception is justified by the significance of the study, (2) determine if procedures other than deception could be used, and (3) provide the subjects with an explanation of the deception as soon as possible. What do you think of this? Do you think these cautions make research involving deception ethical? Or, do you see these cautions as attempts to justify what is simply an unethical practice?

ipate, speak as little as possible. To get a better idea of how apprehensive you are when speaking, you may wish to pause here and take the self-test, "How Apprehensive Are You in Public Speaking?" on page 381.

General and Specific Apprehension

If you have a general apprehension that manifests itself in all communication situations, you have *trait apprehension*–a fear of communication generally, regardless of the specific situation. Your fear would appear in conversations, small group settings, and public speaking situations.

If you are like most people, and experience apprehension in only certain communication situations, you have *state apprehension*—a fear that is specific to a given communication situation. For example, you may fear public communication but have no difficulty in talking with two or three people. Or, you may fear job interviews but have no fear of public communication. State apprehension is extremely common. Most

Can you articulate a theory that would attribute speaker apprehension to cultural values and beliefs?

people experience it for some situations. As you probably guessed, public communication provokes the most apprehension.

Degrees of Apprehension

Speaker apprehension exists on a continuum. Some people are extremely apprehensive and are unable to function in communication. They suffer greatly in a society oriented around communication where success often depends on the ability to communicate effectively. Other people are so mildly apprehensive that they appear to experience no fear at all. They actively seek out communication experiences and rarely feel even the slightest apprehension. Most of us fall between these two extremes.

For some people, apprehension is debilitating and hinders personal effectiveness in professional and social relationships (Comadena & Prusank 1988). For others, apprehension is motivating and may actually help in achieving one's goals.

Positive Apprehension

Although you may at first view apprehension as harmful, that is not necessarily the case. In fact, apprehension can energize you; it may motivate you to work a little harder to produce a speech that will be better than it might have been. Further, the audience cannot see the apprehension symptoms that you might experience. Even though you may think that the audience can hear your heart beat faster and faster, they cannot. They cannot see your knees tremble. They cannot sense your dry throat—at least not most of the time.

Culture and Speaker Apprehension

Speaker apprehension is universal, though its degree varies with the culture. For example, in an investigation of shyness (closely akin to speaker apprehension but more general) among Japanese, Taiwanese, and Jewish students living in the United States, the Japanese and Taiwanese indicated much greater shyness than the Jewish students (Carducci with Zimbardo 1995). In further studies in Japan, Taiwan, and Israel, the differences were even greater. Only 30 percent of the Israeli students said they were shy but 60 percent of the Japanese and Taiwanese said they were shy. The researchers speculate that one of the key factors accounting for this difference is that in Japan and Taiwan the child gets little credit for his or her success;

SELF TEST

how apprehensive are you in public speaking?

This questionnaire is composed of six statements concerning your feelings about public speaking. Indicate in the space provided the degree to which each statement applies to you by marking whether you: 1 = strongly agree, 2 = agree, 3 = are undecided, 4 = disagree, 5 = strongly disagree. There are no right or wrong answers. Many of the statements are similar to other statements; do not be concerned about this. Work quickly; record your first impression.

_____ 1. I have no fear of giving a speech.
_____ 2. Certain parts of my body feel very tense and rigid while giving a speech.
_____ 3. I feel relaxed while giving a speech.
_____ 4. My thoughts become confused and jumbled when I am giving a speech.
_____ 5. I face the prospect of giving a speech with confidence.
_____ 6. While giving a speech, I get so nervous that I forget facts I really know.

Thinking Critically About Apprehension in Public Speaking To obtain your public speaking apprehension score, use the following formula:

18 plus scores for items 1, 3, and 5

minus scores for items 2, 4, and 6

The result is your apprehension score for public speaking. A score above 18 indicates some degree of apprehension, which is quite normal for public speaking. Most people score above 18 in the public speaking context, so if you scored relatively high, you are among the vast majority of people who experience fear in this relatively formal communication situation. In public speaking you are the sole focus of attention and are usually being evaluated on your performance. Therefore, experiencing fear or anxiety is not strange or unique. You may wish to compare your apprehension score on this test with those for the previous tests. Research shows that your public speaking score should be higher than the scores for conversation (see Unit 13), group discussions (see Unit 17), and meetings (see Unit 19) (Richmond & McCroskey 1996). Research has not yet compared these apprehension tests with the employment apprehension test (see Unit 20). What do you think would be found? How would you go about comparing apprehension in these several contexts?

Source: James C. McCroskey *Introduction to Rhetorical Communication,* 6th ed. (Upper Saddle River, NJ: Prentice-Hall, 1993).

instead the credit goes to the parents for raising such a wonderful child. A failure on the other hand might result in a loss of face for the child and perhaps even for his or her family. As a result, the child may become shy. This pattern seems common in collectivistic cultures. In Israel the child gets rewarded just for trying, a practice that is considerably more popular in individualistic cultures.

As might be expected, speaker apprehension is heightened in intercultural situations. Intercultural communication can create uncertainty, fear, and anxiety, all of which are intimately related to speaker apprehension (Stephan & Stephan 1985). When you are in an intercultural situation—say your audience is composed largely of people of cultures very different from your own—you are more uncertain about the situation and about their possible responses. Not surprisingly, most people react negatively to high uncertainty and develop a decreased attraction for these other people (Gudykunst & Nishida 1984; Gudykunst, Yang, & Nishida 1985). When you are sure of the situation and can predict what will happen, you are more likely to feel comfortable and at ease. When the situation is uncertain, however, and you cannot predict what will happen, you become more apprehensive (Gudykunst & Kim 1992).

Intercultural situations can also engender fear (see Unit 6). You might, for example, fear saying something that will prove offensive or reveal your own prejudices or ethnocentrism. The fear easily translates into apprehension.

Intercultural situations often create anxiety, a feeling very similar to apprehension. You may feel anxiety for a number of reasons (Stephan & Stephan 1985). For example, your *prior relationships* with members of a culturally different group will influence your apprehension. If your prior relationships were few or if they were unpleasant, then you are likely to experience greater apprehension when dealing with these members than if these prior experiences were numerous and positive.

Your *thoughts and feelings* about the group will also influence your apprehension. For example, if you have little knowledge of the other culture, hold stereotypes and prejudices, are highly ethnocentric, or if you feel that you are very different from these others, then you are likely to experience more apprehension than if you saw these people as similar to you.

The *situation* you are in can also exert influence. If, for example, you feel that members of another group are competing with you or evaluating you, then you are likely to experience more apprehension than if the situation were more cooperative and equal. Similarly, unstructured and ambiguous situations create more anxiety because you are not quite sure what is expected of you. Also, your status relative to the others in the group will influence your anxiety; if you are lower in status, you are likely to experience greater anxiety than if you were higher in status.

Factors Influencing Public Communication Apprehension

THINK ABOUT

Think about the factors that influence public communication anxiety (Beatty 1988; also see Ayres 1990). In reviewing these factors visualize yourself in a specific communication situation, say, giving a speech to your communication class. How will these factors come into play? How can their effects be lessened?

- *Perceived novelty.* Situations that are new and different from those with which you are familiar contribute to anxiety. As the novelty of the situation is reduced (as you gain experience in public communication), your anxiety is also reduced.
- *Subordinate status.* When you feel that others are better speakers than you or that they know more about the topic than you do, anxiety increases. Thinking more positively about yourself and being thorough in your preparation are helpful techniques for reducing this particular cause of anxiety.
- *Conspicuousness.* When you feel you are the center of attention, as you normally are in public communication, your anxiety may increase. Thinking of public communication as a type of conversation may help reduce this feeling of conspicuousness.
- *Dissimilarity.* The more different you feel from your listeners, the more apt you are to experience fear in public communication. Therefore, emphasize your similarity with your listeners as you prepare your public speeches as well as during the presentation of the actual speech.
- *Prior history.* A prior history of apprehension is likely to increase anxiety. Your positive public communication experiences should help reduce this cause of anxiety.

Theories of Speaker Apprehension and Its Management

What causes speaker apprehension? Can it be controlled or managed effectively? Following communication researchers Virginia Richmond and James McCroskey (1996) we can distinguish three theoretical (and eminently practical) approaches to understanding speaker apprehension and how it may be managed or controlled: cognitive restructuring, systematic desensitization, and skill acquisition.

Cognitive Restructuring

Cognitive restructuring holds that your own unrealistic beliefs generate a fear of failure. Because you set yourself unachievable goals (Everyone must love me, I have to be thoroughly competent, I have to be the best in everything), you logically fear failure. This fear of failure (and the irrational beliefs behind it) are at the foundation of your apprehension (Markway,

Carmin, Pollard, & Flynn 1992 among others). Cognitive restructuring, then, advises you to change your irrational beliefs and substitute more rational ones (It would be nice if everyone loved me but I don't need that to survive. I can fail. Although it would be nice, I don't have to be the best in everything.) Your last step is to practice your new more rational beliefs (Ellis & Harper 1975; Ellis 1988; Watson & Dodd 1984).

The process may go something like this: unrealistic beliefs give rise to anxiety because you know you can never achieve these unrealistically high goals and that you'll fail at some point. There's not a speaker in the world who wouldn't fail given these unrealistic beliefs. You then focus on the inevitable failure; you can almost see yourself failing. This image leads to a loss of confidence and further visions of failure.

A special type of cognitive restructuring is *performance visualization,* designed specifically to reduce the outward manifestations of speaker apprehension and also to reduce negative thinking (Ayres & Hopf 1993; Ayres, Hopf, & Ayres 1994). This technique, not surprisingly, has been shown to be significantly more effective with those who can create vivid mental images (Ayres, Hopf, & Ayres 1994). The first part of performance visualization is to develop a positive attitude and a positive self-perception. This involves visualizing yourself in the role of the effective public speaker. Visualize yourself walking to the front of the room—fully prepared and totally confident. You scan the audience and slowly begin your speech. Throughout the speech you are fully in control of the situation. The audience is at rapt attention and as you finish, burst into wild applause. Throughout this visualization, avoid all negative thoughts.

As you visualize yourself giving an effective public speech, take special note of how you walk, look at your listeners, handle your notes, respond to questions, and especially how you feel about the whole experience.

The second part of performance visualization is designed to help you model your performance on that of an especially effective speaker. Here you would view a particularly competent public speaker on video and make a mental movie of it. As you review the actual and the mental movie, you begin to shift yourself into the role of the effective speaker. You, in effect, become this effective speaker.

Systematic Desensitization

Systematic desensitization is a technique for dealing with a variety of fears, including those involved in public communication (Wolpe 1957). The general assumption of systematic desensitization is that apprehension was learned, and because it was learned, it can be unlearned. The procedure involves creating a hierarchy of behaviors leading up to the desired but feared behavior (say, speaking before an audience). One specific hierarchy might look like this:

- giving a speech in class
- introducing another speaker to the class
- speaking in a group in front of the class
- answering a question in class
- asking a question in class

You would begin at the bottom of this hierarchy and rehearse this behavior mentally over a period of days until you can clearly visualize asking a question in class without any anxiety. Once you can accomplish this, you can move to the second level. Here you would visualize the somewhat more threatening behavior, answering a question. Once you can do this, you can move to the third level, and so on until you get to the desired behavior.

Skill Acquisition

The third general approach to speaker apprehension holds that you develop apprehension largely from having inadequate skills—because you have inadequate skills, you logically fear failing. The strategy for managing apprehension, therefore, is to acquire the specific skills involved in any given behavior. For example, the skills of public communication would involve a number of more specific skills. These more specific skills would be mastered individually and then put together into the process of preparing and delivering an effective speech. For example, some such skills would include gaining attention, analyzing and adapting to the specific audience, using voice and bodily action to reinforce the message, reading and adapting to audience feedback, and using language to communicate the desired meaning clearly. Other types of skills might be using deep breathing to engender a sense of relaxation, creative visualization so that you can see yourself as successful, or self-affirmation, which helps you feel more positively about yourself.

With mastery, the task—in this case public communication, but it could just as logically be any behavioral task—becomes less forbidding and hence less anxiety provoking. With mastery also comes successful experiences. These successes help build your confidence and lessen anxiety.

THE AUDIENCE IN PUBLIC COMMUNICATION

In public communication—as in other forms of communication—the audience and the speech (the message and the listener) are really inseparable. Public communication audiences vary greatly. Thousands of people at Yankee Stadium listening to Billy Graham, 30 students in a classroom listening to a lecture, and 5 people listening to a street corner orator are all audiences. The characteristic that seems best to define such audiences is common purpose. An audience is a group of individuals gathered together to hear a speech.

You deliver a speech to inform or persuade your audience. A teacher lectures on Gestalt psychology to increase understanding. A minister speaks against adultery to influence behaviors and attitudes. A football coach gives a pep talk to motivate the team. All of these persons are trying to produce change. If they are to be successful, then they must know their audience.

The first step in audience analysis is to construct an audience profile in which you analyze the sociological or demographic characteristics of the audience. These characteristics help you to estimate the attitudes, beliefs, and values of the audience. If you want to effect changes in these attitudes, beliefs, and values, you have to know what they are.

Attitude refers to your tendency to act for or against a person, object, or position. If you have a positive attitude toward the death penalty, you are likely to act in favor of instituting the death penalty (for example, by voting for a candidate who supports the death penalty) or argue in favor of the death penalty. If you have a negative attitude toward the death penalty, then you are likely to act against it or argue against it. Attitudes influence how favorable or unfavorable listeners will be toward speakers who support or denounce the death penalty.

Belief refers to the confidence or conviction you have in the existence or truth of some proposition. For example, you may believe that there is an afterlife, that education is the best way to rise from poverty, that democracy is the best form of government, or that all people are born equal.

If your listeners believe that the death penalty is a deterrent to crime, for example, then they will be more likely to favor arguments for (and speakers who support) the death penalty than would listeners who do not believe in the connection between death penalty and deterrence.

Value refers to the relative worth you place on an object, person, or position. Technically, value can refer to either positive or negative worth. In popular usage, however, we often reserve the term for positive evaluation. If your listeners place a high positive value on crime deterrence, then they will also view arguments that will help achieve this goal positively.

As you can readily see from this example of the death penalty, the attitudes, beliefs, and values that your listeners have will greatly influence how receptive they will be to your topic, your point of view, and your evidence and arguments.

Audience Sociology (Demographics)

THINK ABOUT

Think about your own audience. How will the sociological or demographic characteristics of your audience impact on your speech? Here six such variables, generally considered essential in understanding any audience, are discussed. Once you understand these variables, you'll be able to make intelligent decisions about how to adapt your speech to this specific group of people. The variables are: (1) age; (2) gender; (3) cultural factors; (4) educational and intellectual levels; (5) occupation, income, and status; and (6) religion. As you read these brief descriptions, try analyzing your class as an audience. If you have the opportunity, compare your analysis with others.

Age

Different age groups have different attitudes, beliefs, and values simply because they have had different experiences. Take these differences into consideration when preparing your speeches. For example, let us say that you are an investment counselor and you want to persuade your listeners to invest their money to increase their earnings. Your speech would have to be very different if you were addressing an audience of retired people (say, in their 60s) and an audience of young executives (in their 30s).

Gender

Gender is one of the most difficult audience variables to analyze. The rapid social changes taking place today make it difficult to pin down the effects of gender. Although we use the shorthand "men" and "women," remember that psychological sex roles may be more significant than biological sex in accounting for these differences.

For example, if you plan to speak on caring for a newborn baby, you would approach an audience of men very differently from an audience of women. With an audience of women, you could probably assume a much greater knowledge of the subject and a greater degree of comfort in dealing with it. With an audience of men, you might have to cover such elementary topics as the type of creams and lotions to use, how to test the temperature of a bottle, and the way to prepare a formula.

Cultural Factors

Nationality, race, and cultural identity and identification are crucial in audience analysis. Largely because of different training and experiences, the interests, values, and goals of different cultural groups will also differ. An American would be ill-advised to include references in a speech given to Japanese citizens to the military capabilities of the United States that can destroy entire cities. Nor would an American be advised to talk about illegal aliens to an audience of Mexicans or religion to Iraqis (Axtell 1993).

Educational and Intellectual Levels

An educated person may not be very intelligent. Conversely, an intelligent person may not be very well educated. In most cases, however, the two go together. When addressing the less educated, use commonly understood words, avoid jargon and technical vocabulary, and make connections between your supporting materials (examples, arguments, evidence, and the like) and your main propositions. Generally, a good guide to follow is to never overestimate the knowledge or education of your audience but never underestimate their intelligence.

Occupation, Income, and Status

Occupation, income, and status, although not the same, are most often positively related. Therefore, we can deal with them together. Job security and occupational pride are strong motivators and are always important in understanding the attitudes and values of an audience. Different socioeconomic groups will view the same issue in very different terms. The issues of welfare reform, universal health insurance, and property taxes, for example, are seen very differently by the poor and by the middle class and the rich.

Religion

Today there is great diversity within each religion. Almost invariably there are conservative, liberal, and middle-of-the-road groups within each religion. As the differences within each religion widen, the differences between and among religions seem to narrow. Different religions are coming closer together on various social and political, as well as moral, issues. A vast number of topics will be influenced by the religion and religious beliefs. Consider, for example, how religious beliefs might influence such issues as these: prayer in the schools, gay and lesbian rights, health care, Middle East conflicts, and women's rights.

Audience Psychology (Psychographics)

THINK ABOUT

Think about your audience also from a psychological point of view. That is, in addition to their sociological characteristics, audiences may be analyzed in terms of their psychographics or psychological characteristics. Audiences may be viewed along such scales as those in Figure 21.2. By indicating on each scale where a particular audience is (or where you think it is), you may construct an audience profile. Since each audience is unique, each audience will have a unique profile.

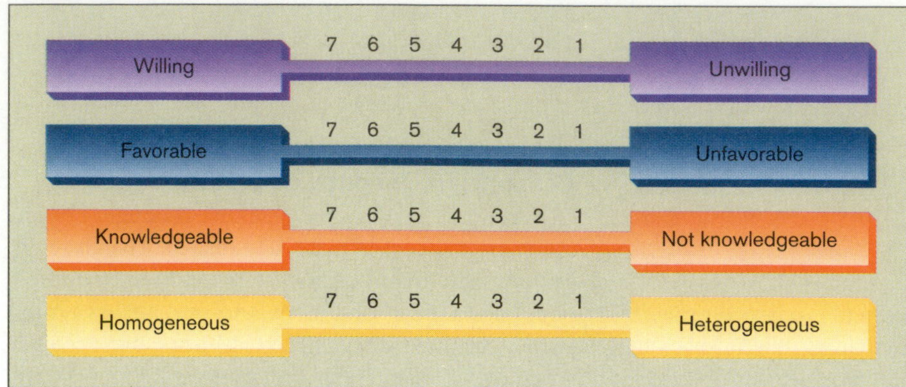

FIGURE 21.2 The dimensions of an audience. These four dimensions are not the only ones that could be mentioned. Such additional dimensions as passive-active, critical-uncritical, and interested-uninterested might also be used. What suggestions could you offer a public speaker for dealing with audiences differing in passivity, criticalness, and interest?

Willingness

Audiences gather with varying degrees of willingness to hear a speaker. Some are anxious to hear the speaker and might even pay substantial admission prices. The "lecture circuit," for example, is a most lucrative aspect of public life. Public figures often earn substantially more from speaking than they do from their "regular jobs."

While some audiences are willing to pay to hear a speaker, others do not seem to care one way or the other. Still other audiences need to be persuaded to listen (or at least to sit in the audience). A group of people who gather to hear Shirley MacLaine talk about supernatural experiences are probably there willingly. They want to be there and they want to hear what MacLaine has to say. On the other hand, some groups gather because they must; for example, a union contract may require members to attend meetings.

Favorableness

Audiences may or may not agree with your thesis or point of view. One group may be in agreement with your speech advocating comprehensive health insurance while another group may be totally against it. If you intend to change your audiences' attitudes, beliefs, or behaviors, you must understand their present position.

Audiences also differ in their attitudes toward you and toward your topic. At times the audience may have no real feeling, positive or negative. At other times they will have very clear feelings that must be confronted. Thus, when Richard Nixon addressed the nation after Watergate, it was impossible to avoid the audience's unfavorable attitude toward him as a person. Sometimes favorableness will be influenced by specific characteristics of the speaker. Thus, a group of police officers may resent listening to a convicted felon argue against unlawful search and seizure. On the other hand, they might be quite favorable toward essentially the same speech given by a respected jurist or criminologist.

Similarly, audiences may have favorable or unfavorable responses to you because of your racial or ethnic origin, religion, or social status.

Knowledge

Listeners differ greatly in the knowledge they have. Some listeners will be quite knowledgeable about the topic. Others will be almost totally ignorant. Mixed audiences are the really difficult ones. If you are unaware of the audience's knowledge, you will not know what to assume and what to explain. You will not know how much information will overload the channels and how much will bore the audience to sleep.

Homogeneity

Audiences vary in homogeneity—the degree to which they have similar characteristics, for example, values, attitudes, knowledge, willingness, and so on. Homogeneous audiences consist of individuals who are very much alike. Heterogeneous audiences consist of widely different individuals.

Obviously, it is easier to address a homogeneous group than a heterogeneous group. If your listeners are alike, your arguments will be as effective for one as for another. The language appropriate to one will be appropriate to another, and so on, through all the elements of the public communication transaction.

With a heterogeneous group, however, this does not hold. The argument that works with one subgroup will not work with another. The language that is appropriate to the educated members will not be appropriate to the uneducated. When you address a heterogeneous audience you will have to make some tough decisions.

SUMMARY

In this unit we introduced the nature of public communication, speaker apprehension, and the public communication audience.

1. Public communication consists of a speaker addressing a relatively large audience with a relatively continuous discourse usually in a face-to-face situation.
2. The essential components of a public speech are speaker, listeners (audience), noise, effect, context, messages and channels, language and style, delivery, and ethics.
3. Speaker apprehension refers to a fear of communication and is extremely common in public communication.
4. Trait apprehension refers to a fear that manifests itself in all communication situations and thus is a type of personality trait; state apprehension refers to a fear that is unique to specific situations, for example public communication or employment interviewing.
5. Speaker apprehension varies in degree from mild to severe, may have positive as well as negative effects, and is greatly influenced by the culture.
6. Three theories focusing on the management of speaker apprehension are: (1) cognitive restructuring: unrealistic beliefs that generate a fear of failure need to be replaced with more logical and more productive beliefs; (2) sysytematic desensitization: apprehension can be unlearned through conditioning positive responses to less threatening behaviors and gradually working up to responding positively to public speaking; and (3) skill aquisition: apprehension results from inadequate skill and is lessened when the appropriate skills are acquired.
7. The audience is central to any conception of public communication and must be analyzed carefully if an effective speech is to be constructed and if you are to understand the ways in which a speech has an effect.
8. A sociological or demographic analysis of the audience consists of analyzing age, gender, cultural factors, education and intellectual levels, occupation, income and status, and religion. In addition, your audience's expectations, relational status, special interests, organizational memberships, and political affiliations often provide useful insight into who they are and what their attitudes and beliefs are.
9. In addition to its demographic characteristics, an audience needs to be examined in terms of its psychological willingness to hear the speech, its favorableness, its knowledge about the speech topic, and its degree of homogeneity.

THINKING CRITICALLY ABOUT THE PRELIMINARIES TO PUBLIC COMMUNICATION

1. What role will public communication play in your professional life?
2. Is your apprehension score in public communication higher than the scores you received in conversations (see Unit 13), group discussions (see Unit 18), meetings (see Unit 19), and interviewing (see Unit 20)? What characteristics of the communication situation most influence your level of apprehension?
3. How satisfied are you with your apprehension scores? If you are not satisfied, what do you intend to do about them?
4. In one study of students of African, African American, and Caribbean descent, the researchers concluded that shyness is experienced differently in different cul-

tures (Breidenstein-Cutspec & Goering 1989). Do you find that members of different cultures have differing levels of apprehension? Or, that different cultures experience apprehension in different situations? Or, that different cultures "teach" their members to experience or not experience apprehension?

5. In a study of high and low communication apprehensive students, it was found that males with high apprehension rated their female communication partners as less attractive and less trustworthy than did low communication apprehensive men. High apprehensives also rated their female partner as less satisfying to interact with than did low apprehensive men (Ayres 1989). Do these findings seem logical to you? If so, what reasons could you give for these findings?
6. What theory of speaker apprehension seems to offer the most insight into how speaker apprehension develops and how it can be managed?
7. How important is your culture in influencing your attitudes, values, and beliefs? A good way to explore this question is to talk with a person from a culture very different from yours about your religious beliefs; attitudes toward relationships, success, or money; and family values, for example.
8. What factors other than those discussed here are important in understanding audience sociology?
9. What psychological profile would your ideal audience have? What profile would your nightmare audience have?
10. How would you go about finding answers to such question as these:
    a. Are men or women more likely to experience high communication apprehension? Are there certain situations in which women would be less apprehensive than men and other situations in which men would be less apprehensive than women?
    b. Do different cultures have different rules for public communication?
    c. Are unfavorable audiences more likely to respond favorably to a speaker who is demographically similar or to a speaker who is dissimilar to them?
    d. How do members of individualistic and collectivistic cultures define "ethical communication"?

twenty-two unit

Principles of Public Communication

unit contents

unit goals

After completing this unit, you should be able to

1. explain the principles for informative speaking: information load, relevance, appropriateness, new to old, several senses, and levels of abstraction
2. explain the principles of persuasion: selective exposure, audience participation, inoculation, and magnitude of change
3. define *argument* and *evidence* and the three general tests of reasoning
4. explain the role of emotion and motivational appeals in motivating behavior
5. define *speaker credibility* and the ways in which credibility impressions may be formed
6. define *criticism,* its values and standards

In this unit we present some principles of public speaking for communicating information and persuasion. These principles are actually applicable to all forms of communication but seem especially appropriate in the public communication context. In addition we consider the three types of proof: appeals based on logic, emotion, and credibility. Last, we look at criticism and its role in public communication.

PRINCIPLES OF INFORMATIVE COMMUNICATION

When you communicate information you tell your listeners something they do not know, something new. You may tell them of a new way of looking at old things or an old way of looking at new things. You may discuss a theory not previously heard of or a familiar one not fully understood. You may talk about events that the audience may be unaware of or about which they may have misconceptions. Regardless of the type of informative speech, the following principles should help.

The Information Load Principle

There is a limit to the amount of information that an audience can take in at one time. Therefore, speakers need to resist overloading the audience with information. Limit the amount of information that you communicate and expand its presentation. It is better to present two new items of information and explain these with examples, illustrations, and descriptions, than to present five items without the needed amplification.

The Relevance Principle

Listeners remember information best when they see it as relevant and useful to their own needs or goals. Notice that as a listener you follow this principle all the time. In class, you attend to and remember information if you feel it is relevant to you, for example, if it's a skill that you can use at work or something that will be on the test. If you want the audience to listen, relate the information to their needs, wants, or goals, throughout the speech.

The Appropriateness Principle

Listeners retain information best when you present it on an appropriate level. Steer a middle course between being too simple—thus boring or insulting the audience—and being too sophisticated—thus confusing the audience. Remember that the audience hears the speech only once and must grasp on first hearing what you may have taken weeks to learn. For example, if you are a philosophy major do not assume that terms that are part of your active vocabulary—such as *existentialism, enlightenment,* and *empiricist*—will be immediately understood by your listeners.

The New to Old Principle

An audience will learn information more easily and retain it longer when it is related to what they already know. Relating the new to the old, the unfamiliar to the familiar, the unseen to the seen, the untasted to the tasted, helps listeners see more clearly what they have never experienced before.

The Several Senses Principle

You will communicate your information best if you present it to your audience through several senses—through hearing, seeing, smelling, tasting, feeling. Use as many of your listeners' senses as you can. If you are describing the layout of a football field (presenting information through hearing), also show a picture of the field (presenting information through seeing as well). If you are giving a speech on stress and you are talking about muscular tension, make the audience feel their own muscle tension by asking them to tighten their leg or stomach muscles.

The Levels of Abstraction Principle

You can discuss freedom of the press in the abstract by talking about the importance of getting information to the public, by referring to the Bill of Rights, and by relating a free press to the preservation of democracy—all on a relatively high level of abstraction. You can also talk about freedom of the press by citing specific examples, about how a local newspaper was prevented from running a story critical of the town council, or about how Lucy Rinaldo was fired from the *Accord Sentinel* after she wrote a story critical of the mayor—all on a relatively low level of abstraction, a level that is specific and concrete. Too many high abstractions without the specifics or too many specifics without the high abstractions will prove less effective than the combination of abstract and specific.

PRINCIPLES OF PERSUASIVE COMMUNICATION

Most of the speeches you hear are persuasive. The speeches of politicians, advertisers, and religious leaders are perhaps the clearest examples. In most of your own speeches, you too will aim at persuasion. You will try to change your listeners' attitudes and beliefs or perhaps change their behaviors. In school you might try to persuade others to (or not to) expand the core curriculum, use a plus-minus or a pass-fail grading system, disband the basketball team, allocate increased funds for the school newspaper, establish competitive majors, or eliminate fraternity hazing. In your job you may be called upon to speak on establishing a union, a wage increase proposal, a health benefit package, or promoting Pat Williams for shop steward.

Success in strengthening or changing attitudes or beliefs and in moving listeners to action will depend on the degree to which the speaker follows the principles of persuasion.

The Selective Exposure Principle

Listeners often follow the *law of selective exposure*. It has two parts:

1. Listeners actively seek out information that supports their opinions, beliefs, values, decisions, and behaviors.
2. Listeners actively avoid information that contradicts their existing opinions, beliefs, attitudes, values, and behaviors.

Generally listeners exercise selective exposure when they have little confidence in their opinions and beliefs. If, on the other hand, listeners are very sure that their opinions and attitudes are logical and valid, then they might not bother seeking supporting information; and, they may not actively avoid nonsupportive messages.

Thus, for example, if as a speaker you intend to persuade an audience that holds very different attitudes from your own, anticipate selective exposure operating and proceed inductively; that is, hold back on your thesis until you have given them your evidence and argument. Only then relate this evidence and argument to your initially contrary thesis.

The Audience Participation Principle

Persuasion is greatest when the audience participates actively in the presentation. In experiments, for example, the same speech is delivered to different audiences. The attitudes of each audience are measured before and after the speech. The difference between their attitudes before and after the speech is taken as a measure of the speech's effectiveness. For one audience the sequence consists of (1) pretest of attitudes, (2) presentation of the persuasive speech, and (3) posttest of attitudes. For another audience the sequence consists of (1) pretest of attitudes, (2) presentation of the persuasive speech, (3) audience paraphrases or summarizes the speech, and (4) posttest of attitudes. It is consistently found that those listeners who participated actively (as in paraphrasing or summarizing) are more persuaded than those who receive the message passively. Demagogues and propagandists who succeed in arousing huge crowds often have the crowds chant slogans, repeat catch phrases, and otherwise participate actively in the persuasive experience. Most of the world's religions have rituals in which the audience actively participates in the communication experiences.

The Inoculation Principle

The principle of inoculation is best explained with the biological analogy on which it is based. Suppose that you lived in a germ-free environment. Upon leaving this germ-free environment and upon exposure to germs, you would be particularly susceptible to infection because your body would not have built up an immunity—it would have no resistance. Resistance, the ability to fight off germs, might be achieved by the body through some form of inoculation. You could, for example, be injected with a weakened dose of the germ so that your body begins to fight the germ by building up antibodies that create an immunity to this type of infection.

The situation in persuasion is similar to this biological process. Some of your attitudes and beliefs have existed in a "germ-free" ("challenge-free") environment. For example, you may have lived in an environment in which the values of a democratic form of government, the importance of education, and the traditional family structure were never challenged. Consequently, you have not been "immunized" against attacks on these values and beliefs. You have no counterarguments (antibodies) prepared to fight off possible attacks on your beliefs. Therefore, if a speaker presents strong arguments against these beliefs, you might be easily persuaded.

Contrast these "germ-free" beliefs with issues that have been attacked and for which you have an arsenal of counterarguments ready. Your attitudes on gays and lesbians in the military, deforestation, abortion, nuclear weapons, and thousands of other issues have been challenged in the press, on television, and in your interpersonal interactions. As a result of this exposure, you have counterarguments ready for any attacks on beliefs concerning these issues. Should someone attempt to change your attitudes on these issues, you would be highly resistant because you have been inoculated and immunized against such attacks.

In addressing an inoculated audience, the speaker has to take into consideration the fact that they have an arsenal of counterarguments ready to fight any persuasive assault. For example, if you are addressing heavy smokers on the need to stop smoking or alcoholics on the need to stop drinking, you might assume that these people have already heard your arguments and that they have already inoculated themselves against the major arguments. In such situations, be prepared, therefore, to achieve only small gains. Don't try to reverse totally the beliefs of a well-inoculated audience. For example, it would be asking too much to get the smokers or the alcoholics to quit their present behaviors as a result of one speech. But, it might not be too much to ask to get them—at least some of them—to attend a meeting of a smoking clinic or Alcoholics Anonymous or to read a pamphlet.

The task is often simpler when trying to persuade an uninoculated audience. The reason is that the speaker does not have to penetrate a fully developed immunization shield. For example, it might be relatively easy to persuade a group of high school seniors about the values of a college core curriculum since they probably have not thought much about the issue and probably do not have arguments against the core curriculum at their disposal.

The Magnitude of Change Principle

The greater and more important the change the speaker wishes to produce in an audience, the more difficult the task will be. The reason is simple: people demand a great number of reasons and lots of evidence before making important decisions—career changes, moving families to another state, or investing life savings in certain stocks.

On the other hand, they may be more easily persuaded (and demand less evidence) on relatively minor issues—whether to take the course Small Group Communication rather than Persuasion, or to give to the United Heart Fund instead of the American Heart Fund.

People change gradually, in small degrees over a long period of time, although there are cases of sudden conversions. Persuasion, therefore, is most effective when it strives for small changes and works over a period of time. For example, a persuasive speech stands a better chance when it tries to get the alcoholic to attend just one AA meeting rather than to give up alcohol for life. If you try to convince your audience to change their attitudes radically or to engage in behaviors to which they are violently opposed, your attempts may backfire.

When you have the opportunity to try to persuade your audience on several occasions—rather than simply delivering one speech—two strategies will prove useful: the foot-in-the-door and the door-in-the-face techniques.

Foot-in-the-Door Technique

This foot-in-the-door technique involves getting your foot in the door first. You first request something small, something with which your audience will easily comply. Once this compliance has been achieved, you then make your real (and larger) request (Cialdini 1984; DeJong 1979; Freedman & Fraser 1966; Pratkanis & Aronson 1991). People are more apt to comply with a large request after they have complied with a similar, but much smaller, request. For example, in one study the objective was to get people to put a "Drive Carefully" sign on their lawn. When this (large) request was made first, only about 17 percent of the people were willing to comply. However, when this request was preceded by a much smaller request (in this case to sign a petition) between 50 and 76 percent agreed to install the sign.

For this strategy to work, the first request must be small enough to gain compliance. If it does not, then the chance to gain compliance with the desired and larger request will be lost.

Door-in-the-Face Technique

This door-in-the-face technique is the opposite of foot-in-the-door (Cialdini 1984; Cialdini & Ascani 1976). In this strategy you first make a large request that you know will be refused (for example, "We're asking most people to donate $100 for new school computers"). Later, you make a more moderate request, the one you really want your listeners to comply with (for example, "Might you be willing to contribute $10?"). In changing from the large to the more moderate request, you demonstrate your willingness to compromise and your sensitivity to your listeners. The general idea here is that your listeners will feel that since you have made concessions, they will also make concessions and at least contribute something. Listeners will probably also feel that $10 is actually quite little, considering the initial request and, research shows, are more likely to comply and donate the money.

For this technique to work, the first request must be significantly larger than the desired request but not so large that it seems absurd and is rejected out of hand.

Compliance-Gaining Strategies

THINK ABOUT

Think about persuasion from the point of view of specific compliance-gaining strategies, tactics that influence others to do what you want them to do. Here are a few that research has identified and that seem especially relevant to public speaking situations—as well as to a variety of other communication situations such as conversation, interviewing, and small group communication (Marwell & Schmitt 1967, Miller & Parks 1982).

- *Liking.* Appear likable to the audience; generally, if people like you they will be more apt to comply with your requests. Smiling, presenting a positive attitude, and demonstrating a genuine concern for the audience will make you appear more likable.
- *Promise and treat.* If you can promise the audience a reward for doing as you suggest ("Invest with X-brand and you'll earn larger profits") or threaten them with a punishment if they do not follow your advice ("You'll miss the opportunity for double-digit earnings") you are likely to gain audience compliance.
- *Positive and negative self-feelings.* Demonstrate that the audience will feel better about themselves if they do as you suggest and worse if they do not. This is a commonly used compliance-gaining strategy by charities that tell you (or Sally Struthers tells you) that you will feel so much better if you help one of these children.
- *Positive and negative altercasting.* Place the audience in the position of the good and responsible citizen (student, manager, friend) and then show them that such a person would definitely do as you suggest. For example, if you can show the audience that a responsible citizen votes, attends PTA meetings, or volunteers as a firefighter (depending on your speech purpose), they are more

likely to see your position as just and are more likely to comply with it. Conversely, you can place the audience into the role of "bad" people and show them how they (the "bad" people) would not do as you suggest.

- *Positive and negative esteem.* If you can show the audience that others will think more highly of them if they do as you suggest or negatively of them if they do not do as you suggest, you will raise your chances of gaining audience compliance. For example, show them that by donating blood their names will be published in the student paper (with the implication that others will, as a result, think more highly of them).

THE THREE PROOFS

Some twenty-three hundred years ago the Greek philosopher Aristotle identified three types of proof in his *Rhetoric,* three types of supporting materials through which speakers could move audiences. These were logic and argument (logos), motivational appeals (pathos), and credibility appeals (ethos). Although these three appeals are considered separately here, in actual public speeches (and, in fact, in all persuasive communications), they are often used simultaneously.

Logos: Logical Appeals

The logical aspect of public communication consists basically of arguments, which in turn consist of evidence (for example, facts) and a conclusion. Evidence, together with the conclusion that the evidence supports, equal an argument. *Reasoning* is the process you go through in forming conclusions on the basis of evidence. For example, you might reason that since college graduates earn more money than nongraduates (evidence), Jack and Jill should go to college if they wish to earn more money (conclusion).

The same principles of logic will prove useful to the speaker in constructing the speech, to the listener in receiving and responding to the speech, and to the critic in evaluating the speech. A poorly reasoned argument, inadequate evidence, and stereotypical thinking, for example, should be avoided by the speaker, recognized and responded to by the listener, and negatively evaluated by the critic. Three general tests of evidence and argument are especially important: recency, corroboration, and fairness.

Recency

The world changes rapidly. Economic strategies that worked for your parents will not work for you. Political strategies in place ten years ago are now considered inappropriate. As the world changes, so must the strategies for coping with it. Therefore, it is important that supporting materials be as recent as possible. Recency alone, obviously, does not make an effective argument. Yet, other things being equal, the more recent the evidence and support, the better.

Corroboration

In drawing a conclusion (or in supporting a thesis) gather evidence and arguments from numerous and diverse sources. When all or most of the evidence points in the same direction, you are on pretty firm ground. If some evidence points to yes and some evidence points to no, then perhaps your conclusion needs to be reevaluated. Just as you would be convinced by evidence all pointing in the same direction, so will your listeners.

Fairness

Each person sees the world through his or her individual filters. You see the world, not objectively, but through your prejudices, biases, preconceptions, and stereotypes. Others see the world through their own filters. No one is totally objective. Consequently, in evaluating evidence, establish how fair or biased the sources are and in what direction they may be biased. A report on the connection between smoking and lung cancer from a tobacco company and one from an impartial medical research institute should be treated very differently. Question research conducted and disseminated by any special interest group. It is always legitimate to ask: To what extent might this source be biased? Might this source have a special interest that leads her or him to offer this evidence or this conclusion?

Pathos: Emotional (Motivational) Appeals

When you use emotional (or motivational) appeals you direct your appeals to your listeners' needs and desires. Although psychological appeals are never totally separate from logical appeals, they are considered separately here. The concern here is with motives, with those forces that energize or move or

Effective public speaking techniques vary widely from one culture to another. In some cultures, speakers are expected to present their arguments logically and dispassionately, whereas in others speakers are expected to present their case with great emotion. Do the principles covered in this unit adequately convey the expectations of your own culture? Can you identify a culture for which these principles would need to be revised?

motivate a person to develop, change, or strengthen particular attitudes or ways of behaving. For example, one motive might be the desire for status. This desire might motivate you to develop certain attitudes about what occupation to enter, the importance of saving and investing money, and so on. It may move you to behave in certain ways—to buy Gucci shoes, a Rolex watch, or a Tiffany ring. As these examples illustrate, appeals to status (or to any motive) may motivate different persons in different ways. Thus, the status motive may lead one person to enter the poorly paid but respected occupation of social work. It may influence another to enter the well-paid but often disparaged world of real estate or diamonds.

Motive Hierarchy

One of the most useful analyses of motives is Abraham Maslow's five-fold classification, reproduced in Figure 22.1. One of the assumptions here is that you would seek to fulfill the need at the lowest level first and only then the need at the next higher level. Thus, for example, you would not concern yourself with the need for security or freedom from fear if you were starving (that is, if your need for food had not been fulfilled). Similarly, you would not be concerned with friendship or affectional relationships if your need for protection and security had not been fulfilled.

In this system certain needs have to be satisfied before other needs can motivate behavior. Thus, you need to determine what needs of the audience have been satisfied and, therefore, what needs might be used to motivate them. In most college classrooms, for example, you may assume that the two lowest levels—physiological needs and safety needs—have been reasonably fulfilled. For many students, however, the third level (love needs) is not fulfilled, and propositions may be linked to these with great effectiveness. Thus, to assure the audience that what you are saying will enable them to achieve more productive interpersonal relationships or greater peer acceptance will go a long way toward securing their attention and receptiveness.

Motive Appeals

THINK ABOUT

Think about the ways in which appeals may be addressed to specific motives. Each audience, of course, is different, and motives that are appropriately appealed to in one situation might be inappropriate or ineffective in another. Here are some of the motives to which speakers (and advertisers) appeal. As you read through the list, you may find it interesting to recall a recent print or television advertisement that makes use of each of these motive appeals.

- *Altruism.* People want to do what they consider the right thing—to help others, to contribute to worthy causes, to help the weak, feed the hungry, and cure the sick.
- *Fear.* People are motivated in great part by a desire to avoid fear, fear of the loss of those things desired, for example, money, family, friends,

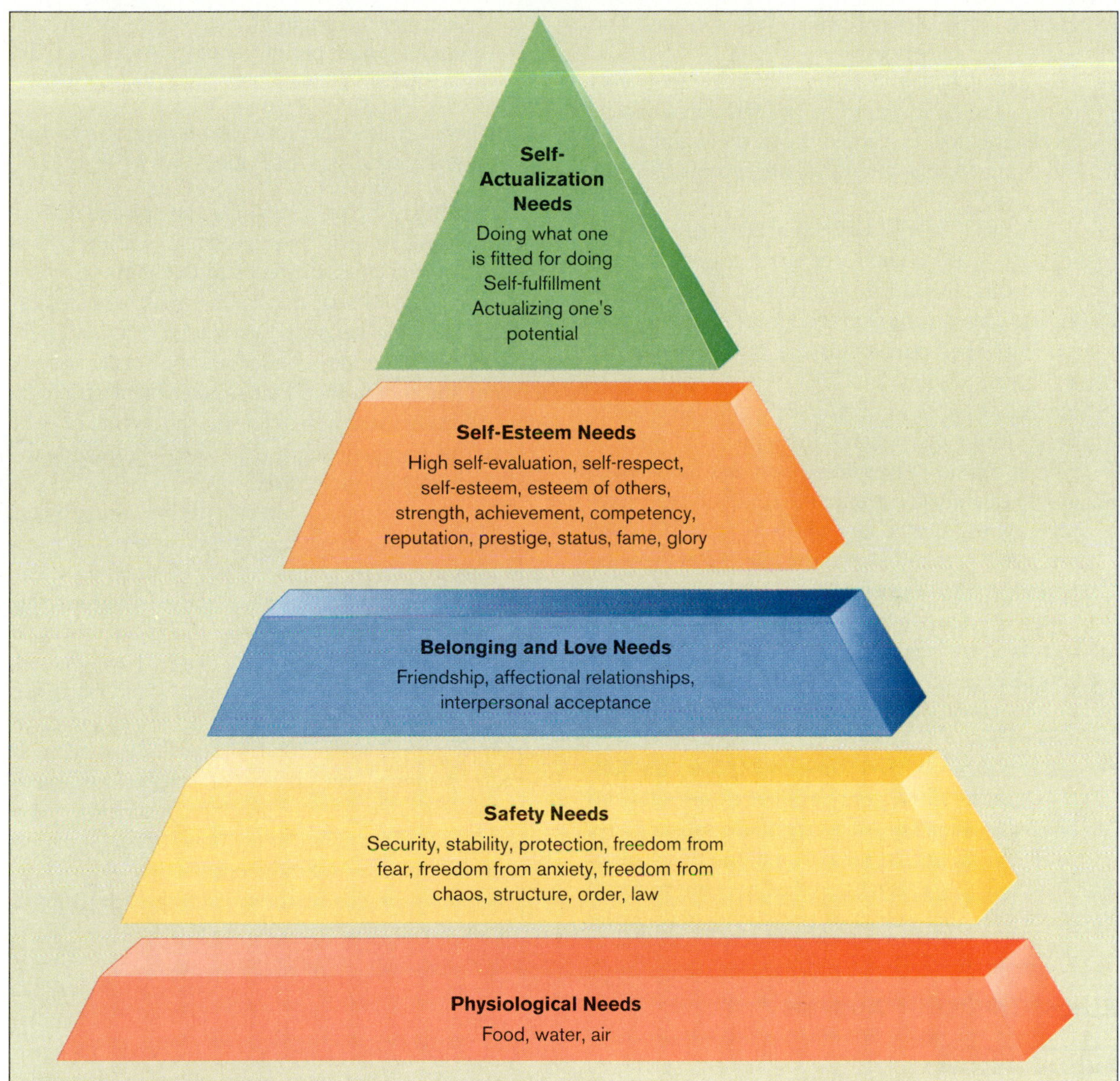

FIGURE 22.1 Maslow's Hierarchy of Needs. According to Maslow satisfied needs do not motivate. For example, if the safety need of an individual is satisfied, that individual will not be motivated to seek further safety. Therefore, appeals to satisfied needs will not be persuasive for this listener. The insights of Maslow—as well as of various other theorists—underlie the principles of motivation discussed in this section.

(*Source:* Based on Abraham Maslow, *Motivation and Personality.* New York: Harper & Row, 1970).

love, attractiveness, health, job, and just about everything now possessed and valued. People also fear punishment, rejection, failure, the unknown, the uncertain, and the unpredictable.

- *Individuality and conformity.* People want to stand out from the crowd and may fear being lost in the crowd, being indistinguishable from everyone else. Yet many also want to conform, to be one of the crowd, to be "in."
- *Power, control, and influence.* People want power, control, and influence over themselves and over their own destinies. People also want control over other persons, to be influential, and to be opinion leaders.
- *Self-esteem and approval.* People want to see themselves as self-confident, as worthy and contributing human beings. Because of this need, inspirational speeches, speeches of the "you are the

greatest" type, never seem to lack receptive and suggestible audiences.

- *Love and affiliation.* People are strongly motivated to love and be loved, to be assured that someone (preferably lots of people) loves them and at the same time to be assured they are capable of loving in return.
- *Achievement.* People want to achieve in whatever they do. They want to be a successful student. They want to achieve as friends, as parents, as lovers. This is why you read books and listen to speeches that purport to tell how to be better achievers.
- *Financial gain.* Most people seem motivated by the desire for financial gain—for what it can buy, for what it can do. Advertisers know this motive well and frequently get people interested in their messages by using such key words as "sale," "50 percent off," "save now," and the like. All of these are appeals to the desire for money.
- *Status.* In American society a person's status is measured by occupation and wealth, but also by competence on the athletic field, from excelling in the classroom, or from superiority on the dance floor.
- *Self-actualization.* According to Maslow, the self-actualization motive only influences attitudes and behaviors after all other needs are satisfied. Yet people all have in some part a desire to self-actualize, to become what they feel they are fit for. If people see themselves as poets, they must write poetry.

Ethos: Credibility Appeals

THINK ABOUT

Think about how believable you are as a speaker. How believable are you apart from any evidence or argument you might advance? What is there about you as a person that makes others believe or not believe you? These are questions of credibility or believability.

You have probably made judgments on many occasions of speakers apart from any arguments, evidence, or motivational appeals they offered. Often you believe or disbelieve a speaker because of who the speaker is, not because of anything the speaker says. You may, for example, believe certain information or take certain action solely by virtue of Lee Iacocca's or Shirley MacLaine's reputation, personality, or character. Alexander Pope put it more poetically in his "Essay on Criticism":

> Some judge of author's names, not works, and then
> Nor praise nor blame the writings, but the men.

Credibility is not something the speaker has or does not have in any objective sense. Rather, it is a quality that a listener attributes to the speaker; it is a quality that the listener thinks the speaker possesses. In reality the speaker may be a stupid, immoral person, but, if the audience perceives the speaker as intelligent and moral, then that speaker has high credibility. Further, research tells us, the audience will believe this speaker. Figure 22.2 displays how credibility impressions are formed.

Everyone seems interested in credibility. Advertisers, for example, are interested because it relates directly to the effectiveness of their ad campaigns. Is Michael Jordan an effective spokesperson for Hanes underwear? Is Susan Lucci an effective spokesperson for Ford? Is Jerry Seinfeld an effective spokesperson for American Express? Politicians are interested in credibility because it determines in great part how people vote. Educators are interested in it because students' perceptions of teacher credibility determine the degree of influence the teacher has on a class. There seems to be no communication situation that credibility does not influence.

Before reading about the specific characteristics of credibility, you may wish to take the self-test, "How Credible Are You?" on page 400.

We can identify three major qualities of credibility: competence, character, and charisma. Generally, in the United States, speakers are advised to stress their credibility and make their audience know that they are competent, of good character, and dynamic or charismatic. In some cultures, however, to stress your own competence or that of your corporation may be taken to mean that your audience members are inferior or that their corporations are not as good as yours. As with any principle of communication, it helps to know something of the culture of your listeners.

Competence

Competence refers to the knowledge and expertise a speaker is thought to have. The more knowledge and expertise the audience perceives the speaker as having, the more likely the audience will be to believe the speaker. For example, we believe a teacher to the ex-

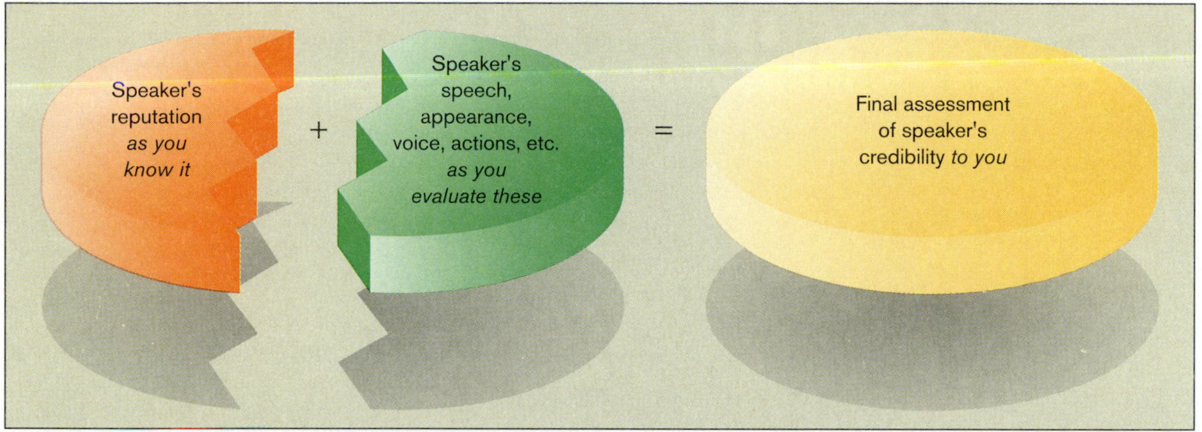

FIGURE 22.2 How we form credibility impressions. We form a credibility impression of a speaker on the basis of two sources of information. First, we assess the reputation of the speaker as we know it. This is initial, or what theorists call *extrinsic*, credibility. Second, we evaluate how that reputation is confirmed or refuted by what the speaker says and does during the speech. This is derived, or *intrinsic*, credibility. In other words, we combine what we know about the speaker's reputation with the more immediate information we get from present interactions and form a collective final assessment of credibility.

tent that we think he or she is knowledgeable on the subject.

Competence is logically subject-specific. Usually, it is limited to one specific field. A person may be competent in one subject and totally incompetent in another. Your political science instructor, for example, may be quite competent in politics but quite incompetent in mathematics or economics.

Often, however, we do not make the distinction between areas of competence and incompetence. Thus, we may see a person who we think competent in politics as competent in general. We will, therefore, perceive this person as credible in many fields. We refer to this as the halo effect—when listeners generalize their perception of competence to all areas (see Unit 4). Listeners see the speaker's competence as a general trait of the individual.

This halo effect also has a counterpart—the reverse halo effect. Here the person, seen as incompetent in, say, mathematics, is perceived as being similarly incompetent in most other areas as well. As a critic of public communication, be particularly sensitive to competence being subject-specific. Be sensitive to both halo and reverse halo effects.

Character

We perceive a speaker as credible if we perceive that speaker as having high moral **character.** Here our concern is with the individual's honesty and basic nature. We want to know if we can trust that person. We believe a speaker we can trust. An individual's motives or intentions are particularly important in judging character. When the audience perceives your intentions as good for them (rather than for your personal gain), they will think you credible, and, they will believe you.

Charisma

Charisma is a combination of the speaker's personality and dynamism as seen by the audience. You perceive as credible or believable speakers you like rather than speakers you do not like. You perceive as credible speakers who are friendly and pleasant rather than aloof and reserved. Similarly, you favor the dynamic over the hesitant, nonassertive speaker. You perceive the shy, introverted, soft-spoken individual as being less credible than the extroverted and forceful individual. The great leaders in history have been dynamic people. Perhaps you feel that the dynamic speaker is open and honest in presenting herself or himself. The shy, introverted individual may be seen as hiding something. As speakers there is much that you can do to increase your charisma and hence your perceived credibility.

CRITICISM IN PUBLIC COMMUNICATION

Criticism is an integral part of all communication. Criticism provides the standards for evaluating the wide variety of communications you'll hear throughout your life. This critical frame of mind will prove

SELF-TEST
how credible are you?

Respond to each of the following phrases as you think members of this class (your audience) see you when you deliver a public speech. Use the following scale:

7 = Very true
6 = Quite true
5 = Fairly true
4 = Neither true nor untrue
3 = Fairly untrue
2 = Quite untrue
1 = Very untrue

_____ 1. Knowledgeable about the subject matter
_____ 2. Experienced
_____ 3. Confident
_____ 4. Informed about the subject matter
_____ 5. Fair in the presentation of material (evidence and argument)
_____ 6. Concerned with the audience's needs
_____ 7. Consistent over time on the issues addressed in the speech
_____ 8. Similar to the audience in attitudes and values
_____ 9. Positive rather than negative
_____ 10. Assertive in personal style
_____ 11. Enthusiastic about the topic and in general
_____ 12. Active rather than passive

Thinking Critically About Your Credibility. This test focuses on the three qualities of credibility: competence, character, and charisma, and is based on a large body of research (for example, McCroskey 1995, Riggio 1987). Items 1 through 4 refer to your perceived *competence:* How competent or capable does the audience see you when you give a public speech? Items 5 through 8 refer to your perceived *character:* Does the audience see you as a person of good and moral character? Items 9 through 12 refer to your perceived *charisma:* Does the audience see you as dynamic and active rather than as static and passive? You may wish to consider what specific steps you can take to change any audience perception with which you may be unhappy.

useful in assessing all communications: the salesperson's pitch to sell the new car, the advertiser's plea to sell Tylenol rather than Excedrin, and the newspaper's or network's editorial. Although our discussion here focuses on criticism in a public speaking context, do realize that the principles are useful in all types of communication.

The term *criticism* comes from the Latin *criticus,* which means "able to discern," "to judge." Note that there is nothing inherently negative about criticism; rather, criticism is a process of judging and evaluating a work of art, a movie, or a public speech.

The major purpose of criticism in education is to improve the students' skills. Constructive criticism is an effective way of teaching and learning the principles of any art. Through criticism, you will be better able to see what works and what doesn't. You'll be able to see what should be kept, enlarged upon, modified, or eliminated. By observing what works and what doesn't and then going beyond that to identify more effective alternatives, the critic offers specific suggestions for achieving greater effectiveness.

Cultural Differences in Criticism

There are vast cultural differences in what is considered proper when it comes to criticism. In some cultures, public criticism—even if it is designed to help teach skills—is considered inappropriate. As already noted in several contexts, some cultures place a heavy

MEDIA WATCH

MEDIA CREDIBILITY

Among many people, the media enjoy enormous credibility. People generally believe what they hear on television or read in the newspapers. In part they believe the media because they believe the media spokespersons, Dan Rather, Ted Koppel, and Diane Sawyer. Many believe what Oprah Winfrey says about relationships and self-esteem, and what Montel Williams says about dealing with problem teenagers. The belief seems to come in part because these personalities are so impressive and because they are on TV.

In a similar way, we believe what we read. We believe our newspapers and magazines. Unless it's marked "editorial" or "advertisement," we assume that what appears in a newspaper or news magazine is accurate and objective. The News Credibility Scale that follows provides an interesting way to look at the credibility of a newspaper and, with modifications, of any media source. It is also an interesting way to think about the factors you take into consideration when you make your judgments of believability.

THE NEWS CREDIBILITY SCALE

Select a specific newspaper and encircle the number for each pair of phrases which best represents your feelings about this newspaper.

Is fair	5 4 3 2 1	Is unfair
Is unbiased	5 4 3 2 1	Is biased
Tells the whole story	5 4 3 2 1	Doesn't tell the whole story
Is accurate	5 4 3 2 1	Is inaccurate
Respects people's privacy	5 4 3 2 1	Invades people's privacy
Does watch after readers' interests	5 4 3 2 1	Does not watch after readers' interests
Is concerned about the community's well-	5 4 3 2 1	Is not concerned about the community's well-being
Does separate fact and opinion	5 4 3 2 1	Does not separate fact and opinion

What level of credibility (competence, character, and charisma) do you attribute to CBS anchor Dan Rather? To other media personalities such as Diane Sawyer, Peter Jennings, Tom Brokaw, Barbara Walters, and Ted Koppel?

Can be trusted	5 4 3 2 1	Cannot be trusted
Is concerned about the public interest	5 4 3 2 1	Is concerned about making profits
Is factual	5 4 3 2 1	Is opinionated
Has well-trained reporters	5 4 3 2 1	Has poorly trained reporters

Thinking Critically About Media Credibility. To compute your score simply add up the circled numbers. The higher the score the greater degree of credibility you perceive this newspaper to have and, more important, the more likely you are to believe what you read in this newspaper. The highest possible score would be 60, the lowest 12, and the midpoint 36. You might wish to try completing this scale for several different newspapers and see if the scores on the test correspond to the degree with which you believe the newspaper.

This scale, although designed for newspapers, can easily be extended to all news media—television, magazines, radio, and the various computerized information sources—and across media; for example, how does the credibility of your local paper compare to CNN news?

Source: Adapted from "Media Watch: Media Credibility" from "Measuring the Concept of Credibility," by C. Gaziano and K. McGrath, *Journalism Quarterly* 63, 1986, pp. 451–462. Reprinted by the Association for Education in Journalism and Mass Communication. [Also see Rubin (1994) and West (1995).]

emphasis on face saving, on allowing the other person to always remain in a positive light (James 1995). In cultures in which face-saving is especially important, therefore, members may prefer not to say anything negative in public and may even be reluctant to say anything positive for fear that the omissions may be construed as negatives. In some cultures, being kind to the person is more important than telling the truth and so its members may say things that are complimentary but basically untrue. In cultures in which face-saving is especially important, such communication rules as the following (stated here in rather extreme form) would prevail:

- don't express negative evaluation in public; instead compliment the person
- don't prove someone wrong, especially in public; express agreement even if you know the person is wrong
- don't correct someone's errors; don't even acknowledge them
- don't ask difficult questions lest the other person not know the answer and lose face or be embarrassed by asking; generally, avoid asking questions

Those who come from cultures that are highly individual and competitive (the United States, Germany, and Sweden are examples) may find public criticism a normal part of the learning process. Those who come from cultures that are more collective and that emphasize the group rather than the individual (Japan, Mexico, and Korea are examples) are likely to find giving and receiving public criticism uncomfortable. Thus, people from individual cultures may readily criticize others and are likely to expect the same "courtesy" from other listeners. After all, this person might reason, "If I'm going to criticize your skills to help you improve, I expect you to help me in the same way."

Persons from collective cultures may feel that it is more important to be polite and courteous than to help someone learn a skill. Cultural rules to maintain peaceful relations among the Japanese (Midooka 1990) and politeness among many Asian cultures (Fraser 1990) may conflict with the classroom cultural norm to express honest criticism.

The difficulties are compounded when you interpret unexpected behavior through your own cultural filters. For example, if a speaker who expects comments and criticism gets none, he or she may interpret the silence to mean that the audience didn't care or wasn't listening. In fact, they may have been listening very intently. They may simply be operating under a different cultural rule, a rule that says it is impolite to criticize or evaluate another person's work, especially in public.

Standards of Criticism

What standards does the critic use in evaluating a speech? How do you measure the excellence of a speech? On what basis do you say that one speech is weak, another is good, and still another is great? Three major standards quickly suggest themselves: effectiveness, universality, and conformity to the principles of the art.

Effectiveness

Effectiveness is the standard the advertiser, political speechwriter, and lawyer would use in evaluating a speech. This standard judges the speech in terms of whether or not it achieves its purpose. If the purpose is to sell soap, then the speech is effective if it sells soap and is ineffective if it doesn't. Increased sophistication in measuring communication effects makes this standard tempting to apply.

There are, however, problems with this approach. In many instances—in the classroom, for example—the effects of a speech cannot always be measured. Sometimes the effect of a speech is long term and you may not be present to see it take hold. Also, some effects are simply not measurable; you cannot always measure changes in attitude and belief.

Sometimes audiences may be so opposed to a speaker's position that even the greatest speech will have no observable effect. It may take an entire campaign to get such an audience to change its position even slightly. At other times audiences may agree with the speaker and even the weakest speech will secure compliance. In situations such as these, the effectiveness standard will lead to inaccurate and inappropriate judgments.

Universality

The historian, social critic, and philosopher would probably look more favorably on the *universality standard* (Murphy 1958). This standard focuses on the extent to which the speech addresses values and issues that have significance for all people in all times. This standard is often the one used in evaluating literature.

By this standard Martin Luther King, Jr.'s "I Have a Dream" speech would be judged positively because it argues for beliefs, values, and actions that most of the civilized world view positively.

A similar standard is that of *historical justification.* This standard looks at the extent to which the speech's thesis and purpose were justified by subsequent historical events. By this standard William Jennings Bryan's famous "Cross of Gold" speech (delivered in 1896)—although it won Bryan the Democratic nomination for president—would be judged negatively because it argued in favor of a rejected monetary standard and against a monetary standard (gold) that the entire world had accepted.

Another similar standard is that of *ethical merit.* This standard focuses on the extent to which the speech argues for what is true, moral, humane, or good. By this standard the speeches of Adolf Hitler would be judged negatively because they supported ideas most people find repugnant. Other situations would not be so easy to judge with the ethical merit standard.

THINK ABOUT

Think about, for example, how different cultures would respond to such theses as the following:

- Try eating beef (or pork, dog, or snake meat).
- Get divorced when things don't work out; marriage is not a "forever" commitment/Never get divorced; marriage is forever.
- Support same-sex marriage proposals/Do not support same-sex marriages.
- Women should be allowed to serve in all military positions and in all positions within any religious organization/Women should be restricted from serving in certain military and religious positions.

Obviously, different cultures will respond with very different attitudes; some will judge some speeches ethical and others unethical while members of another culture may do exactly the opposite.

Conformity to the Principles of the Art

For instructional purposes, a more useful standard is to evaluate a speech on the basis of its conformity to the principles of the art. With this standard a speech is positively evaluated when it follows the principles of public speaking established by theorists and critics and negatively evaluated when it deviates from these principles. The great advantage of this standard (especially in a learning situation such as this) is that it will help you master the principles of public communication. When your speech is measured by its adherence to these principles, you will be learning the principles by applying them to your unique situation.

This standard is of course not totally separate from the effectiveness standard since the principles of public communication are largely principles of effectiveness. When you follow the principles of the art, your speech will in all likelihood be effective.

The discussion presented in this unit and the previous one will serve as a firm foundation for the preparation and presentation of public speeches. The specific steps for this are covered in the next unit.

SUMMARY

In this unit we looked at the principles for communicating information and for persuading, at the three means of proof, and at criticism.

1. Among the principles for communicating information effectively are to limit the amount of information, stress relevance and usefulness, present information at the appropriate level, relate new information to old, present information through several senses, and vary the level of abstraction.
2. Among the principles of persuasion are the principles of selective exposure, audience participation, inoculation, magnitude of change, and compliance-gaining strategies.
3. Logical appeals consist of evidence and argument which lead to a conclusion. General tests of evidence include recency, corroboration, and fairness.
4. Emotional appeals are directed at the motives that energize people. Motives are often conceived of as existing in a hierarchy such that the lower level needs (for example, food and water) must be satisfied before higher level needs (for example, status or friendship) become motivating
5. Speaker credibility refers to the audience's perception of the speaker's believability, and consists of judgments of competence (the knowledge and expertise a speaker is seen to possess), character (the speaker's perceived morality), and charisma (the speaker's dynamism).
6. Speech criticism refers to making a judgment or evaluating (both positively and negatively) a public speech.
7. The major standards for speech criticism are effectiveness, universality, and the extent to which the principles of the art have been followed.

THINKING CRITICALLY ABOUT THE PRINCIPLES OF PUBLIC COMMUNICATION

1. What principles for communicating information have you found useful? What principles for communicating information do your instructors seem to follow?
2. How would the principles of informative and persuasive speaking be of value to the individual supervising a large group of workers in an organization? Could you rephrase these principles as suggestions for effective organizational communication?
3. How do the principles for communicating information differ for a college instructor, an advertiser, a politician, and a talk show host?
4. What principles of persuasion can you find in a print advertisement?
5. How important is logic and argument in contemporary advertising? Are some products advertised logically and others nonlogically?
6. What is the relative importance of logic versus emotion in getting people to change their toothpaste or their laundry detergent?
7. Many people will probably argue that they are not swayed by the credibility of the speaker or the media source; they will claim that they look at the evidence and not at the image of the source. Advertisers and the media generally think differently. They believe (and base multimillion dollar advertising campaigns on this belief) that the credibility of the spokesperson and the medium in which they place their advertisements are crucial to persuasion. Are you influenced by the

image of the speaker? Are you persuaded by people because of who they are, apart from anything they may say? Are you persuaded more when information comes from one media source than another? What general principles can explain why you give certain sources high credibility and other sources less credibility?

8. What standard of criticism would you prefer be applied to your communication efforts in general and to your public speaking efforts in particular?
9. What critical standards do you use in evaluating conversations? Informal group meetings and discussions? Job interviews?
10. How would you go about finding answers to such questions as these:
    a. Are college-educated people more critical in evaluating an argument than those who didn't go to college?
    b. Do men and women differ in their susceptibility to emotional appeals?
    c. Do members of different cultures evaluate the credibility of a public speaker similarly? Do they use the same standards?
    d. Is one's self-concept (see Unit 5) correlated with one's credibility? With one's perceived self-credibility?

twenty-three unit

Preparing and Presenting the Public Speech

unit contents

unit goals

After completing this unit, you should be able to:

1. explain the ten steps for preparing and presenting a public speech
2. follow the ten steps in preparing and presenting a public speech

Now that the nature of public speaking and its essential principles have been identified, you can devote attention to the process of putting all this knowledge to practical use. The ten steps discussed here (see Figure 23.1) will provide guidelines to enable you to prepare and present a wide variety of public speeches. Our focus here is on informative and persuasive speeches with some lesser consideration of special occasion speeches.

STEP 1. SELECT YOUR TOPIC AND PURPOSE

The first step in preparing a speech is to select the topic (or subject) and the purposes you hope to achieve. Let us look first at the topic.

The Topic

Perhaps the question beginning public speakers most often ask is, "What do I speak about?" Suggestions are everywhere. Surveys (regularly appearing in magazines and newspapers) and news items (especially editorials) are especially useful because they tell you what people are interested in and what they are thinking about. Or, try brainstorming with yourself by following the general principles for idea generation discussed in Unit 17. Here are a few guidelines to follow in selecting your topic:

- Select a topic that addresses significant issues, issues that have consequences for you and your listeners.
- Select a topic that you are interested in and that you want to learn more about. You will not only acquire new knowledge but also will discover how to learn more about the topic, for example, the relevant journals, the noted authorities, and so on. Another advantage is that your interest in your topic will show through during your presentation and will help establish your credibility and make your delivery less effortful. If you select a topic you are not interested in, you will have an extremely difficult time concealing this from the audience.
- Select a topic that the audience will be interested in; try to see potential topics from the audience's perspective. Find out what they are interested in and what they care about. It's a lot easier to hold the attention of the audience when they are interested in the topic.
- Select a topic that is limited in scope. Probably the major problem for beginning speakers is attempting to cover a huge topic in too short a time. A limited topic covered in detail is almost always more effective than a broad topic covered superficially.
- Select a topic with the culture of your audience in mind. Culture plays an important role in the topics people consider appropriate or worthwhile. For example, it would be considered (generally but not always) inappropriate for an American businessperson to speak on a wide variety of topics in different cultures. Table 23.1 identifies several examples that Roger Axtell, in *Do's and Taboos Around the World* (1993), recommends visitors from the United States avoid. These examples are not intended to be exhaustive, but rather should serve as a reminder that each culture defines what is and what is not an appropriate topic of conversation.

The Purpose

The three major or general purposes of public speeches are to inform, to persuade, and to serve some ceremonial or special occasion function:

- The informative speech creates understanding; the speaker clarifies, enlightens, corrects misunderstandings, demonstrates how something works.
- The persuasive speech influences attitudes or behaviors; the speaker strengthens or changes the existing attitudes or gets the audience to take action.
- The special occasion speech, containing elements of information and persuasion, serves varied purposes; for example, the speaker might introduce another speaker or a group of speakers, present a tribute, secure the goodwill of the listeners, or entertain the audience.

Your speech will also have a specific purpose. For example, specific informative purposes might include: to inform the audience of the proposed educa-

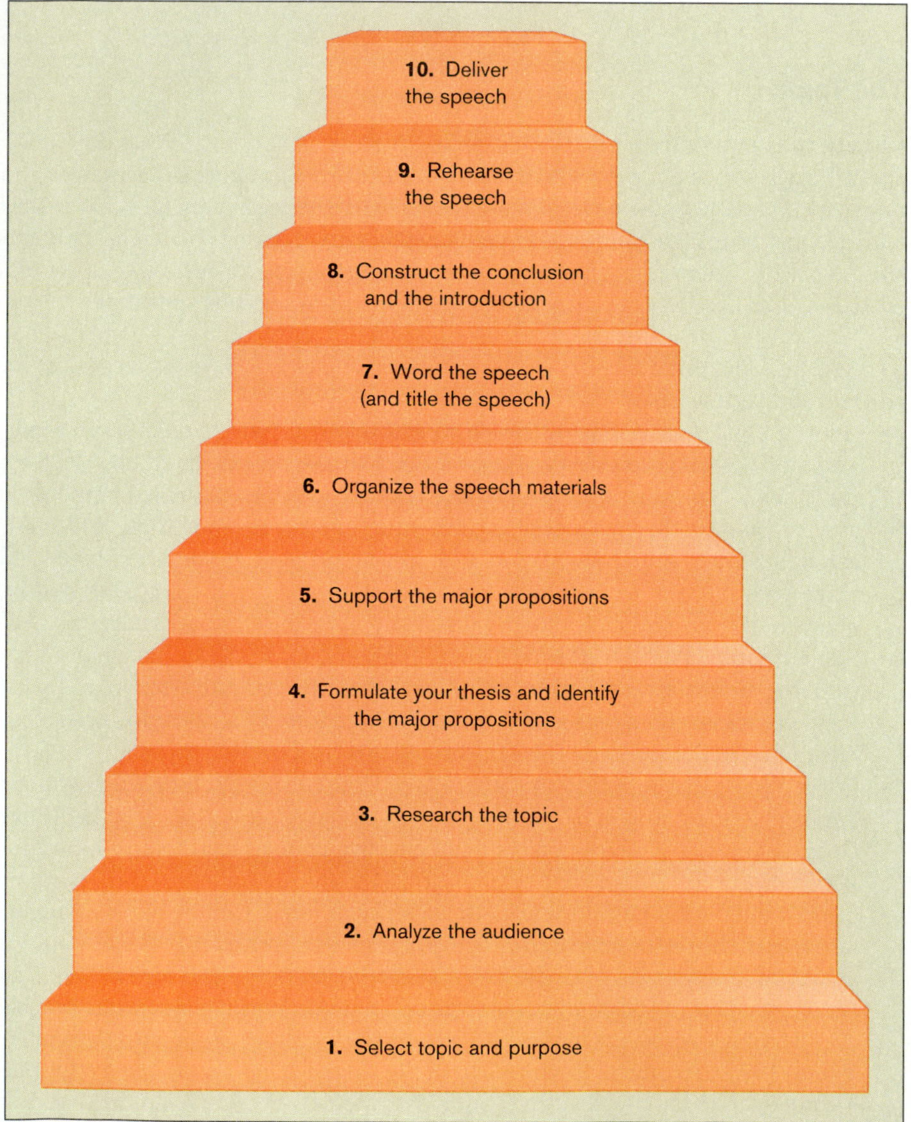
10. Deliver the speech
9. Rehearse the speech
8. Construct the conclusion and the introduction
7. Word the speech (and title the speech)
6. Organize the speech materials
5. Support the major propositions
4. Formulate your thesis and identify the major propositions
3. Research the topic
2. Analyze the audience
1. Select topic and purpose

FIGURE 23.1 The steps in preparing and delivering a public speech. In your actual preparation you will probably not progress simply from Step 1, to 2, to 3, and so on. Instead, your progression might go more like this: Step 1 (to select your topic), Step 2 (to analyze your audience), back again to Step 1 (to modify your topic), Step 3 (to research your topic), back again to Step 2 (to get more information on your audience), and so on throughout the preparation of your speech. Going from one step to another and then back again should not throw you off track. This is the way most people prepare speeches and written communications. So, although we present the steps in the order a speaker normally follows, remember that you are in charge of the process. Use the order of these steps as guidelines but break the sequence as needed. As long as you cover all ten steps thoroughly, you should accomplish your goal.

TABLE 23.1
taboo topics around the world

Because you are all college students, you can assume—to some extent—that the topics you are interested in will also prove interesting to your classmates. But, beyond this exceptionally accepting atmosphere—an atmosphere you are not likely to meet any time after college—the culture will always play a role in the selection of the topic.

Culture	Taboo Topics
Belgium	Politics, language differences between French and Flemish, religion
Norway	Salaries, social status
Spain	Family, religion, jobs, negative comments on bullfighting
Egypt	Middle-Eastern politics
Nigeria	Religion
Libya	Politics, religion
Philippines	Politics, religion, corruption, foreign aid
Iraq	Religion, Middle-Eastern politics
Japan	World War II
Pakistan	Politics
South Korea	Internal politics, criticism of the government, socialism or communism
Bolivia	Politics, religion
Colombia	Politics, criticism of bullfighting
Mexico	Mexican-American war, illegal aliens
Caribbean	Race, local politics, religion

tion budget or the way a television pilot is audience-tested. Specific persuasive purposes might include: to persuade the audience to support the proposed budget or to vote for Smith. Specific purposes for special occasion speeches might include introducing the latest Nobel Prize winner who will speak on advances in nuclear physics or defending a company policy of an all-male board of directors to the shareholders.

STEP 2. ANALYZE YOUR AUDIENCE

In public speaking, your audience is central to your topic and purpose. In most cases you will be thinking of both your audience and your topic at the same time; it is difficult to focus on one and not the other. Your success in informing or persuading an audience rests largely on the extent to which you know them and to which you have adapted your speech. The factors identified in Unit 21 (age; gender; cultural factors; education and intellectual levels; occupation, income, and status; and religion) need to be taken into account here. Ask yourself: How will the age of your audience impact on your topic? How will gender? How can you incorporate into your speech adaptations to your specific audience?

Similarly, such psychological factors as the willingness, favorableness, knowledge, and degree of homogeneity of your audience need to be considered. How will these psychological dispositions influence the way your audience receives your message? How can you adjust your message so that your audience will be more willing to listen and more favorable to your purpose?

STEP 3. RESEARCH YOUR TOPIC

If the speech is to be worthwhile and if you and the audience are to profit from it, you must research the topic. First read some general source—an encyclopedia article or a general article in a journal or magazine. You might pursue some of the references in the article or seek out a book or two in the library. For some topics, you might want to consult individuals: professors, politicians, physicians, or people with specialized information are useful sources.

Or, you might begin with accessing a database, assembling a bibliography, and reading the most general source first and continuing with increasingly specific articles.

STEP 4. FORMULATE YOUR THESIS AND MAJOR PROPOSITIONS

Your thesis is the main idea you want your audience to retain. It is the essence of what you want your audience to get out of your speech. If your speech is an informative one, then your thesis is the main idea that you want your audience to understand. Examples of such theses would be: "Human blood consists of four major elements" or, "The new computerized billing system is easy to understand."

If your speech is to be a persuasive one, then your thesis is the central idea that you wish your audience to accept or act on. Examples of such theses would be: "We should support Grace Moore for Union Representative" or "We should contribute to the college athletic fund."

Theses for special occasion speeches vary widely. In introducing a speaker it may be something like, "Pat Perez is worth listening to." In a speech of tribute it might be "Chris Ward was a model citizen" or "President Kennedy deserves an important place in history."

Once you word the thesis statement, ask yourself—as would an audience—questions about the thesis in order to identify its major components. For an informative speech, the most helpful questions are "What?" or "How?" Therefore, to the thesis, "Human blood consists of four major elements," the logical question seems to be, "What are they?" To the thesis, "The new computerized billing system is easy to understand," the logical question seems to be, "Why is it easy?" or "How is it easy?" The answers to these questions identify the major propositions that you should cover in your speech. The answer to the question, "What are the major elements of human blood?" in the form of a brief speech outline, would look like this:

Thesis: "There are four major elements in human blood." (What are they?)

I. Plasma

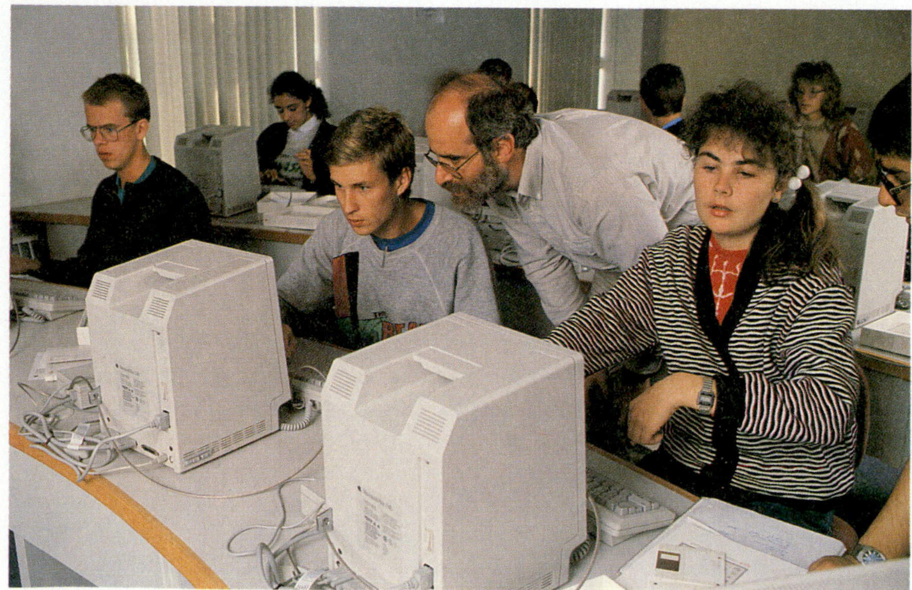

What kind of online research facilities are available on your campus? What databases would you access if you were researching a speech on abortion? On high blood pressure? On the flat tax? On toxic waste? On air transportation?

II. Red blood cells (erythrocytes)
III. White blood cells (leukocytes)
IV. Platelets (thrombocytes)

In a persuasive speech, the question an audience would ask would more often be of the Why? type. If your thesis is, "We should support Grace Moore for Union Representative," then the inevitable question is, "Why should we support Grace Moore?" Your answers to this question will then enable you to identify the major parts of the speech, which might look like this:

Thesis: "We should support Grace Moore." (Why should we support Grace Moore?)

I. Grace Moore is an effective negotiator.
II. Grace Moore is honest.
III. Grace Moore is knowledgeable.

STEP 5. SUPPORT YOUR MAJOR PROPOSITIONS

Once your thesis and your major propositions are identified, turn your attention to how to support each of them. You must tell the audience what it needs to know about the elements in human blood. You need to convince the audience that Grace Moore is, in fact, honest, knowledgeable, and an effective negotiator.

In the informative speech, your support primarily amplifies—describes, illustrates, defines—the various concepts you discuss. You want the "causes of inflation" to come alive for the audience. You want them to see and feel the drug problem, the crime, or the economic hardships of the people about whom you are talking. Amplification accomplishes this. Specifically, you might use examples and illustrations and the testimony of others to explain a concept or issue. Presenting definitions helps the audience to understand specialized terms. Definitions breathe life into concepts that may otherwise be too abstract or vague. Statistics (summary figures that explain various trends) are essential for certain topics.

In a persuasive speech, your support is proof—material that offers evidence, argument, and motivational appeal and that establishes your credibility, topics covered in detail in Unit 22. Proof helps you convince the audience to agree with you. Let us say, for example, that you want to persuade the audience to believe that Grace Moore is an effective negotiator (your first major proposition as noted earlier). To do this you need to give your audience good reasons for believing in Moore's effectiveness as a negotiator. Your major proposition might be supported as illustrated here:

I. Grace Moore is an effective negotiator.
   A. Moore effectively negotiated the largest raise we ever received.
   B. Moore prevented management from reducing our number of sick days.
   C. Moore has been named "Negotiator of the Year" for the past three years by our own union local.

You can also support your position with motivational appeals. For example, you might appeal to the audience's desire for status, for financial gain, or for increased self-esteem. You also add persuasive force through your own personal reputation or credibility. If the audience sees you as competent, of high moral character, and as charismatic, they are likely to believe what you say.

In public speaking you have the opportunity to use audiovisual aids—charts, maps, actual objects, slides, films, audiotapes, records, and so on—to enliven normally vague concepts. A pie chart to make your statistics clearer, a picture of the forest that is being destroyed, or a map showing military bases are important forms of support that will make your ideas more appealing, informative, and persuasive.

STEP 6. ORGANIZE YOUR SPEECH MATERIALS

Organize your materials to help your audience understand and retain what you say. You might, for example, select a simple topical pattern. This involves dividing your topic into its logical subdivisions or subtopics. Each subtopic becomes a main point of your speech and each is given approximately equal time. You would then organize the supporting materials under each of the appropriate points. The body of the speech, then, might look like this:

I. Main point I
   A. Supporting material for I
   B. Supporting material for I

II. Main point II

CRITICAL LISTENING

This entire unit is devoted to the practical part of preparing and presenting a speech. Keep in mind, however, that an effective speech also requires an effective listener. Part of that listening effectiveness depends on listening critically. Of course, critical listening is relevant to all forms of communication, but is traditionally taught in connection with public speaking. Listening critically depends on your ability to see distortions that speakers may introduce.

The first four distortions were first introduced in *The Fine Art of Propaganda,* prepared for the Institute for Propaganda Analysis in the 1940s (Lee & Lee 1972, 1995). The last three are taken from a more contemporary study of persuasive techniques (Pratkanis & Aronson 1991). The unethical persuader (one who distorts the truth) uses these techniques to gain compliance without logic or evidence. Learn to identify these devices so that you will not be fooled by them.

NAME-CALLING

In **name-calling** the speaker gives an idea, a group of people, or a political philosophy a bad name ("atheist," "Neo-Nazi"). In this way, the persuader tries to make you condemn the idea without analyzing the argument and evidence.

The purpose here is to give listeners a negative impression of the person or the person's proposal and to turn their attention away from analyzing the issues to responding only to the negative label.

In the opposite of name-calling the speaker tries to make you accept some idea by associating it with things you value highly ("democracy," "free speech," "academic freedom"). By using *virtue words,* the speaker tries to get you to ignore the evidence and simply approve of the idea.

TESTIMONIAL

The **testimonal** involves using the image associated with some person to gain your approval (if you respect the person) or your rejection (if you do not respect the person). This is the technique of advertisers who use people dressed to look like doctors or plumbers or chefs to sell their products. And, it seems, the technique works. Sometimes this technique takes the form of using only vague and general "authorities." For example, we frequently hear such appeals as "experts agree," "scientists say," "good cooks know," or "dentists advise." Exactly who these experts are or how many of them have agreed is seldom made clear. The advertisers hope, however, that you will simply remember that "experts agree" (with the commercial).

Sometimes the testimonials are from people who have no recognizable authority in the field in which they are speaking. Does Bill Cosby have a specialized knowledge of Jell-O or of photography? Does Angela Lansbury have specialized knowledge of painkillers?

CARD-STACKING

The speaker using **card-stacking** selects only the evidence and arguments that support the case. The speaker might even falsify evidence and distort the facts to better fit the case. Despite these lies, the speaker presents the supporting materials as "fair" and "impartial." For example, when advertisers say, "90 percent of the dentists surveyed endorse WhiterWhite Toothpaste as an effective cleansing agent," what are they really saying? Are they saying that WhiterWhite is better than any other toothpaste on the market? Or, are they saying that 90 percent of the dentists endorse WhiterWhite compared to not brushing your teeth at all?

BANDWAGON

When using the **bandwagon** method, the speaker persuades the audience to accept or reject an idea or proposal because "everybody is doing it." The persuader might also try to show that the "right" people are doing it. The propagandist persuades by convincing you to jump on this large and popular bandwagon. This is a popular technique in political campaigns, in which results of polls are used to get undecided voters to jump on the bandwagon with the candidate leading in the polls. After all, the implication goes, you don't want to vote for a loser.

GRANFALLON

Granfallon is a term taken from a novel by Kurt Vonnegut and refers to the tendency of people to see themselves as constituting a cohesive and like-minded group because they are given a label. The name might be religious: "As Christians (Jews, Muslims, Hindus) we know that . . ." or cultural: "As Native Americans (African Americans, Hispanics, Arabs) we should . . . ." Or, the label might be occupational: "As teachers (blue-collar workers, artists, journalists, athletes) we should agree that . . . ."

The problem with this line of reasoning is that it tends to divide the world into "we" and "they," which inevitably simplifies the situation and ignores the vast individual differences in any group covered by such broad labels.

AGENDA-SETTING

In **agenda-setting** a speaker might argue that XYZ is the issue and that all other matters are unimportant and insignificant. This appeal is heard frequently: "Balancing the budget is the key to the city's survival." "There is only one issue confronting elementary education in our largest cities and that is violence."

In almost all situations, however, there are many issues and many sides to each issue. Often the person proclaiming "X is the issue" really means "I'll be able to persuade you if you focus solely on X and ignore the other issues."

ATTACK

Attack involves accusing another person (usually an opponent) of some serious wrongdoing so that the issue under discussion never gets examined. "Arguments" such as "How can we support a candidate who has been unfaithful (smoked pot, avoided the military)" are heard often in just about any political discussion today.

A person's personal reputation and past behavior are often relevant. When, however, personal attack is used to draw attention away from other issues, then it becomes fallacious and should be identified as such by the critical listener.

Can you find examples of these fallacies in contemporary political speechmaking? In advertising?

- A. Supporting material for II
- B. Supporting material for II
- C. Supporting material for II

III. Main point III
- A. Supporting material for III
- B. Supporting material for III

Other patterns appropriate to informative speeches are time and space patterns, in which you organize, say, the history of the Civil War in a time pattern or the structure of the earth's surface in a spatial pattern.

For a persuasive speech you may wish to consider other organizational patterns. For example, a problem-solution pattern might be effective for a number of topics. Let us say you want to persuade your listeners that medical schools should require communication courses. You might use a problem-solution pattern. Your speech in outline form might look like this:

I. Doctors cannot communicate. (problem)
- A. They are inarticulate in expressing ideas. (problem 1)
- B. They are ineffective listeners. (problem 2)
- C. They do not see beyond the literal meaning. (problem 3)

II. Medical schools should require communication courses. (solution)
- A. Communication courses will train doctors to express themselves. (solution 1)
- B. Communication courses will train doctors in listening skills. (solution 2)
- C. Communication courses will train doctors to listen for meaning beyond the literal. (solu tion 3)

STEP 7. WORD YOUR SPEECH

Because the audience hears your speech only once, make sure that they readily understand everything you say; be instantly intelligible. Do not speak down to your audience, but do make your ideas, even complex ones, easy to understand at one hearing.

Use words that are simple rather than complex, concrete rather than abstract. Use personal and informal rather than impersonal and formal language. For

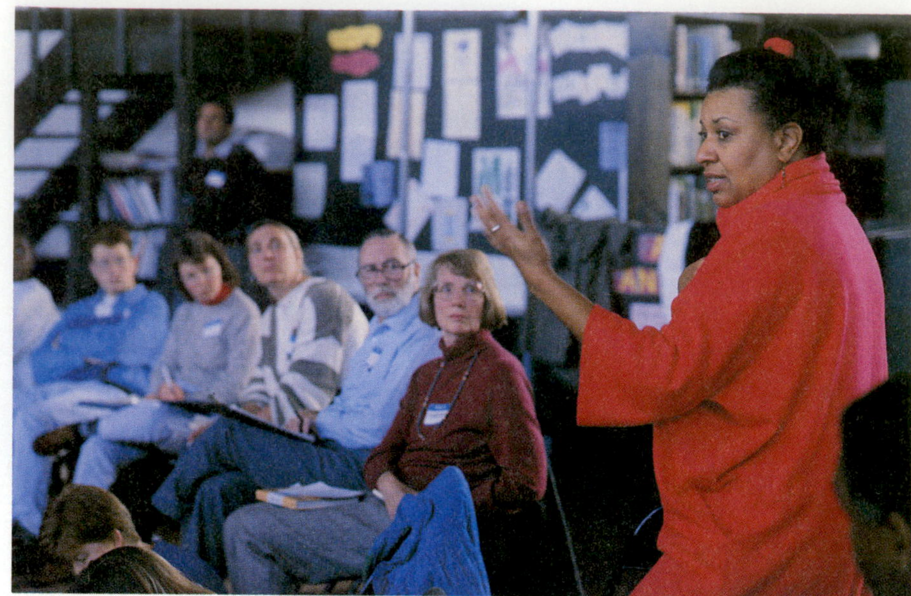

Do you find that women and men are likely to use different persuasive strategies? If so, which strategies are women more likely to use? Which are men more likely to use? How would you go about investigating gender differences in using persuasive strategies?

example, use lots of pronouns (*I, me, you, our*) and contractions (*can't* rather than *cannot, I'll* rather than *I will*). Use simple and direct rather than complex and indirect sentences. Say, "Vote in the next election," instead of, "It is important that everyone vote in the next election."

In wording the speech, be careful not to offend members of your audience. Remember that not all doctors are men. Not all secretaries are women. Not all persons are or want to be married. Not all persons love parents, dogs, and children. The hypothetical person does not have to be male.

Perhaps the most important advice is: do not write out your speech word-for-word. This will only make you sound like you are reading a text to your audience. You will thus lose the conversational quality that is so important in public speaking. Instead, outline your speech and speak *with* your audience, using this outline to remind you of the main ideas and the order in which you want to present them.

Title the Speech

In some ways the title of a speech is a kind of frill. On the other hand, the title may be effective in gaining the interest of the audience and, perhaps, stimulating them to listen. In more formal public speech presentations, the title helps to gain audience attention and interest in announcements publicizing the speech.

Create a title that is relatively short (so it's easy to remember), attracts the attention and arouses the interest of the listeners, and has a close and clear relationship to the major purpose of the speech.

STEP 8. CONSTRUCT YOUR CONCLUSION, INTRODUCTION, AND TRANSITIONS

Give special attention to your conclusion, introduction, and transitions. The conclusion and the introduction are often the parts that are remembered best and so need to be carefully constructed. The transitions will help to hold the speech together. They will help the audience see the speech as a coherent unit.

Conclusion

In concluding your speech do at least two things. First, summarize the speech. Identify the main points again and sum up what you have told the audience:

> Let's all support Grace Moore. She's our most effective negotiator; she's honest; and she knows what negotiation and our union are all about.

Second, wrap up your speech. Develop an appropriate closure, a crisp ending. Do not let the speech hang. End the speech clearly and distinctly.

> I hope then that when you vote on Tuesday, you'll vote for Moore. She's our only real choice.

Introduction

Because you must know in detail all you are going to say before you prepare the introduction, construct your introduction last. Your introduction should immediately gain the attention of the audience. Most often, your coming to the front of the room will attract their attention. As you start to speak, however, you may lose them if you do not make a special effort to hold their attention. A provocative statistic, a little-known fact, an interesting story, or a statement explaining the topic's significance will help secure this initial attention.

Second, establish a relationship among yourself, the topic, and the audience. Tell audience members why you are speaking on this topic. Tell them why you are concerned with the topic and why you are competent to address them. Here is one example of how this might be done.

> You may be wondering why a 25-year-old woman with no background in medicine or education is talking to you about AIDS education. I'm addressing your today as a mother of a child with AIDS and I want to talk with you about my child's experience in class—and about every child's experience in class, your own children as well as mine.

Third, orient the audience. Tell them what you are going to say and the order in which you are going to say it.

> I'm going to explain the ways in which war movies have changed through the years. I'll discuss examples of movies depicting World War II, the Korean War, and Vietnam.

Transitions

After you have completed the introduction, review the entire speech to make sure that the parts flow into one another and that the movement from one part to another (say, from the introduction to the first major proposition) will be clear to the audience. Transitional words, phrases, and sentences will help you achieve this smoothness of movement. These linguistic devices are often called *connectives* because they connect pieces of the speech to each other. Here are a few suggestions:

- Connect your introduction's orientation to your first major proposition: "*Let's now look at the first of these three elements,* the central processing unit, in detail. The CPU is the heart of the computer. It consists of . . . ."
- Connect your major propositions to each other: *But, not only is* cigarette smoking dangerous to the smoker, *it is also* dangerous to the nonsmoker. Passive smoking is harmful to everyone . . . .
- Connect your last major proposition to your conclusion: *As we saw,* there were three sources of evidence against the butler. He had a motive; he had no alibi; he had the opportunity.

STEP 9. REHEARSE YOUR SPEECH

A speech is prepared to be presented to an audience, so work on achieving the most effective presentation possible. Rehearse your speech, from start to finish, out loud, at least four times before presenting it. During these rehearsals, time your speech so that you stay within the specified time limits.

Practice any terms that you may have difficulty with; consult a dictionary to resolve any questions about pronunciation. Include in your outline any notes that you want to remember during the actual speech—notes to remind you to use your visual aid or to read a quotation.

STEP 10. PRESENT YOUR SPEECH

In your actual presentation, use your voice and bodily action to reinforce your message. Make it easy for your listeners to understand your speech. Any vocal or body movements that draw attention to themselves (and away from what you are saying) obviously should be avoided. Here are a few major guidelines that will prove helpful.

MEDIA WATCH

REVERSING THE PROCESS: INFLUENCING THE MEDIA

Although the media are generally analyzed for their effects on the individual, recognize that viewers and readers also exert influence on each other and may ultimately affect the media. For example, you may influence your friends or your family. They, in turn, will influence others who will influence still others. Through these interpersonal channels, the influence of one person can be considerable. The larger and more influential these groups become, the more influence they will exert on the media through their selective attention and their buying habits. You may also influence the media more directly. The principles and insights of public speaking, those for communicating information and for persuading, will provide you with essential tools for talking back to the media—for expressing your point of view and advancing your position to your media audience.

Kathleen Hall Jamieson and Karlyn Kohrs Campbell, in their perceptive *Interplay of Influence* (1992), for example, suggest that you can effectively influence the media in several important ways (see also Postman & Powers 1992).

Register individual complaints. You may write letters to (or call) a television station or to an advertiser expressing your views on the content of a program or topics to which you think more attention should be given. You can also write letters to a public forum, such as to the editor of a newspaper, or call in to a television talk show. You can also write letters to the Federal Communication Commission or to other regulatory agencies that in turn will exert pressure on the media.

These letters and phone calls count a great deal more than most people realize. Because most people do not write or call, the media give such messages, when they do receive them, considerable weight. Phone calls, for example, may also help other audience members crystallize their own thinking and, depending on your persuasiveness, may even convince them to believe and to act as you do.

Group pressure. When you join with others who think the same way, group pressure can be brought to bear on television networks, newspapers, advertisers, and manufacturers. Threatening a boycott or legal action (and potentially at least damage the economic base of an organization) can quickly gain attention and often some measure of compliance.

Protest through an established organization. Obviously the larger the organization you use to influence the media, the better. Similarly, the more economically powerful, the more persuasive your appeal will be. The AIDS epidemic has led to the creation of a wide variety of organizations that have exerted pressure for increased research funding and services to people with AIDS. ACT UP (AIDS Coalition to Unleash Power) is perhaps the most visible of such organizations.

Protest with a social movement. This technique has been used throughout history to gain civil rights for minority groups and for women. Forming such movements or aligning yourself with an established movement can enable you to secure not only a large number of petitioners but also the accompanying media coverage, which would enable you to put forth your own position.

Create legislative pressure. You can exert influence on the state or federal level by influencing your local political representatives (through your own voting, calls, and letters), who will in turn influence representatives on higher levels of the political hierarchy. Of course you can also help to influence the groups to which you belong to exert influence.

Do recall that communication is inevitable and that silence communicates just as surely as do words and gestures—principles covered throughout this text and especially in the Media Watch box, the Spiral of Silence (in Unit 10). Therefore, when you do not talk back to the media, your silence is interpreted by the media as basic approval. If approval is not what you wish to register, then you have little choice but to talk back.

When called on to speak, approach the front of the room with enthusiasm; even if, as do most speakers, you feel nervous, show your desire to speak with your listeners. When at the front of the room, don't begin immediately; instead, pause, engage your audience eye-to-eye for a brief moment and then begin to talk directly to the audience. Talk at a volume that can be easily heard without straining.

Throughout your speech maintain eye contact with your entire audience; avoid concentrating on only a few members or looking out of the window or at the floor.

Many public speaking situations are followed by a question-and-answer period. Be prepared to answer questions after your speech. Here are a few suggestions for making this question-and-answer session more effective:

- Consider if you need to repeat the question. If you suspect the audience did not hear it, then repeat it.
- Control any tendency to get defensive. Don't assume that the question is an attack. Assume, instead, that the question is an attempt to secure more information or perhaps to challenge a position you have taken.
- If appropriate, thank the person for asking the question or note that the question is a particularly good one.
- Don't bluff. If you are asked a question and you don't know the answer, say so.
- As you develop your public speaking skills, you'll find many instances in which you'll be able to connect the question with one or more of your major assertions or points of view: "I'm glad you asked about child care because that is exactly the difference between the two proposals we're here to vote on."

Here are four learning aids to explain further the process of preparing a public speech:

- a complete preparation outline with annotations to illustrate the entire structure of a public speech and some of its major elements
- a delivery outline to illustrate the type of outline you should use when you actually present the speech to your audience
- a skeletal outline to provide a type of template of a speech outline to remind you of its major parts
- a complete speech to illustrate what a good speech looks like and to summarize the major parts of a speech and the principles of public speaking

Learning Aid One. A Sample Outline with Annotations

Here is a relatively detailed outline similar to the ones you might prepare in constructing your speech. The sidenotes should clarify both the content and the format of a full sentence outline.

Have You Ever Been Culture Shocked?

Thesis: Culture shock can be described in four stages.

General Purpose: To inform

Specific Purpose: To inform my audience of the four phases of culture shock

Generally the title, thesis, general, and specific purpose of the speech are prefaced to the outline. When the outline is an assignment that is to be handed in, additional information may be requested.

Note the general format for the outline; note that the headings are clearly labeled and that the indenting helps you to see clearly the relationship that one item bears to the other. For example, in Introduction II, the outline format helps you to see that A, B, C, and D are explanations (amplification, support) for II.

Note that the Introduction, Body, and Conclusion are clearly labeled and separated visually.

Introduction

IV. Many of you have or will experience culture shock.

  A. Many people experience culture shock, that reaction to being in a culture very different from what you were used to.

The speaker assumes that the audience knows the general nature of culture shock and therefore does not go into detail as to its definition. Just in case some audience members do not know, and to refresh the memory of others, the speaker includes a brief definition.

B. By understanding culture shock, you'll be in a better position to deal with it if and when it comes.

Here the speaker attempts to connect the speaker, audience, and topic by stressing intercultural experiences and an abiding interest in the topic. Also, the speaker makes the topic important to the audience by referring to their everyday surroundings.

II. Culture shock occurs in 4 stages (Oberg 1960).
   A. The Honeymoon occurs first.
   B. The Crisis occurs second.
   C. The Recovery occurs third.
   D. The Adjustment occurs fourth.

Note that references are integrated throughout the outline just as they would in a term paper. In the actual speech, the speaker might say: "Anthropologist Kalervo Oberg, who coined the term *culture shock*, said it occurs in four stages."

The introduction serves the two functions noted: it gains attention (by involving the audience and by stressing the importance of the topic to the audience's desire to gain self-understanding) and it orients the audience as to what is to follow. This particular orientation identifies both the number of stages and their names. If this speech were a much longer and more complex one, the orientation might also have included brief definitions of each stage.

[Let's follow the order in which these four stages occur and begin with the first stage, the honeymoon.]

This transition cues the audience into a four-part presentation. Also, the numbers repeated throughout the outline will further aid the audience in keeping track of where you are in the speech. Most important, it tells the audience that the speech will follow a temporal thought pattern.

Body

Notice the parallel structure throughout the outline. For example, note that I, II, III, and IV in the body are all phrased in exactly the same way. Although this may seem unnecessarily redundant, it will help your audience follow your speech more closely and will also help you in logically structuring your thoughts.

I. The Honeymoon occurs first.
   A. The honeymoon is the period of fascination with the new people and culture.
   B. You enjoy the people and the culture.
      1. You love the people.
         a. For example, the people in Zaire spend their time very differently from the way New Yorkers do.
         b. For example, my first 18 years living on a farm was very different from life in a college dorm.
      2. You love the culture.
         a. The great number of different religions in India fascinated me.
         b. Eating was an especially great experience.

Notice that there are lots of examples throughout this speech. These examples are identified only briefly in the outline and would naturally be elaborated on in the speech.

Notice too the internal organization of each major point. Each main assertion in the body contains a definition of the stage (IA, IIA, IIIA, and IVA) and examples (IB, IIB, IIIB, and IVB) to illustrate the stage.

[But, like many relationships, life is not all honeymoon; soon there comes a crisis.]

II. The Crisis occurs second.
   A. The crisis is the period during which you begin to experience problems.
      1. One-third of American workers abroad fail because of culture shock (Samovar & Porter 1991, p. 232).
      2. The personal difficulties are also great.

Because this is a specific fact, some style manuals require that the page number should be included.

B. Life becomes difficult in the new culture.
   1. Communication is difficult.
   2. It's easy to offend people without realizing it.

[As you gain control over the crises, you begin to recover.]

III. The Recovery occurs third.
   A. The recovery is the period during which you learn how to cope.
   B. You begin to learn intercultural competence (Lustig & Koester 1996).
      1. You learn how to communicate.
         a. Being able to go to the market and make my wants known was a great day for me.
         b. I was able to ask for a date.
      2. You learn the rules of the culture.
         a. The different religious ceremonies each have their own rules.
         b. Eating is a ritual experience in lots of places throughout Africa.

Note that each statement in the outline is a complete sentence. You can easily convert this outline into a phrase or key word outline for use in delivery. The full sentences, however, will help you see more clearly relationships among items.

[Your recovery leads naturally into the next and final stage, the adjustment.]

IV. The Adjustment occurs fourth.
   A. The adjustment is the period during which you come to enjoy the new culture.
   B. You come to appreciate the people and the culture.

The transitions are inserted between all major parts of the speech. Although they may seem too numerous in this abbreviated outline, they will be appreciated by your audience because the transitions will help them follow your speech.

[Let me summarize the stages you go through in experiencing culture shock.]

Conclusion

I. Culture shock can be described in four stages.
   A. The Honeymoon is first.
   B. The Crisis is second.
   C. The Recovery is third.
   D. The Adjustment is fourth.

Notice that these four points correspond to I, II, III, and IV of the body and to II A, B, C and D of the introduction. Notice how the similar wording adds clarity.

II. By knowing the four stages, you can better understand the culture shock you may now be experiencing on the job, at school, or in your private life.

This step provides closure; it makes it clear that the speech is finished. It also serves to encourage reflection on the part of the audience as to their own culture shock.

References

This reference list includes just those sources that appear in the completed speech.

Lustig, Myron W. and Jolene Koester (1996). *Intercultural Competence: Interpersonal Communication Across Cultures,* 2nd ed. New York: HarperCollins.

Oberg, Kalervo (1960). Culture Shock: Adjustment to New Cultural Environments. *Practical Anthropology* 7:177–182.

Samovar, Larry A. and Richard E. Porter (1991). *Communication Between Cultures.* Belmont, CA: Wadsworth.

Learning Aid Two. The Skeletal Outline

Here is a skeletal outline—a kind of template for structuring a speech. This particular outline would be appropriate for a speech using a temporal, spatial, or topical organization pattern. Note that in this skeletal outline there are three major propositions (I, II, and III in the Body). These correspond to the IIA, IIB, and IIC in the introduction (in which you would orient the audience) and to the IA, IB, and IC in the conclusion (in which you would summarize your major propositions). The transitions are signaled by square brackets. As you review this outline—the faintly printed watermarks will remind you of the functions of each outline item—you will be able to see how it can be adapted for use with other organization patterns, for example, problem-solution, cause-effect, or the motivated sequence.

Thesis: *your main assertion; the core of your speech* ______.

General Purpose: *your general aim (to inform, to persuade, to entertain)* ______.

Specific Purpose: *what you hope to achieve from this speech* ______.

Introduction

I. *gain attention* ______.

II. *orient audience* ______.

  A. *first major proposition; same as I in Body* ______.

  B. *second major proposition; same as II in Body* ______.

  C. *third major proposition; same as III in Body* ______.

[Transition: *connect the Introduction to the Body* ______]

Body

I. *first major proposition* ______.

  A. *support for I (the first major proposition)* ______.

  B. *further support for I* ______.

[Transition: *connect the first major proposition to the second* ______]

II. *second major proposition* ______.

  A. *support for II (the second major proposition)* ______.

  B. *further support for II* ______.

[Transition: *connect the second major proposition to the third*]

III. *third major proposition*.

A. *support for III*.

B. *further support for III*.

[Transition: *connect the third major proposition (or all major propositions) to the Conclusion*]

Conclusion

I. *summary*.

A. *first major proposition; same as I in body*.

B. *second major proposition; same as II in body*.

C. *third major proposition; same as III in body*.

II. *closure*.

References

1.

2.

3.

Learning Aid Three. The Delivery Outline

Resist the temptation to use your preparation outline to deliver the speech. If you use your preparation outline, you will tend to read from the outline, instead of presenting an extemporaneous speech, during which you attend to and respond to audience feedback. Instead, construct a brief delivery outline, one that will assist rather than hinder your delivery of the speech. Here is a sample delivery outline constructed from the preparation outline on culture shock, presented previously. Note these features in the following sample outline:

- It is brief enough that you will be able to use it effectively without losing eye contact with the audience. It uses abbreviations (for example, CS for culture shock) and phrases rather than complete sentences.
- It is detailed enough to include all essential parts of your speech, including transitions.
- It contains delivery notes specifically tailored to your own needs, for example, pause suggestions and guides to using visual aids.
- It is clearly divided into Introduction, Body, and Conclusion and uses the same numbering system as the preparation outline.

PAUSE!

LOOK OVER THE AUDIENCE!

I. Many experience CS

A. CS: the reaction to being in a culture very different from your own

B. By understanding CS, you'll be better able to deal with it

PAUSE—SCAN AUDIENCE

II. CS occurs in 4 stages (WRITE ON BOARD)

A. Honeymoon

B. Crisis

C. Recovery

D. Adjustment

[Let's examine these stages of CS]

PAUSE—STEP FORWARD

I. Honeymoon

A. fascination w/people and culture

B. enjoyment of people and culture

1. Zaire example

2. farm to college dorm

[But, life is not all honeymoon—the crisis]

II. Crisis

A. problems arise

1. $^1/_3$ U.S. Am workers fail abroad

2. personal difficulties

B. life becomes difficult

1. communication

2. offend others

[As you gain control over the crises, you learn how to cope]

PAUSE

III. Recovery

A. period of learning to cope

B. you learn intercultural competence

1. communication becomes easier

2. you learn the culture's rules

[As you recover, you adjust]

IV. Adjustment

A. learn to enjoy (again) the new culture

B. appreciate people and culture

[These then are the four stages; let me summarize]

PAUSE BEFORE STARTING CONCLUSION

I. CS occurs in 4 stages: honeymoon, crisis, recovery, & adjustment

II. By knowing the 4 stages, you can better understand the culture shock you may now be experiencing on the job, at school, or in your private life.

PAUSE, ASK FOR QUESTIONS

Learning Aid Four. A Sample Speech with Annotations

This sample speech, a particularly good one, will illustrate what a finished speech looks like. The marginal questions will give you an opportunity to apply your newly acquired public speaking skills. The speech was presented by Rebecca Witte, a student from the University of Missouri, St. Louis, Missouri. She was coached by Sherry LaBoon and Tom Preston.

America's Youth in Crisis

Rebecca Witte
University of Missouri-St. Louis, Missouri
Coached by Sherry LaBoon and Tom Preston

I am a seven letter word. I destroy friends, families, neighborhoods and schools. I am the biggest killer among teenagers today. I am not alcohol. I am not cocaine. I am suicide.

The title, "America's Youth in Crisis," gives you a general idea of the nature of the speech but doesn't reveal the specific topic. *(1) What does the title mean to you? Does it gain your attention? What would have been other suitable titles? What would you have titled it?*

The opening lines are designed to gain attention by posing a kind of riddle. The speaker anticipates that the listeners will interact and try to identify what the topic is. The speaker then rules out the two major anticipated topics (alcohol and cocaine) and then identifies her topic,

According to the American Suicide Prevention Association, 85% of all teenagers between the ages of 15 and 18 consider committing suicide. Of that 85%, 50% of them will attempt and roughly 32% will succeed.

suicide. *(2) Did the opening lines gain your attention? Did they involve you in the speech by withholding the topic while you think of what this seven-letter word might be? (3) What other attention-gaining devices might the speaker have used?*

Obviously, suicide kills thousands of high school teenagers every year. In fact, the ASPA says that over 3,000 teenagers died in 1993 from suicide alone. Why is it then that the high schools aren't doing anything? Why is it that high schools do not have mandatory suicide prevention programs as a part of their everyday curriculum? Those are very good questions and that is why I am here today. First, we'll establish why teenagers commit suicide; next, we'll compare the schools that have a prevention program to those that do not; and finally, look at what we can do to help decrease the number of suicides every year.

Continuing to hold the attention of the audience and to emphasize the importance of the topic, the speaker presents some pretty startling statistics. *(4) Did these help to maintain your attention? (5) Did they help to establish the importance of the speech topic? (6) What thoughts and feelings did these statistics arouse in you?*

(7) What is the specific purpose of this speech? The thesis? (8) Are they sufficiently narrow and limited in scope?

According to Psychiatrist, Glenda Taber, in her book, **Suicide: The Teenage Death Syndrome,** "Teens are under more stress today than ever before." This stress stems from such things as drug [or] alcohol abuse, abusive parents and abusive boyfriend or girlfriend, pressure to have sex, failure, be it on the job or in school, even homosexuality. Taber says that when these teens are so low that they are actually considering suicide, they have what is known as tunnel vision, meaning that they can see no other option other than the one in front of them. They can't even see the light at the end of the tunnel. Dr. Michael Gleason, a Psychiatrist at Christian Northwest Hospital in St. Louis, Missouri, says that suicide is such an easy option for teenagers because they aren't taught the correct ways to deal with the stressors in their lives. So they don't. Instead, they continue to build up one stressor on top of another until they all come toppling over. Suicide then becomes an easy, permanent answer to a difficult, temporary situation. Dr. Gleason puts it this way, "Picture it. These teens are dealing with multitudes of problems every day, and one little thing promises to take it all away." A national organization called TREND or Turning Reactional Excitement in New Directions, has published a pamphlet entitled, "Getting Out or Getting Help." In this pamphlet it states that teens need to be taught that there are other options beside suicide. It goes on to say that every community across the United States has a suicide hotline number. Unfortunately, for these troubled teens the primary place for them to get this vital information is at school.

The speaker uses the authority and credibility of a psychiatrist and author to establish the proposition that "teens are under more stress today than ever before" and then connects this stress to suicide. *(9) How effectively does the speaker establish this connection? What else might the speaker have done?*

The speaker cites a pamphlet by "a national organization called TREND." *(10) What credibility do you ascribe to TREND? (11) How do you compare the credibility of this pamphlet,* Newsweek, *the* St. Louis Post Dispatch, *and the* San Francisco Tribune*?*

Then why is it that high schools refuse to do anything? TREND itself has given them two options of what to do: publish the suicide hotline number and teach teenagers other options beside suicide. What is holding them back? According to a study conducted by **Newsweek,** June, 1992, superintendents and principals seem to possess a fear of suicide. They interviewed over 2,000 high school principals. Only 22% of those interviewed claimed to discuss suicide in any way, shape or form.

The speaker provides additional startling statistics in her discussion of the attitudes of high school principals toward suicide. *(12) Are you surprised at the principals' attitudes toward suicide information? What does it lead you to think about high school programs in suicide prevention? (13) Is the speaker beginning to convince you that this is a real problem?*

This includes prevention programs in class, assemblies, publication of the community's suicide hotline number and any advertisement that the school has suicide counseling available. That leaves 80% of the high school students in America to fend for themselves. One superintendent went so far as to say, "Hey if we discussed everything that affects teenagers today, we'd have to add on another month to the school year." What he doesn't understand is that unless he decides to face this problem he will lose many of his students before the year 2000.

This fear that high school authorities have of suicide often snowballs into disaster. According to the **St. Louis Post Dispatch,** August, 1992, a newspaper editor of a small school in St. Charles County, Missouri, wanted to publish an article about suicide in her school's paper. She dealt with the issues honestly and carefully, providing some statistics, some things to look for in friends and their community's suicide hotline number. The Principal, however, would not allow the article to be published, saying his school did not have a problem with suicide. The article went unpublished, as did the suicide hotline number. Later that year, the editor graduated. And two days after her graduation, her best friend shot himself in the head. Two weeks after that, an alum from the school from two years before shot himself in the head. And two weeks after that, the Principal's son shot himself in the head. Three suicides from a school where "suicide is not a problem."

The specific example, from the *St. Louis Post Dispatch,* is a good balance to the survey statistics cited from *Newsweek. (14) Would you have used the specific example before the survey statistics or would you have presented the case essentially as did this speaker? What reasons can you give for the effectiveness of one order of presentation over the other? (15) What effect did the* St. Louis Post Dispatch *article have on you? What does it lead you to think?*

The real problem is that the story is true and is happening to schools all across the country. Another problem is that the story does not end here. The small community found out about the editor's article and demanded the Principal's resignation, blaming him for the three deaths. He resigned and moved on to another high school, initiating a suicide prevention program there. And at the small school . . . well, suicide still isn't a problem. You see, even the communities are afraid of suicide. They are afraid that by admitting suicide is a problem, they're giving in to it.

(16) What type of audience is the speaker addressing? For example, does the speaker address the concerns of parents and grandparents of teen-aged children as well as, say, college students in their early twenties? If you were giving this speech to parents and grandparents, what changes would you make?

Admittance is the first step. Unfortunately, most programs are not initiated until after the school has suffered great suicidal loss. According to the **San Francisco Tribune,** March, 1993, North High School in San Francisco had the highest suicide average in a ten-year period. Their average death rate was five deaths a year with an additional 15 attempts. A new principal came in and decided to stop the death and initiated a program. In the past three years their average death rate has dropped from five deaths a year to less than one and from 15 attempts to about three.

(17) Does the San Francisco Tribune *article convince you that suicide prevention programs work? What other evidence might you want?*

Obviously, these programs work. And they work for three reasons. The first is because most often these programs are interspliced with health class. Health class is a mandatory class every public high school student must take in order to graduate. By making it mandatory, the schools are guaranteeing these stu-

The speaker used a variety of research sources in her speech. *(18) Would you consider this research adequate for a speech on this topic if delivered to your Human Communication class? What did you like about the research? How might it have been improved?*

dents will take the class. I mean, what student is going to pick "Death 101" over Home Ec or Shop. The second reason they work is because the books that deal with suicide do so in a down-to-earth personal manner. This appeals to teenagers making them want to learn. So, they do. The final reason they work is because teenagers are able to take this new information throughout the rest of their lives. This is beneficial to you and I because these students are graduating with this vital information. They know the statistics, they know the signs to look for in friends and they know the community's suicide hotline number. They know what to do when suicide comes knocking not only at their doors, but at our doors as well.

The programs work, but it takes a superintendent who is willing to face the issues. Without our help this could take years and many lives. So what can we do to help take years and many lives. So what can we do to help decrease the numbers of suicidal deaths? There are many things, but first and foremost, make sure every person you know knows your community's suicide hotline number. It's very easy to find, simply open up the *Yellow Pages* and look up "suicide." Secondly, check with the high schools in your area and see if they have a suicide prevention program. If they don't, make them. We all know that with enough arguing, enough petitioning, enough phone calls, something has to be done. Talk to the parents, talk to the students, talk to the school board if you have to, but do something to stop the death in your area. Remember, just because you don't hear about it, doesn't mean it doesn't happen.

The speaker offers a variety of solutions to the problem, for example, integrating suicide information into high school courses and using books that discuss suicide in a "down-to-earth personal manner." *(19) How would you evaluate these solutions? Would they be acceptable to an audience such as your Human Communication class? (20) What other solutions might you have advanced if your were giving this speech?*

This speech was very clearly and effectively organized. *(21) What organizational pattern did the speaker use? Did the speaker clue the audience into the organizational pattern to be used? (22) What other organizational patterns would have been appropriate?*

Finally, because suicide does not just affect teenagers, because it affects every age group across the spectrum, check for some of these possible suicide signs in friends of yours as published in **Health** from Heath Publishing in 1993:

1. Severe depression
2. Giving away personal possessions
3. Buying a weapon
4. Talking about suicide
5. A decrease in energy
6. A sudden increased use of drugs or alcohol
7. Wanting to continually be alone

We all know why teens commit suicide. We all know what happens to the schools that do nothing compared to those that do. And now, we know what we can do to decrease the numbers of suicides every year. The next suicide victim could be someone you know. You may hold their life, their future, in the palms of your hands.

As discussed in Unit 22, we can use a variety of standards to evaluate this speech. *(23) Using the effectiveness standard, was this speaker effective? That is, are you going to comply with the speaker's recommendations—to look up the phone number and to check with the local high schools? If not, why not? (24) Do you consider the speech to have universal merit? (25) Does this speech follow the principles of the art as discussed in this unit?*

Generally, the conclusion should summarize and close the speech. Another function often mentioned is that of motivating the audience. *(26) What functions did this conclusion serve? Where they effectively served?*

(27) Can you identify any transitions the speaker used? Were these sufficient in number? Were they effective in achieving their purpose?

(28) What one thing did you like best about this speech? (29) What one suggestion would you make to improve this speech?

SUMMARY

In this unit we covered the practical steps in preparing and delivering a speech.

1. Topics for public speeches should be worthwhile and limited in scope. The purpose should be clearly and specifically defined.
2. The speech needs to be appropriate to and adapted to your specific audience.
3. The speech topics should be thoroughly researched, using the best materials available.
4. The speech should have one clearly identifiable thesis that all the major propositions support.
5. The major propositions should be adequately supported so that they are clear and, if appropriate, persuasively presented.
6. The speech should be organized into a logical progression of ideas that will aid audience comprehension.
7. The speech should be worded so that it is instantly intelligible by listeners who will hear the speech only once.
8. The conclusions should summarize and close the speech and the introduction should gain attention and orient the audience. The parts of the speech need to be connected adequately with transitions.
9. The speech should be rehearsed to the point where you are comfortable giving it to an audience.
10. In delivering the speech, voice and bodily action should reinforce the message.

THINKING CRITICALLY ABOUT PREPARING AND PRESENTING THE PUBLIC SPEECH

1. What topics would you like to hear other students speak on? What topics would you definitely not like to hear about? What accounts for your likes and dislikes?
2. Do men and women differ in what they consider an appropriate or an interesting topic in public speaking? In what ways has your culture influenced your thinking concerning what should be or what should not be an appropriate topic for public speaking?
3. How would you describe your class as an audience?
4. Visit the library and select one research source (in print, video, audio, or electronic form) that you think would be useful to students preparing speeches for this class. What types of information does this reference source contain? Why do you think this would prove useful?
5. Select a recent television show or movie and identify its thesis. Are there subordinate theses?
6. What types of supporting materials would you find most useful in explaining to children the nature of advertising? In persuading class members to contribute blood?
7. What thought pattern would you use to describe your college campus to a group of high school students who have never seen a college campus? To persuade your audience to follow a healthy diet?
8. What suggestions for using language more effectively would you offer your typical college instructor? Are these suggestions useful to students preparing public speeches?

9. What three principles of public speaking can you find illustrated in the sample speech provided at the end of this unit?
10. How would you go about finding answers to such questions as these:
    a. Do men and women respond differently to attention-gaining strategies?
    b. Are speakers who use a personal and informal style of speaking more effective than speakers who use an impersonal and formal style of speaking?
    c. Is a speech without transitions any less effective than a speech with transitions?
    d. Do men and women differ in their critical listening?

glossary of concepts and skills in human communication

Included here are definitions of some of the major terms used in this text and, where appropriate, the corresponding skills appear in italics.

Abstraction. A general concept derived from a class of objects; a part representation of some whole.

Abstraction process. The process by which a general concept is derived from specifics; the process by which some (never all) characteristics of an object, person, or event are perceived by the senses or included in some term, phrase, or sentence. See *Level of abstraction.*

Accent. The stress or emphasis placed on a syllable when pronounced.

Acculturation. The processes by which a person's culture is modified or changed through contact with or exposure to another culture.

Active listening. A process of putting together into some meaningful whole the listener's understanding of the speaker's total message—the verbal and the nonverbal, the content and the feelings. *Listen actively by paraphrasing the speaker's meanings, expressing an understanding of the speaker's feelings, and asking questions to enable you to check the accuracy of your understanding of the speaker. Express acceptance of the speaker's feelings and encourage the speaker to explore further his or her feelings and thoughts and thereby increase meaningful sharing.*

Adaptors. Nonverbal behaviors that, when emitted in private (or in public without being seen) serve some kind of need and occur in their entirety—for example, scratching one's head until the itch is eliminated. *Avoid adaptors that interfere with effective communication and that reveal your discomfort or anxiety.*

Adjustment principle. The principle of verbal interaction claiming that communication can take place only to the extent that the parties communicating share the same system of signals. *Expand the common areas between you and significant others; learn each other's system of communication signals and meanings in order to increase understanding and interpersonal communication effectiveness.*

Affect displays. Movements of the facial area and body that convey emotional meaning—for example, anger, fear, and surprise.

Affinity-seeking strategies. Behaviors designed to increase your interpersonal attractiveness and make another person like you more. *Use the various affinity-seeking strategies, as appropriate to the interpersonal relationship and the situation, to increase your own interpersonal attractiveness.*

Agape. A selfless, altruistic love.

Agenda-setting. The effect of the media in focusing attention on certain issues and problems. This media attention or inattention influences people to see various issues as important or unimportant; generally, the more media attention given an issue, the more will people think it is important. Also, a persuasive technique in which the speaker identifies his or her agenda as the significant issue and others as insignificant.

Aggressiveness. See *Verbal aggressiveness.*

Allness. The assumption that all can be known or is known about a given person, issue, object, or event. *End statements with an implicit* etc. (et cetera) *to indicate that more could be known and said; avoid allness terms and statements.*

Altercasting. A statement that places the listener in a specific role for a specific purpose and asks that the listener consider the question or problem from this role's perspective. *Putting another person or yourself into the role of another is often a useful way of gaining new perspectives.*

Ambiguity. The condition in which a word or phrase may be interpreted as having more than one meaning.

Analogy, reasoning from. A type of reasoning in which you compare like things and conclude that since they are alike in so many respects that they are also alike in some previously unknown respect.

Apology. A type of excuse in which you acknowledge responsibility for the behavior, generally ask forgiveness, and claim that this will not happen again.

Appeals for the suspension of judgment. A type of disclaimer in which the speaker asks listeners to delay their judgments.

Appraisal interview. A type of interview in which the interviewee's performance is assessed by management or by more experienced colleagues.

Apprehension. See *Speaker apprehension.*

Arbitrariness. The feature of human language that refers to the fact that there is no real or inherent relationship between the form of a word and its meaning. If we do not know anything of a particular language, we could not examine the form of a word and thereby discover its meaning.

Argot. The language of a particular class, generally an underworld, or criminal class, which is difficult and sometimes impossible for outsiders to understand.

Argument. Evidence (for example, facts or statistics) and a conclusion drawn from the evidence.

Argumentativeness. A willingness to argue for a point of view, to speak your mind. Distinguished from verbal aggressiveness. *Cultivate your argumentativeness, your willingness to argue for what you believe, by, for example, treating disagreements as objectively as possible, reaffirming the other, stressing equality, expressing interest in the other's position, and allowing the other person to save face.*

Articulation. The physiological movements of the speech organs as they modify and interrupt the air stream emitted from the lungs.

Artifactual messages. Communication that takes place through the wearing or arrangement of various artifacts—for example, clothing, jewelry, buttons, or the furniture in your house.

Assertiveness. A willingness to stand up for your rights but with respect for the rights of others. *Increase assertiveness (if desired) by analyzing the assertive and nonassertive behaviors of others, analyzing your own behaviors in terms of assertiveness, recording your behaviors, rehearsing assertive behaviors, and acting assertively in appropriate situations. Secure feedback from others for further guidance in increasing assertiveness.*

Assimilation. The process of message distortion in which messages are reworked to conform to your own attitudes, prejudices, needs, and values. *Recognize this tendency and make a conscious effort to remember as objectively as possible.*

Attack. A persuasive technique that involves accusing another person (usually an opponent) of some serious wrongdoing so that the issue under discussion never gets examined. *Avoid it.*

Attention. The process of responding to a stimulus or stimuli.

Attitude. A predisposition to respond for or against an object or person or assertion.

Attraction. The state or process by which one individual is drawn to another by having a highly positive evaluation of that other person.

Attraction theory. A theory holding that we form relationships on the basis of our attraction for another person which involves physical and personality attractiveness, proximity, and similarity.

Attribution. A process through which we attempt to understand the behaviors of others (as well as our own), particularly the reasons or motivations for these behaviors. *In attempting to identify the motivation for behaviors, examine consensus, consistency, and distinctiveness. Generally, low consensus, high consistency, and low distinctiveness identify internally motivated behavior; high consensus, low consistency, and high distinctiveness identify externally motivated behavior. Also inquire into controllability and stability judgments.*

Audience participation principle. A principle of persuasion stating that persuasion is achieved more effectively when the audience participates actively.

Authoritarian leader. A group leader who determines the group policies or makes decisions without consulting or securing agreement from group members.

Avoidance. An unproductive conflict strategy in which we take mental or physical flight from the actual conflict.

Backchanneling cues. Responses made by a listener during a conversation that acknowledge the speaker or the speaker's message rather than request a turn as speaker. *Respond to backchanneling cues as appropriate to the conversation. Use backchanneling cues to let the speaker know that you are listening.*

Bandwagon. A persuasive technique by which the speaker tries to gain compliance by saying that "everyone is doing it" and urges you to join in.

Barriers to communication. Those factors (physical or psychological) that prevent or hinder effective communication.

Behavioral approach to organizations. An approach to organizations holding that increases in worker satisfaction lead to increases in productivity; the function of management is to keep workers happy and satisfied so that workers, in turn, will be productive; also referred to as *humanistic* or *organic.*

Behavioral synchrony. The similarity in the behavior, usually nonverbal, of two people. Generally, behavioral synchrony is an index of mutual liking.

Belief. Confidence in the existence or truth of something; conviction.

Beltlining. An unproductive conflict strategy in which we hit the other person with insults below his or her level of tolerance—that is, below the belt.

Blame. An unproductive conflict strategy in which we attribute the cause of the conflict to the other person or devote our energies to discovering who is the cause and avoid tackling the issues causing the conflict.

Blind self. The part of the self that contains information about the self that is known to others but unknown to oneself.

Boundary markers. Markers separating territories—for example, the armrests in a theater that separate one person's space from another's.

Brainstorming. A technique for generating ideas among people.

Breadth. The number of topics about which individuals in a relationship communicate.

Bypassing. A pattern of misevaluation in which people fail to communicate their intended meaning. Bypassing may take either of two forms: (1) when two people use different words but give them the same meaning, resulting in apparent disagreement that hides the underlying agreement; and (2) when two people use the same words but each gives them different meanings, resulting in apparent agreement that hides the underlying disagreement. *Recognize that the same word may be given different meanings by different people and that different words may be used to mean the same thing. Look for meaning in the person and use active listening techniques to combat possible bypassing.*

Cant. The conversational language of any nonprofessional (usually noncriminal) group, which is generally understood only by its own members.

Card-stacking. A persuasive technique in which the speaker selects only the evidence and arguments that build a case and omits or distorts any contradictory evidence.

Causes and effects, reasoning from. A form of reasoning in which you reason that certain effects are due to specific causes or that specific causes produce certain effects.

Central markers. Items placed in a territory that are intended to reserve it for us—for example, a jacket left on a library chair.

Certainty. An attitude of closed-mindedness that creates a defensiveness among communication participants. Opposed to *provisionalism.*

Channel. The vehicle or medium through which signals are sent.

Character. One of the qualities of credibility; the individual's honesty and basic nature; moral qualities.

Charisma. One of the qualities of credibility; the individual's dynamism or forcefulness.

Cherishing behaviors. Small behaviors that we enjoy receiving from a relational partner—for example, a kiss, a smile, a gift of flowers.

Chronemics. The study of communicative nature of time—how we treat time and how we use it to communicate. Two general areas of chronemics are usually distinguished: *cultural time* and *psychological time.*

Civil inattention. Polite ignoring of others so as not to invade their privacy.

Clearance. The quality that identifies the other person as being available for an interpersonal interaction.

Cliché. Overused phrase that has lost its novelty and part of its meaning, and that calls attention to itself because of its overuse.

Closed-mindedness. An unwillingness to receive certain communication messages.

Code. A set of symbols used to translate a message from one form to another.

Coercive power. Power dependent on one's ability to punish or to remove rewards from another person.

Cognitive disclaimer. A disclaimer in which the speaker seeks to confirm his or her cognitive capacity, for example, "You may think I'm drunk, but I'm as sober as anyone here."

Cognitive restructuring. A theory for substituting logical and realistic beliefs for unrealistic ones; used in reducing communication apprehension and in raising self-esteem.

Cohesiveness. The property of togetherness. Applied to group communication situations, it refers to the mutual attractiveness among members; a measure of the extent to which individual members of a group work together as a group.

Collectivist orientation. A cultural orientation in which the group's rather than the individual's goals and preferences are given greater importance. Opposed to *individual orientation.*

Colloquy. A small group format in which a subject is explored through the interaction of two panels (one asking and one answering questions) or through the panel members responding to questions from audience members.

Communication. (1) The process or act of communicating; (2) the actual message or messages sent and received; and (3) the study of the processes involved in the sending and receiving of messages. The term *communicology* (q.v.) is suggested for the third definition.

Communication network. The pathways of messages; the organizational structure through which messages are sent and received.

Communicology. The study of communication and particularly that subsection concerned with human communication.

Competence. In communication, the rules of the more social or interpersonal dimensions of communication, often used to refer to those qualities that make for effectiveness in interpersonal communication; one of the qualities of credibility that encompasses a person's ability and knowledge.

Complementarity. A principle of attraction holding that one is attracted by qualities one does not possess or one wishes to possess and to people who are opposite or different from oneself. *Identify the characteristics that* *you do not find in yourself but that you admire in others and that therefore might be important in influencing your perceptions of complementarity.* Opposed to *similarity.*

Complementary relationship. A relationship in which the behavior of one person serves as the stimulus for the complementary behavior of the other; in complementary relationships, behavior differences are maximized.

Compliance-gaining strategies. Tactics that are directed to gain the agreement of others; behaviors designed to persuade others to do as we wish. *Use the various strategies to increase your own persuasiveness.*

Compliance-resisting strategies. Tactics used to resist or refuse to do as asked. Nonnegotiation, negotiation, identity management (positive or negative), and justification are four types of compliance-resisting strategies. *Use such strategies as identity management, nonnegotiation, negotiation, and justification as appropriate in resisting compliance.*

Confidence. The absence of social anxiety; the communication of comfortableness in social situations. One of the qualities of effective interpersonal communication. *Communicate a comfortable, at-ease feeling with the interaction through appropriate verbal and nonverbal signals.*

Confirmation. A communication pattern in which we acknowledge the presence of the other person and also indicate our acceptance of this person, this person's definition of self, and our relationship as defined or viewed by this other person. Opposed to *disconfirmation. Avoid those verbal and nonverbal behaviors that disconfirm another person. Substitute confirming behaviors, behaviors that acknowledge the presence and the contributions of the other person.*

Conflict. A difference of opinion or disagreement. In popular usage, an extreme form of competition in which a person tries to bring a rival to surrender; a situation in which one person's behaviors are directed at preventing, interfering with, or harming another individual. See *Interpersonal conflict.*

Congruence. A condition in which both verbal and noverbal behaviors reinforce each other.

Connotation. The feeling or emotional aspect of meaning, generally viewed as consisting of the evaluative (for example, good-bad), potency (strong-weak), and activity (fast-slow) dimensions; the associations of a term. *Recognize that connotations for the same term will vary widely from one person to another and especially among persons from different cultures.* See *Denotation.*

Consciousness-raising group. A supportive group in which people discuss their feelings and in doing so raise their level of intrapersonal and interpersonal awareness.

Consensus. A principle of attribution through which we attempt to establish whether other people react or behave in the same way as the person on whom we are now focusing. If the person is acting in accordance with the general consensus, then we seek reasons for the behavior outside the individual; if the person is not acting in accordance with the general consensus, then we seek reasons that are internal to the individual.

Consistency. (1) A perceptual process that influences us to maintain balance among our perceptions; a process that influences us to see what we expect to see and to be uncomfortable when our perceptions contradict our expectations; (2) a principle of attribution through which we attempt to establish whether this person behaves the same way in similar situations. If there is consistency, we are likely to attribute the behavior to the person, to some internal motivation; if there is no consistency, we are likely to attribute the behavior to some external factor. *Recognize the human tendency to seek and see consistency even where it does not exist—to see our friends as all positive and our enemies as all negative.*

Contact. The first stage of an interpersonal relationship in which perceptual and interactional contact occurs. *In establishing contact keep the following nonverbal guidelines in mind: establish eye contact, signal interest and positive responses, concentrate your focus, establish physical closeness, maintain an open posture, respond visibly, reinforce positive behaviors, and avoid overexposure. Also, keep the following verbal guidelines in mind: introduce yourself, focus the conversation on the other person, exchange favors-rewards, be energetic, stress the positives, avoid negative and too intimate self-disclosures, establish commonalities, and avoid yes/no questions and answers and rapid-fire questions.*

Contamination. A form of territorial encroachment that renders another's territory impure.

Content and relationship dimensions. A principle of communication holding that messages refer both to content (the world external to both speaker and listener) and to relationship dimensions (the relationship existing between the individuals interacting).

Context of communication. The physical, social-psychological, and temporal environment in which communication takes place. *Assess the context in which messages are communicated and interpret that behavior accordingly; avoid seeing messages as independent of context.*

Controllability. One of the factors considered in judging whether or not a person is responsible for his or her behavior. If the person was in control, then you judge that he or she was responsible. See *Attribution theory.*

Conversation. Relatively informal talk in which the roles of speaker and listener are exchanged freely and frequently.

Conversational maxims. The rules that conversation is expected to follow and which differ from one culture to another. *Discover and try not to violate (and if appropriate, follow) the conversational maxims of the culture in which you are communicating.*

Conversational turns. The changing (or maintaining) of the speaker or listener role during a conversation. These turns are generally signaled nonverbally. Four major types of conversational turns may be identified: turn-maintaining, by which we indicate our desire to continue in the role of speaker; turn-yielding, by which we indicate our desire to change roles from speaker to listener; turn-requesting, by which we indicate our desire to speak; and turn-denying, by which we indicate our desire not to assume the role of speaker. *Respond to conversational turn cues from the other person and use conversational cues to signal your own desire to exchange (or maintain) speaker or listener roles. Become sensitive to and respond appropriately to conversational turn cues such as turn-maintaining, turn-yielding, turn-requesting, and turn-denying cues.*

Cooperation principle. An implicit agreement between speaker and listener to cooperate in trying to understand what each is communicating. A management strategy for dealing with power plays. *Try managing power plays cooperatively by expressing your feelings, describing the behavior you object to, and stating a cooperative response.*

Counseling interview. A type of interview in which the interviewer tries to learn about the interviewee in an attempt to provide some form of guidance, advice, or insight.

Credentialing. A type of disclaimer in which the speaker acknowledges that what is about to be said may reflect poorly on himself or herself but will say it nevertheless (usually for quite positive reasons).

Credibility. The degree to which a receiver perceives the speaker to be believable.

Critical thinking. Reasoned and reasonable thinking and decision making.

Critical thinking hats technique. A technique developed by Edward deBono by which a problem or issue is viewed from six distinct perspectives.

Criticism. The reasoned judgment of some work; although often equated with faultfinding, criticism can involve both positive and negative evaluations.

Cultivation theory. A theory of mass communication effects which claims that the media, largely television, teach us our culture.

Cultural approach to organizations. A view of organizations as a society or culture with its own rules for appropriate behavior, rituals, heroes, and values.

Cultural imperialism. As a theory of media, it holds that the media from a few dominant cultures, being so powerful and so pervasive, influences and dominates other cultures.

Cultural time. The communication function of time as regulated and as perceived by a particular culture. Generally, three types of cultural time are identified: technical time refers to precise scientific time; formal time refers to the divisions of time that a culture makes (for example, dividing a semester into 14 weeks); and informal time refers to the rather loose use of such time terms as *immediately, soon,* and *right away.*

Cultural transmission. The feature of language referring to the fact that human languages (at least in their outer surface form) are learned. Unlike various forms of animal language, which are innate, human languages are transmitted traditionally or culturally. This feature of language does not deny the possibility that certain aspects of language may be innate. Also referred to as cultural transmission.

Culture. The relatively specialized life-style of a group of people—consisting of their values, beliefs, artifacts, ways of behaving, and ways of communicating—that is passed on from one generation to the next.

Culture shock. The psychological reaction one experiences at being placed in a culture very different from one's own or from what one is used to.

Date. An extensional device used to emphasize the notion of constant change and symbolized by a subscript: for example, Joan $Smith_{1991}$ is not Joan $Smith_{1997}$.

Deception cues. Verbal or nonverbal cues that reveal the person is lying.

Decoder. What takes a message in one form (for example, sound waves) and translates it into another code (for example, nerve impulses) from which meaning can be formulated. In human communication, the decoder is the auditory mechanism; in electronic communication, the decoder is, for example, the telephone earpiece. See *Encoder.*

Decoding. The process of extracting a message from a code—for example, translating speech sounds into nerve impulses. See *Encoding.*

Defensiveness. An attitude of an individual or an atmosphere in a group characterized by treats, fear, and domination; messages evidencing evaluation, control, strategy, neutrality, superiority, and certainty are assumed to lead to defensiveness. Opposed to *supportiveness.*

Delphi method. A type of problem-solving group in which questionnaires are used to poll members on several occasions in an effort to arrive at a group decision on, say, the most important problems a company faces or activities a group might undertake.

Democratic leader. A group leader who stimulates self-direction and self-actualization of the group members.

Denotation. Referential meaning; the objective or descriptive meaning of a word. See *Connotation.*

Depenetration. A reversal of penetration; a condition in which the breadth and depth of a relationship decreases. See *Social penetration theory.*

Depth. The degree to which the inner personality—the inner core of an individual—is penetrated in interpersonal interaction.

Deterioration. A state in an interpersonal relationship in which the bonds holding the individuals together are weakened.

Dialogue. A form of communication in which each person is both speaker and listener; communication characterized by involvement, concern, and respect for the other person. Opposed to *monologue. Treat conversation as a dialogue rather than a monologue; show concern for other, and for the relationship between you, with other-orientation.*

Direct speech. Speech in which the speaker's intentions are stated clearly and directly. See *Indirect speech. Use direct requests and responses (1) to encourage compromise, (2) to acknowledge responsibility for your own feelings and desires, and (3) to state your own desires honestly so as to encourage honesty and openness in others.*

Disclaimer. Statements that ask listeners to receive what the speaker says as intended without it reflecting negatively on the speaker's image or reputation. *Avoid using disclaimers that may not be accepted by your listeners (they may raise the very doubts you wish to put to rest), but do use disclaimers when you think your future messages might offend your listeners.*

Disconfirmation. A communication pattern in which we ignore the presence of the other person as well as this person's communications. Opposed to *confirmation.*

Dissolution. The breaking of the bonds holding an interpersonal relationship together. *If the relationship ends: (1) break the loneliness-depression cycle, (2) take time out to get to know yourself as an individual, (3) bolster your self-esteem, (4) remove or avoid uncomfortable symbols that may remind you of your past relationship and may make you uncomfortable, (5) seek the support of friends and relatives, (6) avoid repeating negative patterns.*

Distinctiveness. A principle of attribution in which we ask whether this person reacts in similar ways in different situations. If the person does, there is low distinctiveness and we are likely to conclude there is an internal cause or motivation for the behavior; if there is high distinctiveness, we are likely to seek the cause in some external factors.

Double-bind message. A particular kind of contradictory message possessing the following characteristics: (1) the persons interacting share a relatively intense relationship; (2) two messages are communicated at the same time, demanding different and incompatible responses; (3) at least one person in the double bind cannot escape from the contradictory messages; (4) there is a threat of punishment for noncompliance.

Downward communication. Communication in which the messages originate at the higher levels of an organization or hierarchy and are sent to lower levels—for example, management to line worker. *Using a language known to both management and workers and providing workers with sufficient information will make downward communication more effective.*

Dyadic communication. Two-person communication.

Dyadic consciousness. An awareness of an interpersonal relationship or pairing of two individuals, distinguished from situations in which two individuals are together but do not perceive themselves as being a unit or twosome.

Dyadic effect. The tendency for the behavior of one person in a dyad to influence a similar behavior in the other person. Used most often to refer to the reciprocal nature of self-disclosure. *Be responsive to the dyadic effect; if it is not operating, consider why.*

Earmarkers. Identifying marks that indicate that the territory or object belongs to you—for example, initials on an attaché case.

Effect. The outcome or consequence of an action or behavior; communication is assumed always to have some effect.

Emblems. Nonverbal behaviors that directly translate words or phrases—for example, the signs for okay and peace.

Emotion. The feelings we have; for example, of guilt, anger, or sorrow.

Empathy. A quality of effective interpersonal communication that refers to the ability to feel another's feelings as that other person does and the ability to communicate that similarity of feeling. *To increase understanding of another's feelings, empathize with others (by sharing experiences, role-playing, and seeing the world from his or her perspective) and express this empathic understanding verbally and nonverbally.*

Employment interview. A type of interview in which the interviewee is questioned to ascertain his or her suitability for a particular job.

Encoder. Something that takes a message in one form (for example, nerve impulses) and translates it into another form (for example, sound waves). In human communication the encoder is the speaking mechanism; in electronic communication the encoder is, for example, the telephone mouthpiece. See *Decoder.*

Encoding. The process of putting a message into a code—for example, translating nerve impulses into speech sounds. See *Decoding.*

Enculturation. The process by which culture is transmitted from one generation to another.

E-Prime. A form of the language that omits the verb to be except when used as an auxiliary or in statements of existence. Designed to eliminate the tendency toward projection, or assuming that characteristics that one attributes to a person (for example, "Pat is brave") are actually in that person instead of in the observer's perception of that person.

Equality. A quality of effective interpersonal communication in which the equality of personalities is recognized, and both individuals are seen as worthwhile, valuable contributors to the total interaction. *Share the speaking and listening; recognize that all parties in communication have something to contribute.*

Equilibrium theory. A theory of proxemics holding that intimacy and physical closeness are positively related; as a relationship becomes more intimate, the individuals will use shorter distances between them.

Equity theory. A theory claiming that we experience relational satisfaction when there is an equal distribution of rewards and costs between the two persons in the relationship.

Erotic love. A sexual, physical love; a love that is ego-centered and given because of an anticipated return.

Etc. (Et cetera). An extensional device used to emphasize the notion of infinite complexity; since one can never know all about anything, any statement about the world or event must end with an explicit or implicit etc. *Use the implicit or explicit etc. to remind yourself and others that there is more to be known, more to be said.*

Ethics. The branch of philosophy that deals with the rightness or wrongness of actions; the study of moral values.

Ethnocentrism. The tendency to see others and their behaviors through our own cultural filters, often as distortions of our own behaviors; the tendency to evaluate the values and beliefs of one's own culture more positively than those of another culture.

Euphemism. A polite word or phrase used to substitute for some taboo or otherwise offensive term.

Evaluation. A process whereby a value is placed on some person, object, or event. *Delay evaluation until you acquire the needed information and have assessed the major options.*

Exclusive talk. Talk about a subject or in a vocabulary that only certain people understand, often in the presence of someone who does not belong to this group and therefore does not understand; use of terms unique to a specific culture as if they were universal. *Use language that is more inclusive and that does not signal the presence of an in-group and an out-group.*

Excuse. An explanation of one's behaviors designed to lessen their negative impact. *Avoid excessive excuse making; too many excuses may backfire and create image problems for the excuse maker.*

Exit interview. A type of interview designed to establish why an employee (the interviewee) is leaving the organization.

Expectancy violations theory. A theory of proxemics holding that people have a certain expectancy for space relationships. When that is violated (say, a person stands too close to you or a romantic partner maintains abnormally large distances from you), the relationship comes into clearer focus and you wonder why this "normal distance" is being violated.

Expert power. Power dependent on a person's expertise or knowledge; knowledge gives an individual expert power.

Expressiveness. A quality of effective interpersonal communication referring to the skill of communicating genuine involvement in the interpersonal interaction. *Communicate involvement and interest in the interaction by providing appropriate feedback, by assuming responsibility for your thoughts and feelings and for your role as speaker and listener, and by appropriate expressiveness, variety, and flexibility in voice and bodily action.*

Extemporaneous speech. A speech that is thoroughly prepared and organized in detail and in which certain aspects of style are predetermined.

Extensional devices. Those linguistic devices proposed by Alfred Korzybski for keeping language as a more accurate means for talking about the world. The extensional devices include the etc., date, and index—the working devices—and the hyphen and quotes—the safety devices. *Use these devices to make language more accurately reflect what is being talked about.*

Extensional orientation. A point of view in which the primary consideration is given to the world of experience and only secondary consideration is given to the labels. See *Intensional orientation.*

Eye communication. Sending and receiving of messages from movements of the eye. Use eye movements to monitor feedback, signal conversational turns, signal the nature of the relationship, and compensate for physical distance effectively. Also see *Pupillometrics.*

Face-saving. The tendency to maintain a positive self-image in the minds of others. *Avoid face-negative messages even in more individualistic cultures where face-saving is less important than it is in collectivistic cultures.*

Facial feedback hypothesis. The hypothesis stating that facial expressions influence the level of physiological arousal.

Facial management techniques. The techniques for communicating emotions facially, for example, to hide certain emotions or to substitute acceptable for unacceptable emotions.

Fact-inference confusion. A misevaluation in which one makes an inference, regards it as a fact, and acts upon it as if it were a fact. *Distinguish facts from inferences; respond to inferences as inferences and not as facts.*

Factual statement. A statement made by the observer after observation, and limited to the observed. See *Inferential statement.*

Fear appeal. The appeal to fear to persuade an individual or group of individuals to believe or to act in a certain way.

Feedback. Information that is fed back to the source. Feedback may come from the source's own messages (as when we hear what we are saying) or from the receiver(s) in the form of applause, yawning, puzzled looks, questions, letters to the editor of a newspaper, increased or decreased subscriptions to a magazine, and so forth. Feedback may vary on the basis of such dimensions as positive-negative, person-focused–message-focused, immediate-delayed, low monitoring–high monitoring, and supportive-critical. *Assess your feedback messages in terms of at least these five dimensions.*

Feedforward. Information sent prior to the regular messages telling the listener something about future messages. *When appropriate, preface your messages in order to open the channels of communication, to preview the messages to be sent, to disclaim, and to altercast. Use feedforward sparingly, be brief, and follow through on your promises. Also, be sure to respond to the feedforward as well as the content messages of others.*

Flexibility. The ability to adjust communication strategies on the basis of the unique situation. *Apply all the principles of effective communication flexibly; remember that each situation calls for somewhat different skills.*

Focus group. A group designed to explore the feelings and attitudes of its individuals and that usually follows a question-and-answer format.

Force. An unproductive conflict strategy in which one attempts to win an argument by physical force or threats of force. *Avoid it.*

Forum. A small group format in which members of the group answer questions from the audience; often follows a symposium. *Use this method, generally, when the speakers are experts and can increase audience understanding by sharing certain information and when you wish to increase audience involvement.*

Free information. Information about a person that one can see or that is dropped into the conversation, and that can serve as a topic of conversation.

Friendship. An interpersonal relationship between two persons that is mutually productive, established and maintained through perceived mutual free choice, and characterized by mutual positive regard. *Learn the rules that govern your friendships and follow these or risk damaging the relationship. Adjust your verbal and nonverbal communication as appropriate to the stages of your various friendships.*

Functional approach to leadership. An approach to leadership that identifies leadership with the performance of specific functions.

Fundamental attribution error. The tendency to attribute a person's behavior to the kind of person he or she is (to the person's personality, say) and not to give sufficient importance to the situation the person is in. *Consider the opposite possibilities in making attributions, especially about those you do not know well.*

Gatekeeping. The process of filtering messages from source to receiver. In this process some messages are allowed to pass through, and others are changed or not allowed to pass at all. *Secure information from varied sources to minimize the inevitable bias created by gatekeeping.*

General semantics. The study of the relationships among language, thought, and behavior.

Gossip. Communication about someone not present, some third party, usually about matters that are private to this third party. *Avoid gossip that breaches confidentiality, that is known to be false, and that is unnecessarily invasive.*

Granfallon. The tendency of people to see themselves as constituting a cohesive and like-minded group because they are given a label. *Apply the extensional device, the index.*

Grapevine. The informal lines through which messages in an organization may travel; these informal lines resemble the physical grapevine, with its unpredictable pattern of branches. *Recognize that grapevine communication is often incomplete but is extremely useful (and generally accurate), therefore it is wise to tap into it.*

Group. A collection of individuals related to each other with some common purpose and with some structure among them.

Group norm. Rules or expectations of appropriate behavior for a member of the group. *Learn norms and break them only after careful consideration of the consequences.*

Groupthink. A tendency observed in some groups in which agreement among members becomes more important than the exploration of the issues at hand. *Look for the symptoms, such as members seeing themselves as invulnerable or the group as moral or in simplistic terms.*

Gunnysacking. An unproductive conflict strategy in which we store up grievances against the other person and unload these during a conflict encounter. *Avoid it.*

Haptics. Touch or tactile communication. See *Tactile communication.*

Hedging. Using a disclaimer in which the speaker disclaims the importance of what he or she is about to say.

Heterosexist language. Language that assumes all people are heterosexual and thereby denigrates lesbians and gay men. *Avoid it.*

Hidden self. The part of the self that contains information about the self known to oneself, but unknown to and hidden from others.

High-context culture. One in which much of the information in communication is in the context or in the person rather than explicitly coded in the verbal messages. *Opposed to low-context culture.*

Home field advantage. The increased power that comes from being in your own territory. *Use the home-field advantage as you would any persuasive strategy.*

Home territories. Territories for which individuals have a sense of intimacy and over which they exercise control—for example, a child's clubhouse.

Hyphen. An extensional device used to illustrate that what may be separated verbally may not be separable on the event or nonverbal level; although one may talk about body and mind as if they were separable, in reality they are better referred to as body-mind. *Use it to indicate that some things cannot be separated, for example, source-receiver.*

Idea-generation group. See *Brainstorming.*

Illustrators. Nonverbal behaviors that accompany and literally illustrate the verbal messages—for example, upward movements that accompany the verbalization, "It's up there."

I-messages. Messages in which the speaker accepts responsibility for personal thoughts and behaviors; messages in which the speaker's point of view is stated explicitly. *Use I-messages to take responsibility for your own feelings and to increase honest sharing.*

Immediacy. A quality of effective interpersonal communication referring to the creation of a feeling of togetherness and oneness with another person. *Communicate immediacy through appropriate word choice, feedback, eye contact, body posture, and physical closeness.*

Implicit personality theory. A theory of personality that each individual maintains, complete with rules or systems, and through which others are perceived. *Be conscious of your implicit personality theories; avoid drawing firm conclusions about others on the basis of these theories.*

Impromptu speech. A speech given without any direct prior preparation.

Improvement group. A type of group used in organizations to seek out areas of possible improvement.

Inclusive talk. Communication that includes all people; communication that does not exclude certain groups, for example, women, lesbians and gays, or members of certain races or nationalities. *Use inclusive language to include everyone present in the interaction (both verbally and nonverbally) so as not to exclude, offend, or fail to profit from the contributions of others.*

Index. An extensional device used to emphasize the notion of nonidentity (no two things are the same) and symbolized by a subscript—for example, $politician_1$ is not $politician_2$. *Use the index to avoid indiscrimination and the tendency to discriminate against someone because of that person's label.*

Indirect speech. Speech that hides the speaker's true intentions; speech in which requests and observations are made indirectly. *Use indirect speech (1) to express a desire without insulting or offending anyone, (2) to ask for compliments in a socially acceptable manner, and (3) to disagree without being disagreeable.*

Indiscrimination. A misevaluation caused by categorizing people or events or objects into a particular class and responding to specific members only as members of the class; a failure to recognize that each individual is an individual and is unique; a failure to apply the index. *Index your terms and statements to emphasize that each person and event is unique; avoid treating all individuals the same because they are covered by the same label.*

Individualistic orientation. A cultural orientation in which the individual's rather than the group's goals and preferences are given greater importance. Opposed to *collective orientation.*

Inevitability. A principle of communication referring to the fact that communication cannot be avoided; all behavior in an interactional setting is communication. *Give attention to all types of messages whether in decoding the meanings of others or encoding your own meanings. See all message behavior as legitimate communication, and respond to the nonverbal as well as the verbal messages.*

Inferential statement. A statement that can be made by anyone, is not limited to the observed, and can be made at any time. *Distinguish this clearly from the factual statement.* See *Factual statement.*

Information. That which reduces uncertainty.

Information interview. A type of interview in which the interviewer asks the interviewee, usually a person of some reputation and accomplishment, questions designed to elicit his or her views, predictions, perspectives, and the like on specific topics.

Information overload. That condition in which the amount of information is too great to be dealt with effectively; the condition in which the number or complexity of messages is so great that the individual or organization is not able to deal with them. Recognize your own as well as the limits of others to deal with information; more information is not always better. *Reconsider the normal tendency to pass on* *information and to keep information that you no longer need or that appears in several different places.*

Information power. Power dependent on one's information and one's ability to communicate logically and persuasively. Also called *persuasion power.*

Information-sharing group. A group designed to share information among its members.

Inoculation principle. A principle of persuasion stating that persuasion will be more difficult to achieve when beliefs and attitudes that have already been challenged previously are attacked, because the individual has built up defenses against such attacks in a manner similar to inoculation. *In addressing an inoculated audience, you will generally need to proceed in small steps.*

Insulation. A reaction to territorial encroachment in which we erect some sort of barrier between ourselves and the invaders.

Intensional orientation. A point of view in which primary consideration is given to the way in which things are labeled and only secondary consideration (if any) to the world of experience. *Recognize that labels are not things; respond to the thing first and then examine the label.* See *Extensional orientation.*

Interaction management. A quality of effective interpersonal communication referring to the ability to control the interpersonal interaction to the satisfaction of both participants. Manage the interaction to the satisfaction of both parties by sharing the roles of speaker and listener, avoiding long and awkward silences, and being consistent in your verbal and nonverbal messages.

Interaction process analysis. A content analysis method that classifies messages into four general categories: social emotional positive, social emotional negative, attempted answers, and questions. *Use this technique to gain insight into the way members interact in a group setting.*

Intercultural communication. Communication that takes place between persons of different cultures or who have different cultural beliefs, values, or ways of behaving. *Recognize the differences between yourself and the culturally different, recognize the differences among the culturally different, see the differences in meaning, recognize and (perhaps) follow the rules and customs of the others, and avoid evaluating differences negatively.*

Interethnic communication. Communication between members of different ethnic groups.

International communication. Communication between nations.

Interpersonal communication. Communication between two persons or among a small group of persons and distinguished from public or mass communication; communication of a personal nature and distinguished from impersonal communication; communication between or among intimates or those involved in a close relationship; often, intrapersonal, dyadic, and small group communication in general.

Interpersonal conflict. A conflict or disagreement between two persons; a conflict within an individual caused by his or her relationships with other people. *A variety of effective conflict strategies are available; here are several. Follow these guidelines to fight more productively: (1) state your position directly and honestly; (2) react openly to the messages of your combatant; (3) own your own thoughts and feelings; (4) address the real issues that are causing the conflict; (5) listen with and demonstrate empathic understanding; (6) validate the feelings of your interactant; (7) describe the behaviors causing the conflict; (8) express your feelings spontaneously rather than strategically; (9) state your position tentatively; (10) capitalize on agreements; (11) view conflict in positive terms to the extent possible; (12) express positive feelings for the other person; (13) be positive about the prospects of conflict resolution; (14) treat your combatant as an equal, avoiding ridicule or sarcasm, for example; (15) involve yourself in the conflict; play an active role as both sender and receiver; (16) grant the other person permission to express himself or herself freely; (17) avoid power tactics that may inhibit freedom of expression.*

Interpersonal perception. The perception of people; the processes through which you interpret and evaluate people and their behaviors.

Interracial communication. Communication between members of different races.

Interview. A particular form of interpersonal communication in which two persons interact largely by question-and-answer format for the purpose of achieving specific goals.

Intimacy. The closest interpersonal relationship; usually used to denote a close primary relationship.

Intimate distance. The shortest proxemic distance, ranging from touching to 6 to 18 inches.

Intrapersonal communication. Communication with oneself.

Invasion. The unwarranted entrance into another's territory that changes the meaning of the territory. See *Territorial encroachment.*

Involvement stage. The stage in an interpersonal relationship that normally follows contact in which the individuals get to know each other better and explore the potential for greater intimacy.

Irreversibility. A principle of communication referring to the fact that communication cannot be reversed; once something has been communicated, it cannot be uncommunicated. *Avoid saying things (for example, in anger or in the heat of passion) that you may wish to retract (but will not be able to) in order to prevent resentment and ill feeling.*

Jargon. The language of any special group, often a professional class, that is unintelligible to individuals not belonging to the group; the "shop talk" of the group. *Avoid jargon terms with those who do not understand them, or explain the terms.*

Johari window. A diagram or model of the four selves: open, blind, hidden, and unknown.

Kinesics. The study of the communicative dimension of face and body movements.

Knowledge gap hypothesis. A theory holding that there is a division between those who are knowledgeable and those who are not; especially relevant in access to and knowledge of the new technologies.

Laissez-faire leader. A group leader who allows the group to develop and progress or make mistakes on its own.

Language relativity hypothesis. The theory that the language we speak influences our perceptions of the world and our behaviors, and therefore persons speaking widely differing languages will perceive and behave differently as a result of the language differences. Also referred to as the *Sapir-Whorf hypothesis* and the *Whorfian hypothesis.*

Lateral communication. Communication among equals—for example, manager to manager, worker to worker. *Recognizing that one's own specialty often involves a technical jargon unknown to others, that one's perspective may be limiting, and that cooperation can probably be increased without any serious loss to the individual should help lateral communication.*

Leadership. That quality by which one individual directs or influences the thoughts and/or the behaviors of others. See *Laissez-faire leader, Democratic leader,* and *Authoritarian leader.*

Legitimate power. Power dependent on the belief that a person has a right, by virtue of position, to influence or control another's behavior.

Level of abstraction. The relative distance of a term or statement from the actual perception; a low-order abstraction would be a description of the perception, whereas a high-order abstraction would consist of inferences about inferences about descriptions of a perception. *Generally, effective communication consists of a combination of different levels of abstraction, though the general problem in much communication is the lack of low-level abstractions (specific terms).*

Leveling. A process of message distortion in which a message is repeated, but the number of details is reduced, some details are omitted entirely, and some details lose their complexity.

Linguistic collusion. A reaction to territorial encroachment in which we speak in a language unknown to the intruders and thus separate ourselves from them.

Listening. An active process of receiving aural stimuli consisting of five phases: receiving, understanding, remembering, evaluating, and responding. *Adjust your listening perspective as the situation warrants between active and passive, judgmental and nonjudgmental, surface and deep, and empathic and objective listening.*

Logic. The science of reasoning; the study of the principles governing the analysis of inference making.

Looking-glass self. The self-concept that results from the image of yourself that others reveal to you.

Loving. An interpersonal process in which one feels a closeness, a caring, a warmth, and an excitement for another person.

Low-context culture. One in which most of the information in communication is explicitly stated in the verbal messages.

Ludus love. Love as a game, as fun; the position that love is not to be taken seriously and is to be maintained only as long as it remains interesting and enjoyable.

Magnitude of change principle. A principle of persuasion stating that the greater and more important the change desired by the speaker, the more difficult its achievement will be.

Manic love. Love characterized by extreme highs and extreme lows; obsessive love.

Manipulation. An unproductive conflict strategy in which open conflict is avoided; instead, attempts are made to divert the conflict by being especially charming and getting the other person into a noncombative frame of mind. *Avoid it.*

Manuscript speech. A speech designed to be read from a script verbatim. *Use this method only when exact wording and timing are more important than the ability to adapt to the audience during the speech.*

Markers. Devices through which we signal to others that a particular territory belongs to us. *Become sensitive to the markers (central, boundary, and ear) of others, and learn to use these markers to define your own territories and to communicate the desired impression.*

Mass communication. Communication addressed to an extremely large audience, mediated by audio and/or visual transmitters, and processed by gatekeepers before transmission.

Matching hypothesis. The assumption that persons date and mate people who are approximately the same as they are in terms of physical attractiveness.

Meaningfulness. A perception principle that refers to your assumption that people's behavior is sensible, stems from some logical antecedent, and is consequently meaningful rather than meaningless.

Mere exposure hypothesis. The theory holding that repeated or prolonged exposure to a stimulus may result in attitude change toward the stimulus object, generally in the direction of increased positiveness.

Message. Any signal or combination of signals that serve as stimuli for a receiver.

Metacommunication. Communication about communication. *Metacommunicate to ensure understanding of the other person's thoughts and feelings by giving clear feedforward, explain feelings as well as thoughts, paraphrase your own complex thoughts, and ask questions.*

Metalanguage. Language used to talk about language.

Metaskills. Skills for regulating more specific skills, for example, the skills of interpersonal communication such as openness and empathy must be regulated by the metaskills of flexibility, mindfulness, and cultural sensitivity. *Use these skills to help you regulate all your communications.*

Micromomentary expressions. Extremely brief movements that are not consciously perceived and that are thought to reveal a person's real emotional state.

Mindfulness and mindlessness. States of relative awareness. In a mindful state we are aware of the logic and rationality of our behaviors and the logical connections existing among elements. In a mindless state we are unaware of this logic and rationality. *Apply the principles of interpersonal communication mindfully rather than mindlessly. Increase mindfulness by creating and re-creating categories, being open to new information and points of view, and not relying too heavily on first impressions.*

Minimization. An unproductive conflict strategy in which we make light of the other person's disagreements or of the conflict as a whole. *Recognize that what appears minor to one person may legitimately be major to another.*

Mixed messages. Messages that contain contradictory meanings, a special type of which is the double-bind message. *Avoid sending mixed messages by focusing clearly on your purposes when communicating and by gaining more conscious control over your verbal and nonverbal behaviors. Detect mixed messages in other people's communications and avoid being placed in double-bind situations by seeking clarification from the sender.*

Model. A physical representation of an object or process.

Monologue. A communication form in which one person speaks and the other listens; there is no real interaction among participants. *Avoid it under most circumstances.* Opposed to *dialogue*.

Motivated sequence. An organizational pattern for arranging the information in a discourse to motivate an audience to respond positively to one's purpose. *Use this pattern for persuasive speeches as appropriate but also consider the importance of gaining attention, establishing need, satisfying the need, visualization, and action regardless of what organizational pattern is used.*

Name-calling. A persuasive technique in which the speaker gives an idea a derogatory name. *Avoid it, and detect it in the persuasive appeals of others.*

Negative feedback. Feedback that serves a corrective function by informing the source that her or his message is not being received in the way intended. Negative feedback serves to redirect the source's behavior. Looks of boredom, shouts of disagreement, letters critical of newspaper policy, and the teacher's instructions how to approach a problem better are examples of negative feedback.

Neutrality. A response pattern lacking personal involvement; encourages defensiveness. Opposed to *empathy*.

Noise. Anything that distorts or interferes with the message in the communication system. Noise is present in communication to the extent that the message sent differs from the message received. Physical noise interferes with the physical transmission of the signal or message—for example, the static in radio transmission. Psychological noise refers to distortions created by such psychological processes as prejudice and bias. Semantic noise refers to distortions created by a failure to understand each other's words. *Combat the effects of physical, semantic, and psychological noise by eliminating or lessening the sources of physical noise, securing agreement on meanings, and interacting with an open mind in order to increase communication accuracy.*

Nominal group. A collection of individuals who record their thoughts and opinions, which are then distributed to others. Without direct interaction, the thoughts and opinions are gradually pared down until a manageable list (of solutions or decisions) is produced. When this occurs the nominal group (a group in name only) may restructure itself into a problem-solving group that analyzes the final list.

Nonallness. An attitude or point of view in which it is recognized that one can never know all about anything and that what we know or say or hear is only a part of what there is to know, say, or hear.

Nonnegotiation. An unproductive conflict strategy in which the individual refuses to discuss the conflict or the disagreement, or to listen to the other person. *Generally, a strategy that should be avoided since it delays resolving the conflict and often creates resentment.*

Nonverbal communication. Communication without words.

Norm. See *Group norm*.

Olfactics. Communication by smell.

Openness. A quality of effective interpersonal communication that refers to (1) the willingness to engage in appropriate self-disclosure, (2) the willingness to react honestly to incoming stimuli, and (3) the willingness to own one's own feelings and thoughts.

Open self. The part of the self that contains information about the self that is known to oneself and to others. *Adjust your open self in light of the total context, disclosing or not disclosing yourself to others as appropriate.*

Opinion leader. Persons looked to for opinion leadership; those who mold public opinion.

Oral style. The style of spoken discourse that, when compared with written style, consists of shorter, simpler, and more familiar words; more qualification, self-reference terms, allness terms, verbs and adverbs; and more concrete terms and terms indicative of consciousness of projection—for example, "as I see it."

Organization. A group of individuals organized for the achievement of specific goals.

Other-orientation. A quality of effective interpersonal interaction referring to one's ability to adapt to the other person's needs and desires during the interpersonal encounter. *Convey concern for and interest in the other person by empathic responses, appropriate feedback, and attentive listening responses.*

Outing. The forced disclosure of one's homosexuality.

Owning feelings. The process by which you take responsibility for your feelings instead of attributing them to others. *Own your feelings; use I-messages; acknowledge responsibility for your own thoughts and feelings to increase honest sharing.*

Panel. A small group format in which expert group members participate informally and without any set pattern of who speaks when.

Paralanguage. The vocal (but nonverbal) aspect of speech. Paralanguage consists of voice qualities (for example, pitch range, resonance, tempo), vocal characterizers (for example, laughing or crying, yelling or whispering), vocal qualifiers (for example, intensity, pitch height), and vocal segregates (for example, *uh-uh* meaning "no," or *shh* meaning "silence"). *Vary paralinguistic elements such as rate, volume, and stress to add variety and emphasis to your communications, and be responsive to the meanings communicated by others' variation of paralanguage features.*

Parasocial relationship. Relationships between a real and an imagined or fictional character, usually used to refer to relationships between a viewer and a fictional character in a television show.

Passive listening. Listening that is attentive and supportive but occurs without talking or directing the speaker in any nonverbal way; also used negatively to refer to inattentive and uninvolved listening.

Pause. A silent period in the normally fluent stream of speech. Pauses are of two major types: filled pauses (interruptions in speech that are filled with such vocalizations as *er* or *um*) and unfilled pauses (silence of unusually long length).

Perception. The process of becoming aware of objects and events from the senses.

Perception checking. A technique for increasing your chances of making accurate perceptions. *Use perception checking to get more information on your impressions: (1) describe what you think is happening and (2) ask if this is correct or in error.*

Perceptual accentuation. A process that leads us to see what we expect to see and what we want to see; for example, we see people we like as better looking and smarter than people we do not like. *Be aware of the influence that your own needs, wants, and expectations have on your perceptions. Recognize that what you perceive is a function both of what exists in reality and what is going on inside your own head.*

Personal distance. The second-shortest proxemic distance, ranging from $1\frac{1}{2}$ to 4 feet.

Personal growth group. A group designed to help members gain greater awareness of themselves and an improved ability to deal with their experiences.

Personal rejection. An unproductive conflict strategy in which the individual withholds love and affection, and seeks to win the argument by getting the other person to break down under this withdrawal.

Persuasion. The process of influencing attitudes and behavior.

Persuasive interview. A type of interview in which the interviewer attempts to change the interviewee's attitudes or behavior.

Phatic communion. Communication that is primarily social; communication designed to open the channels of communication rather than to communicate something about the external world; "Hello," and "How are you?" in everyday interaction are common examples.

Pitch. The highness or lowness of the vocal tone.

Polarization. A form of fallacious reasoning by which only the two extremes are considered; also referred to as "either-or" thinking. *Use middle terms and qualifiers when describing the world; avoid talking in terms of polar opposites (rich and poor, good and bad) in order to describe reality more accurately.*

Positive feedback. Feedback that supports or reinforces behavior along the same lines as it is proceeding—for example, applause during a speech.

Positiveness. A quality of effective interpersonal communication referring to the communication of positiveness toward the self, others, and the communication situation generally, and willingness to stroke the other person as appropriate. *Verbally and nonverbally communicate a positive attitude toward yourself, others, and the situation with smiles, positive facial expressions, attentive gestures, positive verbal expressions, and the elimination or reduction of negative appraisals.*

Power. The ability to control the behaviors of others. *When appropriate, communicate power through forceful speech, the avoidance of weak modifiers and excessive body movement, and the demonstration of your knowledge, preparation, and organization of the matters at hand. Also, use the several power bases such as expert, legitimate, and reward.*

Power play. A type of game or manipulative strategy by which someone repeatedly tries to control another's behavior. *Identify the power plays that people use on you, especially Nobody Upstairs, You Owe Me, Metaphor,*

Yougottobekidding, and Thought Stoppers, and respond to these power plays with appropriate cooperative management responses in an effort to stop them.

Pragma love. Practical love; love based on compatibility; love that seeks a relationship that will satisfy each person's important needs and desires.

Pragmatic implications. Assumptions that are made that are logical but not necessarily true. *Distinguish between pragmatic and logical implications and recognize that our memories often confuse the two. In recalling situations and events, ask yourself if your conclusions are based on pragmatic or on logical implications.*

Primary affect displays. The communication of the six primary emotions: happiness, surprise, fear, anger, sadness, and disgust/contempt. See *Affect displays.*

Primacy effect. The condition by which what comes first exerts greater influence than what comes later or more recently. *Beware of first impressions serving as filters that prevent you from perceiving other and perhaps contradictory behaviors and changes in situations and especially in people. Recognize the normal tendency for first impressions to leave lasting impressions and to color what we see later and the conclusions we draw. Be at your very best in first encounters. Also, take the time and effort to revise your impressions of others on the basis of new information.* See *Recency effect.*

Problem-solving group. A group whose primary task is to solve a problem, but more often to reach a decision.

Problem-solving sequence. A logical step-by-step process for solving a problem frequently used by groups and consisting of defining and analyzing the problem, establishing criteria for evaluating solutions, identifying possible solutions, evaluating solutions, selecting the best solution, and testing the selected solutions. *Use this sequence (or some similar sequence) for effective problem solving.*

Process. Ongoing activity; nonstatic communication is referred to as a process to emphasize that it is always changing and always in motion.

Projection. A psychological process whereby we attribute characteristics or feelings of our own to others; often used to refer to the process whereby we attribute our own faults to others.

Pronunciation. The production of syllables or words according to some accepted standard, as presented, for example, in a dictionary.

Protection theory. A theory of proxemics holding that people establish a body-buffer zone to protect themselves from unwanted closeness, touching, or attack.

Provisionalism. An attitude of open-mindedness that leads to the creation of supportiveness. Opposed to *certainty.*

Proxemics. The study of the communicative function of space; the study of how people unconsciously structure their space—the distance between people in their interactions, the organization of space in homes and offices, and even the design of cities. *Adjust spatial (proxemic) distances as appropriate to the specific interaction; avoid distances that are too far, too close, or otherwise inappropriate, which might falsely convey, for example, aloofness or aggression. Recognize the wide cultural differences in what is considered appropriate distance.*

Proximity. As a principle of perception, the tendency to perceive people or events that are physically close as belonging together or representing some unit; physical closeness; one of the qualities influencing interpersonal attraction.

Psychological time. The importance that we place on past time, in which particular regard is shown for the past and its values and methods; present time, in which we live in the present for the enjoyment of the present; and future time, in which we devote our energies to planning for the future. *Recognize the significance of your own time orientation to your ultimate success and make whatever adjustments you think desirable.*

Public communication. Communication in which the source is one person and the receiver is an audience of many persons.

Public distance. The longest proxemic distance, ranging from 12 to over 25 feet.

Punctuation of communication. The breaking up of continuous communication sequences into short sequences with identifiable beginnings and endings, or stimuli and responses. *See the sequence of events punctuated from perspectives other than your own in order to increase empathy and mutual understanding.*

Pupillometrics. The study of communication through changes in the size of the pupils of the eyes. *Detect pupil dilation and constriction, and formulate hypotheses concerning their possible meanings. Use perception checking when appropriate.*

Purr words. Highly positive words that express the feelings of the speaker rather than refer to any objective reality. Opposed to *snarl words.*

Pygmalion effect. The condition in which one makes a prediction and then proceeds to fulfill it; a type of self-fulfilling prophecy but one that refers to others and to our evaluation of others rather than to ourselves.

Quality circles. Groups designed to improve quality in the workplace.

Racist language. Language that denigrates a person or group because of their race. *Avoid it.*

Rate. The speed with which we speak, generally measured in words per minute. *Let your speech rate reflect the meanings you wish to communicate; variation rather than sameness is generally more effective.*

Receiver. Any person or thing that takes in messages. Receivers may be individuals listening or reading a message, a group of persons hearing a speech, a scattered television audience, or a machine that stores information.

Recency effect. The condition in which what comes last (that is, most recently) exerts greater influence than what comes first. See *Primacy effect.*

Redefinition. An unproductive conflict strategy in which the conflict is given another definition so that the source of the conflict disappears.

Redundancy. A message's quality that makes it totally predictable and therefore lacking in information. A message of zero redundancy would be completely unpredictable; a message of 100 percent redundancy would be completely predictable. All human languages contain some degree of built-in redundancy, generally estimated at about 50 percent. *Use redundancy to reinforce messages, especially in public speaking. Generally, avoid excess redundancy in writing.*

Referent power. Power dependent on one's desire to identify with or be like another person.

Regulators. Nonverbal behaviors that regulate, monitor, or control the communications of another person.

Reinforcement/packaging, principle of. The principle of verbal interaction holding that in most interactions, messages are transmitted simultaneously through a number of different channels that normally reinforce each other; messages come in packages.

Rejection. A response to an individual that rejects or denies the validity of an individual's self-view.

Relationship communication. Communication between or among intimates or those in close relationships; term used by some theorists as synonymous with interpersonal communication.

Relationship deterioration. The stage of a relationship during which the connecting bonds between the partners weaken and the partners begin drifting apart.

Relationship repair. Attempts to reverse the process of relationship deterioration. *If you wish to repair a deteriorating relationship, take positive action by recognizing the problem, engaging in productive conflict resolution, posing possible solutions, affirming each other, integrating solutions into normal behavior, and being willing to take risks.*

Reward power. Power dependent on one's ability to reward another person.

Rigid complementarity. The inability to change the type of relationship between oneself and another even though the individuals, the context, and a host of other variables have changed.

Role. The part an individual plays in a group; an individual's function or expected behavior.

Round table. A small group format in which group members, arranged in a circular pattern, share information or solve a problem without any set pattern of who speaks when.

Scientific approach to organizations. An approach to organizations holding that scientific methods should be applied to the organization to increase productivity; through the use of scientifically controlled studies, management can identify the ways and means for increasing productivity and ultimately profit.

Selective exposure principle. A principle of persuasion stating that listeners will actively seek out information that supports their opinions and actively avoid information that contradicts their existing opinions, beliefs, attitudes, and values.

Self-attribution. A process through which we seek to account for and understand the reasons and motivations for our own behaviors.

Self-awareness. One's level of intrapersonal knowledge.

Self-concept. An individual's self-evaluation; an individual's self-appraisal. *Increase self-awareness by asking yourself about yourself, listening to others, actively seeking information about yourself from others by carefully observing their interactions with you and by asking relevant questions, seeing yourself from different perspectives (see your different selves), and increasing your open self.*

Self-disclosure. The process of revealing something significant about ourselves to another individual or to a group—something that would not normally be known by them. *Self-disclose selectively; regulate your self-disclosures as appropriate to the context, topic, and audience; and carefully assess the potential rewards and the potential risks that may result from the disclosure. Also, self-disclose when the motivation is to improve the relationship, when the context and the relationship are appropriate for the self-disclosure, when there is an opportunity for open and honest responses, when the self-disclosures will be clear and direct, when there are appropriate reciprocal disclosures, and when you have examined and are willing to risk the possible burdens that the self-disclosure might entail. In responding to the disclosures of others, listen actively: paraphrase the speaker's thoughts and feelings, express understanding of the speaker's feelings, and ask relevant questions to ensure understanding and to signal attention and interest.*

Self-esteem. Personal self-esteem refers to the value one places on oneself, one's self-evaluation and feeling of worth. Group self-esteem refers to one's evaluation of oneself as a member of a particular racial or ethnic group. *Increase your self-esteem by attacking self-destructive beliefs, engaging in self-affirmation, seeking out nourishing people, and working on projects that will result in success.*

Self-fulfilling prophecy. The situation in which we make a prediction or prophecy and fulfill it ourselves—for example, expecting a class to be boring and then fulfilling this expectation by perceiving it as boring. *Avoid fulfilling your own negative prophecies and seeing only what you want to see. Be especially careful to examine your perceptions when they conform too closely to your expectations; check to make sure that you are seeing what exists in real life, not just in your expectations or predictions.*

Self-monitoring. The manipulation of the image that we present to others in our interpersonal interactions. High self-monitors carefully adjust their behaviors on the basis of feedback from others so that they can project the desired image. Low self-monitors do not consciously manipulate their images. *Self-monitor as appropriate to the specific communication situation.*

Self-serving bias. A bias that operates in the self-attribution process and leads us to take credit for the positive consequences and to deny responsibility for the negative consequences of our behaviors. *In examining the causes of your own behavior, beware of the self-serving bias, the tendency to attribute negative behaviors to external factors and positive behaviors to internal factors. In self-examinations of your behaviors, ask yourself if and how the self-serving bias might be operating.*

Semantics. The area of language study concerned with meaning.

Sexist language. Language derogatory to one sex, generally women. *Whether man or woman, avoid sexist language, for example, terms that presume maleness as the norm (policeman or mailman); avoid masculine pronouns when referring to both sexes.*

Sexual harassment. Behavior that proves annoying or is offensive in a sexual way. *Avoid any indication of sexual harassment by beginning with the assumption that others at work are not interested in sexual advances and stories, listen for any negative reactions to any sexually explicit discussions, and avoid behaviors that you think might prove offensive. If confronted with sexual harassment consider talking to the harasser, collecting evidence, using appropriate channels within the organization, or filing a complaint.*

Sharpening. A process of message distortion in which the details of messages, when repeated, are crystallized and heightened.

Shyness. The condition of discomfort and uneasiness in interpersonal situations. *Try the suggestions for reducing apprehension.* See *Speaker apprehension.*

Sign, reasoning from. A form of reasoning in which the presence of certain signs (clues) are interpreted as leading to a particular conclusion.

Silence. The absence of vocal communication; often misunderstood to refer to the absence of any and all communication. *Use silence to communicate feelings or to prevent communication about certain topics. Interpret silence as meaningful message.*

Silencers. Unproductive conflict strategies that literally silence the other person—for example, crying, or feigning emotional or physical disturbance. *Generally, avoid them.*

Similarity. A principle of attraction holding that you are attracted to qualities similar to those you possess and to people who are similar to you. Opposed to *complementarity.*

Sin licenses. A disclaimer in which the speaker acknowledges that he or she is about to break some normally operative rule; the speaker asks for a license to sin (that is, to break a social or interpersonal rule of behavior).

Situational approach to leadership. An approach that views leadership as having two main functions (to accomplish the task and to ensure member satisfaction) which vary depending on the specific situation.

Slang. The language used by special groups, which is not considered proper by the general society; the language made up of the argot, cant, and jargon of various subcultures, known by the general public. *Generally, avoid slang especially in relatively formal communications.*

Small group communication. Communication among a collection of individuals, small enough in number that all members may interact with relative ease as both senders and receivers, the members being related to each other by some common purpose and with some degree of organization or structure among them. *Use small group communication to generate ideas, share information, gain support and insight, and solve problems.*

Snarl words. Highly negative words that express the feelings of the speaker rather than refer to any objective reality. Opposite to *purr words.*

Social comparison processes. The processes by which we compare ourselves (for example, our abilities, opinions, and values) with others and then assess and evaluate ourselves.

Social distance. The third proxemic distance, ranging from 4 to 12 feet; the distance at which business is usually conducted.

Social exchange theory. A theory claiming that we develop and maintain relationships in which the rewards or profits are greater than the costs.

Social penetration theory. A theory concerned with relationship development from the superficial to the intimate levels and from few to many areas of interpersonal interaction.

Source. Any person or thing that creates messages. A source may be an individual speaking, writing, or gesturing or a computer solving a problem.

Speaker apprehension. A fear of engaging in communication transactions; a decrease in the frequency, strength, and likelihood of engaging in communication transactions. *Identify the causes of your own apprehension, considering, for example, lack of communication skills and experience, fear of evaluation, conspicuousness, unpredictability of the situation (ambiguity, newness), and your history of prior successes or failures in similar and related situations. Manage your own communication apprehension by acquiring the necessary communication skills and experience, preparing and practicing for relevant communication situations, focusing on success, familiarizing yourself with the communication situations important to you, using physical activity and deep breathing to relax, and putting communication apprehension in perspective. In cases of extreme communication apprehension, seek professional help.*

Specific instances, reasoning from. A form of reasoning in which several specific instances are examined and then a conclusion about the whole is formed.

Speech. Messages utilizing a vocal-auditory channel.

Speech accommodation theory. The theory holding that speakers adjust their speaking style to their listeners to gain social approval and achieve greater communication effectiveness.

Spiral of silence theory. A theory of mass media that claims that people assess the popularity of their positions (largely on the basis of media coverage) and speak up if they are in the majority and keep silent if they are in the minority. As more people with minority positions keep silent and those with majority positions speak out, a spiral forms with the majority opinion gaining exposure and the minority opinion losing exposure.

Static evaluation. An orientation that fails to recognize that the world is characterized by constant change; an attitude that sees people and events as fixed rather than as constantly changing.

Status. The relative level one occupies in a hierarchy; status always involves a comparison, and thus one's status is only relative to the status of another. In our culture, occupation, financial position, age, and educational level are significant determinants of status.

Stereotype. In communication, a fixed impression of a group of people through which we then perceive specific individuals; stereotypes are most often negative (Martians are stupid, uneducated, and dirty), but may also be positive (Venusians are scientific, industrious, and helpful). *Avoid stereotyping others; instead, see and respond to each person as a unique individual.*

Storge love. Love based on companionship, similar interests, and mutual respect; love that is lacking in great emotional intensity.

Strategy. The use of some plan for control of other members of a communication interaction that guides one's own communications; encourages defensiveness.

Supportiveness. A quality of effective interpersonal communication in which one is descriptive rather than evaluative, spontaneous rather than strategic, and provisional rather than certain. *Exhibit supportiveness to others by being descriptive rather than evaluative, spontaneous rather than strategic, and provisional rather than certain.*

Symmetrical relationship. A relation between two or more persons in which one person's behavior serves as a stimulus for the same type of behavior in the other person(s). Examples of such relationships include situations in which anger in one person encourages or serves as a stimulus for anger in another person, or in which a critical comment by one person leads the other to respond in like manner.

Symposium. A small group format in which each member of the group delivers a relatively prepared talk on some aspect of the topic.

Symposium-forum. A small group format consisting of a symposium (with prepared speeches) and a forum (with questions from the audience and responses by the speakers).

Systematic desensitization. A theory and technique for dealing with a variety of fears (such as communication apprehension) in which you gradually desensitize yourself to behaviors you wish to eliminate.

Systems approach to organizations. An approach to organizations that stresses the interaction of all parts of the organization; each part influences each other part. The organization should be seen as an open system in which the physical and physiological factors and the social and psychological factors interact, each influencing the other.

Taboo. Forbidden; culturally censored. Taboo language is what is frowned upon by "polite society." Themes and specific words may be considered taboo—for example, death, sex, certain forms of illness, and various words denoting sexual activities and excretory functions. *Avoid taboo expressions in order to avoid negative evaluations by others; substitute more socially acceptable expressions or euphemisms where and when appropriate.*

Tactile communication. Communication by touch; communication received by the skin. *Use touch when appropriate to express positive affect, playfulness, control, and ritualistic meanings, and to serve task-related functions. Respond to touch patterns of others in light of their gender and culture and not exclusively through your own.*

Task group. Usually, a group designed to serve a specific function or task and then disbanded.

Territorial encroachment. The trespassing on, use of, or appropriation of one's territory by another. The major types of territorial encroachment are violation, invasion, and contamination. *Generally, avoid territorial encroachment; give others the space they need; remember, for example, that people who are angry or disturbed need more space than usual.*

Territoriality. A possessive or ownership reaction to an area of space or to particular objects. *Establish and maintain territory nonverbally by marking or otherwise indicating temporary or permanent ownership. Become sensitive to the territorial behavior of others.*

Testimonial. A persuasive technique in which the speaker uses the authority or image of some positively evaluated person to gain your approval or of some negatively evaluated person to gain your rejection.

Theory. A general statement or principle applicable to a number of related phenomena.

Thesis. The main assertion of a message—for example, the theme of a public speech.

Touch avoidance. The tendency we have to avoid touching and being touched by others. *Recognize that some people may prefer to avoid touching and being* *touched. Avoid drawing too many conclusions about people from the way they treat interpersonal touching.*

Traits approach to leadership. An approach to leadership that attributes leadership to specific qualities or traits, for example, intelligence or creativity or dominance.

Transactional. The relationship among elements in which each influences and is influenced by each other element; communication is a transactional process, since no element is independent of any other element.

Turf defense. The most extreme reaction to territorial encroachment through which one defends one's territory and expels the intruders.

Two-valued orientation. A point of view in which events are seen or questions are evaluated in terms of two values—for example, right or wrong, good or bad. Often referred to as the fallacy of black-and-white and polarization. *Recognize that the vast majority of instances are between the opposites; use middle terms and qualifiers to reflect reality more accurately.*

Uncertainty reduction. The process by which uncertainty or ambiguity about another person is reduced. *Increase your accuracy in interpersonal perception by using all three uncertainty reduction strategies: passive, active, and interactive.*

Universal of communication. A feature of communication common to all communication acts.

Unknown self. That part of the self that contains information about the self that is unknown to oneself and to others, but that is inferred to exist on the basis of various projective tests, slips of the tongue, dream analyses, and the like.

Upward communication. Communication in which the messages originate from the lower levels of an organization or hierarchy and are sent to upper levels—for example, line worker to management. *Establishing a nonthreatening system with convenient channels and cultivating an openness to criticism and a willingness to listen should help improve upward communication.*

Uses and gratifications. A theory of mass media that seeks to explain the influence of the media in terms of the uses to which people put the media and the gratifications they derive from those uses.

Value. Relative worth of an object; a quality that makes something desirable or undesirable; ideals or customs about which we have emotional responses, whether positive or negative.

Verbal aggressiveness. A method of winning an argument by attacking the other person's self-concept. *Avoid verbal aggressiveness since it means inflicting psychological pain on the other person to win an argument.*

Violation. Unwarranted use of another's territory. See *Territorial encroachment.*

Volume. The relative loudness of the voice. *Use volume (and especially appropriate variation in volume) to complement the meanings you wish to communicate.*

Withdrawal. (1) A reaction to territorial encroachment in which we leave the territory. (2) A tendency to close oneself off from conflicts rather than confront the issues.

Written style. See *Oral style.*

You-messages. Messages in which the speaker denies responsibility for his or her thoughts and behaviors; messages that attribute what is really the speaker's perception to another person; messages of blame. Opposed to *I-messages.*

bibliography

Abt, Vicki (1995). Cited in Thats' Psychotainment. *Psychology Today* 28 (March/April):18.

Acuff, Frank L. (1993). *How to Negotiate Anything with Anyone Anywhere Around the World.* New York: American Management Association.

Adams, Linda with Elinor Lenz (1989). *Be Your Best.* New York: Putnam.

Adams, R. G. (1987). Patterns of Network Change: A Longitudinal Study of Friendships of Elderly Women. *The Gerontologist* 27:222–227.

Addeo, Edmond G. and Burger, Robert E. (1973). *Egospeak: Why No One Listens to You.* New York: Bantam.

Adler, Mortimer J. (1983). *How to Speak, How to Listen.* New York: Macmillan.

Adler, Ronald B. (1977). *Confidence in Communication: A Guide to Assertive and Social Skills.* New York: Holt, Rinehart and Winston.

Agee, Warren K., Phillip H. Ault, and Edwin Emery (1994). *Introduction to Mass Communications*, 11th ed. New York: HarperCollins.

Akert, Robin M. and Abigail T. Panter (1988). Extraversion and the Ability to Decode Nonverbal Communication. *Personality and Individual Differences* 9:965–972.

Akinnaso, F. Niyi (1982). On the Differences between Spoken and Written Language. *Language and Speech* 25 (Part 2):97–125.

Albert, Rosita and Gayle L. Nelson (1993). Hispanic/Anglo American Differences in Attributions to Paralinguistic Behavior. *International Journal of Intercultural Relations* 17 (Winter):19–40.

Albert, S. M., and M. Moss (1990). Consensus and the Domain of Personal Relationships Among Older Adults. *Journal of Social and Personal Relationships* 7:353–369.

Alessandra, Tony (1986). *How to Listen Effectively, Speaking of Success* (Video Tape Series). San Diego, CA: Levitz Sommer Productions.

Alexander, Susan and Keith Baker (1992). Some Ethical Issues in Applied Social Psychology: The Case of Bilingual Education and Self-Esteem. *Journal of Applied Social Psychology* 22 (November):1741–1757.

Alisky, Marvin (1985, January 15). *Vital Speeches of the Day* 51, 208–210.

Allen, Richard K. (1977). *Organizational Management Through Communication.* New York: Harper & Row.

Altman, Irwin (1975). *The Environment and Social Behavior.* Monterey, CA: Brooks/Cole.

Altman, Irwin and Dalmas Taylor (1973). *Social Penetration: The Development of Interpersonal Relationships.* New York: Holt, Rinehart and Winston.

Andersen, Peter (1991). Explaining Intercultural Differences in Nonverbal Communication. In Larry A. Samovar and Richard E. Porter, eds., *Intercultural Communication: A Reader,* 6th ed. (pp. 286–296) Belmont, CA: Wadsworth.

Andersen, Peter A. and Ken Leibowitz (1978). The Development and Nature of the Construct Touch Avoidance. *Environmental Psychology and Nonverbal Behavior* 3:89–106.

Angier, Natalie (1995). "Scientists Mull Role of Empathy in Man and Beast." *New York Times* (May 9):C1, C6.

Applebaum, Richard P. and William J. Chambliss (1995). *Sociology.* New York: HarperCollins.

Argyle, Michael (1986). Rules for Social Relationships in Four Cultures." *Australian Journal of Psychology* 38 (December):309–318.

Argyle, Michael (1988). *Bodily Communication,* 2nd ed. New York: Methuen.

Argyle, Michael and J. Dean (1965). Eye Contact, Distance and Affiliation. *Sociometry* 28:289–304.

Argyle, Michael and Monika Henderson (1984). The Rules of Friendship. *Journal of Social and Personal Relationships* 1 (June):211–237.

Argyle, Michael and Monika Henderson (1985). *The Anatomy of Relationships: And the Rules and Skills Needed to Manage Them Successfully.* London: Heinemann.

Argyle, Michael and R. Ingham (1972). Gaze, Mutual Gaze and Distance. *Semiotica* 1:32–49.

Arliss, Laurie P. (1991). *Gender Communication.* Upper Saddle River, NJ: Prentice-Hall.

Armstrong, Cameron B. and Alan M. Rubin (1989). Talk Radio as Interpersonal Communication. *Journal of Communication* 39 (Spring):84–94.

Arnold, Carroll C. and John Waite Bowers, eds. (1984). *Handbook of Rhetorical and Communication Theory.* Boston: Allyn & Bacon.

Aron, Arthur and Elaine N. Aron (1986). *Love and the Expansion of Self: Understanding Attraction and Satisfaction.* New York: Hemisphere.

Aron, Arthur and Elaine N. Aron (1995). Love. In Weber and Harvey (1995), pp. 131–152.

Aronson, Elliot (1980). *The Social Animal,* 3rd ed. San Francisco: W. H. Freeman.

Aronson, Elliot, Timothy D. Wilson, and Robin M. Akert (1994). *Social Psychology: The Heart and the Mind.* New York: HarperCollins.

Asante, Molefi (1987). *The Afrocentric Idea.* Philadelphia, PA: Temple University Press.

Asch, Solomon (1946). Forming Impressions of Personality. *Journal of Abnormal and Social Psychology* 41:258–290.

Aune, R. Kelly and Linda L. Waters (1994). Cultural Differences in Deception: Motivations to Deceive in Samoans and North Americans. *International Journal of Intercultural Relations* 18 (Spring):159–172.

Aune, R. Kelly and Krystyna Strzyzewski Aune (1994). The Influence of Culture, Gender, and Relational Status on Appearance Management. *Journal of Cross Cultural Psychology* 25 (June):258–272.

Aune, R. Kelly and Toshiyuki Kikuchi (1993). Effects of Language Intensity Similarity on Perceptions of Credibility, Relational Attributions, and Persuasion. *Journal of Language and Social Psychology* 12 (September):224–238.

Authier, Jerry and Kay Gustafson (1982). Microtraining: Focusing on Specific Skills. In Eldon K. Marshall, P. David Kurtz, and Associates, *Interpersonal Helping Skills: A Guide to Training Methods, Programs, and Resources* (pp. 93–130). San Francisco: Jossey-Bass.

Axtell, Roger E. (1990a). *Do's and Taboos Around the World,* 2nd ed. New York: Wiley.

Axtell, Roger E. (1990b). *Do's and Taboos of Hosting International Visitors.* New York: Wiley.

Axtell, Roger E. (1992). *Do's and Taboos of Public Speaking: How to Get Those Butterflies Flying in Formation.* New York: Wiley.

Axtell, Roger E. (1993). *Do's and Taboos Around the World.* 3rd ed. New York: Wiley.

Aylesworth, Thomas G. and Virginia L. Aylesworth (1978). *If You Don't Invade My Intimate Zone or Clean Up My Water Hole, I'll Breathe in Your Face, Blow on Your Neck, and Be Late for Your Party.* New York: Condor.

Ayres, Joe. (1983). Strategies to Maintain Relationships: Their Identification and Perceived Usage. *Communication Quarterly* 31:62–67.

Ayres, Joe (1986). Perceptions of Speaking Ability: An Explanation for Stage Fright. *Communication Education* 35:275–287.

Ayres, Joe (1989). The Impact of Communication Apprehension and Interaction Structure on Initial Interactions. *Communication Monographs* 56 (March):75–88.

Ayres, Joe (1990). Situational Factors and Audience Anxiety. *Communication Education* 39:283–291.

Ayres, Joe and Janice Miller (1986). *Effective Public Speaking,* 2nd ed. Dubuque, IA: Wm. C. Brown.

Ayres, Joe & Tim Hopf (1993). *Coping with Speech Anxiety.* Norwood, NJ: Ablex Publishing Company.

Ayres, Joe, Tim Hopf, & Debbie M. Ayres (1994). An Examination of Whether Imaging Ability Enhances the Effectiveness of an Intervention Designed to Reduce Speech Anxiety. *Communication Education* 43 (July):252–258.

Bach, George R. and Peter Wyden (1968). *The Intimate Enemy.* New York: Avon.

Bach, George R. and Ronald M. Deutsch (1979). *Stop! You're Driving Me Crazy.* New York: Berkley.

Backrack, Henry M. (1976). Empathy. *Archives of General Psychiatry* 33:35–38.

Bader, Lars (1995). Free Speech Dilemma. *New York Times* (June 30):A26.

Baird, John E., Jr. (1977). *The Dynamics of Organizational Communication.* New York: Harper & Row.

Baker, Paul Morgan (1983). The Friendship Process: A Developmental Model of Interpersonal Attraction. *Sociological Spectrum* 3 (July–December):265–279.

Bales, Robert F. (1950). *Interaction Process Analysis: A Method for the Study of Small Groups.* Cambridge, MA: Addison-Wesley.

Banks, Jack (1995). "MTV as Gatekeeper and Censor: A Survey of the Program Service's Attempts to Impose Its Standards on U.S. Popular Music," paper presented at the Eastern Communication Association Convention (Pittsburgh, April 27–30).

Baran, Stanley and Dennis K. Davis (1995). *Mass Communication Theory: Foundations, Ferment, and Future.* Belmont, CA: Wadworth.

Barbato, Carole A. and Elizabeth M. Perse (1992). Interpersonal Communication Motives and the Life Position of Elders. *Communication Research* 19:516–531.

Barge, J. Kevin (1994). *Leadership: Communication Skills for Organizations and Groups.* New York: St. Martin's Press.

Barker, Larry L. (1990). *Communication,* 5th ed. Upper Saddle River, NJ: Prentice-Hall.

Barker, Larry, R. Edwards, C. Gaines, K. Gladney, and F. Holley (1980). An Investigation of Proportional Time Spent in Various Communication Activities by College Students. *Journal of Applied Communication Research* 8:101–109.

Barna, LaRay M. (1991). Stumbling Blocks in Intercultural Communication. In Larry A. Samovar and Richard E. Porter, eds., *Intercultural Communication: A Reader,* 6th ed. (pp. 345–352). Belmont, CA: Wadsworth.

Barnard, Chester (1938). *The Functions of the Executive.* Cambridge, MA: Harvard University Press.

Barnlund, Dean C. (1970). A Transactional Model of Communication. In J. Akin, A. Goldberg, G. Myers, and J. Stewart, compliers *Language Behavior: A Book of Readings in Communication.* The Hague: Mouton.

Barnlund, Dean C. (1975). Communicative Styles in Two Cultures: Japan and the United States. In A. Kendon, R. M. Harris, and M. R. Key, eds., *Organization of Behavior in Face-to-Face Interaction.* The Hague: Mouton.

Barnlund, Dean C. and Shoko Araki (1985). Intercultural Encounters: The Management of Compliments by Japanese and Americans. *Journal of Cross Cultural Psychology* 16 (March):9–26.

Baron, Robert A. and Donn Byrne (1984). *Social Pscyhology: Understanding Human Interaction,* 4th ed. Boston: Allyn and Bacon.

Barrett, Karen (1982). Date Rape. *Ms.* (September):48–51.

Barrett, Lennard and T. Godfrey (1988). Listening. *Person Centered Review* 3 (November):410–425.

Barry, Andrew (1993). Television, Truth and Democracy," *Media, Culture, and Society* 15 (July):487–496.

Bartholomew, Kim (1990). Avoidance of Intimacy: An Attachment Perspective. *Journal of Social and Personal Relationships* 7:147–178.

Basso, K. H. (1972). To Give Up on Words: Silence in Apache Culture. In Pier Paolo Giglili, ed., *Language and Social Context.* New York: Penguin.

Bateson, Gregory (1972). *Steps to an Ecology of Mind.* New York: Ballantine.

Baxter, Leslie A. (1983). Relationship Disengagement: An Examination of the Reversal Hypothesis. *Western Journal of Speech Communication* 47:85–98.

Baxter, Leslie A. (1986). Gender Differences in the Heterosexual Relationship Rules Embedded in Break-up Accounts. *Journal of Social and Personal Relationships* 3:289–306.

Baxter, Leslie A. (1988). A Dialectical Perspective on Communication Strategies in Relationship Development. In Steve W. Duck, ed., *Handbook of Personal Relationships.* New York: Wiley.

Baxter, Leslie A. (1990). Dialectical Contradictions in Relationship Development. *Journal of Social and Personal Relationships* 7 (February): 69–88.

Baxter, Leslie A. and Eric P. Simon (1993). Relationship Maintenance Strategies and Dialectical Contradictions in Personal Relationships. *Journal of Social and Personal Relationships* 10 (May):225–242.

Baxter, Leslie A., and W. W. Wilmot (1984). "Secret Tests": Social Strategies for Acquiring Information About the State of the Relationship. *Human Communication Research* 11:171–201.

Beall, Anne E. and Robert J. Sternberg (1995). The Social Construction of Love. *Journal of Social and Personal Relationships* 12 (August):417–438.

Beatty, Michael J. (1988). Situational and Predispositional Correlates of Public Speaking Anxiety. *Communication Education* 37:28–39.

Beck, A. T. (1988). *Love Is Never Enough.* New York: Harper & Row.

Becker, Samuel L. and Churchill L. Roberts (1992). *Discovering Mass Communication,* 3rd ed. New York: HarperCollins.

Beebe, Steven A. and John T. Masterson (1986). *Family Talk: Interpersonal Communication in the Family.* New York: Random House.

Beebe, Steven A. and John T. Masterson (1994). *Communicating in Small Groups: Principles and Practices,* 4th ed. New York: HarperCollins.

Beier, Ernst (1974). How We Send Emotional Messages. *Psychology Today* 8 (October):53–56.

Bell, Robert A. and John A. Daly (1984). The Affinity-Seeking Function of Communication. *Communication Monographs* 51:91–115.

Benne, Kenneth D. and Paul Sheats (1948). Functional Roles of Group Members. *Journal of Social Issues* 4:41–49.

Bennett, Mark (1990). Children's Understanding of the Mitigating Function of Disclaimers. *Journal of Social Psychology* 130 (February):29–37.

Bennis, Warren and Burt Nanus (1985). *Leaders: The Strategies for Taking Charge.* New York: Harper & Row.

Berg, John H. and Richard L. Archer (1983). The Disclosure-Liking Relationship. *Human Communication Research* 10:269–281.

Berger, Charles R. and James J. Bradac (1982). *Language and Social Knowlege: Uncertainty in Interpersonal Relations.* London: Edward Arnold.

Berger, Charles R. and Steven H. Chaffee, eds. (1987). *Handbook of Communication Science.* Thousand Oaks, CA: Sage.

Berger, P. L. and T. Luckmann (1980). *The Social Construction of Reality.* New York: Irvington.

Berman, John J., Virginia Murphy-Berman, and Purnima Singh (1985). Cross-Cultural Similarities and Differences in Perceptions of Fairness. *Journal of Cross Cultural Psychology* 16 (March):55–67.

Bernstein, W. M., W. G. Stephart, and M. H. Davis (1979). Explaining Attributions for Achievement: A Path Analytic Approach. *Journal of Personality and Social Psychology* 37:1810–1821.

Berry, John W., Ype H. Poortinga, Marshall H. Segall, and Pierre R. Dasen (1992). *Cross-Cultural Psychology: Research and Applications.* Cambridge: Cambridge University Press.

Berscheid, Ellen and Elaine Hatfield Walster (1978). *Interpersonal Attraction,* 2nd ed. Reading, MA: Addison-Wesley.

Bettinghaus, Erwin P. and Michael J. Cody (1987). *Persuasive Communication,* 4th ed. New York: Holt, Rinehart and Winston.

Bettinghaus, Erwin P. and Michael J. Cody (1994). *Persuasive Communication,* 5th ed. Chicago: Harcourt, Brace.

Bierhoff, Hans W. and Renate Klein (1991). Dimensionen der Liebe: Entwicklung einer Deutschsprachigen Skala zur Erfassung von Liebesstilen. *Zeitschrift for Differentielle und Diagnostische Psychologie* 12 (March):53–71.

Blieszner, Rosemary and Rebecca G. Adams (1992). *Adult Friendship.* Thousand Oaks, CA: Sage.

Blumstein, Philip and Pepper Schwartz (1983). *American Couples: Money, Work, Sex.* New York: Morrow.

Bochner, Arthur (1978). On Taking Ourselves Seriously: An Analysis of Some Persistent Problems and Promising Directions in Interpersonal Research. *Human Communication Research* 4:179–191.

Bochner, Arthur (1984). The Functions of Human Communication in Interpersonal Bonding. In Carroll C. Arnold and John Waite Bowers, eds., *Handbook of Rhetorical and Communication Theory* (pp. 544–621). Boston: Allyn and Bacon.

Bochner, Arthur and Clifford Kelly (1974). Interpersonal Competence: Rationale, Philosophy, and Implementation of a Conceptual Framework. *Communication Education* 23:279–301.

Bok, Sissela (1978). *Lying: Moral Choice in Public and Private Life.* New York: Pantheon.

Bok, Sissela (1983). *Secrets.* New York: Vintage Books.

Borden, George (1991). *Cultural Orientation: An Approach to Understanding Intercultural Communication.* Upper Saddle River, NJ: Prentice-Hall.

Borisoff, Deborah and Lisa Merrill (1985). *The Power to Communicate: Gender Differences as Barriers.* Prospect Heights, IL: Waveland Press.

Bosmajian, Haig (1974). *The Language of Oppression.* Washington, DC: Public Affairs Press.

Bourland, D. D., Jr. (1965–66). A Linguistic Note: Writing in E-prime. *General Semantics Bulletin* 32–33:111–114.

Bradac, James J., John Waite Bowers, and John A. Courtright (1979). Three Language Variables in Communication Research: Intensity, Immediacy, and Diversity. *Human Communication Research* 5:256–269.

Bravo, Ellen and Ellen Cassedy (1992). *The 9-to-5 Guide to Combating Sexual Harassment.* New York: Wiley.

Breidenstein-Cutspec, Patricia and Elizabeth Goering (1989). Exploring Cultural Diversity: A Network Analysis of the Communicative Correlates of Shyness within the Black Culture. *Communication Research Reports* 6 (June):37–46.

Bremner, John B. (1980). *Words on Words: A Dictionary for Writers and Others Who Care About Words.* New York: Columbia University Press.

Brennan, Maire (1991). Mismanagement and Quality Circles: How Middle Managers Influence Direct Participation. *Employee Relations* 13:22–32.

Brilhart, John and Gloria Galanes (1992). *Effective Group Discussion,* 7th ed. Dubuque, IA: Brown & Benchmark.

Brody, Jane F. (1991). How to Foster Self-Esteem. *New York Times Magazine* (April 28):26–27.

Brougher, Toni (1982). *A Way with Words.* Chicago, IL: Nelson-Hall.

Brown, Jane D. and Laurie Schulze (1990). The Effects of Race, Gender, and Fandom on Audience Interpretations of Madonna's Music Videos. *Journal of Communication* 40 (Spring):88–102.

Brown, Penelope. and S. C. Levinson (1987). *Politeness: Some Universals of Language Usage.* Cambridge: Cambridge University Press.

Brown, Penelope (1980). How and Why Are Women More Polite: Some Evidence from a Mayan Community. In Sally McConnell-Ginet, Ruth Borker, and Mellie Furman, eds., *Women and Language in Literature and Society.* (pp. 111–136) New York: Praeger.

Brownell, Judi (1987). Listening: The Toughest Management Skill. *Cornell Hotel and Restaurant Administration Quarterly* 27:64–71.

Bruneau, Tom (1985). The Time Dimension in Intercultural Communication. In Larry A. Samovar and Richard E. Porter, eds., *Intercultural Communication: A Reader,* 4th ed. (pp. 280–289). Belmont, CA: Wadsworth.

Bruneau, Tom (1990). Chronemics: The Study of Time in Human Interaction. In Joseph A. DeVito and Michael L. Hecht, eds., *The Nonverbal Communication Reader* (pp. 301–311). Prospect Heights, IL: Waveland Press.

Bugental, J. and S. Zelen (1950). Investigations into the "Self-Concept," I. The W-A-Y Technique. *Journal of Personality* 18:483–498.

Bull, Peter and Lesley Frederikson (1995). Non-verbal Communication. In Michael Argyle and Andrew M. Colman, eds., *Social Psychology.* (pp. 78–98) New York: Longman.

Buller, David B. and R. Kelly Aune (1992). The Effects of Speech Rate Similarity on Compliance: Application of Communication Accommodation Theory. *Western Journal of Communication* 56 (Winter):37–53.

Buller, David B., Beth A. LePoire, Kelly Aune, and Sylvie Eloy (1992). Social Perceptions as Mediators of the Effect of Speech Rate Similarity on Compliance. *Human Communication Research* 19 (December):286–311.

Bumiller, Elisabeth (1995). *The Secrets of Mariko: A Year in the Life of a Japanese Woman and Her Family.* New York: Times Books/Random House.

Burgoon, Judee K. (1978). A Communication Model of Personal Space Violations: Explication and an Initial Test. *Human Communication Research* 4:129–142.

Burgoon, Judee K. (1991). Relational Message Interpretations of Touch, Conversational Distance, and Posture. *Journal of Nonverbal Behavior* 15 (Winter):233–259.

Burgoon, Judee K., David B. Buller, Amy S. Ebesu, & Patricia Rockwell (1994). Interpersonal Deception: V. Accuracy in Deception Detection. *Communication Monographs* 61 (December):303–325.

Burgoon, Judee K., David B. Buller, and W. Gill Woodall (1989). *Nonverbal Communication: The Unspoken Dialogue.* New York: Harper & Row.

Burke, N. Denise (1993). Restricting Gang Clothing in the Public Schools. *West's Education Law Quarterly* 2 (July):391–404.

Burleson, Brandt R., W. Samter, and A. E. Luccetti (1992). Similarity in Communication Values as a Predictor of Friendship Choices: Studies of Friends and Best Friends. *Southern Communication Journal* 57:260–276.

Burleson, Brant R., Adrianne W. Kunkel, and Jennifer D. Birch (1994). Thoughts about Talk in Romantic Relationships: Similarity Makes for Attraction (and Happiness, Too). *Communication Quarterly* 42 (Summer):259–273.

Buss, David M. and David P. Schmitt (1993). Sexual Strategies Theory: An Evolutionary Perspective on Human Mating. *Psychological Review* 100 (April): 204–232.

Busse, Wilfried M. and Janice M. Birk (1993). The Effects of Self-Disclosure and Competitiveness on Friendship for Male Graduate Students Over 35. *Journal of College Student Development* 34 (May):169–174.

Butler, Pamela E. (1981). *Talking to Yourself: Learning the Language of Self-Support.* New York: Harper & Row.

Callan, Victor J. (1993). Subordinate-Manager Communication in Different Sex Dyads: Consequences of Job Satisfaction. *Journal of Occupational and Organizational Psychology* 66 (March):13–27.

Camden, Carl, Michael T. Motley, and Ann Wilson (1984). White Lies in Interpersonal Communication: A Taxonomy and Preliminary Investigation of Social Motivations. *Western Journal of Speech Communication* 48:309–325.

Canary, Daniel J. and Laura Stafford (1994). *Communication and Relational Maintenance.* Orlando, Fla.: Academic Press.

Canary, Daniel J., Laura Stafford, Kimberly S. Hause, & Lisa A. Wallace (1993). An Inductive Analysis of Relational Maintenance Strategies: Comparisons Among Lovers, Relatives, Friends, and Others. *Communication Research Reports* 10 (June): 5–14.

Canary, Daniel J. & Laura Stafford (1994). Maintaining Relationships Through Strategic and Routine Interaction. In *Communication and Relational Maintenance,* edited by D. J. Canary and L. Stafford. New York: Academic Press.

Cappella, Joseph N. (1987). Interpersonal Communication: Definitions and Fundamental Questions. In Charles R. Berger and Steven H. Chaffee, eds., *Handbook of Communication Science* (pp. 184–238). Thousand Oaks, CA: Sage.

Cappella, Joseph N. (1993). The Facial Feedback Hypothesis in Human Interaction: Review and Speculation. *Journal of Language and Social Psychology* 12 (March–June):13–29.

Carducci, Bernardo J. with Philip G. Zimbardo (1995). Are You Shy? *Psychology Today* 28 (November/December):34–41, 64–70, 78–82.

Care, R, J. Henton, J. Koval, R. Christopher, and S. Lloyd (1982). Premarital Abuse: A Social Psychological Perspective. *Journal of Family Issues* 3:79–90.

Carle, Gilda (1995). 10 Reasons Why Talk Shows Are Good for You. *All Talk* (Spring):27.

Carroll, John B., ed. (1956). *Language, Thought and Reality: Selected Writings of Benjamin Lee Whorf.* New York: Wiley.

Carroll, John B. and Joseph B. Casagrande (1958). The Functions of Language Classifications in Behavior. In Eleanor E. Maccoby, Theodore M. Newcomb, and Eugene L. Hartley, eds. *Readings in Social Pscyhology,* 3rd ed. (pp. 18–31). New York: Holt, Rinehart and Winston.

Cathcart, Dolores and Robert Cathcart (1985). Japanese Social Experience and Concept of Groups. In Larry A. Samovar and Richard E. Porter, eds., *Intercultural Communication: A Reader,* 4th ed. (pp. 190–197). Belmont, CA: Wadsworth.

Cathcart, Robert S., Larry A. Samovar, and Linda Henman (1996). *Small Group Communication: A Reader,* 7th ed. Dubuque, IA: Brown & Benchmark.

Chadwick-Jones, J. K. (1976). *Social Exchange Theory: Its Structure and Influence in Social Psychology.* New York: Academic.

Chaney, Robert H., Carolyne A. Givens, Melanie F. Aoki, and Michael L. Gombiner (1989). Pupillary Responses in Recognizing Awareness in Persons with Profound Mental Retardation. *Perceptual and Motor Skills* 69 (October):523–528.

Chanowitz, B. & Ellen Langer (1981). Premature Cognitive Commitment. *Journal of Personality and Social Psychology* 41:1051–1063.

Chen, Guo-Ming (1990). Intercultural Communication Competence: Some Perspectives of Research. *The Howard Journal of Communication* 2 (Summer):243–261.

Chen, Guo Ming (1992). "Differences in Self-Disclosure Patterns Among Americans versus Chinese: A Comparative Study," paper presented at the annual meeting of the Eastern Communication Association (Portland, ME).

Chesebro, James, ed. (1981). *Gayspeak.* New York: Pilgrim Press.

Chisholm, Shirley (1978, August 15). *Vital Speeches of the Day* 44.

Cialdini, Robert T. (1984). *Influence: How and Why People Agree to Things.* New York: Morrow.

Cialdini, Robert T. and K. Ascani (1976). Test of a Concession Procedure for Inducing Verbal, Behavioral, and Further Compliance with a Request to Give Blood. *Journal of Applied Psychology* 61:295–300.

Clair, Robin Patric (1994). Resistance and Oppression as a Self-Contained Opposite: An Organizational Communication Analysis of One Man's Story of Sexual Harassment. *Western Journal of Communication* 58 (Fall):235–262.

Clark, Herbert (1974). The Power of Positive Speaking. *Psychology Today* 8:102, 108–111.

Clement, Donald A. and Kenneth D. Frandsen (1976). On Conceptual and Empirical Treatments of Feedback in Human Communication. *Communication Monographs* 43:11–28.

Cline, M. G. (1956). The Influence of Social Context on the Perception of Faces. *Journal of Personality* 2:142–185.

Coalition Commentary, a Publication of the Illinois Coalition against Sexual Assault (1990). Urbana, IL (Spring):l–7.

Coates, Jennifer (1986). *Women, Men and Language.* New York: Longman.

Cody, Michael J., P. J. Marston, and M. Foster (1984). Paralinguistic and Verbal Leakage of Deception as a Function of Attempted Control and Timing of Questions. In R. M. Bostrom, ed., *Communication Yearbook/7* (pp. 464–490). Thousand Oaks, CA: Sage.

Cohen, C. E. (1983). Inferring the Characteristics of Other People: Categories and Attribute Accessibility. *Journal of Personality and Social Psychology* 44:34–44.

Collier, Mary Jane (1991). Conflict Competence Within African, Mexican, and Anglo American Friendships. In Stella Ting-Toomey and Felipe Korzenny, eds., *Cross-Cultural Interpersonal Communication* (pp. 132–154). Thousand Oaks, CA: Sage.

Collins, Caroline L. and Odette N. Gould (1994). Getting to Know You: How Own Age and Other's Age Relate to Self-Disclosure. *International Journal of Aging and Human Development* 39:55–66.

Comadena, Mark E. (1984). Brainstorming Groups: Ambiguity Tolerance, Communication Apprehension, Task Attraction, and Individual Productivity. *Small Group Behavior* 15:251–254.

Comadena, Mark and Diane Prusank (1988). Communication Apprehension and Academic Achievement among Elementary and Middle School Students. *Communication Education* 37:270–277.

Condon, John C. and Fathi Yousef (1975). *An Introduction to Intercultural Communication.* Indianapolis: Bobbs-Merrill.

Cook, Mark (1971). *Interpersonal Perception.* Baltimore: Penguin.

Cooley, Charles Horton (1922). *Human Nature and the Social Order,* rev. ed. New York: Scribner's.

Coupland, Nikolas, Justine Coupland, Howard Giles, Karen Henwood. et al. (1988). "Elderly Self-Disclosure: Interactional and Intergroup Issues. *Language and Communication* 8:109–133.

Coupland, Nikolas, Karen Grainger, and Justine Coupland (1988). Politeness in Context: Intergenerational Issues. *Language in Society* 17 (June):253–262.

Cozby, Paul (1973). Self-Disclosure: A Literature Review. *Psychological Bulletin* 79:73–91.

Cozby, Paul (1993). *Methods in Behavioral Research,* 5th ed. Mountain View, CA: Mayfield.

Cragan, John F. and David W. Wright (1990). Small Group Communication Research of the 1980's: A Synthesis and Critique. *Communication Studies* 41 (Fall):212–236.

Crohn, Joel (1995). *Mixed Matches.* New York: Fawcett.

Dainton, M., & Laura Stafford (1993). Routine Maintenance Behaviors: A Comparison of Relationship Type, Partner Similarity, and Sex Differences. *Journal of Social and Personal Relationships* 10:255–272.

Danna, Sammy R., ed. (1992). *Advertising and Popular Culture: Studies in Variety and Versatility.* Bowling Green, OH: Bowling Green State University Popular Press.

Darwin Charles (1872). *The Expression of the Emotions in Man and Animals.*

Davis, Flora (1973). *Inside Intuition.* New York: New American Library.

Davis, Keith (1977). The Care and Cultivation of the Corporate Grapevine. In Richard Huseman, Cal Logue, and Dwight Freshley, eds., *Readings in Interpersonal and Organizational Communication,* 3rd ed. (pp. 131–136). Boston: Holbrook.

Davis, Keith (1980). Management Communication and the Grapevine. In Stewart Ferguson and Sherry Devereaux Ferguson, eds., *Intercom: Readings in Organizational Communication* (pp. 55–66). Rochelle Park, NJ: Hayden Book.

Davis, Keith E. (1985). Near and Dear: Friendship and Love Compared. *Psychology Today* 19:22–30.

Davis, Murray S. (1973). *Intimate Relations.* New York: Free Press.

Davis, Ossie (1967). The English Language Is My Enemy. *American Teacher,* pp. 13–15. Reprinted in DeVito (1973), pp. 164–170.

Davitz, Joel R., ed. (1964). *The Communication of Emotional Meaning.* New York: McGraw-Hill.

Deal, James E. and Karen Smith Wampler (1986). Dating Violence: The Primacy of Previous Experience. *Journal of Social and Personal Relationships* 3:457–471.

deBono, Edward (1976). *Teaching Thinking.* New York: Penguin.

deBono, Edward (1987). *The Six Thinking Hats.* New York: Penguin.

DeCecco, John (1988). Obligation versus Aspiration. In *Gay Relationships,* John DeCecco, ed., New York: Harrington Park Press.

DeFleur, Melvin (1987). The Growth and Decline of Research on the Diffusion of the News: 1945–1985. *Communication Research* 14:109–130.

DeFleur, Melvin L. and Sandra Ball-Rokeach (1989). *Theories of Mass Communication,* 5th ed. New York: Longman.

DeFrancisco, Victoria (1991). The Sound of Silence: How Men Silence Women in Marital Relations. *Discourse and Society* 2:413–423.

DeJong, W. (1979). An Examination of Self Perception Mediation of the Foot-in-the Door Effect. *Journal of Personality and Social Psychology* 37:2221–2239.

Delia, Jesse G. (1977). Constructivism and the Study of Human Communication. *Quarterly Journal of Speech* 63:66–83.

Delia, Jesse G., Barbara J. O'Keefe, and Daniel J. O'Keefe (1982). The Constructivist Approach to Communication. In Frank E. X. Dance, ed., *Human Communication Theory: Comparative Essays* (pp. 147–191). New York: Harper & Row.

Derlega, V. J., B. A. Winstead, P. T. P. Wong, and S. Hunter (1985). Gender Effects in an Initial Encounter: A Case Where Men Exceed Women in Disclosure. *Journal of Social and Personal Relationships* 2:25–44.

Derlega, Valerian J., Barbara A. Winstead, Paul T. P. Wong, and Michael Greenspan (1987). Self-Disclosure and Relationship Development: An Attributional Analysis. In Michael E. Roloff and Gerald R. Miller, eds., *Interpersonal Processes: New Directions in Communication Research* (pp. 172–187). Thousand Oaks, CA: Sage.

Derlega, Valerian J., Sandra Metts, Sandra Petronio, and Stephen T. Margulis. (1993). *Self-Disclosure.* Thousand Oaks, CA: Sage.

DeStephen, R. and R. Hirokawa (1988). Small Group Consensus: Stability of Group Support of the Decision, Task Process, and Group Relationships. *Small Group Behavior* 19:227–239.

DeTurck, Mark A. (1987). When Communication Fails: Physical Aggression as a Compliance-Gaining Strategy. *Communication Monographs* 54:106–112.

DeTurck, Mark A. and Gerald R. Miller (1985). Deception and Arousal: Isolating the Behavioral Correlates of Deception. *Human Communication Research* 12 (Winter):181–201.

DeVito, Joseph A. (1965). Comprehension Factors in Oral and Written Discourse of Skilled Communicators. *Communication Monographs* 32:124–128.

DeVito, Joseph A. (1969). Some Psycholinguistic Aspects of Active and Passive Sentences. *Quarterly Journal of Speech* 55:401–406.

DeVito, Joseph A. (1970). *The Psychology of Speech and Language: An Introduction to Psycholinguistics.* New York: Random House.

DeVito, Joseph A. (1973) *Language: Concepts and Processes.* Upper Saddle River, NJ: Prentice-Hall.

DeVito, Joseph A. (1974). *General Semantics: Guide and Workbook,* rev. ed. DeLand, FL: Everett/Edwards.

DeVito, Joseph A. (1976). Relative Ease in Comprehending Yes/No Questions. In Jane Blankenship and Herman G. Stelzner, eds., *Rhetoric and Communication* (pp. 143–154). Urbana: University of Illinois Press.

DeVito, Joseph A. (1986). *The Communication Handbook: A Dictionary.* New York: Harper & Row.

DeVito, Joseph A. (1986, June). Teaching as Relational Development. In Jean Civikly, ed., *Communicating in College Classrooms* (New Directions for Teaching and Learning), No. 26 (pp. 51–60). San Francisco: Jossey-Bass.

DeVito, Joseph A. (1989). *The Nonverbal Communication Workbook.* Prospect Heights, IL: Waveland Press.

DeVito, Joseph A. (1995). *The Interpersonal Communication Book,* 7th ed. New York: HarperCollins.

DeVito, Joseph A. (1996a). *Brainstorms: How to Think More Creatively about Communication (or About Anything Else).* New York: HarperCollins.

DeVito, Joseph A. (1996b). *Messages: Building Interpersonal Communication Skills,* 3rd ed. New York: HarperCollins.

DeVito, Joseph A. (1997). *The Elements of Public Speaking,* 6th ed. New York: HarperCollins.

DeVito, Joseph A., Jill Giattino, and T. D. Schon (1975). *Articulation and Voice: Effective Communication.* Indianapolis: Bobbs-Merrill.

DeVito, Joseph A. and Michael L. Hecht, eds. (1990). *The Nonverbal Communication Reader.* Prospect Heights, IL: Waveland Press.

DeVries, Mary A. (1994). *International Yours: Writing and Communicating Successfully in Today's Global Marketplace.* Boston: Houghton Mifflin.

Dindia, Kathryn (1987). The Effects of Sex of Subject and Sex of Partner on Interruptions. *Human Communication Research* 13:345–371.

Dindia, Kathryn and Mary Anne Fitzpatrick (1985). Marital Communication: Three Approaches Compared. In Steve Duck and Daniel Perlman, eds., *Understanding Personal Relationships: An Interdisciplinary Approach.* (pp. 137–158). Thousand Oaks, CA: Sage.

Dindia, Kathryn, and Leslie A. Baxter (1987). Strategies for Maintaining and Repairing Marital Relationships. *Journal of Social and Personal Relationships* 4:143–158.

Dion, Kenneth L. and Karen K. Dion (1993). Gender and Ethnocultural Comparisons in Styles of Love. Special Issue: Gender and Culture. *Psychology of Women Quarterly* 17 (December):463–473.

Dodd, Carley H. (1991). *Dynamics of Intercultural Communication,* 3rd ed. Dubuque, IA: Wm. C. Brown.

Dodd, David H. and Raymond M. White, Jr. (1980). *Cognition: Mental Structures and Processes.* Boston: Allyn and Bacon.

Dolgin, Kim, G., Leslie Meyer, and Janet Schwartz (1991). Effects of Gender, Target's Gender, Topic, and Self-Esteem on Disclosure to Best and Midling Friends. *Sex Roles* 25:311–329.

Dominick, Joseph R. (1974). The Portable Friend: Peer Group Membership and Radio Usage. *Journal of Broadcasting* 18:161–170.

Dominick, Joseph R. (1994). *The Dynamics of Mass Communication,* 4th ed. New York: McGraw-Hill.

Donohue, William A. with Robert Kolt (1992). *Managing Interpersonal Conflict.* Thousand Oaks, CA: Sage.

Dosey, M. and M. Meisels (1976). Personal Space and Self-Protection. *Journal of Personality and Social Psychology* 38:959–965.

Dreyfuss, Henry (1971). *Symbol Sourcebook.* New York: McGraw-Hill.

Driskell, James, Beckett Olmstead, and Eduardo Salas (1993). Task Cues, Dominance Cues, and Influence in Task Groups. *Journal of Applied Psychology* 78 (February):51–60.

Drucker, Susan J. and Gary Gumpert (1991). Public Space and Communication: The Zoning of Public Interaction. *Communication Theory* 1 (November):294–310.

Duck, Steve and Robin Gilmour, eds. (1981). *Personal Relationships. 1: Studying Personal Relationships.* New York: Academic Press.

Duncan, Barry L. and Joseph W. Rock (1991). *Overcoming Relationship Impasses: Ways to Initiate Change When Your Partner Won't Help.* New York: Plenum Press [Insight Books].

Duncan, S. D., Jr. (1972). Some Signals and Rules for Taking Speaking Turns in Conversation. *Journal of Personality and Social Psychology* 23:283–292.

Duran, Robert L. and L. Kelly (1988). The Influence of Communicative Competence on Perceived Task, Social, and Physical Attractiveness. *Communication Quarterly* 36:41–49.

Dworetsky, T.A. (1994). Roadmap to the Information Highway. *Modern Maturity* 37 (February-March): 24–31.

Edelstein, Alex S. (1993). Thinking About the Criterion Variable in Agenda-Setting Research. *Journal of Communication* 43:85–99.

Eden, Dov (1992). Leadership and Expectations: Pygmalion Effects and Other Self-Fulfilling Prophecies in Organizations. *Leadership Quarterly* 3 (Winter):271–305.

Ehrenhaus, Peter (1988). Silence and Symbolic Expression. *Communication Monographs* 55 (March): 41–57.

Eibl-Eibesfeldt, I. (1972). Similarities and Differences Between Cultures in Expressive Movements. In R. A. Hinde, ed., *Non-Verbal Communication* (pp. 297–311). Cambridge: Cambridge University Press.

Eisenberg, Nancy and Janet Strayer, eds. (1990). *Empathy and its Development.* New York: Cambridge University Press.

Ekman, Paul (1965). Communication through Nonverbal Behavior: A Source of Information about an Interpersonal Relationship. In S. S. Tomkins and C. E. Izard, eds., *Affect, Cognition and Personality.* New York: Springer.

Ekman, Paul. *Telling Lies* (1985). New York: W. W. Norton.

Ekman, Paul and W. V. Friesen (1969). The Repertoire of Nonverbal Behavior: Categories, Origins, Usage, and Coding. *Semiotica* 1:49–98.

Ekman, Paul, Wallace V. Friesen, and Phoebe Ellsworth (1972). *Emotion in the Human Face: Guidelines for Research and an Integration of Findings.* New York: Pergamon Press.

Ekman, Paul, Wallace V. Friesen, and S. S. Tomkins (1971). Facial Affect Scoring Technique: A First Validity Study. *Semiotica* 3:37–58.

Elgin, Suzette Haden (1993). *Genderspeak: Men, Women, and the Gentle Art of Verbal Self-Defense.* New York: Wiley.

Elliott, Deni (1993). Ethics and Mass Communication. In Hunt and Ruben (1993), pp. 148–151.

Ellis, Albert (1988). *How to Stubbornly Refuse to Make Yourself Miserable about Anything, Yes Anything.* Secaucus, NJ: Lyle Stuart.

Ellis, Albert and Robert A. Harper (1975). *A New Guide to Rational Living.* Hollywood: Wilshire Books.

Escobar, Arturo, David Hess, Isabel Licha, Will Sibley, Marilyn Strathern, and Judith Sutz. (1994). *Current Anthropology* 35 (June):211–223.

Esten, Geri and Lynn Willmott (1993). Double-Bind Messages: The Effects of Attitude Towards Disability on Therapy. *Women and Therapy* 14:29–41.

Exline, R. V., S. L. Ellyson, and B. Long (1975). Visual Behavior as an Aspect of Power Role Relationships. In P. Pliner, L. Krames, and T. Alloway, eds., *Nonverbal Communication of Aggression.* New York: Plenum.

Faber, Adele and Elaine Mazlish (1980). *How to Talk so Kids Will Listen and Listen so Kids Will Talk.* New York: Avon.

Farrell, M. P., and S. D. Rosenberg (1981). *Men at Midlife.* Westport, Conn.: Auburn House.

Fengler, A. P. (1974). Romantic Love in Courtship: Divergent Paths of Male and Female Students. *Journal of Comparative Family Studies* 5:134–139.

Festinger, L., S. Schachter, and K. W. Back (1950). *Social Pressures in Informal Groups: A Study of Human Factors in Housing.* New York: Harper & Row.

Festinger, Leon (1954). A Theory of Social Comparison Processes. *Human Relations* 7:117–140.

Field, R. H. G. (1989). The Self-Fulfilling Prophecy Leader: Achieving the Metharme Effect. *Journal of Management Studies* 26 (March):151–175.

Filley, Alan C. (1975). *Interpersonal Conflict Resolution.* Glenview, IL: Scott, Foresman.

Fischer, C. S. and S. J. Oliker (1983). A Research Note on Friendship, Gender, and the Life Cycle. *Social Forces* 62:124–133.

Fisher, B. Aubrey (1980). *Small Group Decision Making: Communication and the Group Process,* 2nd ed. New York: McGraw-Hill.

Fiske, Susan T. and Shelley E. Taylor (1984). *Social Cognition.* Reading, MA: Addison-Wesley.

Fitzpatrick, Mary Anne (1983). Predicting Couples' Communication from Couples' Self-Reports. In *Communication Yearbook 7,* edited by R. N. Bostrom, 49–82. Thousand Oaks, CA: Sage.

Floyd, James J. (1985). *Listening: A Practical Approach.* Glenview, IL: Scott, Foresman.

Foddy, Margaret and Ian Crundall (1993). A Field Study of Social Comparison Processes in Ability Evaluation. *British Journal of Social Psychology* 32 (December):287–305.

Folger, Joseph P. and Marshall Scott Poole (1984). *Working Through Conflict: A Communication Perspective.* Glenview, IL: Scott, Foresman.

Foss, Sonja K. (1996). *Rhetorical Criticism Exploration and Practice,:* 2nd ed. Prospect Heights, IL: Waveland Press.

Fox, M., M. Gibbs and D. Auerbach (1985). Age and Gender Dimensions of Friendship. *Psychology of Women Quarterly* 9:489–501.

Fraser, Bruce (1990). Perspectives on Politeness. *Journal of Pragmatics* 14 (April):219–236.

Freedman, Jonathan (1978). *Happy People: What Happiness Is, Who Has It, and Why.* New York: Ballantine Books.

Freedman, J. and S. Fraser (1966). Compliance Without Pressure: The Foot-in-the Door Technique. *Journal of Personality and Social Psychology* 4: 195–202.

French, J. R. P., Jr., and B. Raven (1968). *The Bases of Social Power.* In Dorwin Cartwright and Alvin Zander, eds., *Group Dynamics: Research and Theory,* 3rd ed., (pp. 259–269). New York: Harper & Row.

Frentz, Thomas (1976). "A General Approach to Episodic Structure," paper presented at the Western Speech Association Convention (San Francisco). Cited in Reardon (1987).

Friedman, Joel, Marcia Mobilia Boumil, and Barbar Ewert Taylor (1992). *Sexual Harassment.* Deerfield Beach, Fla.: Health Communications, Inc.

Friedman, Meyer and Ray Rosenman (1974). *Type A Behavior and Your Heart.* New York: Fawcett Crest.

Frye, Jerry K. (1980). *FIND: Frye's Index to Nonverbal Data.* Duluth: University of Minnesota Computer Center.

Frymier, Anne B. and Catherine A. Thompson (1992). Perceived Teacher Affinity-Seeking in Relation to perceived Teacher Credibility. *Communication Education* 41 (October):388–399.

Furnham, Adrian and Nadine Bitar (1993). The Stereotyped Portrayal of Men and Women in British Televison Advertisements. *Sex Roles* 29 (August):297–310.

Furnham, Adrian and Stephen Bochner (1986). *Culture Shock: Psychological Reactions to Unfamiliar Environments.* New York: Methuen.

Furnham, Adrian and T. Dowsett (1993). Sex Differences in Social Comparison and Uniqueness Bias. *Personality and Individual Differences* 15 (August):175–183.

Galvin, Kathleen and Bernard J. Brommel (1996). *Family Communication: Cohesion and Change.* 4th ed. Glenview, IL: Scott, Foresman.

Gao, Ge (1991). Stability of Romantic Relationships in China and the United States. In Stella Ting-Toomey and Felipe

Korzenny, eds., *Cross-Cultural Interpersonal Communication* (pp. 99–115). Thousand Oaks, CA: Sage.

Gaziano, C. and K. McGrath (1986). Measuring the Concept of Credibility. *Journalism Quarterly* 63:451–462.

Gelles, R. (1981). The Myth of the Battered Husband. In R. Walsh and O. Pocs, eds. *Marriage and Family 81/82,* New York: Guilford.

Gelles, R. and C. Cornell (1985). *Intimate Violence in Families.* Thousand Oaks, CA: Sage.

George, Diana and John Trimbur (1995). *Reading Culture: Contexts for Critical Reading and Writing,* 2nd ed. New York: HarperCollins.

Gerbner, George, L. P. Gross, M. Morgan, and N. Signorielli (1980). The "Mainstreaming" of America: Violence Profile No. 11. *Journal of Communication* 30:10–29.

Gergen, K. J., M. S. Greenberg, and R. H. Willis (1980). *Social Exchange: Advances in Theory and Research.* New York: Plenum.

Gibb, Cecil A. (1969). Leadership. In G. Lindsey and E. Aronson, eds. *The Handbook of Social Psychology,* 2nd ed., vol. 4 (pp. 205–282). Reading, MA: Addison-Wesley.

Gibb, Jack (1961). Defensive Communication. *Journal of Communication* 11:141–148.

Giles, Howard, Anthony Mulac, James J. Bradac, and Patricia Johnson (1987). Speech Accommodation Theory: The First Decade and Beyond. In Margaret L. McLaughlin, ed., *Communication Yearbook 10* (pp. 13–48). Thousand Oaks, CA: Sage.

Gill, Mary M. and William J. Wardrope (1992, June). To Say or Not: To Do or Not—Those Are the Questions: Sexual Harassment and the Basic Course Instructor. In Lawrence W. Hugenberg, ed., *Basic Communication Course Annual,* Vol. 4. Boston: Academic.

Gilmour, Robin and Steve Duck, eds. (1986). *The Emerging Field of Personal Relationships.* Hillsdale, NJ: Lawrence Erlbaum.

Giordano, Joseph (1989). *Telecommuting and Organizational Culture: A Study of Corporate Consciousness and Identification.* Unpublished doctoral dissertation, University of Massachusetts, Amherst, MA.

Glucksberg, Sam and Joseph H. Danks (1975). *Experimental Psycholinguistics: An Introduction.* Hillsdale, NJ: Lawrence Erlbaum.

Goffman, Erving (1967). *Interaction Ritual: Essays on Face-to-Face Behavior.* New York: Pantheon.

Goffman, Erving (1971). *Relations in Public: Microstudies of the Public Order.* New York: Harper Colophon.

Golden, James L., Goodwin F. Berquist and William E. Coleman (1993). *The Rhetoric of Western Thought,* 5th ed. Dubuque, IA: Kendall/Hunt.

Goldhaber, Gerald (1990). *Organizational Communication,* 5th ed. Dubuque, IA: Wm. C. Brown.

Gonzalez, Albert, Marsha Houston, and Victoria Chen. (1994). *Our Voices: Essays in Culture, Ethnicity, and Communication: An Intercultural Anthology.* Los Angeles, CA: Roxbury Publishing Company.

Gonzalez, Alexander and Philip G. Zimbardo (1985). Time in Perspective. *Psychology Today* 19:20–26.

Goodale, James G. (1992). *One to One: Interviewing, Selecting, Appraising, and Counseling Employees.* Upper Saddle River, NJ: Prentice-Hall.

Gordon, Thomas (1975). *P.E.T.: Parent Effectiveness Training.* New York: New American Library.

Goss, Blaine (1989). *The Psychology of Communication.* Prospect Heights, IL: Waveland Press.

Goss, Blaine, M. Thompson, and S. Olds (1978). Behavioral Support for Systematic Desensitization for Communication Apprehension. *Human Communication Research* 4:158–163.

Gould, Stephen Jay (1995). No More 'Wretched Refuse." *New York Times* (June 7):A27.

Gouran, Dennis S. and Randy Y. Hirokawa (1986). Counteractive Functions of Communication in Effective Group Decision-Making. In Randy Y. Hirokawa and M. S. Poole, Eds., *Communication and Group Decision-Making* (pp. 81–90). Thousand Oaks, CA: Sage.

Graham, E. E. (1994). Interpersonal Communication Motives Scale. In R. B. Rubin, P. Palmgreen, and H. E. Sypher, eds., *Communication Research Measures: A Sourcebook* (pp. 211–216). New York: Guilford.

Graham, E. E., C. A. Barbato, and E. M. Perse (1993). The Interpersonal Communication Motives Model. *Communication Quarterly* 41:172–186.

Grant, August E., K. Kendall Guthrie, Sandra J. Ball-Rokeach (1991). Television Shopping: A Media System Dependency Perspective. *Communication Research* 18 (December):773–798.

Gratus, Jack (1988). *Successful Interviewing: How to Find and Keep the Best People.* New York: Penguin.

Greeley, Andrew (1988). Letter to the Editor. *New York Times* (August 14):21.

Greenberg, J. H., ed. (1963). *Universals of Language.* Cambridge, MA: MIT Press.

Grice, H. P. (1975). Logic and Conversation. In P. Cole and J. L. Morgan, eds., *Syntax and Semantics Vol. 3, Speech Acts* (pp. 41–58). New York: Seminar Press.

Griffin, Em (1991). *A First Look at Communication Theory.* New York: McGraw-Hill.

Griffin, Em and Glenn G. Sparks (1990). Friends Forever: A Longitudinal Exploration of Intimacy in Same-Sex Friends and Platonic Pairs. *Journal of Social and Personal Relationships* 7:29–46.

Gronbeck, Bruce E., Raymie E. McKerrow, Douglas Ehninger, and Alan H. Monroe (1994). *Principles and Types of Speech Communication,* 12th ed. Glenview, IL: Scott, Foresman.

Gross, Larry (1991). The Contested Closet: The Ethics and Politics of Outing. *Critical Studies in Mass Communication* 8 (September):352–388.

Grossin, William (1987). Monochronic Time, Polychronic Time and Policites for Development. *Studi di Sociologia* 25 (January–March):18–25.

Grove, Theodore G. (1991). *Dyadic Interaction: Choice and Change in Conversations and Relationships.* Dubuque, IA: Wm. C. Brown.

Gudykunst, William B., ed. (1983). *Intercultural Communication Theory: Current Perspectives.* Thousand Oaks, CA: Sage.

Gudykunst, William B. (1989). Culture and the Development of Interpersonal Relationships. In J. A. Andersen, ed. *Communication Yearbook/12,* (pp. 315–354). Thousand Oaks, CA: Sage.

Gudykunst, W. B. (1991). *Bridging Differences: Effective Intergroup Communication.* Thousand Oaks, CA: Sage.

Gudykunst, W. and T. Nishida (1984). Individual and Cultural Influence on Uncertainty Reduction. *Communication Monographs* 51:23–36.

Gudykunst, W., S. Yang and T. Nisida (1985). A Cross-Cultural Test of Uncertainty Reduction Theory: Comparisons of

Acuaintance, Friend, and Dating Relationships in Japan, Korea, and the Untied States. *Human Communication Research* 11:407–454.

Gudykunst, William B. and Y. Y. Kim (1990). *Communicating with Strangers: An Approach to Intercultural Communication,* 2nd ed. New York: McGraw-Hill.

Gudykunst, W. B. and Y. Y. Kims, eds. (1992). *Reading on Communication with Strangers: An Approach to Intercultural Communication.* New York: McGraw-Hill.

Gudykunst, W. B. and Stella Ting-Toomey with Elizabeth Chua (1988). *Culture and Interpersonal Communication.* Thousand Oaks, CA: Sage.

Guerrero, L. K., S. V. Eloy, and A. I. Wabnik (1993). Linking Maintenance Strategies to Relationship Development and Disengagement: A Reconceptualization. *Journal of Social and Personal Relationships* 10:273–282.

Guerrero, Laura K. and Peter A. Andersen (1994). Patterns of Matching and Initiation: Touch Behavior and Touch Avoidance Across Romantic Relationship Stages. *Journal of Nonverbal Behavior* 18 (Summer):137–153.

Gumpert, Gary and Susan J. Drucker (1995). Place as Medium: Exegesis of the Cafe Drinking Coffee, The Art of Watching Others, Civil Conversation—with Excursions into the Effects of Architecture and Interior Design. *The Speech Communication Annual* 9 (Spring):7–32.

Guo-Ming, Chen and William J. Starosta (1995). Intercultural Communication Competence: A Synthesis. *Communication Yearbook/19,* ed., Brant R. Burleson. Thousand Oaks, CA: Sage.

Hackman, Michael Z. and Craig E. Johnson (1996). *Leadership: A Communication Perspective,* 2nd ed. Prospect Heights, IL: Waveland Press.

Haferkamp, Claudia J. (1991–92). Orientations to Conflict: Gender, Attributions, Resolution Strategies, and Self-Monitoring. *Current Psychology Research and Reviews* 10 (Winter):227–240.

Haga, Yasushi (1988). Traits de Langage et Caractere Japonais. *Cahiers de Sociologie Economique et Culturelle* 9 (June):105–109.

Haggard, E. A. and K. S. Isaacs (1966). Micromomentary Facial Expressions as Indicators of Ego Mechanisms in Psychotherapy. In L. A. Gottschalk and A. H. Auerbach, eds., *Methods of Research in Psychotherapy.* Upper Saddle River, NJ: Prentice-Hall.

Halberstadt, Amy G., Kirk D. Grotjohn, Cheryl A. Johnson, Meredith S. Furth, et al. (1992). Children's Abilities and Strategies in Managing the Facial Display of Affect. *Journal of Nonverbal Behavior* 16 (Winter):215–230.

Hall, Edward T. (1959). *The Silent Language.* Garden City, NY: Doubleday.

Hall, Edward T. (1963). System for the Notation of Proxemic Behavior. *American Anthropologist* 65:1003–1026.

Hall, Edward T. (1966). *The Hidden Dimension.* Garden City, NY: Doubleday.

Hall, Edward T. (1976). *Beyond Culture.* Garden City, NY: Anchor Press.

Hall, Edward T. (1983). *The Dance of Life: The Other Dimension of Time.* New York: Anchor Books/Doubleday.

Hall, Edward T. and Mildred Reed Hall (1987). *Hidden Differences: Doing Business with the Japanese.* New York: Doubleday [Anchor Books].

Hall, Joan Kelly (1993). Tengo una Bomba: The Paralinguistic and Linguistic Conventions of the Oral Practice Chismeando. *Research on Language and Social Interaction* 26:55–83.

Hall, Judith A. (1984). *Nonverbal Sex Differences.* Baltimore: Johns Hopkins University Press.

Hambrick, Ralph S. (1991). *The Management Skills Builder: Self-Directed Learning Strategies for Career Development.* New York: Praeger.

Hammer, M. R. (1989). Intercultural Communication Competence. In M. K. Asante and W. B. Gudykunst, eds., *Handbook of International and Intercultural Communication.* (pp. 247–260). Thousand Oaks, CA: Sage.

Han, Sang-pil and Sharon Shavitt (1994). Persuasion and Culture: Advertising Appeals in Individualistic and Collectivistic Societies. *Journal of Experimental Social Psychology* 30 (July):326–350.

Haney, William (1973). *Communication and Organizational Behavior: Text and Cases,* 3rd ed. Homewood, IL: Irwin.

Hart, R. P., R. E. Carlson, and W. F. Eadie (1980). Attitudes Toward Communication and the Assessment of Rhetorical Sensitivity. *Communication Monographs* 39:75–91.

Hart, R. P. and D. M. Burks (1972). Rhetorical Sensitivity and Social Interaction. *Communication Monographs* 39:75–91.

Hashimoto, I. (1986). The Myth of the Attention-Getting Opener. *Written Communication* 3:123–131.

Hastorf, Albert, David Schneider, and Judith Polefka (1970). *Person Perception.* Reading, MA: Addison-Wesley.

Hatfield, Elaine and Jane Traupman (1981). Intimate Relationships: A Perspective from Equity Theory. In Steve Duck and Robin Gilmour, eds., *Personal Relationships. 1: Studying Personal Relationships* (pp. 165–178). New York: Academic Press.

Hayakawa, S. I. and A. R. Hayakawa (1989). *Language in Thought and Action,* 5th ed. New York: Harcourt Brace Jovanovich.

Hays, Robert B. (1989). The Day-to-Day Functioning of Close Versus Casual Friendships. *Journal of Social and Personal Relationships* 6:21–37.

Heap, James L. (1992). Seeing Snubs: An Introduction to Sequential Analysis of Classroom Interaction. *Journal of Classroom Interaction* 27:23–28.

Hecht, Michael L. (1978a). The Conceptualization and Measurement of Interpersonal Communication Satisfaction. *Human Communication Research* 4:253–264.

Hecht, Michael L. (1978b). Toward a Conceptualization of Communication Satisfaction. *Quarterly Journal of Speech* 64:47–62.

Hecht, Michael L., Mary Jane Collier, and Sidney Ribeau (1993). *African American Communication: Ethnic Identify and Cultural Interpretation.* Thousand Oaks, CA: Sage.

Hecht, Michael L. and Sidney Ribeau (1984). Ethnic Communication: A Comparative Analysis of Satisfying Communication. International *Journal of Intercultural Relations* 8:135–151.

Heiskell, Thomas L. and Joseph F. Rychiak (1986). The Therapeutic Relationship: Inexperienced Therapists' Affective Preference and Empathic Communication. *Journal of Social and Personal Relationships* 3:267–274.

Hellweg, Susan A. (1992). Organizational Grapevines. In Kevin L. Hutchinson, ed., *Readings in Organizational Communication* (pp. 159–172). Dubuque, IA: Wm. C. Brown.

Henderson, M. and A. Furnham (1982). Similarity and Attraction: The Relationship Between Personality, Beliefs, Skills, Needs, and Friendship Choice. *Journal of Adolescence* 5:111–123.

Hendrick, Clyde, Susan Hendrick, Franklin H. Foote, and Michelle J. Slapion-Foote (1984). Do Men and Women Love Differently? *Journal of Social and Personal Relationships* 1:177–195.

Hendrick, Susan S. and Hendrick, Clyde (1992). *Romantic Love.* Thousand Oaks, CA: Sage.

Henley, Nancy M. (1977). *Body Politics: Power, Sex, and Nonverbal Communication.* Upper Saddle River, NJ: Prentice-Hall.

Herbert, Robert K. and Stephen H. Straight (1989). Compliment-Rejection Versus Compliment-Avoidance: Listener-Based Versus Speaker-Based Pragmatic Strategies. *Language and Communication* 9:35–47.

Hernandez, Robert D. (1994). Reducing Bias in the Assessment of Culturally and Linguistically Diverse Populations. *Journal of Educational Issues of Language Minority Students* 14 (Winter):269–300.

Hersey, Paul and Ken Blanchard (1988). *Management of Organizational Behavior: Utilizing Human Resources.* Upper Saddle River, N J: Prentice-Hall.

Hess, Ekhard H. (1975). *The Tell-Tale Eye.* New York: Van Nostrand Reinhold.

Hess, Eckhard H., Allan L. Seltzer, and John M. Schlien (1965). Pupil Response of Hetero-and Homosexual Males to Pictures of Men and Women: A Pilot Study. *Journal of Abnormal Psychology* 70:165–168.

Hess, Ursula, Arvid Kappas, Gregory J. McHugo, John T. Lanzetta, et al. (1992). The Facilitative Effect of Facial Expression on the Self-Generation of Emotion. *International Journal of Psychophysiology* 12 (May):251–265.

Hewitt, John and Randall Stokes (1975). Disclaimers. *American Sociological Review* 40:1–11.

Hickson, Mark L. and Don W. Stacks (1993). *NVC: Nonverbal Communication: Studies and Applications,* 3rd ed. Dubuque, IA: Wm. C. Brown.

Hirokawa, Randy Y. (1985). Discussion Procedures and Decision-Making Performance: A Test of a Functional Perspecive. *Human Communication Research* 12:203–224.

Hirsch, P. (1980). The "Scary World" of the Nonviewer and Other Anomalies: A Reanalysis of Gerbner et al.'s Findings on Cultivation Analysis. *Communication Research* 7:403–456.

Hocker, Joyce L. and William W. Wilmot (1985). *Interpersonal Conflict,* 2nd ed. Dubuque, IA: Wm. C. Brown.

Hockett, Charles F. (1977). *The View from Language: Selected Essays, 1948–1974.* Athens: University of Georgia Press.

Hofstede, Geert (1984). *Culture's Consequences: International Differences in Work-Related Values.* Thousand Oaks, CA: Sage.

Hoft, Nancy L. (1995). *International Technical Communication: How to Export Information about High Technology.* New York: Wiley.

Hoijer, Harry, ed. (1954). *Language in Culture.* Chicago: University of Chicago Press.

Holden, Janice M. (1991). The Most Frequent Personality Priority Pairings in Marriage and Marriage Counseling. *Individual Psychology Journal of Adlerian Theory, Research, and Practice* 47 (September):392–398.

Holmes, Janet (1986). Compliments and Compliment Responses in New Zealand English. *Anthropological Linguistics* 28:485–508.

Holmes, Janet (1995). *Women, Men and Politeness.* New York: Longman.

Honeycutt, James (1986). A Model of Marital Functioning Based on an Attraction Paradigm and Social Penetration Dimensions. *Journal of Marriage and the Family* 48 (August): 51–59.

Hopper, Robert, Mark L. Knapp, and Lorel Scott (1981). Couples' Personal Idioms: Exploring Intimate Talk. *Journal of Communication* 31:23–33.

Hosman, Lawrence A. (1989). The Evaluative Consequences of Hedges, Hesitations, and Intensifiers: Powerful and Powerless Speech Styles. *Human Communication Research* 15:383–406.

Hunt, Todd and Brent D. Ruben (1993). *Mass Communication: Producers and Consumers.* New York: HarperCollins.

Huseman, Richard C. (1977). The Role of the Nominal Group in Small Group Communication. In Richard C. Huseman, Cal M. Logue, and Dwight L. Freshley, eds., *Readings in Interpersonal and Organizational Communication,* 3rd ed. (pp. 493–502). Boston: Holbrook Press.

Hutchinson, Kevin L., ed. (1992). *Readings in Organizational Communication.* Dubuque, IA: Wm. C. Brown.

Iizuka, Yuichi (1993). Regulators in Japanese Conversation. *Psychological Reports* 72 (February):203–209.

Imahori, T. Todd and William R. Cupach (1994). A Cross-Cultural Comparison of the Interpretation and Management of Face: US American and Japanese Responses to Embarrassing Predicaments. *International Journal of Intercultural Relations* 18 (Spring):193–219.

Infante, Dominic A. (1988). *Arguing Constructively.* Prospect Heights, IL: Waveland Press.

Infante, Dominic A. and Andrew S. Rancer (1982). A Conceptualization and Measure of Argumentativeness. *Journal of Personality Assessment* 46:72–80.

Infante, Dominic A., Andrew S. Rancer, and Deanna F. Womack (1993). *Building Communication Theory,* 2nd ed. Prospect Heights, IL: Waveland Press.

Infante, Dominic A. and C. J. Wigley (1986). Verbal Aggressiveness: An Interpersonal Model and Measure. *Communication Monographs* 53:61–69.

Infante, Dominic A. and Andrew S. Rancer (1995). Argumentativeness and Verbal Aggressiveness: A Review of Recent Theory and Research. *Communication Yearbook/9,* ed., Brant R. Burleson. Thousand Oaks, CA: Sage.

Insel, Paul M. and Lenore F. Jacobson, eds. (1975). *What Do You Expect? An Inquiry into Self-fulfilling Prophecies.* Menlo Park, CA: Cummings.

Jablin, Fred M. (1981). Cultivating Imagination: Factors that Enhance and Inhibit Creativity in Brainstorming Groups. *Human Communication Research* 7:245–258.

Jablin, Fred M. (1990). Organizational Communication. In Gordon L. Dahnke and Glen W. Clatterback, eds. *Human Communication: Theory and Research.* Belmont, CA: Wadsworth, pp. 156–182.

Jacobs, A. J. (1995). Talkin' Trash. *Entertainment Weekly,* No. 304 (December 8):42–43.

Jaksa, James A. and Michael S. Pritchard (1994). *Communication Ethics: Methods of Analysis.* Belmont, CA: Wadsworth.

Jaleshgari, Ramin P. (1995). "Taking Life's Big Step: Marriage (Arranged)." *New York Times* (August 13): 1.

James, David L. (1995). *The Executive Guide to Asia-Pacific Communications.* New York: Kodansha International.

Jamieson, Kathleen Hall and Karlyn Kohrs Campbell (1992). *The Interplay of Influence,* 3rd ed. Belmont, CA: Wadsworth.

Jandt, Fred E. (1995). *Intercultural Communication.* Thousand Oaks, CA: Sage.

Jang, Ha Yong and George A. Barnett (1994). Cultural Differences in Organizational Communication: A Semantic Network Analysis. *Bulletin de Methodologie Sociologique* 44 (September):31–59.

Janis, Irving (1983). *Victims of Group Thinking: A Psychological Study of Foreign Policy Decisions and Fiascoes,* 2nd ed., rev. Boston: Houghton Mifflin.

Jassem, Harvey and Roger Jon Desmond (1984). "Theory Construction and Research in Mass Communication: The Implications of New Technologies," paper delivered at the Eastern Communication Association Convention (Philadelphia, Pennsylvania).

Jaworski, Adam (1993). *The Power of Silence: Social and Pragmatic Perspectives.* Thousand Oaks, CA: Sage.

Jecker, Jon and David Landy (1969). Liking a Person as a Function of Doing Him a Favor. *Human Relations* 22:371–378.

Jensen, J. Vernon (1985). Perspectives on Nonverbal Intercultural Communication. In Larry Samovar and Richard E. Porter, eds., *Intercultural Communication: A Reader,* 4th ed. (pp. 256–272). Belmont, CA: Wadsworth.

Johannesen, Richard L. (1991). *Ethics in Human Communication,* 4th ed. Prospect Heights, IL: Waveland Press.

Johnson, F. L. and E. J. Aries (1983). The Talk of Women Friends. *Women's Studies International Forum* 6:353–361.

Johnson, Geri M. (1992). Subordinate Perceptions of Superior's Communication Competence and Task Attraction Related to Superior's Use of Compliance-Gaining Tactics. *Western Journal of Communication* 56 (Winter):54–67.

Johnson, M. P. (1973). Commitment: A Conceptual Structure and Empirical Application. *Sociological Quarterly* 14:395–406.

Johnson, M. P. (1982). Social and Cognitive Features of the Dissolution of Commitment to Relationships. In *Personal Relationships 4: Dissolving Personal Relationships,* ed. Steve Duck. New York: Academic Press, pp. 51–73.

Johnson, M. P. (1991). Commitment to Personal Relationships. In *Advances in Personal Relationships,* ed., W. H. Jones and D. Perlman, vol. 3. London: Jessica Kingsley, pp. 117–143.

Johnson, Otto, ed. (1994). *The 1994 Information Please Almanac.* New York: Houghton Mifflin.

Johnson, Scott, A. (1993). *When "I Love You" Turns Violent: Emotional and Physical Abuse in Dating Relationships.* Far Hills, NJ: New Horizon Press.

Jones, E. E., et al. (1984). *Social Stigma: The Psychology of Marked Relationships.* New York: W. H. Freeman.

Jones, E. E. and K. E. Davis (1965). From Acts to Dispositions: The Attribution Process in Person Perception. In L. Berkowitz, ed., *Advances in Experimental Social Psychology,* Vol. 2. (pp. 219–266). New York: Academic Press.

Jones, Stanley (1986). Sex Differences in Touch Communication, *Western Journal of Speech Communication* 50:227–241.

Jones, Stanley and A. Elaine Yarbrough (1985). A Naturalistic Study of the Meanings of Touch. *Communication Monographs* 52:19–56. A version of this paper appears in DeVito and Hecht (1990), pp. 235–244.

Jourard, Sidney M. (1966). An Exploratory Study of Body-Accessibility. *British Journal of Social and Clinical Psychology* 5:221–231.

Jourard, Sidney M. (1968). *Disclosing Man to Himself.* New York: Van Nostrand Reinhold.

Jourard, Sidney M. (1971a). *Self-disclosure.* New York: Wiley.

Jourard, Sidney M. (1971b). *The Transparent Self,* rev. ed. New York: Van Nostrand Reinhold.

Kalichman, Seth C., David B. Sarwer, Jennifer Johnson, Syed-Akram Ali, et al. (1993). Sexually Coercive Behavior and Love Styles: A Replication and Extension. *Journal of Psychology and Human Sexuality* 6:93–106.

Kanner, Bernice (1989). Color Schemes. *New York Magazine* (April 3):22–23.

Kanter, Arnold B. (1995). *The Essential Book of Inteviewing: Everything You Need to Know from Both Sides of the Table.* New York: Random House [Times Books].

Kapoor, Suraj, Arnold Wolfe, and Janet Blue (1995). Universal Values Structure and Individualism-Collectivism: A U.S. Test. *Communication Research Reports* 12 (Spring): 112–123.

Kashima, Yoshihisa, Michael Siegal, Kenichiro Tanaka, and Hiroko Isaka (1988). Universalism in Lay Conceptions of Distributive Justice: A Cross-Cultural Examination. *International Journal of Psychology* 23:51–64.

Katz, Elihu (1957). The Two-Step Flow of Communication: An Up-to-Date Report on an Hypothesis. *Public Opinion Quarterly* 21:61–78.

Kealy, D. J. and R. D. Ruben (1983). Cross-Cultural Personnel Selection Criteria, Issues, and Methods. In D. Landis and R. W. Brislin, eds. *Handbook of Intercultural Training,* Vol. 1. (pp. 155–175). New York: Pergamon.

Kelley, H. H. (1967). Attribution Theory in Social Psychology. In D. Levine, ed., *Nebraska Symposium on Motivation* (pp. 192–240). Lincoln: University of Nebraska Press.

Kelley, H. H. (1973). The Process of Causal Attribution. *American Psychologist* 28:107–128.

Kelley, H. H. (1979). *Personal Relationships: Their Structures and Processes.* Hillsdale, NJ: Erlbaum.

Kelley, H. H. and J. W. Thibaut (1978). *Interpersonal Relations: A Theory of Interdependence.* New York: Wiley/Interscience.

Kennedy, C. W. and C. T. Camden (1988). A New Look at Interruptions. *Western Journal of Speech Communication* 47:45–58.

Kersten, K. and L. Kersten (1988). *Marriage and the Family: Studying Close Relationships.* New York: Harper & Row.

Kesselman-Turkel, Judi and Franklynn Peterson (1982). *Note-Taking Made Easy.* Chicago: Contemporary Books.

Keyton, Joann (1995). Sexual Harassment: A Multidisciplinary Approach. *Communication Yearbook/19,* ed., Brant R. Burleson. Thousand Oaks, CA: Sage.

Kim, Ken I., Hun-joon Park, and Nori Suzuki (1990). Reward Allocations in the United States, Japan, and Korea: A Comparison of Individualistic and Collectivistic Cultures. *Academy of Management Journal* 33 (March):188–198.

Kim, Min Sun (1994). Cross-Cultural Comparisons of the Perceived Importance of Conversational Constraints. *Human Communication Research* 21 (September):128–151.

Kim, Min Sun and William F. Sharkey (1995). Independent and Interdependent Contruals of Self: Explaining Cultural Patterns of Interpersonal Communication in Multi-Cultural Organizational Settings. *Communication Quarterly* 43 (Winter):20–38.

Kim, Sung Hee and Richard H. Smith (1993). Revenge and Conflict Escalation. *Negotiation Journal* 9 (January):37–43.

Kim, Young Yun, ed. (1986). *Interethnic Communication: Current Research.* Thousand Oaks, CA: Sage.

Kim, Young Yun (1988). Communication and Acculturation. In Larry A. Samovar and Richard E. Porter, eds., *Intercultural Communication: A Reader,* 4th ed. (pp. 344–354). Belmont, CA: Wadsworth.

Kim, Young Yun (1991). Intercultural Communication Competence. In Stella Ting-Toomey and Felipe Korzenny, eds., *Cross-Cultural Interpersonal Communication* (pp. 259–275). Thousand Oaks, CA: Sage.

Kim, Young Yun and William B. Gudykunst, eds. (1988). *Theories in Intercultural Communication.* Thousand Oaks, CA:Sage.

King, Robert and Eleanor DiMichael (1992). *Voice and Diction.* Prospect Heights, IL.: Waveland Press.

Kirkpatrick, C. and T. Caplow (1945). Courtship in a Group of Minnesota Students. *American Journal of Sociology* 51:114–125.

Klein, Jeremy, ed. (1992). Special Issue: The E-Prime Controversy: A Symposium. *Etc.: A Review of General Semantics* 49, No. 2.

Kleinfield, N. R. (1992). The Smell of Money. *New York Times* (October 25), 9:1, 8.

Kleinke, Chris L. (1978). *Self-Perception: The Psychology of Personal Awareness.* San Francisco: W. H. Freeman.

Kleinke, Chris L. (1986). *Meeting and Understanding People.* New York: W. H. Freeman.

Klineberg, O. and W. F. Hull (1979). *At a Foreign University: An International Study of Adaptation and Coping.* New York: Praeger.

Klopf, Donald W., Catherine A. Thompson, Satoshi Ishii, and Aino Sallinen-Kuparinen (1991). Nonverbal Immediacy Differences Among Japanese, Finnish, and American University Students. *Perceptual and Motor Skills* 73 (August):209–210.

Knapp, Mark L. (1984). *Interpersonal Communication and Human Relationships.* Boston: Allyn and Bacon.

Knapp, Mark L., Donald Ellis, and Barbara A. Williams (1980). Perceptions of Communication Behavior Associated with Relationship Terms. *Communication Monographs* 47:262–278.

Knapp, Mark and Judith Hall (1992). *Nonverbal Behavior in Human Interaction,* 3rd ed. New York: Holt, Rinehart and Winston.

Knapp, Mark L., Roderick P. Hart, Gustav W. Friedrich, and Gary M. Shulman (1973). The Rhetoric of Goodbye: Verbal and Nonverbal Correlates of Human Leave-Taking. *Communication Monographs* 40:182–198.

Knapp, Mark L. and Gerald R. Miller, ed. (1995). *Handbook of Interpersonal Communication,* 2nd ed. Thousand Oaks, CA: Sage.

Knapp, Mark L. and Eric H. Taylor (1994). Commitment and Its Communication in Romantic Relationships. In Ann L. Weber and John H. Harvey, eds., *Perspectives on Close Relationships* (pp. 153–175). Boston: Allyn and Bacon.

Knapp, Mark L. and Anita L. Vangelisti (1992). *Interpersonal Communication and Human Relationships,* 2nd ed. Boston: Ailyn and Bacon.

Knodt, Gerrit J. (1994). Do Your Homework . . . Don't Assume . . . and Use 'Fingerspitzengefuehl' or . . . How to Survive and Prosper as a Business Person in Another Culture. *Organization Development Journal* 12 (Summer):41–43.

Kochman, Thomas (1981). *Black and White: Styles in Conflict.* Chicago: University of Chicago Press.

Korzybski, Alfred (1933). *Science and Sanity.* Lakeville, CT: The International Society for General Semantics.

Kramarae, Cheris (1974a). Folklinguistics. *Psychology Today* 8:82–85.

Kramarae, Cheris (1974b). Stereotypes of Women's Speech: The Word from Cartoons. *Journal of Popular Culture* 8:624–630.

Kramarae, Cheris (1977). Perceptions of Female and Male Speech. *Language and Speech* 20:151–161.

Kramarae, Cheris (1981). *Women and Men Speaking.* Rowley, MA: Newbury House.

Kramer, Ernest (1963). Judgment of Personal Charactristics and Emotions from Nonverbal Properties. *Psychological Bulletin* 60:408–420.

Kreps, Gary L. (1990). *Organizational Communication,* 2nd ed. New York: Longman.

Krivonos, P. D. and M. L. Knapp (1975). Initiating Communication: What Do You Say When You Say Hello? *Central States Speech Journal* 26:115–125.

Kupersmidt, Janis B., Melissa E. DeRosier, and Charlotte P. Patterson (1995). *Journal of Social and Personal Relationships* 12 (August):439–452.

Kurdek, Lawrence A. (1994). Areas of Conflict for Gay, Lesbian, and Heterosexual Couples: What Couples Argue About Influences Relationship Satisfaction. *Journal of Marriage and the Family* 56 (November):923–934.

Kurdek, Lawrence A. (1995). Developmental Changes in Relationship Quality in Gay and Lesbian Cohabiting Couples. *Developmental Psychology* 31 (January):86–93.

LaBarre, W. (1964). Paralinguistics, Kinesics, and Cultural Anthropology. In T. A. Sebeok, A. S. Hayes, and M. C. Bateson, eds., *Approaches to Semiotics* (pp. 191–220). The Hague: Mouton.

Lacey, Colin and David Longman (1993). The Press and Public Access to the Environment and Development Debate. *Sociological Review* 41 (May):207–243.

LaFrance, M. and C. Mayo (1978). *Moving Bodies: Nonverbal Communication in Social Relationships.* Monterey, CA: Brooks/Cole.

Laing, Milli (1993). Gossip: Does It Play a Role in the Socialization of Nurses? *Journal of Nursing Scholarship* 25 (Spring):37–43.

Laing, Ronald D., H. Phillipson, and A. Russell Lee (1966). *Interpersonal Perception.* New York: Springer.

Lambdin, William (1981). *Doublespeak Dictionary.* Los Angeles, CA: Pinnacle Books.

Langer, Ellen J. (1978). Rethinking the Role of Thought in Social Interaction. In J. H. Harvey, W. J. Ickes, and R. F. Kidd, eds., *New Directions in Attribution Research,* Vol. 2 (pp. 35–58). Hillsdale, NJ: Lawrence Erlbaum.

Langer, Ellen J. (1989). *Mindfulness.* Reading, MA: Addison-Wesley.

Lanzetta, J. T., J. Cartwright-Smith, and R. E. Kleck (1976). Effects of Nonverbal Dissimulations on Emotional Experience and Autonomic Arousal. *Journal of Personality and Social Psychology* 33:354–370.

Larsen, Randy J., Margaret Kasimatis, and Kurt Frey (1992). Facilitating the Furrowed Brow: An Unobtrusive Test of the Facial Feedback Hyopothesis Applied to Unpleasant Affect. *Cognition and Emotion* 6 (September):321–338.

Larson, Charles U. (1995). *Persuasion: Reception and Responsibility,* 7th ed. Belmont, CA: Wadsworth.

Lazarsfeld, Paul F., Bernard Berelson, and Helen Gaudet (1944). *The People's Choice.* New York: Duell, Sloan and Pearce.

Lazarsfeld, Paul F. and Robert K. Merton (1951). Mass Communication, Popular Taste, and Organized Social Action. In Lyman Bryson, ed., *The Communication of Ideas* (pp. 95–118). New York: Harper & Row.

Leathers, Dale G. (1992). *Successful Nonverbal Communication: Principles and Applications,* 2nd ed. New York: Macmillan.

Lederer, William J. (1984). *Creating a Good Relationship.* New York: Norton.

Lederman, Linda (1990). Assessing Educational Effectiveness: The Focus Group Interview as a Technique for Data Collection. *Communication Education* 39:117–127.

Lee, Alfred McClung and Elizabeth Briant Lee (1972). *The Fine Art of Propaganda.* San Francisco, CA: International Society for General Semantics.

Lee, Alfred McClung and Elizabeth Briant Lee (1995). "The Iconography of Propaganda Analysis," *ETC.: A Review of General Semantics* 52 (Spring):13–17.

Lee, John Alan (1973). Styles of Loving. *Psychology Today* 8:43–51.

Lee, John Alan (1976). *The Colors of Love.* New York: Bantam.

Lee, Raymond L. M. (1984). Malaysian Queue Culture: An Ethnography of Urban Public Behavior. *Southeast Asian Journal of Social Science* 12:36–50.

Leon, Joseph J., Joseph L. Philbrick, Fernando Parra, Emma Escobedo, et al. (1991) Love Styles among University Students in Mexico. *Psychological Reports* 74 (February):307–310.

Leung, Kwok (1987). Some Determinants of Reactions to Procedural Models for Conflict Resolution: A Cross-National Study. *Journal of Personality and Social Psychology* 53:898–908.

Leung, Kwok (1988). Some Determinants of Conflict Avoidance. *Journal of Cross Cultural Psychology* 19 (March):125–136.

Leung, Kwok and M. H. Bond (1984). The Impact of Cultural Collectivism on Reward Association. *Journal of Personality and Social Psychology* 47:793–804.

Leung, Kwok and M. H. Bond (1988). The Impact of Cultural Collectivism on Reward Allocation. *Journal of Personality and Social Psychology* 4:793–-804.

Leung, Kwok and Saburo Iwawaki (1988). Cultural Collectivism and Distributive Behavior. *Journal of Cross Cultural Psychology* 19 (March):35–49.

Lever, Janet (1995). The 1995 Advocate Survey of Sexuality and Relationships: The Women, Lesbian Sex Survey. *The Advocate* 687/688 (August 22):22–30.

LeVine, R. and K. Bartlett (1984). Pace of Life, Punctuality and Coronary Heart Disease in Six Countries. *Journal of Cross Cultural Psychology* 15:233–255.

Lewin, Kurt (1947). *Human Relations.* New York: Harper & Row.

Lewis, Peter H. (1995). The New Internet Gatekeepers. *New York Times* (November 13): D1, D6.

Likert, Rensis (1961). *The Human Organization.* New York: McGraw-Hill.

Linver, Sandy (1994). *Speak and Get Results: The Complete Guide to Speeches and Presentations that Work in Any Business Situation.* New York: Fireside.

Littlejohn, Stephen W. (1995). *Theories of Human Communication,* 5th ed. Belmont, CA: Wadsworth.

Littlejohn, Stephen W. and David M. Jabusch (1987). *Persuasive Transactions.* Glenview, IL: Scott, Foresman.

Livingstone, Donia M. and Peter K. Lunt (1992). Expert and Lay Participation in Television Debates: An Anaylsis of Audience Discussion Programmes. *European Journal of Communication* 7 (March):9–35.

Loftus, Elizabeth F. and J. C. Palmer (1974). Reconstruction of Automobile Destruction: An Example of the Interaction Between Language and Memory. *Journal of Verbal Learning and Verbal Behavior* 13:585–589.

Lomax, Crystal M. et al. (1994). "Proxemics in Public: Space Violations as a Function of Dyad Composition," paper presented at the Southeastern Psychological Association (New Orleans).

Luce, Gay Gaer (1971). *Body Time: Physiological Rhythms and Social Stress.* New York: Pantheon.

Luft, Joseph (1969). *Of Human Interaction.* Palo Alto, CA: Mayfield.

Luft, Joseph (1984). *Group Processes: An Introduction to Group Dynamics,* 3rd ed. Palo Alto, CA: Mayfield.

Lujansky, H. and G. Mikula (1983). Can Equity Theory Explain the Quality and Stability of Romantic Relationships? *British Journal of Social Psychology* 22:101–112.

Lukens, J. (1978). Ethnocentric Speech. *Ethnic Groups* 2:35–53.

Lumsden, Gay and Donald Lumsden (1993). *Communicating in Groups and Teams.* Belmont, CA: Wadsworth.

Lund, Philip R. (1974). *Compelling Selling: A Framework for Persuasion.* New York: American Management Association.

Lurie, Alison (1983). *The Language of Clothes.* New York: Vintage.

Lustig, Myron W. (1988). Cultural and Communication Patterns of Saudi Arabians. In *Intercultural Communication: A Reader,* 5th ed., ed. Larry A. Samovar and Richard E. Porter (pp. 101–103). Belmont, CA: Wadsworth.

Lustig, Myron W. and Jolene Koester (1996). *Intercultural Competence: Interpersonal Communication Across Cultures,* 2nd ed. New York: HarperCollins.

Lyman, Stanford M. and Marvin B. Scott (1967). Territoriality: A Neglected Sociological Dimension. *Social Problems* 15:236–249.

MacLachlan, John (1979, November). What People Really Think of Fast Talkers. *Psychology Today* 13:113–117.

Mahl, George F. and Gene Schulze (1964). Psychological Research in the Extralinguistic Area. In T. A. Sebeok, A. S. Hayes, and M. C. Bateson, eds., *Approaches to Semiotics.* The Hague: Mouton.

Main, Frank and Ronald Oliver (1988). Complementary, Symmetrical, and Parallel Personality Priorities as Indicators of Marital Adjustment. *Individual Psychology Journal of Adlerian Theory, Research, and Practice* 44 (September):324–332.

Malandro, Loretta A., Larry Barker, and Deborah Ann Barker (1989). *Nonverbal Communication,* 2nd ed. New York: Random House.

Malinowski, Bronislaw (1923). The Problem of Meaning in Primitive Languages. In C. K. Ogden and I. A. Richards, *The Meaning of Meaning* (pp. 296–336). New York: Harcourt Brace Jovanovich.

Mallardi, Vincent (1978). *Biorhythms and Your Behavior,* rev. ed. Philadelphia, PA: Running Press.

Manes, Joan and Nessa Wolfson (1981). The Compliment Formula. In Florian Coulmas, ed., *Conversational Routine* (pp. 115–132). The Hague: Mouton.

Mao, LuMing Robert (1994). Beyond Politeness Theory: "Face" Revisited and Renewed. *Journal of Pragmatics* 21 (May):451–486.

Marin, Gerardo (1985). The Preference for Equity When Judging the Attractiveness and Fairness of an Allocator: The Role of Familiarity and Culture. *Journal of Social Psychology* 125 (October):543–549.

Markman, Howard J., Louise Silvern, Mari Clements, and Shelley Kraft-Hanak (1993). Men and Women Dealing with Conflict in Heterosexual Relationships. *Journal of Social Issues* 49 (Fall):107–125.

Marks, Mitchell Lee (1986). The Question of Quality Circles. *Psychology Today* 20 (March):36–38, 42–46.

Markway, Barbara G., Cheryl N. Carmin, C. Alex Pollard, and Teresa Flynn. *Dying of Embarrassment: Help for Social Anxiety and Phobia.* Oakland, CA: New Harbinger Publications, 1992.

Marsh, Peter (1988). *Eye to Eye: How People Interact.* Topside, MA: Salem House.

Marshall, Evan (1983). *Eye Language: Understanding the Eloquent Eye.* New York: New Trend.

Marshall, Linda L. and Patricia Rose (1987). Gender, Stress, and Violence in the Adult Relationships of a Sample of College Students. *Journal of Social and Personal Relationships* 4:299–316.

Marston, Peter J., Michael L. Hecht, and Tia Robers (1987). True Love Ways: The Subjective Experience and Communication of Romantic Love. *Journal of Personal and Social Relationships* 4:387–407.

Martel, Myles (1989). *The Persuasive Edge.* New York: Fawcett.

Martin, Matthew M. and Carolyn M. Anderson (1995). Roommate Similarity: Are Roommates Who Are Similar in Their Communication Traits More Satisfied? *Communication Research Reports* 12 (Spring):46–52.

Martin, Scott L. and Richard J. Klimoski (1990). Use of Verbal Protocols to Trace Cognitions Associated with Self- and Supervisor Evaluations of Performance. *Organizational Behavior and Human Decision Processes* 46:135–154.

Marwell, G. and D. R. Schmitt (1967). "Dimensions of Compliance-Gaining Behavior: An Empirical Analysis," *Sociometry* 39, 350–364.

Marwell, Gerald and David R. Schmitt (1990). An Introduction. In *Seeking Compliance: The Production of Interpersonal Influence Messages,* ed. James Price Dillard (pp. 3–5). Scottsdale, AZ: Gorsuch Scarisbrick.

Matsumoto, David (1991). Cultural Influences on Facial Expressions of Emotion. *Southern Communication Journal* 56 (Winter):128–137.

Matsumoto, David (1994). *People: Psychology from a Cultural Perspective.* Pacific Grove, CA: Brooks/Cole.

Mayer, Michael, William Gudykunst, Norman Perrill, and Bruce Merrill (1990). A Comparison of Competing Models of the News Diffusion Process. *Western Journal of Speech Communication* 54:113–123.

Maynard, Harry E. (1963). How to Become a Better Premise Detective. *Public Relations Journal* 19:20–22.

McCarthy, B. and S. W. Duck (1976). Friendship Duration and Responses to Attitudinal Agreement-Disagreement. *British Journal of Clinical and Social Psychology* 15:377–386.

McCombs, Maxwell E. and Donald L. Shaw (1972). The Agenda–Setting Function of Mass Media. *Public Opinion Quarterly* 36:176–185.

McCombs, Maxwell E. and Donald L. Shaw (1993). The Evolution of Agenda-Setting Research: Twenty-five Years in the Marketplace of Ideas. *Journal of Communication* 43:58–67.

McCormack, Steven A. and Malcolm R. Parks (1990). What Women Know That Men Don't: Sex Differences in Determining the Truth Behind Deceptive Messages. *Journal of Social and Personal Relationships* 7:107–118.

McCroskey, James C. (1993). *An Introduction to Rhetorical Communication,* 6th ed. Upper Saddle River, NJ: Prentice-Hall.

McCroskey, James C. and Virginia P. Richmond (1995). Correlates of Compulsive Communication: Quantitative and Qualitative Characteristics. *Communication Quarterly* 43 (Winter):39–52.

McCroskey, James C., Virginia P. Richmond, and Robert A. Stewart (1986). *One on One: The Foundations of Interpersonal Communication.* Upper Saddle River, NJ: Prentice-Hall.

McCroskey, James C. and Lawrence Wheeless (1976). *Introduction to Human Communication.* Boston: Allyn and Bacon.

McEwen, William (1975). Communication, Innovation, and Change. In G. Hannenman and W. McEwen, eds., *Communication and Behavior* (pp. 197–217). Reading, MA: Addison-Wesley.

McGill, Michael E. (1985). *The McGill Report on Male Intimacy.* New York: Harper & Row.

McGregor, Douglas (1960). *The Human Side of Enterprise.* New York: McGraw-Hill.

McGuire, William J. (1964). Inducing Resistance to Persuasion: Some Contemporary Approaches. In Leonard Berkowitz, ed., *Advances in Experimental Social Psychology,* Vol. 1 (pp. 191–229). New York: Academic Press.

McKee, Michael B., Stuart F. Hayes, and Renee I. Axiotis (1994). Challenging Heterosexism in College Health Service Delivery. *Journal of American College Health* 42 (March):211–216.

McLaughlin, Margaret L. (1984). *Conversation: How Talk Is Organized.* Thousand Oaks, CA: Sage.

McLoyd, Vonnie and Leon Wilson (1992). Telling Them Like It Is: The Role of Economic and Environmental Factors in Single Mother's Discussions with Their Children. *American Journal of Community Psychology* 20 (August):419–444.

McLuhan, Marshall (1964). *Understanding Media: The Extensions of Man.* New York: McGraw-Hill.

Medley, H. Anthony (1978). *Sweaty Palms: The Neglected Art of Being Interviewed.* Belmont, CA: Wadsworth Lifetime Learning Publications.

Mehrabian, Albert (1976). *Public Places and Private Spaces.* New York: Basic Books.

Mehrabian, Albert (1978). *How We Communicate Feelings Nonverbally* (A *Psychology Today* Cassette). New York: Ziff–Davis.

Mella, Dorathee L. (1988). *The Language of Color.* New York: Warnerr.

Mencken, H. L. (1971). *The American Language.* New York: Knopf.

Merrill, John C., John Lee, and Edward Jay Friedlander (1994). *Modern Mass Media,* 2nd ed. New York: HarperCollins.

Merrill, John C. and Ralph L. Lowenstein (1979). *Media, Messages, and Men: New Perspectives in Communication.* New York: Longman.

Merton, Robert K. (1957). *Social Theory and Social Structure.* New York: Free Press.

Messick, R. M. and K. S. Cook, eds. (1983). *Equity Theory: Psychological and Sociological Perspectives.* New York: Praeger.

Metts, Sandra (1989). An Exploratory Investigation of Deception in Close Relationships. *Journal of Social and Personal Relationships* 6 (May):159–179.

Meyer, Janet R. (1994). Effect of Situational Features on the Likelihood of Addressing Face Needs in Requests. *Southern Communication Journal* 59 (Spring):240–254.

Midooka, Kiyoshi (1990). Characteristics of Japanese Style Communication. *Media, Culture and Society* 12 (October):477–489.

Millar, Frank E. and L. E. Rogers (1987). Relational Dimensions of Interpersonal Dynamics. In Michael E. Roloff and Gerald R. Millar, eds., *Interpersonal Processes: New Directions in Communication Research* (pp. 117–139). Thousand Oaks, CA: Sage.

Miller, Dale T., William Turnbull, and Cathy McFarland (1988). Particularistic and Universalistic Evaluation in the Social Comparison Process. *Journal of Personality and Psychology* 55 (December): 908–917.

Miller, George A. and David McNeill (1969). Psycholinguistics. In Gardner Lindzey and Elliot Aronson, eds. *The Handbook of Social Psychology,* 2nd ed. Vol. III. (pp. 666–794). Reading, MA: Addison-Wesley.

Miller, Gerald R. (1978). The Current State of Theory and Research in Interpersonal Communication. *Human Communication Research* 4:164–178.

Miller, Gerald R. and Malcolm R. Parks (1982). Communication in Dissolving Relationships. In Steve Duck, ed., *Personal Relationships. 4: Dissolving Personal Relationships.* New York: Academic Press.

Miller, J. G. (1984). Culture and the Development of Everyday Social Explanation. *Journal of Personality and Social Psychology* 46:961–978.

Miller, Katherine (1995). *Organizational Communication: Approaches and Processes.* Belmont, CA: Wadsworth.

Miner, Horace (1956). Body Ritual Among the Nacirema. *American Anthropologist* 58:503–507.

Mir, Montserrat (1993). "Direct Requests Can Also Be Polite," paper presented at the Annual Meeting of the International Conference on Pragmatics and Language Learning (Champaign, IL).

Mishra, Jitendra M. (1990). Managing the Grapevine. *Public Personnel Management* 19 (Summer):213–228.

Moghaddam, Fathali M., Donald M. Taylor, and Stephen C. Wright (1993). *Social Psychology in Cross-Cultural Perspective.* New York: W. H. Freeman.

Mole, John (1990). *When in Rome . . . A Business Guide to Cultures and Customs in 12 European Nations.* New York: American Management Association.

Molloy, John (1975). *Dress for Success.* New York: P. H. Wyden.

Molloy, John (1977). *The Women's Dress for Success Book.* Chicago: Foilet.

Molloy, John (1981). *Molloy's Live for Success.* New York: Bantam.

Mongeau, Paul A., Jerold L. Hale, and Marmy Alles (1994). An Experimental Investigation of Accounts and Attributions Following Sexual Infidelity. *Communication Monographs* 61 (December):326–344.

Montagu, Ashley (1971). *Touching: The Human Significance of the Skin.* New York: Harper & Row.

Montana, Patrick (1991). *Management.* New York: Barron's.

Moore, Q. L. (1993/1994). A "Whole New World" of Diversity. *Journal of Intergroup Relations* 20 (4): 28–40.

Morales, Jorge (1995). London: Death by Outing. *The Advocate* 680 (May 2):20–22.

Morgan, Michael and James Shanahan (1991). Televison and the Cultivation of Political Attitudes in Argentina. *Journal of Communication* 41 (Winter):88–103.

Morland, David (1995). Paper delivered at the Academy of Management, cited in *Psychology Today* 28 (March/April):16.

Morris, Desmond (1967). *The Naked Ape.* London: Jonathan Cape.

Morris, Desmond (1972). *Intimate Behaviour.* New York: Bantam.

Morris, Desmond (1977). *Manwatching: A Field Guide to Human Behavior.* New York: Abrams.

Morris, Desmond (1985). *Bodywatching.* New York: Crown.

Morris, Desmond (1994). *Bodytalk: The Meaning of Human Gestures.* New York: Crown.

Morris, Desmond, Peter Collett, Peter Marsh, and Marie O'Shaughnessy (1980). *Gestures: Their Origins and Distribution.* New York: Stein and Day.

Morrow, Gregory D., Eddie M. Clark, and Karla F. Brock (1995). Individual and Partner Love Styles: Implications for the Quality of Romantic Invovlements. *Journal of Social and Personal Relationships* 12 (August):363–387.

Mulac, A., J. M. Wiemann, S. J. Widenmann, and T. W. Gibson (1988). Male/Female Language Differences and Effects in Same-Sex and Mixed-Sex Dyads: The Gender-Linked Language Effect. *Communication Monographs* 55:315–335.

Mullen, Brian, Anthony Tara, Eduardo Salas, and James E. Driskell (1994). Group Cohesiveness and Quality of Decision Making: An Integration of Tests of the Groupthink Hypothesis. *Small Group Research* 25 (May):189–204.

Murata, Kumiko (1994). Intrusive or Co-operative? A Cross-Cultural Study of Interruption. *Journal of Pragmatics* 21 (April):385–400.

Murphy, Richard (1958). The Speech as Literary Genre. *Quarterly Journal of Speech* 44 (April): 117–127.

Murstein, Bernard I., Joseph R. Merighi, and Stuart A. Vyse (1991). Love Styles in the United States and France: A Cross-Cultural Comparison. *Journal of Social and Clinical Psychology* 10 (Spring):37–46.

Naifeh, Steven and Gregory White Smith (1984). *Why Can't Men Open Up? Overcoming the Fear of Intimacy.* New York: Clarkson N. Potter.

Naisbitt, John (1984). *Megatrends: Ten New Directions Tranforming Our Lives.* New York: Warner.

Nakanishi, Masayuki (1986). Perceptions of Self-Disclosure in Initial Interaction: A Japanese Sample. *Human Communication Research* 13 (Winter):167–190.

Napier, Rodney W. and Matti K. Gershenfeld (1989). *Groups: Theory and Experience,* 4th ed. Boston: Houghton Mifflin.

Nash, Nathaniel C. (1995). Advertising. *The New York Times* (July 7):D6.

Neimeyer, R. A. and G. J. Neimeyer (1983). Structural Similarity in the Acquaintance Process. *Journal of Social and Clinical Psychology* 1:146–154.

Neimeyer, Robert A. and Kelly A. Mitchell (1988). Similarity and Attraction: A Longitudinal Study. *Journal of Social and Personal Relationships* 5 May: 131–148.

Neugarten, Bernice (1979). Time, Age, and the Life Cycle. *American Journal of Psychiatry* 136:887–894.

Nichols, Ralph (1961). Do We Know How to Listen? Practical Helps in a Modern Age. *Communication Education* 10:118–124.

Nichols, Ralph and Leonard Stevens (1957). *Are You Listening?* New York: McGraw-Hill.

Nicotera, Anne Maydan and Andrew S. Rancer (1994). The Influence of Sex on Self-Perceptions and Social Stereotyping of Aggressive Communication Predispositions. *Western Journal of Communication* 58 (Fall):283–307.

Nierenberg, Gerald and Henry Calero (1971). *How to Read a Person Like a Book.* New York: Pocket Books.

Nierenberg, Gerald and Henry Calero (1973). *Metatalk.* New York: Simon and Schuster.

Noble, Barbara Presley (1994). The Gender Wars: Talking Peace. *New York Times* (August 14): 21.

Noelle-Neumann, Elisabeth (1973). Return to the Concept of Powerful Mass Media. In H. Eguchi and K. Sata, eds., *Studies in Broadcasting: An International Annual of Broadcasting Science* (pp. 67–112). Tokyo: Nippon Hoso Kyokai.

Noelle-Neumann, Elisabeth (1980). Mass Media and Social Change in Developed Societies. In G. C. Wilhoit and H. de Bock, eds., *Mass Communication Review Yearbook,* vol. 1, (pp. 657–678). Thousand Oaks, CA: Sage.

Noelle-Neumann, Elisabeth (1991). The Theory of Public Opinion: The Concept of the Spiral of Silence. In James A. Anderson, *Communication Yearbook/14,* (pp. 256–287) Thousand Oaks, CA: Sage.

Noller, Patricia (1982). Couple Communication and Marital Satisfaction. *Australian Journal of Sex, Marriage, and Family* 3:69–75.

Noller, Patricia (1993). Gender and Emotional Communication in Marriage: Different Cultures or Differential Social Power? Special Issue: Emotional Communication, Culture, and Power. *Journal of Language and Social Psychology* 12 (March–June):132–152.

Noller, Patricia and Harley Hiscock (1989). Fitzpatrick's Typology: An Australian Replication. *Journal of Social and Personal Relationships* 6:87–92.

Noller, Patricia and Mary Anne Fitzpatrick (1993). *Communication in Family Relationships.* Upper Saddle River, N.J.: Prentice Hall.

O'Hair, Dan, M. J. Cody, B. Goss, and K. J. Krayer (1988). The Effect of Gender, Deceit Orientation and Communicator Style on Macro-Assessments of Honesty. *Communication Quarterly* 36:77–93.

O'Hair, Dan and Gustav W. Friedrich (1992). *Strategic Communication in Business and the Professions.* Boston: Houghton Mifflin.

O'Neil, Barbara and Richard Phillips (1975). *Biorhythms: How to Live with Your Life Cycles.* Pasadena, CA: Ward Ritchie Press.

Oberg, Kalervo (1960). Cultural Shock: Adjustment to New Cultural Environments. *Practical Anthropology* 7:177–182.

Oggins, Jean, Joseph Veroff, and Douglas Leber (1993). Perceptions of Marital Interaction Among Black and White Newlyweds. *Journal of Personality and Social Psychology* 65 (September):494–511.

Olday, David and Beverly Wesley (1990). Intimate Relationship Violence Among Divorcees. *Free Inquiry in Creative Sociology* 18 (May):63–71.

Orbe, Mark P. (1995). African American Communication Research: Toward a Deeper Understanding of Interethnic Communication. *Western Journal of Communication* 59 (Winter):61–78.

Osborn, Alex (1957). *Applied Imagination,* rev. ed. New York: Scribners.

Osborn, Michael and Suzanne Osborn (1991). *Speaking in Public,* 2nd ed. Boston: Houghton Mifflin.

Ouchi, William (1981). *Theory Z.* New York: Avon.

Palmer, M. T. (1989). Controlling Conversations: Turns, Topics, and Interpersonal Control. *Communication Monographs* 56:1–18.

Parlee, Mary Brown (1979). The Friendship Bond. *Psychology Today* 13 (October):43–54, 113.

Patton, Bobby R., Kim Giffin, and Eleanor Nyquist Patton (1989). *Decision-Making Group Interaction,* 3rd ed. New York: Harper & Row.

Pearce, W. Barnett and Steward M. Sharp (1973). Self-Disclosing Communication. *Journal of Communication* 23:409–425.

Pearson, Judy C. (1980). Sex Roles and Self Disclosure. *Psychological Reports* 47:640.

Pearson, Judy C. (1993). *Communication in the Family: Seeking Satisfaction in Changing Times,* 2nd ed. New York: HarperCollins.

Pearson, Judy C. and B. H. Spitzberg (1990). *Interpersonal Communication: Concepts, Components, and Contexts,* 2nd ed. Dubuque, IA: Wm. C. Brown.

Pearson, Judy C., Richard West, and Lynn H. Turner (1995). *Gender and Communication,* 3rd ed. Dubuque, IA: Wm. C. Brown.

Pease, Allen (1984). *Signals: How to Use Body Language for Power, Success and Love.* New York: Bantam Books.

Peck, Janice (1995). TV Talk Shows as Therapeutic Discourse: The Ideological Labor of the Televised Talking Cure. *Communication Theory* 5 (February):58–81.

Penfield, Joyce, ed. (1987). *Women and Language in Transition.* Albany: State University of New York Press.

Pennebacker, James W. (1990). *Opening Up: The Healing Power of Confiding in Others.* New York: Morrow.

Peplau, Letitia Anne (1988). Research on Homosexual Couples: An Overview. In *Gay Relationships,* edited by John De-Cecco, 33–40. New York: Harrington Park Press.

Peplau, Letitia Anne and Daniel Perlman, eds. (1982). *Loneliness: A Sourcebook of Current Theory, Resarch and Therapy.* New York: Wiley/Interscience.

Perlman, Daniel and Letitia Anne Peplau (1981). Toward a Social Psychology of Loneliness. In Steve Duck and Robin Gilmour, eds., *Personal Relationships. 3: Personal Relationships in Disorder* (pp. 31–56). New York: Academic Press.

Perse, Elizabeth M. and Rebecca B. Rubin (1989). Attribution in Social and Parasocial Relationships. *Communication Research* 16 (February):59–77.

Peters, Roger (1987). *Practical Intelligence: Working Smater in Business and the Professions.* New York: HarperCollins.

Peters, Thomas J. and Robert H. Waterman, Jr. (1982). *In Search of Excellence: Lessons from American's Best-Run Companies.* New York: Harper & Row.

Petrocelli, William and Barbara Kate Repa. (1992). *Sexual Harassment on the Job.* Berkeley, CA: Nolo Press.

Petronio, Sandra and Charles Bantz (1991). Controlling the Ramifications of Disclosure: Don't Tell Anybody But . . ." *Journal of Language and Social Psychology* 10:263–269.

Petronio, Sandra and Judith Martin (1986). Ramifications of Revealing Private Information: A Gender Gap. *Journal of Clinical Psychology* 42:499–506.

Petronio, Sandra, Jess K. Alberts, Michael L. Hecht, and Jerry Buley, eds. (1993). *Contemporary Perspectives on Interpersonal Communication.* Dubuque, IA: Brown and Benchmark.

Phillips, Pamela A. and Lyle R. Smith (1992). The Effect of Teacher Dress on Student Perceptions. ERIC Document No. ED347151.

Philogene, Gina (1994). "African American" as a New Social Representation. *Journal of the Theory of Social Behaviour* 24 (June):89–109.

Pilkington, Constance J. and Deborah R. Richardson (1988). Perceptions of Risk in Intimacy. *Journal of Social and Personal Relationships* 5:503–508.

Pilotta, Joseph J., Timothy Widman, and Susan A. Jasko (1988). Meaning and Action in the Organizational Setting: An Interpretive Approach (with commentaries by Stanley Deetz and Sue DeWine). In James A. Anderson, ed., *Communication Yearbook/11* (pp. 310–355). Thousand Oaks, CA: Sage.

Piot, Charles D. (1993). Secrecy, Ambiguity, and the Everday in Kabre Culture. *American Anthropologist* 95 (June):353–370.

Pittenger, Robert E., Charles F. Hockett, and John J. Danehy (1960). *The First Five Minutes.* Ithaca, NY: Paul Martineau.

Place, Karen S. and Judith A. Becker (1991). The Influence of Pragmatic Competence on the Likeability of Grade School Children. *Discourse Processes* 14 (April–June):227–241.

Plank, Gary A. (1994). What Silence Means for Educators of American Indian Children. *Journal of American Indian Education* 34 (Fall):3–19.

Pollack, Andrew (1995). A Cyberspace Front in a Multicultural War. *New York Times* (August 7):D1, D4.

Porter, J. R. and R. E. Washington (1993). "Minority Identity and Self-Esteem," *Annual Review of Sociology* 19:139–161.

Porter, R. H. and J. D. Moore (1981). Human Kin Recognition by Olfactory Cues. *Physiology and Behavior* 27:493–495.

Postman, Neil and Steve Powers (1992). *How to Watch TV News.* New York: Penguin.

Potter, Ellen F. and Sue V. Rosser (1992). Factors in Life Science Textbooks That May Deter Girls' Interest in Science. *Journal of Research in Science Teaching* 29 (September):669–686.

Potter, W. James (1986). Perceived Reality and the Cultivation Hypothesis. *Journal of Broadcasting and Electronic Media* 30:159–174.

Potter, W. James (1990). Adolescents' Perceptions of the Primary Values of Television Programming. *Journalism Quarterly* 67 (Winter):843–851.

Potter, W. James and Ik Chin Chang (1990). Television Exposure Measures and the Cultivation Hypothesis. *Journal of Broadcasting and Electronic Media* 34:313–333.

Powers, William G. (1993). The Effects of Gender and Consequences upon Perceptions of Deceivers. *Communication Quarterly* 41 (Summer):328–337.

Pratkanis, Anthony and Elliot Aronson (1991). *Age of Propaganda: The Everyday Use and Abuse of Persuasion.* New York: W. H. Freeman.

Prisbell, Marshall (1994). Students, Perceptions of Teachers, Use of Affinity-Seeking and Its Relationship to Teachers' Competence. *Perceptual and Motor Skills* 78 (April):641–642.

Prosky, Phoebe S. (1992). Complementary and Symmetrical Couples. *Family Therapy* 19:215–221.

Prusank, Diane T., Robert L. Duran, and Dena A. DeLillo (1993). Interpersonal Relationships in Women's Magazines: Dating and Relating in the 1970s and 1980s. *Journal of Social and Personal Relationships* 10 (August):307–320.

Pullum, Stephen J. (1991). Illegal Questions in the Selection Interview: Going Beyond Contemporary Business and Professional Communication Textbooks. *Bulletin of the Association for Business Communication* 54 (September):36–43.

Putnam, Linda and M. Pacanowsky, eds. (1983). *Communication and Organizations: An Interpretive Approach.* Thousand Oaks: CA: Sage.

Qubein, Nido R. (1986). *Get the Best from Yourself.* New York: Berkley.

Rabinowitz, Fredric E. (1991). The Male-to-Male Embrace: Breaking the Touch Taboo in a Men's Therapy Group. *Journal of Counseling and Development* 69 (July–August):574–576.

Ramsey, S. J. (1981). The Kinesics of Femininity in Japanese Women. *Language Sciences* 3:104–123.

Rancer, Andrew S., Roberta L. Kosberg, and Robert A. Baukus (1992). Beliefs about Arguing as Predictors of Trait Argumentativeness: Implications for Training in Argument and Conflict Management. *Communication Education* 41 (October):375–387.

Rankin, Paul (1929). Listening Ability. *Proceedings of the Ohio State Educational Conference's Ninth Annual Session.*

Raven, R., C. Centers, and A. Rodrigues (1975). The Bases of Conjugal Power. In R. E. Cromwell and D. H. Olson, eds., *Power in Families* (pp. 217–234). New York: Halstead Press.

Rawlins, William K. (1983). Negotiating Close Friendship: The Dialectic of Conjunctive Freedoms. *Human Communication Research* 9 (spring): 255–266.

Rawlins, William K. (1989). A Dialectical Analysis of the Tensions, Functions, and Strategic Challenges of Communication in Young Adult Friendships. *Communication Yearbook/12,* edited by James A. Anderson, 157–189. Newbury Park, Calif.: Sage.

Rawlins, William K. (1992). *Friendship Matters: Communication, Dialectics, and the Life Course.* Hawthorne, NY: Aldine DeGruyter.

Reardon, Kathleen K. (1987). *Where Minds Meet: Interpersonal Communication.* Belmont, CA: Wadworth.

Redmond, Mark V., ed. (1995). *Interpersonal Communication: Readings in Theory and Research.* Fort Worth, TX: Harcourt Brace.

Reik, Theodore (1944). *A Psychologist Looks at Love.* New York: Rinehart.

Reilly, Mary Ellen, Bernice Lott, Donna Caldwell, and Luisa DeLuca (1992). Tolerance for Sexual Harassment Related to Self-Reported Sexual Victimization. *Gender and Society* 6 (March):122–138.

Reivitz, Linda (1985). *Vital Speeches of the Day* 52 (November 15):88–91.

Rich, Andrea L. (1974). *Interracial Communication.* New York: Harper & Row.

Richards, I. A. (1951). Communication Between Men: The Meaning of Language. In Heinz von Foerster, ed., *Cybernetics, Transactions of the Eighth Conference.*

Richmond, Virginia P. and James C. McCroskey (1996). *Communication: Apprehension, Avoidance, and Effectiveness,* 4th ed. Scottsdale, AZ: Gorsuch Scarisbrick.

Richmond, Virginia P., J. C. McCroskey, and Steven Payne (1991). *Nonverbal Behavior in Interpersonal Relationships,* 2nd ed. Upper Saddle River, NJ: Prentice-Hall.

Riggio, Ronald E. (1987). *The Charisma Quotient.* New York: Dodd, Mead.

Ringer, R. Jeffrey (1994). *Queer Words, Queer Images: Communication and the Construction of Homosexuality.* New York: New York University Press.

Roach, David K. (1991). The Influence and Effects of Gender and Status on University Instructor Affinity-Seeking Behavior. *Southern Communication Journal* 57 (Fall):73–80.

Roberts, Wes (1987). *Leadership Secrets of Attila the Hun.* New York: Warner.

Robinowitz, Fredric E. (1991). The Male-to-Male Embrace: Breaking the Touch Taboo in a Men's Therapy Group. *Journal of Counseling and Development* 69 (July–August):574–576.

Robinson, W. P. (1972). *Language and Social Behavior.* Baltimore: Penguin Books.

Robinson, W. Peter (1993). Lying in the Public Domain. *American Behavioral Scientist* 36 (January):359–382.

Rodriguez, Maria (1988). Do Blacks and Hispanics Evaluate Assertive Male and Female Characters Differently? *Howard Journal of Communication* 1: 101–107.

Rogers, Carl (1970). *Carl Rogers on Encounter Groups.* New York: Harrow Books.

Rogers, Carl and Richard Farson (1981). Active Listening. In Joseph A. DeVito, *Communication: Concepts and Processes,* 3rd ed. (pp. 137–147). Upper Saddle River, NJ: Prentice-Hall.

Rogers, E. M. and F. Shoemaker (1971). *Communication of Innovations,* 2nd ed. New York: Free Press.

Rogers, Everett M. (1983). *Diffusion of Innovations,* 3rd ed. New York: Free Press.

Rogers, Everett M. and Rekha Agarwala Rogers (1976). *Communication in Organizations.* New York: Free Press.

Rogers, L. E. and R. V. Farace (1975). Analysis of Relational Communication in Dyads: New Measurement Procedures. *Human Communication Research* 1:222–239.

Rogers, William T. (1978). The Contribution of Kinesic Illustrators toward the Comprehension of Verbal Behavior within Utterances. *Human Communication Research* 5:54–62.

Rogers-Millar, Edna and Frank E. Millar (1979). Domineeringness and Dominance: A Transactional View. *Human Communication Research* (Spring):238–246.

Rosenfeld, Lawrence (1979). Self-disclosure Avoidance: Why I Am Afraid to Tell You Who I Am. *Communication Monographs* 46:63–74.

Rosenfeld, Lawrence B. and Gary L. Bowen (1991). Marital Disclosure and Marital Satisfaction: Direct-Effect versus Interaction-Effect Models. *Western Journal of Speech Communication* 55 (Winter):69–84.

Rosenfeld, Lawrence, Sallie Kartus, and Chett Ray (1976). Body Accessibility Revisited. *Journal of Communication* 26:27–30.

Rosengren, Karl (1987). Introduction to "A Special Issue on News Diffusion." *European Journal of Communication* 2:135–142.

Rosenthal, Robert and B. M. DePaulo (1979). Sex Differences in Accommodation in Nonverbal Communication. In Robert Rosenthal, ed., *Skill in Nonverbal Communication: Individual Differences.* (pp. 68–103). Cambridge, MA: Oelgeschlager, Gunn and Hain.

Rosenthal, Robert and L. Jacobson (1992). *Pygmalion in the Classroom,* rev. ed. New York: Irvington.

Rossiter, Charles M., Jr. (1975). Defining "Therapeutic Communication." *Journal of Communication* 25:127–130.

Rotello, Gabriel (1995). The Inning of Outing. *The Advocate* 679 (April 18):80.

Rothwell, J. Dan (1982). *Telling It Like It Isn't: Language Misuse and Malpractice/What We Can Do About It.* Upper Saddle River, NJ: Prentice-Hall.

Rothwell, J. Dan (1995). *In Mixed Company: Small Group Communication.* Fort Worth, TX: Harcourt Brace Jovanovich.

Ruben, Brent D. (1985). Human Communication and Cross-Cultural Effectiveness. In Larry A. Samovar and Richard E. Porter, eds., *Intercultural Communication: A Reader,* 4th ed. (pp. 338–346). Belmont, CA: Wadsworth.

Ruben, Brent D. (1988). *Communication and Human Behavior,* 2nd ed. New York: Macmillan.

Rubenstein, Carin (1993). Fighting Sexual Harassment in Schools. *New York Times* (June 10), C8.

Rubenstein, Carin and Philip Shaver (1982). *In Search of Intimacy.* New York: Delacorte.

Rubenstein, Eric (1992). *Vital Speeches of the Day* (April 15):401–404.

Rubin, Alan M. (1979). Television Use by Children and Adolescents. *Human Communication Research* 5:109–120.

Rubin, Alan M. (1994). News Credibility Scale. In R. B. Rubin, P. Palmgreen, and H. E. Sypher, eds., *Communication Research Measures: A Source Book.* New York: Guilford Press.

Rubin, Alan M. Elizabeth Perse, and Robert Powell (1985). Loneliness, Parasocial Interaction, and Local Television News Viewing. *Human Communication Research* 12:155–180.

Rubin, D. C., E. G. Groth, and D. J. Goldsmith (1984). Olfactory Cuing and Autobiographical Memory. *American Journal of Psychology* 97:493–505.

Rubin, Rebecca B. (1982). Assessing Speaking and Listening Competence at the College Level: The Communication Competency Assessment Instrument. *Communication Education* 31 (January):19–32.

Rubin, Rebecca B. and Michael McHugh (1987). Development of Parasocial Interaction Relationships. *Journal of Broadcasting and Electronic Media* 31:279––292.

Rubin, Rebecca B., Elizabeth M. Perse, and Carole A. Barbato (1988). Conceptualization and Measurement of Interpersonal Communication Motives. *Human Communication Research* 14:602–628.

Rubin, Rebecca B., C. Fernandez-Collado, and R. Hernandez-Sampieri (1992). A Cross-Cultural Examination of Interpersonal Communication Motives in Mexico and the United States. *International Journal of Intercultural Relations* 16:145–157.

Rubin, Rebecca B. and Alan M. Rubin (1992). Antecedents of Interpersonal Communication Motivation. *Communication Quarterly* 40:305–317.

Rubin, Rebecca B. and M. M. Martin (1994). Development of a Measure of Interpersonal Communication Competence. *Communication Research Reports* 11:33–44.

Rubin, Theodore Isaac (1983). *One to One: Understanding Personal Relationships.* New York: Viking.

Rubin, Zick (1973). *Liking and Loving: An Invitation to Social Psychology.* New York: Holt.

Rubin, Zick and Elton B. McNeil (1985). *Psychology: Being Human,* 4th ed. New York: Harper & Row.

Ruesch, Jurgen and Gregory Bateson (1951). *Communication: The Social Matrix of Psychiatry.* New York: Norton.

Ruggiero, Vincent Ryan (1987). *Vital Speeches of the Day* 53:671–672.

Rundquist, Suellen (1992). Indirectness: A Gender Study of Flouting Grice's Maxims," *Journal of Pragmatics* 18 (November):431–449.

Rusbult, Caryl E. and Bram P. Buunk (1993). Commitment Processes in Close Relationships: An Interdependence Analysis. *Journal of Social and Personal Relationships* 10 (May):175–204.

Sabatelli, Ronald M. and John Pearce (1986). Exploring Marital Expectations. *Journal of Social and Personal Relationships* 3:307–321.

Saegert, Susan, Walter Swap, and Robert B. Zajonc (1973). Exposure, Context, and Interpersonal Attraction. *Journal of Personality and Social Psychology* 25:234–242.

Salminen, Simo and Timo Glad (1992). The Role of Gender in Helping Behavior. *Journal of Social Psychology* 132 (February):131–133.

Samovar, Larry A. and Richard E. Porter (1995). *Communication Between Cultures,* 2nd ed. Belmont, CA: Wadsworth.

Samovar, Larry A. and Richard E. Porter, eds. (1994). *Intercultural Communication: A Reader,* 7th ed. Belmont, CA: Wadsworth.

Samovar, Larry A., Richard E. Porter, and Nemi C. Jain (1981). *Understanding Intercultural Communication.* Belmont, CA: Wadsworth.

Sanders, Judith A., Richard L. Wiseman, and S. Irene Matz (1991). Uncertainty Reduction in Acquaintance Relationships in Ghana and the United States. In Stella Ting-Toomey and Felipe Korzenny, eds., *Cross-Cultural Interpersonal Communication* (pp. 79–98). Thousand Oaks, CA: Sage.

Sapadin, Linda A. (1988). Friendship and Gender: Perspectives of Professional Men and Women. *Journal of Social and Personal Relationships* 5:387–403.

Sapir, Edward (1929). *Language: An Introduction to the Study of Speech.* New York: Harcourt, Brace & World.

Sargent, J. F. and Gerald R. Miller (1971). Some Differences in Certain Communication Behaviors of Autocratic and Democratic Leaders. *Journal of Communication* 21:233–252.

Sarwer, David B., Seth C. Kalichman, Jennifer R. Johnson, Jamie Earl, et al. (1993). Sexual Aggression and Love Styles: An Exploratory Study. *Achives of Sexual Behavior* 22 (June):265–275.

Sashkin, Marshall and William C. Morris (1984). *Organizational Behavior: Concepts and Experiences.* Reston, VA: Reston Publishing/Prentice-Hall.

Sayre, Shay (1992). "T-shirt Messages: Fortune or Folly for Advertisers?" In Danna (1992), 73–82.

Schafer, R. B. and P. M. Keith (1980). Equity and Depression Among Married Couples. *Social Psychology Quarterly* 43:430–435.

Scherer, K. R. (1986). Vocal Affect Expression. *Psychological Bulletin* 99:143–165.

Schoenhals, Martin (1994). Encouraging Talk in Chinese Classrooms. *Anthropology and Education Quarterly* 25 (December):399–412.

Schramm, Wilbur (1988). *The Story of Human Communication: Cave Painting to Microchip.* New York: Harper & Row.

Schramm, Wilbur and William E. Porter (1982). *Men, Women, Messages and Media: Understanding Human Communication.* New York: Harper & Row.

Schultz, Beatrice G. (1996). *Communicating in the Small Group: Theory and Practice,* 2nd ed. New York: HarperCollins.

Schwartz, Marilyn and the Task Force on Bias-Free Language of the Association of American University Presses (1995). *Guidelines for Bias-Free Writing.* Bloomington: Indiana University Press.

Seidman, I. E. (1991). *Interviewing as Qualititative Research: A Guide for Researchers in Education and the Social Sciences.* New York: Teachers College.

Sergios, Paul A. and James Cody (1985). Physical Attractiveness and Social Assertiveness Skills in Male Homosexual Dating Behavior and Partner Selection. *Journal of Social Psychology* 125 (August):505–514.

Severin, Werner J. with James W. Tankard, Jr. (1988). *Communication Theories,* 2nd ed. New York: Longman.

Shaffer, David R., Linda J. Pegalis, and David P. Cornell (1992). Gender and Self-Disclosure Revisited: Personal and Contextual Variations in Self-Disclosure to Same-Sex Acquaintances. *Journal of Social Psychology* 132 (June): 307–315.

Shannon, J. (1987). Don't Smile When You Say That. *Executive Female* 10:33, 43. Reprinted in DeVito and Hecht (1990), 115–117.

Shaw, D. L. and M. E. McCombs, eds. (1977). *The Emergence of American Political Issues: The Agenda-Setting Function of the Press.* St. Paul, MN: West.

Shaw, Marvin E. (1955). A Comparison of Two Types of Leadership in Various Communication Nets. *Journal of Abnormal and Social Psychology* 50: 127–134.

Shaw, Marvin E. (1981). *Group Dynamics: The Psychology of Small Group Behaviors,* 3rd ed. New York: McGraw-Hill.

Shaw, Marvin E. and Dennis S. Gouran (1990). Group Dynamics and Communication. In *Human Communication: Theory and Research*, Gordon al. Dahnke and Glen W. Clatterbuck, eds. Belmont, CA: Wadsworth.

Shimanoff, Susan B.(1980). *Communication Rules: Theory and Research.* Thousand Oaks, CA: Sage.

Shimanoff, Susan B. (1985). Rules Governing the Verbal Expression of Emotions Between Married Couples. *Western Journal of Speech Communication* 49 (Summer):147–165.

Shockley-Zalabak, Pamela (1991). *Fundamentals of Organizational Communication: Knowlede, Sensitivity, Skills, Values,* 2nd ed. White Plains, NY: Longman.

Siegert, John R. and Glen H. Stamp (1994). "Our First Big Fight" as a Milestone in the Development of Close Relationships. *Communication Monographs* 61 (December):345–360.

Signorielli, Nancy and Margaret Lears (1992). Children, Television, and Concepts about Chores: Attitudes and Behaviors. *Sex Roles* 27 (August):157–170.

Signorile, Michelangelo (1993). *Queer in America: Sex, the Media, and the Closets of Power.* New York: Random House.

Sillars, Alan L. and Michael D. Scott (1983). Interpersonal Perception Between Intimates: An Integrative Review. *Human Communication Research* 10:153–176.

Sincoff, Michael Z. and Robert S. Goyer (1984). *Interviewing.* New York: Macmillan.

Singer, Marshall R. (1987). *Intercultural Communication: A Perceptual Approach.* Upper Saddle River, NJ: Prentice-Hall.

Skopec, Eric William. (1986) *Situational Interviewing.* Prospect Heights, IL: Waveland Press.

Slade, Margot (1995). We Forgot to Write a Headline. But It's Not Our Fault. *New York Times* (February 19):5.

Snyder, C. R. (1984). Excuses, Excuses. *Psychology Today* 18:50–55.

Snyder, C. R., Raymond L. Higgins, and Rita J. Stucky (1983). *Excuses: Masquerades in Search of Grace.* New York: Wiley.

Snyder, Mark (1987). *Public Appearances, Private Realities.* New York: W. H. Freeman.

Snyder, Maryhelen (1992). A Gender-Informed Model of Couple and Family Therapy: Relationship Enhancement Therapy." *Contemporary Family Therapy: An International Journal* 14 (February):15–31.

Sommer, Robert (1969). *Personal Space: The Behavioral Basis of Design.* Upper Saddle River, NJ: Prentice-Hall/Spectrum.

Spitzberg, Brian H. (1991). Intercultural Communication Competence. In Larry A. Samovar and Richard E. Porter, eds., *Intercultural Communication: A Reader* (pp. 353–365). Belmont, CA: Wadsworth.

Spitzberg, Brian H. and William R. Cupach (1984). *Interpersonal Communication Competence.* Beverly Hills, CA: Sage.

Spitzberg, Brian H. and William R. Cupach (1989). *Handbook of Interpersonal Comptence Research.* New York: Springer-Verlag.

Spitzberg, Brian H. and Michael L. Hecht (1984). A Component Model of Relational Competence. *Human Communication Research* 10:575–599.

Sprague, Jo and Douglas Stuart (1996). *The Speaker's Handbook,* 4th ed. Chicago, IL: Harcourt Brace.

Sprecher, Susan, and Sandra Metts (1989). Development of the "Romantic Beliefs Scale" and Examination of the Effects of Gender and Gender-Role Orientation. *Journal of Social and Personal Relationships* 6:387–411.

Staines, Graham L., Kathleen J. Pottick, and Deborah A. Fudge (1986). Wives' Employment and Husbands' Attitudes Toward Work and Life. *Journal of Applied Psychology* 71:118–128.

Steil, Janice M. and Hillman, Jennifer L. (1993). The Perceived Value of Direct and Indirect Influence Strategies: A Cross-Cultural Comparison. *Psychology of Women Quarterly* 17 (December):457–462.

Steil, Lyman K., Larry L. Barker, and Kittie W. Watson (1983). *Effective Listening: Key to Your Success.* Reading, MA: Addison-Wesley.

Steiner, Claude (1981). *The Other Side of Power.* New York: Grove.

Stephan, Walter G. and Cookie White Stephan (1985). Intergroup Anxiety. *Journal of Social Issues* 41:157–175.

Stephan, Walter G., Cookie Stephan, Brenda Wenzel, and Jeffrey Cornelius (1991). Intergroup Interaction and Self-Disclosure. *Journal of Applied Social Psychology* 21 (August):1370–1378.

Sternberg, Robert J. (1988). *The Triangle of Love: Intimacy, Passion, Commitment.* New York: Basic Books.

Sternberg, Robert J. with Catherine Whitney (1991). *Love the Way You Want It: Using Your Head in Matters of the Heart.* New York: Bantam.

Stewart, Charles J. and William B. Cash, Jr. (1988). *Interviewing: Principles and Practices,* 4th ed. Dubuque, IA: Wm. C. Brown.

Stewart, Lea P., A. D. Stewart, S. A. Friedley, and P. J. Cooper (1990). *Communication Between the Sexes,* 2nd ed. Scottsdale, AZ: Gorsuch Scarisbrick.

Stohl, Cynthia (1986). Quality Circles and Changing Patterns of Communication. In Margaret L. McLaughlin, ed., *Communication Yearboook/9* (pp. 511–531). Thousand Oaks, CA: Sage.

Stohl, Cynthia (1987). Bridging the Parallel Organization: A Study of Quality Circle Effectiveness. In Margaret L. McLaughlin, ed., *Communication Yearboook/10* (pp. 416–430). Thousand Oaks, CA: Sage.

Strauss, George and Leonard R. Sayles (1980). *Behavioral Strategies for Managers.* Upper Saddle River, NJ: Prentice-Hall.

Strecker, Ivo (1993). Cultural Variations in the Concept of "Face." *Multilingua* 12:119–141.

Sunnafrank, Michael (1989). Uncertainty in Interpersonal Relationships: A Predicted Outcome Value Interpretation of Gudykunsts's Research Program. In James A. Anderson, ed., *Communication Yearbook/12.* Thousand Oaks, CA: Sage.

Tannen, Deborah (1990). *You Just Don't Understand: Women and Men in Conversation.* New York: Morrow.

Tannen, Deborah (1994a). *Gender and Discourse.* New York: Oxford University Press.

Tannen, Deborah (1994b). *Talking from 9 to 5: How Women's and Men's Conversational Styles Affect Who Gets Heard, Who Gets Credit, and What Gets Done at Work.* New York: William Morrow.

Taraban, Carolyn Beth and Clyde Hendrick (1995). Personality Perceptions Associated with Six Styles of Love. *Journal of Social and Personal Relationships* 12 (August):453–461.

Taylor, D. M. and V. Jaggi (1974). Ethnocentrism and Causal Attribution in a South Indian Context. *Journal of Cross Cultural Psychology* 5:162–171.

Taylor, Dalmas A. and Irwin Altman (1987). Communication in Interpersonal Relationships: Social Penetration Processes. In M. E. Roloff and G. R. Miller, eds., *Interpersonal Processes: New Directions in Communication Research* (pp. 257–277). Thousand Oaks, CA: Sage.

Taylor, Frederick W. (1911). *The Principles of Scientific Management.* New York: Harper and Brothers.

Tersine, Richard J. and Walter E. Riggs (1980). The Delphi Technique: A Long-Range Planning Tool. In Stewart Ferguson and Sherry Devereaux Ferguson, eds., *Intercom: Readings in Organizational Communication* (pp. 266–373). Rochelle Park, NJ: Hayden.

Thibaut, John W. and Harold. H. Kelley (1986). *The Social Psychology of Groups.* New Brunswick, NJ: Transaction Books.

Thorne, Barrie, Cheris Kramarae, and Nancy Henley, eds. (1983). *Language, Gender and Society.* Rowley, MA: Newbury House Publishers.

Tichenor, P. J., G. A. Donohue, and C. N. Olien (1970). Mass Media Flow and Differential Growth in Knowledge. *Public Opinion Quarterly* 34:159–170.

Ting-Toomey, Stella (1985). Toward a Theory of Conflict and Culture. *International and Intercultural Communication Annual* 9:71–86.

Ting-Toomey, Stella (1986). Conflict Communication Styles in Black and White Subjective Cultures. In Young Yun Kim, ed. *Interethnic Communication: Current Research* (pp. 75–88). Thousand Oaks, CA: Sage.

Ting-Toomey, Stella and Felipe Korzenny, eds. (1991). *Cross-Cultural Interpersonal Communication.* Thousand Oaks, CA: Sage.

Tolhuizen, James H. (1989). Communication Strategies for Intensifying Dating Relationships: Identification, Use and Structure. *Journal of Social and Personal Relationships* 6:413–434.

Torbiorn, I. (1982). *Living Abroad.* New York: Wiley.

Trager, George L. (1958). Paralangauge: A First Approximation. *Studies in Linguistics* 13:1–12.

Trager, George L. (1961). The Typology of Paralanguage. *Anthropological Linguistics* 3:17–21.

Trenholm, Sarah (1991). *Human Communication Theory,* 2nd ed. Upper Saddle River, NJ: Prentice-Hall.

Trower, P. (1981). Social Skill Disorder. In S. Duck and R. Gilmour, ed., *Personal Relationships 3,* (pp. 97–110). New York: Academic Press.

Truax, C. (1961). "A Scale for the Measurement of Accurate Empathy," Wisconsin Psychiatric Institute Discussion Paper No. 20. Madison: Wisconsin Psychiatric Institute.

Ueleke, William, et al. (1983). Inequity Resolving Behavior as a Response to Inequity in a Hypothetical Marital Relationship. *A Quarterly Journal of Human Behavior* 20:4–8.

Ullmann, Stephen (1962). *Semantics: An Introduction to the Science of Meaning.* New York: Barnes & Noble.

UNESCO [United Nations Education, Scientific, and Cultural Organization] (1993). *World Education Report.* Paris, France: UNESCO Publishing.

Uris, Auren (1986). *101 of the Greatest Ideas in Management.* New York: Wiley.

Van Yperen, Nico W. and Bram P. Buunk (1991). Equity Theory and Exchange and Communal Orientatioin from a Cross-National Perspective. *Journal of Social Psychology* 131 (February):5–20.

VanHyning, Memory (1993). *Crossed Signals: How to Say No to Sexual Harassment.* Los Angeles: Infotrends Press.

Veenendall, Thomas L. and Marjorie C. Feinstein (1996). *Let's Talk About Relationships: Cases in Study,* 2nd ed. Prospect Heights, IL: Waveland Press.

Vernon, JoEtta A., J. Allen Williams, Terri Phillips, and Janet Wilson (1990). Media Stereotyping: A Comparion of the Way Elderly Women and Men Are Portrayed on Prime-Time Television. *Journal of Women and Aging* 4:55–68.

Victor, David (1992). *International Business Communication.* New York: HarperCollins.

Viswanath, K., et al. (1993). Motivation and the Knowledge Gap: Effects of a Campaign to Reduce Diet-Related Cancer Risk. *Communication Research* 20 (August):546–563.

Viswanath, K. and John R. Finnegan, Jr. (1995). The Knowledge-Gap Hypothesis: Twenty-Five Years Later. *Communication Yearbook/19,* ed., Brant R. Burleson. Thousand Oaks, CA: Sage.

Walster, E. and G. W. Walster (1978). *A New Look at Love.* Reading, MA: Addison-Wesley.

Walster, Elaine, G. W. Walster, and Ellen Berscheid (1978). *Equity: Theory and Research.* Boston: Allyn & Bacon.

Walters, Lilly (1993). *Secrets of Successful Speakers: How You Can Motivate, Captivate, and Persuade.* New York: McGraw-Hill.

Wardhaugh, Ronald (1985). *How Conversation Works.* New York: Basil Blackwell.

Watson, Arden K. and Carley H. Dodd (1984). Alleviating Communication Apprehension through Rational Emotive Therapy: A Comparative Evaluation. *Communication Education* 33:257–266.

Watzlawick, Paul (1977). *How Real Is Real? Confusion, Disinformation, Communication: An Anecdotal Introduction to Communications Theory.* New York: Vintage Books.

Watzlawick, Paul (1978). *The Language of Change: Elements of Therapeutic Communication.* New York: Basic Books.

Watzlawick, Paul, Janet Helmick Beavin, and Don D. Jackson (1967). *Pragmatics of Human Communication: A Study of Interactional Patterns, Pathologies, and Paradoxes.* New York: Norton.

Weber, Ann L. and Harvey, John H., eds. (1995). *Perspectives on Close Relationships.* Boston, MA: Allyn & Bacon.

Weinstein, Eugene A. and Paul Deutschberger (1963). Some Dimensions of Altercasting. *Sociometry* 26:454–466.

Werner, Elyse K. (1975). *A Study of Communication Time.* M. A. thesis, University of Maryland, College Park. Cited in Wolvin and Coakley (1982).

West, Daniel V. (1995). "Further Validity Assessment of the News Credibility Scale," paper presented at the Eastern Communication Association Convention (Pittsburgh, April 27–30).

Wetzel, Patricia J. (1988). Are "Powerless," Communication Strategies the Japanese Norm? *Language in Society* 17:555–564.

Wheeless, Lawrence R. and Janis Grotz (1977). The Measurement of Trust and Its Relationship to Self-Disclosure. *Human Communication Research* 3:250–257.

Whitham, Cynthia (1993). When a Child Needs to Be Heard: How Mirroring Soothes and Solves. *PTA Today* 18 (March):8–9.

Whitman, Richard F. and John H. Timmis (1975). The Influence of Verbal Organizational Structure and Verbal Organizing Skills on Select Measures of Learning. *Human Communication Research* 1:293–301.

Wichstrom, Lars, Arne Holte, Ragnhild Husby, and Lyman C. Wynne (1993). Competence in Children at Risk for Psychotherapy Predicted from Confirmatory and Disconfirmatory Family Communication. *Family Process* 32 (June):203–220.

Wiemann, John M. (1977). Explication and Test of a Model of Communicative Competence. *Human Communication Research* 3:195–213.

Wiemann, John M. and Philip Backlund (1980). Current Theory and Research in Communicative Competence. *Review of Educational Research* 50:185–199.

Wiemann, John M., A. Mulac, D. Zimmerman, and S. K. Mann (1987). "Interruption Patterns in Same-Gender and Mixed-Gender Dyadic Conversations," paper presented at the Third International Conference on Social Psychology and Language (Bristol, England). Cited in Mulac, Wiemann, Widenmann, and Gibson (1988).

Wilcox, Joanne (1994). Gestures and Language: Fair and Foul in Other Cultures. *Mosaic* 2 (Fall 1994):10–13.

Williams, Andrea (1985). *Making Decisions.* New York: Zebra.

Williams, Frederick, ed. (1970). *Language and Poverty: Perspectives on a Theme.* Chicago: Markham.

Williams, Frederick (1983). *The Communications Revolution.* New York: New American Library.

Williams, Frederick (1987). *Technology and Communication Behavior.* Belmont, CA: Wadsworth.

Williams, Frederick (1991). *The New Telecommunications.* New York: Free Press.

Williams, Frederick (1992). *The New Communications,* 3rd ed. Belmont, CA: Wadsworth.

Wilmot, William W. (1987). *Dyadic Communication,* 3rd ed. New York: Random House.

Wilson, A. P. and Thomas G. Bishard (1994). Here's the Dirt on Gossip. *American School Board Journal* 181 (December): 27–29.

Wilson, Glenn and David Nias (1976). *The Mystery of Love.* New York: Quadrangle/The New York Times Book Co.

Wilson, R. A. (1989). Toward Understanding E-prime. *Etc.: A Review of General Semantics* 46:316–319.

Winhahl, Sven and Benno Signitzer with Jean T. Olson (1992). *Using Communication Theory: An Introduction to Planned Communication.* Thousand Oaks, CA: Sage.

Wiseman, Richard, ed. (1995). *Intercultural Communication Theory.* Thousand Oaks, CA: Sage.

Wolf, Florence I., Nadine C. Marsnik, William S. Tacey, and Ralph G. Nichols (1983). *Perceptive Listening.* New York: Holt, Rinehart and Winston.

Wolfson, Nessa (1988). The Bulge: A Theory of Speech Behaviour and Social Distance. In J. Fine, ed., *Second Language*

Discourse: A Textbook of Current Research (pp. 21–38). Norwood, NJ: Ablex.

Wolpe, Joseph. (1958). *Psychotherapy by Reciprocal Inhibition.* Stanford, CA: Stanford University Press.

Wolvin, Andrew D. and Carolyn Gwynn Coakley (1982). *Listening.* Dubuque, IA: Wm. C. Brown.

Won-Doornink, Myong Jin (1985). Self-Disclosure and Reciprocity in Conversation: A Cross-National Study. *Social Psychology Quarterly* 48:97–107.

Won-Doornink, Myong Jin (1991). Self-Disclosure and Reciprocity in South Korean and U.S. Male Dyads. In Stella Ting-Toomey and Felipe Korzenny, eds., *Cross Cultural Interpersonal Communication* (pp. 116–131). Thousand Oaks, CA: Sage.

Wood, Julia T. (1994). *Gendered Lives: Communication, Gender, and Culture.* Belmont, CA: Wadsworth.

Woodward, Gary C. and Robert E. Denton (1996). *Persuasion and Influence in American Life,* 3rd ed. Prospect Heights, IL: Waveland Press.

Wright, J. W. and L. A. Hosman (1983). Language Style and Sex Bias in the Courtroom: The Effects of Male and Female Use of Hedges and Intensifiers on Impression Formation. *Southern Speech Communication Journal* 48: 137–152.

Wright, Paul H. (1978). Toward a Theory of Friendship Based on a Conception of Self. *Human Communication Research* 4:196–207.

Wright, Paul H. (1984). Self-Referent Motivation and the Intrinsic Quality of Friendship. *Journal of Social and Personal Relationships* 1:115–130.

Wright, Paul H. (1988). Interpreting Research on Gender Differences in Friendship: A Case for Moderation and a Plea for Caution. *Journal of Social and Personal Relationships* 5:367–373.

Yancy, George and Sarah Berglass (1991). Love Styles and Life Satisfaction. *Psychological Reports* 68.3 part 1 (June): 883–890.

Yerby, Janet, Nancy Buerkel-Rothfuss, and Arthur P. Bochner (1990). *Understanding Family Communication.* Scottsdale, AZ: Gorsuch Scarisbrick.

Yoshida, Akihiro (1992). On the Why-What Phenomenon: A Phenomenological Explication of the Art of Asking Questions. *Human Studies* 15 (January):35–46.

Zajonc, Robert B. (1968). Attitudinal Effects of Mere Exposure. *Journal of Personality and Social Psychology, Supplement 9,* No. 2, Pt. 2.

Zakahi, Walter R. and Blaine Goss (1995). Loneliness and Interpersonal Decoding Skills. *Communication Quarterly* 43 (Winter):75–85.

Zamanou, Sonia and Susan R. Glaser (1994). Moving Toward Participation and Involvement: Managing and Measuring Organizational Culture. *Group and Organization Management* 19 (December):475–502.

Zima, Joseph P. (1983). *Interviewing: Key to Effective Management.* Chicago: Science Research Associations, Inc.

Zimmer, Troy A. (1986). Premarital Anxieties. *Journal of Social and Personal Relationships* 3:149–159.

Zincoff, M. Z. and Robert S. Goyer (1984). *Interviewing.* New York: Macmillan.

Zuckerman, M., R. Klorman, D. T. Larrance, and N. H. Spiegel (1981). Facial, Autonomic, and Subjective Components of Emotion: The Facial Feedback Hypothesis Versus the Externalizer-Internalizer Distinction. *Journal of Personality and Social Psychology* 41:929–944.

Zunin, Leonard M. and Natalie B. Zunin (1972). *Contact: The First Four Minutes.* Los Angeles: Nash.

index

Note: t indicates a text table; *f* indicates a figure; numbers in **bold** indicate a glossary term.